African Women in Law

African Women in Law

A Comparative Perspective

J. JARPA DAWUNI, *PH.D.*

Full Professor of Political Science, Howard University, Washington, DC, USA

OXFORD
UNIVERSITY PRESS

OXFORD
UNIVERSITY PRESS

Oxford University Press is a department of the University of Oxford.
It furthers the University's objective of excellence in research, scholarship,
and education by publishing worldwide. Oxford is a registered trade mark of
Oxford University Press in the UK and in certain other countries.

Published in the United States of America by Oxford University Press
198 Madison Avenue, New York, NY 10016, United States of America.

Library of Congress Cataloging-in-Publication Data
Names: Dawuni, J. Jarpa author
Title: African women in law : a comparative perspective / J. Jarpa Dawuni.
Description: New York : Oxford University Press, 2026. |
Includes bibliographical references and index.
Identifiers: LCCN 2025048953 (print) | LCCN 2025048954 (ebook) |
ISBN 9780197795064 hardback | ISBN 9780197795071 epub | ISBN 9780197795088 updf |
ISBN 9780197795095 online
Subjects: LCSH: Women lawyers—Africa. | Women judges—Africa. |
Sex discrimination against women—Law and legislation—Africa. |
Women—Legal status, laws, etc.—Africa. | Comparative law—Africa. |
Practice of law—History.
Classification: LCC KQC51 .D39 2026 (print) | LCC KQC51 (ebook)
LC record available at https://lccn.loc.gov/2025048953
LC ebook record available at https://lccn.loc.gov/2025048954

DOI: 10.1093/9780197795095.001.0001

Printed by Integrated Books International, United States of America

The manufacturer's authorized representative in the EU for product safety is
Oxford University Press España S.A. of Parque Empresarial San Fernando de Henares,
Avenida de Castilla, 2–28830 Madrid (www.oup.es/en or product.safety@oup.com).
OUP España S.A. also acts as importer into Spain of products made by the manufacturer.

Note to Readers

This publication is designed to provide accurate and authoritative information in regard to the subject matter covered. It is based upon sources believed to be accurate and reliable and is intended to be current as of the time it was written. It is sold with the understanding that the publisher is not engaged in rendering legal, accounting, or other professional services. If legal advice or other expert assistance is required, the services of a competent professional person should be sought. Also, to confirm that the information has not been affected or changed by recent developments, traditional legal research techniques should be used, including checking primary sources where appropriate.

(Based on the Declaration of Principles jointly adopted by a Committee of the American Bar Association and a Committee of Publishers and Associations.)

Praise Page

An essential book that explores the influence of historical, institutional, and social factors on African women working as lawyers, judges, and legal academics. It examines how shifts in local and global trends create both opportunities and challenges, and how women develop strategies to succeed. This book will serve as a valuable resource for African and international policymakers, as well as organizations committed to increasing women's representation in leadership and decision-making roles.

Elizabeth Adu, Former Deputy General Counsel, Operations, World Bank

Dawuni's maiden monograph has laid a strong foundation for the study of African women in law. It stands as a seminal work, offering an in-depth examination of African women's roles across the three key sectors: the bar, the bench, and the legal academy.

Professor Raymond Akongburo Atuguba, Professor of Law and Former Dean, University of Ghana School of Law

African Women in Law: A Comparative Perspective explores the histories, challenges, and achievements of African women in the legal profession—at the bar, on the bench, and within the legal academy. Grounded in postcolonial feminism, intersectionality, and matri-legal feminism, the book examines how women have navigated colonial legacies and gendered barriers to transform law and justice. Through comparative analysis and rich historical insight, it celebrates the resilience, intellect, and leadership of African women who continue to shape the continent's legal and social futures. Ultimately, the book offers a comprehensive analysis that bridges historical context with contemporary evaluation, advancing understanding and guiding future research.

Professor Oluyemisi Bamgbose, SAN, Deputy Vice-Chancellor, Research Innovation and Strategic Partnerships, University of Ibadan, Nigeria

An exceptional work driven by determination, passion, and a rigorous empirical understanding of African women's experiences in law. Dawuni once again demonstrates her standing as a scholar of the highest caliber. This is a must-read for anyone interested in law, history, good governance, access to justice, and organizational theory.

Professor Babacar Kantè, Former Law Dean at Gaston Berger; Former Judge of the Constitutional Court of Senegal

This book is built on a strong intellectual foundation and makes a significant contribution to socio-legal scholarship by introducing a new theoretical framework: *matri-legal feminism.* This innovative approach serves as an analytical tool for examining African legal systems through the lens of lived experiences, matrilineal strengths, and the agency of African women. By moving beyond existing Western feminist paradigms, matri-legal feminism seeks to reshape our understanding and conceptualization of gender, womanhood, and law within African contexts.

Dr. Willy Mutunga, PhD, Chief Justice and President of the Supreme Court of Kenya, 2011–2016; Professor of Law at Kabarak Law School

Across Africa and globally, significant disparities persist between men and women in terms of basic rights and the power to shape the future. This book underscores the importance of examining gender, public policy, and development through a historical lens. It challenges the dominant narrative that portrays African women as inescapable victims of patriarchy by tracing their pre-colonial positionality and agency through to their current participation in the legal profession. Despite their late entry into the field and the gendered challenges they encounter, African women have made remarkable contributions to the profession. With discussions on ideas, resources, experiences, and best practices, this book is an essential read for scholars and policymakers committed to designing policies that promote gender equality.

Muna Ndulo, William Nelson Cromwell Professor of International and Comparative Law, Cornell Law School, USA; Elizabeth and Arthur Reich Director of the Leo and Arvilla Berger International Legal Studies Program, Cornell Law School

Dr. Dawuni has produced a historically grounded, empirically rich, deeply insightful, and highly analytical account of the inspiring triumphs—amid tribulations and challenges—of African women in law. The book is as theoretically sophisticated as it is firmly rooted in the diverse contexts that shape the lives and careers of the accomplished women it examines. It is no surprise that this outstanding work breaks new ground on an understudied topic. A remarkable and invaluable addition to the literature.

Professor Obiora Chinedu Okafor, Edward B. Burling Chair in International Law and Institutions, Johns Hopkins University School of Advanced International Studies; Former UN Independent Expert on Human Rights and International Solidarity; Former Chair of the UN Human Rights Council Advisory Committee

The author takes readers on a journey from Africa's precolonial justice systems and women's roles in law, through various domestic contexts, to the global stage where African women continue to influence law, justice, and good governance. Written with zeal and compassion and supported by robust empirical, qualitative, and quantitative data, this work offers a dignified, scholarly, and long-overdue account of the rich and distinctive contributions African women have made to the bar, the bench, and the legal academy.

Justice Albie Sachs, Former Justice of the Constitutional Court of South Africa

Drawing on postcolonial feminism, intersectionality, and her own theory of *matri-legal feminism*, Professor Dawuni introduces theoretical innovations rooted in the diverse and nuanced lived experiences of women in law. Employing terms such as "gender-norm conformists" and "gender-norm disruptors," and introducing concepts like female "workhorses" and male "racehorses," the book explores strategies for surviving, navigating, and challenging gendered power structures. These contributions significantly advance the study of women in law—both across African contexts and globally. This book is poised to serve as a key reference for research on African women in law for years to come.

Professor Margaret L. Satterthwaite, Professor of Law, New York University School of Law; UN Special Rapporteur on the Independence of Judges and Lawyers

Jarpa Dawuni offers a deeply researched exploration of the experiences of African women in the legal profession, creating a rich contextual knowledge base—the first of its kind. Her feminist insights and comprehensive survey make this book an invaluable resource for aspiring legal professionals. It is also a practical tool for policymakers advocating for gender justice, while remaining accessible to the general reader.

Professor Sylvia Tamale, Former Law Dean and Feminist Law Professor

This book is dedicated to my ABCs-Afrys, Bebe, and Chichi
Live, Love, Laugh

and to Jeanne Maddox Toungara, Ph.D., and
Babacar Kanté, Ph.D., great mentors

Contents

Figures

Tables

Foreword by Dr. Justice Willy Mutunga

Reimagining Justice: African Women and the Future of Law

I am pleased to write the foreword for Professor J. Jarpa Dawuni's groundbreaking book, *African Women in Law: A Comparative Perspective.* The research supporting this book was meticulously conducted, employing multiple methods across several countries and involving over 150 informants from the three main areas of the legal field—the bar, the bench, and legal academia. The book begins with a detailed historical account of women's often-overlooked entry into the African legal profession and their contributions to law, justice, and democracy. This book is not merely a historical narrative; it is a comprehensive intellectual exploration of the lives of women legal professionals, drawing on detailed interview stories to craft a compelling narrative that highlights the shared struggles and significant contributions of women in law.

This book is built on a solid intellectual foundation and makes a significant contribution to socio-legal scholarship by introducing a new theoretical framework called *matri-legal feminism.* This innovative framework acts as an analytical tool that examines African legal systems through the lens of the lived experiences, matrilineal strengths, and agency of African women. By moving beyond existing Western feminist standards, the matri-legal feminist theory aims to reshape our understanding and conceptualization of gender, womanhood, and the law within African contexts. The theory also promotes the decolonization of law, offering a new perspective on how legal systems intersect with social norms to influence the experiences of African women in law.

Professor Dawuni provides a broad framework for understanding how scholars can rethink the rigidity of legal norms in women's professional interactions. Using the concepts of *gender norm conformists and non-conformists*, the book helps readers see how historical, institutional, and social norms socialize women into specific behaviors (conformists) and how others challenge these norms by breaking away (non-conformists). These distinctions foster a deeper understanding of a key point in the book—the importance of moving beyond simple and essentialist views of the lives of "African women" and instead recognizing the individual realities that shape collective imagination, action, and mobilization within the profession.

In expanding our understanding of African women in law, the book confidently looks to the future by introducing the concept of *Sankofa Futurisms*, a term derived from the Akan principle of looking backward to move forward. The author encourages us to learn from the past struggles and achievements of African women in law, thereby creating a new vision of what a fair and equitable future for women in the legal field could be. *African Women in Law* is more than just a book; it is a powerful intellectual blueprint for rethinking and reimaging the roles of African women in law. It reminds us that although progress has been made in the brief historical span of women's emergence in law, more work is necessary to fully integrate women into the legal profession.

The arguments, methodological approaches, and main assumptions in this book deeply resonate with my own feminist journey. My feminist thinking and praxis as a legal scholar, judge, and human rights advocate are deeply rooted in African knowledge systems shaped by feminist thinkers and colleagues like Micere Githae Mugo, Sylvia Tamale, Wangui wa Goro, Jessica Horn, Mumbi Mugo, Eunice Sahle, Monica Aleman, Nawal al Sadawi, Ama Ata Aidoo, Feminista Mwikali, Zarina Patel, Ousseina Alidou, Tazim Elkington, and Faith Kasina, among others. These thinkers have helped me to see feminism and overall liberated sexualities as sites of struggle in the implementation of transformative constitutions.

Exposure to various genres of feminist legal and literary thought has profoundly shaped my understanding of how deeply rooted historical, institutional, and sociocultural patriarchal biases converge to exclude women from decision-making and leadership roles. My tenure as Chief Justice and President of the Supreme Court of Kenya provided a unique platform to translate my scholarly insights into judicial and institutional practices. Deliberate efforts were made to promote substantive justice by applying the Constitution of Kenya and other regional and legal instruments that address women's rights. Within the institution of the Judiciary itself, this mission was part of the Judiciary Transformation Framework.

African Women in Law: A Comparative Perspective has strong potential to become the foundational book that defines the field of African women in law. It will serve as a seminal textbook for students, scholars, practitioners, and policymakers alike. It provides a rich historical overview of the legal profession in Africa, categorizes women's entry into the profession into five phases, and offers an in-depth comparative discussion of the three sectors—bar, bench, and academy. It concludes on an optimistic note by highlighting how women have developed strategies to survive and succeed in the profession. It ends with an inspiring outlook on the future possibilities of a legal profession that is just and inclusive. I proudly commend Professor Dawuni for her exceptional scholarship and for the gift of this book that will inspire, educate, and provoke deep conversations for years to come in the fields of law, sociology, politics, and interdisciplinary studies.

Willy Mutunga, PhD
Chief Justice and President of the Supreme Court of Kenya, 2011–2016
Professor of Law at Kabarak Law School

Foreword by Professor Margaret L. Satterthwaite

Breaking Barriers: Women's Leadership in African Law

As I entered the gracious event space at the hotel in Accra, I was accompanied by several of Ghana's most promising law students, who led me to a reserved seat. I was struck immediately by the great diversity of those awaiting the commencement of the day's events. Law students chatted with lawyers of all generations. Women, and some men, sat side by side. In the front row, the leaders of the bench and bar made final changes to their prepared remarks. Individuals in suits sat next to those in high-fashion dress attire stitched from the handmade cloth of multiple nations. This was the launch of the Gender Equality in Law Campaign, a continent-wide advocacy effort to advance women in the bench, bar, and legal academy. The brainchild of Professor Jarpa Dawuni, the campaign was led by the Institute for African Women in Law and was built on research carried across a variety of African countries. The data presented, the words of the Chief Justice of the Supreme Court, and the advice to women and their male allies united those present in a commitment to ensuring women's leadership in the law. It was an honor to take part in my role as the UN Special Rapporteur on the Independence of Judges and Lawyers.

This scholarly volume provides an incomparable academic foundation for understanding women's equality and leadership in the law across Africa. Drawing on work conducted over a decade, Professor Dawuni uses a mixed-methods approach to analyze data from in-depth interviews in six countries and from hundreds of surveys across more than 20 countries. From these primary data, Professor Dawuni constructs narratives that convey the daily realities for women in the legal profession, uncovering the strategies women have used to overcome formal and informal barriers, and examining the influence women have had on the legal systems they have entered.

Those who come fresh to this topic may be surprised to learn that Africa is the continent with "the highest number of women chief justices and presidents of constitutional courts worldwide." After all, African women did not enter the formal legal profession until comparatively recently, much later than their male counterparts. How did they achieve such eminent leadership positions so quickly? As Professor Jarpa Dawuni demonstrates in this seminal volume, women's leadership did not spring forth from nowhere. It grew out of the fertile soil of women's histories in African societies, where "the legal profession, characterized by systems, processes, practices, and the regulation of human interactions, has always existed." This recognition, of the long history of women in the law in the many, diverse polities on the Continent, alongside an examination of the colonial-era laws, practices, and imposed traditions that restricted women's access to formal legal education and the profession, allows Professor Dawuni to build both historical accounts and theoretical frameworks that scholars will utilize for years to come.

Drawing on postcolonial feminism, intersectionality, and her own theory of matri-legal feminism, Professor Dawuni offers theoretical innovations that are grounded in the nuanced and varied daily experiences of women in the law. As she explains in the introduction, the goal is for readers "to understand the nuances within the diversity of legal systems" while keeping the focus on women's equality. To accomplish this goal, Professor Dawuni expands on her earlier work setting out the theory of matri-legal feminist theory, here demonstrating its ability to make sense of "the interconnected influences of history, institutions, and social systems on women's representation in legal professions" across the continent. Thus grounded, the book makes three main arguments: first, that women's roles in the law across Africa result from historically influenced institutional rules and norms as they interact with social elements. Second, as diverse women confront historical, institutional, and social barriers, they demonstrate common forms of resilience, agency, and drive to succeed. Finally, generational shifts among women in legal professions can be observed, which allow for a deeper understanding of how gender equality is achieved.

Deploying the terms "gender-norm conformists" and "gender-norm disruptors," and introducing the figures of female "workhorses" and male "racehorses," the book also examines strategies for surviving, navigating, and unsettling gendered power structures. Separately, these analyses provide new theoretical, argumentative, and terminological insights and suggest frameworks for periodizing women in African legal professions. Taken together, these are major contributions to the study of women in the law—both in the varied contexts of African countries and beyond. This book will be a cornerstone for research on African women in law for years to come.

As the UN Special Rapporteur on the Independence of Judges and Lawyers, much of my time is spent studying the ways that judges, prosecutors, and lawyers are hindered in their work. I have spent a great deal of time creating taxonomies of attack against justice operators, identifying emerging challenges to independent justice actors, and recommending ways to end the most severe forms of abuse. I rarely have sufficient time to look deeply into the ways that those facing obstacles overcome them. This book makes a compelling case for why studying resilience and continuity in the face of difficulty is more important than ever. As they have done for apex court judges, African women in the law are leading us toward new horizons across legal institutions.

Professor Margaret L. Satterthwaite
Professor of Law, NYU
UN Special Rapporteur on the Independence of Judges and Lawyers

Acknowledgments

It takes a village to raise a child is a popular African saying. I will paraphrase that into it takes a village to write a book.

Ten years, thousands of air miles, countless conversations, and years spent writing. Beneath these experiences lie the joy of discovery, the thrill of theorizing, and the exhilaration of finally seeing your labor come to life. This journey also demanded a significant investment of time, resources, and both psychological and physical discipline to bring this book to fruition. However, my personal stories of this journey would not have been possible without the support of my village—all the people I encountered as I navigated the academic wilderness, seeking knowledge to produce knowledge.

I am forever grateful to all the women lawyers, judges, and academics who willingly shared their time and expertise in answering my research questions. Often, these interviews occurred after their work hours, extending their workday, but they graciously met with me. I remain eternally thankful. To the countless foot soldiers who helped me connect with the right people, find the right data sources, and engage in conversations about the local context, thank you for enriching my knowledge and this body of work.

Country visits often began with detailed pre-travel planning, including reaching out to hosts, finding suitable research assistants, and sometimes interpreters and translators. I am thankful for the translations provided in Senegal by Mamadou Diop, in the Ivory Coast by David Koudiao, and in Cape Verde by Monica Coelho. Through long days and running from one office to another, we built friendships, and in turn, they learned about women in the legal profession in their respective countries. I treasure the moments I shared with the countless drivers who transported me from place to place; they served as the cultural ambassadors of their countries and cities.

Gathering data in African countries can sometimes be like searching for a needle in a haystack. Many people helped me by connecting me to the right contacts and, in some cases, searching for the data on my behalf. I have a long list of in-country social and academic ambassadors who assisted during the country visits: Judge Babacar Kantè, Professor Abdoulai Barry, Professor Mbye Cham, Dr. Myma Belo-Osagie, Judge Amina Augie, Judge Aristides Lima, Dr. Joshua Bamfo, Dr. Brice Bado, Dr. Adjoua Ntakpa, Madam Abibatou Siby, Ms. Gloria Akpore, Ms. Isabelle Sokolo Boni. My student assistants were outstanding and supported me each time I called on them. Moustapha Hoyeck, Babajide Tella, Tamia McDonald, and Ama Forson—thank you for your exceptional research assistance.

After years of staring at my computer and obsessively editing the same data, I turned to my village of academic warriors for help. My peer reviewers were as diligent as any blind reviewer could be. The deep insights, corrections, and suggestions I received initially felt overwhelming, but once I stepped back and looked at the mountain of feedback, I realized I had uncovered a treasure trove of knowledge. I raise a toast to my peer reviewers—Dr. Justice Amy Tsanga, Ms. Anita Schmied, Dr. Alice

Kang, Professor Judge Babacar Kanté, Professor Dakas C. J. Dakas, SAN, Professor Gretchen Bauer, Professor Jeanne Maddox Toungara, Dr. Maureen Mapp, Dr. Maame Efua Adaddzi-Koom, Professor Muna Ndulo, Mr. Ralph Madlalate, and Ms. Shannon Johnson. I am forever grateful to each of you.

Who can navigate life without the support of a group of mentors guiding you along the way? My academic and nonacademic mentors were always there to offer guidance, cheer me on, and challenge me to reach the finish line. They encouraged me, offered words of wisdom when I was exhausted, and some of them patiently and gently reviewed very rough drafts of my work. Special thanks to Professor Babacar Kanté, Professor Jeanne Maddox Toungara, Professor Florence Bonner, Professor Gretchen Bauer, Professor Muna Ndulo, Professor James Thuo Gathii, and Professor Obiora Okafor.

This project has taken me to many countries and continents. I have been fortunate to receive several influential fellowships that were crucial during each research and writing phase. In 2023, I spent my academic sabbatical at the French Institute for Advanced Studies (IMERA) in Marseille, France, where I held the Chair in Sustainable Development. The pristine campus at IMERA radiated an academic atmosphere beyond words. The opportunity to spend hours working alongside an interdisciplinary group of scholars from different countries and career stages was invaluable. The beauty of Marseille, filled with a Mediterranean vibe and a city alive with diverse cultures and people, offered a refreshing break from my computer. Walking and meditating along the Mediterranean Sea each evening helped renew my mind, body, and spirit.

In 2022, I served as a Fellow at the Stellenbosch Institute for Advanced Studies (STIAS) in South Africa, working on this project. I felt physically and mentally refreshed by the beautiful and peaceful campus, the excellent staff, the calm surroundings, and the valuable conversations and interactions with my co-fellows. That fellowship was priceless because it allowed me to travel with my family, forge bonds, and make memories, even though I was often focused on my computer day and night.

Engaging in transnational comparative research requires both time and resources. I have been fortunate to receive various forms of financial support for the extensive and costly travel across multiple countries in Africa. I am grateful to Howard University, especially through my department chair, the Dean of the College of Arts and Sciences, and the Provost and Chief Academic Officer, Dr. Anthony Wutoh. Each of these offices supported my efforts through the start-up faculty grant, the pre-tenure grant, and other means to facilitate my travel. I also thank the staff and administrators who managed several of my travel authorizations—I appreciate your efforts.

The lengthy and rigorous process of getting my initial proposal approved by Oxford University Press (OUP) was eased by my excellent Acquisitions Editor, Robert Cavooris, whose quick responses to my follow-up emails helped reduce my anxiety while waiting. To my Project Editor, Paulina dos Santos Major, and the editorial team at OUP, thank you for the outstanding work in bringing this book to life.

My family's support made this possible. The love, patience, kindness, encouragement, trust in me, and holding me up whenever I was down—inspiring me to stand and keep moving when I wanted to give up—you mean the world to me. Thank you!

Abbreviations

AALS	American Association of Law Schools
ACHPR	African Commission on Human and Peoples' Rights
ACtHPR	African Court on Human and Peoples' Rights
AWLA	African Women Lawyers Association
APT	Appointments and Promotions Committee
AJS	Association de Juristes Senegalaise
BAME	Black, Asian, and Minority Ethnic
CEDAW	Convention on the Elimination of All Forms of Discrimination Against Women
CLE	Continuing Legal Education
CPD	Continuous Professional Development
EACJ	East African Court of Justice
ECOWAS	Economic Community of West African States
ECCC	Extraordinary Chambers in the Courts of Cambodia
FLAG	Female Lawyers Association of Gambia
FIDA	Federación Internacional de Abogadas
GELC	Gender Equality in Law Campaign
GBAWF	Ghana Bar Association Women's Forum
HISP	History, Institutions, Social (norms), and Position(ality)
IAWJ	International Association of Women Judges
IAWL	Institute for African Women in Law
ICC	International Criminal Court
ICTR	International Criminal Tribunal for Rwanda
ICTY	International Criminal Tribunal for the Former Yugoslavia
INFJ	Magistrature of the National Institute of Judicial Training
IPU	Interparliamentary Union
IRB	Institutional Review Board
ISCJS	Higher Institute of Legal and Social Sciences
JSCs	Judicial Services Commissions
LSK	Law Society of Kenya
LPPC	Legal Practitioners Privileges Council
MICT	Mechanism for International Criminal Tribunals
NBA	Nigerian Bar Association
NIALS	Nigerian Institute for Advanced Studies
NORHED	Norwegian Programme for Capacity Development in Higher Education and Research for Development
ODPP	Office of the Deputy Public Prosecutor
QC	Queen's Counsel

SAG	Senior Advocates of Ghana
SAN	Senior Advocates of Nigeria
SAWL	South African Women Lawyers Association
SCSL	Specialized Court for Sierra Leone
SEARCWL	Southern and Eastern African Regional Centre for Women's Law
TWAIL	Third World Approaches to International Law
UNOAU	United Nations Office to the African Union
WiLDAF	Women in Law and Development in Africa
WLEA	Women and the Law in Eastern Africa
WLSA	Women and the Law in Southern Africa
WLWA	Women and the Law in West Africa
WLUML	Women Living Under Muslim Laws
ZWLA	Zambia Women Lawyers Association
ZWLA	Zimbabwe Women Lawyers Association

1
Studying Women in Law Across Africa: The Lion(Ness) and the Hunter

I. Introduction

"*If the lion(ness) does not tell their story of the hunt, the tale of the hunt will always glorify the hunter*" is an African proverb emphasizing the importance of retelling the historical account of events to provide a complete perspective on current or recurring issues. From an academic perspective, and for the purposes of this book, the story of the hunt is understood through multiple frameworks, including standpoint theory, intersectional storytelling, and comparative historical narratives that incorporate the voices of the women about whom we are telling the legal stories and from whose realities we are building the theories. The book has three main goals: first, to *explore* the history of African women in law and provide context for current developments; second, to examine their *present* status, highlighting demographic diversity, contributions, challenges, and survival strategies; and third, to suggest directions for future research. This book is an academic hunting expedition—to tell the story of the lioness (the woman in law) and lay the groundwork for future theorizations on African women in law.

In 2023, South Africa celebrated 100 years since officially allowing women to practice law under the Women Legal Practitioners Act 7 of 1923. Inspired by the British Sex Disqualification (Removal) Act of 1919, the South African law highlights how historical events continue to influence and shape the representation of women in law across South Africa, with ripple effects in several jurisdictions throughout southern Africa. Colonial institutional norms, practices, and policies exported from the British, French, and Portuguese mother countries to their African colonies set the foundation for the legal profession, especially concerning the role of women. These colonial policies historically created institutional and social barriers that limited women's access to legal education compared to men, which significantly hindered and delayed women's entry into the legal field.

The rise of women in law across Africa took place within a historical context shaped by deliberate colonial policies that restricted access to legal education. In some cases, such as in South Africa, laws were enacted that banned women from pursuing legal careers. Other barriers to women's educational opportunities included adherence to sociocultural and religious norms that discouraged women from seeking education in Muslim-majority regions like Northern Nigeria, Mali, Senegal, and Niger (Ibrahim, 2016). Additionally, Christian missionary policies influenced girls to avoid professional careers in various British colonies, including Kenya, Uganda, Tanzania, and Ghana (Tripp, 2004).

African Women in Law. J. Jarpa Dawuni, Oxford University Press. © Oxford University Press 2026.
DOI: 10.1093/9780197795095.003.0001

As discussed later in Chapter 2, the practice of justice and law is not new to Africa. Precolonial systems of dispute resolution, adjudication, reparation, and punishment—the essential elements of what lawyers and judges do—existed across Africa before colonization. Consequently, this book argues that the legal profession, characterized by systems, processes, practices, and the regulation of human interactions, has always existed in Africa. Joining other African scholars who challenge the periodization of Africa into pre- and postcolonial phases, this book adopts a long durational approach, centering African lived experiences and histories as a continuous thread supported by historical precedents of diverse experiences. African legal systems and processes of law and justice should not be sacrificed to colonial hegemonic erasure or reemerge as a fictitious product of the colonial enterprise.

Recognizing the existence of law, justice, and traditional lawyers and judges in African systems, this book traces the development of the Western legal profession, beginning in South Africa, where African male lawyers appeared in colonial cities in the late 1800s (Ngcukaitobi, 2018); however, it took several decades for women to join the legal field. Some historical records mention Irene Geffen as the first woman advocate in 1923, followed by Zainunnisa "Cissie" Gool, who made history in 1963 as the first "colored" woman lawyer, and then Constance Hall in 1967, the first Black woman in South Africa to be called to the bar (Sasinsky, 2020). Across the continent, pioneering women lawyers were admitted to the bar in colonial cities during colonial rule, several years after the first male lawyers from Nigeria (Adewoye, 1982a), Ghana (Luckham, 1976), and Kenya, Tanzania, and Uganda (Ghai, 1981).

The first group of women magistrates south of the Sahara appeared in the 1940s, and the first law professors emerged in the early 1970s. In The Gambia, it wasn't until 1979 that the first woman lawyer was admitted to the bar. The women trailblazers in West Africa included Stella Marke Thomas from Nigeria, who was called to the English Bar in 1933 (and later admitted to the Nigerian Bar in 1935), making her the first African woman magistrate south of the Sahara. She was followed by Frances Claudia Wright from Sierra Leone in 1941 and Essie Matilda Forster from Ghana, who was called to the English Bar in 1945 (and later admitted to the Gold Coast Bar in 1947). In eastern and southern Africa, the first women lawyers and judges came much later than in South Africa and West Africa (see Table 3.1 in Chapter 3).

In contrast to women entering the professions in early 1800s Europe and America (Mossman, 2006; Schultz & Shaw, 2003), it took over a century until the mid-1920s for women to join the bar, the bench, and legal academies across Africa. Despite this delayed entry, Africa stands out as the continent with the highest number of women chief justices and presidents of constitutional courts worldwide (Institute for African Women in Law, n.d.-a). As of 2023, Africa had appointed more women judges to the International Criminal Court (ICC) than other regions. In some major law firms, there has been an increase in the number of women managing partners (Institute for African Women in Law, 2023a). Furthermore, the number of deans of law schools and law faculties continues to rise steadily. How did these developments happen? What insights do we have into the historical factors that paved the way for women's leadership roles, and how have these advancements surpassed those in some Western societies, where women entered the legal professions much earlier than in Africa?

1. The Research Questions

Three goals guide the development of the research questions for this book. The first goal is to explore the history of African women in law to enhance our understanding of current and ongoing developments. The second goal involves a comparative analysis of the present situation of African women in law, highlighting their demographic diversity, contributions, challenges, and survival strategies. The third goal points to new directions for future research on African women in law. As the first comprehensive comparative study on this topic, the findings from this work establish a baseline and foundation for future research, generating new questions, methodologies, and theories in the study of African women in law.

Five major questions frame the discussion in the book:

1. What are the historical and current pathways for women entering the legal profession?
2. What professional transformations have occurred with women entering the professions, and what do these changes signify for the rule of law, access to justice, women's rights, human rights, and good governance?
3. What intersectional challenges do women in the legal profession face?
4. What strategies have women implemented to navigate gendered power hierarchies in the profession?
5. What factors explain the positionalities of women in law, and what implications do these have for the future of legal professions?

Figure 1.1 illustrates these questions, demonstrating the interconnectivity of each major variable and how they influence women's positionalities in law. The connectivity can also be presented as a formula: P = C-C + S = P. Where P (women's presence) equals the C (contributions they make) minus C (the challenges they face) plus S (the strategies they adopt) equals P (their position and achievements).

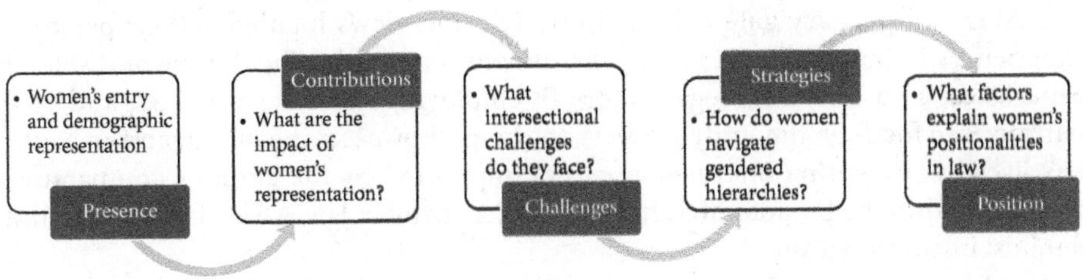

Figure 1.1 *Interactivity and Connectivity of the Main Research Questions*

To answer these questions, the book uses a comparative historical method (Mahoney, 2004) by analyzing the ongoing effects of historical continuities, institutional policies, and social norms on African women in roles such as lawyers, judges, and legal academics. It looks at these issues from the perspective of an African feminist legal scholar, drawing on a broad range of African feminist scholarship from a diverse group of scholars, practitioners, and activists. Linking this goal to the subtitle of this chapter, the stories and experiences of African women in law are best shared by the women themselves (the lionesses) to challenge interpretations that diminish their agency, voice, and actions.

Guided by a comparative methodological approach, the book argues that telling the stories of African women in law is the starting point for theory development. To achieve this, the book uses various strategies, including legal narratives, to create a literary depiction of the lived experiences of African women in law. It explores the factors that have contributed to women's rise as lawyers during a global era when they were still barred from entering the profession in major cities and often denied access to basic education in colonies. It investigates how women navigated institutional rules and sociocultural norms to enter fields such as law, judging, and academia. Connecting the past to the present, the book evaluates the changes that have occurred in these legal fields since pioneering women entered the profession. It traces the increasing number of women in the field and how they are influencing and reshaping its landscape. Finally, it outlines the strategies women have used to navigate deeply rooted gendered and institutional hierarchies to become successful and equal participants in these careers.

The book results from 10 years of primary data collection, including 153 in-depth interviews conducted across six African countries and 249 survey responses from 21 nations. This mixed-methods approach provides the most comprehensive understanding of women's experiences across various countries and regions on the continent so far. The book employs three theoretical frameworks to ensure that the narratives accurately reflect the real lives of African women in both theory and practice. First, *postcolonial feminism* examines the impact of colonial rule on the historical development of women's roles in society; second, *intersectionality* highlights the overlapping structural challenges and barriers women face; and third, *matri-legal feminism* emphasizes women's individual and collective agency to succeed. These theories were chosen to best illustrate how historical, institutional, and social power structures shape women's experiences as lawyers, judges, and legal scholars.

To deepen our understanding of the complexities of women's lives, a comprehensive review of primary data collected through interviews highlights their personal experiences in law, while the survey instruments emphasize the diverse and shared experiences across the three legal sectors. By employing feminist legal praxis and legal narratives to focus on the study subjects, the book showcases the uniqueness of women's lives by presenting interview excerpts, supported by the author's comparative analyses within the broader literature on women, gender, law, African feminism, and feminist institutionalism.

The discussions in each chapter explore the nuances of legal traditions, institutional norms, and sociocultural systems, and their impact on women in the profession. This chapter is divided into five sections, starting with this introductory part. Section II introduces the innovative *historical, institutional, social, and positionality* (HISP) framework, specifically designed to analyze the complex phenomenon of women in law by examining the research questions asked, the methods used, and the theories applied. This section examines how history, institutions, and social systems influence women's roles in law. Section III provides context for the comparative framework by clarifying key terminology and classifications used in the study. Section IV highlights significant findings and major contributions of the book. Finally, section V outlines the structure of the following chapters.

II. Developing a Practical Framework for Complex Phenomena

With few exceptions, such as Cynthia Fuchs Epstein's *Women in Law* (1981), most single-authored books on women in law mainly focus on one aspect of the profession: women as lawyers, judges, or academics. This book is an ambitious project; it not only aims to compare these three sectors but also does so across a diverse continent with various geographic regions, unique historical links to imperialism, multiple cultures, and different legal systems that oversee these professions. As the first comparative study of African women in law, this project seeks to create a practical framework for future research on the complex legal landscape—a complexity further highlighted by the limited literature on African women in law and the lack of accessible quantitative data, including demographic information, income levels, and hiring and promotion policies, among other factors.

This book uses two interconnected frameworks—location and profession—to manage the complexity of covering a continent. The first framework is *location*. While the book refers to "Africa," it is important to note that Africa is a continent made up of 54 nation-states, and this work does not aim to cover all those countries. Doing so would require significant time and resources. In my effort to create a book worthy of the continent's name in its title, I include interviews and survey responses from 21 African nations, along with existing and digitally accessible literature on women in law from various countries across the continent, much of which is included in my edited collection of five books on African women judges. This location framework—both spatially and intellectually—provides a comprehensive understanding of African women in law.

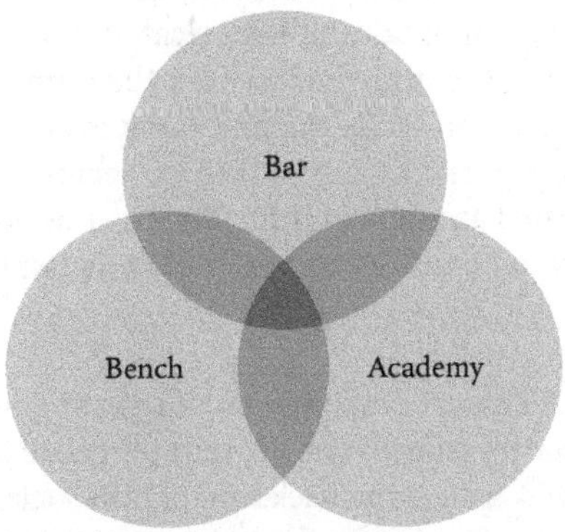

Figure 1.2 *The Trilogy of Women in Law*

The second framework is *profession*. I categorize women in law using a trilogy by focusing on three sectors of the profession. The first sector is the bar, the initial battleground where women had to break through ceilings to gain entry. The second sector is the bench, the middle ground where many pioneering women lawyers often entered due to factors that will be explored in the book. The third sector is the legal academy, viewed as the final battleground for women's representation. Certainly, women have expanded their focus and areas of specialization within the law to include other fields, such as notaries, leaders in the executive and legislative branches of government, and roles in civil society and international law and governance. The book focuses on these three as the profession's main field from which other sectors have emerged. **Figure 1.2** illustrates this tripartite conceptualization of women in law. The overlapping and intersecting points of convergence demonstrate that these three sectors are not mutually exclusive; individuals can transition between them. For example, lawyers may move into the judiciary or academia and vice versa.

The difficulty of studying the trilogy across Africa arises not only from the vast geography but also from the challenge of accessing detailed historical data and research on pioneering women in law. In *The First Women Lawyers: A Comparative Study of Gender, Law, and the Legal Professions*, covering six countries, Mary Jane Mossman (2006, p. 18) discusses the challenges of obtaining archival data to piece together the full stories of the first women. She notes:

> Overall, although the study does not represent a comprehensive history of the first women lawyers all over the world, it offers some impressive insight into the contexts in which women in a number of different jurisdictions actively sought to become lawyers at the turn of the twentieth century, and some reflections on their strategies and experiences as the first women in law. To some extent, the selection of jurisdictions in which women sought admission to the bar was defined for this study by the availability of individual personal records concerning women's quests to become lawyers.

Contextual realities and data access shape the practical yet scientific methods researchers use to produce informed and meaningful findings from available data. In addition to the challenge of obtaining historical and archival records of the first women in law across Africa, this study had to limit the number of countries analyzed due to time and budget constraints. As the first book to compare women's representation in law across various jurisdictions and three sectors, it was wise to develop a framework that incorporated as much existing literature as possible.

Arguing for the contextual consideration of women's issues, in an earlier volume, I emphasized that

> [a]ny discussion of the historical development of legal and judicial systems, and of subsequent constitutional transformation projects propelled by the tide of democratization, must be analyzed against the backdrop of how socially constructed gender norms affect what is perceived as gender equity or equality by the law, the courts, and judges (Dawuni, 2021c, p. 2)

The two quotes highlight the complexity and challenges of studying subjects when limited data access hinders observation and analysis of social constructions and the diverse, intersecting contexts of women's experiences. To address the difficulties in gathering both qualitative and quantitative data, the book presents a framework for analyzing complex phenomena by exploring three interconnected questions: First, what research questions should be asked? Second, which methodological approaches are appropriate? Third, what theoretical frameworks should guide the study? Each question is briefly examined.

1. What Research Questions Should Be Asked?

This book's inquiry approach is guided by the challenge posed by Bennett and Tamale (2011) concerning the necessity of high-quality documentation of women's lives, experiences, and feminist activism:

> A major weakness that continues to affect much feminist activism on the continent is the lack of high-quality documentation. We generally do not give documentation the attention it deserves. And yet, documentation is an important and necessary element in the overall struggle of any social movement; it captures the complexity of historical process and social change and it is from this that people and movements can reflect and learn. Bennett & Tamale (2011, p. 2)

To avoid the weakness mentioned earlier, this study focuses on the types of questions and inquiry methods used to examine the lives of African women in law. This book moves away from treating Western women's experiences as the standard for feminist practice. It scientifically uses research questions, variables, and methodologies that reflect the realities faced by African women in law. Before the publication of the coedited book, *Gender and the Judiciary in Africa: From Obscurity to Parity?* (Bauer & Dawuni, 2016), there had not been a comprehensive edited volume on women judges across Africa. As a pioneering work on this subject, the editors aimed to lay a foundation that truly captures the lived experiences of African women while connecting them to existing studies on women judges from Europe and North America.

The foundational questions that shaped the analyses in *Gender and the Judiciary in Africa: From Obscurity to Party?* (Bauer & Dawuni, 2016) also guide this current study. To create a comprehensive, historically grounded, and contemporary view of women in law across Africa, this book explores how and when women entered the legal professions. This historical approach necessitates understanding the development of the legal professions throughout much of the continent. Chapter 3 details the history of women's entry into these professions by examining how gender and race influenced women's access. Guided by the historical context and aware of the current presence of women in these fields, *the five key questions* that drive this project are outlined earlier in this chapter's introductory section. By adopting a decolonial perspective grounded in African feminist research methods, theories, and approaches, these questions inform the discussions in each chapter and across the three main areas.

Analyzing responses to these questions through a cross-sectoral comparative approach takes into account the context in which the questions were asked. For instance, due to historical ties to various colonial administrations, the experiences of women in Anglophone Africa differ from those of women in Francophone and Lusophone

Africa. Moreover, while women's experiences across the three sectors share similarities, they also differ due to the interaction with the theoretical framework discussed in the next section. For example, when applying intersectionality, race has a greater predictive effect in South Africa than in Nigeria. Despite different historical backgrounds, politics, and legal systems, some questions reveal similar experiences. A common theme throughout these experiences is the intersection of gendered patriarchal power imbalances embedded in institutional and specific social processes related to women's roles as legal professionals.

2. What Methodological Approaches Should Be Used?

Chapter 2 provides a detailed overview of the methodology used in this study. The complexity of African women's lives resists simple generalizations; therefore, the study employs a historical–comparative approach that explores women's experiences within legal traditions, across various professions, and in different fields. The research analyzes individual experiences through interviews and collective experiences through the survey tool.

The dependent variable (*what is being explained*) in this study is the position(ality) of African women in law, while the three independent variables (*which explain the observed phenomena*) are history, institutions, and social systems. To establish a strong methodological foundation for this study and for future researchers interested in exploring various questions about the lives of African women in law, this study introduces an innovative framework to assess the intersectional impact of history, institutions, and social systems on women's positions in law—the HISP framework. Ancillary questions rooted in a decolonial feminist framework guide each of the four variables in the HISP framework.

a. ***History:*** How do we situate the agency of African women in the precolonial context as a crucial factor in explaining the postcolonial continuities of women's agency in public life? This variable examines the impact of colonization and double jeopardy on women's emergence as legal professionals—the intersection of racial and gender exclusions. By exploring history, the study reveals how the importation of imperial patriarchy from the metropole excluded Western women from both the legal academy and legal professions. This historical approach highlights the masculinized foundations of legal professions across Africa and the role of pioneering women in law in creating opportunities for women in the professions.
b. ***Institutions:*** What normative and regulatory frameworks shape women's work experiences? Do gendered constructs influence formal and informal rules, practices, and processes? The institutional variable examines how imported, male-centered institutional practices from the metropole interact with the domestic context in the colonies to create gendered experiences for women in law. It evaluates findings from existing studies on the profession's regulatory frameworks (Abel & Lewis, 1989), the political economy of the legal professions (Dias et al., 1981), and contemporary issues such as the impact of globalization and

neoliberalism on the profession (Garth & Shaffer, 2020; Nelson et al., 2023; Khanna et al., 2017).

c. ***Social (norms):*** How do socially constructed gender norms, perceptions, and practices shape sociocultural systems that influence and determine women's presence in the legal profession? How do the sociocultural expectations related to the intersection of identities—such as age, gender, marital status, and more—impact women in law? In examining this variable, the book uses survey data to assess women's experiences in the legal field. By using an intersectional framework, the social variables investigated in this study do not cover all categories and identities represented by women. This allows future research to explore additional categories, including sexuality and (dis)ability.
d. ***Position(ality):*** What is the personal experience of women lawyers, judges, and legal academics? Is there a collective position that women in law share? What factors influence their roles within the profession in relation to their other identities? The personal decisions women make to enter the profession, along with how they navigate historical, institutional, and systemic factors, shape both their individual and collective roles in the field. The ongoing struggle with the challenges they face informs the strategies various women adopt to remain, thrive, and succeed. Exploring the positional situatedness of women leads to categorizing ***gender-norm disruptors*** and ***gender-norm conformists,*** which will be discussed later. Figure 1.3 provides a visual representation of the HISP framework.

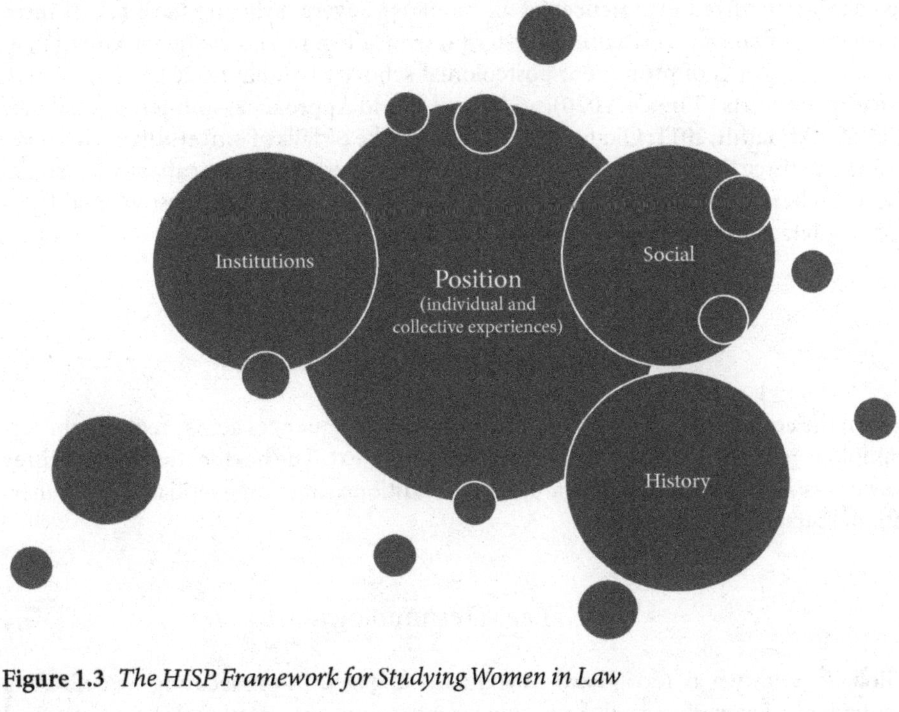

Figure 1.3 *The HISP Framework for Studying Women in Law*

The dotted bubbles in **Figure 1.3** illustrate the intervening variables that exist outside the three main variables: history, institutions, and social factors. The largest bubble is the position, indicating that women's lived experiences are central to the other variables that influence them. As a methodological model, the HISP framework clarifies women's *emergence* and *experiences* in the legal profession by emphasizing the interactive nature of these three key variables. These variables are neither linear nor independent; they interact at various levels and points of intersection. The individual and collective outcomes observed depend on the extent of interaction among the variables.

History and time influence these variables. For example, the immediate effects of historical racial and gender discrimination and exclusion have shaped the experiences of the first generation of women in law more than those of later generations. Likewise, social factors, such as cultural expectations of women's societal roles, are fluid and change over time, creating different experiences for women across generations in law. Although these variables intersect at other points, they also evolve. The external pressures from each layer at any given moment can directly and indirectly impact the lives of women in law. Therefore, the effects are experienced differently by women depending on which variables are active, and their combined impacts are the main themes highlighted in the findings.

3. What Theoretical Frameworks Are Appropriate in Framing the Study?

To what extent are theoretical frameworks universal? Should there be universal theories? Who decides what is considered universal for observing, predicting, and explaining the lived experiences of all humans? Several scholars have raised these questions, often those critiquing Western universalism in knowledge production, as seen in the works of prominent postcolonial scholars (Mohanty, 2013; Said, 2003), African feminists (Tamale, 2020), and Third World Approaches to International Law (TWAIL) (Gathii, 2011; Okafor, 2008). To avoid the pitfalls of universalism, this book combines three theoretical approaches with the greatest predictive capacity to explain women's lived experiences in law. Chapter 2 will further examine postcolonial feminism, intersectionality, and matri-legal feminism.

III. The Comparative Framework: On Terminology and Classifications

Given the continent's diversity and the different legal nuances across regions, the terminology in this book needs to be explained in context. The next section defines three key terms: legal terminology, legal systems/traditions, and nonessentialist intergenerational categorization.

1. Legal Terminology

Globally, a lawyer is recognized as someone engaged in prosecuting or defending individuals. Lawyers may also provide legal services not strictly related to criminal matters. Despite common practices, the terminology used to describe lawyers varies. For instance, in the United States, they are called attorneys or counsel. In the United Kingdom, the profession is divided into roles such as barristers and solicitors. In France, lawyers are commonly called *avocats*. The influence of the French (civil-law) and British (common-law) systems has led to the adoption of similar terms for lawyers in other countries. Therefore, terms like "lawyer," "barrister," or "counsel" are used in former British colonies such as Nigeria, Ghana, Kenya, and Uganda. In South Africa, which follows the British model of a split legal profession, individuals must train as either solicitors (attorneys) or barristers (advocates), with their titles based on their qualifications. In former French colonies like Senegal, Ivory Coast, Mali, and Niger, lawyers are often simply called *avocats*.

Across judiciaries, we see similar differences in terminology. Judges in common-law countries are mainly divided into two groups: judges and magistrates. The term "judge" refers to justices of the peace serving in higher courts, often starting with the High Court, the Court of Appeals, and the Supreme and Constitutional Courts. Conversely, magistrates preside over lower courts, such as circuit, magistrate, district, or other specialized courts. In civil-law countries, the terms for a judge are either *juge* or *magistrat*. Since court structures vary greatly across countries, the use of *judge* or *magistrate* is not always consistent. For example, in Senegal and the Ivory Coast, which follow the civil-law tradition, the term *magistrat* can describe most judicial officers.

Additionally, in civil-law countries, a judge may be called a *procureur* (prosecutor) because of the investigative duties they perform, while in common-law countries, a prosecutor is usually a lawyer in the Ministry of Justice responsible for prosecuting cases on behalf of the state (Schultz, 2013). In civil-law countries, judges take on a prosecutorial role as investigating judges. In contrast, in common-law countries, the term "prosecutor" generally refers to lawyers representing the state, often working in the Office of the Attorney General.

The legal academy also uses different terminology to describe various ranks and functions. Most common-law countries employ titles such as Assistant Lecturer, Lecturer, Senior Lecturer, Associate Professor, and Full Professor. In civil-law countries, we encounter the terms *Assistant, Maître Assistant* (assistant professor), *Maître de conférences* (similar to senior lecturer or associate professor), and *Professor titulaire/agrégé* (full professor).

The complexity of colonial legacies, changing globalization patterns, and the impact of American-style legal education and classifications have led to diverse terms for describing lawyers, judges, legal scholars, and other legal professionals (Bartie & Sandomierski, 2021). Recognizing this complexity in legal terminology, Hammerslev and Sommerlad (2020, p. 4) noted, "While culturally specific terms such as 'attorney,' 'barrister,' and 'solicitor' serve to indicate structural and functional differences, this proliferation of designations and categories has hindered the identification of commonalities in the social and political meaning of the profession."

This book uses the term "lawyer" to refer to all legal professionals who appear in court or serve as in-house counsel. The term "judge" includes all justices of the peace in higher courts and magistrates overseeing lower courts. For legal scholars, I simplify this by calling them law professors or academics without specifying their ranks unless the context requires it. **Table 1.1** offers a general overview of common terminology across the three sectors and the different approaches to their application.

Table 1.1 *Classification of Terminology Across the Three Sectors*

Sector	Terminology/Classifications	Approaches
Bar	• Lawyers vs. attorneys • Advocates/barristers vs. solicitors • Bar Association vs. Law Society • Prosecutor in common-law vs. *avocat* in civil-law countries	• Differences in how to become a lawyer—years of training, internship, pupillage, clerkship, articles. • Fused or split legal profession (barristers vs. solicitors; attorneys vs. advocates). • Diversity in the areas of practice—public, private, and other legal sectors. • Differences in regulatory standards, professional ethics, and disciplinary measures.
Bench	• Higher vs. intermediate courts • Superior vs. inferior courts • Judge vs. magistrate (English-common law) • Juge vs. magistrat (French-civil law)	• Diversity in court structures and jurisdictional powers. • Diversity in selection methods for the bench. • Diversity in promotion policies. • Differences in regulatory standards, professional ethics, and disciplinary measures.
Academy	• Law professor vs. law lecturer • Law faculty vs. law school	• Diversity in law school structures. • Diversity in the role of lecturers. • Different academic rank classifications. • Differences in regulatory standards—tenure and promotion.

2. Legal Systems/Traditions

Legal systems and traditions greatly shape how women enter and participate in legal professions (Auchmuty et al., 2021; Schultz & Shaw, 2003, 2013). Worldwide, legal systems are mainly classified into two types—civil law and common law. The civil-law tradition, which comes from Roman–Dutch law, covers most of continental Europe and, by extension, countries and territories colonized by European powers, including France, Portugal, Spain, and the Netherlands. Major features of civil law include the codification of laws. Judges interpret these codes as written, while lawyers work to establish their clients' innocence, and judges often act as prosecutors in criminal cases (Schultz, 2013).

Common law, which originated from Roman law, is practiced in the United Kingdom, Scotland, and Ireland. Because of British colonization, it is also applied in the United States, Canada, and various countries in Asia and Africa that were colonized by the British Empire. The main features of the common-law tradition include the development of law through legal precedents and judges' rulings in prior cases. Prosecutors carry the burden of proof to establish the guilt of the accused, while judges serve as neutral arbiters in a case (Schultz, 2013). Located between these two legal traditions is a third system called the hybrid legal system, practiced in some southern African countries—such as South Africa, Namibia, and Botswana—that preserve elements from Dutch and British colonization.

Despite the dominance of these legal systems and traditions, most African countries operate hybrid legal systems that blend traditional or customary laws and religious (Sharia) laws and norms with the prevailing civil or common law, depending on which country colonized them. The spread of colonial legal systems across Africa complicates efforts to neatly categorize African countries into one of the two main legal traditions worldwide. Therefore, while recognizing the diversity of legal systems and traditions across the continent, this book will focus on the two dominant legal traditions, as the legal professions we know today developed from the European legal systems that were introduced and enforced during colonization.

3. Nonessentialism and Intergenerational Categorization

Women are not identical despite sharing experiences. Feminist discussions on antiessentialism highlight the complexities within and among women's lived experiences (Kenney, 2013a). Examining women's experiences at the bar, on the bench, and in the legal academy in the countries covered in this book does not aim to present a single story or narrative. Instead, it seeks to identify parallels within and across these experiences, relying heavily on personal narratives gathered from interviews and collective insights from surveys. By adopting an antiessentialist approach, this study aims to clarify the nuances of women's lived experiences while respecting their shared journeys. For analytical purposes, "women in law" refers to a group of women whose individual experiences come together into a collective experience that goes beyond gender and age. Importantly, women's experiences at one point in history can differ from those at another, although some shared continuities can be traced over time.

In this study, women in law are divided into five generations, as shown in **Table 1.2**, each with distinct features and characteristics from specific historical periods. To understand the timeline of the issues discussed in the book, the five generational phases allow for a deeper look at the contextual factors in each phase and how they differently impact women in law. Using two-decade intervals also supports longitudinal observations. This generational periodization is neither fixed nor isolated, as issues and changes in the legal profession develop from one period to the next.

By dividing the rise of women in law into five generations starting in 1930, we can trace the career paths of pioneering women from two main perspectives: exclusionary and accommodationist views. First, the *exclusionary view* saw women as unfit for the legal profession. This perspective stemmed from deeply rooted patriarchal beliefs and the dominant idea in the colonizing metropole that women were not suited for the demands of a legal career, which at the time often involved litigation in land and commercial cases (Adewoye, 1982a; Ghai, 1981; Luckham, 1981). These views shaped the types of careers women pursued and the challenges they faced in gaining acceptance into the profession.

Second, the *accommodationist view* aimed to include women in the profession by drawing on cultural ideas that valued them as leaders. However, this perspective

Table 1.2 *Intergenerational Categorization of Women in Law*

Phase	Generations	Period	Political economy
First	Pioneer women	1930–1950	**Colonial:** marked by few women in law, often trained in the colonial metropole.
Second	Independence cohort	1951–1970	**Independence to state formation:** the beginning and peak of independence from colonization, marked by the establishment of law faculties and law schools.
Third	Growth cohort	1971–1990	**Resistance to authoritarian rule and the push for political liberalization:** The post-independence phase, marked by political instability, one-party states and authoritarianism.
Fourth	Accelerator cohort	1991–2010	**Diffusion and expansion in the profession:** Marked by the return to democratic rule through elections and civil society participation in politics and law.
Fifth	Expansionist cohort	2011–present	**Global expansionism:** Increased globalization, free markets, neoliberal educational policies and the expansion of global legal markets and frontiers.

remained limiting as women entered the bureaucratic civil service model in the ministries of justice and judiciary, which were often seen as "suitable" careers for women. Many of the first female lawyers transitioned from the bar to become the first women magistrates and judges, a topic explored in Chapter 3. The accommodationist view thrived on the prevailing belief that a career on the bench was flexible enough to allow women to better balance work and family obligations than actively pursuing litigation (Houghton, 1981). While these two classifications emerge from a close reading of historical documents, they do not represent the only viewpoints. Although the accommodationist view may have helped facilitate women's entry, the institutional practices and policies rooted in both perspectives did not support women's full integration and upward mobility within the profession. These two views continue to influence the legal profession today, and women have not remained silent bystanders.

Building on these two perspectives—exclusion versus accommodation—the book introduces the concepts of *gender-norm conformists* and *gender-norm disruptors.* While not comprehensive, these categories classify how women navigate the gendered institutional and systemic hierarchies that influence their roles as legal professionals. Gender-norm disruptors are women who oppose institutional and social gender stereotypes and actively assert their rights as equals within the profession. Their stories will be featured in the upcoming chapters. Although gender-norm disruptors may appear more activist-oriented, women in this group use various actions and resistance strategies to defend their legal rights, potentially opening more opportunities for other women in law.

For "gender conformists," the term does not mean a lack of agency; instead, it describes the survival strategies used by different groups to navigate existing power structures. Gender-norm conformists are individuals who may or may not recognize the gender norms and social influences that contribute to workplace biases and stereotypes. This group does not openly or aggressively oppose gender norms but instead follows them. The term "conformist" is not meant to be offensive; it simply shows that this group accepts the norms as they have been socialized to believe or feel pressured to follow due to institutional policies beyond their control.

IV. Major Contributions and Key Findings

Writing a book of this scope—aimed at establishing a foundation for future research on African women in law—requires a strategy and methodology that are both broad and specific. Covering the entire continent isn't feasible, nor can this book alone address the complexities of legal professions across regions and countries. However, by using a comparative approach and collecting extensive primary data through interviews and surveys, the findings provide a more solid comparative base than many books claiming to discuss Africa.

When I started writing this book, my goal was clear: to establish a foundation for studying women in law across Africa through decolonial and intersectional feminist perspectives, while recognizing that no single "African feminism" exists. By integrating interdisciplinary research on African feminism(s) (Dosekun, 2020; Tamale, 2020), I developed the matri-legal feminist framework to analyze women in law (Dawuni, 2019). This book builds on a "logic of appropriateness" (Chappell, 2006) by situating lived experiences, identities, social practices, and norms related to women's representation in law. The aim is for readers to understand the nuances within the diversity of legal systems, professional structures, and the complex, intersectional realities of women's lives.

To clarify expectations, I will briefly outline what this book covers and what it does not. Essentially, this book is a comparative study of the experiences of African women as legal professionals in three sectors: the bar (lawyers), the bench (judges), and the academy (academics). It does not aim to present a single African narrative, nor does it seek to tell "the women's story," as women's experiences vary within, across, and among regions, countries, professions, and ranks. Furthermore, this book is not about the difference women make; they should not carry the additional burden of proving their impact as a basis for their inclusion. Navigating hierarchical structures, masculinized workplace cultures, and the demands of domestic and communal life is already challenging—women should not have to bear the extra burden of constantly proving themselves.

Building on this understanding, the following chapters explore women's presence, contributions, and impacts to highlight their lived experiences across different sectors. The current analysis is not framed through a "difference" lens; instead, I reemphasize the often overlooked but obvious truth—women are changemakers and vital contributors to society at multiple levels. Moreover, the book does not present a one-sided narrative of the challenges women in law face. Instead, it highlights their

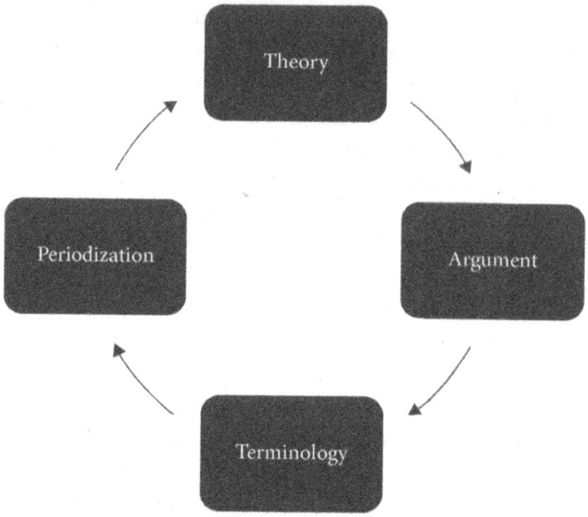

Figure 1.4 *Major Contributions of the Book*

contributions to law, justice, and national development while demonstrating their agency through the politics of survival and strategies for success. The book significantly expands existing scholarship on women in law within the African context across three dimensions: argument, theory, and terminology, as shown in **Figure 1.4.**

1. Theory

The book expands on earlier ideas of matri-legal feminist theory and a decolonial feminist approach to illustrate women's experiences within the legal system. It also presents the HISP framework to show the interconnected influences of history, institutions, and social systems on women's representation in legal professions across Africa. Ultimately, matri-legal feminism serves as a foundation for future research on women in law throughout the continent.

2. Argument

The book makes a significant contribution to the literature on women in law by outlining three main arguments in each chapter. First, *historical influences* shape *institutional rules and norms*, interacting with social *factors* that define women's legal roles. Second, detailed accounts of women's experiences show common patterns of resilience, personal agency, and a desire to succeed despite historical, institutional, and social obstacles. Third, the changing institutional rules, including constitutions, laws, and various frameworks that promote gender equality, have driven generational shifts toward creating a gender-inclusive environment for women in law within specific contexts.

3. Terminology

In establishing the context for studying women in law, the book introduces several key concepts. First, it distinguishes between *exclusionary and accommodationist perspectives on* women's acceptance in the legal professions, highlighting the inherent challenges of each stance. Second, it contrasts *gender norm conformists with gender norm disruptors from both institutional and social viewpoints* to show how different women navigate the complexities of social and institutional patriarchy. *Third, within the institutional framework, the book presents the concepts of women's other-bar (lawyers) and women's other-bench (judges)* as strategies women in law use to meet their unique needs within the profession. While these associations demonstrate women's agency, they also expose a deeper issue, suggesting that primary organizations are not fully addressing women's concerns. *Fourth, the book differentiates between workhorses and racehorses* to reveal a gendered pattern of labor and recognition. *The* dominance of women in the lower and middle ranks of law firms points to gendered organizational practices and cultures that favor male work ethics, leading to men being promoted faster than their female peers. Therefore, while women often serve as the *workhorses* of many large law firms, men are viewed as *racehorses* and traditionally have advantages when senior partners consider promotions, salary increases, and bonuses. The complexities of promotion decisions and the limitations within those processes are examined further in Chapter 4.

4. Periodization

To provide clear guidelines for the upcoming discussions in the substantive chapters, the book uses a generational framework to contextualize the rise of women in law within the formal legal professions across the continent. It emphasizes the term "formal" because, as Chapters 2 and 3 show, African communities had established justice, law, and dispute resolution systems before colonial rule began, with women playing important roles during this period. Since politics and the economy are closely linked as signs of the colonial enterprise's exploitative nature, the generational framework connects to the continent's political economy, divided into five phases. Each phase represents women's emergence in law as *pioneer women, second cohort, growth cohort, accelerator cohort, and expansionist cohort.* These phases are interconnected, as different countries experienced various developments within each of the five phases and the classification of the political economy.

Overall, the findings reaffirm that there is no single narrative for women in law—various historical, institutional, structural, and positional factors contribute to diverse experiences and outcomes. What unites these discussions is the central argument presented in this book: the nonessentialized accounts of women's lives in law reveal *intersecting* patterns of strength, personal agency, and determination to succeed despite historical, institutional, and social challenges. While addressing three major sectors in a single book is ambitious, the original intent was not to cover the entire continent of 54 nation-states. Additionally, limited access to longitudinal data on the demographics of lawyers, judges, and academics, along with the relatively sparse peer-reviewed research on African women in law, required constructing the data and arguments from the ground up. The various challenges faced during the 10 years of data collection and analysis for this work can be addressed by future studies that build on the foundation established here.

V. Structure and Plan of the Book

The book assesses the main argument of this project using a framework that allows for both within-sector and across-sector comparisons of variables in the HISP model. Building on this introductory chapter, Chapter 2 uses a historical–methodological approach to explore the origins of legal professions in selected African countries. Drawing heavily on existing research, the analyses in Chapter 2 highlight the historical roots of inherited legal professions and their influence on the profession's development and women's status. Additionally, Chapter 2 outlines the three theoretical frameworks that support the book: postcolonial feminism, intersectionality, and matri-legal feminism, and also discusses the methodology.

Chapter 3 provides an exhaustive overview of women in law, tracing the historical evolution of women's entry into the profession, their current demographic representation, and their contributions to law and justice. While centering the African woman's experiences, it connects with the global scholarship on women in law by drawing commonalities and differences to highlight global linkages among women in law.

The three substantive chapters on women in the professions are divided into three periods—first, middle, and last frontier—to illustrate the phases during which women entered the legal profession (bar) and how they advanced into the remaining two sectors—the bench and the legal academy. Chapter 4 is the first substantive chapter that covers women's entry into the profession and outlines the challenges (battles) women faced in entering a field traditionally considered to be the sole domain of men. It is from the bar, or becoming a lawyer, that women then move into other sectors of the profession, such as the bench and legal academia. The chapter offers a comprehensive overview of women's entry, representation, challenges, and contributions to law, justice, and the profession.

Chapter 5 is viewed as the second professional entry point or middle stage where women entered the legal field. As will be seen, the pioneer women magistrates often moved directly from law school to the magistracy, sometimes with only a few years of experience at the State Attorney's or Attorney General's office. In countries like Nigeria and Sierra Leone, the first women lawyers also became the first women magistrates and eventually the first women judges.

Chapter 6 explores the representation and influence of women in the legal academy. Although there has been progress in the number of women joining the legal academy, their numbers remain low compared to women in the first two sectors—the bar and bench—and reflect the broader trends and patterns of women entering higher education institutions as faculty. Each of the three substantive chapters begins by outlining women's entry into the profession and provides demographic information about women in the sector. Additionally, each chapter examines women's contributions, challenges, and strategies for success.

Chapter 7 examines the three substantive chapters by highlighting their similarities and differences across each sector. By creating a comparative narrative of women's shared experiences, the chapter provides a detailed discussion of the strategies women have used, both individually and collectively, to confront their challenges.

Chapter 8 takes readers back to the book's origins. Titled "Women in Law, Sankofa Futurisms, and Learning from the Past to Move Forward," this chapter revisits core themes and offers a forecast for women's representation in law across Africa. Despite historical policies of gender exclusion and segregation, like a phoenix rising, African women in law have challenged the intersection of colonial patriarchy and domestic gender norms to emerge and succeed in the legal profession, despite ongoing obstacles.

2

The Legal Profession in Africa: History, Theory, and Methods

I. Introduction

Major historical events have influenced the development of legal professions across Africa. Drawing on developments across various jurisdictions in sub-Saharan Africa, this chapter aims to provide a comprehensive overview that contextualizes how the legal profession has evolved. While offering a general synthesis of this evolution, the main goal is to highlight how historical and institutionalized racial- and gender-based exclusion practices have influenced women's emergence and experiences in the field.

By adopting a comparative historical approach that highlights similarities and differences between and within cases (Mahoney, 2004), the chapter examines the tensions embedded in the colonial machinery and how the law and legal professionals served as extensions of the colonial metropole—mainly as tools and agents of exploitation, extraction, and exclusion. Following independence from colonial rule, these harmful practices were later adopted by the newly emergent governments, which, often confronted by growing economic hardships and citizen demands for their economic, social, civil, and political rights, reverted to the colonial administration's strategies of violence as a means of social control (Adewoye,1982a; Luckham, 1981). These practices would divide lawyers, judges, and academics into several camps, marked by the obvious fault lines between those who supported the autocratic state and those who opposed the excesses of state control (Kapinga,1992). Lawyers and judges opposing the autocratic state machinery faced violent purging, while those who supported these governments benefited from their subservience to authority (Mutua, 2001; VonDoepp, 2013).

The chapter further demonstrates that the legal profession has been in constant change due to efforts to regulate it, sometimes marked by executive overreach in setting the regulatory frameworks. Some of these frameworks—such as expanding educational training, introducing legal clinics, and standardizing the processes for becoming a lawyer, judge, or legal academic—have gendered impacts that are often overlooked during rule formulation; these impacts are examined in the following detailed chapters. Section II provides a brief overview of precolonial forms of law and justice in Africa, arguing that the "legal profession," defined by its actors, systems, procedures, and regulatory processes, existed before colonization. Section III traces the evolution of the legal profession across Africa, analyzing the effect of early educational policies on access to legal education and careers. Finally, section IV discusses the theoretical and methodological foundations underlying the book.

African Women in Law. J. Jarpa Dawuni, Oxford University Press. © Oxford University Press 2026.
DOI: 10.1093/9780197795095.003.0002

II. Law and Justice in Precolonial Africa

Africa had a rich history before colonial powers took control, leading to the systematic erasure and rewriting of its history, cultures, and legal systems. Legal and judicial systems, later called customary or native law, were in place to regulate morality, law, justice, and order (Mamdani, 2018). Ideas of justice, law, and order were rooted in morality and traditional beliefs heavily shaped by religion. Although laws were man-made, they mostly came from beliefs in deities, and this strong link to religion meant that a higher authority governed society through humans.

Precolonial justice systems were mainly based on consensual participation. For example, in the Igbo justice system in Nigeria, Elechi (2008) argues that law violations were not seen as offenses against individuals (victims) but rather as crimes against society. The accused was considered to be disrupting social and community harmony, and the best way to restore this harmony was through reparation instead of punishment, comparing punishing the accused with rewarding and restituting the victim (and society) and rehabilitating the accused. This highlights the importance of community peace. The desire for restoration across communities is clear in the principles of ubuntu (in South Africa) and utu (among Eastern African communities), which emphasize community and belonging. These principles laid the foundation for adopting restorative justice, which gained worldwide recognition during South Africa's Truth and Reconciliation Commission after apartheid (Kinyanjui, 2009), as well as in the Sierra Leone criminal tribunals, the Rwandan *gacaca* courts after the genocide, and more recently in Gambia's reconciliation following the removal of dictator Yahya Jammeh. The debates about African diverse legal systems—whether concepts of justice existed before colonial contact and whether the roles of "judges" and "lawyers" in Africa were introduced through colonization—have long been scrutinized (Mamdani, 2018).

How were these ideas of justice managed? Who were the enforcement agents, and what roles did the different actors play? Drawing on Indigenous precolonial legal practices, Inameti (2013) classifies the king or chief as the ultimate arbiter of law—both lawmaker and enforcer. The distribution of legislative and judicial powers is shared among the king or chief, his council of advisers, and subchiefs. The king and chiefs acted as traditional judges, and this division of power created a hierarchy that allowed for different levels of appeals, similar to today's court and judicial systems. These judicial hearings for crimes, whether criminal or civil, were open to public participation, and the sites of judicial hearings could be anywhere, including the chief's compound, under trees, or other public places where the crimes took place (Freddie & Koketso, 2013).

In exploring criminal justice in West Africa, Dalgleish (2005) examines the complex connections between economic, judicial, and religious powers in the Songhai Empire, a kingdom that included modern-day Senegal, Gambia, Mali, and Guinea-Bissau. The king appointed judicial officers, often religious leaders, who had the authority to resolve disputes and issue judgments. While the king and chiefs served as judicial figures, both the accused and victims had legal representation; they could either represent themselves or have a family member present their case. These "traditional" lawyers sometimes represented more than one person, which led to the development of the role of defense counsel. Legal rules based on religion and morality were overseen by the chief or king, who was responsible for ensuring justice was fairly administered to community members (Ojo & Ekhator, 2020). Later, colonial authorities used these "traditional lawyers" to create what they called "native" courts for case adjudication, exercising control over society to support the colonial agenda. As Adewoye (1982a) notes, these "native courts" were managed by a group of indigenous "lawyers" derogatorily called "bush lawyers" by the colonial enterprise.

These individuals were not trained in Western legal institutions. However, they had developed the art and skill of judging cases, drawing mainly on precolonial legal and judicial systems that existed before colonial rule. The passage of discriminatory laws that undermined traditional customs, practices, and forms of governance through "repugnancy clauses," along with segregation policies, were tactics used by colonial administrators to reduce the influence of traditional authority, law, and justice (Mamdani, 2018). Traditional judges (chiefs) and lawyers (the accused or their representatives) were bound by the norms of court procedures and evidence rules upheld within their communities or ethnic groups. Victims and perpetrators had rights, including the right to appear, be heard, call witnesses, present evidence, and plead for mercy. The severity and type of punishment depended on several factors, such as the evidence presented and the impact of the alleged crime on social harmony. As a result, Novak (2018) concluded that the death sentence, regarded as the ultimate punishment, was rarely imposed.

What roles did women play in precolonial justice and legal systems? Did the same laws equally bind women, and did they have the same rights as men? Could women serve as legal actors—such as traditional judges and lawyers? Exploring the power of women in precolonial African societies, Ogbomo (2005) notes that women held varying levels of political, economic, and religious power, which enabled them to play vital roles in enforcing justice, law, and morality. These powers differed across communities, ethnic groups, and nations, with specific restrictions on what women could or could not do in different contexts. While recognizing the presence of patriarchy and power hierarchies, Ogbomo (2005) concludes that women often acted as influential intermediaries in criminal justice enforcement mechanisms. Drawing from traditional roles of women in justice and administration, Diye (2022) examines the significant roles women played among the Podogo of Cameroon in dispute resolution, which was sometimes intertwined with religious or spiritual beliefs surrounding the head woman/chief, who possessed mystical religious powers. Thus, in such communities, the rights and powers of women as leaders were closely connected to the religious or spiritual realm—the legal authority was ultimately derived from the super deity, rather than being a strictly gendered construct.

Evaluating the complex power of women in customary law, Ndulo (2011) noted that, despite women's inherent power in various communities, laws were often gender-biased and frequently disadvantaged women's rights in social, economic, customary, and political contexts. Women in precolonial African societies were both creators and recipients of the law, actively engaging in legal systems. African feminist scholars (Achebe, 2020; Day, 2020) have extensively documented women's roles as legal and political leaders, such as chiefs and queens. Women's participation in dispute resolution shows they served as traditional judges in various courts (Obiora,

2020; Weeks, 2022). Moreover, women acted as traditional legal advocates, defending their own rights or those of others—often children—during judicial proceedings. While Ndulo (2011) states that women's rights were generally subordinate to men's rights, this view reflects the situation of women's rights in Western societies during the colonial period. It also continues to mirror the current global situation, where women are still fighting for fundamental rights. Though this discussion is not intended to be comparative, it is important to emphasize that African laws and judicial systems are not the only systems that discriminate against women.

The preceding discussion shows that precolonial African systems had a legal "profession"—characterized by laws, actors, systems, and processes similar to those in modern legal systems and professions. The examples provided demonstrate that precolonial African polities maintained strong and diverse justice systems, shaped by various structures, sources of law, and actors. Women held positions of authority; although their rights and powers might have been limited in some cases, matri-legal feminist theory suggests that the rise of women in modern African legal systems and professions can be traced back to precolonial ideas and realities regarding women's roles in law, rights, and justice.

III. Development of the Legal Professions Across Africa

This section explores two main pillars of the HISP (history, institutions, social systems, and position) framework—the historical and the institutional—by assessing how these factors influenced the development, structure, and practices of the legal profession across much of sub-Saharan Africa. A closer look at these developments reveals how the intersection of colonial-era race policies and postcolonial gendered institutional policies shapes women's roles in law. The history, practices, and regulations of the legal profession has long been a focus for sociolegal scholars. The sociology of law and lawyering has generated extensive research, with some works focusing on the legal profession by examining how lawyers are trained and what their job involves (Abel et al., 2020; Abel & Lewis, 1995). Other studies have investigated how professional regulations impact the roles and responsibilities of lawyers (Abdullahi, 2017; Dezalay & Garth, 2021; Fong et al., 2019; Lumumba, 2014; Wilkins, 1992).

In recent years, scholarly focus has shifted to the impacts of neoliberalism and globalization on educational models, the worldwide spread of legal practices, and the tensions between the dominant influence of American legal education (Bartie & Sandomierski, 2021) and the rise of global legal fields and superpowers in China (Fong et al., 2019) and India (Khanna et al., 2017). Amid these major developments, other scholars have highlighted the ongoing inequality within the legal profession in key markets like the United States (Nelson et al., 2023). Most of these studies concentrate on legal professions in the Global North. For instance, some foundational comparative studies on lawyers by Abel and Lewis (1989, 1995) did not include any African jurisdictions. Later efforts aimed to address this gap through an expanded two-part series published in 2020, which featured four cases from Africa: Burundi, Nigeria, Zimbabwe, and South Africa (Abel et al., 2020). As a result, research on the legal profession in the Global North has largely shaped the sociology of law and legal professions. Some of this work has explored the colonial legacies linking the metropole and formerly colonized nations without addressing the racialized and gendered experiences of lawyers in these regions (Abel & Lewis, 1988; Dezalay, 2020; Dias et al., 1981).

Legal systems have been adopted worldwide due to various factors, including colonization, legal education, and the law and development movements of the 1980s (Bartie & Sandomieski, 2021). In many cases, these imported legal systems were never meant to promote the rights of indigenous inhabitants (Ghai & McAuslan, 1970; Gower, 2014; Mann & Roberts, 1991), grant rights to indigenous peoples (Mamdani, 2018), or introduce legal education (Madlalate, 2022; Oloka-Onyango, 2021; Tshuma, 1991). The transplantation of legal traditions and laws significantly changed existing legal and justice systems by redefining and reshaping the legal status of individuals and groups. In several African countries, such changes included the infantilization of women, often reducing them to the property of their husbands, which contradicted customary practices that viewed marriage as a union between families (Roberts, 2013). The colonial discriminatory systems created classifications of individuals with different rights and privileges, erasing elements of several pre-colonial structures that fostered cohesive community living and recognized women's rights as leaders in political, social, religious, and economic decision-making (Oyewumi, 1997).

Colonial laws and legal systems were thus used for social, political, and economic control. Colonial laws and policies focused on extraction, exploitation, and exclusion to shape society, including redefining gender roles, and served as a tool of extraction by regulating how systems operated to promote colonial interests. In all these uses and abuses of law, women were often marginalized, erased, and controlled by these laws and policies (Banda, 2005; Ndulo, 2011). It was through this combination of imperial patriarchal control and customary gender-discriminatory norms that the legal professions across Africa developed.

1. The Accidental Emergence of Legal Education

The development of legal professions across much of the continent was unintentional and unplanned. The legal and educational systems were subsequently modeled after those of the colonizing countries, including French and Portuguese civil law and Great Britain's common law (Murphy, 1991). Although the introduction of these foreign laws and legal systems created a diversity of laws, the customary and religious laws that governed most citizens' lives in the colonies were given lower priority by colonial administrators, who focused instead on the foreign colonial laws (Ghai, 1987).

Inspired by earlier experiences in India—another British colony—the colonial policy of not establishing higher education institutions and law schools in African colonies stemmed from the fear that lawyers would push for civil and political rights, which could lead to independence movements (Adewoye, 1982a; Dias et al., 1981; Ghai, 1981; Harvey, 1966; Luckham, 1981). As a result, by the late 20th century, Burgis-Kasthala (2022, pp. 129–130), citing Samoff and Carrol (2004, p. 77), states: "In 1950 out of thirty-four countries, only eleven had a university, yet by 1962, twenty-eight did. Over the same period, university numbers tripled from sixteen to forty-one along with a 600 percent increase in student enrollments."

In East Africa, Ghai (1987, p. 752) noted similar dismal numbers of lawyers:

> In 1960, for example, there was only one African lawyer in Tanganyika (as it was then known); only 10 out of 300 qualified lawyers in Kenya were African, while in Uganda the figures were 20 out of 150. In West Africa there were 1300 African lawyers.

Similar developments occurred in other southern African countries, including Zambia, Malawi, Botswana, and Namibia, all of which were affected by apartheid in South Africa, sharing the common feature of a late emergence of Black lawyers (Karekwaivanane, 2016; Madlalate, 2022; Tshuma, 1991). In Zimbabwe, as in several other African nations, law was not taught at the university level until the introduction of the Bachelor of Laws (LL.B.) degree through the University of London. The formal establishment of legal education in Zimbabwe began in 1968 with the introduction of a postgraduate diploma that led to qualification as an attorney. After several changes since 1981, Zimbabwean legal education eliminated the distinction between attorneys and advocates (Karekwaivanane, 2020). Except for South Africa, which has maintained the British distinction between barristers and solicitors (known as advocates and attorneys in South Africa), nearly all jurisdictions across the continent have unified the legal profession.

The colonial enterprise strongly opposed the creation of law schools, often using racialized explanations for why Blacks could not pursue law degrees. In Zimbabwe, these racialized experiences led Tshuma (1991, p. 172) to conclude:

> To justify their imagined superiority over Blacks, Rhodesian settlers went out of their way to prove that Blacks were incapable of achieving what Whites could achieve. It comes as no surprise that at independence, very few Blacks had managed to make it through the Department of Law. Very few survived the alienation, humiliation and racial prejudice that was the order of the day.

Faced with a limited number of lawyers trained in the metropolis, the British colonial administration established the Denning Committee to advise on the development of legal education in the colonies. While the Denning Report focused its recommendations on producing indigenous and locally trained lawyers who understood the context of their countries, legal education soon became a site of experimentation (Ghai, 1987). From the beginning of legal education, influences from the British, French, and American legal educational systems were integrated into the practical approaches favored by Denning and early independence leaders such as Kwame Nkrumah of Ghana, Julius Nyerere of Tanzania, and Kenneth Kaunda of Zambia (Ghai, 1987). Ghana led the way in establishing legal education with the law faculty at the University of Ghana in 1958 and the Ghana School of Law (for practical training before call to the bar) in 1959 (Harvey, 1966).

In 1960, Lord Denning chaired a committee tasked with reviewing the legal education of Africans in the United Kingdom. Among other significant findings, the report noted the need for training lawyers who could perform important administrative and bureaucratic tasks once these countries transitioned from colonial rule. In East Africa, the Denning Report of the Committee on Legal Education for Students from Africa recommended establishing a single law school for the region, which was initially known as the University of East Africa. Later, the University of East Africa led to the creation of the Faculty of Law at the University of Dar es Salaam in 1961, followed by the University of Nairobi in Kenya and Makerere University in Uganda (Ghai, 1987).

Many of the pioneering lawyers from Tanzania, Kenya, and Uganda graduated from the University in Dar es Salaam. Similar committees were formed in other regions, including the Hughes Parry Report of 1951, which recommended establishing a law faculty in Ghana, and the Unsworth Report, which advised creating law faculties in Nigeria (Adewoye, 1982a; Harvey, 1966). When these countries gained independence from colonial rule, several lacked institutions to train legal professionals. Lawyers educated in the common-law system in Great Britain had limited practical experience applying customary laws (Adewoye, 1969). Newly independent governments, needing qualified and politically aware lawyers, took various measures to address the gap left by colonial administrators. In Ghana, this involved establishing the first law faculty at the University of Ghana in 1958 and transforming the existing program linked to the University College of London into a full law faculty (Dawuni, 2021b). In Zimbabwe, after gaining independence from British control in 1980, the new government faced decades of racial segregation policies that characterized Rhodesian settler practices and barred Blacks from education. In Zambia, Zimbabwe, and Malawi, there were no Black-trained lawyers before independence. After independence, Zimbabwe's government temporarily allowed lawyers who qualified abroad without practical training in Zimbabwe to practice until 1985. This temporary opportunity for lawyers soon changed, as the legal profession established the Legal Practitioners Act (1981) to regulate the field (Karekwaivanane, 2016).

In tracing the evolution of the legal profession in East Africa (Kenya, Uganda, and Tanzania) and West Africa (Ghana and Nigeria), Ghai (1987) explains how different colonial extractive policies delayed the emergence of lawyers. In East Africa, the colonial administration focused on using migrant labor, mainly from India, for administrative work, while East African citizens were exploited for plantation-based production. Under this exploitative labor system, no scholarships were offered to train Africans abroad in law. However, the West African coast was different, as peasant farming allowed native Africans to control access to land and the means of production, enabling them to fund their children's education abroad. In West Africa, lawyers could also work in rural areas, applying customary laws related to land. With the gradual domestic training of lawyers, a group of legal practitioners emerged who had better access to citizens. These lawyers were sensitive to the operations of unjust capitalist land exploitation by colonial administrators. Their involvement in fighting illegal land grabbing by colonial enterprises fostered a vibrant legal market for lawyers (Dias et al., 1981; Luckham, 1976). In both East and West Africa, the rise of lawyers posed a significant challenge to colonial policies, reaffirming the colonial administration's initial fear of not establishing institutions for legal training.

Realizing the erosion of their control over law and justice, colonial administrators made sure that the newly emerging African lawyers were not fully integrated into the legal practices and associations regulating the profession. Later, in countries such as Kenya, Tanzania, Ghana, South Africa, and Zimbabwe, what different scholars called the "Black Bar" appeared—a separate group of Indigenous lawyers working alongside the colonial lawyers (Adewoye, 1982a; Ghai, 1987; Harvey, 1963; Karekwaivanane, 2015). These racial exclusions boosted the demand for more locally trained lawyers. A new movement to establish law schools quickly emerged alongside the push for independence from colonial rule. As the first law faculty established in sub-Saharan Africa, the University of Ghana saw President Kwame Nkrumah strongly emphasize the importance of legal education. Nkrumah's vision was motivated by the need for lawyers who could advance both national and Pan-African development agendas.

> Our lawyers, therefore, if they are to understand the spirit of our laws, must understand the basic principles upon which the state is directed and why certain laws are enacted, repealed or amended by Parliament. The teaching of law is totally incomplete if it is not accompanied by a background of economic, social and political science, and even politics, science and technology. (Nkrumah 1962, p. 103)

It was this combination of developments and the need for lawyers in different countries under various colonial administrations that led to the founding of the first faculties and schools of law across Africa, as shown in **Table 2.1.**

Across sub-Saharan Africa, the gradual move to establish law schools and faculties required significant resource investments, provided by newly independent governments, former colonial powers, and philanthropic organizations. At first glance, this renewed focus on supporting legal education appeared to be a good plan, but beneath the surface of generosity lay intentional efforts to influence and transplant the legal systems and educational practices of the investing countries (Dawuni & Badejogbin, 2021). A thorough review by Krishnan (2012) highlights how colonial governments strategically positioned themselves by consolidating control over legal practices through investments in scholarships, research funding, and the recruitment of academics to teach in the countries receiving these investments. Despite these efforts, major challenges persisted in legal education and the type of lawyers being produced, due to the disconnect between imported legal principles and the practical issues often rooted in customary laws and practices (Ghai, 1987; Manteaw, 2008; Ndulo, 2011; Oloka-Onyango, 2021).

In this emerging legal academy, the impact on women was even more significant, affecting all social, political, and administrative spheres. As Nnaemeka (1994: 139) notes, "The sexual politics and Victorian ideals of colonial education created a hierarchy privileging men by virtually erasing any meaningful female presence." A review of the existing literature on efforts to establish legal education, the training of emerging lawyers in the metropolis, and the tensions between lawyers and the colonial enterprise remains silent on the role of women. This is not surprising, given the poor records of colonizing countries regarding women's participation in professional and public life.

Oloka-Onyango and Tamala's (2000, p. 3) poignant observation of women's entry into higher education institutions highlights endemic colonial practices of that era, with lasting negative effects.

Table 2.1 *List of Law Schools and Dates of Establishment*

Country	Year of independence	First law faculty	Year established	First law school	Year established
South Africa	1910	Faculty of Law, University of Cape Town	1859	Wilfred and Jules Kramer Law School	1859
Ghana	1957	Kwame Nkrumah	1958	Ghana School of Law	1959
Nigeria	1960	Faculty of Law, Enugu Campus	1960	Nigerian Law School	1962
Senegal	1960	Faculty of Law, Cheikh Anta Diop, Dakar	1957	Senegal Law School	1957
Ivory Coast	1960	Faculty of Law, Pigier Côte d'Ivoire	1956	Pigier School of Law and Jurisprudence	1956
Tanzania	1961	University College of Dar-es-Salaam	1961	Dar-es-Salaam School of Law	1961
Rwanda	1962	Faculty of Law, Kigali Independent University	2001	Kigali School of Law	2001
Uganda	1962	Faculty of Law, Makerere University	1973	Makerere School of Law	2011
Kenya	1963	Faculty of Law, University of Nairobi	1970	Parklands Campus	1970
Zambia	1964	Faculty of Law, University of Zambia	1967	Zambian School of Law	1967
Malawi	1964	Faculty of Law, University of Malawi	1970	Chancellor College	1970
Gambia	1965	University of Gambia Faculty of Law	2007	Gambian Law School	2007
Botswana	1966	Gaborone University College of Law and Professional Studies	2006	Gaborone University College of Law and Professional Studies	2006
Cape Verde	1975	Faculty of Law, Universidade de Mindelo	2002	Mindelo Law School	2002
Zimbabwe	1980	Faculty of Law, Midlands State University	2007	Midlands State Law School	2007

Note. The countries are arranged chronologically by year of political independence.

Source: The data in this table were collected from the institutions' websites. While all efforts were made to verify the dates, some institutions have multiple listed dates. The author chose the most recurring date. Most of these institutions have undergone different phases, including rebranding and renaming from the Faculty of Law to the School of Law.

> The concept of academic freedom itself has not been free of gender bias, particularly since women have not only been discriminated against in access to institutions of learning but also with regard to what they can study and research. This basis of such an insidious demarcation is deeply rooted in the colonial history of our continent. Women in Africa (as is the case the world over) generally entered academics later than their male counterparts. A systemic and deliberate colonial policy ensured that African women were excluded from the various 'ivory towers' that dotted the continent.

Across several colonizing cities in France, the United Kingdom, Portugal, and the United States, women continued fighting for recognition as equals to their male counterparts. While women gained access to legal education and professions much earlier than their counterparts in Africa, those in the global north were still working toward full integration (Schultz & Shaw, 2013). Therefore, this overview of the development of legal education in much of Africa shows that women faced dual exclusion from the profession—first, because of racial segregation, and second, because of gender-based discrimination both at home and abroad.

2. Lawyers, the Colonial Enterprise, and State Relations

The previous discussions highlight the historical context of a racially and gender-segregated legal education system from which lawyers across Africa emerged. Over time, these emerging lawyers evolved into different roles. Some served as facilitators and intermediaries between the colonial enterprise and the new states, while others aligned with the new states and their citizens, advocating for the rights and dignity of the colonized people. With the advent of independence, lawyers have played crucial roles as statesmen during the political development of these new nations. From colonial autocracy to post-independence state-building, political resistance against autocratic one-party states, and military dictatorships leading up to the start of democratization in the early 1990s, lawyers have been at the forefront of regulating state–society relations (Edsman, 1979; Harvey, 1966; Kapinga, 1992; Karekwaivanane, 2017; Oguamanam & Pue, 2007; Ojo, 1987; Oko, 1997; Prempeh, 2007). In South Africa, the limited number of Black lawyers—Henry Sylvester Williams, Alfred Mangena, Ngcubu Poswayo, George Montsioa, Nelson Mandela, and Oliver Tambo—were trained in South Africa and played significant roles in the struggles against apartheid (Ngcukaitobi, 2018).

Despite being victims of discriminatory colonial policies, many of the new lawyers became influential intermediaries and supporters of the colonial enterprise. From the beginning, the law and the legal profession were not designed for the Indigenous inhabitants of the colonies. The law operated within a framework of conflicting tensions, promoting civil rights only when it benefited the colonial agenda (Mamdani, 2018; Oguamanam & Pue, 2007). Lawyers—mostly white, with some Black male lawyers—primarily worked to advance the business interests of various traders along the coast and to support the colonial goals of the metropole (Adewoye, 1982a; Dezalay, 2017). Since the establishment of the profession in much of sub-Saharan

Africa, the role of lawyers has been to serve the state, thus giving the colonial government the legal legitimacy for its actions and decisions (Dias et al., 1981; Ghai & McAuslan, 1970; Gower, 2014).

Since most early lawyers were trained in the colonial metropole, they understood the law as it was passed down to them and often returned to their home countries as extensions of the colonial enterprise. Their social class and status were elevated, granting them privileges that only a few could attain, which put them in a compromised position to carry out the will of the colonial enterprise (Adewoye, 1982a; Dezalay, 2017; Karekwaivanane, 2015). However, not all lawyers accepted this elevated status; for many, what they learned about the law in the metropole—law as a tool for universal democratization and the protection of individual rights and freedoms—was not reflected in the colonies. The law as practiced in the British colonies served to oppress citizens' rights, suppress indigenous laws, and extract resources and rents from chiefs and the people (Mann & Roberts, 1991). Several lawyers began advocating for the rights they had been taught in the colonies. Their demands for decolonizing legal, administrative, and bureaucratic structures included granting legal, political, social, and civil rights. This group of lawyers formed the anticolonial lawyers' brigade, advocating for self-rule and citizens' rights (Gower, 2014; Harvey, 1963; Karekwaivanane, 2015).

These anticolonial lawyers formed alliances to demand equal rights for citizens. For them, the arbitrary distinction between citizens—those with legal rights—and subjects—those governed by legal rights—was no longer acceptable (Dias et al., 1981; Ghai & McAuslan, 1970; Mamdani, 2018). Challenging the simple story of colonialism, Mamdani (2018) traces the effects of the colonial division between *citizens* under colonial laws and *subjects* governed by customary laws, what British colonial administrators called the "Native Authorities." This division created tensions that still influence the judicial and legal systems of many postcolonial African countries today. Lawyers (primarily white) played a key role in creating oppressive colonial policies, which were formalized through laws and enforced by agents of the colonial system, including lawyers, judges, and police. The colonial suppression of Indigenous citizens' rights did not automatically lead to postcolonial reforms or justice—it was a struggle led by an expanding alliance of anticolonial lawyers, politicians, and social movement leaders (Adewoye, 1982a; Dias et al., 1981; Ghai & McAuslan, 1970; Luckham, 1981; Rwelamira, 1981; Salman, 1981).

Efforts to rapidly transform the legal profession to meet the needs of the newly independent states led to the implementation of "Africanization" in Zimbabwe and Kenya (Kamau, 2020; Karekwaivanane, 2015) and "indigenization" initiatives in Ghana (Dawuni, 2021b). The legal community played a crucial role, often acting as intermediaries between the colonial system and the newly independent states by negotiating an end to colonial rule. In other cases, the legal sector served as a mediator between the new government and its citizens as the new administrations aimed to develop new understandings of the law's role as a tool for social change while emphasizing social cohesion (Dias et al., 1981; Ghai & McAuslan, 1970; Harvey, 1962; Kapinga, 1992). Revolutionary post-independence leaders such as Kwame Nkrumah of Ghana, Julius Nyerere of Tanzania, and Leopold Sedar Senghor of Senegal made it their goal to quickly break away from the colonial legacies that had shaped African nations for centuries. Despite the best intentions and revolutionary goals of these efforts, isolating

countries and an entire continent already deeply entrenched in the capitalist system of exploitation and extraction proved nearly impossible (Luckham, 1981). Years later, the challenges of reforming legal education systems and the legal profession continue to resonate across various parts of the continent (Bonnin, 2019; Kamau, 2020; Klaaren, 2020; Madlalate, 2022; Manteaw, 2008; Ndulo, 2002).

Fast forward from the early postcolonial era into the democratization phase, and lawyers played essential roles at various stages of political development in African states. In the postdemocratic period, lawyers were crucial in helping implement the transformative development agenda of the newly independent nations (Adewoye, 1982a; Ghai & McAuslan, 1970; Kapinga, 1992; Karekwaivanane, 2015; Rwelamira, 1981; Salman, 1981). Over time, the lingering effects of colonial policies became evident—an unprepared civil service, a predominantly uneducated population, and the law being used as a tool of oppression for social control—leading to weaknesses in the enforcement of civil and political rights. In efforts to better control the growing populations and address social and economic underdevelopment challenges, many governments adopted autocratic control methods (Okoth-Ogendo, 1988; Widner, 2001). The violation of civil and political rights through illegal activities, such as the unlawful seizure of communal lands, which had been common under colonial administrations, continued, and lawyers often found themselves at the center of legal conflicts (Adewoye, 1982b; Ghai & McAuslan, 1970; Harvey, 1963).

Legislatures were often co-opted and turned into tools that merely rubber-stamped the wishes of the executive. Parliaments were used to pass laws and legislation that infringe on citizens' rights (Fombad, 2011; Prempeh, 2007; Shomade, 2022). The co-optation of judiciaries to serve the interests of the executive became common in many African countries, shattering the post-independence hope for multiparty democratic states. These countries quickly fell into one-party autocracies, using the state's apparatus to tightly control social and political life, just as the colonial administration had done (Ghai, 1981; Mutua, 2001).

These autocratic tendencies caused divisions within the legal profession, splitting it into pro-government and antigovernment factions. Several lawyers aligned themselves with autocratic regimes, assisting these governments in enforcing restrictive laws on their citizens. Some judges were effectively co-opted to interpret laws that supported the oppressive state's agenda (Gathii, 1994; Ross, 1992). Antigovernment lawyers and judges advocated for justice and acted as strong mediators between the state and the people, utilizing legal and judicial tools to uphold the rule of law (Karekwaivanane, 2015; Widner, 2001). Others served as intermediaries between the law and the state, working to enforce justice and protect equality for the communities they represented (Karekwaivanane, 2015). The legal academy also became a battleground for political tensions and conflicts. Legal scholars who taught from a human rights perspective and exposed the oppressive nature of state actions often faced intimidation and were detained without trial. Many were forced into exile (Harrington & Manji, 2021b; Kapinga, 1992).

Between 1960 and 1990, during the period of authoritarian military dictatorships in much of West Africa, judiciaries in several African countries gained notoriety as extensions of executive power. Many analysts saw the judiciary as obeying the will of the executive rather than protecting the rule of law. The co-optation of large parts of the judiciary benefited many judges who acted as instruments of executive control, while those who opposed could easily be framed and removed from their positions (Gathii, 1994; Mutua, 2001; Odenyo, 1979). This simple division of pro- and anti-government factions was not the only way to describe the profession, however; many other factions and groups existed between these two main divisions.

Successive military dictatorships quickly became the norm in political development, often resulting from coup d'états supported by foreign governments and allies. Law and order, good governance, the rule of law, and the protection of citizens' rights fell into neglect (Fombad, 2011; Okoth-Ogendo, 1988; Oloka-Onyango, 2017; Prempeh, 2007). In some countries, the legal profession, represented by the Bar Association or Law Society, made steadfast efforts to be the voice of hope, often leading to the imprisonment of their leaders, such as Sam Okudzeto of Ghana (Okudzeto, 2018), Willy Mutunga of Kenya (Kang'ara et al., 2021), and Orton and Vera Chirwa of Malawi (Chirwa, 2007; Ross, 1992).

Recognizing the important role of bar associations in promoting public advocacy for civil and political rights, governments often infiltrated the leadership of these organizations. In Ghana, despite initial support from Kwame Nkrumah in establishing a legal profession aimed at encouraging national development, the latter part of his term was overshadowed by one-party state politics, leading to tensions with the legal profession. In response to these tensions, the Ghana Bar Association decided not to hold any formal meetings or elections that could have resulted in the election of an executive board sympathetic to the Nkrumah government (Luckham, 1981, p. 115). In Nigeria, the conflicts within the Nigerian Bar Association during the 1992 elections for the bar executive illustrate how governments infiltrate the leadership of bar associations that oppose their dictatorial tendencies (Ajayi, 2017). Similar oppressive control tactics were used against judges who issued rulings challenging the powers of the executive in Zimbabwe (Karekwaivanane, 2015), Kenya (Gathii, 1994; Ghai, 1981; Odenyo, 1979), and Tanzania (Widner, 2001).

Since the 1990s, several African countries have moved toward different forms of democratic governance (Shomade, 2022). While some of these governments display traits of illiberal and semiauthoritarian democracies (Oloka-Onyango, 2021; VonDoep, 2013), many focus on strengthening democracy. In this context, lawyers remain vital, with many parliamentary seats held by legal professionals. This period also experienced economic growth, and some lawyers have used state power for personal financial gain. However, challenges within the legal and judicial professions persist in various forms. In South Africa, efforts have been made to reform the legal and judicial sectors to address significant inequalities in the representation of Black South Africans in these fields (Klaaren, 2020; Madlalate, 2022). Still, the racial transformation agenda has faced criticism for overshadowing the importance of gender transformation and for promoting equitable and inclusive professional institutions both at the bar and on the bench (Albethyn & Bonthuys, 2016; Masengu, 2015; Mocumie, 2022; Sasinsky, 2020). Despite the move toward democracy, lawyers across different jurisdictions continue to face major challenges in their efforts to support democratic governance, including ongoing insecurity, widespread corruption, poorly managed public institutions, and declining standards of democratic and legal ethics (Lumumba, 2014; Oko, 2008).

3. Legal Institutional Frameworks and Professional Regulatory Practices

Tracing the regulation of legal professions in common- and civil-law countries, Hammerslev and Sommerlad (2020, p. 4) distinguished between regulation based on who may qualify as a lawyer (entry regulation) and regulation based on the functions and institutional practices of the profession (functional regulation). In common-law countries, the legal profession appears to have higher levels of regulatory independence, while in civil-law countries, the bureaucratic model of the profession means that the government has more control over the entry and functional regulations of lawyers and the judiciary (Abel & Lewis, 1989).

Across Africa, different political eras have created unique opportunities and challenges for legal professionals. Depending on the political period, lawyers have faced varying institutional rules, norms, and practices. These regulations may be lifted or enforced based on the preferences of the current government. For example, when regulations were needed to support the colonial system, formal qualifications for lawyers were not strictly enforced, and individuals with legal knowledge were organized into the "Native Authorities and Bodies" as "bush lawyers" (Adewoye, 1982b). In South Africa and much of southern Africa—Zambia, Malawi, and Zimbabwe—the legal profession was tightly controlled to prevent Black individuals from becoming lawyers, and the few who did were not allowed to serve as advocates—the more prestigious position (Chanock, 1985; Madlalate, 2022; Odenyo, 1979; Tshuma, 1991).

Similar patterns of regulatory trends appeared across East and West Africa. In Kenya, a former British settler colony, the social class structure established by the colonial administration favored white lawyers and Asian migrant communities over native Black citizens (Ghai & McAuslan, 1970). In several countries, the regulation of legal professions dates back to the colonial era, even though these associations were not formalized and included only men. For example, the Gold Coast Bar, a precursor to the Ghana Bar, was established in 1904 in the United Kingdom (Luckham, 1981). The composition of the regulatory bodies of various associations and societies was formalized after independence, adopting either the term "Bar Associations" (mainly used in West Africa) or "Law Societies" (primarily used in eastern and southern Africa). The Law Society of Kenya was created by an Ordinance in 1948, which was repealed in 1992 and replaced by the Law Society Act of 2014 (Kamau, 2020). In Ghana, however, the Ghana Bar Association was formalized in 1958; prior to that, it operated as an informal gathering of "gentlemen at the bar" with no formal structure, officers, or internal regulatory instruments (Harvey, 1963).

Across the continent, the legal and judicial professions are governed by various rules, including Acts passed by Parliament, statutory instruments, regulations, and other professional guidelines. Most of these regulatory systems are not as effective as they were intended to be. The decline in legal education standards has been blamed for the drop in ethical standards among professionals, further worsened by increased bribery, taking shortcuts to legal solutions, and a general sense of protectionism among lawyers and judges (Kamau, 2020; Karekwaivanane, 2020; Klaaren, 2020). In Nigeria, Abdullahi (2017) concludes that the legal profession suffers from a "brother's keeper syndrome," where legal practitioners and judges cover for each other's misconduct.

Although nearly all legal and judicial professions are overseen by regulatory bodies, codes, and enforcement committees, the enforcement of operational rules for professional regulation has been ineffective. Proper oversight of these bodies will be vital for the survival of the legal profession (Ghai & Ghai, 2014; Kameri-Mbote, 2014). While pioneering lawyers and judges have observed the decline in professional regulation and ethical standards, gender-based discrimination in the legal and judicial fields has not received as much attention in mainstream discussions and scholarship. These topics will be further explored in the upcoming chapters. Efforts to improve standards in the legal professions across countries include integrating law clinics into curricula to provide practical training for aspiring lawyers. The establishment of Judicial Training Institutes and Institutes for Advanced Legal Studies has also been pursued as measures to provide essential training to strengthen legal and judicial professions (Manteaw, 2008; Masabo, 2021; Ndulo, 2002; Rukuba-Ngaiza, 2021). While most of these clinics and institutes focus on various areas of law, many do not offer curricula specifically centered on women and gender issues within the professions.

IV. Studying African Women in Law: Theories and Methods

This section thoroughly examines the foundational theoretical and methodological frameworks that support this project. Evaluating women, law, and gender requires interdisciplinary theoretical frameworks. From a feminist perspective, women's lived experiences differ from those of men and other gender identities, making it essential to apply an intersectional gender lens. Women's experiences in law across Africa cannot be grouped into a single explanation, and no single theoretical framework can fully and accurately capture the complexities and nuances of cultural diversity, legal traditions, and lived experiences. To represent the diversity and breadth of the issues discussed, the book combines three theoretical frameworks, leveraging the strengths of each to address the research questions. Employing these three approaches, the aim is to strengthen the argument of this book by illustrating and clarifying the interconnectedness and impact of historical continuities in shaping institutional norms and practices, which, along with structural factors, influence women's standing in the legal professions.

1. Theoretical Frameworks

The initial theoretical framework is postcolonial feminism, which offers a valuable starting point by critiquing traditional feminist theories, examining the relationality and positionality of African women, and analyzing various gendered power hierarchies to decolonize African feminist thought, locations, and identities (Tamale, 2020). By engaging with postcolonial feminist theory, I explore how imported legal doctrines intersect with cultural realities in this context—in this case, Africa—and how these intersections influence women's lived experiences within the legal system. Through this critical perspective, the book underscores the importance of contextual applicability as a discursive method for understanding the outcomes women face in legal professions.

Second, intersectionality (Crenshaw, 1989) is a theoretical framework that reveals the categorical structures of power and gender hierarchies at the *macro* (institutional), *meso* (professional), and *micro* (domestic/private) levels. Through intersectionality, I construct a counternarrative about how gender categories lead to different outcomes for women by examining how overlapping power structures shape women's roles as actors and agents of the law. The third theoretical framework, matri-legal feminism, is a novel theory I developed in 2019 to analyze assumptions about the study of women in law in Africa. Matri-legal feminism aligns with postcolonial feminism and intersectionality theory as a critical legal framework that emphasizes and amplifies African women's previously marginalized and silenced voices in law by highlighting their individual and collective agency, voice, and action.

This book broadly defines feminism as a framework and theory that supports gender equality in all areas of society. The origins of feminism, along with its assumptions, key figures, and demands, remain debated, mainly depending on the different waves and strands that have developed in feminist movements since the 1960s (Beoku-Betts et al., 2005). Tensions among women from various regions, along with the tendency to prioritize some women's experiences over others, have led to disputes within the global feminist movement and the idea of global sisterhood (Mohanty et al., 1991). Scholars like Amadiume (1987), Mohanty (2013), Oloka-Onyango and Tamale (1995), and Oyewumi (1997) have criticized the focus on and universalization of Western women's experiences as the global standard for studying women. Furthermore, these scholars criticize their colleagues in the Global North for attempting to appropriate and claim ownership of the term "feminism," thereby excluding the lived realities, agency, activism, and mobilization of the "others"—especially non-Western women.

African and postcolonial feminist theories and scholarship have undergone rapid growth (Achebe, 2013; Beoku-Betts et al., 2005). These studies utilize diverse theoretical, methodological, and ontological approaches that challenge dominant discourses about African women's lives, which are often viewed through a Western feminist lens that tends to homogenize (Mohanty, 2013). Postcolonial feminist scholars such as Mohanty (2013) have questioned the prevailing narratives by exposing the gendered, racialized, and capitalist silences, erasures, and representations of women from regions outside the Western world. Many African feminist scholars have also engaged in theorization as acts of resistance against racial dominance in knowledge production (Arowosegbe, 2016; Banda, 2005; Bennett & Tamale, 2011; Kameri-Mbote & Wekesa, 2018; Masola, 2020; Stewart & Tsanga, 2011). Emphasizing African feminist practice has been crucial to ongoing efforts to decolonize knowledge. The integration of decolonizing scholarship and practice has played a vital role in movements like "Fees Must Fall" and "Rhodes Must Fall" in South Africa. The current waves of decolonial knowledge and decolonization are built upon the work of several scholars from the African negritude and renaissance movements (Diop, 1996; Sesanti, 2016).

African feminist scholarship, therefore, sits at the crossroads of several important issues, including the need to decolonize knowledge systems and the urgency of degendering and deracializing knowledge production (Carastathis, 2016; Mohanty et al.,

1991; Nesiah, 2003; Tamale, 2020; Wing, 2000). By degendering, I mean the feminist effort to challenge the gender neutrality of laws, norms, institutions, and practices that uphold and reinforce global, national, and societal patriarchy. In their analysis of comparative feminist methodology as a way to denaturalize the state, Āse and Wendt (2019) emphasize the importance of questioning the boundaries of accepted knowledge systems, which fosters agency and drives change in social, political, and legal spheres.

Theory is essential to the academic process of creating knowledge. Regardless of the methodological approach used, theory serves as the guiding compass for describing social phenomena scientifically. The mistaken belief in theoretical neutrality and scientific objectivity arises from socialization and educational systems influenced by powerful decision makers and academic gatekeepers. Decades of theorization have primarily occurred in the Global North, often led by men who see the universal male as the standard and model for explaining social phenomena. As women entered academia, efforts aimed to challenge a male-centered approach to explaining social phenomena. Feminist scholars argued that women's experiences, gender roles, and expectations should be included in explanations of social phenomena. The development of feminist legal theory is one of several methods feminists use to describe women's experiences within the law (Stanley & Wise, 1993).

Despite efforts to include women's experiences and voices, early feminist theorists' initiatives in deconstructing maleness overlooked the significance of race, ethnicity, social class, and other identity categories in understanding women's lives. Most women around the world live outside the Western hemisphere. This neglect has caused ongoing criticism and activism from feminists who believe that women in non-Western contexts often face gender, racial, and ethnic silencing and exclusion (Mohanty et al., 1991; Oloka-Onyango & Tamale, 2000; Oyewumi, 1997). There are different strands of feminism—liberal, radical, dominant, postmodern, and many others—each with limitations in addressing and considering the cultural context of women from various regions, including Africa.

Considering the diversity of feminist thought, a single theoretical approach cannot fully explain the complexities of women's lives in law across Africa. I draw on multiple genealogies of feminist theories, guided by inclusion as a feminist comparative methodology that enhances our understanding of the phenomena we compare (Lopez, 1999). Dosekun's (2020) exploration of "African feminisms" highlights the work of notable African women scholars in developing theoretical models that reflect the cultural, historical, and political contexts of African women's lives. These scholarly genealogies analyze women's roles in history through letters, using them as a literary means to understand women's literary and political agency before, during, and after colonial times (Masola, 2020). Given this extensive body of knowledge on women's theorization from both global and African-specific perspectives, I rely on three main theoretical approaches to support the arguments in this book—matri-legal feminism, postcolonial feminism, and intersectionality. These core approaches are supplemented by secondary frameworks such as feminist legal theory and feminist institutionalism. I will now briefly discuss each of these frameworks.

A. Matri-Legal Feminism

Matri-legal feminism, a theory that offers a counternarrative to dominant discourses and theories about women's representation as actors and subjects in law, was developed as an African feminist response to international law (Dawuni, 2019). It reengages with Indigenous African women's activist, collective, and law-enforcing roles to deepen our understanding of how the matriarchal ethos of gender duality functions within the legal sphere. Matri-legal feminism is an emancipatory theory that restores voice and agency to African women's roles in shaping legal discourse (academics), interpreting the law (judges), and enforcing or challenging legal norms (lawyers). In providing a counternarrative, matri-legal feminism should not be misunderstood as implying that African women in law are uniform and perform identical functions; rather, it aims to elevate the African woman's voice and rights. It recognizes and highlights the diversity and differences among African women.

The main idea of matri-legal feminism is to challenge the gaps and blind spots in global feminist legal scholarship concerning the lived experiences, positionality, and involvement of African women in law. Arguing from a nonessentialist perspective, matri-legal feminism recognizes the diversity of differences among women on the continent. It rejects using terms like "African women" or "African woman" to make broad, overgeneralized explanations of women's lives in law. Building on critical legal studies and postcolonial feminist theories, it promotes understanding women's lives in law through African matriarchal systems. African feminist scholars have led in developing and refining the concepts of matri-force and matrilineal customs and practices across various cultural contexts in different countries. Research by Adésínà (2010), Amadiume (1987, 2000), Dipio (2019), Goettner-Abendroth (2012), and Oyewumi (1997) represents just a small part of the extensive work that shaped this theory. Efforts by scholars like Eller (2000) to deconstruct and downplay the idea of matriarchy as a central feminist concept show a lack of awareness about the lived experiences and realities of women outside the ethnocentric view through which she perceives the women's movement.

Contrary to the misunderstandings of some scholars like Eller (2000), African matriarchy is not a counterforce to patriarchy; instead, it highlights the importance of communalism over individualism, agency over hierarchical power, and consensus over imposition. Matriarchy, in its various forms and expressions, embodies core values that showcase women's leadership at home, in the community, and at work (Dashú, 2005). Through matriarchy, the boundaries of the Western feminist public–private divide are less defined in favor of a collective environment that nurtures and recognizes the complementarity of gender roles.

Three assumptions form the core of matri-legal feminism. The first assumption is *non-equal subordination,* which recognizes that women's challenges and subordination in law vary across time and place. For example, the patriarchal restrictions that once prevented women from attending law school or pursuing legal careers in the Western world do not account for the effects of imperial colonization, which limited educational access for women throughout Africa. The second assumption is the principle of *gender duality* inherent in matriarchal systems, allowing women to use cultural ideas of motherhood and spiritual leadership to navigate the gender binary of male and female. Gender duality helps women in many African societies attain positions of power and leadership, grounded in traditional and cultural views of their roles in spiritual and economic contexts. The third assumption, *cultural difference and diversity*, emphasizes nonessentialist views to highlight the importance of recognizing differences among women both as a category and *within* different cultures and periods. This assumption underscores the need to view women's lives in law through intersectional lenses that reveal various forms of exclusion and privilege (Dawuni, 2019). Understanding different cultural contexts is crucial for comprehending women's power and agency.

Building on the work of earlier feminist scholars, matri-legal feminism contributes to African legal feminist thought by advocating for

> [a] renewed commitment to documenting the lives, experiences, and contributions of individual women of African descent, and the collective of African women in leadership at the domestic, regional, and international spheres. Such theorizing must proceed from a positionality that considers the identity, location, and experiences of women across the continent as quite independent and variegated along multiple and intersecting identities. (Dawuni, 2019, p. 445)

Through matri-legal feminism, I argue that systems of gender duality among women and cultural matriarchal positionality clarify women's abilities and mobility within the legal professions. Why is it that, despite the over 100-year gap since the emergence of the first women lawyers and judges in major colonizing countries such as the United Kingdom, France, and Portugal, women in several African countries have managed to catch up to—and in some cases, even surpass—the rise of women in leadership positions (Dawuni & Kang, 2015)? Gender duality also offers strong explanatory potential, helping us understand how, despite historical, institutional, and structural challenges, women continue to navigate legal professions to assert their authority in decision-making roles in law and related fields. Building on this argument, matri-legal feminism emphasizes the maternal and caregiving roles of African women as vital for sustaining societies and communities. As will be discussed later in the book, concepts of motherhood rooted in matrilineal power show why many women in law are committed to improving access to justice for other women, children, and marginalized groups in society.

B. Postcolonial Feminism

Postcolonial feminism critiques the dominant Western discourse about women from regions outside the Western or Global North. It responds to both broader postcolonial studies (Fanon, 1963; Said, 2003; Spivak, 1988) and Western hegemonic theories, viewing both as excluding women's experiences and agency (Nesiah, 2003). In legal studies, postcolonial theory from an African perspective led to the development of the Third World Approaches to International Law (TWAIL). TWAIL emerged as a response to the violence, control, silencing, and marginalization imposed on people outside the Western world through war and conquest. These practices and marginalizations were further reinforced by hegemonic legal norms, practices, and institutions that served as tools to continue oppressing and silencing "Third World" peoples. TWAIL scholars (as members of this school of thought are known) engage in academic theorization to challenge previous erasures and to expose ongoing exclusion, marginalization, and minimization of the experiences and contributions of the "Third World" (Anghie, 2005; Gathii, 2011; Mutua, 2000; Okafor, 2008). Drawing on the work of postcolonial feminist legal scholars (Natarajan et al., 2016; Nesiah, 2003; Nyamu, 2000; Tamale, 2020), I use a decolonial lens to highlight the voices and experiences of the women I interviewed by observing and challenging the impacts of colonial policies and practices on the construction of the legal profession and the gendered norms, practices, and expectations within institutions.

C. Intersectionality

Intersectionality is a theoretical framework developed from critical legal studies and critical race studies (Crenshaw, 1989; Collins, 2000; Collins & Bilge, 2016; Wing, 2000). It deepens our understanding of how women's identities, their contexts, and their experiences across different categories interact in complex and additive ways. Intersectionality highlights the lived experiences of racial and other minority groups to provide context for their stories and to build theory from them. The intersection of gender (woman) and race (Black) offers explanatory power for women in South Africa and other southern African countries such as Zimbabwe, Botswana, and Namibia, as well as the experiences of foreign African women judges in these nations (Bauer & Ellett, 2016). In this book, I focus on women as a socially constructed binary category. Using McCall's (2005) intracategorical approach, which dissects differences among women in relation to other women, I examine how age and generational effects shape the practices and experiences of women in law.

When considering marital and family status, I examine differences among married women, married women with children, single women, and those in the early stages of their careers. In the African context, additional research is needed to explore the importance of identity categories relevant to Africa, such as ethnicity, religion, geographical region, age, sexual identity, and disability. Analyzing these categories in the current study was challenging due to the lack of disaggregated quantitative data. However, I expand the traditional concept of intersectionality, which usually focuses on the personal attributes and identities of women or other subjects under study. In this research, I broaden the concept of intersectionality to include not only individual identities (positionality) but also the ways historical, institutional, and structural factors intersect to shape women's experiences within the law. From organizational and institutional perspectives, intersectionality highlights the roles of norms, practices, and processes as sources of exclusion, allowing for a more comprehensive evaluation of systems that can be improved to address discrimination and promote social justice and gender equality.

In an earlier study on women's access to justice, I expanded on intersectionality by arguing that "a contextualized framing of intersectionality within the African context must be viewed through a decolonial lens, to better situate the experiences of women across the continent of Africa" (Dawuni, 2022b, p. 8). In the present study, I reaffirm my earlier conclusions by stating that historical, institutional, and social factors mutually reinforce each other, and their convergence with customary laws and practices creates and maintains both new and old forms of power hierarchies that influence women's status in law. Despite these gendered hierarchies, women across Africa are using their traditional sources of gender power to challenge, dismantle, and contest these hierarchies, rising to prominent leadership positions. By employing three theoretical approaches, the book establishes a strong conceptual framework for understanding women's roles as agents of law across different countries, professions, and legal systems. Emphasizing the specific contexts of women in Africa, it highlights the diversity of historical, political, social, and cultural influences and tensions in the lives of African women in law.

2. Methodological Framework

This section provides a thorough overview of the processes, methods, and design thinking that guided the study. It explains these processes to help future research benefit from the approaches used to create the first book on women's perspectives in law across Africa. The project adopts a sociolegal approach to understand, trace, and analyze women's pathways into the legal profession through a mixed-methods strategy (Banakar, 2019). First, it uses qualitative methods by conducting elite interviews with women judges, lawyers, and law professors in the seven countries where fieldwork was conducted (Smart, 2009). Second, it incorporates secondary data sources by analyzing information and archival materials located in libraries and national archives in the countries visited during fieldwork. The third phase involves data analysis, employing process tracing to systematically identify patterns among current and past causal variables (Hesse-Biber, 2010). Additionally, a survey was carried out in 2021 to collect data from women in the three sectors. Respondents were given the option to reply anonymously to enhance the reliability of data on sensitive topics, such as sexual harassment.

Comparative methodological approaches enable comparisons across different variables and units of analysis. These comparisons can involve various cases, such as lawyers in *Country X* versus lawyers in *Country Y*, or within the same case, like corporate lawyers versus public-sector lawyers (Abel, 1985; Dogan & Pelassy, 2001). For the judiciary, special attention was given to selecting judges from different judicial levels, including the supreme, constitutional, appeals, high, and magistrates' courts. The diversity among these court levels provided different experiences that contributed to the findings. The choice of comparison method depends on the dependent and independent variables, the questions asked, and the interdisciplinary nature of the study (Husa, 2022). The case study method involves a detailed analysis of a specific case or set of cases, allowing the researcher to gather information that can be compared with other cases to develop broad comparative insights and conclusions (Johnson, 1997).

Social phenomena reflecting women's lives are complex and not always easily explained by scientific methods. Therefore, the intersectionality of women's experiences requires the use of feminist methodological approaches that prioritize and center women's experiences across multiple analytical dimensions, integrating various strategies. According to Lopez (1999), using a comparative approach to understand and explain women's lived realities involves the comparativist grasping the cultural context, establishing a framework to identify this context, and applying different critical theories to interpret what legal frameworks mean for women. To gain a comprehensive understanding of the nuances of the subjects' lives in this study, I employ comparative and case study methods. I compare within cases (e.g., women as lawyers in corporate, private, and public sectors) and across cases (women as judges, lawyers, and academics). To facilitate a deeper in-sector comparison, three chapters use the case study method to trace and analyze women's experiences in law across the bar, bench, and academia. I conduct a comparative cross-sector analysis to identify the similarities, differences, and outliers in women's experiences within each legal sector. Using the case study method, I illustrate women's experiences in law through brief analyses of the profiles of pioneering women featured in each chapter.

Feminist research methodology emphasizes reflexivity as an approach that centers power in the voices of the individuals telling their stories (Lopez, 1999; Stanley & Wise, 1993). Although some academic methods may not prioritize this approach, a key tactic of feminist methodological writing is to deconstruct hierarchies in knowledge production while highlighting the narrator's voice through an inclusive narrative technique (Chadha & Thomas, 2023). Situating this study within feminist methodology, I rely heavily on direct narratives and interview transcripts. By prioritizing the interviewee's voice, I aim to provide a clearer picture of their lived experiences, followed by an academic analysis from the researcher. Feminist reflexivity is crucial for defining research boundaries. It both empowers the narrator and guides the researcher's analysis of the interviewee's lived experiences (Alidou, 2002; Macbeth, 2001). At the same time, it limits the researcher's ability to interpret the interviewee's lived reality without misrepresenting their life story.

A. Case Selection

This book is based on 10 years of qualitative data collection through in-depth interviews with women in law across six West African countries—Ghana, Nigeria, Senegal, Ivory Coast, The Gambia, and Cape Verde—and one East African country, Kenya. The cases were selected to represent the two main legal traditions on the continent: civil- and common-law systems introduced through colonization. Before colonization, Africa's dominant legal systems were reflected in the customary laws, practices, and norms of its diverse populations. With the arrival of Islamic conquests from the Middle East and European colonization, African nations developed mixed legal systems, often called pluralistic. Generally, almost all African legal systems operate within a blend of these frameworks, heavily relying on those inherited from European colonization.

In this book, I focus on three legal systems: French civil law, Portuguese civil law, and British common law. I recognize the challenges of classifying African countries based on their colonial histories and understand that this approach needs reconsideration. However, for this project, I rely on the classification currently used by the African Union to categorize countries on the continent. **Table 2.2** presents the classification of the countries included in this study by legal tradition. Throughout the book, I aim to adopt a comparative approach by examining the three sectors across and within countries, as well as between different legal traditions and professions. Besides ensuring diversity in legal traditions, the selection of countries presented in **Table 2.2** was designed to maximize regional diversity but was limited by access to

Table 2.2 *Countries Where Fieldwork Was Conducted*

Country	Region	Classification	Legal tradition
Ghana	West	Anglophone	Common law
Nigeria	West	Anglophone	Common law
The Gambia	West	Anglophone	Common law
Kenya*	East	Anglophone	Common law
Senegal	West	Francophone	Civil law (French)
Ivory Coast	West	Francophone	Civil law (French)
Cape Verde	West	Lusophone	Civil law (Portuguese)

*In Kenya I conducted one focus group with 15 women judges

data, interview networks, travel costs, and time constraints. Future research can investigate regions and countries that remain underexplored.

To provide a detailed explanation and cover as much of the continent as possible, I relied heavily on the growing scholarship about women in law in Africa. Most of these studies are included in the four books I edited on women judges. One of my main goals for this project has been to build on existing scholarship about African women in law through a decolonial feminist approach (Ampofo et al., 2008; Dawuni, 2019 Tamale, 2020). Decolonial feminist approaches critique Western knowledge production by emphasizing the voices, narratives, analytical critiques, and imaginaries of formerly colonized peoples and places. Understanding the cultural context through women's lived experiences adds depth to knowledge production. Therefore, while I reference dominant Western discourses on women in law, this book aims to highlight scholarship by African and Africanist scholars on this topic.

The coronavirus pandemic disrupted travel plans to South Africa and Rwanda in 2020 for conducting in-depth interviews. To expand the scope and regional focus of this project, I relied heavily on a four-nation research initiative on women in law and leadership, which I designed and coordinated as the executive director of the Institute for African Women in Law (IAWL). This project produced 10 reports on women's representation in law and leadership at the bar, bench, and legal academia in Nigeria, Kenya, South Africa, and Senegal. **Table 2.3** presents country-specific studies from my edited books, offering valuable opportunities to broaden the regional focus beyond West Africa to include countries from eastern, southern, and other parts of the continent.

This study used data triangulation to gather multiple data points for a comprehensive analysis, as shown in **Table 2.3**, which indicates the countries where desktop research was conducted. First, quantitative data on women's symbolic and descriptive representation were collected by counting the number of women in three main areas of the study: women at the bar, on the bench, and in the legal academy. To obtain data on the bar in each country, I contacted bar associations or law societies to get the latest statistics on the number of lawyers currently enrolled. Data on judges were

Table 2.3 *Secondary Countries Where Research Studies Were Consulted*

Country	Region	Classification	Legal tradition
Algeria	North	Francophone	Islamic/Civil
Botswana	Southern	Anglophone	Hybrid (common & civil)
Benin	West	Francophone	Civil
Ethiopia	East	Italian influence	Civil
Egypt	North	Francophone	Civil
Kenya	East	Anglophone	Common
Malawi	Southern	Anglophone	Common
Namibia	Southern	Anglophone	Common
Rwanda	East	Anglophone	Common
South Africa	Southern	Anglophone	Hybrid (common & civil)
Tanzania	East	Anglophone	Common
Tunisia	North	Francophone	Islamic/Civil
Uganda	East	Anglophone	Common
Zambia	Southern	Anglophone	Common
Zimbabwe	Southern	Anglophone	Common

Note. This list includes countries where my five edited books have covered the experiences of women in law.

often obtained directly from officials overseeing the judiciary, usually the judicial secretary or registrar. Similarly, data were collected from deans of law schools and faculties for law institutions. When I received no response to my data requests, I estimated the numbers by reviewing the websites of these organizations, assuming the publicly displayed data was current or nearly so. All data were sorted by gender. Although intersectionality advocates for examining other identities like race, ethnicity, sexual orientation, and (dis)ability, among others (Collins & Bilge, 2016; Crenshaw, 1989), most bar associations and law societies do not collect such demographic information; however, in South Africa, race data are often gathered (Mabokela & Mawila, 2004; Meer and Muller, 2017).

Second, the qualitative data for this research were collected through 153 in-depth interviews and one focus group with participants from the six countries where I conducted fieldwork. **Table 2.4** provides a breakdown of the respondents who took part in the interviews. An additional source of qualitative data was obtained from an extensive review of existing scholarly literature on women in the legal professions in Africa and globally. Since qualitative research involves human subjects, it is governed by strict institutional rules. At my home institution, Howard University, there are rigorous protocols for obtaining approval from the Institutional Review Board (IRB), which I secured before starting my fieldwork.

Third, **Table 2.5** displays the number of responses from a 2021 survey of women lawyers, judges, and academics, which received 249 responses. **Table 2.6** offers a detailed breakdown of those 249 responses, including the countries they originated from. The survey was conducted during the COVID-19 pandemic, allowing for a

Table 2.4 *Number of Women in Law Interviewed*

Country	Judges/magistrates	Lawyers	Professors/lecturers
Ghana	20	21	6
Nigeria	5	16	6
Senegal	8	7	4
Ivory Coast	5	7	5
Gambia	5	6	1
*Kenya	15	0	0
Cape Verde	6	9	1
Total per sector	64	66	23
Total number of interviewees			**153**

*In Kenya, I only conducted a focus group of women judges due to health challenges during my visit to the country. I draw heavily on the studies I conducted later, which resulted in the IAWL reports on women at the Kenyan bar and legal academy.

Table 2.5 *Survey Responses*

Sector	Number of responses
Bar	122
Bench	79
Academy	48
Total	***249***

question about how women in law were being affected by it. The survey results are discussed in later chapters.

The survey responses increased the diversity of voices, experiences, and regions, thereby enhancing the study's validity and representativeness. To ensure internal validity and gender diversity in the data sources (Johnson, 1997), I interviewed 10 men in each of the three professional categories to gain insight into the male perspective on some of the women's experiences.

The method involved a diverse approach to gather opinions from each of the three sectors. Before traveling to each country for interviews, a preliminary list of potential participants was compiled and contacted via email to schedule interviews. In all countries except Ghana, I relied on one or two contacts to connect with potential respondents. The snowball effect was used by asking respondents to introduce me to other potential interviewees. To ensure diverse responses, I started with a list of individuals representing different levels within the profession. For example, in compiling the list of judges, efforts were made to include a variety of ranks, from lower to highest courts. When selecting interviewees, careful consideration was given to differences in legal traditions and judge classifications. For instance, in civil-law countries, judges often serve both judicial and prosecutorial roles (Cohen, 2018; Schultz &

Table 2.6 *Countries Represented in the Survey Responses*

Region	Countries
North	Algeria Egypt
East	Ethiopia Kenya Tanzania Uganda
West	Ghana Nigeria Cameroon Benin
Southern	Botswana Malawi Mozambique South Africa Zambia Zimbabwe
Diaspora	United States United Kingdom The Netherlands Germany Australia

Shaw, 2013). In the common-law system, a judge applies the law without investigating the case, so the judge is not part of the prosecutorial team (Schultz & Shaw, 2013). Due to these differences, the study paid closer attention to the questions asked about their roles as judges.

On the other hand, the legal profession was more complex. To gather diverse responses, I recruited lawyers from various sectors, including those actively practicing in litigation, corporate law, and as general counsel, as well as those employed by public or government agencies, such as the Attorney General and Ministries of Justice. The same approach was used in academia by interviewing both junior and senior faculty members, including female deans and department heads. To ensure the experiences reflected the diversity of women, I emphasized the importance of intergenerational representation to capture intercategorical differences (McCall, 2005) and the lived experiences of my informants. For each sector, respondents were selected across the entire career spectrum—from early to midlevel and senior positions.

Conducting a comparative study like this, which integrated various legal systems across three sectors in six countries, required careful planning, diplomacy, strong networks, and flexibility. This study greatly benefited from the generosity and willingness of the professional women who set aside time from their busy schedules to participate in interviews. Most interviews took place at their workplaces, with some respondents arriving early to meet with me before their workday started, while others stayed late to accommodate our meetings. I appreciated their openness in answering my questions and their readiness to share additional resources, such as reports. The interviews lasted about an hour; at times, conversations extended well beyond the formal interview. Those informal discussions became some of the most valuable sources of information, providing deeper insights into the lived experiences of my informants, the institutional contexts in which they worked, the gendered hierarchies they challenged, and the difficulties of balancing their personal and professional lives.

Following approval from my university's IRB and to safeguard the privacy and safety of the informants, none of the interviewees is named. I refer to them by profession, court, rank, or country to showcase the diverse voices, nations, and occupations. Sometimes, I omit the country to reduce the risk of identification. When I do mention individuals by name, it is because they are the first woman in a particular position (which is public information). Other name references come from published sources, such as news articles or oral stories from the Amandla African Women in Law Speaker Series curated by the Institute for African Women in Law. For data analysis, I use a thematic framework to identify key themes and patterns.

B. A Note on Quantitative Data

Sourcing data from Africa for research can be very challenging and sometimes even impossible. Access to reliable and valid quantitative data on legal professionals across Africa is a major obstacle most researchers encounter. Since 2016, I have edited five books on women judges and have seen firsthand how data inaccessibility hampers the ability to conduct the sociolegal research needed to properly understand women's representation in law.

Access to reliable and readily available data is often hindered by poor recordkeeping, a common institutional issue in many regions. When data are accessible, they may be outdated, inaccurate, or incomplete. In several countries, data aren't broken down by gender, race, ethnicity, or religion, making it difficult to see intersectional representation. Unlike the United States and many European Union countries, where data are easily accessible on organizational websites or online databases, this isn't the case in many other parts of the continent. Even when data exist, they are often outdated and inaccurate.

These challenges in obtaining accurate data greatly increased my interest in conducting fieldwork and collecting qualitative data through interviews, which I find to be reliable and current—at least according to my interviewees. I was also lucky to meet several wonderful individuals eager to help me gather the data needed for my quantitative analyses. Sometimes, I had to depend on my networks and contacts in high offices to access information. Due to the difficulties of collecting data over the nine years of this study, I have not been able to update some records to reflect the most recent information. As a result, the data in this book may have different cut-off points and dates due to the data-collection challenges I mentioned. I hope that, over time, this data scarcity issue will be resolved, speeding up research on the legal professions in Africa.

3

Studying Women in Law Across Africa: A Conceptual Framework

I. Introduction

Globally, the development of the legal profession has reinforced a binary view of male dominance, as shown in research in this area. Feminist and sociolegal scholars in the Global North continue to explore masculinities within legal professions (Mossman, 2006; Schultz & Shaw, 2003; Sommerlad, 1994). While feminist legal scholars have made important progress in deconstructing maleness in the law, mainstream legal feminists have done little to examine the intersection of gender and race within existing scholarship. In response to this epistemological gap, Black feminist scholars and women of color increasingly contribute to illuminating these dual erasures (Blackburne-Rigsby, 2009; Crenshaw, 1989; Melaku, 2019; Pratt, 2012).

Amidst a historical and social backdrop marked by multiple exclusions—gender, race, class, and global hegemony—women's entry into the legal professions across Africa took place. The long-standing masculinization of the legal field and the tendency to consider maleness as the standard for professionalism in both past and present institutional norms and practices explain why there are even fewer scholarly works on African women in law. For some exceptions, see Albethyn and Bonthuys (2016), Andrews (2021), Aura-Odhiambo (2018), Bauer and Dawuni (2016), Cowan (2013), Kamau (2013), Kameri-Mbote (2014), Masengu (2016), and Stewart (2012). This chapter draws on emerging interdisciplinary African feminist legal scholarship to examine questions regarding the position of African women within these professions.

As outlined in Chapter 1, this book does not aim to cover the entire continent. The discussion provided offers data-rich narratives that establish a foundation for future case studies to evaluate the assumptions, hypotheses, and arguments presented here. To provide a nuanced examination of African women in law, this chapter combines historical process tracing with the current lived experiences of women in the legal field. In the next section, I contextualize the positionality of African women within a precolonial framework, presenting evidence to support my argument that women in African social systems held significant social, economic, religious, and legal roles, which explains the ongoing continuities in women's positions in law. Section III examines women in law from a global perspective, engaging in a cross-national comparison of the similarities and differences in women's experiences. Section IV shifts the focus back to Africa by outlining five phases of women's entry into the legal profession. Section V discusses the variables that influence women's pathways into the profession. Section VI uses an intersectional and intergenerational framework of women's identity categories to demonstrate how these identities shape their individual

African Women in Law. J. Jarpa Dawuni, Oxford University Press. © Oxford University Press 2026.
DOI: 10.1093/9780197795095.003.0003

and collective roles within the professions. Section VII highlights the lives and contributions of pioneering women in law, and section VIII concludes the chapter.

II. Women, Agency, and Justice in Precolonial African Systems

The existence of Africans did not start with a "discovery" by European explorers and conquests. Before any encounters between these two worlds, the landmass now known as Africa was home to diverse groups of people with their own unique cultures and ways of life. The inhabitants of this continent developed their political, economic, judicial, and legal systems through which they governed their communities, traded with each other, settled disputes, and established binding laws and norms (Akyeampong & Obeng, 2005; Amadiume, 2000; Oyewumi, 1997).

An evaluation of various interdisciplinary research from sociology, literature, politics, and history, among others, using historical and archival methods, shows that most (pre)colonial African societies had practices, norms, and belief systems that emphasized the roles and agency of women. Colonial rule weakened these areas of female power by reinforcing men's dominance, thus empowering men at women's expense. Colonial rule was a male-dominated enterprise. Christianity also did not provide relief; it introduced rules requiring women to obey their husbands. European colonial systems imported European models of patriarchy into African societies by placing patriarchal control in the hands of African men through assigning them menial administrative and commercial roles.

In much of precolonial Africa, matriarchal and matrilineal systems were common. Although women still had gendered domestic roles, these systems enabled women to hold important positions, blurring the line between public and private spheres. These systems were transplantations of colonial influence (Amadiume, 2000; Day, 2020; Diop, 1989). Drawing on the call by feminist scholars to theorize from African cultural perspectives, geopolitical context, and ideological viewpoints (Nnaemeka, 2003; Tamale, 2020), I connect the role of African women in law by linking the present to a historical past of women's agentic positions.

Using historical comparative analysis reveals the continuities we see today and the vital role of tracing African matriarchal power in understanding women's roles in law. Examining women's histories in law should not start with the rise of formal legal systems in the common-and civil-law traditions established by the British, French, and Portuguese. I argue that to truly understand the status of women in law, we need to expand the historical framework beyond colonial perspectives and Western feminist theories. This detailed historical analysis and comprehensive review of women's roles before colonization offers a broader perspective from which we can trace women's agency and potential in law. Therefore, this book aims to show how historical factors highlight the way African women consistently resist the multiple layers of patriarchy—imported from the West and existing in precolonial societies—while progressing through professional leadership hierarchies.

Research on the early, precolonial roles of women's leadership and representation in law shows the important roles women played in social, political, religious, and economic decision-making within communities. In several communities and ethnic groups across precolonial and colonial Africa, including Kenya, women had varying levels of access to and control over property, which they could pass down as inheritance to their children. This economic power also gave them the authority to participate in dispute resolution related to property rights (Hay, 1982).

In her writing on women's roles in Zimbabwe (formerly Southern Rhodesia), Chanock (1982) analyzes the strategies used by colonial administrators to establish and formalize "customary" legal systems that stripped women of most of their traditional rights. In these conditions, the fall of colonial rule did not erase these tensions, which had, by the end of the colonial era, become ingrained in the laws and practices, allowing their continuation by the new leaders. Many of these colonial conflicts and gender-based discriminatory practices still exist today, impacting some of the major gender rights issues women face across the continent (Banda, 2005; De Souza et al., 2014.

I am not arguing that patriarchy did not exist in African societies before colonization. Instead, I offer a counternarrative that shifts the focus from the negative effects of patriarchy to highlighting the roles of matriarchal systems in showcasing women's power and decision-making abilities. This is not an attempt to conduct a relational analysis where Western feminism serves as the basis for understanding the lives of African women. Several African feminists have worked to deconstruct and detach Western feminism's dominance as the standard for explaining women's experiences worldwide (Amadiume, 2000; Day, 2020; Dosekun, 2020; Obiora, 1993; Oyewumi, 1997).

This chapter aims to highlight emerging themes and patterns of women's agency in law across Africa, rather than creating a narrative of "sameness" or an essentialist view of African women's lives. The analysis recognizes the differences that exist *within* and *between* various regions, countries, communities, and locales. These differences are primarily influenced by intersectional factors, including ethnicity, religion, economics, sociocultural aspects, class, disability, and many other vectors of difference. These varied vectors of power, privilege, and exclusion come together to shape African women's unique and shared experiences at the bar, on the bench, and in the legal academy.

A substantial body of knowledge demonstrates the significant roles women played in precolonial Africa as political leaders (Amadiume, 1987; Oyěwùmí, 1997; Tsikata, 1989). In *African Women: Traditional Chiefs and Rulers*, Day (2020) provides a comprehensive overview of women's leadership roles across various regions of the continent during the precolonial and colonial eras. She further explores how colonial rule disrupted and diminished the power and agency of African women as political leaders, economic powerhouses, spiritual mediums, and legal intermediaries. By examining the lives of women in different communities across Nigeria, Uganda, Sierra Leone, Swaziland, and Ghana, Day's (2020) historical review highlights how contemporary understandings of women's leadership roles often differ from historical narratives that emphasize their agency as leaders in precolonial times. Building on this historical agency, several scholars have referenced women's past leadership roles to explain the continuities in women's significant roles in modern peace movements during and after conflicts (Anyidoho et al., 2020; Kang, 2015; Tripp, 2000).

Women's roles and contributions in politics and decision-making are clear across the continent. From warriors like Queen Yaa Asantewaa, the Ejusi Queenmother among the Akan people of Ghana, who fought against the British, to market women who organized during the Aba War of 1929 to protest unfair colonial taxes (Achebe, 2020; Akyeampong & Obeng, 2005), their impact is undeniable. In Ghana, women also played vital roles in economic decision-making, as seen in their involvement in cocoa hold-ups and strikes against colonial administrators' exploitative pricing and market control policies (Tsikata, 1989). In Senegal, within the Wolof and Serer kingdoms, women held positions as governors and chiefs, often called *Jee*. Prominent figures like Ndaté Yalla Mbodj and Aline Sitoe Diatta are recognized as powerful matriarchs and priestesses who led women's communities in revolt against the French in 1855 (Gierczynski-Bocandé, 2013). Women's influence also extended into judicial and legal matters. Among the Podoko in Cameroon, women played roles in the judiciary, especially in customary laws used during dispute resolutions (Diye, 2022). Recognizing women's crucial roles, some countries have aimed to incorporate customary law practices that foster peace and justice into formal laws. In South Africa, Weeks (2022) examined the need for gender diversity among traditional court members through the Traditional Courts Bill (B1D-2017), which was eventually enacted as Act 9—The Traditional Courts Act—in 2022 after years of stagnation in Parliament.

Drawing on their roles as mothers, grandmothers, sisters, and aunts, women played a vital role in uniting communities through dispute resolution, thereby promoting peace and harmony. They acted as key mediators and arbitrators in both individual and community conflicts. The positions of women as powerful social, political, economic, and legal intermediaries were violently interrupted by the clash between customary patriarchy and the imperial patriarchal policies of colonization. In line with an agenda of exploitation, extraction, and exclusion rooted in Western patriarchy, African men were pushed into the economic and capitalist sectors as the sole holders of power and controllers of the means of production (Akyeampong & Obeng, 2005; Zeleza, 2005). Women's contributions to economic development and community well-being were diminished and regarded as inferior to the decision-making roles of men (Rodney, 2012). In a clear assessment of the impact of colonial laws on women's presence and participation in the public sphere, Obiora (2020, p. 173) summarized it:

> In jurisdictions where the British common law was applicable, ideological axioms, normative precepts, and judicial precedents converged to encode patriarchal imperatives as authoritative. Notorious historical antecedents of the inscription and legitimation of gender differentiation in the legal system include the promulgation of protectionist legislation, which further restricted women's labor market participation.

Over 300 years of colonial occupation, exploitation, extraction, and exclusion have negatively affected the institutional, cultural, political, and legal restructuring of African societies. These impacts have harmed women's roles within these societies and continue to influence many of today's legal practices. Despite these upheavals to women's agency, their active participation persisted throughout the struggles for independence. Recognizing women's roles as influential mediators, visionary leaders like Kwame Nkrumah created opportunities for women's involvement in formal politics during the post-independence government. Nkrumah was unapologetic about the roles women played in uniting the political party (Mama, 2023; Nkrumah, 1959). He secured women's representation in governance and decision-making by reserving seats for them in the new government (Mama, 2023; Prah, 2004; Tsikata, 1989).

Unfortunately, across Africa, independence from colonial rule did not fully free women from patriarchal control. Throughout the continent, the rise of "statesmen" as the standard for bureaucratic and administrative authority undermined women's traditional power and leadership (Tsikata, 1989). Despite these challenges to women's organizational efforts, women across the continent continued to draw on their historical roles to fight for their rightful place in decision-making through collective activism, social movements, and participation in global initiatives to promote women's rights (Amadiume, 1987; Mama, 2020; Tripp, 2000).

In this book, I argue that while the marginalization and exclusion of African women result from the colonial transplantation of patriarchy merging with customary patriarchy, a thorough review of women's precolonial power remnants is essential for understanding their entry into legal professions. A return to the historical roots of African women's agency and leadership roles is necessary to frame this study on women in law. As Sesanti (2016, p. 494) notes, "the traditional African culture that gave African women recognition and respect must constitute the core and center of the African renaissance project." *However*, the precolonial African system should not be romanticized; while African cultures have many positive aspects, they also include practices that continue to undermine women's rights today. Cultural norms regarding marriage and inheritance often prioritize men's rights over those of women. By recognizing this dissonance between rights and their violations, matri-legal feminism highlights the maternal and nurturing roles of African women as essential to uniting societies and communities. I argue that it is this role of motherhood, along with the importance of matrilineality and matriarchal power, that enables women to navigate male-dominated fields like the legal professions, while challenging power hierarchies to expand access to justice for other women, children, and vulnerable groups in society.

III. Women in Law: Global Perspectives

Before examining the rise of African women in the legal profession, it is important to outline how women are positioned in the legal fields in other regions around the world. This context allows for a deeper analysis of the similarities, differences, and points of convergence and divergence in women's experiences worldwide, helping to illuminate the circumstances surrounding the emergence and current status of African women lawyers. The masculinization of the legal profession and the emphasis on maleness as the norm are global issues. In the Global North, women have actively fought for their rights to legal education, to join the bar (Epstein, 1981; Letswaart, 2003; Malleson, 2003; Menkel-Meadow, 1986; Mossman, 2006; Rhodes, 2003; Sanderson & Sommerlad, 1998; Thornton, 1996), serve on the bench (L'Heureux-Dubè, 2001; Rackley, 2013; Röwekamp, 2013; Schultz & Shaw, 2013), and participate equally with their male counterparts in the legal academy (Auchmuty et al., 2021; Paquin, 2021; Schultz, 2021a, 2021b; Thornton, 1989; West, 2018).

Along with the gender challenges women often face, racial segregation has created an intersectional hierarchy with multiple layers of exclusion that women from racially minoritized groups must navigate. This context helps explain the later involvement of racial minorities in law (Blackburne-Rigsby, 2009; Brown et al., 2020; McLeod, 2016; Melaku, 2019; Pratt, 2012). As the initial gateway into the professions, the bar has traditionally been an exclusionary, masculine, elitist, and classist club, often called a "gentleman at the bar." In the United Kingdom, where common law developed and was spread worldwide through colonization, minority women lawyers and judges face both masculinized and racialized obstacles. Despite claims of equal opportunities in hiring racial minorities, there has been little focus on the institutional rules these groups must follow. Essentially, racial minorities are drawn into institutions that have not changed their rules of engagement (Sommerlad, 2013).

Despite the different structures, functions, qualifications, and experiences of women across the three professions, several common features have shaped the research agenda and questions in these fields. First, scholars aimed to answer questions that explain the reasons women are excluded from entering these professions and how they overcame barriers to gain acceptance. The impact of the European wars, culminating in World War I and World War II, fueled advocacy for civil and political rights. Women's movements that arose after these wars, especially during the first and second waves of feminism, helped develop practical demands for women's equality and representation in public life, including in legal professions (Schultz & Shaw, 2003). In many Western countries, removing formal barriers to entry did not eliminate all the professional obstacles women faced in the legal field (Epstein, 1981).

In the United Kingdom, the Sex Disqualification (Removal) Act of 1919 finally allowed women to join the legal profession. However, they quickly faced another barrier—the split bar—which favored men joining the roll of barristers while women entered as solicitors—a structure partly designed to uphold the perceived privilege of a traditionally male-dominated profession (McGlynn, 2003; Sanderson & Sommerlad, 1998). Different countries allowed women to enter the legal field at different times, leading to a gradual rise in the number of female lawyers. Some of the first women lawyers appeared in 1900 (France), 1905 (Australia), 1903 (The Netherlands), 1918 (Portugal), 1920 (UK), and 1922 (Germany) (Schultz & Shaw, 2003, p. xxxiv). With new opportunities to qualify as lawyers, women pursuing judicial careers had to navigate male-dominated legal and judicial hierarchies, often rooted in masculinized institutional norms and practices.

Limited employment options shaped the careers of early women law professors in the Global North. In her writing on the experiences of pioneering women academics in the United States, Carle (2021) argues that the persistent lack of opportunities for women academics forced these trailblazers to apply to less prestigious law schools. Once admitted, they still encountered challenges related to gendered segregation in the courses they were permitted to teach. In tracing the entry of women into the legal profession in the United States, Kay (1991) found that although the first group of women lawyers appeared by 1879, it was not until 1970 that there was a significant rise in the number of women law professors. Despite the slow acceptance of women in the legal field, women in the legal academy were not fully regarded as equals to men. Women academics with credentials equal to or better than those of their male colleagues were often employed as law librarians and, in some cases, held dual roles as law professors and in other departments, such as economics and political science (Carle, 2021; Kay, 1991). These persistent discriminatory practices led the American Association of Law Schools (AALS) to establish a program in 1970 to eliminate sex-based discrimination by AALS member universities in law school admissions and faculty hiring (Kay, 1991).

In all three sectors of the legal profession, gaining access was one challenge, but fitting into institutional structures was a different battle. For many women, this meant facing noninclusive work environments that valued long hours, navigating a masculinized, competitive culture where standing out was necessary for promotion, and dealing with limited areas of specialization in legal practice. Schultz and Shaw (2013) observed a gendered career pattern emerging from institutional norms and practices that assigned women specific job tasks in the judiciary. Women judges reportedly faced challenges such as a gendered assignment of cases (with women often being assigned family and divorce cases), slow promotions, and limited opportunities for professional development. Although women have since entered fields once thought to be exclusively male, intersectional exclusions still exist in the hiring of Black women and other minority groups in the United States (Deo, 2019; Dubin, 2000). In this context of gender-based employment discrimination, the intersection of gender and race means that racial minorities experience higher levels of gender-based discrimination, racial scrutiny, and unequal treatment (Melaku, 2019; Pratt, 2012).

Another key question in research on women in law concerns the impact women have on the profession. Increased opportunities for women to enter the field were not enough to ensure their equal status in a profession that upheld justice and equity. Women also needed to justify their inclusion and representation in these roles. Feminist legal scholars heavily referenced debates on "difference," especially the work of sociologist Carol Gilligan (1982). This scholarship on "difference" often highlights women's traits, such as being relational, conflict-avoidant, attentive, and guided by an ethic of care that considers the whole person rather than just the individual. Most studies argue that women must be seated on the bench because they play a vital role in advancing women's rights, law, and justice (Baines, 2013; Hunter, 2008).

The *difference* debate is especially prominent in studies about women judges. Many studies highlight the "ethic of care" women bring to cases and the expectation that they will offer a more compassionate perspective in judicial decision-making (Röwekamp, 2013). These studies suggest that women may be less prone to corruption (Cardinal, 2013) and more supportive of women in divorce and alimony cases (Dijksterhuis, 2013). However, an academic consensus on the influence of women remains elusive, and many scholars question why women feel the need to demonstrate a difference to gain full acceptance in the profession. To expand the discussion beyond just difference, some attention has shifted to feminist adjudication, often based on the idea that women judges could bring feminist reasoning by asking the "woman question" and highlighting gendered blind spots in the law (Baines, 2013; Hunter, 2008). Despite the diversity among women and judges, it is unreasonable to expect all women judges to think and act alike. Many women judges do not openly identify with their gender, and in discussing the Argentine judiciary, Kohen (2013) explains how many women judges resist being labeled as feminine or categorized as feminist judges. Several scholars have challenged framing women's participation in the profession solely around the "difference" they make. Rhodes (2003, p. 7) observed:

> A more effective strategy is neither to exaggerate nor deny gender differences. We can avoid sweeping claims about women's essential nature, while noting that particular groups of women under particular social conditions practice their professions based on different expectations and experiences than men. . . . In short, we can advocate visions of professionalism that resonate with women's experiences but on the basis of feminist commitments, not biological categories.

Although there is a growing focus on feminist anti-essentialism, it is undeniable that women, regardless of their social class and context, tend to face similar patterns of gender-based professional challenges. These issues start with entering and integrating into their careers, where women struggle to adapt to masculine work cultures (Liebenberg & Scharf, 2019; Sterling & Chanow, 2021). Additional challenges come from balancing social responsibilities with a work environment that values male-centric work ethics, often requiring long hours for lawyers. For women with caregiving duties, these masculine institutional structures become especially burdensome (Nayak & Tabassum, 2021). Women also often earn less due to the undervaluation of their work (Schultz & Shaw, 2003). Income disparities and the gender wage gap are especially severe for minority women in academia (Deo, 2019) and private legal practice (Nelson et al., 2023). Sexual harassment remains common in law firms and frequently contributes to high turnover rates within these organizations (Letswaart, 2003).

Women judges have not been immune to gender-based discrimination. The judiciary's hierarchy makes it especially vulnerable to the "othering" of women. Judicial deference to higher courts in common-law countries means that women are likely to face unfavorable power dynamics, as they tend to be underrepresented at the higher levels of the court hierarchy. The introduction of affirmative action quotas, Judicial Services Commissions (JSCs), and selection panels are various efforts by different judiciaries to promote greater transparency in appointment processes, aiming to break down barriers to gender diversity (Kamau, 2013; Malleson, 2003; Mossman, 2013; Rackley, 2013). In several countries, it has taken decades for women to be accepted and fully integrated into the judiciary, with ongoing sources of exclusion making full equality nearly impossible (L'Heureux-Dubè, 2001; Schultz & Shaw, 2003). In France, the feminization of the judiciary has not removed the glass ceiling, and women continue to be underrepresented in court leadership (Boigeol, 2013; Cohen, 2018).

Research on women in the legal academy shows similar patterns of gender discrimination and exclusion. Across much of Europe, the first female legal academics came from middle-class families committed to higher education, often connected to the law through fathers, husbands, or other family members (Auchmuty et al., 2021). One might expect that women's progress in the legal academy would mark a turning point in the deep-rooted perceptions of inequality faced by women in the legal field. Even though female professors teach male students, it is still paradoxical that these students continue to see women academics as less competent than their male colleagues. These attitudes underscore the ongoing presence of gender stereotypes in higher education and law schools. The experiences of female law professors show that ingrained social misconceptions about women's abilities in law stay with law students throughout their education and into their careers, sustaining a cycle of gender stereotypes.

Women's experiences with gender-based discrimination in the legal academy go beyond their interactions with colleagues. Women legal academics receive lower scores on student evaluations and are cited less often in academic publications (Deo, 2019; Paquin, 2021). The situation for women in legal academia in leadership roles mirrors the general patterns seen among women at the bar and on the bench. Fewer women are appointed as full professors, endowed chair holders, or deans. In the legal academy, gendered career expectations often place the main responsibility for mentoring students on women academics (Auchmuty et al., 2021).

Emerging regional and country-specific studies focus on women in law. While some of these studies by Western scholars aim to "diversify" their scope in edited volumes, others serve as stand-alone books centered on women judges. Lindbekk and Sonneveld's (2017) edited volume on women judges in the Middle East and North Africa offers a comparative overview of women judges in a region that has received relatively little scholarly attention. Shen's (2017) book, *Women Judges in Contemporary China: Gender, Judging, and Living*, provides an insightful analysis of the professional choices and lives of women judges in China. By examining women's entry into the Chinese judiciary, Shen (2017) highlights the challenges of navigating not only a male-dominated profession but also the additional burden of functioning within a command economy state.

In their comparative study of women in high courts, Escobar-Lemmon et al. (2021) examined the effects of women in the pipeline, institutional factors, and international influences on the advancement of women in high courts. Focusing on five countries—Canada, Ireland, the United States, Colombia, and South Africa—the authors aimed to apply their findings to a broader global context. Recent studies on women at the bar have adopted an intersectional framework to explore the experiences of Black women lawyers (American Bar Association, 2006; Blackburne-Rigsby, 2009; Melaku, 2019; Norwood, 2020; Pratt, 2012). Others have highlighted the significant and groundbreaking contributions of Black women lawyers to social movement issues related to race and equality (Smith, 2000; Wing, 2000). Additionally, country-specific studies have examined women's representation in law. Ballakrishnen (2019, 2021) investigates the impact of globalization on the work of women lawyers in India, leading to what she describes as the emergence of a group of "accidental feminist lawyers"—a scenario of gender parity among women in top law firms that is not necessarily the result of any feminist or gender interventions, but instead driven by the demand for high skills, family connections, and firm policies.

In examining women's representation in law in Sri Lanka, Samararatne (2020) challenges dominant discourses and theories, such as the "legal complex theory," which universally silences the experiences of diverse women in the legal field. Sharif (2015) highlights the glass ceiling effect on the experiences of women lawyers in Malaysia, while da Gloria Bonelli (2013) investigates how gender and other categorical differences impact women lawyers and judges in Brazil. These examples of existing scholarship from contexts outside the Global North are not exhaustive, nor do they cover the full range of intriguing questions and research being explored. However, these emerging studies indicate a global movement regarding women's representation in law and emphasize the need for ongoing research on the challenges women in law continually face.

The preceding discussion has established a context and framework for understanding the role of African women as leaders and decision makers during the precolonial and colonial periods. It has also offered a global perspective and summarized key issues from existing literature on women in law. The next section applies matri-legal feminist theory to explain how women have emerged in law across the continent. Since matri-legal feminism focuses on the lived experiences of its subjects, this discussion mainly draws from and emphasizes the personal stories of the women interviewed, grounding the findings in specific country and continental contexts. This section uses legal narratives and storytelling methods to create a mosaic that illustrates how the *HISP* (*history, institutions, and social interactions*) *framework* shapes women's *positionalities (P)* through their experiences and life stories in the legal profession.

IV. Along Came the Women: Mapping Women's Representation in Law Across Africa

Similar to global trends in women's entry into the legal profession, the late entry of women across Africa can be linked to two main historical factors: colonial racial anti-education policies and prevalent sociocultural gender discrimination favoring male education over female. The emergence of women in the formal legal field does not diminish the important roles they played in precolonial justice systems and dispute resolution mechanisms that existed before formal legal professions arrived. Christopher Sapara Williams made history as the first Nigerian lawyer called to the English Bar in 1879. However, it took another 50 years for the first woman, Stella Thomas Marke, to be called to the English Bar in 1933. Stella Jane Thomas Marke later joined the judiciary, becoming Nigeria's first magistrate in 1943. In Sierra Leone, Frances Claudia Wright became the second woman called to the bar in West Africa in 1943, despite conflicting reports about the first male Sierra Leonean called to the bar (Dawuni, 2020).

In Ghana, a similar pattern appeared. While John Mensah Sarbah was called to the English Bar in 1887, it was not until 1946 that Essie Matilda Forster became the first woman lawyer in the Gold Coast (as it was then called) (Dawuni, 2021b). Annie Jiagge was called to the bar at Lincoln's Inn in 1945, and she became the first woman magistrate in Ghana in 1954 and later the first woman to serve as a High Court judge in British West Africa (Dawuni, 2012). In much of southern Africa—Zimbabwe, Namibia, Botswana, and Zambia—the winds of apartheid South Africa created a chilling barrier to education for Black individuals with a few exceptions of some Black people who were able to be trained in the metropole (Ngcukaitobi, 2018). The radical movements to overthrow apartheid and the changes happening after apartheid explain the much later emergence of women as lawyers, judges, and scholars.

The goal of this section of the chapter is to trace and explain the gradual entry of women into the legal professions. Given the close connection between the legal field and politics, I use a historical comparative approach and rely on the categorization established in Chapter 1, dividing the major evolutionary trends into five phases—the

Table 3.1 *List of First Women Lawyers in Sub-Saharan Africa*

Country	Name	Year called
South Africa	Constance May Hall (first White woman)	1926
Zimbabwe	Phyllis Mackendrick	1929
Nigeria	Stella Jane Thomas	1935
Sierra Leone	Frances Claudia Wright	1943
Ghana	Essi Matilda Forster	1945
Angola	Maria do Carmo Medina	1948
Liberia	Angie Brooks	1949
Mauritius	Laure Pillay	1955
Malawi	Vera Chirwa	1959
Uganda	Princess Elizabeth Bagaya of Toro	1966
South Africa	Desiree Finca (first Black woman)	1967
Zambia	Lombe Chibesakunda	1968
Kenya	Effie Owuor	1968
Cameroon	Miriam Weledji	1969
Benin	Hélène Aholou Keke	1974
Senegal	Mame Bassine Niang	1975
Namibia	Maria Catharina Greeff	1977
Eswatini	Qinisile Mabuza	1978
The Gambia	Mariam Jack-Denton	1979
Somalia	Caasha-Kin Duale	1979
Mauritania	Fatimata M'Baye	1985
Chad	Nadingar Ekoue Thérèse	1992
Burundi	Espérance Musirimu	1995
Burkina Faso	Antoinette Ouédraogo	N/A
Cabo Verde	Evelyse de Melo Monteiro	N/A
Comoros	Harimia Ahmed	N/A
Cote d'Ivoire	Kwassi Béatrice Cowplli-Boni	N/A
Gabon	Marylise Issembé	N/A
Madagascar	Berthe Raharijaona	N/A
Niger	Adji Fati Kountche	N/A
Tanzania	Julie Manning	N/A
Togo	Acouetey Massan Lorette	N/A

Source: This list was compiled from multiple sources, and attempts were made to verify the dates. Some of these dates may show up in other databases with different dates designated as the year of their call to the bar. N/A is used for names where it was impossible to find multiple data points of validation.

colonial period (1930–1950), pre-independence to state formation (1950–1970), resistance and liberalization (1970–1990), diffusion and bar expansion (1990–2010), and global expansionism (2010–present). Due to the strong link between law and politics, these phases are shaped by major political developments across the continent, while also considering the connections between continental and global trends in the legal professions. **Table 3.1** displays data on the first women called to the bar in countries where such data are available.

The ensuing analysis evaluates the data presented in **Table 3.1** to contextualize the periods during which these women were called to the bar. A synthesis of the different periods outlined here must be understood against the backdrop of colonial and political developments, as well as the evolution of legal education and the legal profession, as discussed in Chapter 2.

1. Phase One: The Colonial Phase (1930–1950)

Historians pinpoint the full colonization of Africa starting from the 1884 Berlin Conference. Before this date, colonial powers had already interacted with the continent, and trade in goods and people was ongoing (Adu-Boahen, 1989). To narrow this discussion to women's entry into the profession, I use 1930 as the starting point to examine the state of the colonies and when the first women lawyers appeared. Before the 1930s, only men could access legal education in the colonial metropole. In Great Britain, which colonized many African territories, the Sex Disqualification (Removal) Act of 1919 marked a turning point for women's participation in public life, including law. Although Eliza Orme is considered the first woman to earn a law degree in 1888, other women enrolled as solicitors in Scotland (1920), England (1922), and Wales (1922) (Schultz & Shaw, 2013). The 100 Years Project, which lists the first women in various legal and judicial sectors in the UK, sometimes provides different dates for these women, often distinguishing between those called to different bars, those enrolled as barristers versus solicitors, and those admitted but not practicing (First Hundred Years, n.d.).

The British law of 1919 was not, however, applicable to the colonies due to the English Law Extent of Application Act, which limited the application of laws to the colonies. Since colonial control was still in effect when women were allowed to enroll as solicitors across the United Kingdom, African women faced the additional burden of racial discrimination on their path to becoming lawyers. The first African women called to the various English bars—Stella Jane Thomas Marke in Nigeria, Frances Claudia Wright in Sierra Leone, and Essi Matilda Forster in Ghana—were called to the English Bar 13, 23, and 25 years, respectively, after the first woman solicitor in Scotland. In most sub-Saharan African countries, except South Africa, I could not find records of formal laws disqualifying women from entering the legal professions. Following the British Sex Disqualification (Removal) Act of 1919, South Africa enacted a similar law—the Women Legal Practitioners Act of 1923—which finally allowed women to join the legal profession. Irene Geffen became the first woman to be enrolled as a lawyer (advocate) in 1926. But due to the ongoing dominance of racial apartheid, it would take 41 years before the first Black woman—Desiree Finca—qualified as a lawyer in 1967 (Sasinsky, 2020).

The legal profession is among the most highly regulated fields worldwide. Access, practice regulations, and the management of ethics and standards of conduct have largely been shaped by men to favor their professional interests (Schultz & Shaw, 2003). These regulatory structures influence institutional norms and practices aimed at limiting entry to the profession and establishing standards for practitioners' work. In the United Kingdom, these norms include creating professional hierarchies through the establishment of the Queen's Counsel (QC) or King's Counsel, depending on the current monarch. The division of the legal system between solicitors and barristers, along with various bars and inns, is intended to control access and advancement within the legal hierarchy (Sommerlad, 1994). In African countries like South Africa, these hierarchies are reflected in a split bar separating attorneys from advocates. Similarly, in Kenya, Uganda, Zambia, and South Africa, the QC has been renamed Senior Counsel to create distinctions among practicing lawyers. In Nigeria, the QC has been renamed Senior Advocates of Nigeria (SAN). All these institutional mechanisms function as gatekeeping tools, with most, if not all, gatekeepers being male.

The dominant gender discriminatory practices prevalent in the colonial powers of Great Britain, France, and Portugal were subsequently transferred to their colonies. These exclusionary regulatory practices led to the development in the metropole of what is commonly known today as the "old boys' club," a network of men promoting their collective interests while excluding others—primarily women. The harmful nature of these gatekeeping practices adversely affects when and how women can enter the legal professions. The patriarchal institutional norms established in the English Bar were ultimately transplanted to Nigeria (and continue to persist), resulting in the phrase "there are no ladies at the bar," with some even referring to women as "gentlemen at the bar" and "gentlemen in skirts" (Cruickshank & Ozobia, 2006).

Embedded within the socially and culturally violent colonial policies was the intersection of race and gender for Indigenous peoples of colonized lands. The colonialists did not believe that Africans were capable of studying law, arriving in the colonies with Western patriarchal ideas that women were unfit to become lawyers or pursue higher education. In tracing the history of legal education in South Africa, Madlalate (2022, p. 163) quotes from Nelson Mandela's biography, discussing the views of one of the deans of the law faculty: "his view was that law was a social science and that women and Africans were not disciplined enough to master its intricacies. He once told me I should not be at Wits but should study for my degree through UNISA" (Mandela, 1995, p. 90). Expressions of educational racism were widespread throughout southern Africa, including Zimbabwe (Tshuma, 1991). Against this contested and racially segregated historical backdrop, the first foreign-educated elite class emerged. The preference for male children from coastal elite families explains the significant gaps between the emergence of the first male lawyer and the first female lawyer. All the women lawyers from this initial period (1930–1950) were educated in the colonizing metropolis, just like the men before them. Similar to the experiences of the first women lawyers in much of Europe, Frances Claudia Wright of Sierra Leone and Essi Matilda Forster of Ghana had fathers who were lawyers. The trend of studying abroad was a major feature of this period due to the lack of law schools in the colonies. Despite the colonial administration's worries that lawyers would lead the movement for decolonization, the natural progression of obtaining basic education and pursuing further studies overseas eventually led to the second phase of lawyer emergence, which coincided with the growth of the bar and more women entering the profession.

2. Phase Two: Independence to State Formation (1951–1970)

Ghana's independence from Great Britain in 1957, the first country in sub-Saharan Africa, triggered a domino effect that encouraged other nations to pursue their own demands for independence. Ghana's independence marked a significant milestone in Africa's quest for self-governance and the rule of law. The postcolonial state-formation agenda required an educated elite capable of taking over remnants of colonial administration and managing efficient bureaucracies. While President Nkrumah of Ghana and other leaders after independence aimed to develop various levels of technical and specialized skills, training lawyers was particularly important within this agenda (Harvey, 1963). Training lawyers abroad was costly, and because these lawyers were educated in British common law and equity, connecting what they learned to the local context could sometimes be a difficult adjustment (Adewoye, 1982b; Dawuni & Badejogbin, 2021; Ghai, 1981; Luckham, 1981).

Most post-independence leaders invested in creating law faculties and law schools in their countries to meet the high demand for lawyers as agents in developing the postcolonial state. These local law schools expanded opportunities for educating more lawyers domestically. The newly established law faculties also allowed women to obtain professional qualifications, including in law. Paradoxically, the growth of law faculties and law schools across the continent did not mean that every law graduate received legal training locally. Many still pursue their legal degrees abroad for various reasons to this day. Many postcolonial leaders aimed to indigenize by integrating local knowledge and professionals. This effort led to the quick creation of law faculties. Shortly after gaining independence from Great Britain, Kwame Nkrumah transformed University College in Ghana (established in 1948 as an extension of University College London) into the University of Ghana in 1957. The law faculty was established in 1958, followed by the Ghana School of Law in 1959. Due to a shortage of instructors for specialized courses, the first cohort had to wait an extra year before enrolling (Harvey, 1966). Among the first lawyers called to the Ghana Bar in 1962, no records indicate that any women graduated in this group.

Following President Kwame Nkrumah's ambitious vision for advancing Pan-African development, the Faculty of Law at the University of Ghana and the Ghana School of Law welcomed students from across the continent who wished to study law. Although legal education was still mainly delivered by foreign (mostly British and American) lawyers and academics, the shift toward indigenizing legal education soon led to the training of Ghanaians as law lecturers (Harrington & Manji, 2021b). In Sierra Leone, Fourah Bay College is recognized as the first university-level institution (then affiliated with the University of Durham) established in sub-Saharan Africa in 1827; however, it wasn't until 1990 that the first law faculty and law school were created (Council of Legal Education, n.d.).

Across the continent, the wave of independence motivated efforts to establish local higher education institutions aimed at training locally skilled experts to fulfill the administrative and bureaucratic needs of the post-independence period. During the opening ceremony of the new School of Law in Accra in 1962, President Nkrumah (1962, p. 103) stated:

> Our lawyers, therefore, if they are to understand the spirit of our laws, must understand the basic principles upon which the state is directed and why certain laws are enacted, repealed or amended by Parliament. The teaching of law is totally incomplete if it is not accompanied by a background of economic, social and political science, and even politics, science and technology.

Although law schools were later established across much of East and West Africa, the apartheid-era restriction of legal educational opportunities for Blacks in South Africa was echoed throughout the southern African region. The apartheid policies of racial and gender discrimination, which spread throughout the South, influenced when and where the first women lawyers appeared in Namibia and Zimbabwe. While this project has not conducted primary archival research, records of the first women lawyers and judges in Zambia, Malawi, Lesotho, Botswana, and Zimbabwe are documented as Black women. A more thorough investigation into the historical archives likely would reveal that the first women called to the bar were often white settler women. This is a research area that others could explore to better understand the history of women in law across the continent.

The establishment of law faculties and law schools varied widely across the continent. In some countries, it took several years, often into the 1990s, before a law faculty or law school was founded. In The Gambia, the first law faculty was established at the University of Gambia in 2007, followed by the first law school in 2011, which became fully operational with statutory approval in 2016 (Gambia School of Law, n.d.). As a result, many lawyers were trained abroad, mainly in England, Nigeria, and Sierra Leone, often through government scholarships and financial support from those countries. It's not surprising that the first female lawyer in The Gambia—Mariam Jack-Denton—was called to the bar in 1979, and the first female High Court judge from The Gambia, Mary Mame Yassin Sey, was appointed in 1998 (Koroma, n.d.). During my fieldwork in The Gambia, I learned from some pioneering legal professionals that it's little known that before Judge Sey's appointment, other women had served in The Gambia's judiciary, including judges from Sierra Leone and other Commonwealth jurisdictions. The first female magistrate in The Gambia, appointed in 1980, was Aminatta Runeni Ngum, a Zimbabwean national who married a Gambian citizen and moved to The Gambia.

In other countries, the establishment of law schools coincided with the third phase of nation-building and expansion. This period accelerated the entry of more women into legal educational institutions, and during this time, the second generation of women lawyers emerged. However, in many countries, the women in this second phase were actually the first women to enter the legal field. Throughout Africa, women played vital roles in the struggles for independence (Mama, 2020; Tsikata, 1989). These contributions significantly supported independence movements and led early leaders to see women as essential to nation-building. For example, in Ghana, Kwame Nkrumah's newly independent government was the first to create a women's wing for his political party, the Convention People's Party (CPP). Ghana was also the first country to endorse the Convention on the Elimination of All Forms of Discrimination Against Women (CEDAW) (Mama, 2023). In Tanzania, President Julius Nyerere's inclusive socialist policies are widely recognized for involving women from all social classes in the nation's development efforts (Ladner, 1971; Peeples, 2019). In Senegal, President Léopold Sédar Senghor is known for fostering a political and social environment that supported women's rights organizations in the early 1970s. The Association of Senegalese Female Lawyers (l'Association des Juristes Sénégalaises—AJS) was established in 1974, advocating for equality and legal rights for women (Scales-Trent, 2010).

Recognizing the impact of colonial social reengineering on women's roles, the significant participation of women in the struggle for decolonization was a catalytic development that led to their reemergence as leaders. Although these advancements have been seen as inadequate and sharply criticized by African feminist scholars (Mama, 2020; Tsikata, 1989), they nonetheless created new opportunities for women seeking to bridge the public/private divide to pursue higher education and engage in political and economic initiatives. Having been constrained by restrictive and anti-woman colonial policies that long confined women to the domestic sphere in many parts of Africa, the immediate postcolonial era brought a renewed awareness of the importance of including women in postcolonial state-building and national development. The complementary roles women held in precolonial societies, often blurring the lines between the domestic/private and the public, began to resurface. The traditional positions of authority that women occupied in societies as chiefs, queens, native doctors, and priestesses (Achebe, 2020; Day, 2020; Ezeanya, 2020) served as crucial foundations for the acceptance of women in roles traditionally reserved for men. Women's mobilization during the independence struggles and separatist movements, along with their organizing efforts for democratic governance, are powerful indicators of how grassroots women's movements have been, and continue to be, essential to centering women as leaders (Kang, 2015; Mougoue, 2019).

Post-independence state formation required the use of all available skilled labor. Justice Annie Jiagge, the first female magistrate and judge in Ghana, received support from President Kwame Nkrumah. Her rise to the high court would not have been possible without the president's political will and recognition of women's roles. Her professional journey—from being appointed a magistrate in 1954 to her appointment to the High Court in 1961 and the Court of Appeal in 1969—not only affirms President Nkrumah's belief in women's leadership potential but also highlights that Ghana, and Africa as a whole, would not accept being second to Great Britain, which colonized Ghana and had not yet appointed a woman to its High Court (Dawuni, 2012). Political leaders' acknowledgment of women's agency in development was crucial in the rise of the first women in law. The push for rapid state-building in the immediate postcolonial and postapartheid periods served as a strong indicator of how institutional factors (in this case, informal appointment and selection processes) are key driving forces behind the expansion of professional opportunity structures for women in law (Escobar-Lemmon et al., 2021).

3. Phase Three: Resistance and Liberalization Phase (1971–1990)

The euphoria that sparked the independence of many African nations was short-lived. Countries like Ghana, which promoted Pan-African hopes of democracy, the rule of law, and good governance, gradually shifted toward authoritarian tendencies. Many states soon became one-party systems, often marked by executive dominance over the government, a lack of separation of powers, and no checks and balances (Fombad & Murray, 2010; Shomade, 2022). As governments moved toward suppressing remaining traces of nation-building, lawyers and the legal profession emerged as strong defenses against growing authoritarianism. In Ghana, several attorneys who opposed the power and excesses of President Kwame Nkrumah's regime ended up in prison (Edsman, 1979; Harvey, 1966; Luckham, 1976; Okudzeto, 2018). Similarly, in Kenya, fear and anxiety among lawyers increased as President Moi's government used executive orders and illegal detentions to silence opposition (Nowrojee, 2014). Oloka-Onyango (2021), writing about Uganda, traced the role of academic institutions like Makerere University in mounting strong opposition to government abuses during transitions to democracy. The judiciary has consistently been targeted by executive overreach (Ellett, 2013; Gathii, 1994; Prempeh, 2007; VonDoepp, 2013). In many other African countries, legal scholars who challenged the authoritarian actions of ruling elites faced the full force of executive power, often forcing some into political exile (Harrington & Manji, 2021b). These political shifts soon led to military dictatorships, causing the 1980s and 1990s to be called the "lost decade" for Africa's development (Adjei et al., 2014).

These politically turbulent periods in the histories of several African countries were marked by strong resistance to military rule from lawyers and bar associations. While some lawyers were corrupted and silenced by political elites, many others stayed committed as voices of morality and hope for citizens. Among this group, the consequences they faced were often harsh, including political detention and, in some cases, even death (Mutua, 2001; Okudzeto, 2018). The resistance demonstrated by certain members of the bar and judiciary positioned these professions as symbols of hope and justice for ordinary people (Karekwaivanane, 2015; Nowrojee, 2014). Although history often overlooks the contributions of women in opposing the ruling regimes, it is noteworthy that during this time, more women pursued careers in law, partly due to the expansion of higher education opportunities, especially in law schools.

Despite the political challenges, many regarded the legal profession as noble—one that could defend citizens' rights while opposing government excesses. The liberalization of the profession allowed more people to join and marked a key turning point in expanding legal opportunities for women. As more men pursued legal education and careers, the likelihood that women would become lawyers increased, supporting Michelson's (2013) assertion that bar expansion leads to the feminization of the profession. The groups of women who entered the profession during this period may have done so for various reasons. However, as will be discussed later, some of these women might have been motivated by a broad interest in justice, especially regarding women's rights. Although they joined the profession much later, outside the historical context of the second phase explored in this book (state formation and expansion, 1950–1970), another example of how political leadership recognized women's abilities is the appointment of Navanethem "Navi" Pillay by President Nelson Mandela as a High Court judge in 1995, making her the first woman of color in South Africa to be appointed to a judicial position (Naidu, 2013).

Several leading advocates for human and women's rights—lawyers and judges—began to stand out during this period of professional liberalization. Among them is Vera Chirwa, the first woman lawyer in Malawi, who, in 1966, became a vocal critic of President Banda's authoritarian regime (Chirwa, 2007). By urging their governments to respect and safeguard human and women's rights, these women lawyers were fundamentally campaigning against authoritarian rule and government excesses. As discussed later, women lawyers and judges emerging during this phase transformed their legal skills, training, and knowledge into activism to advance women's rights. In Zimbabwe, like many other parts of Africa, perceptions persisted until independence that women were unfit for the legal profession, even though women had fought on the battlefield for independence and faced racial barriers. After independence, they had to continue their fight against gender discrimination. As Karekwaivanane (2020, p. 556) points out:

> Whereas prior to independence black lawyers struggled to get white clients, who believed them to be less competent than white lawyers, after independence it was primarily black women lawyers who had to fight the perception that they were less competent than their male counterparts. As a result, many black women who entered private practice in the 1980s and early 1990s found themselves serving mainly female clients, whose concerns dealt mostly with family law issues such as child custody, divorce, and abusive partners. It was this environment that prompted a group of lawyers, including Virginia Mudimu, Elizabeth Gwaunza, Sara Moyo and Catherine Msipa, to discuss creating what would become Zimbabwe Women Lawyers Association (ZWLA).

Despite the widespread belief that the legal profession is liberal and inclusive of women without formal restrictions (except in South Africa), women who enter the field still face challenges, especially in being fully accepted as equals by their colleagues and clients. Women lawyers faced similar issues in Ghana (Houghton, 1981), Kenya (Kamau, 2020), and Nigeria (Ozobia & Cruickshank, 2006). Although the intersectional nature of these challenges—gender, race, ethnicity, class, and other identities—has improved over time, the latter part of this chapter shows that some of these issues still exist, appearing both openly and secretly.

4. Phase Four: Diffusion and Bar Expansion (1990–2010)

The mid-1990s marked a turning point toward political liberalization, characterized by the emergence of the fourth wave of democratization across the continent. The economic disasters caused by military dictatorships from the late 1970s to the early 1990s led to economic and political turmoil. With increasing global pressure for political liberalization and democratization, several African countries began to take steps toward constitutional and electoral democracy (Prempeh, 2007; Shomade, 2022).

Democratic governance required the drafting of new constitutions and the creation of new institutions to uphold the rule of law and safeguard human rights. Once again, lawyers played a crucial role in advancing this new agenda (Mutunga, 2014).

While most lawyers who survived the authoritarian takeovers of the legal profession and bar associations remained leaders in activism against political dictatorship, there was renewed interest in legal education as a way to develop skills needed to strengthen democracy (Ndulo, 2002; Oloka-Onyango, 2021). The demand for more expertise in public interest litigation and human rights law prompted changes in legal education (Ghai & Ghai, 2014). However, the increasing need for public interest litigation was not the only reason for establishing new law schools, as economic factors also influenced this move. The entry of women into the profession during this time exemplifies what I call the *role-model effect*. The steady rise in the number of women lawyers in the first and second generations, along with their accomplishments in the courtroom and judiciary, sent clear signals that the legal field was no longer an exclusive domain for men. With the successful careers of these pioneering women professionals, many young women and girls began to see their potential and started to view the legal profession as a real career option.

The symbolic representation of early women lawyer role models shattered traditional perceptions that women were only suited for careers in the so-called feminine professions of nursing, teaching, and catering. With the incremental impact of the first three generations, the fourth generation of women lawyers has led to the number of women at the bar in most countries now reaching the 30% critical mass target often cited by the United Nations and women's rights organizations (Krook & McKay, 2011). This indicates that institutional and cultural shifts are underway, as the descriptive and symbolic presence of women has opened the doors for more women and girls to consider the legal profession as a viable career option. In addition to the symbolic representation of women, there are substantial outcomes from their presence at the bar. In many countries, women have ascended to leadership roles as chief justices, law deans, attorneys general, partners in law firms, and heads of major corporations. Collectively, the increasing trend of women in leadership positions has helped demystify the law as a male-dominated profession. The expansion of educational opportunities, the rising number of women role models, and the strong educational performance of girls have combined to create a critical mass of young women pursuing legal education and entering the legal professions.

5. Phase Five: Global Expansionism (2011–Ongoing)

According to scholars such as Fong, Trubek, and Wilkins (2019), the globalization of the legal profession has been ongoing since the 1990s. For this project, considering the delayed entry of Africans into the legal field, I identify 2010 as the year when the continent started experiencing the effects of global changes in the sector. The rise of global liberalization—marked by international trade, increased corporate mergers and acquisitions, technological influence on financial markets, and the rise in human rights violations and environmental issues—has together boosted the demand for lawyers and legal expertise. The interconnectedness of legal systems worldwide has created a need for diverse skills and knowledge. In several African countries, the liberalization of education has led to a surge in law schools and faculties (Oloka-Onyango, 2021). The growth of these institutions, driven by capitalist expansion and the rising demand for lawyers, has also caused unintended effects, including a decline in ethical standards among lawyers, law firms, educational institutions, and judicial bodies (Abdullahi, 2017; Lumumba, 2014). Cross-border business deals and law firm mergers have expanded opportunities for diversity in hiring skilled lawyers, increasing entry points for women.

Over time, the culmination of the four phases discussed above has led to a significant increase in the number of women lawyers across the continent. The current phase of global liberalization is fueled by expanded educational opportunities for girls, international efforts advocating for the right to education and women's rights (including the United Nations' Sustainable Development Goals 4 and 5 on equal educational opportunities and gender equality), and cultural shifts within countries toward girls' education. The challenge of obtaining current and reliable data makes it difficult to provide accurate projections on the number of women in legal professions in many countries, let alone across the entire continent. This represents a research project that will require a substantial investment of resources and time, beyond the scope of the current effort. The following discussion aims to weave together various narratives from my fieldwork while referencing existing literature to illustrate the factors that influenced women's decisions to pursue careers in law.

V. Pathways to the Profession: Explaining Career Choices

Examining the emergence of women in law through five distinct phases provides both a historical and intergenerational view of their entry into the profession. These phases highlight how barriers to women's representation have evolved, how institutional practices among professional organizations have shifted, and how societal norms and expectations about women's roles have changed over time. These intergenerational shifts have collectively expanded the opportunities available to women entering the field. However, despite the rise in the number of women, institutional norms have not adapted quickly enough, leading to workplace practices that are neither inclusive nor supportive of women. Changing social and gender expectations, such as women's caregiving roles, remains a challenge, as will be illustrated later through women's stories in these fields. Additionally, intersecting socially constructed categories, identities, and expectations influences women differently, resulting in a variety of outcomes.

Women's diverse lived experiences within socially constructed categories and identities lead to different outcomes, as expected given the antiessentialist view of women across the continent—shared along a spectrum of differences within countries and across various professions. Despite these challenges, and inspired by the role model effect, the legal field has seen steady growth in the symbolic presence of women as lawyers, judges, and academics. To develop a broader narrative about women's roles in the legal professions, I used an intergenerational approach by interviewing women from the second to the current fifth generation of women in law, as shown in Chapter 1. While individual circumstances, motivations, and choices vary, patterns emerged that enabled thematic analysis of different pathways into the profession and the varied experiences within it. Pursuing a career in law requires years of education and the gradual development of skills. For many women, the time needed to establish a career can be challenging due to gendered social and cultural expectations related to marriage and childbirth.

Why and how did women enter professional fields? What factors explain their choices to become lawyers, judges, or academics? As mentioned earlier in Chapter 1, there is no single explanation for the experiences discussed in this book. While some common patterns emerge, women's experiences and career decisions are influenced by personal choices, experiences, and encounters throughout their careers. These patterns are neither mutually exclusive nor an exhaustive list of factors that shape career paths. As you read the narratives, you may notice that multiple factors influence the motivation to pursue a law degree and ultimately a legal career. Before examining the qualitative interview responses, **Table 3.2** shows data from 249 survey respondents to highlight the variety in their decisions to pursue a law degree. A significant 71.3% of lawyers, 65.8% of judges, and 77.1% of academics said their choice was personal, but the detailed narratives and analyses that follow provide the details of what influenced these decisions.

Table 3.2 *Survey Responses on Career Choices*

Motivation	Lawyers ($n = 122$)	Judges ($n = 79$)	Academics ($n = 48$)
Family legacy (a parent or both parents are lawyers)	9.8%	10.1%	8.3%
Personal choice	71.3%	65.8%	77.1%
Encouragement by a peer or friend	8.25	7.6%	14.6%
Encouragement by a pioneer woman in law	7.4%	15.2%	6.3%
No particular reason	13.1%	11.4%	4.2%

*The total in each category may add up to more than 100% because respondents were given the option to choose more than one reason.

1. Changing Educational Opportunity Structures

In several countries across the continent, the return to democratic governance has led to new constitutional frameworks designed to uphold the principles of equality and nondiscrimination based on gender and other social categories. For instance, the 1996 Constitution of South Africa and the 2010 Constitution of Kenya have been praised for their progressive provisions on gender equality (Albethyn & Bonthuys, 2016; Kamau, 2013). In various other nations—as noted by Ibrahim (2016) in Nigeria, Dawuni (2016a) in Ghana, and Kang (2016) in Benin—specific provisions for nondiscrimination exist in national constitutions; however, the impact on women's access to public office, particularly within the legal profession, has been gradual. Driven by the evolving political and historical landscape, the second phase of women's entry into the legal profession marks a significant moment. This phase is characterized by increasing opportunities for pursuing legal education through personal choice and government-funded programs. Other scholars attribute the rising demand for qualified legal practitioners to fill expanding roles and improved selection methods that recognize women's merit as factors explaining the increasing number of women in the profession (Albethyn & Bonthuys, 2016; Kamau, 2013).

The historical and intergenerational changes occurring during these periods are illustrated by two narratives of women lawyers in Cape Verde. In Cape Verde, a first-generation woman judge pursued her dream of legal education and a legal career despite the lack of educational opportunities.

> At age 15, there weren't many opportunities to study law on my island. I could have changed my mind and chosen a different profession. When I got the chance, I went to Portugal to study law, and I have been a lawyer my entire life. If I had to do it again, I would still choose to be a lawyer. All my fight for women and human rights is connected to my original feelings about life and law. When I was in Lisbon, I was the first and only person from Cape Verde studying law. There was another woman from Mozambique and another from Angola.

For a prosecutor in Cape Verde, the decision to pursue a law degree was made possible through government investment in education. The newly independent government offered scholarships for citizens to study abroad because there were no higher education institutions in the former Portuguese colony. Her journey to the bench resulted from the government's need for qualified personnel to fill various positions.

> The Minister of Justice decided that I should study law, and I enjoyed it. I went to Portugal to attend the University of Lisbon from 1984 to 1989 because I was interested in law and did not want to become a teacher or scientist. After graduating in 1989, I worked as a trainee lawyer. Usually, we are required to attend the School of Magistrature, but because of the shortage of judges, I was appointed as a judge in 1992. Later, in 1993, I returned to Portugal to officially qualify as a judge.

The stories of many women from Cape Verde across the first to fourth generations in law are similar because the first university and law faculty in the country were not established until much later, in the 2000s. Although Cape Verde gained independence from Portugal in 1975, it did not follow the same pattern as other African countries by establishing law schools early on. University education and pursuing a legal career were expensive and often required traveling abroad—usually to Portugal.

In other regions, having qualifications as a legal or judicial professional nearly guaranteed employment, especially for those who chose to work in the public sector, often in the judiciary or the Attorney General's office. A second-generation woman in law (a judge) in Ghana remarked:

> The pattern shows that most women go to the Attorney General's office or commercial banks, while some join the litigation departments of law firms and later move up

> in the corporate sector. Regarding equal pay for equal work, I'm unsure if it's a major issue in Ghana. In government jobs, women earn the same as men. When many women start their families, they prefer working in government positions for job security; notably, many department heads at the Attorney General's office are women, which is appropriate.

The need for development in the early post-independence period significantly created professional opportunities for women. Despite ongoing cultural and systemic norms that women had to contend with, Uzebu-Imarhiagbe (2020b, p. 11) concludes that in Nigeria:

> The history of women in the legal profession is not a history of exclusion but of reception and advancement. In the admission and appointment of women lawyers into the bar and the bench, there was no deliberate consensus or policy by government to achieve gender integration. The driving force was need, the need for qualified legal practitioners.

Despite women's qualifications, the phenomenon of "male flight" from the judiciary created new opportunities for women. As previously mentioned, in several countries throughout sub-Saharan Africa, the era of one-man rule and military authoritarianism led to state capture by the authoritarian executive, making attacks on judicial independence common. Judges' salaries and allowances were often withheld to exert greater control over the judiciary, and no improvements were made to their working conditions (Oloka-Onyango, 2017; Widner, 2001). This caused male judges to leave the judiciary as they sought more lucrative careers at the bar (Uzebu-Imarhiagbe, 2020b). This notable "male flight" opened up new positions for women. A retired High Court judge in Nigeria reflects on this historical context.

> During military rule, judges' salaries were low, and the economy stagnated. It was terrible, so I thank God I had a husband who could feed us. Most men went into the private sector, and women remained in public service. Women started to advance through the ranks. Now that conditions have improved, the men want to return.

For other judges, the path to the bench resulted from changes in selection methods that allowed lawyers in practice to be appointed to the bench. A Supreme Court judge described her journey to the court and the tough decisions she had to make.

> Until the day I was offered a seat on the Supreme Court, I had never thought about joining the bench; no one ever discussed it with me. I was successful as a private lawyer, and the judiciary wasn't an option for me when it was first mentioned. However, after some reflection, I realized it might be a great opportunity to help develop the law. When I talked about it with my late uncle, he said, "it may be one of the ways things are happening to you. It has come your way, and it is such a great honor. How many people are offered a Supreme Court seat straight from private practice?" I accepted it as both a duty and an honor, understanding it would come with significant financial and social sacrifices, as I found myself suddenly changing my way of life.

Regardless of the key moments that led women to enter the legal professions, their choices were driven by the growing opportunities created by changes in their countries' political economy and institutional frameworks. Each woman's final decision to pursue the profession was a personal choice.

2. Family Tradition

Globally, the legal profession often runs through family generations, similar to other fields like the judiciary and academia. While not every lawyer can trace a long family lineage of lawyers, for many, this tradition has greatly influenced their decision to pursue a legal career. Accessible archival data on the first women lawyers in most African countries is limited. I found it challenging to discover information on the motivations and personal stories behind why the pioneering women chose to study law. Concerning Essi Matilda Forster, the first female lawyer in Ghana, I was lucky to interview her daughter, Estelle Appiah, who is also a lawyer, and she shared a detailed account of her mother's life story. In an interview published in "*Essi Matilda Forster: First Woman Lawyer in Ghana,*" Estelle Appiah recounted (Institute for African Women in Law, 2022, p. 2):

> Essi Matilda was born in 1922, and she was sent to school in England in 1927, at the age of five. When she left the Gold Coast, she did not speak English and when she returned to the Gold Coast in 1947, she had lost her mother tongue. Essi's mother, Mami Abba French, did not see her for the duration of that period, from 1927 to 1947, however she saw her father frequently, because he would visit the UK in connection with his legal work and also his business. He was a businessman as well as a politician. In 1940, Essi Christian had to decide on what career path she was going to follow. She was very much influenced by her father as well as her older brother, Howard and decided to become a lawyer. In 1942, she entered Gray's Inn to study to become a barrister and she qualified as a barrister in 1945.

For a lawyer and women's rights advocate in Cape Verde, even though her decision to become a lawyer was partly influenced by her father's profession, it was a second choice because there were no educational opportunities for her to train as a social worker focused on children. As she explains:

> Law was not my first interest. I always enjoyed being around children and wanted to work with them. However, at the time, studying children was not well-developed, so my father was against it and believed I should pursue a university degree. Then, I decided I wanted to become a lawyer because my father was one.

Although the respondent mentioned above had the option to choose a different career, her final decision to pursue law was influenced by her familiarity with the profession through her father. For others, following a legal education was shaped by their parents' choices. In The Gambia, a country on the West coast of Africa, a prominent lawyer explained that her father decided she should become a lawyer, hoping she would follow in his footsteps. To her, it felt like a natural step in her life—and luckily, she enjoyed practicing law. Looking back on her journey, she said that her decision to become a lawyer "was not driven by any grand idea of changing the world or anything."

Some judges were motivated to join the bench primarily through family ties—mostly through their fathers. Because law has historically been seen as a male profession rooted in patriarchal traditions, I did not find many first- or second-generation women lawyers whose mothers were also lawyers (although some do exist. For example, Estelle Appiah, called to the English Bar at Gray's Inn in 1976, is the daughter of Essi Matilda Forster, the first woman lawyer in Ghana). Given this history, it's not surprising that most respondents' decisions to become lawyers or judges were influenced by their fathers, with none attributing their careers to their mothers. A Cape Verdean magistrate shared her motivations:

> I joined the bench because of my father. Although he never spoke about his job, as a little girl, I would accompany him to court, and I understood what he did. Even during my judicial training in Portugal, I was uncertain whether I wanted to be a prosecutor or a magistrate. My father was a judge and a prosecutor general, and he taught us that being a judge wasn't a big deal; he emphasized respecting any work we did.

The story above shows how a parent's career can indirectly affect a child's career choices. An important point in this story is that the father did not put any pressure on the respondent. By saying, "he taught us that being a judge was not a big deal; he taught us to respect whatever work we did," it is clear that the father let the child choose naturally. Still, the father's position did influence her eventual decision to become a magistrate.

In Nigeria, another magistrate shared the influence of watching her father in his judicial career and the impact on her personal choice to become a judge:

> My father was a High Court judge, and I followed him everywhere. I loved the legal profession and watched him rise through the ranks to become a high court judge, which made me eager to pursue that path in my career and reach the pinnacle of success.

In addition to the bar and the bench, parental influence has significantly shaped certain career paths to the legal academy. A law lecturer in Nigeria confirms how parental influences affect career choices:

> I was motivated to study law since I was 16. My dad earned a doctorate and worked as an academic before becoming a judge. Initially, I pursued nursing, where I discovered my true self. I then studied archaeology before transitioning to law, which has been beneficial for me. After earning my degree in archaeology, I completed my master's in law (LLM) with a focus on African Studies. Each degree has helped me develop the concept of African feminist theory in my teaching and research.

> I appreciate the flexibility of academia; you are your own boss and set your own pace. I feel more comfortable conducting research.

Lastly, for some women, the path to the legal profession was not necessarily because they followed their parents' footsteps, mostly their fathers. For one judge in Kenya, her father encouraged her to pursue a legal career because he never had the chance to study law himself. This judge represents the second generation of women legal professionals, growing up in the early post-independence era when educational opportunities for girls were limited. It is important to note that, against the backdrop of a colonial environment that restricted educational access, some parents chose to send their daughters to school and let them pursue any career, even those considered a "man's profession" at the time. One could argue that the father hoped to live vicariously through his daughter by encouraging her to earn a law degree, as he had not been given that opportunity. His belief that a girl (his daughter) had the right to pursue a career in law was enough to jumpstart her legal and later judicial career.

The narratives above show that while a parent can influence a child's career choices, most of the women interviewed had the freedom to make their own decisions, many of whom were encouraged by their fathers. For instance, the legal academic from Nigeria, despite her varied experiences before studying law, had the opportunity to become a judge like her father; however, she chose academia, partly because her father was also an academic before becoming a judge.

3. Personal Choice (Intentional Lawyers)

The survey responses show that an overwhelming 71.3% of women chose to join the bar voluntarily. For women judges, the percentage is 65%, and for academics, it's 77.1%. The reasons behind these choices vary, and while they are personal decisions, other factors like family, role models, and encouragement likely played important roles. For some legal professionals, the decision to pursue a career in law was purposeful and influenced by traits they naturally possessed, such as being outspoken or argumentative. For others, it was shaped by socialization that fostered the belief they could succeed as lawyers because of their ability to resolve conflicts. A lawyer in Ivory Coast shared her motivation:

> It wasn't about social justice (laughs). I've always wanted to be a business lawyer, so I simply followed that path. As an introvert, I had to work on overcoming my shyness. Our training to become lawyers includes various types of legal practice, which helped me gain some litigation experience. Eventually, I became an associate at a law firm and gained all the experience I needed before starting my own firm.

In Cape Verde, a self-ascribed "problem-solver" shared that:

> I've been interested in law since I was nine years old. My uncle is a lawyer, and I admire his work. I also enjoy working with people, and I realized that earning a law

degree would enable me to connect with them and help them with their challenges. I can relate to their issues and contribute to solving them.

The motivational factors expressed by this lawyer originate from a mix of her family's influence, especially her uncle, who is also a lawyer, and her personal realization of what she could accomplish with a law degree. This story highlights both internal and external factors that shape a career in law, further confirming that there is no single path or critical factor in pursuing a legal profession. For a superior court judge in Cape Verde, the journey to earning a law degree and becoming a judge "was always my dream. Before I finished secondary school, I knew I wanted to be a judge. I did not know any judges or even anything about the law."

Further east of Cape Verde, a judge in Senegal also expressed her long-standing ambition to become a judge, which she always knew she wanted to pursue, partly influenced by her family (uncle). Her passion and ambition for becoming a judge developed early in life, and the difficulty of the entrance exam did not deter her from chasing her goal.

I've always wanted to be a judge. My uncle was a magistrate, and as a kid, I used to pretend I was in court holding make-believe trials. Getting into college was easy, but the exam to become a judge was tough, and you had to be well-prepared. I succeeded on my second try. You're only allowed to take the exam three times.

Another judge and court president in Senegal recounts her decision to become a judge as the better choice between the two options she had—either to become a lawyer or a judge.

From an early age, I was drawn to law, but I was not eager to become a lawyer because the process is quite bureaucratic. I was also not interested in pursuing money, as active practice does not offer stable employment for women. Very few women work as *attorneys*. I earned a master's degree in commercial law and a second master's in cybercrime. At 24, I was the youngest member of my cohort at the Judicial Training Institute for Judges.

In The Gambia, a first-generation judge has always nurtured her passion for earning a law degree. She started her career as a high school teacher until she decided to pursue her master's in education. She shared:

I also obtained a form and applied to study law. I told my supervisor that I was eager to pursue law rather than a master's in education, and she agreed to transfer me from the Ministry of Education to the Ministry of Justice for one year. In 1980, I received a full scholarship to study law at the University of Wales, which I completed in 1983. I later joined the judiciary in 1988 as a magistrate and applied to join the bar in 1989. I was then invited to join the bench as a high court judge in 1998.

For some professionals, even though they planned to pursue a legal career, the unpredictable twists of fate and decisions that led them to the bench were not what they had anticipated, and sometimes this brought on early doubts about whether they had chosen the right path. From the experience of a High Court judge in Ghana:

> My goals included joining the bench or the foreign service through a political route. I wrote a book about business in Ghana, and when they decided to establish the Commercial Court, I gave the Chief Justice a copy. This caught his attention, and I was invited to join the bench. My family and support network thought it was a good idea. Initially, I felt miserable because I believed I had limited my options. Before joining the bench, I was actively involved in litigation after being called to the bar in 1987, primarily practicing corporate and business law before starting my own firm.

The motivations were deeply personal for some legal professionals pursuing an academic career. In Senegal, one respondent explained that becoming an academic involves several steps: submitting an application, attending an interview, giving a teaching demonstration, and assessing one's composure and interactions with students.

> I always wanted to be a teacher. I had several chances to work as a lawyer, but I wanted a career that would give me practical work experience without obstacles. During the selection process, there were 15 candidates, and they picked two of us based on merit.

In Ghana, a law lecturer shared her pathway to the academy:

> I have always aspired to become a teacher, and the highest academic rank is usually achieved at the university level. After earning my law degree, I immediately pursued my Master of Laws (LLM), and my first job was as a law lecturer. I also work part-time as a legal practitioner; I don't believe in solely theoretical teaching. Being a part-time practitioner allows me to provide practical instruction to my students who ask questions about real-life scenarios. Combining the roles of lawyer and academic helps me answer their questions more effectively.

A third-generation law lecturer in Ghana also shared her motivations:

> I started teaching at the law faculty in 1991, and I have remained passionate about it ever since. After earning my first degree, my professors expected more from me, so I pursued my master's in law (LLM). When I returned, it felt almost natural to come back to the law faculty. I served my national service as a teaching assistant, where the dean encouraged me to teach. Initially, I chose this path because I wasn't interested in litigation, but I have stayed here ever since.

Finally, for some, the personal desire to join the legal academy was rooted in practical considerations of how to balance their careers and personal responsibilities as parents effectively:

> Writing and research fueled my interest in pursuing an academic career. I doubted that practicing law would satisfy that passion. Additionally, when I reflected on the litigation environment, I questioned whether I could balance family responsibilities, legal work, and teaching. Managing everything has been difficult due to the demands of teaching and caring for a young child. I gained more wisdom and began choosing daytime classes, teaching less in the evenings. You still spend a lot of time away from home, and even finding time for research remains difficult.

4. Accidental Lawyers (Unintentional Lawyers)

The legal profession has not always been the top career choice for some women. Unlike the family and intentional decisions mentioned earlier, for many others, choosing to study law might be viewed as unplanned or even accidental. Most women in this group lacked prior knowledge of the legal field and had no family members, female role models, or career counselors to guide them.

A lawyer in Cape Verde started her career working at a supermarket. Getting married young limited her chances for personal growth. Years later, after divorcing her wealthy husband, she was encouraged to pursue further education, which led her to study law at the University of Lisbon. Another lawyer in Cape Verde chose law after realizing she couldn't follow her original dream of a career in foreign service. The story of a Gambian woman lawyer was not only unexpected but also seemed nearly impossible at that time, as she recalls.

> I was planning to study English literature and had also applied for a scholarship. My professor suggested I consider law, which seemed impossible at the time, but I decided to give it a shot. I was the first in my family to attend college, and I had never received any career advice.

The lack of career guidance for most young women (and men) during the first and second generations was a common problem. Judge Florence Mumba, the first female High Court judge in Zambia, shares her unpredictable and tough journey to studying law:

> At the University, I wanted to study theology, unfortunately, it was not offered. In my search for something new to study, I came across the Law School and decided to register there. Some of my friends discouraged me saying that some male students in the Law School were failing because law studies were difficult. I challenged them that I would follow those who passed their law courses. I was fortunate in that some of the senior male students were helpful, they shared their textbooks with me. At that time, it was not easy to find law textbooks in Zambia. In my class, I was the only girl. I always faced teasing from the male students and some of our lecturers who felt that I was in the wrong class as they did not expect women to qualify as lawyers. (Mumba, 2018, p. 30)

In the early post-independence period, many girls were advised to pursue careers considered suitable and feminine. Effie Owuor, the first woman lawyer and magistrate in Kenya, shares her experience of being discouraged from choosing a career in law and the creative methods her father used to motivate her to study law.

> I attended Alliance Girls School, an institution focused on leadership, and I considered myself fortunate to be accepted. While at Alliance High School, I hadn't yet decided that I wanted to pursue law. Unfortunately, since it was a missionary school, my wonderful headmistress, Mrs. Bruce, would hear none of it. A decent girl didn't aspire to study law; instead, she could become a secretary—though even that was too much for her to accept—become a nurse, or pursue a career in teaching. At that time, because we were so few and Dar-es-Salaam University was just starting, they sent someone to inform us about the university. I vividly remember that one of my professors, McAuslan, went to Alliance Boys School, the boys' equivalent of our girls' school, to speak to the boys. Mrs. Bruce wouldn't allow him to come speak to me, even after I expressed my desire to become a lawyer. When my father, who was visiting town, heard that the headmistress was preventing me from seeing Professor McAuslan, my brother visited the school with a friend and proposed to take me out since I was studying Advanced (A) levels and could leave campus. I went into town with my father, who had arranged for me to meet with Professor McAuslan. He was very interested in helping me get to Dar-es-Salaam to study law. I applied, and fortunately, I was accepted. Attending the University of Dar-es-Salaam was a significant milestone for me. Not only did the Kenyan government provide me with an air ticket, but they also granted a dressing allowance and pocket money because this was quite an opportunity. The government was eager to ensure that we trained as lawyers.

Effie Owuor and Florence Mumba eventually became the first female high court judges in Kenya and Zambia, respectively. However, as the narrative above shows, their journeys to studying law were nearly blocked by the colonial missionary educational system and sociocultural norms that fostered the idea that women could not study law. The spread of patriarchy through missionary education affected many young girls' career choices across the continent (Tripp, 2004). It required the determination of parents—mainly fathers—to let their daughters challenge these colonial missionary ideas of womanhood and gender roles.

In the case of a High Court judge in Nigeria, joining the judiciary was not an initial decision—it came about because of her passion to show how justice could be handled differently and effectively:

> My father was a High Court judge, and he inspired me to pursue a career in law initially. He encouraged me to choose a profession that would stay with me for the rest of my life unless I decided to do something else. I felt discouraged when I started attending court and saw how some courts operated. I resolved that if I became a judge, I would show how things could be done differently. I worked for a government corporation for 14 years before moving to the Ministry of Justice, and within four years, I was appointed to the High Court bench in 1994.

A comparable experience in Nigeria illustrates how the dysfunctional judicial system inspired the decision to become a judge:

> From law school until I joined the bench, I did not have that goal in mind. My father encouraged me to pursue a judicial career, but I refused. During my practice, I prosecuted a copyright infringement case in which we filed an injunction; however, the judge failed to rule on it despite numerous delays! The court's inaction frustrated me, and I asked myself, why not go somewhere where I am in charge of my court? That was how my journey to the bench began. In 2008, there was an advertisement for magistrates, and my dad informed me because I was out of state at that time. I applied at a moment when most people hesitated to pursue the magistracy due to low pay and a heavy workload. Given my frustrations with the delays in the judicial system, I handled my cases swiftly as a magistrate, earning a reputation through word of mouth. So, when the opportunity for judgeship arose, I applied. Those coming to court knew that I was not willing to waste anyone's time, which also helped me qualify for the High Court bench.

Interestingly, and in an antithetical way, in the case of a magistrate from Nigeria, her decision to join the judiciary was not because of the dysfunction of the courts, but rather how impressed she was by courts that functioned well:

> During my years as a lawyer, I visited many courts across different states, including the Court of Appeal, the Supreme Court, and occasionally the customary courts. I observed that some courts seem disinterested in administering timely justice—not due to laziness, as the administration back then was different from today—which can be disheartening. However, I noticed that judges were actively engaged in other courts with their caseloads. I was impressed by this and decided to apply to become a judge.

The three different stories from Nigeria about choosing to join the judiciary show an antiessentialist view of women's career paths. Women's different opinions and experiences in law can lead to the same career, even if their motivations and initial interests are different. The career paths of legal academics also shed light on accidental or unintended routes. A fourth-generation law professor in Senegal describes her journey into academia as guided by destiny. When asked why she decided to join the legal academy, she remarked:

> I believe it is destiny. When I was younger, I aspired to be a medical doctor, but the reality is that you might want to pursue something, yet the system guides you elsewhere. I was admitted to Cheikh Anta Diop University (UCAD) in the science faculty, and I switched to the law faculty. I stayed in law because my father wanted me to continue in that profession. I truly wanted to be a magistrate, but that didn't work out. Teaching wasn't my first choice, but it turned out well. After earning my first degree, I pursued my doctorate in France, worked there for five years, and returned to Senegal in 2005. That year, I began working and teaching at various private schools

> and collaborated with a non-governmental organization just to secure a job. I joined the law faculty in 2007 as a substitute teacher and was officially hired in 2008.

Based on interviews conducted in the two Francophone countries of Senegal and the Ivory Coast, the magistracy appears to be the main career choice for most women. The transition to other professions, such as becoming a lawyer, is reflected in another account from the Ivory Coast.

> After completing my degree, I worked and later took the exam to become a magistrate but did not succeed. Initially, I believed that a career in the judiciary was the best path for me because it would allow me to apply the knowledge I had gained to solve real-world problems. Additionally, being a magistrate comes with a certain social status; it provides job stability along with good pay and benefits. The magistrate exam is very competitive, and only a few candidates pass. When I did not succeed, I decided to continue my education and pursue an advanced degree at the doctoral level. I earned my second master's degree and then traveled to France for further studies. Upon returning, I received my Ph.D. here in Abidjan.

In Nigeria, an academic describes her pathway to the academy as accidental:

> I started by chance. I was offered an administrative position, but the director looked at my CV and thought I might fit better in academia. They changed my role to that of a research assistant, and that's how I got started. I love research, but I hadn't planned on going into academia. My passion for research has kept me here. I enjoy sharing knowledge. No matter what I'm facing in life, when I'm teaching, all those worries seem to disappear.

The love for research is also present in the narrative of a law lecturer in a private university in the Ivory Coast:

> When I first started my legal education, I didn't want to become a professor; I wanted to be a magistrate. However, as I began tutoring, I discovered my interest in research and what I could accomplish in this field. Some of my peers who pursued magistracy returned to the faculty to improve their skills, which made me realize that I had the potential to develop my basic research abilities.

5. Justice and Problem-Solving as Driving Forces

There is a common belief that everyone in the legal profession is motivated by a shared commitment to justice and the rule of law. While this may be true for many, it cannot be applied uniformly to all individual career paths. However, some people's career choices are genuinely driven by a strong passion for justice. Many of these individuals refer to themselves as "problem-solvers," motivated by a desire to tackle social justice issues through their work. Most of the women I interviewed for this book project, including both lawyers and judges, cited their dedication to justice as the main reason for pursuing legal or judicial careers. For many, the idea of justice versus injustice began early in life, and one lawyer described it as almost a form of defiance against her parents, who worked in the medical field.

> It's all about my personality. Even as a young girl, I aspired to be a lawyer. My father was a doctor, and my mother was a pharmacist; they assumed I would follow in their footsteps, which made it hard to tell them I wouldn't pursue that path. When I decided to go against my parents' wishes, we argued often, and they couldn't understand my decision. I was constantly surrounded by discussions of health, and I grew tired of it. I dislike injustice; even when I see it on the streets, I stop to confront it. I chose to follow my passion for justice.

Personal experiences of injustice also appear to have significantly influenced others' decisions to study law. As narrated by a lawyer in Cape Verde:

> As a young girl, I developed a strong sense of justice that greatly shaped me. Moreover, certain life experiences influenced my perspective—my mother, a medical doctor, went to specialize in Portugal, and I encountered significant racism at just eight years old. This deeply rooted the ideas of right and wrong within me, and I wanted to help others who, because of poverty, faced discrimination and were treated as inferior. I believed that becoming a lawyer would enable me to make a small but meaningful difference in the world.

For many other women who considered themselves "problem-solvers," a career in law was a great opportunity to test their skills. When asked about her motivations for becoming a lawyer, a second-generation lawyer in Nigeria said:

> I never imagined doing anything other than practicing law, and I truly enjoyed my work. The gift of hindsight lets me reflect that I love solving people's problems and the research involved in handling court cases. For me, litigation was a way to combine my two interests. Through litigation, I connected with people, which added a human element to the law.

For a superior court judge in Cape Verde, even though pursuing a judicial career was accidental, she came to accept the law as both a passion and a way to give back to her country:

> I never thought I would become a judge. On my island, people fear judges because folklore suggests that when a judge dies, they turn into a ghost. As a child, I was frightened by the idea of being a judge. I've always had a natural sense of justice and couldn't tolerate injustice, even though it wasn't a conscious decision. After finishing my legal education, I wanted to be a lawyer and trained as an advocate. However, after graduating in 1998, I worked for several years as a lawyer. In 1999, I got the chance to become a judge—life took me in that direction. Even at home, I serve as a judge, and sometimes my husband reminds me not to take on that role there. I feel that being a judge is my way of giving back to my country. I believe I can contribute

> more to society as a criminal judge because I prefer to see people change. I hold onto the hope that I can do anything to improve society.

Many lawyers who choose law to fight societal injustices realize that changing society is beyond one person's power. Achieving social justice needs a group effort involving different parts of the justice system, a functioning rule of law, and good governance. Still, women in law continue to work hard to help fight injustice as lawyers and judges—whether in the private or public sector, which will be covered in the upcoming section on women's contributions to the profession.

6. Role Models

The fourth generation (1990–2010), known as the diffusion and growth phase, shows how women's symbolic representation as role models positively impacts their legal career choices. The gradual shift across generations in attitudes toward women as legal professionals has been key in changing social and institutional beliefs about women's ability to enter fields once considered exclusive to men. Some women interviewed for this book chose to pursue law because of unexpected or chance mentoring opportunities through encounters with women lawyers and judges. This role model effect, whether intentional or unintentional, was significant for second- and third-generation women in law who entered the profession when very few women were practicing. Often, the decision to pursue a legal career was influenced by the symbolic presence of trailblazing women lawyers and judges. These role models affected the career ambitions of the young women they met, as shared by a lawyer in Ghana.

> During my advanced level (high school), the goal was to pursue a profession rather than just study individual subjects. I was inspired by some women lawyers who didn't even know me; one of them was Professor Akua Kuenyehia, the first female law lecturer and an advocate for women's rights, who spoke on television. I told my family that I would be on TV one day. I also met another woman lawyer, and while I don't remember her exact words, she did encourage me.

For a lawyer in Nigeria, her career choice was not to become a lawyer. "I wanted to be a pilot, but my dad took me to court one day, and when I saw a female lawyer's submission before the judge, I decided I wanted to be just like that." Whether in the courtroom, on television, or during a chance meeting with a woman lawyer, it seems that unintended career mentorship and women serving as role models have positively influenced young women's career choices in law. Interestingly, the role models were not always lawyers. For some women, seeing a woman in a profession typically considered only for men was enough to inspire them. Justice Kellelo Mafoso-Guni, the first woman appointed as a judge in Lesotho, shares her experience as captured by Ellett (2018, p. 111):

> One time . . . we were attended to by a female doctor. She was called Dr. Mahabane. We were flabbergasted. We had never seen a female doctor. The medical profession

> was membered by only males. We could not believe our eyes . . . It was generally believed that girls go to school to be nurses or teachers. Our sight of a female doctor brought into our minds possibilities of women becoming doctors . . . It was possible I could be a doctor . . . Studying law never entered my mind during my first days even or up to University. It is a miracle that I ended up as a lawyer who even proceeded to be a judge.

Although the above discussion of women's career paths is neither comprehensive nor unique, the interview stories highlight various factors that influence individual women. Collectively, these stories suggest interactions among different variables. For example, someone from a family of lawyers might pursue a legal career, whether intentionally or by accident. Likewise, a person who chooses law purposefully might do so because they were inspired by a role model and motivated by their passion for justice and problem-solving. There is no single route to the legal profession, and women make these decisions based on logical calculations that match their aspirational goals.

No matter what factors influence a person's choice to pursue a legal career, women bring their unique personal experiences that shape their individual and collective paths in the profession. The next section provides an intersectional view of women in law, based on the emerging themes found in the interviews.

VI. Women in Law: An Intersectional and Intergenerational Framing of Presence

Understanding women's experiences in the legal profession requires answering several questions that explore different factors along the career path. Do women in law have equal chances to enter the field? What influences when and how a woman joins the profession? Once inside, do women receive fair treatment compared to men? What factors affect the way women are treated relative to men? What influences the treatment women receive compared to other women? Addressing these questions requires an intersectional approach to women's lives through a decolonial and feminist lens.

In *Intersectionality and Women's Access to Justice in Africa* (Dawuni, 2022b, p. 6), I argued that "the relative privilege of an educated woman judge does not always shield her from the multiple and intersecting dimensions of exclusion she may experience due to gender, culture, ethnicity, class, religion, and other identities or categories she embodies." In that book, I challenged the common assumption that access to justice is an issue faced only by women litigants in the courtroom and those seeking other forms of justice outside it. Using the courtroom as both a physical and symbolic space, I argued that women judges also seek access to justice for themselves. For women judges, access to justice means *equal opportunities* to enter the profession (descriptive representation) and fair *treatment* once they are in the profession (substantive representation).

With this framework in mind, I expand the argument to include not only judges but also lawyers and legal scholars—the three groups discussed in this book. *Equal opportunity for entry* and fair *treatment within these professions* is shaped by the HISP

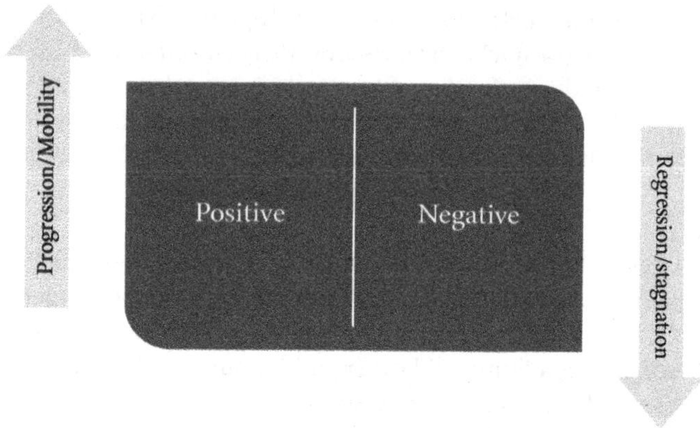

Figure 3.1 *Interactive Model of Positive and Negative Experiences for Women in Law*

framework introduced in Chapter 1—the historical, institutional, social, and positionality factors. These factors interact with each other, producing outcomes experienced both at entry and during treatment. As shown in **Figure 3.1**, the interplay of the four factors can create different opportunities and obstacles. Once inside the profession, a person's experience of fair and positive treatment is closely linked to their career progression. Conversely, negative treatment caused by intersecting positionalities can lead to setbacks, stagnation, or departure from the profession. Additionally, these positive and negative factors can combine to produce mixed outcomes for some women at various points in their careers.

Examining the intersectional identities of women in law deepens our understanding of their roles and substantive representation in the field. Creating a thorough and inclusive list of the intersectional identities and categories women embody is often difficult due to varying situational and cultural backgrounds, along with the presence of invisible identities and categories. The intersectional identities outlined below stem from interviews, highlighting the different levels of importance that respondents assign to their lived experiences. Although sexual identity is an important intersectional factor, none of my respondents identified as a sexual minority, which limits how much the following analyses address sexuality as an intersectional identity.

Growing out of the fields of critical race studies and Black feminist studies, intersectionality challenges us to analyze how socially constructed categories, labels, and identities can supposedly serve to position Black women as the "outsider" or "other." The expansion of intersectionality theory to include categories beyond race and gender is widely recognized in the growing body of scholarly and policy work that applies the theory to other identity categories such as age, disability, sexual orientation, and more (Cooper, 2016; Gillborn, 2015).

In this book, I draw on my earlier framing of intersectionality theory as applied to African women in law (Dawuni, 2022b, p. 10):

> I theorize layered intersectionality, not as distinct from intersectionality as we know it, but rather as an approach that allows us to see that one does not have to stand

> at the intersection of multiple oppressions. One's experience of oppression can be layered. Layered oppression implies that a person experiences the outcomes of oppression indirectly rather than directly. The guise of privilege (as a judge) does not shield a woman from experiencing discrimination in her own courtroom, within the judicial institutions she works in, and through the societal rules that inform her daily existence.

In this earlier framing of layered intersectionality, I examined five variables: gender, race/ethnicity, religion and culture, class/socioeconomic status, and institutional patriarchal norms. Building on layered intersectionality, this book employs the HISP framework to illustrate the interactive, additive, and cumulative effects of these different identities on women's positionality in the profession. Throughout their life cycles, women embody and experience multiple intersecting and competing identities within diverse contexts of production, reproduction, exclusion, and social expectations. The six identity categories discussed here are neither comprehensive of all identities nor exclusive to women in law. They are based on patterns that emerged from the interviews.

1. Sex/Gendered Constructions and Expectations

The social construction of gender and the expectations linked to the male and female binary consistently challenge women more than men. When the legal profession emerged in the Global North, the gender identity tied to manhood and masculinity was seen as an advantage that helped men enter legal fields long before women gained equal opportunities (Schultz & Shaw, 2003). This early focus on patriarchy or male-centered views often ignored other categories. Worldwide, social and cultural ideas of gender are diverse, changing, and flexible, shaped by various factors such as history, culture, religion, race, ethnicity, and economic conditions (Meer & Muller, 2017).

The matri-legal feminist framework emphasizes how, in different African societies, women can navigate social hierarchies and power structures that may privilege their gendered roles as women. For example, works by several African feminist scholars, including Oyewumi (1997), Amadiume (1987), and Achebe (2020), show that among the Yoruba and Igbo communities of Nigeria, women's femininity can be redefined as masculine because of the political, economic, family, or religious leadership positions they hold. These fluid, socially constructed gender categories enable women to move vertically from the realm of the female (less power and privilege) to that of the male (more power and privilege). This gender mobility is associated with increased respect, social privileges, and honorific titles, and such matrilineal privileges are found in many other cultures across the continent (Diop, 1989; Goettner-Abendroth, 2012).

Connecting gender fluidity to women's experiences in law further highlights the realities of the first and second generations of women in this field, as discussed earlier. Traditionally, law has been seen as a profession for men, and women who earned a law degree were viewed as challenging the norms and boundaries of femininity—thus being labeled as "male." For many women, this led to greater social recognition of their societal roles. Acceptable gender relations are reflected in comments from interviews with women from the first and second generations in law, who describe their interactions with male colleagues as *cordial* and *respectful*. A second-generation woman judge from Ghana was nicknamed Yaa Asantewaa (the woman warrior among the Akan) because, as she expressed, "I could do whatever I wanted to do." These early, though limited, self-descriptions of women's professional and social experiences in law support the findings of African feminist scholars that gender, as a social construct in many African contexts, is highly fluid—allowing women to hold and exercise varying levels of power and privilege (Dosekun, 2020).

The stories of first- and second-generation women in law discussed in this book reflect a small sample of many stories that still need to be fully documented through archival research. In this book, I share accounts from my interviews with women, some of whom remain representative of first- and second-generation women in law due to the delayed entry of women into these professions in certain countries. The insights gained from these interview narratives offer a comparative framework for analyzing the experiences of early women in law in the Global North versus the Global South—especially in sub-Saharan Africa. As this reasoning unfolds in the main chapters, it will become clear that categorizing gender identities into male and female, masculine and feminine, helps explain women's career paths and experiences throughout their journeys. Stories of discrimination and problematic experiences continue to be common, and women must constantly navigate the layers of intersectional discrimination—some overt, others less visible.

A thorough analysis of the narratives from the interviews for this book clearly indicates that many women judges, lawyers, and academics continue to encounter male bias and sexist and chauvinistic treatment within their professions and society. Women aiming to rise above these gender stereotypes must constantly challenge social perceptions and expectations linked to their femininity within a system still rooted in historical patriarchal practices and policies that favor men. These women need to demonstrate that they are just as capable, if not more so, than their male colleagues.

In Nigeria, the gender-discriminatory phrase "there are no women at the bar," borrowed from the British legal system, is still in use. A senior second-generation lawyer recounted her experience:

> Women face pressure to conform to the "man's world" or the "old boys' club." They must constantly resist these pressures, and it would help if everyone recognized that the profession is open to both men and women. Here in Nigeria, some men still insist that there are no women at the bar! I responded during a case at the Court of Appeal, telling my colleague not to refer to me as "*brother silk*." I said, "I am a lady, unless you are blind."

This was the experience of a woman at the peak of her career as a SAN, sometimes QC in the British system, known for their "silks." The experiences of younger women lawyers are probably even more challenging, and some of these will be discussed in the chapter on the bar. A nonessentialist analysis shows that women's experiences differ, and some women lawyers do not see their gender as negatively affecting their work, as shared by a senior second-generation woman lawyer in The Gambia.

> The truth of the matter for me is that I have never felt I was a woman. There is no difference for me, I don't know if it was because my dad was a lawyer. I started working with my dad when I finished law school, I guess we were a novelty.

However, this story shows that an intervening variable—her father—might have placed her in a different class from other women lawyers of her time. The recognition tied to her name and her father's standing could have given her additional familial privilege and protection against gender-based discrimination, which not all women experience.

The gendered perceptions and expectations extend beyond the bar. An academic shared her colleague's experience:

> There is a perception in our society that men generally receive more respect than women. My colleague once had a visitor who came looking for her husband. The gardener told the visitor, "Dr. X *is not home, but madam is home*," when my friend was actually the doctor, not her husband. In my own experience, my driver kept referring to me as "aunty," but I had to correct him and ask him to call me "professor." I questioned him if he would have called a male colleague who is a professor with the familial term "uncle." You must assert your authority as a woman and not assume that people will automatically give it to you.

2. Age

Most of the women lawyers and judges from the first generation (1930–1950) have passed away, except for those whose emergence as the "first" in their countries occurred during the second and third generations. In several jurisdictions where I conducted fieldwork, sex-disaggregated data are unavailable, and I had to guess a person's sex based on their names, which can lead to inaccuracies. The expansion of educational opportunities and the rise in both public and private universities have increased law school graduation rates. Analyzing reports from law school graduation ceremonies shows that graduates are getting younger, often in their early 20s, and that more women are graduating. **Table 3.3** indicates that surveyed women are mostly in the 31–40 age range among lawyers (41%) and academics (43.8%). However, among judges, 49.4% of respondents are over 50 years old.

It would be difficult to find lawyers over 70 who are still actively practicing among the top tier of currently practicing attorneys. Biological age usually correlates with years in practice. Consequently, younger women are likely to face additional intersectional barriers, such as lower pay, greater vulnerability to sexual harassment and bullying, and a higher chance of being subjected to gender-based stereotypes that doubt their competence. Additionally, younger women often receive less professional support from law firms that see them as a "risk" because of personal decisions they might make later, like getting married or having children.

Table 3.3 *Age of Survey Respondents*

Age range	Lawyers ($n = 122$)	Judges ($n = 79$)	Academics ($n = 48$)
20–24	1.6%	0%	0%
25–30	23%	1.3%	10.4%
31–40	41%	20.3%	43.8%
41–50	22.10%	29.1%	31.3%
Above 50	13.1%	49.4%	14.6%

** The numbers do not add up to 100% because some people opted not to provide their age.

In this context, I define age as a binary variable—biologically and professionally—indicating how long someone has been in the field. Women at the higher end of the age spectrum are just as vulnerable to age discrimination. A second-generation female lawyer in Ghana shared her experience of realizing that, despite her many years at the bar and extensive experience at the law firm, the male clerk (who had no law degree) was paid more than she was as a lawyer. This perspective reflects the common belief at that time (and still present in some sectors) that women do not deserve higher wages because their husbands or male partners are seen as the primary breadwinners in the family.

Women who enter the profession at a young age and have children early must navigate challenges related to their biological age—often being perceived as inexperienced—while managing professional responsibilities early in their careers. Some benefits may arise as they progress along their career path. A prosecutor from the Ivory Coast shared her experience as follows:

> Initially, it was very challenging because my husband worked in different countries. Since the children were young, I would move with him and return every three weeks, spending two weeks working before heading back to my job. I honestly don't know how I managed—it was really tough. When my kids moved to France, I stayed here in Abidjan, while my husband came weekly since his work's headquarters was here, allowing him to visit once a month. I felt like I had no roots; I was all over the place. I was fortunate to have a supportive husband.

In Senegal, an academic alluded to the increase in the number of younger faculty joining academia but commented on the different experiences of younger versus older women:

> We have younger faculty now, and most of the time, male students show more respect to female faculty than female students show to male faculty. However, if you are older, they will respect you regardless of your gender.

Age may also predispose women to other forms of harm in the profession, as narrated by a lawyer in Nigeria:

> In the early stages of my career, finding a job after graduation was tough. Instead of being recognized as the professional I am, I faced significant sexual harassment. When I rejected the advances, senior men frustrated me, which led me to leave the job. Many young lawyers are struggling. Nothing is being done—women hesitate to come forward, and there are no prosecutions. We, as women, haven't been able to challenge these atrocities; there is a passive acceptance of them even among women.

Despite these different opinions, the intersectional and different experiences of women in law still stand out. In a survey of women lawyers in South Africa, which sought to understand whether age was a disadvantage in their ability to rise to leadership positions, 30.8% strongly agreed that age was a hindrance, while the majority (53.9%) disagreed (Institute for African Women in Law, 2023o).

3. Ethnicity and Race

Ethnic identity is a demographic category that appears in most studies about Africa. The continent is home to thousands of ethnic groups, often within a single country. One can examine the ethnic diversity of a country's legal profession from a regional perspective. For example, in Nigeria and Ghana, most lawyers from the "Northern" regions entered the legal field later due to colonial administrative policies that provided no educational opportunities in those areas (Adewoye, 1982b; Ghai, 1981). In his study of the development of legal practice in southern Nigeria, Adewoye (1982b) noted the geographic advantage of ethnic groups from the "Southern" belt, which had greater representation among lawyers thanks to better access to colonial education, mainly available in coastal cities. In many African countries, the concentration of colonial administrations in coastal areas and the rise of trading and commercial activities helped shape the development of commercial law early in the profession. The availability of educational opportunities along the coast allowed those from coastal regions to benefit more from initial efforts to expand legal education, showing similar trends in Nigeria, Kenya, Tanzania, and Ghana (Adewoye, 1982b; Ghai, 1981; Harvey, 1963).

With the expansion of educational opportunities in the post-independence era and ongoing internal migration, ethnic minority groups have gained access to basic education and, consequently, to higher education—including legal education. While references to some lawyers based on their ethnic origins may be common, ethnicity is not always a reliable indicator of a person's ability or likelihood of becoming a lawyer. However, ethnicity may influence employment prospects if ethnic networks are prioritized over merit. In some societies, ethnic profiling results in stereotypical classifications of individuals working in specific jobs or industries, but this is changing over time, and many are able to break out of these confines.

Racial identity is a crucial social category, especially in southern Africa, with many scholars emphasizing the impact of race on opportunities for upward mobility within the bar (Chitapi, 2018; Sasinsky, 2020), the bench (Andrews, 2021; Masengu, 2016), and academia (Mabokela, 2000). Although Black South Africans now have better access to the profession, the lingering effects of apartheid still affect the legal field, heavily shaping perceptions of incompetence, particularly for Black women (Institute for African Women in Law, 2023o). In Kenya, British policies that favored men over women and Asians over Blacks explain why the country's first lawyers were mainly of Asian descent. Meanwhile, in various parts of southern Africa, including Namibia, Zimbabwe, Zambia, and Botswana, the earliest female lawyers were mostly white or nonnatives (Karekwaivanane, 2020).

Compared to other identities that women in law embody, ethnicity appears to have the least impact on who can attend law school and how quickly they can progress within the profession. The effect of race on women's career advancement seems to align with other studies on the intersectional impact of race on Black women's mobility in the legal field (Deo, 2019; Melaku, 2019; Pratt, 2012).

4. Marital and Family Status

Marital and family status are categories that can directly influence women's experiences within the legal system. I refer to the distinction between marital and family status because not everyone with a child is married, and not everyone who is married has children. Furthermore, due to the extended family systems common in many African contexts, both unmarried women and married women without children may still carry multiple obligations to their extended families, including grandparents, uncles, aunts, and other nonnuclear relatives. In many African societies, marriage determines a woman's status, with married women often receiving more respect than single or unmarried women. According to the data in **Table 3.4**, women who are married with children among lawyers and judges make up a little over 30%, with the highest percentage being 43.8% among academics. The highest proportion of single women is found among young lawyers, at 32.8%, compared to 12.7% among judges and 27.1% among academics. While these numbers may be affected by the demographics of those who responded to the survey, they still show that more lawyers are unmarried—which has implications for their vulnerability to sexual harassment, gender biases, and stereotypes in the workplace, as will be discussed later.

A woman lawyer's marital status can have positive or negative impacts on her professional trajectory, as described by a lawyer in Ghana:

Table 3.4 *Marital and Family Status of Survey Respondents*

Marital status	Lawyers ($n = 122$)	Judges ($n = 79$)	Academics ($n = 48$)
Married	24.6%	25.3%	18.8%
Married with children	33.6%	31.6%	43.8%
Divorced	4.1%	17.7%	8.3%
Single	32.8%	12.7%	27.1%
Widow	n/a	6.3%	n/a

> The challenges vary at different stages. During childbearing years, your commitment to work may be limited, making it harder to advance as quickly as desired. Your priorities might shift, and there will be times when you need to choose between family and career. I always choose family.

Many women shared the difficulty of managing a family with young children who need significant parental supervision and care. Although the need for attention may lessen as these children grow, parenting remains a continuous responsibility—its challenges change with each stage, from toddlerhood to adolescence and into adulthood. In Senegal, when discussing challenges in legal practice, most lawyers I interviewed frequently mentioned the rising divorce rates among women lawyers. I was curious to understand why and how, in a culturally and religiously conservative country like Senegal, divorce rates for women seem to be increasing. I asked one lawyer whether the divorce rates were actually going up among women lawyers.

> Yes, that [increased divorce rates] is happening. Maybe it's cultural, reflecting society's expectations about the roles of women and men; women's dual responsibilities [as wife and worker] can impact a relationship. If you don't have a supportive and understanding husband, then you may face challenges. In our society, there's a stereotype that "it's dangerous to be married to a woman lawyer." We knew from the start that we would face many expectations and a heavy workload, but we didn't realize we wouldn't always have time to devote to our relationships and family.

The stereotype that women lawyers do not marry is quite common and persistent. In one of the few early works on women in law in Ghana, Houghton (1981) examined the various challenges married women lawyers face. Because of their relatively high level of education and awareness of their rights, women lawyers often assert their civil and marital rights within a marriage. Often, men interpret these actions as threats and use this as a baseless reason for engaging in extramarital affairs or leaving the marriage. Given the high social status associated with marriage, many women stay in less-than-ideal marriages for the sake of their children or the perceived dignity of their family. Considering these challenges, Houghton (1981, pp. 138–139) concludes:

> Thus, the woman lawyer has three choices in what amounts to a "no-win situation" to generalize her assertiveness and risk her marriage; to generalize to the work and the home situation qualities of dependency and deference, in which case she violates the norms of the work situation; or to try to change masks between work and home, which is at best a difficult task and one which may placate neither audience. Her best alternative is to marry an older, well-established man of higher income than she, who has ceased to have outside affairs. This possibility is however exceedingly small.

Houghton's (1981) description of the various scenarios and options available to women lawyers in the early 1990s, when she wrote this chapter, cannot be applied to all women in law, as their experiences go beyond the legal field. It is also an overly broad generalization to claim that marrying an older man will result in fewer affairs. A cheater is a cheater; no matter how submissive a woman may be to a man who chooses to cheat, he will still seek extramarital relationships. Women face different marital stereotypes, whether they are married or single. In Cape Verde, a lawyer shared her experiences with these stereotypes:

> But there are others who will reject a woman and assume that being a woman lawyer means you are bossy. When I tell people I'm single, they ask why, and I explain that I'm a lawyer, so no one wants to marry me (laughs). I think the same situation is happening here in Cape Verde, with more women getting divorced because they don't have enough time at home. Many insecure men may struggle with being with a woman who is a lawyer.

Yet many women are married and capable of managing their family and marital responsibilities, and the narratives above do not necessarily reflect the experiences of all women. Marriage, as an institution, might not be the key factor; instead, intersecting sociocultural beliefs about what is expected of a married woman could push some toward divorce. A study on the different divorce rates among women lawyers might offer further insight.

To conclude this section, the stories of intersectional challenges discussed above are not limited to one group of women in law or the younger generation of women in law. A leading female corporate lawyer in Nigeria shared how her male driver often refused to follow her instructions, believing that her husband had the final say in the family's decisions. Together with her husband, they decided she would be the one to give him his salary at the end of each month. This move was meant to show him that she was just as much the boss as her husband was. Her experience clearly shows that there is no single story that captures the complex effects of intersectional identities. In this case, her age, marital status, and professional role did not shield her from the socially constructed view of women as the "weaker" or "less powerful" gender. This example demonstrates that there is no one-size-fits-all story about how gender influences women in law. The layering of intersecting identities makes it harder to determine which identity might be working against a woman at any given moment. The study did not explore the influence of sexuality and disability. Both identities are crucial and can have combined effects on women who belong to these groups. Future research could investigate how each of these identities, along with others, shapes women's positions in law.

VII. Pioneer Women in Law: Individual Lives, Shared Experiences

The pioneer women in law (first and second generation) were trailblazers in their careers, and many of them became the first in various roles, often serving as magistrates and judges, such as Stella Marke Thomas in Nigeria and Effie Owuor in Kenya. Annie Jiagge of Ghana was the second woman lawyer (after Essi Matilda Forster), but she went on to become the first woman magistrate and judge in Ghana (Dawuni, 2012). In The Gambia, the first woman lawyer, Mariam Jack-Denton, was later appointed as the first woman speaker of the National Assembly after the 2016 national elections (Karki, n.d.). A few pioneering women lawyers made their mark in law and politics, including Vera Chirwa, the first woman lawyer in Malawi, who courageously opposed President Banda's dictatorship, which led to a death sentence before she was eventually released from political detention (Chirwa, 2007).

Detailed, peer-reviewed or scholarly biographical accounts of the experiences of the first generation of women judges are scarce, and those that do exist are not easily accessible to a broader audience through online databases. The Institute for African Women in Law has created a digital archive to document the lives and experiences of women in the legal field. Using legal narratives as a storytelling method, the Pioneer African Women in Law project traces the professional paths of women in law, emphasizing pioneering figures. The Amandla Women in Law Speaker Series adopts a standpoint approach where women in law share their stories and experiences of resistance and resilience, rooted in their personal voices. Meanwhile, the African Women in Law Legacy Project functions as a video archive of interviews with women judges across the continent. *International Courts and the African Woman Judge: Unveiled Narratives* is the first academic book to use legal narratives to document the lives of African women in international courts (Dawuni & Kuenyehia, 2018).

Through these narratives, certain patterns emerge that help us piece together the lived experiences of pioneering women across different countries. Using the HISP framework introduced in this book, some stories highlight how historical contexts shaped the emergence and experiences of women in various professions. For example, in countries like South Africa and Namibia, high levels of racism affected women's experiences in unique ways, influencing when the first Black woman became a lawyer or judge. These historical factors also shaped the institutional landscape, determining whether women were seen as equals to men. In Zimbabwe, Namibia, and South Africa, women first had to confront racial challenges before they could address gender issues (Karekwaivanane, 2020; Kariseb, 2022; Masengu, 2015; Sasinsky, 2020; Stewart, 2012).

The institutional arrangements and professional regulations that determined who could qualify as an advocate or attorney were closely linked to the racial class hierarchies present in these countries at that time. While the fourth and fifth generations of women in law in these three countries may be somewhat removed from the racial prejudices of the past, they are not free from gendered challenges or the sociocultural context, as their positions span various and intersecting identities they embody. With a few notable exceptions, such as South Africa, women across Africa were not legally barred from entering the legal profession. For the first generation of women lawyers and judges, the most common career path appeared to be public service—mainly within the judiciary. Moreover, women's opportunities in public service were influenced by their willingness to accept lower salaries and inadequate benefits associated with government roles, largely due to stereotypes that they were not the primary breadwinners in their families.

I categorize the career paths of pioneering women into two approaches: the *accommodationist* and the *exclusionist.* First, the *accommodationist* approach sought to "accommodate" women into the profession, because the institutional and bureaucratic settings were seen as suitable for their needs. This approach thrived on the widespread belief that a career on the bench was flexible enough to let women better balance work and family obligations than engaging in active litigation. Therefore, women were accommodated as long as they were considered capable of doing the job or because there was a need to fill those roles. The *exclusionist* approach was linked to common perceptions and the prevailing idea that women were not well-suited for the demands of a legal career—most of which during this period involved litigation in land and commercial cases (Adewoye, 1982b; Ghai, 1981; Luckham, 1981). As a result, women were excluded from these professions from the colonial era through the early postcolonial period.

The scarcity of women in law during the first and second generations may have elevated the social and elite status of the few women in the profession. The widespread admiration for these women gained them respect from both society and their colleagues. Several of these women describe their experiences in the profession and their interactions with male colleagues as "cordial" and "respectful." These experiences of African women in law sharply contrast with those of women in much of Western Europe and the United States, where scholars have documented various levels of professional and personal discrimination faced by early women in law—as law students and later as lawyers and judges (Carle, 2021; Schultz & Shaw, 2003).

Did the experiences of African women in law differ? There isn't a single explanation for their experiences. The principles of matri-legal feminism offer strong insights into the lives and experiences of women in law, thanks to the matriarchal ethos that promotes respectability for women in society. Some of the interviewees also reflect these experiences. A retired Supreme Court judge from Ghana shared her experiences as a young lawyer in the Attorney General's department, working as a public prosecutor:

> During our time, I don't think anyone could tell the difference between men and women. We all worked together, and cases weren't assigned based on gender. There were only a few of us in Koforidua, [the city where she worked at that time], and I was the only woman. When I worked under a man, I didn't have any issues, and I didn't have any problems when I was the boss either.

I followed up with a question about whether there were barriers to women entering law school, and she responded, "No, not at all; in my class, we had 35 students, and only four were women. The atmosphere was good; we played and joked all the time, like schoolchildren." The experiences of Vera Duarte, the first woman lawyer and judge in Cape Verde, illustrate the societal respect women enjoyed due to their active participation in the liberation wars of independence. During the interview, she recounted:

> After returning from my studies in Lisbon, I was appointed as a prosecutor since there were no lawyers available at the time. We began recruiting and nominating individuals to become prosecutors. Later, in 1985, I returned to Portugal to receive formal training for judges. Upon my return, I was elected to the Supreme Court. I've always maintained a positive outlook and never saw myself as a victim, so even if there was some discrimination, it didn't affect me. There were many offhand comments, and some colleagues would look at me and ask, "What is a beautiful woman doing as a prosecutor?" I often wore dresses and appeared youthful, so I stopped wearing

> them and chose pants instead, which I still wear today. They would remark, "She is beautiful yet tough," though I believe many of these comments were unconscious or caused by a lack of awareness. At that time, men were quite cautious, and women had already become aware of their rights after independence—because while our society still retained much patriarchy, things were different in the legal field. I am proud to have been the first woman in this role, and now we have achieved parity—the only profession with full parity is the judiciary. I'm grateful that I opened the door.

The story of Vera Duarte, the first woman lawyer and judge in Cape Verde, offers multiple interpretations. Initially, she dismisses the idea that she faced discrimination in her career, attributing her resilience to her personal character, which helped her ignore exclusionary attitudes and avoid seeing herself as a "victim." However, as her story unfolds, it becomes evident that sexist or gendered comments about her looks and appearance were made about her. The frequency of these comments, which caused her to stop wearing dresses, clearly shows the impact of social expectations on women and the effect these remarks had on her.

She had to change her dress style to present herself as an equal to her male colleagues who wore pants. Her reflections led her to conclude that these comments stemmed from unconscious gender bias. However, within the cultural context of Cape Verde and many other parts of the continent, remarks regarding a woman's appearance or clothing are often seen as complimentary rather than discriminatory. In Cape Verde, as in other regions of Africa, women's rights began to develop during the early postcolonial era, which may have influenced how her male colleagues and others viewed women's roles socially and professionally. Still, the fact that a woman needed to choose her clothing to fit into a male-dominated profession highlights the institutional and social norms of that time, the control over women's bodily autonomy, and how such control can affect their positions—shaping their clothing choices and how they choose to present themselves.

A second-generation superior court judge from Ghana shares similar sentiments on how the intersection of her personality and family socialization may explain her experiences of non-discrimination:

> Throughout my career, even right after law school, I never faced gender-based challenges; I didn't encounter any. It's in the cases I handle that I observe discrimination and inequality. When a situation arises, I draw on my wisdom to decide how I can help address this inequality. Sometimes, it's not so much about discrimination as it is about foolish remarks, but I always manage to stop those men and warn them never to say that again. Coming from a home with four brothers and seven sisters, the men didn't stand a chance. My father was a reverend minister, and the choice to send the girls to school was equal to that of the boys. My mom was a strong woman who made sure that the work we did at home was shared equally. In the law firms where I gained experience, it seemed that the women who wanted to stay in private practice had equal opportunities to remain and advance within the ranks.

In The Gambia, I asked the first woman judge what it was like for her to work with her male colleagues:

> My appointment as the first woman judge surprised everyone because the judiciary only had female magistrates. People were pleased to see a woman on the high court. I have always enjoyed being among men, and they treated me well during that time—this was in 1998. Before that, I believe Justice Patricia McCauley from Sierra Leone came to The Gambia and sat on the High Court bench (possibly in 1996), but she was not a Gambian.

In Ghana, another second-generation judge describes societal perceptions about her and how that influenced her work and experience as a judge:

> In Kumasi, my nickname was Yaa Asantewaa (the Queenmother of the Ejisu people of Ghana, who led the war against the British colonial administration) because I could do nearly everything the men did. I believe the lawyers were satisfied with my work. The few women who reached out to me (lower court judges) all looked up to me. I was the only woman in the minority in some of the decisions I made. People consider me courageous, but I believe that is simply the right choice, and people continue to call me Yaa Asantewaa.

A second-generation lawyer in Nigeria shared similar experiences of friendliness and respect during her time as a law student and as a practicing lawyer. Her story offers an interesting viewpoint, filled with suggestions that being younger than her classmates may have led to her favorable treatment. However, she shows that age has not always been a shield for others, as some senior advocates fail to show respect to younger women lawyers. Equally insightful is her mention that her strong work ethic might have protected her from discrimination—highlighting the challenges women face, often needing to work twice or even three times as hard as men to earn respect. Ultimately, her intergenerational story shifts from her personal experiences to those of today's young women, emphasizing her efforts to ensure they get the respect they deserve.

> When I was in law school, only 8 of the 57 students were women. I was the youngest at 21 years old and was treated like a little sister, with no signs of discrimination. When I started practicing law, about 15 women lawyers were at the bar when I joined. Most of the time, women served as magistrates and judges, while some worked at the Ministry of Justice. I didn't experience any discrimination—maybe because of my work ethic. I often went to court to observe many cases. Some SANs look down on women, but when I'm around, I tell them not to do that. I know many women face discrimination today, and they need to stand up against it. Men sometimes sit back, counting the number of women they respect. But women hold their own. Perhaps our small numbers and the fact that the men were older gave us an advantage back then.

The stories of first- and second-generation women lawyers and judges show that earning a law degree took determination, and practicing law involved courage while navigating power structures in the profession. These women faced colleagues and clients with gendered expectations about women's abilities as lawyers. Through their shared experiences, they found solidarity and respect from their peers on the bench, with many societies being impressed by the idea of women engaging in what was historically considered "men's work." Notably, in the African context described earlier, even though the legal profession was seen as "men's work," women who dared to challenge this male-dominated barrier were welcomed and consistently earned respect from colleagues and communities. This unique aspect of African women's experiences in the legal field supports findings from African feminist scholars on gender fluidity and women's capacity to rise in social structures and navigate power hierarchies (Achebe, 2020; Amadiume, 1987; Oyewumi, 1997).

Claiming that women's entry into the legal profession was always easy would create an overly simplified story. For many women, their presence was not welcomed with open arms. In 1995, Kellelo Mafoso-Guni was appointed the first woman judge in Lesotho. Before this, her call to the bar as an advocate in 1970 made her the first female lawyer in Lesotho. Mafoso-Guni's journey to becoming a judge faced strong opposition mainly because of her gender. To illustrate the events leading to her appointment, Ellett (2018, pp. 113–114) provides a detailed account of an interviewee's recollection of the process.

> At the time of Judge Mafoso-Guni's appointment in 1995, there were no other women judges in the High court which made her a pioneer. The period leading to her appointment was characterized by the predominance of men in major decision-making positions, both in government and the private sector. Judge Mafoso-Guni was a Lesotho national who had just come back from Zimbabwe where she had built around an illustrious legal career and acquired impeccable credentials. When her name was put before the Law Society for endorsement, they were strongly opposed to her appointment arguing she was not a "fit and proper person" for the position . . . [t]he formal reason advanced for the negative attitude was that although her credentials, which included references, were beyond reproach, she was not sufficiently well known as she had only recently been back in Lesotho after many years of practice internationally. Informally, however, our colleagues stated categorically that they were not convinced that a woman could cope with the demands of the taxing job of being a judge. A plethora of "reasons" were advanced, including that she was not a Mosotho (I suppose from those who did not know her at all and made their judgment on the basis of her surname).

Mafoso-Guni's role as a pioneer woman lawyer and judge, and later as the first woman from Lesotho to serve on the bench of an international court—the African Court on Human and Peoples' Rights—was characterized by numerous instances of resistance. This experience powerfully illustrates how patriarchal institutional and social norms converge to create significant integration challenges for women entering the profession and their experiences while in the position. The sociocultural acceptance of women as equal to men and competent lawyers remains a challenge, but it was an even tougher battle during the early stages of women entering legal practice. In Malawi, Tujilane Chizumila shares her experience with an elderly male client who came to her office but walked out when he discovered that she was the lawyer the receptionist had referred to him. The client left her office saying, "Sorry, it's the wrong office," and when he was redirected to return to that same office, he sat down and asked, "Where is the lawyer?" As Judge Chizumila recounts:

> When I responded that I was the lawyer, he roared "*What, you are a lawyer*? My case is too complicated for a woman. It needs a tough man!" I patiently and plainly explained to him that the same teachers teach both female and male lawyers, write the same exams and are treated equally. I promised to handle his case without the requisite deposit until the day I won his case. He stood up, shook his head then sat down again and narrated his matter to me. It was a simple land trespass. The day I won the case, he sat glued to the court bench, shaking his head. When I approached him, he stood up and said in disbelief, "Madam, you have won my tough case? ***You are a man***!" Then he shook my hand. He faithfully paid my fee note and better still for over two years I received several clients from his village all referred to me by him (Institute for African Women in Law, Amandla, n.d.- d).

The early cohort of women lawyers in Kenya shared similar experiences. As narrated by a respondent (Institute for African Women in Law, 2023i, p. 20):

> It took a long time for the courts, clients, and the public to accept that I was a lawyer. This was because people were not accustomed to having women in the profession. I remember attending a magistrate's court to represent a client and taking a seat on one of the benches reserved for advocates. The magistrate looked at me and informed me that bench was reserved for counsels. He did not believe I was one. In the office, when clients were referred to me, they would say they had come to see a lawyer. In their minds, I could not possibly be a lawyer. Even male colleagues in court often finish sentences for women as if they might forget what to say. This occurs all the time. It does not matter how smart a lawyer you are; this happens to women advocates consistently.

The widespread belief that the legal profession was a "man's job" has gradually changed, but these ideas still persist in the minds of some litigants and certain male lawyers, prompting Masengu (2016) to conclude that the legal field remains "a man's world." Many of these trailblazing women had to fight for their rights, paving the way for numerous others to follow. As discussed later in the chapter on the judiciary, Justice Julia Sebutinde of Uganda, Justice Mary Mame Yassin Sey of The Gambia, and Justice Mable Agyeman of Ghana all faced harsh scrutiny from authoritarian leaders because they stood up for justice. The first woman law lecturer in Ghana, Akua Kuenyehia, built her career as a passionate advocate for women's rights while also fighting for her own. By opposing the policy that barred women from applying for a passport without their husband's or father's consent, Akua Kuenyehia broke barriers for other women trying to obtain passports in Ghana. The upcoming chapters will offer further insights into the experiences of these pioneering women in law.

Aside from a few women leaders—such as Ghana's three female chief justices—many current and recent female chief justices have been pioneers or the first to hold these positions (Dawuni & Kang, 2015). For women, being a pioneer in any field often brings heightened expectations to lead effectively and create pathways for others. Specifically, social expectations are linked to an ethic of care, along with assumptions that women will combine their private caregiving roles with their professional duties in the public workforce, adding more layers of professional demands. The previous discussion has highlighted the opportunities and challenges faced by pioneering women in law through various examples drawn from interviews and existing research. The following section provides brief summaries of the contributions made by these trailblazing women in law, setting the stage for discussions in the substantive chapters focused on women at the bar, on the bench, and in the legal academy.

VIII. Contributions of the Pioneer Women in Law

Whatever influenced the career choices of the first- and second-generation women in law, they made significant contributions to the legal profession and to women's rights overall. The next section highlights some of these contributions by examining their position as role models, representing their countries at international forums, and expanding access to justice through their work as women and human rights advocates. Women continue to make contributions to the bar, bench, and legal academia, which will be discussed in the following substantive chapters.

1. Changed Gender Norms and Perceptions

The pioneering women in law fought many battles to establish their place in the profession and, in the process, changed perceptions and norms for women, even if the change was slow. Standing at the edge of the early post-independence era, they had to navigate a mix of imported Western patriarchy and traditional local practices. Colonial laws were deeply rooted in gender-biased practices. As some of these women pioneers recalled, interviewers often asked about their marital status, plans for children, and whether they needed any allowances (based on the belief that married women were supported by their husbands). While some of these questions still appear in interviews today, these women fought to change these institutional practices—such as Judges Effie Owuor and Joyce Aluoch advocating for equal pay for women judges in the Kenyan judiciary. They were clearly a minority in the professional spaces they occupied, taking on a bigger burden in challenging gender norms and perceptions. Even with the increasing number of women in law, these norms and perceptions still exist in various forms, which will be examined later in the chapters covering the bar, bench, and academy.

2. Role Models and the Diffusion Effect

Several pioneering women in law—lawyers, judges, and legal academics—came from modest backgrounds, although some had fathers who were prominent attorneys. These women learned to carve out their career paths, sometimes receiving support from their male colleagues. Many of them faced institutional patriarchy and developed the ability to stand their ground. The early group of women admitted to the bar in various African countries often became the first magistrates and eventually the first women to serve in higher courts, although a few chose to continue practicing as lawyers. As the public service arm of the legal profession, the judiciary was seen as more welcoming to women, due to the belief that standard working hours, benefits, and other work conditions suited women's dual roles as professionals and caregivers at home. Additionally, in some regions, there was a view that the legal profession, which was mainly litigation-focused at the time, was unsuitable for women because of the masculine culture that characterized these institutions. As women started entering the bar as lawyers, it laid the groundwork for their expansion into other parts of the legal field. The symbolic presence of women undoubtedly influenced the slow shift in institutional perceptions about their role in law. More importantly, these women served as role models; their presence proved impactful enough to spark a chain reaction, inspiring young girls and women to pursue similar careers.

3. Women's and Human Rights Activists

Justice Annie Jiagge of Ghana joined the magistracy in 1953, was promoted to the High Court in 1961, and to the Court of Appeal in 1969. In addition to her work as a judge, Annie Jiagge played a vital role in establishing the national framework for women's rights in Ghana (Dawuni, 2012). Her contributions as a judge and her activism for women's rights gained international recognition. From 1962 to 1972, she served as a member of the United Nations Commission on the Status of Women and was part of the team that drafted the Convention on the Elimination of All Forms of Discrimination Against Women (CEDAW). Additionally, she played key roles in establishing micro-credit schemes that later developed into Women's World Banking (Dawuni, 2012).

Several other women have followed Justice Jiagge's example, advocating for women's rights at both national and international levels. Major organizations supporting women's rights in African countries often include legal groups. A prominent example of such an organization with local and global reach is the International Federation of Women Lawyers (FIDA). The national chapters of these groups are led by women lawyers who are committed activists for women's rights, offering free legal support to underserved women and children. In Ghana, the Ark Foundation, founded by women's rights lawyer Dr. Angela Dwamena-Aboagye, runs the only operational shelter for women victims of domestic violence in the country. Several regional organizations have also emerged across the continent, including the Women in Law and Development In Africa (WiLDAF) and the Southern and Eastern African Regional Centre for Women's Law (SEARCWL) (Kameri-Mbote & Wekesa, 2018).

Furthermore, women lawyers formed women's sections within national bar associations to tackle issues that affect women in the profession. However, a closer look at these groups reveals that much of their effort has been outward-focused, emphasizing expanding access to justice for women and children rather than meeting the professional needs of women in the legal field. In Senegal, the Association Juristes de Sénégal (AJS) has played a leading role in advocating for women's rights nationwide. Founded by a group of pioneering women lawyers and judges, the organization has significantly influenced the national dialogue on women's rights and has also made a global impact by guiding the government in international and regional delegations and committees dedicated to women's rights (Scales-Trent, 2010). Many lawyers from the first and second generations combined their legal work with advocacy for human and women's rights.

4. International Representatives

Several first- and second-generation pioneer women lawyers emerged as their countries gained independence from colonial rule. They were often among the few educated elites who their governments could depend on. In many cases, these women lawyers and judges also represented their national governments at international meetings and forums on women's issues. For example, Annie Jiagge of Ghana was a key legal and judicial pioneer, contributing to both Ghana's legal system and international law within the United Nations frameworks for women's rights (Dawuni, 2012).

In Senegal, the first female prosecutor, Dior Sow Fall, played a key role in leading foreign missions for the Senegalese government. Her career also included serving as the Senior General Counsel at the International Criminal Tribunal for Rwanda (ICTR) (Institute for African Women in Law, n.d.-a). Concerned about women's rights under the Senegalese Family Code, four women lawyers—Mame Madior Boye, Madeline Déves Senghor, Tamaro Tourè Diallo, and Maimouna Ndongo Kane—founded the Association Juristes de Senegal (AJS) in 1973. Through their activism for women's rights, these women later held prominent international positions. In 1976, Maimouna Ndongo Kane was appointed Secretary of State for the Status of Women in Senegal, becoming the first woman to hold that position (Scales-Trent, 2010). Mame Madior Boye later served as Prime Minister of Senegal from 2001 to 2002 (Institute for African Women in Law, n.d.-b).

As the first female lawyer and magistrate in Cape Verde, Vera Duarte was a human rights advocate whose efforts led to several legal and judicial reforms that expanded women's rights. She fought to abolish laws and penal codes that discriminated against women. As the first female magistrate, she accompanied the Prime Minister on international delegations, including attending the Summit of the Non-Aligned Movement held in Havana, Cuba. Her other international roles included being elected in 1993 as the first woman and later the first female chair of the African Commission on Human and Peoples' Rights (ACHPR). Duarte's regional activism also included her active involvement as a drafter of the Additional Protocol to the African Charter on Human and Peoples' Rights on the Rights of Women in Africa (Maputo Protocol) (Duarte, 2022).

Other pioneering women jurists who have made significant contributions to international law and justice include Justice Florence Ndepele Mwachande Mumba, the first female High Court judge in Zambia. Justice Mumba's judicial career ultimately led her to the International Criminal Tribunal for the Former Yugoslavia (ICTY), the International Criminal Tribunal for Rwanda (ICTR), and later to the Extraordinary Chambers in the Courts of Cambodia (ECCC) (Mumba, 2018). Through her judicial decisions, she made substantial contributions to international law. While presiding over *The Prosecutor v. Anton Furundzija*, IT-95-17/1 (*Furundzija Case*), and *The Prosecutor v. Dragoljub Kunarac, Radomir Kova, and Zoran Vukovic*, IT-96-23-T (*Kunarac Case*), she delivered the first judgments from the ICTY that classified sexual violence and rape as war crimes and crimes against humanity (Mumba, 2018). Among several accolades, in 2023, Justice Mumba received the Jessup Alumni Award from White & Case, a law firm based in Washington, DC, USA, in recognition of her global advocacy for justice and the rule of law. Judge Navanethem "Navi" Pillay of South Africa is another trailblazing woman who served on an international court—the International Criminal Tribunal for Rwanda (ICTR) and later as part of the inaugural cohort of judges for the International Criminal Court (ICC). Her numerous contributions to law and justice include the decision in the *Akayesu* case at the ICTR, which defined rape as an act of genocide (Naidu, 2013).

Several women lawyers across the continent have made significant contributions to the work of regional human rights bodies and mechanisms, such as the African Commission on Human and Peoples' Rights (ACHPR), which is a regional organization tasked with promoting human rights and ensuring gender-balanced representation. The first- and second-generation women judges also played key roles in establishing global organizations like the International Association of Women Judges (IAWJ). Trailblazing women judges from Africa participated actively in the association's efforts at both national and international levels. Many of these efforts are documented in *International Courts and the African Woman Judge: Unveiled Narratives* (Dawuni & Kuenyehia, 2018).

IX. Conclusion

This chapter establishes a solid foundation for the arguments in this book. Using a historical comparative approach, it identifies and analyzes the precolonial, colonial, and postcolonial experiences of women in law across various sub-Saharan African countries. Drawing on existing literature about the legal profession in Africa, the chapter focuses on African women's experiences as they navigate intersectional exclusions and hierarchies within society and the legal field. By emphasizing scholarship from African scholars, it challenges the common tendency to compare African experiences with those of the West. While recognizing critiques about the limited references to Western scholarship, this chapter affirms that the goal of decolonizing the African woman's experiences in law and amplifying her voice is attainable.

4
Women at the Bar: The First Battleground

I. Introduction

As shown in Chapter 2, laws and various conflict-resolution methods existed in Africa before colonialism. The imposition of legal systems through colonial rule unfairly sidelined and reduced African justice and conflict resolution practices. As discussed in Chapter 3, the long and turbulent development of the common- and civil-law professions across the continent reveals that women have faced different challenges in various contexts to gain full recognition as legal professionals. An example of this imposed system is the British disqualification of women from joining the bar, which was enforced in South Africa, resulting in a ban on women entering the legal profession. It has been over 100 years since women were legally permitted to practice law in South Africa, following the passage of the Women Legal Practitioners Act of 1923.

In West Africa, women's entry into the legal profession began with Stella Marke Thomas of Nigeria, who was called to the English Bar in 1933, followed by Frances Claudia Wright of Sierra Leone in 1941 and Essi Matilda Forster of Ghana in 1945. Since these pioneering women first entered the legal arena, many developments have occurred across the continent, including the independence of former British, French, and Portuguese colonies, the establishment of domestic institutions for higher education and legal training, the expansion of opportunities in public service, including the judiciary, and the globalization of legal practice (Dawuni, 2021b).

Across Africa, the legal profession is expanding as more women enter the field each year. As discussed in Chapter 3, the intergenerational dialogue about women's advancement in the legal sphere provides a framework for understanding the connection between evolving political economies and the societal demand for lawyers. As the book's first substantive chapter on women in law across the three sectors (bar, bench, academy), I conceptualize the bar as the initial "battleground" for women's entry into these professions. While the term "battleground" may seem strong, it accurately reflects the historical male dominance in the established legal profession and the gender-exclusionary institutional practices that subsequently shaped the structure of the bar and legal profession across different jurisdictions. The chapter also highlights how women have successfully navigated the profession's institutional rules and the social structures within their unique cultural and personal contexts, enabling them to pursue legal education, enter the workforce, and continually challenge the deeply rooted gender hierarchies.

The chapter is divided into seven sections. Following this introduction, section II presents a discussion of the structure and context of the African bar, drawing examples from different regions and countries. Relying on qualitative data gathered through interviews and surveys, section III discusses the different pathways and motivations for women joining the bar. Section IV presents a detailed discussion of

African Women in Law. J. Jarpa Dawuni, Oxford University Press. © Oxford University Press 2026.
DOI: 10.1093/9780197795095.003.0004

women's representation at the bar, with the goal of highlighting significant changes in the number of women, their working conditions, and their representation in leadership. Section V engages in a detailed analysis of the contributions women are making to the profession. Section VI explores the new and persisting challenges women continue to face in the profession, and section VII brings the chapter to a close.

II. Structure and Context of the Bar

Chapter 2 offered a broad overview of how the legal profession has developed across the continent. Without going into specifics for each country, this section summarizes general trends in the current structure of law firms, drawing on practices and observations from selected jurisdictions. The main points include clarifying terminology, regulating lawyers, areas of specialization, the size and organization of law firms, and the geographic distribution of firms.

In several legal markets across Africa, legal professions still retain core elements of their inherited structure and form from the metropolitan model—such as the civil-law system from France and Portugal, or the common-law components from Britain. However, over time, some changes have taken place due to shifting domestic political economies, an increase in the number of lawyers, the development of new legislation or policies regulating the professions, client demands, and the impacts of globalization, which have fostered open markets and borders for legal practitioners (Dezalay, 2020; Kamau, 2020; Ghai & Ghai, 2014; Karekwaivanane, 2020; Klaaren, 2020; Oloka-Onyango, 2021).

In this chapter, I use the term "bar" to describe the legal profession, a term borrowed from English usage to explain the organization of the profession (Hammerslev & Sommerlad, 2020). Bars are structured differently across countries, often reflecting the type of legal tradition present—whether civil law, common law, or the hybrid system of Roman–Dutch civilian law and English common law, as seen in countries like South Africa. In civil-law countries, the association of lawyers may have different names; for example, *ordre des avocats* is used in Senegal and several Francophone countries. In contrast, most common law countries in West Africa refer to it as a "bar association," while those in Eastern and Southern Africa prefer the term "law society." The development and usage of these terms trace back to the colonial experience (Ghai & McAuslan, 1970; Harvey, 1966). Nonetheless, regardless of the terminology used, the "bar" and "law society" refer to the group of lawyers qualified to practice law within the country.

A key aspect of the legal profession is whether the bar is unified or divided (split). Drawing from the traditional English common-law system, a divided or split profession distinguishes between lawyers—barristers or advocates, who are qualified to appear in court, and solicitors or attorneys, who usually handle in-house work and do not appear in court (Abel & Lewis, 1989). Hammerslev and Sommerlad (2020) demonstrate that the legal profession in England and Wales has gradually evolved, enabling barristers and solicitors to work more closely together in legal disciplinary partnerships and, in some cases, with nonlawyers in alternative business structures.

In the fused profession model common in most African legal markets, all lawyers can perform both roles (appearing in court as attorneys or working in-house as solicitors) and may be called lawyers, attorneys, or advocates. For example, South Africa employs the split profession model (advocates versus attorneys), while most common-law countries have moved away from the split model and combined the professions—possibly due to the globalization of the American legal profession (Bartie & Sandomierski, 2021). The South African split bar model has faced criticism as a gatekeeping system that excludes minorities—Black, mixed-race, and women—from the perceived prestigious status of advocates.

Another characteristic of the legal profession is the regulation of lawyers, which is vital for maintaining professional standards. Various laws and policies often govern this regulation. Across the continent, the main bodies responsible for regulating the bar are organized differently and have distinct powers. Their roles may include determining how lawyers are trained, setting standards for those eligible to be called to the bar, outlining procedures for disciplinary actions due to ethical breaches, managing lawyer-client relationships, and more (Bonnin, 2019; Lumumba, 2014; Kamau, 2020). These regulatory bodies work closely with bar associations and law societies to develop standards for the profession, meet the needs of lawyers, and address other issues related to the rule of law. Additionally, legal regulatory bodies are expanding their roles by offering ongoing legal training to ensure lawyers stay current on legal developments and practice trends. In 2024, the Ghana Bar Association introduced a new requirement under the Legal Profession (Professional Conduct and Etiquette) Rules 2020, LI 2423, mandating that lawyers complete at least twelve hours of Continuous Professional Development (CPD) as part of renewing their practice licenses (Ghana Bar Association, n.d.). Similar initiatives are underway in other countries to keep lawyers informed about the law as well as ethical rules and procedures.

As global markets expand, fields of legal specialization are also growing, giving lawyers in different countries more options. Since many African nations have smaller legal markets, most law firms start as generalists, handling various types of civil and criminal cases. Over time, lawyers begin to develop expertise in specific areas of law and may change their practices accordingly. Additionally, some lawyers focus on the public sector, especially those working as state attorneys, for personal and strategic reasons. Evidence from fieldwork shows that women often dominate the public or government sector, particularly in attorney general offices and ministries of justice, partly because male attrition occurs due to low salaries. Women might choose to work in the Ministry of Justice because it offers a bureaucratic system with benefits, leave, and set working hours, helping them balance work and personal life. An increasing number of lawyers are also starting to specialize in what can be called the third sector, mainly those in civil society who focus on public interest litigation involving human rights, women's rights, environmental law, and others (Ghai & Ghai, 2014; Oloka-Onyango, 2017). These specialization areas are not always clearly defined, and with globalization and the rise of new fields like technology and artificial intelligence, diversity in practice areas is expected to grow even more. With this trend, in-house counsel could play crucial roles in the legal landscape—an area that offers many opportunities for future research.

A related aspect is the growth in law firm sizes. Most law firms in the countries studied for this project remain small, ranging from solo practitioners to firms with multiple lawyers. The larger the law firm, the more likely it is to organize its work into teams focused on litigation, commercial transactions, arbitration, and other areas. While smaller law firms, typically with 6 to 10 lawyers, are common, larger markets like South Africa, Nigeria, and Kenya more often feature firms with 15 to 40 lawyers. A key reason for the larger law firms in these countries is the result of mergers and partnership practices, where global firms collaborate with or acquire midsized firms to expand their presence in Africa. Notable examples include ENSafrica, DLA Piper, and Dentons, located in South Africa, Nigeria, and Kenya, respectively. In medium-sized markets such as Ghana, Tanzania, and Ethiopia, larger law firms generally consist of 15 to 20 lawyers. These firms are often recognized as part of the loosely defined "top law firms," since there are no standardized criteria for what qualifies as a "top law firm." Larger firms usually have a broader global presence, with lawyers attending international meetings of the International Bar Association and regional gatherings of the African Bar Association and the Pan-African Lawyers Association. Additionally, these "top" law firms are often nominated and sometimes ranked in global listings like the Chambers Global Legal Guide.

Depending on the firm's size, different models are used to organize law firms hierarchically. The "Americanization" of legal education and practice (Bartie & Sandomierski, 2021; Khanna et al., 2017) has shaped the internal structure of law firms, with medium to large firms often adopting setups that may include managing partners, partners, senior and junior associates, and other key roles. Additionally, law firms have updated their administrative systems to include practice managers, accounting departments, human resources, and other essential staff to support the administrative sustainability of law firms in today's global legal market. Related to these various hierarchical models, many law firms keep written policies on hiring and promotion, while others do not, which can sometimes lead to negative outcomes for women lawyers, as will be discussed later.

Finally, the geographic location of law firms matters. As discussed in Chapter 2, the historical development of the legal profession was partly influenced by the colonial administration's need to regulate trade and commercial activities along the coastal regions of the colonies (Adewoye, 1982b; Ghai, 1981; Luckham, 1976). As a result, lawyers have maintained a strong presence mainly in the capital cities of these former colonies. With the increase in the number and diversity of individuals called to the bar, along with the rising demand for legal services that extend beyond applying customary laws—which are more common outside the capital due to legal pluralism—lawyers have expanded their operations beyond major cities. Although lawyers are present in various locations, they often do not have a permanent base in smaller towns, villages, and communes, usually traveling there to appear before courts when representing clients. Some lawyers and law firms provide legal services to rural areas, sometimes with the help of paralegals. The distribution of lawyers outside the main capital cities, which typically have better public service amenities and schools, often results in lower representation of women in these areas unless they are local residents, married to someone from the area, or their spouse works there.

The previous discussion of the structure and context of the legal profession is based on observations from my fieldwork and supported by existing scholarship. More research is necessary to understand these evolving dynamics in specific countries. For this project, the structural variables outlined here have significant gendered implications for women, which will be explored in more detail in the rest of the chapter.

III. Pathways to the Bar

Earlier in Chapter 3, a general overview was provided on how and why women entered the legal professions across the continent, categorizing them into five entry phases and cohorts. The discussion on intergenerational pathways also offered a detailed analysis of the various motivational factors for joining the profession. In recent years, demographic shifts in the total number of newly enrolled lawyers across different countries have correlated with global increases in the number of women called to the bar each year, confirming Michelson's (2013) argument that bar expansion leads to a feminization of the profession. The difficulty in accessing longitudinal data on the total number of lawyers since law faculties were established in different African countries limits how effectively this chapter can trace these demographic changes over time and accurately assess the number of women lawyers across Africa.

Given the "accidental" emergence of legal education in much of Africa, as discussed in Chapter 2, the pioneering women lawyers were called to the bar, but not in their home countries—this includes Stella Marke Thomas of Nigeria in 1933, Frances Claudia Wright of Sierra Leone in 1941, and Essi Matilda Forster of Ghana in 1945. All three women were admitted to the English bar. Many others followed this example, including several who were called to the bar in the second generation in Senegal, Uganda, Zambia, and Zimbabwe. In other areas, such as The Gambia, Mariam Jack-Denton became the first woman called to the bar in 1979 (Karki, n.d.). In much of Southern Africa, the harmful effects of apartheid segregation policies meant that Black women entered the legal profession much later than white women (Sasinsky, 2020).

Throughout much of the Western coast of Africa, colonial policies of deprioritizing formal education meant that, in the rare cases when education was provided, these opportunities were mainly given to elites—primarily coastal chiefs acting as intermediaries for the colonial administration under the British indirect rule system. The main recipients of these limited educational opportunities were mostly the male children of chiefs and elites (Adewoye, 1982b; Luckham, 1976). Over time, a few female children began to gain access to education, mostly within the colonies, while those lucky enough to travel to England, France, or Portugal received their education there, since there were no educational facilities in the colonies (Ghai & McAuslan, 1970). Even when girls had access to educational opportunities, the social hierarchy was reinforced because girls continued to be educated by missionaries who upheld the private–public divide. This divide led to girls being trained to perform domestic tasks and take on roles in professions seen as the exclusive domain of women, such as nursing, teaching, and other caregiving roles associated with women (Duke-Bryant, 2020; Tripp, 2004; Whitehead, 2005).

By situating this chapter's analysis within the history of legal professions across the continent, the following discussion provides a clear overview of the methods and pathways for entering the legal field. Drawing on the work of various scholars, I use matri-legal feminist theory to evaluate the gendered dimensions of these selection processes and the tensions between opportunities and capabilities. From this evidence, I conclude that when institutional mechanisms are transparent and accessible, women display high levels of merit that make them suitable candidates for joining the bar and achieving notable success.

Influenced by the world's major legal traditions, the division of the legal profession into civil- and common-law systems (including some hybrid versions) significantly shapes the process of becoming a lawyer. In most common-law countries, this process begins with earning a Bachelor of Laws (LL.B) degree from the law faculty of an accredited university. In several jurisdictions, university graduates may need to pass an entry exam to enroll in a professional training program at a "School of Law" for one to two years to gain practical experience. After completing the program and passing the exam, candidates might be required to undergo mandatory training (pupillage) for six months to a year with an accredited law firm before receiving final approval from a regulatory body to practice law (Dawuni, 2021b; Manteaw, 2008). In many countries, obtaining a law degree does not automatically qualify someone to practice law. They may have to take professional courses, such as a postgraduate diploma in Legal Practice, to be eligible for bar admission. These courses might be taken at a law school like the Kenya School of Law (Kamau, 2020; Kameri-Mbote, 2014) the Law Development Centre of Uganda (Oloka-Onyango, 2021), the Nigerian Law School (Dawuni & Badejogbin, 2021), or the Institute of Legal Practice and Development in Rwanda (Kamatali, 2016).

In South Africa's split legal profession, choosing between becoming an advocate or an attorney involves completing "articles" with a law firm to qualify as an advocate. These highly competitive articles include multiple requirements, networks, and connections, often disqualifying many candidates early on. Some critics have argued that the process is gendered and racialized, aiming to exclude marginalized groups from the bar (Centre for Applied Legal Studies, 2014; Chitapi, 2018). In South Africa, the distinction between attorneys and advocates—who are considered more prestigious—leads to fewer women and even fewer Black women being selected as candidate attorneys (Sasinsky, 2020).

In civil-law countries, the typical process for becoming a lawyer usually starts with a four- or five-year undergraduate degree in law from an accredited university's law school. This degree qualifies a person to be called a *juriste* and makes them eligible to work in a legal environment. However, becoming fully licensed as a lawyer, or *avocat*, requires passing a competitive entrance exam and completing a demanding apprenticeship with a law firm for three years or more. In civil-law systems, the competitive entrance exam has often acted as a double-edged sword for women. In Senegal, respondents noted that while women perform well on the written exam, they often struggle with the oral part due to gendered socialization that limits women's public speaking. As a result, women face higher dropout rates and lower pass rates on the bar exam.

In the Ivory Coast, women tend to excel in the entrance examination due to the merit-based evaluation process. Several respondents mentioned that women's ability to study and perform well on the exam explains the increasing number of women at the Ivorian bar. After analyzing field research data comparing these two Francophone countries, sociocultural factors appear to influence Senegal more significantly than the Ivory Coast, partly because of the effects of religion and cultural socialization in Senegal. In both common- and civil-law systems, the pupillage or apprenticeship period presents the biggest challenge for all candidates, especially women. Most candidate attorneys do not receive compensation during pupillage, and when they do, the stipends are minimal. In Senegal, interview respondents noted that many female law students prioritize marriage and family over pursuing a legal career due to strong sociocultural pressure related to marriage and family, resulting in women facing familial expectations to marry and start a family.

These entry requirements are constantly changing, and the discussion here should be seen as reflective of shifting criteria. Generally, women across different countries on the continent have gained nearly equal access to law school and the profession. Although entry requirements and opportunities may be inclusive and equitable, the inherent challenges within the profession lead to different outcomes for women once they enter the field. These challenges will be addressed in the following sections. Overall, women lawyers have made notable progress, evolving from the early days of colonial racial segregation policies to today's institutional norms and practices that create opportunities yet also present challenges to their full integration and advancement. The next section offers a detailed overview of the status of women at the bar, based on the countries where I conducted fieldwork and supported by existing studies. Using the HISP (*history*, *institutions*, *social (norms)*, and *position(ality)*) framework, the discussion emphasizes how changing institutional entry requirements have expanded pathways for women to join the profession, while still presenting hurdles to their advancement and positioning.

IV. Representation at the Bar: No More "Gentlemen in Skirts"

A patriarchal belief rooted in the British legal tradition has long maintained that the legal profession is only for men, leading to the description of women as "gentlemen in skirts"—a term still used by some lawyers in Nigeria. While many have moved away from this language, others still cling to it, reaffirming the idea that women are unsuitable for the legal profession. In Chapter 2, I quote a senior second-generation lawyer who shared her experience in court one day.

> Women are pressured to conform to the "man's world" or the "old boys' club." They must continually resist such pressures, and it would be beneficial if everyone recognized that the profession is open to both men and women. Here in Nigeria, some men still insist that there are no women at the bar! I responded during a case at the Court of Appeal, telling my colleague not to refer to me as "*brother silk*." I said, "*I am a lady, unless you are blind*."

Although women have asserted their rights to full representation, the changing demographic landscape presents opportunities and challenges for their complete integration and inclusion. Unfortunately, in the Nigerian context, some women lawyers and judges still prefer to be addressed with masculine titles, such as "My Lord" for judges, as discussed in Chapter 5. Evidence from interviews with women lawyers strongly suggests an increase in the number of women lawyers across various jurisdictions due to shifting and expanding social and educational opportunities. The rising enrollment of girls in higher education, evolving social expectations, an increasing number of professional women role models, and the strong performance of young women in law schools have all contributed to these demographic shifts.

In Cape Verde, a lawyer explained that there were initially no restrictions when the legal profession was developing in the country, and women had equal opportunities to join. Emphasizing the government's investment in education, she highlighted that entering the profession depended on an individual's determination and competence. She also mentioned that

> [i]n Cape Verde, whenever a job opportunity is based on merit, women are often in the forefront. The people of Cape Verde trust women, and they do not choose which lawyer to hire based on gender; instead, they consider name recognition. If you are a good lawyer, this demonstrates that our community is willing to support women, as more women are showing their capabilities. However, when the selection for public offices involves nomination or election, women face challenges because they often lack the connections or the popularity needed to win elections.

Although this story highlights how merit influences appointments, it doesn't fully reflect the realities faced in many parts of the continent. In this case, the lawyer may have missed the fact that, even with the government's investment in education, not all children or women have equal access. For instance, in Cape Verde, the first law school wasn't established until 2007. Before that, all lawyers and judges had to train in Portugal, which many could not afford. While women have the right to education and possess the necessary merit and qualifications, lingering institutional structures and cultural gender norms continue to restrict women's upward mobility.

1. General Demographic Patterns

Earlier in Chapter 3, I provided a detailed analysis of changing demographic patterns among women in law. The discussion centered on the intersectional effects of age, ethnicity, race, and marital and family status, giving an overview of how women manage these identity categories while balancing their careers. Of the 122 survey respondents, 41% were aged 31 to 40, 23% were between 25 and 30, 22.1% were aged 41 to 50, and 13.1% were over 50. Regarding marital status, 33.6% were married with children, 32.8% were single, 24.6% were married without children, and 4.1% were divorced. The evidence and conclusions from this discussion indicate that younger women are entering the profession, and most women are married. However, a significant number remain single or divorced, often taking on various caregiving roles, as family status includes not only raising biological children but also caring for aging parents and supporting extended family members.

2. Changing Trends in Women's Representation

There is no doubt that the number of women lawyers across the continent has grown since the first generation of women lawyers entered the profession in the mid-1930s. According to the five generational phases described in this book, the current phase is the fifth, marked by increased legal education institutions, shifting perceptions of women's leadership abilities, and greater freedom for women to pursue their chosen legal careers. As mentioned in Chapter 1 regarding data accessibility, the challenge throughout this project has been obtaining accurate data on the number of women compared to men who have been admitted to national bars. Building a comprehensive database of correct and current quantitative data requires time and resources, which are beyond the scope of this project.

The number of women lawyers varies greatly across countries, and recent data from law faculty and law school graduation ceremonies show that women make up a large share of those called to the bar. Across Africa, systemic, policy, and cultural changes explain the increasing presence of women at the bar. First, shifts in cultural perceptions about women's roles in society seem to have led to greater acceptance of girls' education and higher education opportunities. Comparing the impact of these cultural shifts, Inglehart and Norris (2001) found that cultural acceptance of roles traditionally seen as belonging to men in politics and decision-making can positively influence and boost the number of women in those roles. This idea of a "cultural shift" is also relevant in the legal field and can be seen in Chapter 2, where pioneering women in law served as role models and agents of societal and cultural change in perceptions.

A second factor explaining the rise in women's representation is related to global educational policy changes (Garth & Shaffer, 2022). These changes have led to the liberalization of education and the expansion of legal educational institutions in Nigeria (Dawuni & Badejogbin, 2021), Ghana (Manteaw, 2008), Zambia (Ndulo, 2002), Kenya (Ghai & Ghai, 2014; Hellum et al., 2019), and Uganda (Oloko-Onyango, 2021; Tibihikirra-Kalyegira, 2010). As the number of lawyers grows, there is a correlation with the number of women entering the profession, supporting the demand-and-supply thesis. In an earlier analysis of women in the legal academy in Ghana, I suggested that as more law faculties gain accreditation, opportunities for women to join the profession increase, with some of these women later returning to academia (Dawuni, 2021a).

In Kenya, as in many other countries on the continent, inclusive educational policies aimed at increasing girls' access to primary education have begun to show long-term effects (Kamau, 2020; Kameri-Mbote, 2014). Across much of southern Africa, the transformation of institutions after apartheid toward equality expanded opportunities for Black and "coloured" individuals to pursue both basic and higher education (Karekwaivanane, 2016; Madlalate, 2022). In South Africa, despite criticisms of the postapartheid transformative agenda as racially biased and less focused on gender (Masengu, 2016; Meyers, 2018), targeted efforts at certain educational institutions to recruit based on race and gender appear to have positively influenced women's access to better education and increased their chances of pursuing legal studies (Klaaren, 2020).

Third, changes in legal and constitutional frameworks have played a vital role in speeding up efforts to increase women's representation in public life. The democratic guarantees of equality found in legal, constitutional, and legislative measures that promote and enforce the rights of women and minorities are key factors in expanding opportunities for women in public office. In Kenya, the passage of the 2010 Constitution, which guarantees equal rights and access to decision-making for women in public life, has greatly boosted advocacy for women's representation (Aura-Odhiambo, 2018; Kamau, 2020; Kameri-Mbote, 2014). Similarly, in South Africa, the 1996 Constitution is known for initiating transformative changes designed to improve race and gender representation (Albertyn & Bonthuys, 2016; Centre for Applied Legal Studies, 2014; Masengu, 2016). Constitutional and legislative tools have been credited with increasing women's representation in public life and the legal field in Rwanda (Kamatali, 2016); Kenya (Aura-Odhiambo, 2018; Murungi & Meroka-Mutua, 2022), Zambia (Masengu, 2021), Zimbabwe (Bonnin & Maunganidze, 2021; Karekwaivanane, 2020; Stewart, 2012), and Malawi (Ellett, 2022). However, the results are mixed. Not all countries with institutions and mechanisms promoting gender equality have succeeded in boosting women's representation in law. For instance, Senegal ranks eleventh globally for women in national assemblies despite having a constitution that guarantees women's representation in public life (Interparliamentary Union, 2024; Tøraasen, 2017). Even with high parliamentary representation, women remain significantly underrepresented at the bar, constituting only 14% of lawyers in the country (Institute for African Women in Law, 2023o).

Another example is Nigeria, the most populous country on the continent, which operates a federal government system divided into 36 states, each with at least one public university and law faculty. Despite constitutional guarantees of equality and nondiscrimination, as well as the enrollment of the first woman lawyer in 1933, the pace of women's representation at the bar has faced numerous patriarchal institutional challenges (Ibrahim, 2016). For instance, the northern regions of Nigeria tend to have fewer girls in schools, which explains the delayed emergence of women lawyers in that area (Ibrahim, 2016). In Nigeria, despite active advocacy by women's rights organizations and ongoing efforts for these rights, several attempts to pass an Affirmative Action Bill into law have stalled (Amnesty International, 2022). Some progress was made when a coalition of women's rights organizations initiated a lawsuit (FHC/ABC/CS/1006/2020) against the government for its failure to implement the law. In 2022, a Federal High Court in Abuja ordered the government to enforce the provision for 35% women's representation in public offices (Ejekwonyilo, 2022).

In Ghana, constitutional guarantees of human rights based on gender have done little to change institutional norms regarding women's rights (Atuguba et al., 2020). Similar attempts to pass an affirmative action bill stalled for several years until the Parliament of Ghana finally passed it in 2024 (Dawuni, 2024a). Despite challenges in legislative support for women's representation in public office, these two West African countries have made modest progress in gradually increasing the number of women lawyers beyond the 30% mark, with a growing number of women assuming leadership roles such as attorneys general (in Ghana) and at the state levels in Nigeria. Additionally, women have served as chief justices in both countries (Dawuni & Kang, 2015).

Fourth, the influence of role models and diffusion on the growing number of women lawyers has been significant. As discussed in Chapter 3, the symbolic representation of women in careers like law, once seen as male-dominated, has positively influenced younger women aspiring to join the legal field. Not only are women entering these professions, but many have also reached top leadership roles in both the private and public sectors, including in the judiciary and academia. Several respondents in this study noted the impact of role models and symbolic women leaders on their decision to pursue a legal career. The various factors discussed here show that the rise in women at the bar varies depending on each country's historical, social, and political context. However, these factors are interconnected and often reflect global trends across jurisdictions beyond Africa (Auchmuty et al., 2021; Schultz & Shaw, 2003, 2013). Moreover, these elements are linked and often work together with other factors to produce different outcomes for individual women lawyers.

3. Diversity in Practice and Areas of Specialization

At the start of the legal profession in much of Africa, legal practice mainly centered on commercial litigation and land disputes, driven by trade in coastal border towns (Adewoye, 1982b; Ghai & McAuslan, 1970; Harvey, 1966). With the creation of administrative and bureaucratic institutions, such as government ministries of justice, judiciaries, and parliaments, lawyers began to explore other fields to use their skills and knowledge. When asked about their specializations, 31% of the 122 survey respondents said they were in litigation, 32% were corporate lawyers, 2.5% were state attorneys, 21% served as general counsel, and 11% were legal officers in international organizations.

In recent years, the expansion of cross-border trade within the continent, connections to the global marketplace, technological advances, and other global developments have broadened the fields of legal practice and lawyer specialties (Khanna et al., 2017). While men have historically led the way into these new areas, women are increasingly moving beyond the traditional focus on public law to pursue emerging opportunities in the private sector and international markets. Despite these major changes, the public sector (government ministries of justice/attorney general's department) remains mostly staffed by women, though they are underrepresented in top leadership roles. A 2023 report on women's representation in law and leadership shows that, although women make up 42% of the Office of the Deputy Public Prosecutor (ODPP) in Kenya, they have only reached the role of deputy director within the leadership structure (Institute for African Women in Law, 2023i). In 2025, Dorcas Agik Oduor was appointed the first female attorney general. In neighboring Uganda, Jane Abodo, a high court judge and former prosecutor, was appointed Director of Public Prosecutions in 2020.

Beverley Houghton's (1981) analysis of women lawyers in Ghana highlighted their preference for the public sector due to specific family-friendly benefits. The public sector continues to attract many women lawyers. Among the variables discussed in Chapter 2 regarding women's choices to enter the profession, the justice/problem-solver variable remains relevant for many women in the public sector. In addition to personal motivational factors, the public sector offers numerous benefits that support women in their roles. First, these jobs provide a stable, standardized income that guarantees a monthly salary, unlike private practice and litigation, where earnings heavily depend on the number of clients and cases handled. Public-sector salaries also include benefits such as health insurance and maternity and family leave policies that support women (Houghton, 1981). Furthermore, the public sector offers standard working hours, typically from 8 am to 5 pm, allowing women to manage and plan their family and personal obligations effectively. Although these observations are based on interviews, they may not apply in all jurisdictions and can vary widely across countries. Regardless of these differences, the public sector continues to offer many advantageous working conditions compared to other legal practice sectors, even though the pay may be lower.

Another factor contributing to the change in the types and varieties of legal practices emerging across the continent is closely linked to the influence of globalization on legal systems. Throughout much of Africa, early legal practices were called "chambers," borrowing from the English system. Law chambers in Africa typically consisted of individual practitioners, usually no more than five. Over time, most law firms have evolved and adopted the term "firms" in line with American legal branding. These changes are part of the social processes happening within African legal markets, similar to those in other regions of the world (Liu, 2013). These shifts may also be connected to the introduction of American legal education (Bartie & Sandomierski, 2021) and the rapid influence of globalization on the legal profession (Drolshammer & Pfeiffer, 2021). Across Africa, most law offices generally range from five practitioners at the low end to large corporate merger firms employing about 50 or more lawyers—primarily in South Africa and Kenya. In these two countries, the merging of law firms from various nations within the continent, as well as those based in Europe and the Americas, has increased competition for lawyers in the legal market (Kamau, 2020; Klaaren, 2020). In this growing legal market, competition can be intense for the limited opportunities to join top law firms, depending on each firm's practice areas. While women are taking opportunities and exploring new areas of legal practice, as will be discussed later, the limited availability of women mentors and sponsors poses a significant obstacle to professional growth.

When asked if women are branching out into new areas of legal practice and specialization, a female partner in one of the leading law firms in the Ivory Coast commented on the chances for women's mobility:

> There are barriers for women that depend on the type of law firm and the woman's agency; she must work hard to earn her colleagues' respect. Unconscious bias and societal stereotypes about women can influence their chances of advancement. However, some law firms assign women challenging briefs when they show their capability and commitment to the work.

Across the continent, women have consistently shown competitive advantages in hiring processes. Many leading law firms have a higher representation of women in associate and senior associate roles; however, their numbers drop at higher levels of the hierarchy—factors explored later in this chapter. The personal choices women make when entering the legal profession partly influence the areas of law they focus on. Early law firms, or "chambers," tended to be generalists, handling a wide range of cases. With the growth of the global legal market and the increasing complexity of emerging legal issues, most law firms are developing niches and specialized expertise over time. Although many law firms still operate as generalists, a few medium-to-large firms have distinct divisions focusing on different sectors of law (Kamau, 2020; Karekwaivanane, 2020; Klaaren, 2020). Based on my review of the law firms in countries where I conducted fieldwork, most have established legal teams or departments dedicated to specific practice areas, such as corporate, litigation, and intellectual property.

Women lawyers are present across various sectors without a clear concentration in any particular area of law. During my fieldwork, I observed law firms in Ghana and Nigeria where women led their litigation departments, challenging the assumption that litigation is not suited for women. While these women expressed their passion for specializing in litigation, they also highlighted the challenges of the field in the African context, such as frequent court adjournments and delays in resolving cases. Many of them also shared experiences of sexism from male counsel, senior lawyers, and some judges, despite their relative seniority in the profession, reinforcing the idea that societal gender constructs do not protect women, regardless of their professional status or background.

Although more women are participating in active litigation, the field remains predominantly male. Women also view litigation as an area where masculine traits, like aggressiveness, are seen as assertive and essential, while women who display similar aggressiveness are labeled as loud and emotional (Bonnin & Maunganidze, 2021; Stewart, 2012). The head of the litigation department at a leading law firm in Ghana remarked:

> In court, you encounter various male lawyers. For some men, being soft-spoken may lead them to perceive you as lacking intelligence or legal knowledge. Additionally, some men like to test you—if they have seen or heard of you as a competent lawyer, they will test you in court to validate their perceptions and beliefs about you.

In some instances where women choose to be in the litigation department of a law firm, their chances may be limited when it comes to case assignment, as shared by a junior lawyer in Nigeria:

> For those of us involved in litigation at this firm, it seems that the men tend to receive the tougher cases. This case assignment may be unconscious, or it might be that the men know how to promote themselves effectively and express their ideas assertively in meetings, capturing everyone's attention, resulting in them getting the challenging cases.

Interview respondents indicated that, early in their legal careers, most women are assigned to practice areas considered "feminine," such as family law. Additionally, more women work as in-house counsel for corporate organizations, including banks. Many women also prefer to work with the government, often serving as prosecutors in the attorney general's department or within the judiciary. The professional and institutional culture partly influences women's choices regarding which legal practice areas to specialize in. Fields such as family law, divorce, and succession matters are still viewed as "soft law," where women can "survive" without facing the harsh rigors of litigation (Houghton, 1981; Kamau, 2020; Meyers, 2018; Stewart, 2012).

The factors shaping women's choices in legal specialties are mainly driven by personal interest. Sometimes, these decisions are influenced by the law firm's requirements, shaped by market dynamics and the aim to carve out a niche. Women working in government may handle challenging cases such as prosecuting high-profile state and criminal cases, which can put their safety at risk. In later parts of this chapter, I present evidence from women prosecutors in Senegal and Cape Verde to demonstrate some of these challenges. I also discuss the assassination of Joan Kagezi, the then Acting Assistant Director of Public Prosecutions and Head of Prosecutions at the International Crimes Division in Uganda (Institute for Security Studies, 2015). Future research should investigate the factors that motivate women to pursue careers in public prosecution and public service.

Some women make pragmatic decisions when choosing their areas of practice. In a small country and legal market like Cape Verde, deciding on the area of legal specialization is not always easy. A lawyer in Cape Verde specializing in construction law confirmed this:

> My partner and I have had this office since 2006, specializing in public law. It was our choice, a calculated risk; we did not want to give in to the market and take on everything. That's why we have so many clients from construction companies and are recognized for our expertise in this area. I believe that with globalization, we must specialize because one cannot excel in every field; otherwise, one risks being superficial. When we first opened the firm, people would approach us with all kinds of cases. Without sounding arrogant, I would explain what we do and refer them to the right lawyer with the appropriate specialization. Since our market is small, I was always careful because people frequently came back to thank me for providing them with a good referral to another lawyer.

Starting in the 1990s, as several African countries gradually shifted back to democratic governments, there has been an increase in foreign direct investment. This growth has created a demand for corporate and infrastructural legal work to advise companies looking to invest in these nations, such as large infrastructure and mining firms. These changes in the political economy have opened new opportunities for women to work in corporate legal settings. A survey of these organizations shows that most heads of legal departments are women. The prevalence of women in these legal roles is partly due to the stability these positions provide, with regular hours, predictable pay, and benefits. Also, these roles tend to be more attractive and less stressful because they usually do not require the long hours often associated with litigation, which is marked by high unpredictability and unnecessary court delays.

Market forces strongly shape the strategic decisions lawyers make about their areas of specialization. Law firms are adapting to these market demands by recognizing the importance of developing specializations and niche legal markets for their services. This requires lawyers and firms to have in-depth knowledge of the law in those specific fields, which decreases the prevalence of generalist legal practices from the past. Recognizing the need for diversity in legal practice, law firms are recruiting the right talent and skill sets. As specialization areas expand, new opportunities emerge for women lawyers to demonstrate their diverse talents and expertise. A female managing partner of a major law firm in Ghana remarked on the changing legal landscape:

> Shifts in the global political economy drive many changes in the structure of law firms. Clients are discerning about the lawyers they engage. They seek firms that provide not only advice but also proactive legal services. They prefer law firms that stay current with developments and maintain continuity in terms of succession—firms staffed with individuals who have institutional memory, rather than just solo practitioners.

As emerging practice areas become more competitive and expand, more women are training and qualifying as certified arbitrators with the Chartered Institute of Arbitrators in the United Kingdom. The global increase in the use of arbitration for international transactions is where women are making their mark. Some of my respondents pointed out that arbitration is exciting for them because it involves less litigation and more consensus-building, a trait often linked to women. Despite this, international arbitration remains predominantly male worldwide, especially among individuals from the Western Hemisphere who serve as gatekeepers in the industry (Pilawa, 2019). In 2021, Diamana Diawara was appointed Director of Arbitration and ADR for the International Chamber of Commerce. Other women who have played key roles in international arbitration include Funke Adekoya, SAN of Nigeria, who served on the World Bank/International Monetary Fund arbitration panel.

These developments in the legal market provide women lawyers with greater flexibility by expanding their options to transition between different legal sectors and areas of specialization. For many women, the corporate sector is an attractive choice, partly because of the benefit of having established working hours. Additionally, for some women, entering the corporate sector may serve as a strategic step toward starting their own legal practice. In a study of women lawyers in South Africa, Sasinsky (2020) found that 81% of the 11 participants transitioned from law firms to corporate roles as in-house legal counsel, which offered them more flexible working conditions. Furthermore, some women lawyers may switch from one law firm to another; for example, in another study on women lawyers in South Africa, Rasivhetshele (2020) discovered that 33% of respondents made lateral moves between law firms due to institutional cultures that did not align with their values.

A lawyer in Ghana explains some of the reasons for these lateral career moves:

> Many women enter the corporate world to earn money before transitioning to start their own businesses. Once they have paid off their loans and mortgages, they leave, gaining the flexibility to spend time with their families. One advantage of working in the corporate world is the steady salary and benefits, which help with planning, but the job and schedule can be demanding.

Despite the perceived flexibility of working in the corporate sector, corporate law remains a field where women must still demonstrate their abilities as lawyers. The head of the corporate department at an international mining company in Ghana stated:

> I've realized that when you demonstrate your expertise and leadership, people naturally listen to you. As women, we need to understand that if men work long hours, we might also have to put in similar hours to earn recognition. It's not just about working more but about achieving different results. We may need to be the top in our field so that no one considers making decisions without our input. Working hard helps others recognize your contributions and value your role. If you stay at the top of your game, there's no reason to doubt your worth—women must keep investing in their own development.

Regardless of the legal practice area a woman chooses to specialize in, various internal and external factors shape her experiences. No single narrative captures these diverse outcomes or explains why one area of specialization might suit women better than others. When comparing corporate practice to litigation, a lawyer in Ghana believes that in the corporate world, attorneys are compensated based on their rank, and women are likely to receive the same pay as their male counterparts. However, she notes that promotions depend on subjective interpretations, as she states:

> The question is whether women in private practice can perform as well as men, as men tend to trust one another with legal work and assign tasks to their male colleagues—creating networking opportunities that women cannot participate in. For instance, men often meet to play golf; sometimes, deals are made there, and you are not included.

Working in the corporate world is definitely challenging for women. Often, women have to justify their qualifications for promotions and pay increases that match their new roles. A lawyer at a mining company in Nigeria shared her frustration about negotiating her new salary and having to explain why she deserved her current pay. Despite taking on the extra duties of a vice president who left the company, there was no talk of a raise or a promotion to VP. She believes that if she were a man, there would have been no debate about her becoming the official vice president. To highlight the gender bias women encounter in salary negotiations, she shared this experience:

> I was told that if I received a 10% salary increase, I would be earning slightly more than two other men who are my juniors in ranking. You could tell that he [the supervisor] believed my age and gender should not entitle me to an increase, regardless of the work I am doing. To be fair, I make more than my boss ever did at my stage, but

> I am doing a lot more work. At every turn, they fall short of logically explaining their arguments. I told them I would not allow them to treat me as if they were doing me a favor; they could not give me extra work and not pay me for it.

Besides salary negotiations and the pay gaps women face, their expertise and effort don't always match the authority and recognition associated with their roles. Often shaped by historical and cultural gender biases, these organizational cultures and structures are frequently judged through a masculine work ethic that tends to favor men during promotions. A top executive at a multinational communications company in Nigeria states that women must work exceptionally hard, juggling roles as lawyers, managers, and caregivers while competing with their male colleagues. While men can often afford to work long hours, women are expected, and often required, to handle their second jobs at home. Women must meet key performance indicators that are often unrealistic within an eight-hour workday. She concludes:

> The men work hard and play hard. While your supervisors seem to understand when you miss deadlines and can't stay long hours, they won't complain, but you see the men advancing. Out of our 11 top executives, only three are women. You must decide on the sacrifices to make—family or work? It's a constant balancing act, which can be very painful for a mother.

Beverley Houghton's (1981) study of women lawyers in Ghana revealed similar sentiments among women. Unfortunately, even decades later, gender-based stereotypes still exist, portraying women as soft and emotional before a judge, inadequate in criminal defense or insurance claims, and always wanting time off for family and children. While the public sector might seem more welcoming for women trying to balance personal and professional life, the corporate and private sectors are just as tough. Women aiming for executive roles or top positions often face a choice between work and family. Several interview respondents said they had to choose between taking annual leave and staying on the job to meet performance goals needed for bonuses and promotions. In some multinational companies, especially in mining, telecommunications, and finance, many women in executive roles are found in what are considered "softer" departments, such as human resources.

Women's experiences in high corporate organizations raise the question: Can women have it all—family, marriage, and a career? The answer may be yes, and for many women, this is achievable. However, research on women in the legal profession shows that women often lose something along the way, as those who reach leadership positions frequently do so at the expense of family, marriage, or other social needs, which they end up sacrificing for their careers (Brown et al., 2020; Liebenberg & Scharf, 2019; Sterling & Chanow, 2021). According to the social variable discussed in Chapter 1, women in law are held to a higher standard than men concerning societal expectations and obligations (Nayak & Tabassum, 2021). These expectations lead to mostly negative impacts on the well-being and welfare of women in the field. Despite these challenges, evidence from fieldwork shows that women are breaking in, building their expertise, and developing legal specializations that make them competitive, sought after by clients, and respected by their male colleagues both in the office and in the courtroom.

4. Women in International Law

Despite the increase in the number of women admitted to the bar in recent years and the expansion of previously mentioned fields of specialization, legal practice in international law remains a field with lower female representation. Traditionally, international law has had a strong male presence, which led to foundational work by Charlesworth et al. (1991) that questioned women's representation in this domain. Since then, many scholars have studied women and gender issues in international law from various perspectives, focusing on the lived experiences of women lawyers appearing before international courts and tribunals rather than symbolic representation alone. African women have consistently participated in international settings and organizations, such as the United Nations and the African Union, taking on roles within legal departments. Others have worked as legal officers in international courts and tribunals, including the International Court of Justice (ICJ), the International Criminal Court (ICC), and the African Court on Human and Peoples' Rights (ACtHPR). In these organizations, women may also hold nonlegal roles, which complicates the assessment of their contributions and positions.

Recognizing the lack of representation of African women in international law, the Institute for African Women in Law (IAWL) held a public discussion in October 2021 on the topic "Where Are the African Women in International Law?" The forum brought together international law experts to explore the causes of and solutions to this underrepresentation. This discussion occurred before the 2021 elections for the International Law Commission (ILC) of the United Nations, where, as of 2020, no woman from Africa had ever served.

Among the explanations shared by the panelists, it was noted that most law schools and faculties across the continent have traditionally offered international law as an elective course, minimizing its importance for many students. Besides legal education practices, limited access for many lawyers to practice in international law settings creates an additional barrier for women lawyers who, often burdened by family responsibilities, may face difficulties traveling and networking to gain the necessary experience. Regarding nominations for appointments to international bodies such as the ILC, the focus on national networks that support nominations, along with the international negotiations needed to secure votes, was also identified as a significant obstacle. Some speakers highlighted the importance of women demonstrating self-agency, having confidence in themselves, and showcasing their ability to be nominated and appointed to these roles. Ambassador Namira Negm, the first woman appointed as the Legal Counsel of the African Union, poignantly remarked (Institute for African Women in Law, 2023g, p. 18):

> The key is always to believe in yourself and demonstrate to the leaders who handle national-level nominations just how capable you are. Although the internal pressures from our upbringing create some doubts at times, we must keep fighting to show our worth so that our governments consider us for international positions, particularly since men predominantly occupy judiciaries and almost all other sectors.

Despite these challenges, in November 2021, Professor Phoebe Okowa made history as the first woman from the African continent, representing Kenya, to be elected to the ILC, thereby increasing the representation of women in the ILC's makeup to 8% (Institute for African Women in Law, 2023g). Since the ILC's founding, women remain underrepresented, as shown in **Figure 4.1.**

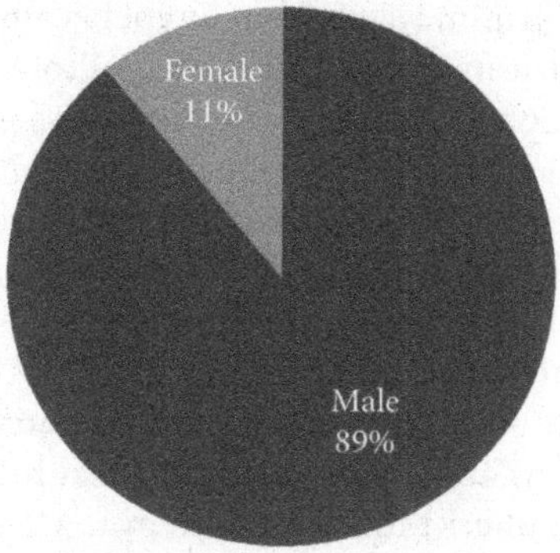

Figure 4.1 *Gender Distribution of African Members of the ILC as of February 2025*
Source: International Law Commission (February 2025).

Women in international courts and tribunals likely represent the area where African women have made the most progress (Dawuni & Kuenyehia, 2018). However, this assessment may be influenced by the available research in this field, leading to a relatively small pool of courts and individuals for analysis and monitoring. While tracking the number of women in international organizations, I encountered European data-sharing restrictions from courts in The Hague and Geneva. The representation of African women can improve through increased mentoring opportunities, greater exposure to international law and institutions, and access to networks within recruiting bodies. Nonetheless, further research is necessary to fully assess the representation of African women in international law institutions and organizations.

5. Women "Normalizing" the Nontraditional Roles

As previously discussed, the first group of women lawyers across the continent mainly took on public service roles such as those in the Ministry of Justice or the judiciary. Earlier studies of this initial group of women lawyers in Ghana (Houghton, 1981), Zimbabwe (Stewart, 2012), and South Africa (Meyers, 2018) showed similar trends, with these women choosing to enter the public sector for many of the same reasons mentioned earlier. As noted in the section on evolving areas of specialization, many other fields of legal practice are seeing women "breaking in." Recently, there has been a notable shift as women explore new areas of legal practice that have traditionally been male-dominated. These emerging fields include law and technology, aviation, maritime law, environmental law, fintech, and artificial intelligence, among others.

In the traditional and quickly changing fields of international law and human rights, women across the continent have achieved significant progress. For example, Fatou Bensouda was the first female prosecutor of the International Criminal Court (ICC), serving from 2012 to 2021. Hilary Gbedemah chaired the United Nations Convention on the Elimination of All Forms of Discrimination Against Women (CEDAW) from 2019 to 2021. In 2017, Dr. Namira Negm from Egypt became the first woman to serve as Legal Counsel of the African Union, followed by Professor Hajer Gueldich from Tunisia in 2024. As mentioned earlier, Kenyan Professor of Law Phoebe Okowa was elected as the first African woman to join the United Nations International Law Commission in 2021. Other notable women in international legal roles include Hanna Tetteh from Ghana, who served as the UN Secretary-General's Special Envoy for the Horn of Africa in 2022. In 2019, she was the Special Representative of the Secretary-General to the African Union and head of the United Nations Office to the African Union (UNOAU). Betty Mould-Iddrisu, also from Ghana, was appointed Head of Legal and Constitutional Affairs at the Commonwealth Secretariat in London in 2003. Professor Patricia Kameri-Mbote from Kenya, a respected legal scholar, became the Director of the Law Division of the United Nations Environment Program (UNEP) in 2022.

Lastly, understanding the diversity of practice areas and engagement among women lawyers is incomplete without recognizing their role in politics. The legal profession often produces many political figures, including presidents and members of parliament. For instance, since Ghana's return to democratic rule in 1992, three of the six presidents have been lawyers (Dawuni, 2021b). A significant percentage of members of parliament are also lawyers. Many women lawyers have served as members of parliament and held ministerial positions. As discussed later, an increasing number of women have taken roles as ministers of justice and public prosecutors. In other regions, women legal professionals have reached the highest levels of political life. In the Ivory Coast, the first female law professor, Jacqueline Lohoues-Oble, ran for president twice (Institute for African Women in Law, n.d.-c). This trend was reflected in Senegal, where in 2012, Professor Amsatou Sidibe Sow, the first female law professor, ran for president (Gierczynski-Bocandé, 2013; Tøraasen, 2017). In Kenya, lawyer and member of parliament Martha Karua, who also served as the Minister of Justice, contested the Kenyan presidential elections in 2013. Although these women were unsuccessful, their courageous bids into politics demonstrate that women in law are no longer restricted by the institutional or structural norms that once confined them to specific roles within the profession.

In Malawi, the inspiring life of Vera Chirwa, the first female lawyer, demonstrates how women's activism can be vital in upholding the rule of law, promoting good governance, and protecting human rights. Chirwa's journey, growing up in colonial Nyasaland, along with her unwavering pursuit of legal education and her career as a lawyer, highlights her determination. Even more remarkable is her partnership with her husband, Orton Chirwa, as they challenged the oppressive regime of Dr. Kenneth Banda. Her political activism ultimately led to a death sentence, years in prison, and the mysterious death (alleged murder) of her husband, who was also jailed (Chirwa, 2007). In The Gambia, Mariam Jack-Denton, the first female lawyer, opposed the authoritarian government of Yahya Jammeh, which resulted in her unlawful arrest and imprisonment. She later became the first woman Speaker of Parliament from 2017 to 2022, serving under the democratically elected government of President Adama Barrow (Karki, n.d.).

These are just a few examples of the many women lawyers involved in politics across the continent. However, politics remains a male-dominated field, and women face numerous challenges, including gender-based political violence, as they navigate the political landscape (Anyidoho et al., 2020; Casimiro et al., 2009; Tsikata, 1989). In Nigeria, Ayisha Osori, a human rights lawyer, provides detailed insights in *Love Does Not Win Elections* about what it means for women aspiring to enter politics in Nigeria (Osori, 2017). In Kenya, Raychelle Omamo, the first female president of the Law Society of Kenya (LSK), achieved other historic milestones, including her role as Kenya's Cabinet Secretary for Foreign Affairs and Minister of Defence, making her the first woman to hold those positions. Among her other political roles, she also served as Kenya's Ambassador to France, Portugal, and Serbia. Many women lawyers from other countries across the continent have also held ambassadorial positions.

Overall, although the legal profession is now open to women, the challenges they face due to the intersection of historical, institutional, and social factors significantly impact their individual experiences. Many of these women may find themselves as double or triple minorities—by race, gender, and age—requiring them to navigate the terrain carefully. For others, being the first woman to hold a position adds a greater burden of responsibility, often forcing them to navigate institutional norms and expectations more carefully, as they face higher levels of scrutiny from both men and women. The "burden of the first" can sometimes lead women to adopt prevailing masculinized institutional norms and practices to avoid challenges within the patriarchal system. In such cases, these women's opportunities to leverage their unique identities and skills may be limited to staying afloat and accomplishing their work with minimal disruptions to institutional norms and standards. As a result, the chances of transforming patriarchal institutional norms decrease, hindering progress toward creating gender-inclusive institutional cultures.

6. Promotion, Leadership, and Managerial Positions

Globally, women still face difficulties in becoming partners at leading law firms. In the United States, a study by the American Bar Association showed that in 2021, women made up only 24% of law firm partners, up from 15% in 1999. This percentage was just 2% for Black women, remaining unchanged for over twenty years. The study also found that within seven years of practicing law, men were two to five times more likely than women to reach partner status, and these chances were even lower for Black women (American Bar Association, 2019; Sterling & Chanow, 2021). Similarly, in the United Kingdom, women are significantly underrepresented in top law firms, with Black and minority women making up an even smaller portion of the female workforce (Bar Council, 2021; Sommerlad, 1994, 2013).

In the survey conducted for this research, respondents were asked if they held a leadership position. **Figure 4.2** shows that over half of the respondents (52%) held some leadership position at work.

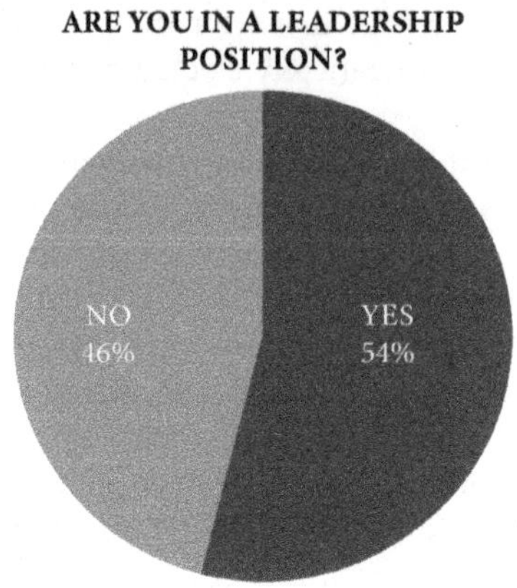

Figure 4.2 *Survey Results on Women in Leadership*
Source: Survey respondents: 122.

Survey respondents were asked about their views on leadership opportunities and whether women had equal chances as men to hold leadership roles. Respondents were asked the question, "Women in my country have equal opportunities as men to leadership; how much do you agree with this statement?" Although 54% held leadership positions, the results from **Figure 4.3** show that a majority, 42.6%, either strongly disagreed or disagreed that women had equal opportunities for leadership as men. A concerning 28.7% remained neutral (neither agreeing nor disagreeing), which suggests that many women may not recognize what constitutes leadership, may be unaware of the qualifications required for leadership, may feel apathetic toward pursuing leadership, or may have simply given up due to institutional barriers. Explanations for some of these observations are drawn from qualitative interviews and elaborated on later in this chapter.

Compared to other surveys, women's perceptions of leadership show inconsistencies. A four-nation study on women in law and leadership—Kenya, Nigeria, Senegal, and South Africa—found that women lawyers' opinions were split and inconclusive.

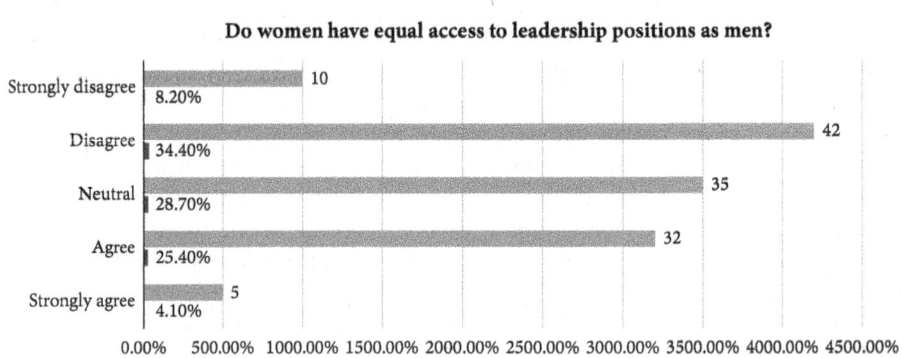

Figure 4.3 *Women's Perceptions of Access to Leadership Roles*
Source: Survey respondents: 122.

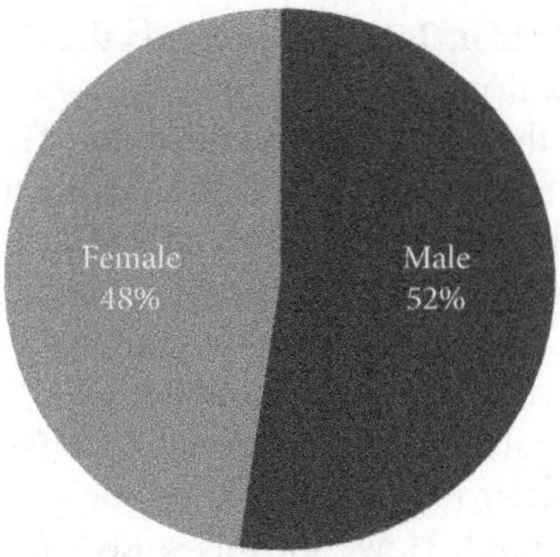

Figure 4.4 *Survey of Law Firms Across Africa*
Source: IAWL gender scorecard, 2023.

In Nigeria, 46% of respondents (from a survey of 449) believed women were well represented in leadership, while 34% disagreed and 20% were unsure or neutral (Institute for African Women in Law, 2023*l*). In South Africa, a sample of 13 respondents showed that 53.9% disagreed that women had equal decision-making power in their law firms. When asked about women's equal presence in top roles, 46.2% disagreed (Institute for African Women in Law, 2023*l*). The International Bar Association (2022) study on women in law highlighted similar patterns, pointing to a shrinking pipeline for women leaders in this field. Contributing factors to higher dropout rates from law firms include long hours, gender stereotypes and biases, sexual harassment, unequal pay and promotions, and personal decisions to move into corporate, academic, or judicial careers (Institute for African Women in Law, 2023a).

The Institute for African Women in Law publishes annual data on women's representation in law and leadership across Africa. The 2022 scorecard surveyed 82 law firms across the continent. Firms with at least 10 associates were selected, and data were gathered from their websites, using photos of associates that could be identified as binary images. Consequently, the data reflect information found on these websites and depend on how often they are updated.

Figure 4.4 illustrates that women comprised 48% of the 2,175 lawyers surveyed, a notable trend in the legal profession. However, when the data are further disaggregated by rank, the number of women in leadership positions drops sharply as one

Table 4.1 *Percentage of Women Law Associates in 82 Law Firms*

Role	Men	Women	Women (%)
Managing partners	43	13	23%
Partners	448	269	38%
Senior associates	209	216	51%
Associates	440	537	55%

Source: IAWL Gender Scorecard, 2023(n.d.-f).

moves up the leadership ladder. Table 4.1 presents the data on the various ranks of women in the surveyed law firms.

Women's dominance in the lower and middle ranks of law firms (at 55%) as shown in **Figure 4.1** highlights the gendered organizational practices and cultures that favor male work ethics. This results in men being promoted at faster rates than their female counterparts. Therefore, while women often serve as the ***workhorses*** of many large law firms, men are seen as the ***racehorses*** and usually take priority when senior partners consider promotions, salary increases, and bonuses.

Despite the growth in legal markets and specialization mentioned earlier, law firms are expected to develop better-organized systems for administrative and human resource policies as they expand. However, this study's findings show that most law firms remain small, with some having only one person and others consisting of 5 to 10 partners and associates. The majority of law firms surveyed for this study lacked written promotion policies or guidelines for moving from associate to senior associate or becoming a partner.

Field data for this project show that the pathway to partnership in law firms is often unclear, with only a few firms having written policies. The absence of clear guidelines on promotions could be a warning sign of a lack of transparency in advancement and pay, potentially leading to inconsistencies. Different law firms have different practices, and although there isn't a simple process to become a partner, I spoke with several managing and senior partners in the countries I visited, and the criteria for promotion decisions were not always documented in policies.

The main criteria for evaluating eligibility to become a partner in a firm include the number of years a person has worked at the firm and annual performance reviews, which assess work output, the number of clients, and the revenue generated for the firm. Other important factors considered are an individual's leadership skills, collegiality, and alignment with the firm's culture. These subjective indicators of leadership, collegiality, and fit allow for different weights to be assigned to various candidates being considered for promotion. The basic procedural requirements involve a nomination by a senior partner and a vote by all partners in the firm.

The absence of written evaluation criteria suggests that different and sometimes incompatible standards may be used to assess work performance. The gendered "reasonable man" remains the standard in law, and women may adjust to this masculine benchmark to meet workplace expectations (Stewart, 2012; Tamale, 2015). Clear promotion policies should outline the criteria for becoming a partner or managing partner in a law firm. In a study on client perceptions of women lawyers' competence in Ghana, Akuffo-Kwapong et al. (2021) found that socially constructed gender stereotypes about women's competence influenced clients' choice of a lawyer. Therefore, the authors highlighted the importance of law firm management considering these gender-biased factors when assessing women's competence as lawyers and aiming for client satisfaction.

Women lawyers provide diverse perspectives on achieving success in their careers and securing positions as partners or managing partners. Insights from interviews show that *personal agency*, *inclusive institutional policies*, and *gender-sensitive work environments* are crucial for women's advancement into leadership roles within a firm. First, regarding *personal agency*, most women leaders attribute their leadership roles to early ambition, starting in high school and continuing through college.

A lawyer at a prominent law firm in Ghana highlighted the importance of hard work, stating that women who put in the necessary hours were "rewarded" with promotions. However, this view assumes that working conditions and evaluation standards are gender-sensitive, especially since many women with caregiving responsibilities may find it difficult to stay late at the office to demonstrate their commitment. As one respondent noted, men often can stay later at work because they usually have a partner at home managing childcare, cooking, and homework for school-aged children—this underscores male privilege.

For women lawyers who may not have caregiving responsibilities (often single women), an extra challenge related to security exists. Several respondents shared that staying late at work and returning home can expose them to unwanted advances from certain male colleagues and pose general safety risks when driving home at night. For some respondents, personal agency's impact on upward mobility toward partnership begins with choosing a supportive life partner who encourages a woman's drive and ambition. Finally, when considering women's self-criticism of their achievements, a respondent from an earlier report on women in leadership explained:

> Being promoted based on merit is essential; the truth will eventually come out if you don't earn a promotion. When you are elevated or promoted, believe in yourself and acknowledge that you genuinely deserve it because no one will give you anything on a silver platter. Every single woman's accomplishment at the law firm is based on merit. Others will find the truth if it's not based on merit. (Institute for African Women in Law, 2023e; p. 9)

This self-critical attitude stemming from widespread gender stereotypes about women in the workplace places a heavy burden on women to prove themselves—an expectation that may not apply when judging men's work.

A second perspective highlights the significance of inclusive *institutional policies.* Feminist institutional theory shows the vital role of gender-inclusive arrangements in supporting women's success (Chappell, 2006; Chappell & Waylen, 2013; Kenny, 2014). No matter how hard a woman works, if her workplace's policies do not align with women's interests, her success may be limited. As law firms specialize and adopt a more business-focused approach to meet global standards, efforts have been made to simplify operational practices and establish policies for promotions and partnerships within the firm. A managing partner of a leading law firm in Ghana remarked:

> Around 2007, the firm lacked a clear policy on how individuals could become partners or even associates. We implemented a system where junior lawyers received training and opportunities to learn, with salaries serving as the main incentive. The firm recognized the importance of retaining talent. Some associates compared our firm to others with different ranks and noticed clearer career progression at those competitors. This prompted us to update compensation and foster a culture of collective belonging within the firm. Over the following years, it became clear that, despite our youth, we were making significant contributions, leading to the adoption of titles like Senior Associate and the responsibility of managing valued clients. This development eventually sparked discussions about partnership. Using the label "partner"

> was also essential for client retention; our valued clients felt reassured knowing they were working with a partner, even without the presence of the senior or managing partner.

The perspective of this partner at a prominent law firm suggests that the firm's reorganization was partly driven by the need to retain talent (lawyers) and clients who wanted assurance that their cases wouldn't be consistently reassigned to different lawyers. This change resulted from practical business decisions aimed at making staff feel their contributions were valued. These adjustments do not appear to be motivated by a desire for gender equality or transparency in pay and promotions. The lack of clear, documented processes and procedures for becoming a partner may also create uncertainties for some women who reach partnership. A lawyer in Nigeria said, "I was the first woman associate to become a partner; there were no written procedures for attaining partner status. I questioned whether I was a token woman or if I was promoted to show colleagues that they could advance through the ranks."

Becoming a partner comes with advantages and disadvantages that women must consider before moving to become a partner. A respondent from the Ivory Coast highlighted this difficulty:

> For a woman to get promoted and contribute more at work, she must consider her family and the age of her children before deciding whether to accept the promotion and leave her family to face the consequences. A man typically does not have to face this issue because he likely has a wife to manage the family's responsibilities. While these concerns are often seen as private and personal, they can affect a woman's professional advancement. Law firms are more likely to promote a woman because of her strong work ethic.

The chances of women becoming partners in law firms will improve when they implement and enforce promotion policies that allow lawyers to assess their readiness for advancement. Although many of the surveyed law firms lack promotion policies, what explains the relative success of women in reaching partner positions? A woman partner in a law firm in the Ivory Coast remarked:

> It depends on the type of law firm and the woman's role. She must respect herself and work diligently. Unconscious bias and social stereotypes about women can influence their chances of advancement. However, some law firms actually assign women challenging briefs when they show their activity and capability.

The response above shifts the burden onto the woman to earn her respect by working hard—and the definition of "working hard" can be highly subjective, varying from firm to firm and from one individual to another.

A third perspective on promotion and leadership involves creating *gender-sensitive work cultures* that acknowledge women's essential contributions to the success of law firms and expand opportunities for them to ascend to leadership roles. Several interviewees highlighted significant challenges women face in law, including primary caregiving duties, gender stereotypes, and imposter syndrome. While women are increasingly entering law firms and breaking the proverbial glass ceiling in other legal areas, the proportion of women serving as managing partners remains low. Becoming a managing partner requires strong skills in business, people, and client management. Like the criteria for becoming a partner, none of the respondents could confirm that their firms had a written standard for reaching the position of managing partner during my fieldwork.

The discussion about promotions within law firms, up to the point of becoming a partner or managing partner, shows that the rules are flexible and unstructured. This flexibility allows for different interpretations of who qualifies for promotion as a senior associate, partner, or managing partner. One way to address this issue is for bar associations and law societies to create general guidelines on promotions within law firms, while still allowing the firms to make the final decisions based on their needs. Some law firms are setting up systems and structures to support women lawyers. In Ghana, Nigeria, and Kenya, several law firms I spoke with had special arrangements for women with newborns, including childcare and flexible work schedules. However, it was not immediately clear whether women would face penalties for taking time off to care for their children while at work. A clear and transparent promotion policy will be crucial for women to confidently advocate for themselves and demonstrate their qualifications for promotion.

Women who have reached the partnership stage emphasize personal agency. Their recommendations include the need for women lawyers to engage in both professional and personal development to build a personal brand and establish a specialization within the law. Additionally, others highlighted the importance of speaking up and standing out beyond the confines of their law firms or workplaces. This involves seizing opportunities to participate in regional and international activities to enhance personal profiles and expand networks.

As the number of women lawyers grows, their representation in leadership roles may also increase. Longitudinal data are needed to monitor law firms with a high number of women as junior associates to see if these numbers rise over time. Without current long-term data, it is hard to determine whether the trickle-up effect is already happening or if the attrition of women from law firms to solo practice or into the public or corporate sectors, as some interviewees suggest, is occurring. This issue requires further research.

7. Salaries and Income

Despite a record number of women entering the legal profession, evidence shows that the rate of feminization is not keeping pace with gender income equality (Chiu & Leicht, 1999; Nelson et al., 2023). Worldwide, the legal field remains hierarchically organized. Viewed through an intersectional lens, it becomes clear that lawyers' experiences differ based on gender, race, ethnicity, class, disability, and other identity categories. A recent publication analyzing over 20 years of data from more than 5,000 lawyers in America reveals that various factors influence lawyers' career paths—and consequently impact income disparities. The gender pay gap and gender inequity continue to be challenges for many women. In all professional fields, women are consistently paid less than men for doing the same work (Field et al., 2023). This issue is no different in law; existing studies show that women in the legal profession are often undercompensated, even when they have higher academic achievements than their male counterparts (Brodherson et al., 2017; Chanow & Sterling, 2021; Liebenberg & Scharf, 2019; Markovic & Plickert, 2022).

Among the many reasons women pursue a legal career, female interviewees noted that their motivation to earn money might differ from men's. The legal profession is viewed as a field with great potential for financial gain, which explains the aggressive tactics of large law firms to dominate the legal market. The American Bar Association (ABA) data on lawyer salaries acts as an important benchmark for assessing legal income (American Bar Association, 2019). However, in nearly all the countries surveyed for this project, including several other African nations, public data on lawyer salaries remains unavailable, making it harder to analyze women's income relative to their male counterparts.

Several demographic factors discussed in Chapter 3 provide valuable insights into women's salaries in law firms. Age—both biological and in terms of years of practice—strongly correlates with a woman's salary. As a junior associate, a woman's ability to negotiate her salary is nearly nonexistent because law firms set salaries at the time of hiring. Often, women have less negotiating power, which puts them at a disadvantage from the start. Income is closely linked to rank within a law firm, and the differences between being a pupil or trainee lawyer and being a junior or senior associate can significantly affect one's earnings.

In law firms across Anglophone and Francophone Africa, new lawyers are classified as pupils, apprentices, or trainee lawyers, where they often face significant economic exploitation. In some jurisdictions, trainee attorneys, called pupils, are traditionally unpaid, with only a few law firms offering modest stipends to cover transportation costs. In Kenya, the experiences of women lawyers clearly highlight the impact of sociocultural beliefs and gender stereotypes that have become institutionalized in how much women should earn. The IAWL report on women lawyers in Kenya includes the following quote from a respondent (2023i, p. 27):

> There appears to be an unspoken rule that women should earn less than their male counterparts. There seems to exist a brotherhood among the gatekeepers in law firms and their male employees, which tends to favor the latter. Typically, women are offered very low salaries, and during tough economic times, they are compelled to accept whatever is offered without negotiating. In contrast, men start at higher salaries and actively negotiate with their employers. This, combined with the different types of work assigned to male and female employees, creates the perception that men work harder and handle more challenging cases, which justifies their better pay. This situation causes unhappiness and discouragement among women lawyers. As a result, many choose to leave law firms in search of greener pastures or establish their own practices.

The situation for lawyers in Nigeria is similar. In the study *Women in Law and Leadership: Nigerian Bar* (Institute for African Women in Law, 2023*l*), respondents were asked whether women received equal pay to men. Of a sample of 449 respondents, 40% agreed, 37% disagreed, and 23% were unsure or neutral. Therefore, even though national and international labor laws regulate and mandate equal pay, women still remain underpaid, even in professions like law, where labor laws should be enforced (Nelson et al., 2023).

Alongside the common belief that women are unfit for certain roles, a significant challenge many women face in demonstrating their workload and capabilities is the need to travel internally to handle cases. In her study of women lawyers in Ghana from 1975 to 1976, Houghton (1981) found that poor road infrastructure made it difficult to travel beyond the capital city. These infrastructure problems caused trips that should normally take one day to often stretch to two days, requiring an overnight stay. This situation remains common today, even with advances in air travel connecting a few major cities. Women with caregiving responsibilities are limited in how long they can be away from their families. For those without family or caregiving duties, the possibility of staying overnight has sometimes left women vulnerable to unwanted advances from senior colleagues. A young Kenyan lawyer shared her distressing experience:

> He [senior partner] ordered me to accompany him to attend court out of Nairobi. After the court session, he refused to drive back to Nairobi and booked one room in the town. I had no money, so I could not get my room, and my protests fell on deaf ears. What happened to me in the room was the most horrible experience I have ever had. I had to fight to [ward] off his sexual advances physically. He slapped me. But thank God I fought hard enough. Of course, that was the end of my job once we returned to the office. I quit. (Institute for African Women in Law, 2023i, p. 29)

For many young women lawyers, the ongoing issue of sexual harassment and unwanted sexual advances often becomes a trap used by unscrupulous senior partners to influence their hiring, pay, and promotion. In some countries, lawyers' incomes are regulated by different rules. For example, in Ghana, *Rule 9(9) of the Legal Profession (Professional Conduct and Etiquette) Rules, 1969 (L.I. 613), which has been replaced by L.I. 2423, set*s the minimum and maximum fees lawyers can charge their clients (Dawuni, 2021b). Regarding Kenya, Kamau (2020) pointed out that the Chief Justice determines the scale of legal fees, and lawyer compensation is governed by the Advocates Remuneration Order of 2014, passed by the Law Society of Kenya (LSK) to allow lawyers to increase their fees.

In some law firms, although all associates receive the same base monthly salary, additional pay and bonuses are based on the types of briefs an associate handles or the clients they bring in. This creates unequal disadvantages for women, especially considering previous discussions about the perception that women may not be seen as "tough" enough or may not work "hard" enough to manage certain types of briefs. Gaining clients is also linked to an individual's ability to network with other lawyers and secure referrals. As will be discussed later, many women have shared their struggles with meeting clients after office hours or on weekends to socialize and close deals. Salary increases are also tied to promotions; therefore, the longer it takes for a woman to be promoted, the more her chances for a salary increase are delayed (Chanow & Sterling, 2021; Melaku, 2019; Schultz & Shaw, 2003).

The size and perceived status of a law firm also influence its potential for income generation. For smaller law firms, solo practices led by women or women-only firms, salaries and incomes tend to be at the lower end of national averages (American Bar Association, 2019; Epstein, 1981). Overall, the type of case or brief determines a lawyer's salary or bonus. Therefore, when gender-based stereotypes prevent women from being assigned rainmaking briefs, their salaries are likely to be lower (Akuffo-Kwapong et al., 2021). Despite the absence of public data on lawyer income, general perceptions gathered from fieldwork support existing research on gender pay inequity among lawyers (Nelson et al., 2023).

8. Women-Only, Women-Dominant, and Women-Solo Law Firms

Various motivational factors influence the structure of law firms. In this analysis, I differentiate between women-only law firms, which are defined as those where 100% of the lawyers are women. Women-dominant law firms are those where approximately 80% of the lawyers are women, while solo-women firms are operated by a single woman without any other associates except for administrative staff. In her seminal book, *Women in Law*, Epstein (1981, pp. 105–106) classified law firms run exclusively by women into two groups.

Feminist law firms can be grouped into various categories. Some are feminist partnerships that focus on serving female clients and addressing women's public interests overall. Others include individual practitioners involved in feminist legal practices. Additionally, there are nonprofit legal organizations dedicated to women's rights, many of which operate within university law schools. According to Epstein (1981), these law firms emerged in the early 1970s in the United States, initially motivated by a feminist ideology advocating for women's rights and a commitment to public service. Because of their specialized focus, most of these firms handled only cases related to women and gender equality issues. While some received support from foundations dedicated to promoting women's rights, others did not. In either case, these small law firms faced significant challenges to their survival.

During the field research for this project, I encountered several women-only, women-majority, and women-led law firms. Some of these firms initially started as women-only but have since hired male lawyers. Unlike Epstein's (1981) research in the United States, I do not categorize these firms as "feminist law firms" because their main reasons for founding were not rooted in feminist ideology. In many cases, they did not focus solely on women's issues. While some of these firms were created with that goal, many developed naturally as women worked together to build and manage law practices led by women.

For a lawyer in South Africa, her motivation to start a *women-only* law firm came from her experience with maternity leave, during which the managing partners at her firm argued over whether she deserved an annual bonus. This personal encounter with maternal and gender discrimination inspired her to create a law firm dedicated to supporting other women. To her, it was a personal goal and a way to help mentor younger women in achieving success in law.

Statistics on the number of women-owned law firms are not easily accessible. According to a report by LexisNexis (2021–2022), the number of women-owned law firms in South Africa grew by 7% from 2021 to 2022. The IAWL report on *Women in Law and Leadership: South African Bar* states that 53.9% of survey respondents said working in a predominantly female firm improved their career progression (Institute for African Women in Law, 2023p).

Starting a law firm from the ground up can be daunting for a newly admitted lawyer and is definitely challenging due to the administrative obstacles and varied environments across different African countries. A second-generation woman lawyer in Ghana, who founded the first women-only law firm, shared her motivation for establishing her firm:

> I'm not sure if there are any barriers preventing women from owning their own law firms. Looking at a firm like ours, we have more women than men because it operates like a corporate entity, whereas most law firms in Ghana do not. Most women prefer structured environments, and we maintain a ratio of 70 percent female to 30 percent male. We focus on hiring the brightest individuals; many men don't stay with us long because they want to start their own firms and earn more money. Luckily, in our region, women's entry into firms hasn't been an issue; as long as you're dedicated and capable of hard work, you won't face problems. There are certain challenges women will encounter regardless of the type of law firm they work at, and they must learn to manage them.

In the narrative above, while the law firm initially operated as a women-only establishment, it has since expanded to include male lawyers. However, it seems that the motivation behind men's departure from the firm is to start their own practices and increase their income.

I asked a lawyer why she chose to work in a women-only law firm:

> After graduation, it felt like a natural fit because I had been interning at the law firm. The connection here mainly involves personality and environment; we have meaningful discussions about our work experiences, and it's not just about how long someone has been at the bar. The firm recognizes the challenges women face, and we all understand what's on each other's docket, which allows us to step in and help when needed. I value the unique atmosphere at this firm and have no plans to move elsewhere.

There is another type of law firm I call *solo-women* firms, which have only one female lawyer. Although these practices are less common now, some still exist and were started for different reasons. I asked one lawyer why she decided to run a solo-women law firm, and her answer was:

> When I graduated from law school, I joined a large law firm and gained a wealth of experience. However, the work environment was not suitable for me as a newly married woman and a mother of a young child. I also found that there was little flexibility

> to specialize in the area of law I desired. With my own law firm, I can set the rules regarding the types of cases I take and how much time I spend with my children. I also don't have to worry about generating enough revenue to pay my junior associates. When my children grow up, I may consider hiring junior associates.

Women-only and women-led law firms face various challenges but also offer unique advantages. In the United States, where these firms originated from feminist activism, Epstein (1981) highlighted the difficulties of managing cash flow due to the types of cases they primarily handled, which focused on women's rights. Additionally, these firms faced obstacles in expanding their practice areas and attracting high-net-worth clients. Managing staff perceptions was another hurdle; as Epstein (1981) notes, some legal staff who joined these firms believed they could produce lower work output compared to what is typically expected in male-led law firms.

In a survey of women lawyers in South Africa, respondents from women-only law firms stated that they did not face issues related to sexual and gender-based discrimination. When asked about career advancement in a female-dominated law firm, 53.9% agreed it was beneficial, 30.8% were neutral, and 15.4% disagreed. However, managing collegial relationships among women was identified as a significant challenge (Institute for African Women in Law, 2023p). Women-only law firms are rare due to gender biases and stereotypes suggesting that male lawyers are better suited to handle certain cases (Akuffo-Kwapong et al., 2021; Stewart, 2012). A partner of a female-dominated law firm I interviewed in Ghana commented:

> We have more women in this firm. The challenge is that male lawyers handle the more difficult cases more easily. It's not about skill; they navigate the terrain better. In terms of caseload, women tend to be more detailed. While men may speak up more, women are more thorough. We can also send men outside of Accra—regardless of the terrain—without concerns about safety or other issues. For the women lawyers, I need to keep *monitoring their safety* when they travel outside the capital for cases.

The response above comes from a woman confirming that men can handle "more robust cases," but it subtly alludes to the fact that the sociocultural and institutional context—which may involve gender biases—shapes the types of cases men are typically assigned. The response also highlights how women-owned or women-led law firms must go to great lengths to remain competitive in a legal market that men largely dominate. The fact that this firm competes on equal footing with men is impressive; however, the added challenge of a partner "monitoring their safety" remains an obstacle women lawyers face in their efforts to operate on equal terms. More research is needed to understand the number, variety, practices, and challenges of women-only and women-majority law firms across the continent.

9. Women in the Hierarchy of the Bar

Despite progress in feminizing the legal profession, it still takes longer to dismantle the structural hierarchies that place men at the top of the professional ladder (Masengu,

2016). To maintain and strengthen the traditional masculine prestige of the bar, the Law Society of England and Wales created a special category within the legal field—the Queen's Counsel (QC) or King's Counsel (KC). These lawyers are often perceived as the elite, primarily comprising white men. The history goes back to the appointment of Francis Bacon as the first Queen's Counsel in 1597 by Queen Elizabeth I. The QC/KC is chosen based on criteria of excellence in advocacy and the ability to handle complex cases with exceptional legal skill (Law Society of UK, n.d.). Seen as an exclusive club, the title was originally limited to barristers until 1996, when solicitors were allowed to join. Known as "Silk," these lawyers enjoy the privileges and rights of the profession, such as sitting at the front of the courtroom, charging higher fees from clients, and serving on important committees and boards (Law Society of UK, n.d.).

According to the 2022 statistics on the British legal profession, the number of legal practitioners (barristers) was 18,026, with women accounting for 39.7%. Of the total practitioners, only 2,016 were QCs, and women accounted for just 19.2%. Looking at racial diversity, the numbers decrease further, with Black, Asian, and Minority Ethnic (BAME) individuals constituting 16.4% of all barristers and 10.5% of all QCs (Bar Standards Board, 2022–2023). In 2021, among the total BAME QCs, there were only 5 Black women, 17 Black men, 16 men of mixed ethnicity, and 9 women of mixed ethnicity. For Asians, the numbers are 60 men and 17 women (Bar Council, 2021). In 2024, a historic milestone was reached when Barbara Mills, KC, was elected as the first Black woman chair of the Bar Council of England and Wales in over 131 years of its existence (Bar Council, n.d.).

It is against the backdrop of a persistent and widespread lack of racial and gender diversity that the system of QC/KC was introduced to former British colonies. In Nigeria, the program was launched in 1975 and later renamed the Senior Advocates of Nigeria (SAN). In 1981, Chief Mrs. Folake Solanke became the first woman to be elevated to the SAN rank. By 2021, only 29 women (95.8%) had been enrolled as SAN, compared to 656 men (95.8%) (Dawuni & Abdul-Rahman, 2022). After interviewing six women SANs, the authors concluded that the reasons for the low number of women included procedural requirements favoring litigation and the number of cases heard before the Supreme Court, as well as the lack of gender diversity on the Legal Practitioners Privileges Council (LPPC), which plays a key role in selecting candidates. These institutional and workplace cultures do not support women's upward mobility, access to influential networks and godfathers, sociocultural demands at home, and prevailing gender biases and stereotypes. Efforts to introduce the Senior Advocates of Ghana (SAG) were unsuccessful. **Table 4.2** presents data on countries with the titles of Senior Counsel or State Counsel. In Zambia, as of 2023, of 53 lawyers who have ever received the title, only 4 have been women, making up just 8%. In Seychelles, the title of Senior Counsel is conferred by the Bar Association to lawyers with more than 20 years of practice who are deemed to be in good standing. Since the title was first awarded in 2004, all seven SCs have been men as of 2023. In South Africa, of 546 Silks, only 63 (12%) are women.

In Kenya, inspired by British tradition, the Senior Counsel (SC) title was established in 2009 after the enactment of the Advocates Act. It is governed by the Senior Counsel Conferment and Privileges Rules (2011) (Kamau, 2020). To earn this title, an individual must have at least 15 years at the bar with an outstanding record in

Table 4.2 *Number of Women Senior Counsel/State Counsel (SC) in Selected Countries*

Country	Title	Percentage of women	Year of data
Nigeria	Senior Advocates of Nigeria	4.2%	2022
South Africa	Senior Counsel	12%	2023
Zambia	State Counsel	8%	2023
Kenya	Senior Counsel	22%	2023
Seychelles	Senior Counsel	0%	2023

Source: Data collected from different law societies and bar associations.

both legal practice and social conduct. As of 2023, the total number of SCs since its inception is 54 males and 12 females. Consequently, women make up only 22% of SCs in Kenya. Although these figures are still low, they show an improvement compared to Nigeria's 4.2% female representation, especially considering Nigeria's longer history with the program. Overall, available data reveal that women remain underrepresented within the professional hierarchy of the special counsel program, which originated in Great Britain and was adopted by other countries. Dawuni and Abdul-Rahman's (2022) study of women senior advocates in Nigeria should be replicated in other jurisdictions to gain a better understanding of the unique features of different contexts.

10. Women Minister of Justice, Attorney General, and Solicitor General

There is limited research on women serving as Attorney General/Minister of Justice and Solicitor General. Depending on the legal tradition and history of a country, an individual may be designated as a Minister of Justice and Attorney General (common in many common law countries), whereas in most civil-law countries, the roles of Minister of Justice and Attorney General are usually separate. Regardless of the titles used, these positions are part of the executive branch and often involve political appointments. Studies on women in legislatures (Bauer, 2021) and women in cabinets (Nwankwor, 2021) indicate that women remain underrepresented in political appointment roles. Some countries have made progress in appointing women as Ministers of Justice or Attorney General. In Ghana, three women have held these positions so far, while at the federal level in Nigeria, no woman has yet been appointed to this role, despite women having been appointed at various state levels. Kenya appointed its first female attorney general in 2025.

11. Women in Leadership—Bar Associations and Law Societies

The earlier discussion in Chapter 3 highlighted how intergenerational shifts from the first generation to current women at the bar have driven changes and diversification in the legal profession's institutional norms and practices. Some of these changes have been deliberate, while others are unconscious acts of resistance by women that have helped to level the playing field for all women at the bar. The patterns and themes of these contributions emerged from the interviews. Specialized bodies are created to regulate the activities of lawyers, and in most countries, the bar association or law society plays vital regulatory roles (Dawuni, 2021b; Kamau, 2020; Karekwaivanane, 2020; Klaaren, 2020). Some bar associations have existed since the colonial era and were formed as extensions of the bar associations or law societies in the colonizing metropole (Adewoye, 1982a; Ghai & Auslan, 1970; Luckham, 1981).

Historically, some of these associations have played vital roles in the decolonization and democratization of African countries. The leaders of these associations wield considerable influence in society, often serving as the voice of civil society in advocating for good governance and the protection of human rights. In countries like Ghana and Kenya, government officials have imprisoned bar association leaders for speaking out against executive overreach and demanding respect for constitutionalism and the rule of law (Nowrojee, 2014; Okudzeto, 2018). Over time, the authority and respect for these associations have diminished, as some have been co-opted to support the executive branch's political agenda. In certain nations, leadership within bar associations has become a steppingstone to future political ambitions. Given the power and influence of bar associations, it is clear why men have traditionally dominated their leadership roles.

Women's right to hold leadership and decision-making roles is legally protected by both domestic and international laws, including the United Nations Convention on the Elimination of All Forms of Discrimination Against Women (CEDAW), the Protocol to the African Charter on Human and Peoples' Rights on the Rights of Women in Africa (Maputo Protocol), and the International Labor Organization (ILO) Equal Remuneration Convention No. 100. Many countries have set up formal mechanisms to boost women's representation in public institutions such as national assemblies and parliaments. Countries like South Africa, Senegal, Namibia, Mozambique, and Kenya have adopted constitutional quota systems to increase opportunities for women in public service (Inter-Parliamentary Union, 2024).

For example, Article 27(8) of the 2010 Constitution of Kenya attempts to promote gender equity by stating that no public body shall consist of more than two-thirds of the same gender, a principle known as the "two-thirds rule." As discussed in Chapter 5 regarding women in the judiciary, the two-thirds rule in Kenya has played a vital role in changing gendered institutional norms. This rule is credited with increasing the number of women in the judiciary, which ultimately led to Justice Martha Koome's appointment in 2021 as Kenya's first female chief justice.

Despite the growing number of women in bars, they remain the silent majority when it comes to leadership positions. Only a few countries have elected women as presidents of their bar associations or law societies. Even as the political influence of bar associations declines, women continue to be historically underrepresented in these leadership roles. **Table 4.3** presents data on countries where women have served as leaders of the bar association or law society.

In Senegal, since the establishment of the bar association (Ordre des Avocats du Sénégal) in 1960, no woman has served as its leader. Nigeria likely hosts the largest

Table 4.3 *Women Presidents of Bar Associations or Law Societies*

No.	Country	*Year bar was established	Name of leader	Election date
1.	Algeria	1848	Ouafya Sidhoum	2014
2.	Ghana	1876	Efua Ghartey	2024
3.	Sierra Leone		Frances Claudia Wright	N/A
4.	Sierra Leone	1904	Eddinia Michaela Swallow	2020
5.	Togo	1930	Loretta Massa Acouetey	1998
6.	Togo	1930	Dopé Kayo Ekoue-Kouvahey	2010
7.	Madagascar	1937	Chantal Razafinarivo	2018
8.	Kenya	1948	Raychelle Awuor Omamo	2001
9.	Kenya	1948	Faith Mony Odhiambo	2024
10.	Tanzania	1954	Joaquine De Mello	2007
11.	Tanzania	1954	Fatma Karume	2018
12.	Uganda	1956	Solomy Balungi Bossa	1994
13.	Uganda	1956	Harriet Diana Musoke	1998
14.	Uganda	1956	Ruth Sebatindira	2013
15.	Uganda	1956	Pheona Nabasa Wall	2020
16.	Mauritius	1957	Narghis Bundhun	2000 2019 2020
17.	Gabon	1960	Marlyse ISSEMBE	2005
18.	Nigeria	1960	Priscilla Kuye	1991
19.	Benin	1965	Hélène Aholou Keke	1989
20.	Mali	1971	Fatoumata Sylla	1998
21.	Zambia	1973	Linda Kasonde	2016
22.	Mauritius	1977*	Zubeida Salajee	2018
23.	Mauritius	1977*	Dya Ghose-Radhakeesoon	2022
24.	Cote d'Ivoire	1959*	Florence Loan Épse Messan	2023
25.	Zimbabwe	1981	Beatrice Mtetwa	N/A
26.	Zimbabwe	1981	Rumbidzai Matambo	2023
27.	Burkina Faso	1990	Antoinette Nongba Ouedraogo	2006
28.	Cameroon	1990	Atangana Bikouna Claire	2021
29.	Congo, Republic of the	1992	Julienne Ondziel Gnelenga	2009
30.	Mozambique	1994	Lucia da Luz Ribeiro	2003

Table 4.3 Continued

No.	Country	*Year bar was established	Name of leader	Election date
31.	Namibia	1995	Elise Angula	2005
32.	South Africa	1998	Esmé du Plessis	1995
33.	South Africa	1998	Mabaeng Denise Lenyai	2022
34.	South Africa	1998	Joanne Anthony-Gooden	2023
35.	Cabo Verde	2000	Lígia Lubrino Dias Fonseca	2001
36.	Cabo Verde	2000	Leida Helena Mauricio dos Santos	2013
37.	Cabo Verde	2000	Sofia Helena de Oliveira Lima	2016
38.	Sao Tome and Principe	2006	Celiza de Deus Lima	2014
39.	Sao Tome and Principe	2006	Célia Posser	2017
40.	Ethiopia	2021	Sinidu Alemu	2021
41.	Djibouti	N/A	Fatouma Mahamoud	2007
42.	Gambia	N/A	Mariam Jack-Denton*	N/A
43.	Gambia	N/A	Amie Bensouda	2006
44.	Gambia	N/A	Neneh M.C Cham	2023
45.	Libya	N/A	Aissatou Zada	2012

Source: Data collected from different online sources. The data may not be reflective of all women who have been elected prior to and after the publication of this book. Some bar associations were established under colonial rule and reconstituted or established after independence from colonial rule; hence countries with an asterisk may be referring to the bar either under colonial rule or after independence. The lack of clarity in existing sources makes it difficult to ascertain the dates accurately.

bar in Africa, and aside from one woman who held the position temporarily for a year in 1991, no woman has served as president of the Nigerian Bar. Recent developments indicate that women are making advancements in leadership roles, highlighted by the election of Linda Bala as first vice president and Amanda Demechi-Asagba as third vice president in 2023–2024. In 2025, the leadership of the Nigerian Bar Association (NBA) included Bolatumi Olasunbo Animashaun as Second Vice President and Zainab Aminu Garba as Third Vice President. Women comprised 50% of the executive leadership positions (Nigerian Bar Association, n.d.).

Examining the history of the legal profession in Ghana, Luckham (1976) highlighted the existence of a Gold Coast Bar Association that dates back to 1904, which regulated the activities of British coastal lawyers. The current Ghana Bar Association was formally established in 1959, and until 2024, 33 men served as presidents. In

2024, the glass ceiling was shattered with the election of Efua Ghartey as the first woman president of the bar, following a vigorous campaign by the Institute for African Women in Law to raise awareness of the historical role of women in bar leadership (Dawuni, 2024b). The 2024 bar election also resulted in Victoria Barth's election as the second woman to serve as vice president. Prior to this, the only woman to hold the position was Felicia Gbesemete, who served from 2004 to 2007. In the Greater Accra regional bar of Ghana, women have also held the position of vice president.

The other success stories on the continent include the election of women in Zambia (Linda Kasonde), South Africa (Mabaeng Lenyai), Cape Verde (Ligia Fonseca), Zimbabwe (Vimbai Nyemba), and Namibia (Retha Steinmann). In Kenya, after the election of Raychelle Omamo in 2011, it took 13 years before the second woman, Faith Odhiambo, was elected president of the LSK in 2024. In some countries, such as Sierra Leone, The Gambia, South Africa, Cape Verde, and Uganda, more than two women have served as president of the bar or law society.

In Cape Verde, the bar association's founding president established the organization in 2001 in response to the need for a unified body of lawyers. I include a significant portion of the interview to highlight her voice and, through this narrative, to contextualize the contributions of women who have started organizations aimed at regulating the legal professions and documenting her achievements as the founding president. For her, the main motivation for creating the association was to ensure that both lawyers and the government recognized the vital roles lawyers play in national development. From the beginning, she ensured that the statute governing the association included provisions requiring it to defend women's rights, human rights, and the rule of law and to monitor government excesses.

> Since this was the first bar association with the mission of holding the government accountable, I was seen as opposing it, and my four years as president were challenging. Now, the bar association is regarded as an important entity, and many aspire to the presidency because when the bar president speaks, their voice cannot be ignored. My focus during these four years was to help the government recognize the importance of lawyers. We aimed to change the perception that lawyers are only accessible to those who can afford them; shifting the government's mindset was not easy. We had to closely monitor parliamentary bills to ensure they wouldn't negatively impact the role of lawyers. My most significant achievement was demonstrating that the Bar Association is an independent and vital organization that makes a substantial contribution to society. The bar association plays a crucial role in upholding the rule of law; there can be no justice without a strong bar association. I believe this was my greatest challenge, and I think I succeeded. I've always said that the first leader shapes what an organization will become.

Overall, although women in many countries have yet to lead bar associations or law societies, more are serving on various committees and, in some cases, as vice presidents or vice chairs, suggesting a shift toward increased women's leadership. During my fieldwork, I aimed to understand how some women overcame male barriers to be elected as presidents and leaders of bar associations and law societies. I asked the question: How did these women attain these roles? In The Gambia, a small country on the West Coast of Africa, Mariam Jack-Denton, the first woman called to the bar in 1979, also served as the first female president of the bar. In my 2018 interview with her, she described her journey this way:

> I was the first female President for two terms. Gambians believe that women are hardworking. The position of bar president was very competitive, but it became a dangerous job under the Yahya Jammeh government, causing more people to shy away from it. Even when I ran for office, I needed some persuasion to do so. I worked hard to maintain balance and avoid trouble. Last year, the bar stood up and spoke out against the government, and civil society followed suit. It was all over the news that the bar had taken a stand, and it is gradually regaining its prestigious status. I suspect that going forward, it will be tougher to be elected, but I believe women can hold their own.

Mariam Jack-Denton's story supports Uzebu-Imarhiagbe's (2020b) analysis that more opportunities for women in certain roles may exist because men choose not to pursue those positions, believing they are less prestigious or require too much work. However, Mariam Jack-Denton was not a token leader of the bar association. As a passionate lawyer, she openly opposed the military dictator Yahya Jammeh and his human rights abuses. This led to her being arrested and unlawfully detained several times (Karki, n.d.). In 2023, Nenneh Cham was elected president of the Gambian Bar Association. Denton's prediction that the bar association will become more competitive for women as it gains prestige remains to be seen.

In Ghana, the first woman to serve as vice president of the Ghana Bar Association shared her journey to that position:

> I had always been actively involved in bar activities. I did not plan to run for office when I became vice president from 2004 to 2007. I didn't want to run for president because I felt I had outgrown the years when I could make an active contribution. I had no intention of even running for vice president, but the person running for president at that time told me he would only run if I agreed to be his running mate. I believe someone else entered the race and then withdrew.

Has women's leadership in bar associations resulted in any continuity or change in how women's leadership in law is viewed? Aside from a few countries, such as Cape Verde, Sierra Leone, The Gambia, and Kenya, where women have served as bar presidents more than once, the idea of women leading bar associations remains a tough challenge in many areas. What does it take for someone to become a leader of a bar association? What will it require to establish women as equals in bar leadership?

In Ghana, the election of the bar president in 2021 was a close race between a woman and a man. Although the woman lost, the rhetoric among lawyers—ironically, including several women lawyers—was that they were voting for the "most qualified" candidate rather than based on the candidate's sex. In other words, most voters believed that men were automatically the "more qualified" candidates. Viewed through a feminist lens, the idea of equating "merit" with masculine standards or traits remains widespread, and a feminist consciousness is necessary to challenge these ideas, even among women (Nayak & Tabassum, 2021).

A second-generation lawyer in Nigeria expressed her observations on the lack of women at the helm of leadership in the Nigerian Bar Association:

> At the Nigerian Bar Association (NBA), no one tries to discourage you because you are a woman. I have always attended the meetings and offered to help the executive committee. In 1980, I ran for the position of Secretary of the NBA, and out of three candidates, one withdrew. It came down to me and another candidate; they asked him to step down, but he refused. I was elected the First Secretary in 1981-1982 and again in 1982-1984. We still don't have a woman president; one woman served as interim president, but she was forced out. It bothers me that no woman has ever led the NBA. I believe that, over time, things will change.

In Nigeria, the hope that "things will change" is not occurring as quickly as women lawyers would prefer. There is still a long journey for women in law in Nigeria to access leadership positions that have been held by men for many years (Institute for African Women in Law, 2023l).

In electing women to the bar leadership, what matters for success? In her 2023 autobiography, *Women, Resilience, and the Will to Lead: A Memoir* (Kasonde, 2023), Linda Kasonde, the first woman president of the Law Association of Zambia (LAZ), talks about her path to leading the legal group. Balancing the male-dominated culture of the legal field with the political challenges of guiding the bar association, Kasonde shares a detailed story of her wins and hardships. One of the toughest struggles she faced was the heartbreaking loss of her child after her election victory. Focusing on resilience, Kasonde's personal story isn't meant to discourage women from seeking leadership roles. Instead, her honest and open analysis offers encouragement and insights that women can and should lead.

What factors influence when and where women are elected as presidents of bar associations or law societies? The varying legal systems and political economies surrounding these roles complicate the explanatory variables. I share a few observations from my interviews. While these explanations might apply in one country, they cannot be generalized to all. Further research is necessary to explore other variables, such as the personality traits of pioneering female leaders.

In most countries where women have not risen as leaders in the bar, the common explanation is that women *do not run for these positions*. The few rare cases where women have contested in multiple electoral cycles (and either lost or won) show that the argument about women not contesting does not apply universally. For instance, women have served as bar presidents four times in Uganda, twice in Kenya, and once each in Sierra Leone and The Gambia. However, a comparison of the number of times men have held these positions versus women reveals that the number of women who have held these roles remains very low.

In Senegal, women made up less than 14% of the bar in 2023 (Institute for African Women in Law, 2023o). The lack of women at the bar shows that the pool of potential female candidates is small, making it harder for women to reach the level of contesting for the bar. The presidency of the bar association is a tough administrative role, with no staff and no salary. One informant in Senegal mentioned that most past presidents leave office in poor health; the position takes a heavy toll on them, and few individuals are willing to face such challenges.

For women already burdened by the demands of their profession and private family obligations, taking on an additional administrative task is not appealing. A woman lawyer in Senegal expressed her frustration:

> This [the election of a woman president of the bar] is an ongoing struggle; leadership knows no gender, and if you are a lawyer, you must be prepared to face everyone. In our society, the legal profession is seen as a man's world, and they often fight among themselves. So, if you are a woman entering this field, you must be ready to fight.

The idea that one must be ready to "fight" makes bar leadership less appealing to many lawyers, especially women, who already face numerous sociocultural challenges, gendered responsibilities, and the widespread belief that law is a male-dominated field. Women have to navigate these masculine institutional cultures (Chappell & Waylen, 2013). In other jurisdictions, the choice not to pursue leadership roles in the bar is connected to the politicization of bar associations and the perception that bar association leaders are often influenced by ruling governments, risking their independence (Kamau, 2020; Karekwaivanane, 2020; Nowrojee, 2014).

Another plausible explanation is that in cases where women contested, they were not voted for. Consider Ghana, where before her election in 2024 as the first female president, she had run in two previous elections. In both of these cases, she was serving as president of the regional bar association; yet she could not secure support at the national level. In the second election, she lost by just a few votes. The situation in Ghana highlights a complex phenomenon in elections, where fieldwork evidence indicated a lack of support from women for female candidates. With the legal profession in most countries comprising 30–40% women, support from women will be crucial for electing women to leadership positions. However, the expectation should not always be that women vote for other women. What are the key leadership traits or qualities that the electorate expects women to display in order to earn their votes?

Elections are inherently popularity contests, and elections for bar association leadership are no exception. In several countries, the political representation of women in Africa within the executive and parliamentary sectors remains low (Bauer, 2021; Mama, 2020; Tripp, 2016). Compared to the judiciaries, some progress has been made in women's leadership within these systems because appointments are based on merit and selection processes that recognize leadership qualities rather than on popularity at the ballot box (Dawuni & Kang, 2015; Dawuni & Masengu, 2019). However, elections for bar leadership are still not the most effective way for women to attain leadership positions, mainly because they are still rooted in a popularity framework.

What does women's underrepresentation as leaders of bar associations reveal about societal perceptions of their leadership abilities? How do jurisdictions differ when women have made progress in the bar compared to areas where such progress has not been achieved? Almost all women interviewed for this project stated that they belong to the national bar association. Although their levels of engagement vary, attending these organizations' annual meetings offers women opportunities to network, meet other lawyers, learn about new practices in the profession, and participate in Continuing Legal Education (CLE) or Continuing Professional Development (CPD). Despite the fact that fewer women have served as president of national bar associations, more women are increasingly participating on various committees within these organizations, which may help some women advance within the leadership pipeline.

Providing leadership training for women at a young age is crucial for building confidence and shaping a career path for women aiming to lead these associations. A comparative study of the leadership and professional journeys of women elected as leaders of bar associations may reveal useful patterns among those who have succeeded in elections. Analyzing leadership outcomes for female and male leaders would provide valuable insights into different leadership styles and their effects.

12. The Women's "Other-Bar" and Women's Forums

In most countries, women lawyers have created women's forums within larger bar associations to address issues specifically affecting women. While the original aim of many of these organizations was to focus on concerns related to women in the profession, they have increasingly shifted their attention to broader challenges that impact women and children in society. My initial idea for this chapter was to call these forums "women's side-bar associations," but a reviewer warned that this terminology might be seen as derogatory. Still, it's important to highlight this topic to show how women need to step outside the main organization to develop forums that serve their specific needs. This demonstrates that mainstream organizations are not fully meeting women's needs—another sign of the dominant idea that "maleness is the norm."

These women's forums are a global phenomenon. In the United States, for example, the umbrella organization for all lawyers—the American Bar Association—established a Commission on the Status of Women in the Profession with the mission to "secure full and equal participation of women in the ABA, the profession, and the justice system." Many state bar associations also have bodies dedicated to women in the profession. As shown by the survey results for this study in **Figure 4.5**, half of the respondents (50%) indicated they belonged to some form of "women-only" associations.

These women-only organizations have played a key role in advancing women's, children's, and human rights. They engage in legal activism at different levels. In a special issue of the *Feminist Africa* journal, Sylvia Tamale and Jane Bennett (2011) examined the challenges and successes of women's legal activism across Africa. In their publication, "Editorial: Legal Voice: Challenges and Prospects in the Documentation of African Legal Feminism," the authors stressed the importance of detailed documentation of women's legal activism. Tracing the development of women's legal activism across the continent, Tamale and Bennett pointed out women's involvement in lobbying governments to pass laws that benefit women, initiating strategic litigation in courts, and winning landmark legal cases that have improved access to justice for

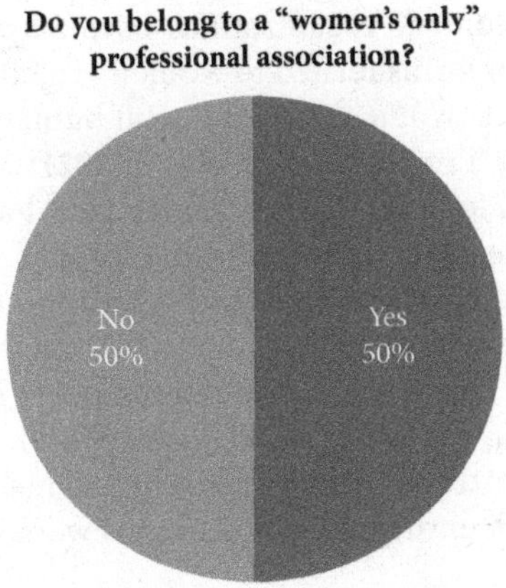

Figure 4.5 *Women's Membership in "Women-Only" Organizations/Associations*

women. Perhaps most importantly for the current discussion, they mention several women's rights organizations that have worked tirelessly, often with limited resources, to promote the expansion of legal rights for women.

In several African countries, women's bar forums include the Ghana Bar Association Women's Forum (GBAWF), the Nigeria Bar Association Women Forum, the Sierra Leone Women Lawyers Forum, and the Female Lawyers Association of Gambia (FLAG). These organizations have different levels of recognition within the main bar association, often functioning as a committee or a recognized branch of the bar. In other countries, however, these groups are entirely independent of the main bar association. Examples include the South African Women Lawyers Association (SAWLA) and the Zambia Women Lawyers Association (ZWLA). In Senegal, the *Association de Juristes Senegalaise* (AJS) was established to address women's societal issues, with limited focus on women in the legal profession, although efforts have been made to support women lawyers and judges (Scales-Trent, 2010).

The African Women Lawyers Association (AWLA) is an organization that was established to address the specific needs of women in the legal profession. A notable organization with roots in various African countries is the Federación Internacional de Abogadas (FIDA), also known as the International Association of Women Lawyers. Founded in 1944 in Mexico City, FIDA has since expanded its global presence, including in several African nations. FIDA primarily aims to tackle women's issues within society, with only a few of its programs directly benefiting women in the profession. Other organizations, such as the Ugandan Women Lawyers Association (FIDA, Uganda), have actively engaged in public interest litigation and lobbied for women's appointments to senior judicial positions. Additional organizations in this field include Women and the Law in Southern Africa (WLSA), Women and the Law in Eastern Africa (WLEA), Women and the Law in West Africa (WLWA), Women Living Under Muslim Laws (WLUML), and Women in Law and Development in Africa (WiLDAF) (Bennett & Tamale, 2011).

In several countries, women's organizations have played a vital role in advocating for legal and judicial reforms related to women's rights. They lobby and push for changes in laws that violate women's fundamental human rights in Senegal, Kenya, and Tanzania (Bennett & Tamale, 2011; Masabo, 2021; Mutua, 2006; Scales-Trent, 2010; Yoon, 2016). Additionally, these organizations have launched strategic litigation in courts to challenge gender-insensitive rulings in Zimbabwe and Malawi (Stewart, 2012) and have conducted research that provides empirical evidence to support policy changes across various countries (Rukuba-Ngaiza, 2021; Scales-Trent, 2010). In a thorough review of the contributions made by women's legal civil society organizations during the 2002 national consultations that led to the adoption of the 2010 Constitution, Athena Mutua (2006) highlighted the influence of women's human rights advocates in ensuring women's rights were incorporated into the new constitution.

Membership in these *women's bar forums* is voluntary, and because they focus on women and gender issues, they mainly attract members interested in advocating for these causes. These women's sidebar organizations and associations provide essential support to women in both the profession and society. They heavily rely on financial contributions from membership dues and philanthropic donations. Relying on these two sources of income creates challenges for sustainably meeting their goals. They also depend on the volunteers' time from leaders to carry out their mission, which further strains the time available for women in law.

I asked interview respondents if they belonged to these *women's bar forums*, and their levels of belonging and engagement with these organizations varied. A lawyer in Cape Verde responded, "I am a member, but I'm not in an active role like I used to be. The association especially helps promote other women in society; it also demonstrates that we [women lawyers] are contributing to society." In the Ivory Coast, a respondent highlighted the importance of having a women's forum to protect the rights of women in law, particularly those still establishing themselves in the profession. She also said, "The fact that we don't have a Women's Lawyers Association may be a sign that it is time to organize ourselves. For example, when a woman lawyer gets pregnant or has a baby during her training or internship, we do not have any maternity benefits."

The reality of women's time constraints makes it hard for many to join and actively participate even when these organizations exist, as a respondent in Senegal pointed out:

> Initially, I was involved with *Femmes Juristes* and networking through the Bar Association. However, because of my busy schedule as a partner in my firm, I had to scale back my participation. We do have women involved in the Bar Association, but no woman has yet served as president. I'm unsure if the association is ready to elect a woman president. In 2006, one woman was close to winning, and since then, several other women have tried to run. The highest leadership role I've observed a woman hold is secretary.

Another respondent in the Ivory Coast noted:

> I got involved in its activities after joining the Bar. I became a member of the Young Lawyers Association and served as treasurer for two years. While other women participate in bar committees, leadership still lacks parity. We have yet to see a female *Batonnier* (president of the bar). Many people are not ready for this change, but it is starting to shift as many are disappointed with male leadership and the numerous unfulfilled promises. Now, there's a growing willingness to elect a woman. Hopefully, a woman will have a strong chance of being elected.

During my interviews, I asked respondents whether they belonged to any women's organizations focused on enhancing their skills as women lawyers, and the overwhelming answer was no. This did not surprise me, since women's caregiving roles go beyond the private sphere (home) and into the public. The professional caregiving roles of women are clear in how these organizations continue to concentrate on helping other women access justice through pro bono legal work, which limits their ability to focus on the professional development of their members.

Despite her interest in joining these associations, the biggest challenge for a female prosecutor in the Ivory Coast has been the time commitment required for their activities.

> I'm not officially engaged, but I participate whenever I have free time. For example, the Rotary Club invited me to speak about my profession and experiences to motivate others to pursue a career in law. Although I don't formally involve myself with women's organizations due to my busy work schedule, I am passionate about taking part in activities that promote gender equality and inspire others. That's why I wanted to meet with you and share my experiences. We need to support those who mentor and conduct research, which is why I enjoy dedicating time to interviews like this one with you.

The previous discussion has focused on identifying themes from interviews with women in the legal profession at various career stages across different countries and legal sectors—both private and public. Connecting these experiences to existing research reveals commonalities among African countries and highlights the contrast between African women's individual and collective experiences and those of women in other jurisdictions outside Africa. The next section highlights some women's contributions to the profession and society.

V. Contributions: The Impact of Sex Diversification

The gradual increase in women's representation at the bar suggests these numbers will continue to rise. What impact has this representation had? Is their symbolic presence leading to meaningful changes in the institutional, social, and positional spheres that women occupy? Are law firms changing their business practices to be more inclusive of women? Where and how are women challenging traditional masculine gender norms, and where do we see the most significant effects? These crucial questions are the focus of this section, which aims to address them through a thematic analysis of field data and connections to existing research. Conducting a longitudinal study of these issues will help track any changes occurring in the third stage (critical actions) and identify areas that require further attention.

1. Sex Diversification (Numbers and Expertise)

The categorization of the five generations of women's entry into the legal profession demonstrates that women's symbolic and descriptive representation across Africa aligns with earlier predictions of global feminization trends in the field (Menkel-Meadow, 1986; Michelson, 2013). I also prefer to refer to the changes in the number of women as sex diversification rather than feminization, as earlier scholars have termed it (Menkel-Meadow, 1986; Michelson, 2013). This is because feminization, by the simple dictionary definition, refers to the changing characteristics that make something feminine. In this case, despite the increasing number of women in the legal professions worldwide, the workplace cultures, expectations, standards, and operational rules remain predominantly masculine—a scenario that contributes to many of the ongoing challenges women in law face.

In this section, drawing from feminist literature on critical mass, I discuss diversity as a dichotomous variable—first, *diversity in numbers (critical mass)* and second, *diversity in expertise (critical actions)*. By examining these two as dichotomous variables, we can better understand the interaction between the symbolic and descriptive representation of women and their substantive contributions. As presented earlier in this chapter regarding demographic shifts in the number of women in law, current statistics indicate that most countries have reached the 30% critical mass threshold, with some exceptions, such as Senegal, where women comprise approximately 14% of the legal bar as of 2023. Based on the figures in Senegal, similar projections can be made for other countries in the Sahel region—Mali, Niger, Chad, and Mauritania—which share characteristics with Senegal concerning the civil-law tradition and the influence of religion on women's social positions.

These changing demographics lead to gender diversity within the bar, and changing the profession at various levels. Some respondents believe that the increase in women's representation is impacting the profession by altering the institutional norms of "business as usual," which have been predominantly masculine. A respondent from a medium-sized law firm in Ghana remarked:

> Women influence the positions they hold simply because they are women. When I make decisions, I consider not only the law but also my common sense and experiences as a woman. For instance, while many men may take significant risks focused on outcomes, I tend to prioritize conflict resolution. Many women are now advancing in their careers and taking on management and in-house positions. These decision-making roles will allow them to shape the law and legal practices within their workplaces and the profession overall.

Numerous studies have examined the benefits of organizational diversity. In their longitudinal review of law firm practices in the United States, Dobbin and Kalev (2022) underscored the significance of diversity initiatives aimed at transforming hiring practices, providing mentoring programs, on-the-job training, and improving work-life support systems. As previously noted, women are increasingly entering various fields of legal practice that were once considered male-dominated, such as law and technology, international investment, and international law. These shifts in women's career choices in law will require the implementation of gender-diverse, gender-inclusive, and gender-sensitive practices.

What exactly does gender diversity in numbers mean for women's experiences in law? The benefits of having more women in the profession and women's contributions were not shared by all the women I interviewed. Some believe that women are not yet transforming the profession. A lawyer in Nigeria observed:

> Women have yet to transform the profession. Many women study law but never pursue it; instead, they remain in their comfort zones. Balancing private practice with family life is challenging. There are few women Senior Advocates of Nigeria (SAN) and women in private practice. We could have more if employers improved working conditions and society provided greater support for women. For instance, when a woman chooses to stay late at the office, she is labeled a "*night crawler*," one of those loose women—such attitudes deter women from practicing law.

For most interviewees, the speed at which women can change the profession depends on how quickly the "old boys' networks" can be broken down, how women are incorporated into these networks, or how they can build their own support systems. These male-exclusive networks serve as channels where men do favors for one another. The women-only sidebars mentioned earlier do not seem to have the same influence as the old boys' networks. Some respondents believe that for women to transform institutional and professional norms, they must assert themselves more and collaborate through real sisterhood and solidarity. Women need to unite to address the collective challenges they face and, if needed, pursue strategic litigation on issues they encounter in the legal field.

2. Changing Gender Norms and Perceptions of Competence

As more women enter the profession, changes in the social and institutional perceptions of women's competence are taking place. The diversity within various groups of women is influencing and transforming societal views on their capacities and capabilities as lawyers. Some female lawyers have distinguished themselves, earning national recognition for their work at the bar. Others have transitioned to different fields, such as diplomacy and international organizations. However, these evolving perceptions come at a cost to the status of women who choose to challenge gender norms. Some of these challenges may be intentional; for instance, a female Senior Advocate in Nigeria shared how she had to raise her voice at a male colleague in court to reject being called "brother silk," referencing the earlier discussion about the scarcity of women Senior

Advocates and the tendency to refer to women lawyers as "gentlemen in skirts." Other acts of disruption may occur unconsciously and may not aim to alter perceptions, though they ultimately have that effect. Regardless of the intent behind the actions that contribute to changing perceptions, women lawyers indicate that they do not shy away from engaging in acts of resistance, resilience, and the pursuit of excellence. Over time, these actions have merged into shifting perceptions regarding women's competence, work ethic, and contributions to the success of the law firms where they are employed.

A lawyer from Cape Verde acknowledged the contributions of earlier generations of women activists to the positive perceptions women enjoy today. Reflecting on the progress women have made, both in numbers and in leadership roles within the bar association, she confidently stated that the increase in women and the changing perceptions would challenge men. She noted that women in the profession are "in a good place" because the bar association has welcomed its third female member, and there are more remarkable women in law. More women are starting their own law firms and excelling in their careers, leading society to trust women lawyers. She concluded her remarks by saying, "I believe that in a few years, men will face a challenge. We owe this progress to the women who came before us; they did an excellent job and paved the way for women today. I don't feel any barriers to being a lawyer or pursuing a career in law."

The shift in perceptions is influenced not only by gender but also by age, an intersectional identity that many women must confront. Another lawyer in Cape Verde remarked poignantly:

> Every day, I interact more with women lawyers than with men; what I've noticed is that in the past, clients preferred older lawyers, who were mostly men. Now, people have become more familiar with women lawyers. These women are competent, so clients choose a lawyer who can effectively manage their case—that's my observation. As lawyers, our primary responsibility is to uphold the Constitution and advocate for equality for all. The challenge lies in defending the rule of law and achieving equality for women. As women lawyers, there is a growing demand for our voices, and we carve out our space through our competence. The bar association was founded by a woman, and subsequent women have stepped up as leaders within the bar association.

Women's perceptions and experiences in legal practice differ. For some women, while they do not view socially constructed gender expectations or their biological sex as obstacles, they employ business strategies to secure the best outcome for their clients, a lawyer from The Gambia shared.

I have never experienced any discrimination due to my gender—not in my work as a lawyer. For instance, earlier in my career, I would receive phone calls at 3 am if someone needed a lawyer, and I had to go. My house was close to the police station, and whenever the police required legal assistance, they would simply knock on my door—they respect me, and so do my clients. I have never found any situation challenging because I am a woman. Indeed, in some cases, when I have male clients, I inform my male colleagues that it's often better for them to handle the case because the clients tend to be more receptive—since we understand how people think. As a dedicated lawyer, I must defend my client to the best of my ability, and if my male colleague might achieve better results, then I would consider that as part of my strategy.

> A lawyer in Cape Verde mentioned that despite the apparent equality in the law and societal admiration for lawyers, women still have to perform extra actions to gain that respect. In Cape Verde, as in many other places, lawyers often need to leave their offices to find clients; if they stay in the office, they won't attract clients. This creates a challenge for women, especially if they lack connections or professional networks.

Historically, criminal law cases were mostly handled by men. As the legal field expanded and women entered different areas of practice, some female lawyers are beginning to make a mark as criminal attorneys. A lawyer's reputation greatly affects the referrals they receive. Several respondents noted that police officers and judges typically refer clients to men; however, some clients specifically ask for female lawyers, though the results are mixed.

> I don't believe women have distinct practice patterns, but in criminal cases, police may favor male lawyers because they are seen as more aggressive. However, in some instances, you might hear someone say, 'I want a woman lawyer because she's a mother and will understand me better.' In one case, I witnessed a judge directing someone to a male lawyer, stating that most of the older lawyers are men with name recognition. The judge told the accused, "I know this lawyer; he can help you because he is a man."

A young lawyer in the Ivory Coast believed that it was all about the perception and reputation a woman builds for herself:

> We are all lawyers, and we do the same work as men. However, women face additional challenges, such as having to stop working when they have a baby. I am not the best person to ask this *because I see myself as a man. I work and think like a man.* Women bring their motherly or nurturing qualities to work, and they are very present and attentive. But a woman can choose whether she wants to handle a brief or not. I don't know if clients choose someone based on sex; it's usually about reputation and recommendation. If you are competent, you will get the recommendation.

This narrative from a young woman lawyer offers various interpretations. First, the respondent claims that women are just as capable as their male colleagues. She also acknowledges that women encounter unique gender-based demands on their time, such as childbearing and caregiving—highlighting the impact of care work on women's roles as lawyers. Her statement, "I work and think like a man," illustrates the widespread belief that men possess a different work ethic, which is often valued more than that of women. Although she does not elaborate on what these attitudes and "working like a man" entail, she aligns with this perception, ultimately undermining her agency and identity as a woman and the strong work ethic that women contribute, which she later describes. Her belief that clients will choose a lawyer based on competence rather than gender reinforces the assumption that women who demonstrate excellence have equal opportunities for client referrals.

Such perceptions and beliefs are deeply rooted in and reinforce the uninformed narrative that the case for gender equality means women are trying to meet standards set by men, rather than focusing on being the best women they can be when given equal opportunities. The reality that equal opportunities may not necessarily lead to equal outcomes raises concerns about intersectionality. Unfortunately, this mindset skews the argument for gender equality in the legal profession, especially in Nigeria, where the narrative that "there are no ladies at the Bar" or that female lawyers are "gentlemen in skirts" implies that female lawyers have achieved the status of gentlemen. Ironically and patronizingly, these narratives are repeated as a celebration of the false perception that there is no discrimination at the bar or that female lawyers have come of age.

What masculine traits do some women adopt to appear competent? Does doing so threaten their socially constructed identities as women? Some respondents believe that women who try to embrace a masculine work ethic risk being labeled as bossy or argumentative.

> In Cape Verde, society values women lawyers; they find it interesting to see a female lawyer, and there is a lot of respect for them. However, some will reject a woman and think that being a female lawyer makes her too assertive. When I tell people I'm single, they ask why, and I tell them that I'm a lawyer and no one wants to marry me (laughs). I believe a similar situation is happening here, with more women getting divorced because they don't spend much time at home. Many insecure men may find it hard to have a partner who is a lawyer.

For many women, the challenges they face regarding perception involve demonstrating to themselves and others that their maternal responsibilities do not conflict with their obligations as lawyers. When asked whether perceptions of women in law are shifting, a corporate lawyer in Nigeria believes it depends on the type of firm and how willing they are to accommodate women's evolving roles and needs. Recognizing the flexibility and support she received from her law firm, she shares that when she had her first child, she chose to extend her maternity leave by taking an additional month without pay. However, with her second child, she worked late into the night to meet deadlines and shortened her maternity leave because she wanted to fulfill her responsibilities. She cautioned women against feeling pressured to prove themselves by rushing back to work. Instead, she encouraged them to focus on their work output to demonstrate their talent.

Perceptions of women's competence may shift, but this often requires them to work twice as hard to earn the same respect and recognition as men. A lawyer in Cape Verde illustrates this by noting that women have historically received greater social respect for their contributions to national development:

> My main goal is to act professionally and manage a firm successfully. In the early 1990s, I observed that people had little confidence in women lawyers. However, over time, when you demonstrate your competence, people learn to trust you. Sometimes,

> you need to be assertive and make your presence known to show that you are capable as a woman. Nevertheless, this issue is gradually decreasing as women in Cape Verde gain empowerment in various fields; we have always been warriors.

Changing client perceptions about women's competence requires shifting institutional norms and practices among decision makers in law firms. It takes time to alter these perceptions, and as more women gain experience and confidence as lawyers, they can develop their own strategies to address situations that challenge clients' gendered views of their abilities. A lawyer in Ghana shared her experience working with a client.

> We have had several clients, both local and international, who expressed a preference for male lawyers. The senior partner remained steadfast in the belief that the female lawyer would manage the case, and she successfully won both cases. This situation places a greater responsibility on you, the female lawyer, to showcase your abilities to such clients. Some clients are simply chauvinistic, making it crucial to know how to handle them. I now understand how to strike a balance between customer service and maintaining respect for the client, and I will not accept certain disrespectful behaviors. The key to addressing such unflattering treatment is to display your competence and assert yourself.

A lawyer in the Ivory Coast shared her experience when I asked if perceptions are changing regarding women's competence. She believes it all depends on individual circumstances. She describes her working relationship with her two partners as respectful, although there is a "certain protective instinct—sometimes, I find it frustrating," indicating a level of patronizing behavior from her male counterparts. An example of this male "protectiveness," which can feel patronizing, occurs when political or criminal law cases arise, and her colleagues attempt to dissuade her from taking on those cases because of their unspoken belief that such cases are too difficult for a woman to handle. She concludes by stating, "It depends on me; I have to stand my ground and choose to take the case myself; there is still that reflexive protectiveness."

For younger women lawyers, the intersection of gender and age can put them in a delicate position, compelling them to constantly demonstrate their competence on two fronts. In the courtroom, some women experience bullying from opposing clients and even judges. Clients often shy away from younger lawyers due to the belief that they lack legal expertise. Consequently, a young woman finds herself at a crossroads, facing two forms of victimization. Some young women lawyers have devised strategies to navigate the implications of their intertwined perceptions of age and gender incompetence, as shared by a young lawyer in Nigeria:

> As a young lawyer with a family, I face a real challenge, but I do everything I can to give special attention to my clients. The key is to stay organized and balance both my work and domestic responsibilities. Sometimes, it requires significant sacrifice. I have a strong support system at home, as my husband helps a lot, which enables me to maintain that balance.

Like other marginalized groups, women often bear the burden of dismantling and changing negative social perceptions based on gender that they did not create. Shifting societal views on women's capabilities as lawyers requires solidarity between women and men. A former president of the Senegalese Women Lawyers Association discussed the challenges women have faced and the potential for changing these perceptions.

> For most women lawyers here in Senegal, a major challenge is balancing domestic and professional responsibilities. The low number of women lawyers stems from a past perception that this profession is solely for men. The socio-cultural expectations placed on women as caregivers and the demanding working conditions necessitate that a woman has a man who understands and supports her. We are fighting to change these societal demands and perceptions of women's roles in our community. I wanted to advocate for women's rights to alter the expectations placed on us, but I did not wish to do that alone; I wanted men to take the lead in this fight for change. It is a collective effort, and men must be interested in collaborating with us.

Despite the mixed social perceptions of women's competence, women lawyers believe that the more women demonstrate their capability and efficiency as lawyers, the more these negative perceptions will gradually change in the legal community and society.

3. Client Satisfaction/Perceptions of Competence

Few studies have examined client perceptions of women's competence (Akuffo-Kwapong et al., 2021; Sasinsky, 2020). Client opinions on women's abilities as lawyers are related to societal beliefs about their roles. The interaction of the four variables discussed in this study significantly helps explain client (dis)satisfaction and perceptions of competence. Historical views of women lawyers influence institutional rules and restrictions that affect their representation. For example, one respondent in Ghana mentioned that in the early years of the profession, women lawyers were not allowed to wear pants in court. These institutional practices stem from sociocultural beliefs and understanding of women's roles. As a result, these gender norms impact women's status in the legal field (Houghton, 1981; Stewart, 2012). Some clients still assume that women lawyers in law firms mainly handle clerical or administrative tasks instead of practicing as attorneys or reaching senior partner roles. Sadly, these perceptions go beyond law firms. The growing number of women lawyers has begun to shift societal views on women's roles and abilities in law. The first and second generations of women lawyers faced major challenges in proving their competence compared to their male peers. In some countries, just the presence of a woman lawyer was almost unthinkable (Stewart, 2012).

Respondents also pointed out the ongoing societal belief that some lawyers, regardless of gender, are corrupt and mainly driven by money, with little concern for their clients' needs. In The Gambia, a second-generation female lawyer noted that clients tend to respond more positively to women lawyers. She then shifts the focus to male lawyers by stating:

> I find that when interacting with clients, they don't outright refuse to work with you just because you're a woman. Some lawyers might avoid collaborating with you because of your gender, especially if they plan to engage in questionable practices and know you would speak out against them. When I think about the major cases that go to court, judges have acknowledged that women handle them effectively. I believe women have built remarkable resilience in this profession.

A study on clients' perceptions of women lawyers found that some clients might prefer female lawyers because they tend to charge lower legal fees, are seen as sincere and attentive to client needs, and show higher levels of client care (Akuffo-Kwapong et al., 2021). In certain cases, clients may specifically request female lawyers, and this request can influence how law firms make hiring decisions to meet changing demographic demands (Sasinsky, 2020). Shifting client perceptions of women's capabilities also rely on male colleagues and supervisors. When a managing partner at a law firm affirms that female lawyers are qualified to handle a case, clients are likely to accept that claim. Such actions by senior management will positively shape social and client perceptions of women's competence as lawyers.

4. Defending Women's Rights

Women are often expected to lead efforts to defend women's rights and oppose gender-based discrimination in society. Women's rights attorneys and organizations have successfully used strategic litigation to promote, defend, and enforce women's rights, as mentioned earlier in the discussion about women's bar forums. There are many women's rights organizations across the continent. A detailed study of the types of organizations, their focus, and the cases they handle would be useful for future research. In this chapter, I focus on the stories from interviewees about the roles women play both individually and together in defending women's rights. Within law firms, an unspoken division of labor exists, with the expectation that women lawyers will advocate for women's rights, as shown by the story of a lawyer in Nigeria.

> They call me "Beijing" because I consistently highlight the gendered implications of the decisions and actions we take, even though I wouldn't label myself a women's rights activist. As the youngest female partner, I've noticed that the men tend to shy away from softer topics, such as personal hygiene, believing it's more acceptable for women to address them. You can see them assigning responsibilities along gender lines, expecting women to manage these issues. Although we may be equals at the table, we still need to demand respect. For instance, during discussions about maternity, when they point out that I'm unmarried and without children, questioning why I would advocate for mothers, they dismiss my contributions as my "Beijing moves."

This narrative emphasizes the importance of women in decision-making roles. Although this lawyer does not identify as a "gender rights activist," her willingness to share her perspective as a woman and advocate for other women's rights is noteworthy. Women lawyers have also founded and joined important organizations dedicated to promoting women's rights and increasing access to justice for women and children. As previously mentioned, women's "sidebar organizations" like FIDA have chapters in various countries. Often led and managed by women, these local chapters have achieved significant progress in advancing the rights of underprivileged women, children, and some men.

Earlier in Chapter 2, the discussion of women's contributions to law and legal advocacy for women's rights highlighted the involvement of women lawyers in both domestic and international arenas, including their roles in drafting post-conflict constitutions (Dawuni, 2021c). These global efforts also included the establishment of regional instruments, such as the Protocol to the African Charter on Human and Peoples' Rights on the Rights of Women in Africa (Maputo Protocol). At the African Commission on Human and Peoples' Rights in Banjul, The Gambia, women make up over 50% of the Commissioners and have held significant rapporteur positions (Alapini-Gansou, 2021). On a global scale, women lawyers from the continent have played key roles within the United Nations system, including serving as Special Rapporteurs.

In Senegal, despite the low number of women lawyers and judges, the AJS has led efforts to advocate for women's rights (Scales-Trent, 2010). In Nigeria, human rights lawyer Hauwa Ibrahim gained international recognition for defending Amina Lawal, who was accused of infidelity and sentenced to death by stoning. Her work was honored in 2005 when she received the European Parliament's Sakharov Prize for Freedom of Thought (PBS, 2003). Across the continent, more women are actively contributing to women's rights, with many taking leadership roles in defending the rights of women and other marginalized groups in society.

VI. Challenges: Navigating Personal and Professional Hurdles

Despite numerous advances in historical, institutional, and social factors, significant barriers and challenges for women in law remain. Gender-based discrimination continues to be a global problem. Workplace discrimination persists, despite international laws like CEDAW, the International Labor Organization (ILO) policies on workplace gender equality, and the Maputo Protocol at the regional level, all of which aim to provide legal protections for women's access to decision-making roles in the workplace with mixed success. Some women see these gender-based challenges as true discrimination, while others view them simply as workplace obstacles without gender implications. Understanding the complex impacts of sex (biological) and gender (socially constructed expectations) on women's experiences in law is best explored through the lived experiences of women lawyers.

The multifaceted and intersecting challenges women in law face are not confined to their career level or rank within a firm or corporate legal sector. For the few women who reach the top of the professional ladder, their challenges do not cease. It seems that women's symbolic presence in leadership is insufficient to prompt gender-appropriate responses throughout the leadership hierarchy. Essentially, without a critical mass of women in leadership positions and a shift in institutional norms and practices toward gender equity, the current bottom-heavy or bell-curve pattern of women's representation in law will not produce significant improvements in women's working conditions. The trickle-up theory of change may take longer to influence women's work environment (Rackley, 2013).

The discriminatory practices and gender-based negative stereotypes that women confront in the legal profession appear in various forms. Cultural expectations shape what is considered discriminatory behavior. Additionally, socialization affects how individuals perceive gender-based discrimination. Is gender-based discrimination so deeply embedded in culture that some women fail to see these actions as discriminatory, or are there women who genuinely remain unaffected by these experiences because of other privileges they hold, such as age or class? For example, in Nigeria, the phrase "*gentlemen in skirts*," used by some women lawyers, undermines gender equality. Furthermore, that some women use this phrase without questioning its gendered implications highlights how gendered socialization influences their vocabulary and self-view. In other words, do these women see themselves as being "elevated" to a man's status because they work in a masculinized profession? Is discrimination considered nonexistent because women have developed coping strategies? The following analysis outlines common patterns of the challenges women face in the profession.

1. Gender-Based Perceptions of Incompetence and Unconscious Bias

Despite evolving perceptions of women's abilities as lawyers, women in law still face various layers of gender stereotypes about their competence in fulfilling their roles as attorneys. The belief that the legal profession, like many other skilled fields, is primarily a man's domain has persisted since the profession's origins in much of Europe and the United States, where women fought numerous battles for admission to the field (Schultz & Shaw, 2003, 2013). In the United States, women were legally barred from attending law school (Mossman, 2013). Sandra Day O'Connor, the first woman appointed to the Supreme Court of the United States, graduated third in her class; however, for many years, she faced challenges in finding work as a lawyer (Kenney, 2013a). The perception of women's assumed incompetence remains widespread in the legal profession, deeply rooted in Europe and the United States, and has spread to other jurisdictions that have adopted those legal traditions (Dawuni & Badejogbin, 2021; Silver, 2013).

The experiences of first-generation women lawyers in African countries have not been systematically documented. The available information highlights some challenges they faced when entering the bar as the first or pioneering women. For example, most of their male peers were educated in British, French, or Portuguese cities, which remained largely patriarchal. In addition to dealing with the patriarchal structures and social norms faced by this first generation of African women trained abroad, they also had to confront both overt and covert racism, facing dual challenges similar to those many African American women in the United States, as well as Black or other minority women in the United Kingdom, continue to face (Melaku, 2019; Pruitt, 2002).

Gender-based discrimination in the workplace continues to be a major concern. According to **Figure 4.6**, when asked if they had experienced workplace

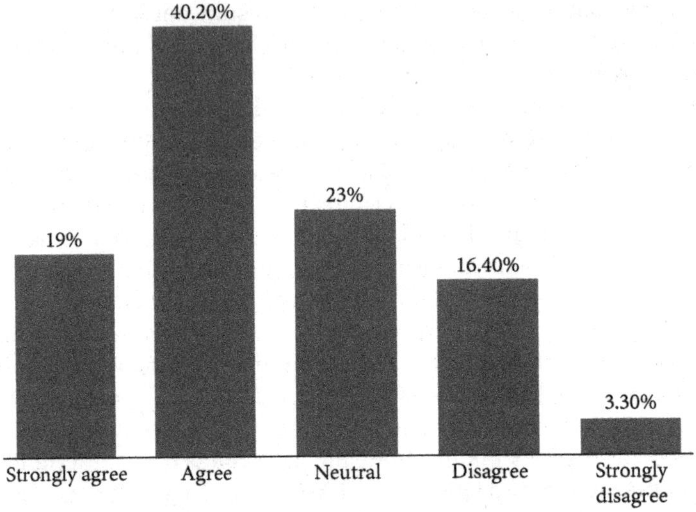

Figure 4.6 *Experience With Workplace Discrimination*
Source: Survey respondents: 122.

discrimination, a significant 59.1% either strongly agreed or agreed with the statement. Meanwhile, 23% expressed neutrality, which highlights the idea that gendered socialization about what constitutes gender discrimination may lead to this neutrality. Additionally, it could be due to challenges with surveys where respondents do not have the opportunity to clarify open-ended questions on the poll.

In a study on the impact of gender stereotypes in managerial roles, Nayak and Tabassum (2021) discovered that gender-based stereotypes encountered at various life stages are shaped by individual, cognitive, family, sociocultural, and organizational factors. These influences have a cumulative effect and can follow a woman throughout her entire life, necessitating different interventions at each phase. At the organizational level, prescribed gender roles and behaviors for women, ingrained masculinities, and persistent networks of male-centered favors can work together to undermine women's potential as leaders and equal partners to their male counterparts. Women must navigate multiple layers of discriminatory gender-based stereotypes rooted in historical and social influences. For women leading the effort to change these perceptions, it can be overwhelming, as described by a lawyer in Nigeria.

> At the start of my career, I worked at a well-established law firm, handling various cases—including real estate, family law, divorce, and debt collection. I mainly focused on litigation in court. We faced some challenges; there were few female attorneys, and I was the first woman to start a private practice in my state. I felt some apprehension because society believed in a man's world, and if you didn't fit into this world [as a man], you might not succeed. So, I had to put in extra effort to prove I could do it, and when I started winning cases, I gained the trust of the people.

Some respondents I spoke with who appeared in court described receiving gender-insensitive treatment from judges. Judges reflect their societal contexts, and in common-law countries, where judges create law through their decisions (*stare decisis*), they play a vital role in judicial outcomes. Judges' biases and perceptions can influence their interactions with women lawyers in court, extending beyond gender to include other intersectional identities. These gender biases can show up in how they allow women lawyers to speak without interruptions from opposing counsel or the presiding judge. A lawyer in Ghana shared her gendered experiences of appearing before a judge.

> Sometimes, the negative experiences you encounter in court may not stem from your gender but rather from your youth and your level of experience as a lawyer. However, once you prove yourself, they will respect you. Some judges may require you to identify as "Ms." or "Mrs.," but why is this necessary when men simply introduce themselves as "Mr."?

Some women have been accused by opposing counsel of having affairs with their clients. There are intersectional effects of gender-based perceptions of incompetence; as a result, a young, unmarried female lawyer may be more likely to face accusations of having an affair with a client, while such claims are less commonly directed at young, unmarried male lawyers. Despite the diverse experiences reported by women, a prevailing perception remains that women's competence will be diminished due to their maternal and family responsibilities. In many cases, women lawyers must prove to their prospective and current employers that they can successfully manage the roles of both lawyer and parent or caregiver. The burden on women to demonstrate that their obligations regarding childbearing and childcare will not hinder their work as lawyers is a challenge faced by women worldwide (Schultz & Shaw, 2003).

Societal perceptions continue to hinder women, regardless of their position—age or marital status often becomes irrelevant. Many employers still see hiring young women as a "risk" because they assume she will marry, start a family, and become less productive. The truth is that while many women choose to have families, the focus should be on what law firms need to do to support women of reproductive age during maternity leave and after they return to work. Some women have reported facing unprofessional questions during interviews, such as inquiries about their plans to start a family soon. A Senior Advocate of Nigeria emphasized the intergenerational perceptions affecting women at all stages of their legal careers.

> Women have increased their presence as in-house counsel and hold top positions in decision-making roles, so no one questions their capabilities. However, challenges remain in private legal practice. There is still a perception that "she is going to leave to care for the family." Also, some believe that women will eventually move out of litigation to become in-house counsel, causing employers to hesitate in investing in them.

Despite women's relative success in the legal profession, navigating the ongoing institutional and structural barriers to full equality still presents many challenges. Whether these negative perceptions, attitudes, and behaviors come from fellow lawyers, judges, or clients, women must constantly navigate different societal power hierarchies. A woman's positionality—shaped by her age, marital status, or social standing—still does not shield her from the persistent effects of gender-based discrimination in the profession.

2. Balancing the Professional and Personal

The global caregiving economy is mainly female. Like other regions, familial and kinship systems in most African countries assign family care responsibilities to women. Despite support from family members and domestic workers, female legal professionals still bear the primary caregiving burden at home. In the broader cultural context of many African systems, the caregiving burden extends beyond the nuclear family to include extended family and communal kinship networks. According to Figure 4.7, 12.3% indicated they find it very challenging to balance their professional and personal responsibilities, while a significant 47.5% agreed it was quite challenging. These responses should be interpreted considering that 41% of the survey respondents were aged 31–40, of which 24.6% were married, while 33.6% were married with children.

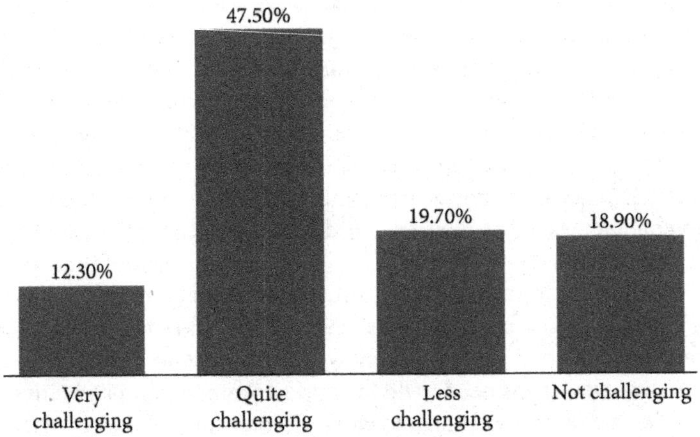

Figure 4.7 *Balancing Personal and Professional Responsibilities*
Source: Survey respondents: 122.

Although opportunities for women in professional work have grown, primary caregiving roles have remained largely unchanged, leaving women still leading household care. Advances in women's access to the workforce have not been matched by changes in workplace policies, which need to better suit women's needs. As a result, most women face a "double bind"—struggling to find a balance between their personal and professional lives.

Women navigate the complex aspects of their lives. The caregiving challenge varies with the age of their children, often decreasing as they get older. Women may also have responsibilities toward aging parents, and some who continue working into their retirement may provide care and support for their grandchildren. For many women, the caregiving cycle seems never-ending. To understand this challenge, I asked interview respondents how they balance their personal and professional obligations. A lawyer from Cape Verde shared her insights on this balancing act:

> It's complicated. I need to find time for myself because I'm always working. I have help at home, but most of the chores still fall on me. I have to balance between the courts, manage the office and household, attend workshops or conferences occasionally, and work late before going back to the office. My life is divided among all these responsibilities.

Recognizing the need to balance multiple obligations, some lawyers must make adjustments in their lives. Another lawyer discussed her decision to balance her work and personal commitments:

> I had to decide whether to move offices, which was a major challenge. My office space was large, but I needed to relocate to a smaller one to be closer to home. I have two daughters—20 and 15—who often complain that I'm never home. I want to be like my colleagues who juggle many responsibilities at once, but I had to choose between being a lawyer and a mother. As a perfectionist, I prefer to do things well rather than just do them poorly.

No matter what changes women make in their lives—such as getting additional help at home, moving their office, or reducing their workload—the balancing act remains challenging. As one lawyer summarized her experience, "*It is hard. There are times when personal or work obligations take precedence. The advantage of being a partner is that I can delegate, which allows me to spend more time on personal matters.*"

Changes in the political economy, community networks, and kinship systems across Africa have diminished the support that extended family systems can provide women in caring for their children. Some women lawyers report that they must forgo family obligations to work late. When they leave the office at closing time while their male colleagues stay behind, it sends a misleading message that women are less committed to their jobs. This perception reinforces stereotypes suggesting that women are not as hardworking as men, a misguided belief that harms women during promotions. Together, these challenges lead to high attrition rates among women in private practice.

3. Perception of Litigation as a Man's Domain

The legal profession has fundamentally shifted into an adversarial system, requiring lawyers to litigate before a judge to defend their clients' rights (Abel & Lewis, 1989). Since this profession is rooted in a masculine work ethic, lawyers are usually expected to be aggressive, self-interested, and unyielding. From Carol Gilligan's (1982) research on the ethic of care, women often show qualities that contrast with the masculine traits considered essential for a successful lawyer. The intersection of the profession's history, the masculine institutional culture of practice, and women's traits leads many female lawyers to feel like outsiders within the professional customs and rules of engagement. As a result, women's career choices often involve adopting assimilation strategies or facing the negative consequences of stagnation or leaving their firms. Analyzing this situation from a feminist institutional perspective shows that women's progress in litigation is a tough journey (Chappell & Waylen, 2013; Nayak & Tabassum, 2021; Thornton, 1996).

Many women are successful litigators; however, while litigation may appear to be gender-neutral, it often has a masculine tone. Women lawyers are expected to maintain a feminine appearance, yet they must also endure evaluations based on masculine vocal standards. They navigate these conflicting expectations from peers, some of whom are socialized to believe that women cannot be effective lawyers. This insidious expectation can be especially strong in law firms with heavy litigation workloads and is most apparent in the courtroom, where litigation practices can be aggressive, abrasive, and confrontational (Akuffo-Kwapong et al., 2021; Chitapi, 2018;; Stewart, 2012). Male lawyers who display such traits are often seen as "good lawyers," while women showing the same characteristics are frequently labeled with less favorable and openly sexist terms. From the perspective of "merit," the qualities that define a good lawyer are inherently biased against women. Some women face a lose–lose situation: if they do not demonstrate those "merit-earning" traits, they are not seen as good lawyers; if they do, they are not regarded as good women.

Trying to fit into the perceived "man's world" of the legal profession also means that women have had to adopt some characteristics displayed by male lawyers. However, this task is not always easy, and women often have to engage in gender role or gender code-switching. What is considered assertive and acceptable behavior for men is seen as aggressive and unacceptable when exhibited by women. As a lawyer in Ghana confirmed:

> Social perceptions are changing, but not as fast as they should. For some, simply being a lawyer means people assume they are confrontational. Because male lawyers tend to raise their voices in court, there's a common expectation that women will do the same. When you start to argue or challenge something, it often becomes a gender issue. This depends on who you're speaking to; even your clients might see you as assertive or domineering.

Survival strategies vary. Some women lawyers criticize the need to "fit in," while others accept it as part of the "game" and learn to navigate by the existing rules. A diverse group of women from different countries reported gender-segregated job levels in law firms. Women are typically assigned cases like divorce, alimony, and debt collection, while high-stakes cases in commercial and corporate litigation are reserved for men.

For some women, the decision not to pursue litigation stems not from the difficulties of the process itself but from the challenges of navigating the courts and the judiciary's complex and slow administrative systems. In many African countries, litigation can take an excessively long time due to poor administrative practices within the courts. Information gathered during fieldwork shows that the time required for a case to be heard can range from a few months to several years. In Nigeria, one lawyer noted that some cases that go to appeal can take six years or more to reach the Supreme Court. The frustrations caused by repeated adjournments, lost dockets, frustrated clients, and missing evidence are not unique to women; men also face these issues. However, the gendered impact is more significant for women, who must navigate institutional challenges and delays to ensure their clients' cases are resolved. Poor caseload management can have serious consequences for cases involving rape and gender-based violence, where preserving the integrity of evidence is essential.

These challenges, among others, influence women's professional choices. The head of litigation at one of Nigeria's top law firms has reflected on her career decisions: "*One of the professional decisions I have been considering is whether to fully or partially leave litigation and transition to corporate work because of how time-consuming litigation is. A corporate project can be completed quickly, allowing one to move on.*" The intersectional challenges faced by younger, unmarried women lawyers impact their ability to navigate power dynamics, such as bullying from senior male colleagues and unwanted sexual advances. Some women report that judges inappropriately influence cases by adjourning them, hoping to frustrate a younger female lawyer resisting their sexual advances.

4. Sexual and Other Forms of Harassment

In 2019, a report in the *Daily Monitor*, a Ugandan newspaper, detailed the story of Samantha Mwesigye, a female lawyer who endured sexual harassment from her superior, Deputy Solicitor General Christopher Gashirabake, for such an extended period that she took legal action in the Industrial Court. While the court delayed in fulfilling its constitutional and statutory duty to ensure a fair and prompt hearing, her harasser was nominated, confirmed, and appointed as a judge of the Court of Appeal. Samantha received backing from women's rights organizations that saw her move as a brave effort to break the silence about the widespread impunity of sexual harassment within both the legal field and society (Musoke, 2024). Sadly, Samantha's case reflects one of thousands of reported and unreported incidents involving women lawyers—including judges and academics—who are victims of silent harassment in the profession. Her case highlights the increasing number of women who have courageously and publicly brought attention to their fight against professional victimization and harassment.

Sexual harassment in the legal profession is a worldwide issue that many women in law have personally experienced or know someone who has been affected. A 2019 global study on lawyers' experiences with bullying and sexual harassment found that 37% of women faced some form of sexual harassment (International Bar Association, 2019). In a 2020 study by the Institute for Women in Law, 64% of respondents from over 14 countries reported experiencing sexual harassment (Institute for Women in Law, 2020). A country-specific study, *Women in Law and Leadership: Nigerian Judiciary*, showed that 77% of the 449 respondents identified sexual harassment as the biggest challenge women in law face (Institute for Women in Law, 2023m). Similar findings were reported in this current study, where 77% of respondents confirmed that women encounter sexual and other types of harassment in the workplace.

Figure 4.8 shows data from the survey of lawyers conducted for this study, revealing that 77% experienced sexual harassment at work. Similar studies in Kenya (Institute for Women in Law, 2023; Wambua, 2013), Zimbabwe (Bonnin & Maunganidze, 2021; Stewart, 2012), Nigeria (Aina-Pelemo et al., 2019), South Africa (Institute for Women in Law, 2023p), and Senegal (Institute for Women in Law, 2023n) confirm

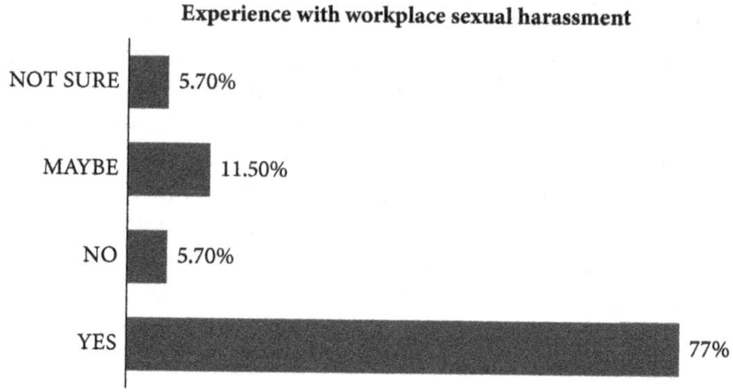

Figure 4.8 *Women's Experience With Sexual and Other Forms of Harassment*
Source: Survey respondents: 122.

the widespread nature of sexual harassment. These behaviors persist despite some legal protections against them. For instance, Rule 75 of the Ghana Legal Profession (Professional Conduct and Etiquette) Rules, 2020 (L.I. 2423), prohibits sexual harassment. A similar law has been enacted by the Nigerian Bar Association (Aina-Pelemo, 2020). Still, many lawyers I interviewed indicated that high levels of sexual harassment continue within the profession.

Sexual harassment, like other forms of gender-based violence, is deeply personal, and many victims hesitate to report it for various reasons, including the social stigma that often accompanies it. Victims' silence also stems from sociocultural contexts and the negative consequences faced by those who experience such violence (Saungweme et.al., 2024). Recognizing how sociocultural factors contribute to victims' silence, I refined the research question by first asking a simple question—whether the respondent had personally experienced it—and then by asking if they knew someone who had faced it. The latter allows respondents to create emotional distance and discuss the experiences as if they belonged to someone else. This interview approach is vital when addressing sexually based crimes and offenses (López, 1999; Subramaniam, 2016).

Some respondents reported incidents of unwanted touching, inappropriate language used to describe them, and, in some cases, the sharing of unsolicited text messages and WhatsApp messages of a sexual nature. Sexual harassment is not limited to the law firm and interactions between colleagues. Some lawyers described unwanted gestures from clients.

> The issue of sexual harassment is always present. You can't reject them outright because you need to respond respectfully to maintain the lawyer-client relationship. A too direct rejection could cause negative consequences. Even with clients, harassment can be subtle; they might ask if you're available for lunch or dinner. Our profession depends heavily on relationships, and you're expected to socialize with clients and partners to keep those connections. For men, this might be easier, but women need to navigate this balance carefully, as closeness with clients and partners can lead to complications.

Social interpretations of what constitutes sexual harassment vary greatly. In Senegal, most women interviewed for this project said they had no direct experience with sexual harassment. I changed my approach by asking in the third person, "*Have you heard of women lawyers experiencing sexual harassment?*" This way of framing the question, as involving someone else, led to a few responses indicating that the problem does exist. However, cultural barriers to discussing it make it a silent issue that many women face. A lawyer in Senegal responded:

> As a single woman, you might meet some men interested in dating you. However, I haven't heard of any reports of sexual harassment. When it happens, it often stays hidden, with many people reluctant to talk about it—victims might choose not to speak out because of fear or stigma. Sometimes, harassment involves someone in a higher position, which makes the victim hesitant to reveal their identity due to concerns about possible repercussions.

In Nigeria, I conducted a focus group with women lawyers in their mid-20s to mid-30s, with an average of five to seven years at the bar. The women unanimously expressed frustration over ongoing harassment they faced. They shared a common story of a young woman lawyer who traveled out of state for a case with her boss, only to find that he had booked a single room for both of them. The lawyer resigned and filed a lawsuit against her former boss. Unsurprisingly, several people, including other lawyers, advised her to drop the case because of his status and the potential risks to her future employment. While some women lawyers are speaking out against harassment, many junior lawyers often suffer in silence. The fear of facing "punishment" from a senior lawyer or partner for rejecting their sexual advances is very real. As one focus group participant painfully observed, "society blames and shames women, and women have to pay the price. Some men feel they have the license to share inappropriate jokes, expecting laughter, and I constantly find myself having to resist such unprofessional behavior."

Reporting mechanisms are weak and often absent. Victim-blaming is common and can lead to a woman being blacklisted for courageously reporting a crime. Bar associations need to address this serious issue of sexual harassment. It's unclear whether this silence results from gender blindness or cultural sensitivities about discussing sexual harassment. In Senegal, when I spoke with the president of the bar association (*Batonnier*), he strongly claimed that sexual harassment was not a problem within the legal profession.

> The Batonnier's office handles cases involving allegations of sexual harassment or other forms of professional misconduct. A committee is assigned to address these issues, and if a case is reported and the individual is found guilty, they may lose their job. We have never received a report of sexual harassment.

The range of sexual and other forms of harassment women face varies. Some young women lawyers intentionally dress down to avoid attracting unwanted sexual advances from clients and colleagues. These views were shared by lawyers

I interviewed in Nigeria and Ghana. The widespread scrutiny of women's bodies and dress codes peaked in 2020 in Ghana when the then-president of the Ghana Bar Association made a statement about women's dress standards.

> Bare legs are never accepted in court, neither are open-toed shoes. Anything flashy such as large gaudy earrings or sandals are also inappropriate. Whether in court or at the office, lawyers should refrain from showing much skin. Bare arms are generally frowned upon in the office and never appropriate in court. Hair and makeup should be conservative. Last, shirts or blouses should always be buttoned, so that the cleavage is never revealed, (Pulse Ghana, n.d.).

While several lawyers shared their opinions on the bar president's statement, some took to the media to oppose the policing of women's bodies within the profession. A female lawyer who responded to the misogynistic remark in a blog commented:

> It was condescending and sexist, reflecting the persistent patriarchal narratives that continue to permeate our discourse in the 21st century. Whenever it suits our whims, we feign offense under the so-called conservativenature of our profession, rebuking others for no apparent reason other than sexism and discrimination. Whose sense of conservatism are we protecting? (Boateng, 2022).

Gender-based sexism and chauvinistic behavior are pervasive and almost institutionalized. The female head of the legal department at an international mining company in Ghana stated:

> Sexual harassment is widespread in this workplace, and even young women feel they cannot report it. When my assistant voiced her concerns about being sexually harassed, she was treated like an outcast. Senior men asked me, "Are you sure she didn't ask for it?" It's a deeply rooted culture. The men believe they are entitled to it, while the women think the men have money.

Along with sexual harassment, many women reported facing intersectional discrimination related to their gender and age. Most said they experienced bullying from senior lawyers and judges, and many victims chose to stay silent out of fear of retaliation.

> Bullying is common in the courtroom, and women must earn respect to avoid mistreatment. A major issue is the professional hierarchy that places judges above lawyers, affecting both men and women. Sometimes, rivalry can develop among women, causing a female judge to treat a female lawyer differently while showing more respect to a male lawyer. It's important to demonstrate that you are an advocate and have a solid understanding of the law.

The transcript above shows that bullying is carried out not only by male lawyers and judges but also by female judges toward women lawyers. A closer look at this transcript reveals that gender-based discriminatory practices and behaviors are intersectional, with perpetrators being either male or female. The widespread and ongoing sexual harassment within the legal profession is shameful. If the legal field, which aims to uphold and protect the rights of women and other vulnerable groups, cannot address sexual harassment within its own ranks, then solving the problem in society will take more effort and a longer time.

Given the serious nature of this issue, I asked the women I interviewed whether their law firms had policies against sexual harassment, and most were unaware of such policies. Where these policies exist, how can they be enforced, especially when a senior partner at the firm commits the harassment? Even in the few cases in Nigeria and Uganda mentioned earlier, where some women have bravely chosen to file a complaint in court, public pressure has forced them to withdraw their cases.

A continent-wide strategy may be needed to raise awareness of gender-based issues in the legal field. One such effort is the Gender Equality in Law Campaign (GELC), launched by the Institute for African Women in Law in 2024. This campaign aims to address four main challenges that women in law frequently encounter: sexual harassment, unequal pay, lack of promotions, and gender biases and stereotypes. Engaging key male allies to publicly commit to resolving these issues will be crucial for fostering attitudinal shifts that could help reduce sexual harassment in the profession.

5. Mentoring, Sponsorship, and Networks

Professional mentorship and sponsorship are crucial for career growth and development (Wallace, 2001). Mentorship plays a vital role in the success and progress of young lawyers, who often graduate from law school with limited practical knowledge of how the law works in real life. It begins in law school, and in institutions lacking academic mentoring, a gap forms in students' understanding of what mentorship involves and how to take full advantage of available opportunities. Based on my experience as a law student, I navigated the process of finding mentors and making the most of those relationships. As a law student in Ghana, I did not participate in any formal academic mentoring, which caused confusion about what a mentor-mentee relationship should involve. For several years, I struggled to understand how mentorship functions. Although I received informal guidance from many individuals along the way, it was not part of a formal or structured mentorship program.

The same is true for most law students across the continent where I conducted interviews. I also notice this in my interactions with law students and young lawyers who are eager to seek mentorship but don't know how to initiate or navigate a mentoring relationship. For young professionals, forming mentoring connections involves negotiating relationships with senior colleagues. As a result, when someone approaches the mentoring process without understanding the rules, they are unlikely to benefit much from it or may be exploited by senior male colleagues.

Several respondents indicated they had never participated in a mentoring relationship, either as mentors or mentees. Most senior lawyers quickly noted that, while they did not participate in formal mentoring programs, they nonetheless mentored junior colleagues on an informal basis. Women often understand the experiences of other women through their lived experiences, but that alone is not always enough for a mentoring relationship. Women must make intentional choices to use their lived experiences as mentoring tools. A partner in a commercial law firm in Nigeria recalls her challenging experience as a young lawyer and how it has influenced her approach to mentoring young women. She remembers working with her first boss, one of the few practitioners in maritime law, an older gentleman who "belonged to the old school and was very disciplined," from whom she learned a lot while adhering to his demanding work hours, which included weekends and late nights. Reflecting on her experience, she shared:

> I saw no reason to ask him to change the hours. I worked for seven years under these conditions. My first pregnancy ended with an emergency hospital visit, and I was placed on bed rest. Because of these experiences, I am very aware of women's issues, and I look out for them; I call to check how they are doing. I encourage them to tell their supervisor about any challenges affecting their work because if they don't speak up, the supervisor might not know. When evaluation time comes, they might be seen as not working hard enough.

Some interviewees believed that certain women are hesitant to help others once they reach the peak of their careers. However, an older female lawyer saw it differently, pointing out that "sometimes women at the top of their careers are still dealing with the loneliness and challenges of their position, leaving them little time to effectively mentor others."

A few of my respondents feel that the younger generation of women lawyers is not open to being mentored. She believes some women may not be receptive to harsh criticism; instead, they tend to withdraw and might not come back, whereas men generally accept critique and mentorship. This suggests that women could potentially miss opportunities for learning and growth. She observes, "most men want to succeed; they don't care if you like them or not; they will persist until the work gets done. I talk to women associates the same way I talk to the guys, but it makes me wonder if I should start addressing them differently."

Another lawyer from Ghana had similar sentiments:

> When I started working here, I used to finish my tasks before my supervisor asked for them. Now, I have to push my junior associates and follow up repeatedly to see if the work is done. Some of them are very capable, but most lack motivation and don't push themselves to excel. How much can you mentor someone who isn't willing to pull themselves up?

Once again, the reluctance or inability of some women to mentor others should not be generalized as a lack of interest in guiding younger women. It's also important to move away from the assumption that women must mentor other women. Typically, power structures are mainly controlled by men; therefore, creating mentoring programs limited to women mentors could disadvantage young women lawyers (mentees) who would benefit from learning from both genders.

For most women lawyers, the challenge isn't finding the right male mentor but navigating the risks of mentoring relationships that can turn into *quid pro quo* deals, where mentors may demand sexual favors. Mentorship in the legal field can open doors for sponsorship, boosting women's career prospects in law beyond their immediate work settings. Attending national, regional, and international professional conferences has sometimes increased chances for both mentoring and sponsorship. Many young women lawyers have used their international experiences to build their own networks and pathways for sponsorship.

6. Workplace Expectations and Rainmaking

The legal profession is known for long working hours and limited vacation time. The situation is even more challenging for solo practitioners and small firms, which usually consist of three to five lawyers, needing extra hours to reach financial goals. These long hours are essential for the survival of both small and large law firms, as global competition and the influence of bigger international firms impact legal markets across Africa (Dezalay, 2020; Kamau, 2020; Klaaren, 2020).

Women face significant challenges in meeting workplace demands for long hours late into the night. First, their family and caregiving responsibilities are greatly impacted. Additionally, working late at night presents security risks for many women, as they must drive home in countries where safety threats are common. A lawyer in Nigeria highlighted the difficulties of retaining clients: "Men can socialize after work and make deals, but you may find yourself as the only woman at the table, often the youngest person. You might not share the same sentiments or values as their discussions and conversations."

The challenges women face with client retention impact their advancement within the firm. A lawyer from the Ivory Coast shared her concern, noting that because her male colleagues attract more clients, they feel empowered to make decisions at the firm with little to no input from women associates or even partners. The perception that men work harder due to their larger client base also creates different expectations for men and women. In a focus group of six lawyers at a law firm in Nigeria, one participant commented:

> The rules are different for men. We, the women, face the harshest backlash even when we are away for a short time. We handle solicitor's work but also have to manage court work or litigation. We've raised our concerns, but it must be done diplomatically; otherwise, we risk being seen as complaining.

Another respondent added:

> After working at this firm for over a year, we didn't get any leave; however, when the new male hires arrived, they received their leave in just six months, which gives the impression that they worked harder! We are not paid the same as our male colleagues, and gender bias might explain this difference. It feels like you are being penalized for being a woman.

Overall, working conditions and expectations have stayed the same despite more women becoming lawyers. Women must either meet these current expectations or find new ways to cope. For many women, the demand to adapt and conform to the norm is unrealistic, leading to higher dropout rates among women lawyers in law firms. Some choose to move into other fields, such as the Ministry of Justice, the judiciary, or the corporate sector, where they can rely on steady hours, fixed monthly pay, and clear promotion standards. For others who stay in law firms, advancement may be possible, as mentioned earlier regarding women reaching partnership. But many find that just meeting the minimum requirements to survive in a law firm results in slow professional growth, which explains why there are still many women associates at the lower levels of the hierarchy.

7. Equal Pay and Promotion

Income disparity in the legal profession continues across different jurisdictions (American Bar Association, 2006; Nelson et al., 2023; Schultz & Shaw, 2003). Unfortunately, data on lawyers' incomes and salaries at law firms were unavailable for this study. Requests for salary range information were often met with excuses, claiming that revealing such details would violate human resource policies. The lack of transparency about salary data between women and men may contribute to a broader lack of clarity surrounding the gender pay gap. There is no established model for lawyers' compensation, except in specific cases like government roles within the judiciary or the Attorney General's Office, which usually follow the bureaucratic civil service model, where salaries are standardized based on rank or level.

The law firms I visited have different pay structures. Most firms give lawyers a base salary plus the chance to earn more through bonuses based on the cases they secure or are assigned by partners. This salary-plus-bonus setup can sometimes put women at a disadvantage, as they often have fewer networking opportunities and find it harder to attract high-paying clients. They may also get fewer challenging cases from senior partners because of stereotypes that suggest men are better suited for those roles. When it comes to case assignments, women have to carefully balance being assertive without appearing overly aggressive. One lawyer in Nigeria said, "women fear promoting themselves to avoid appearing aggressive, while men are unafraid of being wrong and often defend their positions. This mindset impacts salary negotiations, as men advocate more effectively for their value."

While assumptions about equal pay often depend on position or rank, they also rely on how women negotiate their salaries when starting a job—a common point of conflict for them. Men are generally seen as more assertive in salary negotiations and in advocating for their worth. Gender stereotypes and biases work against women, fueled by the belief that they are the primary caregivers at home. A senior female lawyer in Nigeria highlighted these perceptions:

> It is probably harder for a younger woman today to make a living from litigation than for a man. Even as a senior counsel, talking to my colleagues, they comment on things like, "What do you need the money for?" The perception is that a woman can be paid less because they believe that, after all, a man is taking care of her.

Linking a person's gross salary to the cases handled by a law firm or assigned to an individual presents several challenges. First, as previously noted, women often lack the professional networks and outside-of-office meeting opportunities needed to attract new clients. After-hours meetings for drinks or weekend outings to socialize with potential clients are usually not feasible for many women due to caregiving responsibilities. Female lawyers are also influenced by prevailing sociocultural perceptions that suggest a woman socializing after hours or late at night is morally "loose." Additionally, for many women with family obligations, the need to return home and care for their families often takes priority over the desire to stay and meet with potential clients.

A second plausible explanation for the challenges of linking one's salary to case files relates to earlier discussions on perceptions of (in)competence. These perceptions are held not only by senior colleagues but also by some clients who refuse to let a woman handle their files. Especially in litigation cases, women are often viewed as lacking the qualifications to manage highly complex cases. This discussion requires nuance to avoid creating an overly broad picture of hostility toward women in litigation. In several law firms where I conducted interviews, the litigation departments were led by women. Therefore, for women who enjoyed litigation and chose that path, there were opportunities to advance and even lead the department.

Given the combined impact of institutional norms that impede women's advancement and structural factors that place demanding caregiving and time-consuming responsibilities on them, some may feel trapped in a cycle of unpreparedness for promotions. Several respondents noted that, compared to their male colleagues, they felt they needed to be particularly well-prepared to be considered for promotions. One respondent shared her experience:

> I was invited to apply for a promotion earlier, but I didn't feel prepared. In 1993, I became a partner and took on the duty of handling mercantile cases. Partnership in a law firm is like a marriage, so we face the ups and downs together. I believe it's not hard for women to rise and become partners. They often stay longer at firms and have better chances of reaching the top. However, they need the confidence to make that upward move.

Women may hesitate to ask for a promotion or a pay raise for several reasons, including fear of backlash. As one lawyer in Nigeria noted:

> Women often hesitate to ask for a raise or promotion because they fear being seen as greedy or aggressive. On the other hand, men frequently gain advantages through supportive male networks. Some women might be reluctant to pursue a promotion, worried that a male supervisor could expect something in return. For young, unmarried individuals without "the protection of the ring," earning respect can be more difficult. Similarly, single women may feel vulnerable, as requesting a promotion might be mistaken for offering sexual favors.

Beneath the surface of equal pay, the timing and criteria for promotions are often influenced by gendered metrics related to the work performed, and perceptions of competence are frequently assigned to men first. As one respondent noted:

> Promotion is not guaranteed, but when supervisors assess based on output, men often perform better. When a woman seeks advancement, she usually has to put in more hours. Women often have more qualifications than men, but in terms of work experience and output, men tend to have the edge. As a result, when the CEO makes promotional decisions, they may favor men. We need to start focusing on the quality of work instead of just the quantity of outputs.

The paradox of women's competence as lawyers, combined with their slow progress in promotions, prompted me to speak with several senior male managing partners from law firms in Nigeria and Ghana. These founding and senior partners consistently recognized that women are hardworking, diligent, and detail-oriented, showing a high level of client care. One managing partner at a prominent law firm in Ghana specifically mentioned that the women at his firm are the ones who work hard and prepare his court briefs, emphasizing that they "make me shine." The disparity between perceptions of women's abilities and their pay and promotion rates needs further investigation. For now, it can be argued that this imbalance results from gender stereotypes and biases that favor a male-centric work ethic over women's contributions to the financial success of law firms.

Some women have spoken out against how they've been treated. A woman who leads the legal department at a foreign mining company in Nigeria explained:

> A male colleague was appointed to a position for which he was unqualified, receiving both a salary increase and a new title. I considered pursuing legal action but ultimately decided not to for several reasons, including my ongoing employment with the company and the lengthy litigation process. I told my boss that I was confident they would listen to me, not because I am a woman, but because I am a lawyer. In this situation, you face challenges on multiple levels—being Black is already difficult, and it's even harder being a woman! I handle work that a new lawyer could manage, and they praise the quality; I often wonder, "What did you expect?"

The widespread belief that women don't need equal pay because men are seen as heads of households is a structural misconception that sustains salary disparities. Gender pay gaps can be startling, as shown in Chapter 2, where a female lawyer found that she was earning less than a male clerk in her office who didn't have a law degree. Similar findings about pay gaps led two pioneering women judges in Kenya to advocate for equal pay for women in the Kenyan judiciary. For many women, including most of those interviewed for this research, there was no clear evidence to show whether they were underpaid compared to their male colleagues. Overall, they believed they were likely earning less because of the cases they were assigned and gender stereotypes about women's work.

8. Professional Stagnation and Attrition

A study by the ABA Commission on the Status of Women in the Profession found that women at various levels in the legal field leave law firms for different reasons.

For senior women, reasons for leaving included high work stress, long hours, constant pressure to increase billable hours, and balancing caregiving responsibilities (Chanow & Sterling, 2021). In contrast, women in lower to middle ranks reported career stagnation, often saying that their skills were underutilized, receiving little recognition for their contributions, facing long and unpredictable hours, and frequently feeling underpaid (Chanow & Sterling, 2021).

While attrition from law firms occurs within the African context, there is a lack of accessible data on the percentage of women leaving law firms or the legal profession as a whole. Evidence collected for this project shows that the stagnation of women in middle- to lower-level positions at law firms is a significant issue due to slower promotion rates. A more detailed analysis could categorize attrition into horizontal and vertical types. Horizontal attrition occurs when women leave their positions at a law firm to start their own practices, join a corporate entity, or transition to the judiciary. In contrast, vertical attrition refers to situations where women leave a law firm to seek promotions to higher roles at another law firm, a corporate entity, the judiciary, or other regional or international organizations. The reasons why some women choose to make these transitions stem from various structural and positional factors that are not always generalizable.

In the IAWL report on *Making the Move from the Bar to Diplomacy* (Institute for African Women in Law, 2023d), women lawyers appointed as ambassadors highlighted their diverse professional experiences in both legal and nonlegal fields as essential qualifications that made them competitive candidates for diplomatic roles. In the report *Making the Move from Academia to the Bench* (Institute for African Women in Law, 2023c), participants shared their personal interests in joining the bench and applying the knowledge and skills they gained as researchers on gender gaps in the law. A common theme among these women in their individual and collective decisions to switch from one career to another was the importance of being well-prepared and highly qualified before applying for a new position.

Changing careers can be challenging. Some women shared the difficulties that led them to leave the legal profession. During my fieldwork, I met several women who were well-established in their careers; some had husbands who were also professionals, and their families were upper-middle class. Most of these women employed housekeepers, drivers, and other support staff at home and work. However, a common theme they expressed was a desire to do more for their children. A managing partner at a law firm with three children under seven years old discussed her ongoing struggle with conflicted feelings about her career compared to her caregiving roles:

> I have been seriously considering quitting my law practice to stay home and watch the kids grow up. Even though I come home exhausted from work, I still need to fulfill my duties as a mother, like checking their homework and supervising the household to make sure everything is done properly. Some days, I feel guilty about leaving them, and other days, I am too tired to worry. It's taking a toll on me, and I have lost a lot of weight.

During my fieldwork, several women expressed similar views to this managing partner: regardless of their children's ages, they still felt guilty about not doing enough for them. Even those who strongly believed they prioritized their family over their work discovered that balancing the competing demands of their professional and personal lives was an ongoing source of tension for them and, at times, for their partners.

The masculinized nature of legal practice, as mentioned earlier, indicates that women and feminine qualities are still not fully accepted in litigation. Women involved in litigation often feel pressured to adopt masculine traits, such as raising their voices or displaying masculine behaviors, to earn respect. Unfortunately, leaving the legal field is not an option for everyone due to various factors that limit their mobility. Many continue through these challenges, sometimes experiencing negative effects on their physical health, mental well-being, and social lives. Women have become adept at developing strategies and coping mechanisms, which are explored in detail in Chapter 7.

9. Intergenerational Differences

The generational classification discussed in Chapter 1 shows that many second-generation women in law remain active today. Changes in the legal profession and standards of conduct suggest that earlier generations of women may find it hard to relate to younger women lawyers. This shift in practices goes beyond women alone. Leaders of regulatory organizations, such as legal practitioners' councils, have expressed concerns about declining standards within the profession. For many women lawyers, newcomers often lack awareness of the lives and struggles of pioneering women who paved the way. That's why I dedicated Chapter 2 to exploring these women's lives and contributions to the law. Some lawyers recognize and value the victories of earlier generations of women lawyers, which now allow them to work with more freedom and inclusivity than previous groups.

Intergenerational differences among women lawyers can create tensions that impact mentorship opportunities. In several interviews, the older generation of women lawyers felt that their younger colleagues were not serious or committed enough to succeed, while younger women saw the older generation as harsh and unsupportive. As one lawyer in Nigeria noted, "Most of the women at the top come from affluent families, so they cannot even relate to what you are talking about." The term "affluent" describes women from families with a history of lawyers, which may have given them easier access to the profession. Although these intergenerational differences also happen among men, there appears to be less tension in their interactions and support. Women in law must address these tensions to promote friendliness and meaningful mentorship. A critical mass of women cannot become influential if they are divided, and real progress cannot happen without solidarity among the different generations of women in law.

VII. Conclusion

Women lawyers have made notable progress since pioneering women entered the bar in England, France, and Portugal. Findings in this chapter show that the number of women lawyers and their variety of specializations are growing. As discussed here, gender integration and diversity in the legal profession across different countries are producing positive results, despite enduring and emerging challenges. This chapter also illustrates how women's presence in the legal field challenges traditional sociocultural gender norms and improves access to justice for both male and female litigants. The qualitative and quantitative data presented here emphasize the ongoing impact of patriarchal institutional practices and sociocultural norms that hinder women's full integration into a profession that was once predominantly male.

The findings from this chapter confirm the interaction of historical, institutional, and social factors affecting women in law. The HISP framework highlights and contextualizes the similarities and differences in the experiences of African women within the legal profession. By adopting an antiessentialist approach, the rich empirical narratives in this chapter represent only a small portion of the range of experiences of women in law across the continent. Despite the challenges, women in law are making significant contributions to the legal field, and further research is needed to understand the ongoing developments within specific countries, regions, and the private and public sectors.

5

Women on the Bench: The Second Frontier

I. Introduction

Since Stella Jane Marke Thomas of Nigeria was appointed in 1943 as the first female magistrate in West Africa, there has been steady progress in the number of women joining and leading judiciaries across the continent (Dawuni & Kang, 2015). This remarkable growth in the number of women judges in domestic courts is reflected internationally, as more women continue to serve as judges in international courts and tribunals (Dawuni & Kuenyehia, 2018).

Compared to women in the bar and legal academy, the literature on women in African judiciaries is more developed, with many scholars addressing this topic in recent years. These developments include four edited volumes by this author, featuring contributions from various writers covering countries as diverse as Ethiopia, Botswana, Rwanda, Uganda, Kenya, Benin, and Cameroon, among others (Bauer & Dawuni, 2016; Dawuni, 2021d, 2022a, 2025; Dawuni & Kuenyehia, 2018). Following the general trend in this book, this chapter offers a comprehensive overview of the representation, contributions, and challenges faced by women judges across selected regions of the continent. Based on the detailed methodology outlined in Chapter 2, this chapter draws on primary interviews with 64 women judges in seven countries, responses from a survey of 79 judges throughout the continent, and extensive reports on women in law and leadership in the Nigerian, Senegalese, Kenyan, and South African judiciaries conducted by the Institute for African Women in Law (2023a).

Applying the HISP (history, institutions, social systems, and position) framework, this chapter discusses how the historical foundations of the judicial profession shaped the development and functioning of judicial institutions across various jurisdictions on the continent. It also examines the interactive impact of these institutional practices, social norms, and cultural expectations on women's roles within the legal system. Grounded in the three main theoretical frameworks guiding this book—matri-legal feminism, intersectionality, and postcolonial theories—the chapter analyzes the structure and evolving demographics of judiciaries. It explores how the intersection of institutional and social factors influences women's representation, contributions, and challenges within these systems. The chapter is divided into five parts. After this introduction, section II offers an overview of different judicial structures and examines pathways women take to join the judiciary. Section III discusses trends and patterns in women's representation as judges. Section IV highlights women's contributions as judges, while section V addresses ongoing challenges they face. Following the method of maintaining respondent anonymity used in this book, no interviewee is identified by name. Some references to countries or court types may be included to provide context, but in other cases, such details are omitted to prevent identification.

African Women in Law. J. Jarpa Dawuni, Oxford University Press. © Oxford University Press 2026.
DOI: 10.1093/9780197795095.003.0005

II. Judicial Structure and Selection Methods

The structure, functions, and makeup of judiciaries differ across and within legal systems. As noted earlier, African legal systems are known for their pluralism, allowing multiple legal frameworks to coexist, including a blend of African customary laws, imported colonial legal traditions, and Islamic law. In systems with legal pluralism, courts can be divided into customary courts—those that apply customary law—and statutory courts—those that apply either civil or common law. In countries with significant Muslim populations, such as Nigeria, Senegal, Mali, and Tanzania, Islamic or Sharia law may also be enforced through specialized courts called Cadi or Khadi courts (Pimentel, 2011; Ubink, 2011).

In this chapter, while acknowledging the importance of customary courts, I focus on statutory courts as defined by the two main legal traditions—the civil law and common law. The continental civil law was primarily exported from France to its African colonies. Another branch of the civil-law tradition is seen in former Portuguese colonies, such as Angola, Cape Verde, and Mozambique. The second legal system is the common law, which originates from the British legal system. There are clear differences between these leading legal systems that influence the court hierarchy and structure, as well as the recruitment, appointment, benefits, promotion, and termination of judicial officers (Escobar-Lemmon et al., 2021). For example, some judicial systems, such as Ghana and South Africa, use a dual-stream approach where judicial officers are classified as either magistrates (lower courts) or judges (higher courts). These structural features can affect who becomes a judicial officer and their standing within the judicial hierarchy (Schultz & Shaw, 2013). In both civil- and common-law traditions, courts may be organized as tribunals, lower or higher courts, courts of first instance, intermediate or high courts, courts of appeal, or courts of final instance (such as a supreme court or constitutional court), along with various combinations in between (Abel & Lewis, 1988, 1989).

Judicial systems evolve, and the type of judicial system, selection methods, number of courts, and the powers and functions of these courts are closely connected to historical, political, institutional, sociocultural, economic, and other situational factors (Oloka-Onyango, 2017). In this chapter, I use the term "judge" to refer to all judicial officers—both magistrates and judges who were interviewed for this project. Although their institutional powers and functions differ, the experiences shared are not very different, as gender remains a constant and connecting variable among their lived experiences. The next section provides a broad overview of different judicial selections primarily in civil- and common-law systems. While this discussion cannot cover all countries across the continent, it aims to offer some specifics in a few countries.

1. Civil Law Selection Methods

In civil-law countries, judiciaries are viewed as part of the bureaucratic structure of public administration. The pathways to become a judge are more streamlined and are considered based on highly meritocratic standards for hiring and promotion (Kenney, 2013b; Mackenzie et al., 2010; Schultz & Shaw, 2013). In this system, judicial selection usually involves a written competitive exam, an interview, and training or apprenticeship before being assigned to a court (Schultz & Shaw, 2013). Judicial officers in civil-law countries perform various roles in the administration of justice and may be called by different titles, including magistrates (*magistrats*) or prosecutors (*procureure/procurer*). Magistrates handle most judicial work in the courtroom, while prosecuting judges carry out investigative functions of cases. Depending on the court's rank within the judicial system, a judicial officer may be called a judge, a title reserved for those serving on higher courts (Schultz & Shaw, 2013).

Scholars have observed that the merit-based selection process in civil-law systems promotes higher representation of women judges in countries like France, Portugal, Spain, Argentina, and Italy (Boeigol, 2013; Cohen, 2018; Schultz & Shaw, 2013). Merit-based exams allow women to succeed, helping to reduce discrimination at the entry level. Although women have a stronger presence on the benches of these countries, this does not result in equal representation across all levels of the judiciary. The percentage of women decreases as one moves up the judicial hierarchy, with fewer women in higher courts and leadership roles, creating a bottom-heavy pyramid (Schultz & Shaw, 2013).

Why do women outperform men in merit selection processes but appear to stall in their advancement within the judicial hierarchy? In a comparative analysis of gender diversification within the judiciaries of civil-law countries, Schultz and Shaw (2013) identify a trend where the diversification of civil-law benches has led to a loss of male judges and a decline in the judiciary's prestige. They also note that as men leave for more lucrative and prestigious roles, women are left to handle tasks previously performed by men, albeit with lower pay. Building on the gender queue theory proposed by Reskin and Roos (1990), several feminist commentators emphasize that the male exodus from judiciaries is a significant trend that reduces the courts' prestige. Consequently, although opportunities for women to join the judiciary are increasing, institutional practices remain patriarchal, and benefits and resources may be shrinking (Cohen, 2018; Ellett, 2022; Masengu, 2021; Schultz & Shaw, 2013; Uzebu-Imarhiagbe, 2020b).

In line with the common practice of the civil-law tradition, civil-law countries in Africa generally appoint judges through competitive exams. The old belief that the legal profession was solely a man's domain has shifted to recognize that women can also serve as judges. During my fieldwork in Senegal and the Ivory Coast in 2016 and 2018, officials at judicial training schools noted a rise in the number of women graduating from these programs. They observed that women consistently scored higher and ranked at the top of their classes. My interview findings suggest these changes result from improved opportunities for women to attend universities, supported by government investments in basic education, the influence of women's rights organizations advocating for women's and girls' rights, and the role model effect, where younger women are choosing careers over the social expectation of early marriage. If these trends continue, there is strong potential for increased female representation in the judiciaries across Francophone African countries.

Despite opportunities for women to join the judiciary through merit-based selection methods, Senegal presents a striking paradox: As of 2023, women accounted for less than 14% of the judiciary. While the country has a quota law for women's representation in the national assembly, this has not resulted in increased women's representation in other areas of public life, including the judiciary Institute or African Women in Law, 2023o). In 1965, Marie Jose Crespin became the first woman judge appointed during the early post-independence era. Following her lead, other women entered the judiciary, with some rising to prominent positions such as president of the Supreme Court (Andresia Vaz), president of the Constitutional Court (Mireille Niang), and the first woman Minister of Justice, who later became Prime Minister (Mame Madior Boye). Despite the notable achievements of some women judges in Senegal, the overall number remains low. In African countries and beyond, the civil-law judiciary attracts women because of its standardized working hours, transparent salary scales based on rank, and various employee benefits, including maternal care and family leave. These factors will be explored in detail when discussing demographic shifts and reasons why women choose to pursue careers in the judiciary. Future studies on the impact of civil law selection methods in Lusophone African countries will offer an interesting comparative framework.

2. Common Law Selection Methods

As outlined in Chapter 3, although only a few women qualified as lawyers and magistrates in the first and second generations of the profession, I argue that what sets African systems apart from Western ones is that the judicial appointment processes used by African governments were based on the principles of matri-legal feminism—the recognition of women's roles in leadership and development (Dawuni, 2019). These early leaders recognized women's contributions to communal and national progress; as a result, women who qualified for magisterial and judicial roles were not discriminated against in favor of men (Uzebu-Imarhiagbe, 2020b).

Common-law systems, by contrast, use various methods for selecting judges. Countries such as Ghana, Nigeria, Kenya, and Sierra Leone have made significant progress in increasing women's representation in their courts compared to England and Wales, from which they inherited key parts of their legal systems. The British judiciary, which follows the common-law system, has remained mostly male-dominated because of traditional judicial selection practices linked to the "tap on the shoulder" phenomenon—a process that allowed men to maintain judicial appointments within a male-centered "old boys' network" (Malleson, 2003; Rackley, 2013; Sommerlad, 2013).

After gaining independence from colonial rule, the establishment of law schools across Africa improved women's access to legal education. Most post-independence governments revised their methods for selecting judges, creating new opportunities for women aspiring to join the judiciary. These revisions involved drafting new constitutions that outlined the judicial selection processes (Andrews, 2021), forming judicial selection bodies or commissions (Kamau, 2013; Masengu, 2021), and, in some cases, implementing competitive examinations (Dawuni & Masengu, 2019).

Judicial selection methods vary among common-law countries in Africa. The processes for appointing judges may be detailed in constitutional documents, legislative acts, or various rules and principles that oversee the administration of justice. In some countries, passing an entrance exam might be required, and nearly all of them may conduct a selection interview. For higher courts, methods can include nomination by the president, confirmation by the legislature, and input from the bar association or other civil society groups. Although these methods are often described in written documents, there is still potential for external interference, including influence from the executive branch, as seen in authoritarian governments (Gathii, 1994; Ghai & Ghai, 2014; Karekwaivanane, 2015; Prempeh, 2007). For instance, when the executive is responsible for nominating candidates, the likelihood of bias within male networks can lead to a preference for selecting men over women (Andrews, 2021; Masengu, 2016).

Some countries have made changes to ensure that judicial selection processes are transparent and inclusive of various genders. Many common-law countries, such as Kenya and South Africa, have implemented public hearings organized by the Judicial Services Commission (JSC), the primary body responsible for interviewing judicial candidates. Over the past decade, judicial appointment commissions have been established in jurisdictions across Africa, including but not limited to Nigeria, Kenya, Zambia, and South Africa. However, evidence from these JSCs indicates that these selectors' composition and demographic makeup can influence the selection outcomes. JSCs serve as major gatekeepers to judicial selection results, and the diversity of the selectors should be considered a critical factor in the legitimacy of judicial selection methods and processes (Aura-Odhiambo, 2018; Dawuni & Masengu, 2019; Masengu, 2016).

JSCs can, however, be a double-edged sword. While they are embraced as mechanisms to increase transparency in judicial appointments, they have also been used against women in some cases. In Kenya, Kamau (2013) describes how female judicial candidates faced intrusive and irrelevant personal questions during their interviews, and Andrews (2021) documented similar experiences that female candidates in South Africa encountered. Masengu (2016) observed that in the South African context, judicial hearings have not always been fair to certain women, and in some cases, the nomination of unprepared female candidates led to negative outcomes, reinforcing gender stereotypes about women's abilities as judges.

Last, besides the role of JSCs, the pool from which judicial candidates are chosen is also important. In some common-law countries, judges may be appointed to higher courts from among legal practitioners in the bar or legal academia. In South Africa, the split profession (advocates and attorneys) allows practicing advocates to be appointed as acting judges or full judges. Historically, women have been underrepresented among advocates, and the number of minority women is even smaller. As a result, the pipeline from the bar to the bench has mainly favored men (Andrews, 2021; Masengu, 2020).

Overall, there is no strong evidence that one type of judicial selection process results in more women judges than another (Kenney, 2013b). The timing of appointing the first female magistrate or judge in a country does not seem to significantly explain the number of women judges in that country, nor does it clarify when a woman might be appointed as a leader of the judiciary (Dawuni & Kang, 2015). Other factors may influence judicial appointment outcomes. For instance, Valdini and Shortell (2018) suggest that open or public processes, rather than closed or "sheltered" ones, might affect whether selection bodies consider gender and racial factors. The number and diversity of selectors (Dawuni & Masengu, 2019), the pool of applicants (Gill, 2012), and the differences between formal and informal processes (Escobar-Lemmon et al., 2021) can all influence the success of women candidates.

3. Impact of Institutional Changes

Since the appointment of the first women judges and magistrates, some African countries have seen significant growth in women's representation, while others have lagged behind. Several proposals have been proposed, and policy measures have been put in place to address the gender gap on the bench. Implementing quotas or affirmative action policies to increase the number of women judges has been suggested as a quick way to bring more women into the judiciary (Murungi & Meroka-Mutua, 2022 1). However, most judges I interviewed opposed quotas as a means of improving women's representation. This view was particularly strong among judges from three civil-law countries: Cape Verde, the Ivory Coast, and Senegal. These respondents believe that the current underrepresentation of women stems from historical trends in judicial representation. They also pointed out that expanding educational opportunities for women and reducing barriers to pursuing judicial careers could help increase the number of women on the bench. Collectively, these judges highlighted the importance of keeping merit-based appointments for judicial roles. They noted that women tend to do well on written exams. Therefore, solutions should focus on strengthening the pipeline of women interested in judicial careers. One judge in the Ivory Coast described the judiciary as a "prestigious profession" and argued that women should be hired based on merit rather than a quota system.

The debate over implementing and enforcing institutional mechanisms for appointing women judges remains a contentious issue. Affirmative action policies have been credited with increasing the number of women judges in some jurisdictions. Several feminist legal scholars (Albethyn & Bonthuys, 2016; Andrews, 2021; Cowan, 2013; Masengu, 2016) attribute South Africa's transformative postapartheid constitution to the expanded opportunities for women's rights and access to public office. The proportion of women judges surged from 1.2% in 1994 to 35% in 2016, while the percentage of Black judges grew significantly from 1.8% to 64% during the same period.

Rwanda exemplifies a nation where the 30% constitutional gender quota for women's representation in the legislature and public offices has positively influenced the increase in the number of women judges. At its peak, the Supreme Court had 50% women in 2012, which slightly dropped to 41% in 2014 before rising again to 50% (Kamatali, 2016). In Kenya, constitutional affirmative action policies have transformed institutional norms and enhanced the recruitment of women in the public sphere, including the judiciary. The introduction of the 2010 Constitution, which stipulates that the same gender can occupy no more than two-thirds of public offices, has had a favorable impact on the recruitment of women judicial officers (Aura-Odhiambo, 2018; Kamau, 2013). By 2024, women comprised over 50% of the judiciary in Kenya, culminating in the historic election of Martha Koome as the first female chief justice in 2021.

Constitutional quotas are not a magic fix for increasing the number of women judges. Such constitutional or legislative quotas do not accurately predict how many women will actually be appointed as judges. Even though Senegal has a transformative provision for 30% women's representation in the national assembly, this gender equality framework has not yet led to equal representation for women on the bench. By the end of 2023, women made up only 14% of judges in Senegal, highlighting the complex social, religious, and cultural factors that influence women's roles in society, often resulting in less favorable outcomes for women's representation in the judiciary (Institute for African Women in Law, 2023o).

In conclusion, applying the HISP framework highlights the roles of three factors—historical, institutional, and social—in the ongoing debate about selection methods. First, the historical factor reflects a country's legal tradition. In civil-law countries, research shows that women have achieved judicial success partly because merit-based entry exams offer better opportunities for women (Gill, 2012; Schultz & Shaw, 2013). However, this trend does not seem to apply in Francophone countries, where women remain underrepresented in the judiciaries of Senegal, Benin, and the Ivory Coast due to historical barriers that restrict educational opportunities and prevent women from pursuing higher education (Institute for African Women in Law, 2023o).

Second, the institutional variable has a strong predictive effect, as several countries have changed their judicial selection methods. Kenya, Tanzania, Zambia, Nigeria, and hybrid nations like Botswana and South Africa use different judicial selection commissions. Other institutional mechanisms in common-law countries often involve the bar association (or law society), parliamentary vetting for higher judicial positions, and nominations by the executive branch. At various points in the appointment process, different gatekeepers may limit opportunities for achieving gender diversity if these gatekeeping bodies lack gender balance. The executive's role is crucial and may hinge on whether presidents choose to nominate women to gain political advantage both domestically and internationally or if they genuinely support gender diversity and equality (Dawuni & Masengu, 2019).

Third, the predictive influence of social variables is connected to societal perceptions of gender roles and expectations. Social expectations influence women's career choices regarding their participation in the judiciary. In both civil- and common-law countries, women still see the judiciary as a career that effectively fits their personal and professional responsibilities. Standardized working hours in civil- and common-law judiciaries enable women to balance their caseloads and domestic duties with fewer interruptions than they would face in active legal practice. Conversely, socio-religious beliefs about women's roles have led to restrictions on their ability to serve as judges in religious Sharia/Khadi courts in some countries (Ibrahim, 2016; Yoon, 2016). With more women being called to the bar, the pool of candidates for judicial positions is likely to keep growing. It is still unclear whether the gender diversification of the judiciary will cause men to leave and, if so, whether that will reduce the prestige of judicial roles, as seen in other European countries. The current demographic situation of women will be key for guiding future comparative analyses of changes in judiciaries across the continent.

III. Women's Representation: Trends and Patterns

This section explores the patterns and trends identified from interviews and the survey. To demonstrate the interactive effect of the HISP model, it thoroughly analyzes survey data to explain (1) demographic diversity among judges, (2) women's numerical representation, (3) diversity in career choices, (4) representation across judicial ranks, (5) representation in various types of courts, (6) women in leadership roles, and (7) women in international courts and tribunals.

1. Demographic Diversity

The increase in opportunities for women to join the judiciary has led to significant demographic shifts. Using the survey results as a baseline, the diversity in marital status, age, and family status highlights the demographic variety among women judges, as shown in **Table 5.1 and Table 5.2.**

While this study recognizes different forms of diversity, including ethnicity, (dis) ability, sexuality, and religion, the survey did not explore these intersectional issues. Some of these identity topics were discussed during interviews and are analyzed in the following sections.

Table 5.1 *Marital Status of Respondents*

Marital status	Percentage
Married	25.3%
Married with children	31.6%
Divorced	17.7%
Single	12.7%
Widow	6.3%

Note. Survey respondents: 79.

Table 5.2 *Age of Respondents*

Age range	Percentage
20–24	0%
25–30	1.3%
31–40	20.3%
41–50	29.1%
Above 50	49.4%

Note. Survey respondents: 79.

2. Diversity in Career Choices

A significant trend in women's representation is the diversity in demographic factors such as age, marital status, and educational qualifications. Lacking a historical baseline for comparison, this study will serve as a vital foundation for future research aimed at evaluating growth and shifts in patterns. Of the 79 judges surveyed for this research, 60.8% identified as judges, while 25.3% identified as magistrates. The survey also asked respondents to share their reasons for choosing a judicial career. As shown in **Figure 5.1**, the majority (65.8%) stated that joining the judiciary was a personal choice. In comparison, 15.2% were inspired by role models (pioneer woman in law), reinforcing the discussion in Chapter 3 about the influence of role models on women's career choices.

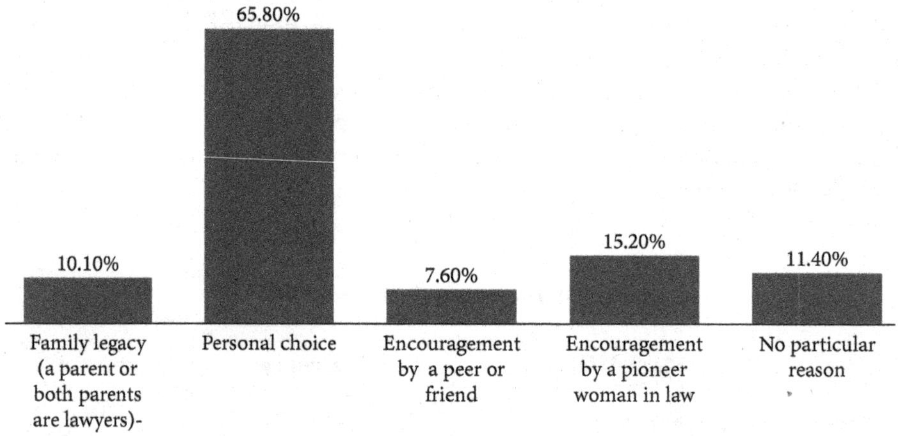

Figure 5.1 *Women's Motivations for Joining the Judiciary*
Source: Survey respondents: 79.

Another notable demographic shift is the growing number of women judges pursuing higher education beyond the bench. **Table 5.3** shows the changing demographic trends, indicating that women judges are increasingly seeking advanced educational opportunities.

Table 5.3 *Graduate Degrees and Educational Qualifications*

Degree	Number	Percentage
Doctorate	7	8.9%
Master of Arts (MA)	6	7.6%
Master of Laws (LLM)	39	49%

Note. Survey respondents: 79

3. Changing Numbers

A significant aspect of the decolonization and independence movements was the establishment of higher education institutions that created new opportunities for women. Chapter 2 examined the effects of decolonization efforts in Africa during the early 1950s to 1960s, which led to new forms of democratic governance (Ghai & Ghai, 2014; Oloka-Onyango, 2017; Prempeh, 2007). Decolonization resulted in increased higher education opportunities, including legal training. Several pioneering women judges and magistrates across the continent were among the first generation of women to pursue legal education and later join the judiciary in the post-independence era.

The second, third, and fourth generations of women judges emerged from the gradual gender diversification of legal education, which influenced the number of women lawyers and judges in various African countries. The lack of accessible data on annual graduation rates from law schools complicates accurate analysis of these ongoing increases. Emerging research in several African countries suggests that the rate of women graduating from law schools may be surpassing the 30% threshold in countries such as Ethiopia (Addadzi-Koom & Gage, 2022), Ghana (Dawuni, 2016a), Cape Verde (Duarte, 2022), Malawi (Ellett, 2022), Zambia (Masengu, 2021), Uganda (Ndagire, 2022), and Nigeria (Uzebu-Imiarhagbe, 2020b). Before discussing the changes in the number of women, **Table 5.4** presents data on the first women judges or magistrates and the years they were appointed to the bench. The year of each country's independence offers context for examining how historical factors—namely, colonial rule- influenced women's access to education, in line with the generational categorizations established in Chapter 1.

In some countries, the late entry of women into the legal professions and the judiciary slowed the number of women obtaining judicial positions. In The Gambia, the delayed indigenization of the bench due to the appointment of expert judges from Commonwealth countries slowed opportunities for Gambian women to join the judiciary (Nabaneh, 2023). Despite the first law faculty being established as late as 2007, women have made significant progress in securing judicial roles. By 2022, women accounted for 53% of superior court judges and 71% of magistrates in lower courts.

The expansion of educational opportunities, investment in girls' education, and women doing well in interviews for judicial positions were all cited by respondents as reasons for the increasing gender diversity in the Gambian judiciary (Nabaneh, 2023). Similar to other West African contexts, improvements in the working conditions for public officials, such as better pay and benefits, housing, and car allowances, seem to attract women to judicial careers (Dawuni, 2016a). The Gambian situation could also reflect what occurs in judiciaries experiencing "male flight"—a phenomenon where men leave the judiciary to pursue more lucrative roles as lawyers in private practice (Ellett, 2022; Masengu, 2021; Uzebu-Imiarghabe, 2020b).

In Cape Verde, despite Vera Duarte being appointed as the first woman judge in 1977, it was not until 2002 that the first law school on the island of Mindelo was established. Until then, all legal professionals in the country were educated in Portugal. In 2015, Fatima Coronel was appointed as the country's first woman chief justice. Like many other African countries, women in Cape Verde have played important roles in both public and private development and were central to the anticolonial movements

Table 5.4 *First Women Judges and Magistrates*

Country	First female magistrate/judge	Year appointed	Year of independence
Nigeria	Stella Marke Thomas	1943	1960
Ghana	Ruth Annie Jiagge	1954	1957
Benin	Elisabeth Kayissan Ekoué Pognon	1965	1960
Sudan	Ihsan Mohamed Fakhri	1965	1956
Senegal	Marie José Crespin	1965	1960
Gabon	Rose Francine Rogombé	1967	1960
Mauritius	Laure Pillay	1967	1968
Democratic Republic of the Congo	Guizela Malanda	1968	1960
South Africa	Leonora van den Heever (Lucy Mailula)	1969	1910
Sierra Leone	Agnes Macaulay	1970	1961
Uganda	Laeticia Kikonyogo	1971	1962
Liberia	Emma Shannon Walser	1971	1847
Kenya	Effie Owuor	1971	1963
Congo, Republic of the	Agathe Pembellot	1973	1960
Tanzania	Julie Manning	1973	1961
Cabo Verde	Vera Duarte	1977	1975
Djibouti	Khadija Abeba	1977	1977
Ethiopia	Atsedeweine Tekle	1978	N/A
Niger	Fatimata Bazeye Salifou	1979	1960
Zambia	Florence Mumba	1980	1964
Zimbabwe	Kelello Justina Mafoso-Guni	1980	1980
Chad	Ngonyam Béradinfar	1983	1960
Seychelles	Matilda Twomey	1987	1976
Malawi	Anastasia Msosa	1993	1964
The Gambia	Mary Maam Yassin Sey	1998	1965
Botswana	Unity Dow	1998	1966
Eswatini	Qinisile Mabuza	2005	1968
Mauritania	Amamah Bint Cheikh Sidya	2013	1960
Togo	Biyémi Brigitte Brym-Kekeh	N/A	1960
Central African Republic (CAR)	Thérèse Dejean	N/A	1960
Sao Tome and Principe	Alice Vera Cruz	N/A	1975
Mozambique	Gita Honwana Welch	N/A	1975
Namibia	Karen Goldblatt Marshall	N/A	1990
Cote d'Ivoire	Mazohin Marguerite	N/A	1960
Lesotho	Kelello Justina Mafoso-Guni	N/A	1966

Note. The data presented in the table were collected from multiple sources, including online sources, articles, and books. When the date could not be verified after multiple source checks, it is left as N/A. Some of the women were first appointed as magistrates, then became judges, while others may have been appointed as judges.

Table 5.5 *Women's Representation in the Judiciaries of Selected Countries in 2023*

Country	Female %	Total female	Total judges
Burkina Faso	18%	130	707
Sierra Leone	22%	18	82
*Nigeria	25%	45	179
Morocco	28%	860	3032
*Ethiopia	30%	120	402
Mozambique	39%	163	416
Algeria	47%	2698	5,711
Kenya	51%	322	627
Lesotho	58%	80	137
Zimbabwe	58%	183	314
TOTAL	***40%***	***4,619***	***11,607***

Source: United Nations Development Program (2024).

*Ethiopia and Nigeria are federal systems and the data for these two countries focus only on the federal courts. These numbers could change drastically when the courts within the states/regions are included.

toward independence (Duarte, 2022). Several judges I interviewed credited traditional public roles women hold as a key factor enabling them to occupy administrative and judicial positions. The civil-law model of competitive entry examinations also explains the success women have had in joining the judiciary in Cape Verde.

Compared to other jurisdictions globally, and notwithstanding women's late entry into the judiciary across Africa, there is evidence of an increasing representation of women in some countries while others lag. **Table 5.5** presents available data on women in selected countries where data were available.

The data presented in the tables above illustrate the diversity of women's representation across various countries on the continent. The number of countries included and the years for which data are available reflect the challenges of data accessibility discussed in Chapter One.

4. Representation in Judicial Ranks

The judicial structure (lower vs. higher courts) and court jurisdiction (civil, criminal, or administrative) may also influence the ranking of women within the judiciary. Women have made significant progress at all levels of courts in most African countries examined in this book. In many cases, African women judges have advanced through court hierarchies more quickly than their counterparts in the colonial metropole. As expected, there is no single or universal pattern in the distribution of women across judicial systems in Africa. A wide variety exists; in some judiciaries, women have successfully reached the highest positions, while others show a greater presence of women at the lower levels. As more women join the judiciary, their representation in higher courts will grow (Dawuni, 2020).

Despite Stella Marke Thomas's appointment as Nigeria's first female magistrate in 1943, making her the first woman in the British-colonized territories of West Africa, women judges accounted for only 25% of all judicial officers at the federal high courts by the end of 2021, up from 18.8% reported in 2016 by Ibrahim. The number of women judges varies significantly across the country's 36 states. In 2016, women made up 60% of judicial officers in Lagos State alone, while their representation in northern territories remained low. Despite the limited presence of women judges in Nigeria, Justice Mariam Mukhtar from the northern region was appointed as the first female chief justice in 2008, breaking gender and ethnic barriers. After Justice Mukhtar's appointment, two other women have served as presidents of the Federal Court of Appeal. In 2014, Justice Zainab Bulkachuwa from Gombe State became the first woman appointed as president of the Federal Court of Appeal. Justice Bulkachuwa was succeeded by Justice Monica Dongban-Mensem in 2020. In 2024, history repeated itself when Justice Tokunbo Kekere-Ekun was appointed Nigeria's second female chief justice. Despite these incremental successes, in other courts, such as the Sharia Court of Appeal and certain state courts, no women had been appointed as judges by 2016 due to religious restrictions on women holding such positions.

Ghana is another West African country where women broke judicial barriers early, starting with Annie Jiagge's appointment in 1951 as a magistrate and later to the court of appeal in 1969, which was the highest court at that time. Women have made significant progress in joining the judiciary, but the numbers have not reached parity. Since Georgina Theodora Wood was appointed in 2007 as the first female chief justice, two other women have led the judiciary. Sophia Akuffo was appointed in 2017, and Gertrude Torkornoo assumed office in 2023. In 2016, women made up 38% of judges on Ghana's Supreme Court. Although that number dropped to 23% in 2018, it increased again to 27% after three more women judges were appointed to the 15-member bench (Dawuni, 2020).

In civil-law countries like Benin, Kang (2016) reported that women made up 28.6% of the constitutional court and 15.4% of the high court as of 2014. By the end of 2014, women accounted for 39% of judges in Rwanda, with 41% representation on the Supreme Court (Kamatali, 2016). In 2004, Aloysie Cyanzayire became Rwanda's first female chief justice, and in 2019, Marie Thérèse Mukamulisa was appointed as the first female deputy chief justice. In Tanzania, despite the presence of a significant number of female judges in the courts, no woman had been appointed to the highest office of chief justice by 2024 (Masabo, 2021; Yoon, 2016). In 1998, Unity Dow made history by becoming the first woman appointed to the Botswana High Court. By 2016, Botswana still had a low percentage of women in the superior courts, with less than 17% representation (Bauer & Ellett, 2016). Although this number has increased significantly, and women are well represented in the lower courts, they continue to struggle to reach the higher courts.

In Uganda, Ndagire (2022) documented women's achievements as judicial officers, with 44% representation across all courts. Women have also held leadership roles in criminal, civil, commercial, and family court divisions, but not as chief judges. Despite these promising figures, Uganda has yet to appoint its first female chief justice. At this time, only one woman—Laeticia Kikonyogo—has ever been appointed deputy chief justice (Ndagire, 2022). Lesotho, Kenya, Zambia, and Zimbabwe have successfully achieved, and even surpassed, gender parity, while in other countries like Malawi, women still face gender-based stereotypes about their suitability and qualifications for higher judicial roles (Ellett, 2022). Women's access to judicial positions, especially in higher courts, continues to be a contentious issue. As Masengu (2021) argues, the prevailing perception is that the increased number of women judges has led to a decline in the perceived prestige of the judiciary (Masengu, 2021).

Overall, the data shown above indicate that women are represented at all levels of the judicial hierarchy, although they are more common in lower courts than in higher courts in some countries. In countries that have exceeded the 50% mark (Kenya, Zambia, Zimbabwe), women are found in similarly high numbers in the higher courts. The data suggest a strong correlation between high female representation on the bench and the rise of female leaders. In other words, female judicial leadership aligns with the overall presence of women in the judiciary.

5. Different Jurisdictions

Women judges are sufficiently represented across various courts with different subject matter jurisdictions. Some courts require specialized training or expertise, and based on the data previously presented regarding postgraduate qualifications, women judges have the necessary academic credentials to hold judicial positions. Generally, religious or Islamic courts have historically excluded women judges due to the common belief that women should not preside over men (Ibrahim, 2016). In countries with large Muslim populations, such as Senegal, The Gambia, Nigeria, and Tanzania, women are often not permitted to serve as judges in religious courts (Khadi) (Ibrahim, 2016; Yoon, 2016). However, these restrictions are gradually easing, with countries like The Gambia now permitting women to serve as judges in Khadi courts (Bah, 2022).

Courts with specific jurisdiction over family matters tend to be staffed with a higher proportion of women than men, and these courts are generally lower courts within the judicial hierarchy. Determining whether this trend is driven by need or the stereotypical "ghettoization" of women into certain courts is challenging. However, interview respondents highlighted the persistence of negative and inaccurate assumptions along with gender biases, suggesting that these courts handle "softer" cases and that women are viewed as more capable of managing such "soft or pink" cases. This stereotype must be challenged, as addressing divorce and other child-related issues is not a "soft" task. The debate over whether women are better suited to handle these cases due to the belief that they possess a different ethic of care has been explored by various scholars (Addadzi-Koom & Nkansah, 2021; Baines, 2013; Gayoye, 2021; Hunter, 2008; Schultz & Shaw, 2013).

Most courts that handle family law issues operate at the circuit and magistrate levels, where there is also a significant number of female judicial officers. These lower courts greatly influence the rights of women and children in family matters. However, in common-law countries, these courts do not establish judicial precedents. It is at the higher court level that the experience gained in family matters can significantly affect precedent-setting cases in common-law nations. Women judges with this expertise from years in lower courts may have the greatest influence if they move up to higher courts (Mensa-Bonsu & Mensa-Bonsu, 2021).

As judiciaries expand their roles and establish specialized courts to address specific issues, qualified women may be appointed to these courts. In common-law countries, choosing judges from the bar and legal academia has proven to be an important way to diversify judicial expertise. In Ghana, I interviewed a high court judge appointed from the bar who had practiced law in commercial cases and authored a book on commercial law in Ghana. In Kenya, in 2023, both the High Court on Environmental Law and the Industrial Court were led by women appointed based on their expertise in the subject (Murungi & Meroka-Mutua, 2022).

The demographic trends described in this section show that the increases in women's representation in various surveyed judiciaries are praiseworthy; however, more efforts are needed to maintain this progress and eliminate ongoing gender biases. Countries with lower representation can learn from those with over 30% female representation. These countries often establish institutional mechanisms that support open and transparent selection processes and adopt constitutional and legislative policies for equal representation, such as quotas. Additional methods include confronting persistent biases about women's abilities, improving working conditions for all judicial staff, and addressing issues of sexual harassment and bullying by senior judicial officials.

6. Women in Leadership

Given that 2023 marked 80 years since the appointment of the first female magistrate—Stella Marke Thomas in West Africa—women have made significant strides in entering the judiciary and, more importantly, advancing to leadership positions within it. The matri-legal feminist framework emphasizes the value that African systems place on educated women, along with traditional beliefs and practices that support women in leadership roles. In many countries across the continent, women have secured prominent judicial positions such as chief justices and presidents of constitutional courts (Dawuni & Kang, 2015). These advances occurred before similar progress was achieved in Great Britain. For example, in Great Britain, Elizabeth Lane was appointed to the High Court in 1965, and Elizabeth Butler-Sloss became the first female "Lord Justice" in 1988 with her appointment to the Court of Appeal. Both appointments in Great Britain came years after Justice Annie Jiagge of Ghana, who was appointed to the High Court in 1951 and to the Court of Appeal in 1969 (Dawuni, 2012). In 2004, Dame Brenda Hale became the first woman appointed to the Appellate Division of the House of Lords (First Hundred Years, n.d.). It was only in 2024 that Justice Carr, Baroness of Walton-on-the-Hill, was appointed as the first female chief justice of the United Kingdom.

In a previous study, Dawuni and Kang (2015) concluded that the strongest predictors of when women are appointed as heads of judiciaries include the selection methods, the nature of the legal system, and the influence of regional trends. Recent research has also shown that women's appointments to top courts are affected by informal processes, such as judicial networks, presidential advisors, and opportunities to serve as acting judges (Escobar-Lemmon et al., 2021). **Table 5.6** presents data on women who have held the top positions in African judiciaries.

Table 5.6 *Women Leaders in African Judiciaries (Chief Justices and Presidents of Constitutional Courts)*

Name	Country	Title	Years
Nigeria	Kudirat Motonmori Olatokunbo Kekere-Ekun	Chief Justice	2024–
South Africa	Mandisa Muriel Lindelwa Maya	Chief Justice	2024–
Ghana	Gertrude Araba Esaaba Sackey Torkornoo	Chief Justice	2023–
Liberia	Sie-A-Nyene Gyapay Yuoh	Chief Justice	2022–
Kenya	Martha Koome	Chief Justice	2021–
Mauritius	Rehana Bbi	Chief Justice	2021–
Cote D'Ivoire	Chantal Camara	President, Cassation Court	2019–
Mozambique	Lúcia da Luz Ribeiro	President, Constitutional Court	2019–
Sudan	Nemat Abdullah Khair	Chief Justice	2019–
Ethiopia	Meaza Ashenafi	President, Federal Supreme Court	2018–
Central African Republic	Danièle Darlan	President, Constitutional Court	2017–
Ghana	Sophia Akuffo	Chief Justice	2017–2019
Zambia	Hildah Chibomba	President, Constitutional Court	2016–
Cabo Verde	Maria de Fátima Coronel	President, Supreme Court	2015–2020
Zambia	Irene Mambilima	Chief Justice	2015–2021
Mali	Manassa Danioko	President, Constitutional Court	2015–2020
Seychelles	Mathilda Twomey	Chief Justice	2015–2020
Lesotho	Nthomeng Majara	Chief Justice	2014–2018
Niger	Kadidiatou Abdoulaye Ly Diori	President, Constitutional Court	2013–
Malawi	Anastasia Msosa	Chief Justice	2013–2015
The Gambia	Mabel Agyemang	Chief Justice	2013–2014
Nigeria	Aloma Mariam Mukhtar	Chief Justice	2012–2014
Sierra Leone	Umu Hawa Tejan–Jalloh	Chief Justice	2008–2015
Ghana	Georgina Wood	Chief Justice	2007–2017
Burundi	Christine Nzeyimana	President, Constitutional Court	2007–2013
Niger	Salifou Fatimata Bazeye	President, Constitutional Court	2007–2009
Mali	Kaïta Kayentao Diallo	President, Supreme Court	2006–2011
Rwanda	Aloysie Cyanzayire	Chief Justice	2004–2014
Guinea-Bissau	Maria Monteiro	President Supreme Court	2004–2012
Senegal	Mireille Ndiaye	Constitutional Court President	2004–2010
Benin	Conceptia Ouinsou	President, Constitutional Court	1998–2008
Liberia	Gloria Musu-Scott	Chief Justice	1997–2003
Liberia	Frances Johnson-Morris	Chief Justice	1996–1997
Benin	Elisabeth Pognon	President, Constitutional Court	1993–1998
Gabon	Marie Mborantsuo	Chief Justice	1991–2001; 2005–Present

Source: Women Chief Justices: wwww.africanwomeninlaw.com/chief-justices

The growing number of women in top judicial leadership roles within African judiciaries has led some analysts to suggest these are merely symbolic appointments. From an African postcolonial feminist perspective, this study warns against simplistic interpretations that undermine African women's leadership, often using explanations that ignore their agency and the respect for women's leadership in their communities. Using the matri-legal feminist framework and previous discussions about the pre-colonial to postcolonial context in Chapters 2 and 3, this study emphasizes African women's long history of agency and leadership as the basis for current judicial leadership. When appointments are based on merit rather than political patronage, African women can reach top positions.

Dawuni and Kang (2015) observed that in several common-law countries, the process of selecting the chief justice follows a tradition known as the "seniority principle," which favors nominating the most senior sitting judge. However, this principle has not always been consistently followed by presidents. In Ghana, Justice Joyce Bamford Addo was appointed to the Supreme Court in 1991. Despite being the longest-serving judge, she was overlooked when President Rawlings nominated another candidate for confirmation by the legislature. In Uganda, Ndagire (2022) emphasized the influence of political interference in judicial appointments, noting that the president often prefers candidates who align with his political beliefs.

In 2022, Justice Mandisa Maya was appointed as South Africa's first female deputy chief justice. Before this, she broke the judicial barrier by becoming the first woman to serve as president of the Supreme Court of Appeal in 2017. While Maya's appointment was historic, some commentators believed she was passed over in favor of a male candidate. The JSC, which handled the public interviews, recommended her for the role; however, the president chose to appoint a male candidate without explaining why the JSC's recommendation was ignored. Ultimately, after Chief Justice Zondo's retirement in 2024, Justice Maya was appointed as South Africa's first female chief justice, highlighting how judicial appointments to top leadership roles can be influenced by political decisions beyond women's control, even if they are more qualified (Dawuni & Kang, 2015).

To determine whether women's ascent to judicial leadership is common across the judicial ranks and not just limited to top positions, this study asked respondents if women have equal leadership opportunities as men. In **Figure 5.2**, 57% reported

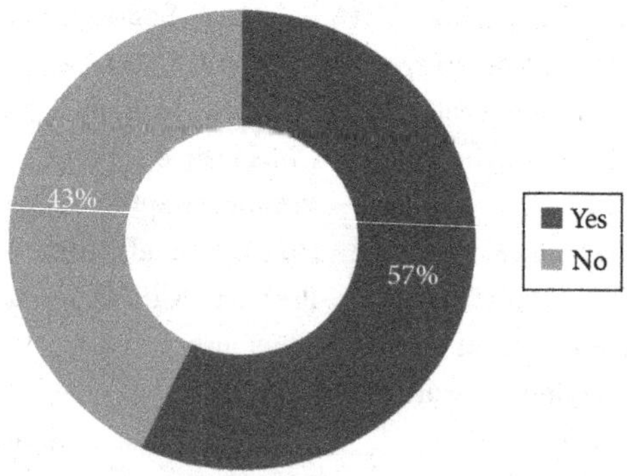

Figure 5.2 *Women in Judicial Leadership Positions*
Source: Survey respondents: 79.

holding a leadership role. This response is significant and indicates that women occupy leadership positions at various levels.

To further explore whether women in leadership are common, the survey asked respondents if women have the same opportunities for leadership as men. The responses in **Figure 5.3** showed that while only 6.3% strongly agreed, 46.8% agreed, bringing the total close to those who reported holding leadership positions. However, 22.8% remained neutral, neither agreeing nor disagreeing, indicating a significant number who either lacked knowledge about leadership roles or felt ambivalent about leadership.

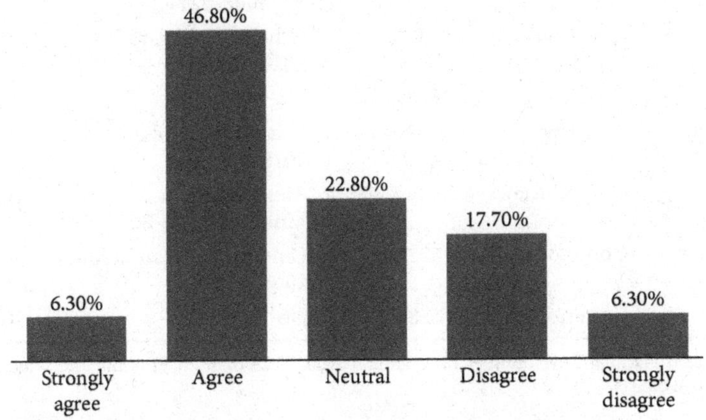

Figure 5.3 *Women's Perspectives on Equal Opportunities for Leadership*
Source: Survey respondents: 79.

To better understand whether there is a correlation between increased representation of women and women leading the court, **Table 5.7** shows data on women in leadership as a proportion of women judges. The findings do not indicate a strong link between numbers and leadership. For example, while several countries with women representing 30% or more have had a woman leader (Ethiopia, Kenya, Lesotho, Mozambique), some countries with less than 30% representation have also had a woman leader (Nigeria and Sierra Leone). More research is needed to explore the relationship between numbers and leadership.

The previous discussion in this section demonstrates that women have made progress in civil, common, and hybrid legal traditions across Africa. Despite their later entry into the judiciary and the challenges posed by judicial selection methods, political will, and balancing professional and personal responsibilities, Africa leads the world in the number of women appointed to top judicial positions, as shown in **Table 5.6.** While this is encouraging, female judges and judicial leaders still face various obstacles, including media portrayal and threats to their authority (Escobar-Lemmon et al., 2016). A detailed analysis of the challenges women judges face will be provided later in this chapter, highlighting the barriers women encounter in the judiciary, especially in leadership roles across the judicial system.

Table 5.7 *Women in Leadership as a Proportion of Women Judges*

Country	Main legal tradition	% of women judges	Woman chief justice/president of constitutional court	Year data collected
Algeria	Civil law	47.2	No	2023
Burkina Faso	Civil law	18%	No	2023
*Ethiopia	Civil law	30%	Meaza Ashenafi, 2018–2023	2023
Kenya	Common law	51%	Martha Karambu Koome, 2021–	2023
Lesotho	Civil law/ Common law	58%	Nthomeng Majara 2014–2019	2023
Morocco	Civil law	28%	No	2023
Mozambique	Civil law	39%	Lucia da Luz Ribeiro 2019–	2023
*Nigeria	Common law	25%	Aloma Mariam Mukhtar, 2012–2014	2023
Sierra Leone	Common law	22%	Umu Hawa Tejan-Jalloh, 2008–2015	2023
Zimbabwe	Common law	58%	No	2023

Source: Uniteed Nations Development Programme, 2024. *The data on Ethiopia and Nigeria represent only the federal courts.

7. Women in Regional and International Courts

International law remains a field where women continue to face obstacles in gaining entry, whether as legal officers, arbitrators, judges, or registrars (Baetens, 2021). Antiessentialist perspectives on women in international courts and tribunals require examining the intracategorical differences among women judges serving on international benches. My research in this area has used a postcolonial feminist lens to explore the distinct pathways and experiences of women from the African continent. In *International Courts and the African Woman Judge: Unveiled Narratives* (Dawuni & Kuenyehia, 2018), we highlighted the importance of recognizing the lived experiences of African women as crucial for understanding how they reached the courts (descriptive and symbolic representation), their experiences as Black or African women judges, and their contributions to international law and jurisprudence (substantive representation).

The rise in the number of women judges in several African countries is creating a ripple effect on the representation of African women in international courts and tribunals (Dawuni, 2018b). These changes are genuine, as research indicates that international benches remain highly competitive, with powerful nations able to leverage their influence to benefit their own candidates (Baetens, 2021). Against this backdrop of global politics, women across Africa are making strides in securing seats on these international courts. Due to the processes for nominating and electing international judges at both the national and international levels, men have generally had an advantage because of their political networks, which give them better access to information and nominators (Baetens, 2021, Mumba, 2018).

The process of selecting members for these courts has been clarified through the stories of women who have reached them. Political networks are crucial as a first step in understanding judicial roles.

However, not all women get support from their governments, nor do they have the political connections needed for nomination in the first place. Grossman (2018, p. 45) recounts the experience of Uganda's first African woman, Judge Julia Sebutinde, as she navigated her path to the International Court of Justice (ICJ) and reflected on whether she would be a suitable addition to a bench that has, for over 70 years, been mainly occupied by white male judges:

> They were typical elderly, white men mostly, probably set in their ways because of their age. You are crazy, I thought to myself if you think that they are ever going to accept you as an equal. Where are you even going to start? Do you really think there is a place for you on this bench? I was thinking, even if I was lucky enough to sit on that bench, would they even listen to me? Would I have anything of value to say to any of them? Many unnerving thoughts went through my head as I contemplated submitting my candidature.

Despite a tough campaign and little support from her home government, Judge Sebutinde was elected to the ICJ, becoming the first African woman to serve on that court. In 2020, she was reelected for her second and final term. She continued to make history when, in 2024, she was elected vice president of the court, further cementing her legacy as the first woman from the continent to hold this position.

The domestic nomination of qualified candidates is a crucial first step for any international bench, and aligning a candidate's qualifications with the nominating body can influence the outcome (Grossman, 2012). As one of three women appointed to the International Criminal Court (ICC) bench in 2003, Akua Kuenyehia from Ghana received support from the women's networks she was part of due to her years of activism as an international women's rights advocate. She recalls that, although Ghana's Minister of Justice initially approached her to be nominated for the ICC position, she declined, citing her lack of interest in pursuing an international role. As the process unfolded, she received encouragement from fellow women's rights advocates. She recounts, "*[T]here had been a Gender Conference here in Accra, and friends of mine who had come from Kenya told me they were lobbying the Ghana government to nominate me—I told them I was not interested in any UN work*" (Dawuni, 2018a, p. 64). Ultimately, Akua Kuenyehia was nominated and elected among the initial set of six judges in the first ballot for the 18 judges on the court.

Alongside the political networks necessary for securing an international judicial position, women's organizations, advocates, and networks can play a vital role in the domestic nomination process. Kelello Mafoso-Guni of Lesotho had a highly contentious journey to the African Court on Human and Peoples' Rights, which also highlighted the essential role of women's organizations in supporting judicial appointments for women (Ellett, 2018). Similarly, Esther Nwanwuri-Thompson's

Table 5.8 *African Women on Selected International Courts and Tribunals (2023)*

Court	Total # of judges on the court	African female judges	African male judges
African Court on Human and Peoples' Rights	11	5 (45%)	6 (55%)
*COMESA Court of Justice	12	5 (42%)	7 (58%)
**ECOWAS Court of Justice	5	1 (20%)	4 (80%)
East African Court of Justice	11	1 (8%)	11 (92%)
Mechanism for International Criminal Tribunals (Africa Group)	25	5 (50%	5 (50%)
International Criminal Court (Africa Group)	15	3 (75%)	1 (25%)
International Court of Justice (Africa Group)	18	1 (33%)	2 (67%)

Source: African women in international courts: https://www.africanwomeninlaw.com/international-court-judges

* COMESA—Common Market of Eastern and Southern Africa.

**ECOWAS—Economic Community of West African States

appointment to the same court emphasizes the significant impact of networks in the nomination process (Badejogbin, 2018).

African women judges are also represented on specialized courts, including the International Criminal Tribunal for the former Yugoslavia (ICTY), the International Criminal Tribunal for Rwanda (ICTR), the Specialized Court for Sierra Leone (SCSL), and the Mechanism for International Criminal Tribunals (MICT). Despite the growing diversity in women's representation, all the courts reviewed in the 2024 Gender Scorecard of the Institute for African Women in Law reveal that women remain significantly underrepresented in some courts. **Table 5.8** shows women's representation on selected courts as of the end of 2024.

Some courts, such as the ICJ, are still working to address the underrepresentation of women. In Africa, the East African Court of Justice (EACJ) has historically had a low number of women since it was founded. While the ECOWAS Court once reached 40%, the current rate of 20% in 2023 shows fluctuations in women's judicial representation and gender-diverse benches. Continued advocacy, training, and development of women are crucial for maintaining progress in these courts. Although women's representation on these benches has varied, many women have also held leadership roles, as shown in **Table 5.9**.

Women judges from Africa have made significant contributions to international law and reshaped norms surrounding important human rights issues, as outlined in *International Courts and the African Woman Judge: Unveiled Narratives* (Dawuni & Kuenyehia, 2018). The first generation of female international court judges started with Navi Pillay from South Africa being appointed to the International Criminal

Table 5.9 *African Women Leaders in Selected International Courts and Tribunals*

Court	Name	Leadership role	Years in leadership
African Court on Human and Peoples' Rights	Sophia Akuffo (2006–2014)	Vice President- President	2008–2012) 2012–2014
	Else Nwanwuri-Thompson (2010–2016)	Vice President	2014–2016
	Imani Daud Aboud (2018–	President	2021–2023 2023–2025
ECOWAS Court of Justice East African Court of Justice	Hansine N. Donli (2001–2009)	President	2001–2007
	Amina Mallé Sanogo (2009–2014)	President	2007–2009
	Maria Do Ceu Silva Monteiro (2014–2018)	President	2014 –2016
East African Court of Justice	Anita Mugeni (2021–	Vice President	2023–
	Sauda Mjasiri (2019–2023	Vice President	2022–2023
	Stella Arach Amoko (2006–2014)	Deputy Principal Judge	2008–2013
	Monica Kalyegira Mugenyi (2013–2020)	Principal Judge	2015–2020
International Criminal Court	Akua Kuenyehia (2003–2015)	First Vice President of the Court	(2003–2009)
	Sanji Monageng (2009–2018)	First Vice President of the Court	(2012–2015)
	Fatoumata Dembele Diarra (2003–2014)	First Vice President,	2009–2012
	Joyce Aluoch (2009–2018)	First Vice President of the Court	(2015–
	Reine Alapini-Gansou (2018–	Second Vice-President,	2024–
International Court of Justice	Julia Sebutinde	Vice President	2024–
International Criminal Tribunal for Rwanda	Navi Pillay (1995–2003)	President,	1995–2003
International Criminal Tribunal for the Former Yugoslavia	Florence Mumba (1997–2003)	Vice President	1999–2001

Source: African Women in Law, International Judges, available at https://www.africanwomeninlaw.com/international-court-judges

Tribunal for Rwanda in 1995, followed by Florence Mumba from Zambia joining the ICTY in 1997. This pioneering group also included Andresia Vaz from Senegal, who was appointed to the International Criminal Tribunal for Rwanda in 2001, as well as Akua Kuenyehia from Ghana and Navi Pillay from South Africa, both among the founding judges of the ICC in 2003. Even after their retirement from the international bench, these judges remain actively involved in judicial training, mentoring, and advocating for women's rights.

IV. Contributions

Significant developments indicate shifts in the symbolic and substantive representation of women in the judiciary. Through their presence, women judges are reshaping gender norms and expectations both on and off the bench. Women judges make meaningful contributions to the law, justice, and women's rights. In this section, the chapter shifts to a discussion of women's roles as judges. This discussion is not intended to evaluate their contributions relative to those of their male counterparts, nor to analyze the differences women judges make, although some of these differences may be apparent. Using thematic analysis and comparisons both within and across cases, this section builds on the analytical methodology outlined in Chapter 2 and employs feminist reflexivity (Stanley & Wise, 1993) to highlight the voices and experiences of the interviewees.

A purely quantitative analysis of the number of women judges in any judiciary provides only part of the picture. A more comprehensive examination of their experiences as judges is essential to understanding what the numbers represent both on and off the bench. In the next section, I engage with existing debates surrounding women judges, using an intersectional framework to highlight the diverse experiences of women as individuals, judges, mothers, wives, and other visible and less visible identities and categories. Employing an intersectional perspective also reinforces McCall's (2005) emphasis on recognizing the intracategorical differences among women as a group.

Drawing from interview data, I categorize women's experiences and conduct situational analyses of how their self-reported experiences, both on and off the bench, create patterns of collective influence and contributions. This observation does not suggest that all women's experiences are the same. However, by clarifying the similarities and differences, it becomes clear where a woman's experience in a specific region of a country or continent may align with or diverge from those of women in other countries or regions. The discussions also highlight women's experiences at various levels within judicial hierarchies and how their positions within the power structure may influence their judicial processes both on and off the bench. Intersectional experiences of women within the court hierarchy (lower courts compared to higher courts), geographical location (urban vs. rural courts), and years of service (years served on the bench) are a few examples that shape one's positionality and experiences. These intersectional identities should be evident to the reader through the analyses of the upcoming interviews.

1. Jurisprudential Contributions

The primary role of a judge in any legal system is to resolve disputes between parties. In common-law countries, a judge's role as an arbiter in deciding cases based on precedent (*stare decisis*) emphasizes the importance of developing jurisprudence, especially in higher courts. Is there a link between the number of women judges and the types of cases and judgments issued by courts? Will more women judges result in more gender-sensitive rulings? These questions have been central to much of the literature on gender and judging, as discussed in Chapter 3 (Alberthyn & Bonthuys, 2016; Cowan, 2013; Kamau, 2013; Kenney, 2013; Schultz & Shaw, 2013; Sommerlad, 2013).

A review of recent scholarship on gender and judging in the African context highlights important legal developments concerning the work of women judges (Gayoye, 2021; Mensa-Bonsu & Mensa-Bonsu, 2021; Mocumie, 2022). Evidence from my interviews with judges shows mixed opinions on whether judges are making a difference in women's rights issues. Some judges quickly stated that they do not consider gender or other factors when making their rulings. For this group, the role of a judicial officer is to act as an impartial umpire in a court of law. Conversely, some judges have indicated that they need to be aware of societal norms and their influence on the cases they hear. In a previous discussion of women judges in Ghana, I distinguished between *gender aware* and *non-gender aware* judges (Dawuni, 2016a). While *gender aware* judges are not necessarily "feminist judges," as Hunter (2008) describes, they are still attentive to women's rights and often use laws that protect these rights as tools for enforcement.

Several studies have examined whether female judges support women's rights. In Kenya, Gayoye (20212) finds that female judges play important roles in enforcing the constitutionally protected property rights of women. In a review of cases related to affirmative action and the registration of children's births, Aura-Odhiambo (2018) emphasizes the role of female judges in promoting the women's rights outlined in the 2010 Constitution of Kenya and international agreements such as the United Nations Convention on the Elimination of All Forms of Discrimination Against Women (CEDAW).

In a study analyzing rape and abortion cases in Rwanda, Kamatali (2016) found insufficient evidence to support the claim that women judges are advocating for women's rights in these cases. Evidence from South Africa is mixed. Albertyn and Bonthuys (2016) found no convincing evidence that the judicial decisions of women judges were advancing women's rights across South Africa. In an earlier study on women judges in South Africa, Cowan (2013) concluded that, whether the cases were gender-coded, the perspectives of women judges—either through their gender-inclusive judging styles or their advocacy for women's rights—were crucial in shaping the jurisprudence of the courts, especially through their dissenting opinions.

Several cases support the argument that male and female judges have worked together to improve women's customary rights in Botswana (Bauer & Ellett, 2016), women's access to property after divorce in Ghana (Mensa-Bonsu & Mensa-Bonsu, 2021), women's rights to maternal and reproductive health in Uganda (Kyobiika, 2021; Ndagire, 2022), general questions about gender minority rights in Namibia

(Kariseb, 2022), and women's constitutional rights to equality in Benin (Kang, 2016). Overall, several of these cases have direct or indirect impacts on women's rights. A systematic review of case law, both within and across countries, will be essential to improving our understanding of whether and how women judges contribute to diversifying jurisprudence and expanding access to justice for women and minority rights issues.

2. Gender-Sensitive Judging or Applying a Feminine Gaze in the Courtroom

Among the key issues in the global scholarship on gender and judging, as discussed in Chapter 3, is whether women judges can be considered feminists (Baines, 2013; Kohen, 2013). While some judges shy away from the label of "feminist judges," others see it as a responsibility to advocate for justice for women. The previous discussion emphasized the importance of feminist jurisprudence in promoting gender-sensitive law. However, what precisely constitutes gender-sensitive judging and how judges should apply it remains a subject of debate, especially given the judge's role as a neutral arbiter in the courtroom. The evolution of legal philosophy and the progress of rights and justice have traditionally reflected the male perspective and lived experience.

Although the fight for women's rights through feminist legal scholarship has made some progress over time, many parts of the law still reflect masculine ideologies that support gendered power hierarchies. These hierarchies exist in the courtroom—a space that is often seen as neutral where laws are tested against evidence to make a judgment. Pioneering women faced deeply rooted masculine structures and hierarchies in the three legal areas discussed in this book. The historical overview of the African legal professions in Chapters 2 and 3 offers important background and context for understanding how the law, the legal and judicial systems, and their institutions were built. Such historical insights are crucial for showing how women judges can work to break down existing gendered power hierarchies.

During my fieldwork, I asked interviewees whether it was the judge's role to change socially constructed norms that influence the rights of women litigants. Some judges who supported women's rights believed it was their responsibility to use the law as a tool to address gender inequities in society, aiming to balance the scales of justice. A judge in Nigeria noted that the social aspects of a judge's life play an integral role in how the law is applied in a courtroom.

> Everything we do centers around the law, but when a woman is presiding, we are, above all, human, and we cannot detach ourselves from our humanity. Most of the time, when people come to court, they just want to win their cases, but a woman judge considers the human perspective and asks questions like, "*What happens when you go back home?*" You are all part of a larger community, and the woman judge may engage with the parties—which I know some men often lack the patience for. The woman judge will strive to resolve the matter so that when the litigants return home, there is peace.

This judge not only addressed the gender aspects of how she and other women may handle gender sensitivities but also the cultural dimensions by citing a Yoruba proverb: "You cannot come to court and go home as friends." This proverb highlights the importance of keeping the community united as a traditional principle and is often central for women who have trained as arbitrators. A court of appeal judge in Cape Verde, who does not identify as a gender activist, nonetheless made significant observations in her review of cases that come on appeal. She describes the variety of cases she hears and how she employs different approaches depending on the situation. For example, in cases where a child victim cannot speak openly in court to avoid being retraumatized, women judges handle these cases differently by using strategies to make the courtroom more welcoming, thus preventing the child from facing the aggressor directly. In cases involving teenagers, defendants may try to stigmatize females by blaming them, and sometimes, some male judges lose focus by asking the victim, "Do you have a boyfriend?" or "How many boyfriends do you have?" She concludes:

> As judges, we must distinguish truth from falsehood. Additionally, there are times when we need to rely on our feminine sensibilities and intuition, which men may not always have. Handling some of these cases isn't easy; for example, people often ask how I manage murder and violent sex crimes. However, with time, it becomes easier, and fear fades.

Some interview respondents believe that women judges consider the practical application of the law to find solutions that promote cohesiveness and the welfare of the parties involved, especially in cases involving children. A high court judge in Ghana noted that it is a judge's responsibility to assess the practicality of the social, economic, and situational context when making decisions. In these situations, when a judge faces issues related to children, some women judges may apply the welfare principle to ensure that the children's welfare takes precedence in deciding which parent should retain custody.

Other judges believe that it is not a judge's role to display their gender sensitivities in the courtroom. In this context, a high court judge in Ghana, who is also a women's rights advocate, emphasizes the law over gender advocacy while on the bench.

> I don't believe gender matters in my role as a judge. When I write my judgments, my main focus is to ensure accuracy; emotions do not influence my decisions, and if they do, it's minimal. If the law supports you, then you face no obstacle. We are individuals, and we have women's rights advocates on the bench, which will have an effect. But for me and others who focus solely on the facts, as long as we handle all cases efficiently, justice can be achieved. For example, in a rape case, why should it take so long to hear a case and deliver a judgment when it doesn't promote justice? Ultimately, a quick decision serves justice to the woman, not necessarily because of any gender issues involved. As a judge, I uphold my oath. Once the law is on your side, why hesitate? To avoid any allegations of corruption or bias, I stick strictly to the law and remove any chance for anyone to claim I am corrupt or biased.

In common-law countries, where precedents strongly influence decision-making, having a solid precedent to support a case is essential. Another judge in Ghana believed that women do not decide cases differently from men.

> I started in the commercial and land court, so I didn't hear many issues related to gender. I only handled one criminal case where the defendant beat his ex-wife to death and received a 35-year sentence; they lost on appeal. The gender of the plaintiff didn't influence me, but I had to consider the two children they had. I believe women judges bring a more compassionate perspective to their judgments.

Some judges believe they should not bring personal idiosyncrasies to the bench; instead, justice must be administered according to the law and the judicial oath of allegiance. While women may better understand the gendered aspects of a case, it is not appropriate judicial practice to favor a woman unless the facts and evidence support her position. Judges are cautious about the influence they exert in a case to avoid accusations of bias, a concern that may be more pronounced in common-law countries, where judges often serve as arbiters, than in civil-law tradition, where judges are more actively involved in the case through investigative questioning (Cohen, 2018; Schultz & Shaw, 2013).

A judge in Cape Verde was emphatic on the need to divorce personal beliefs from the bench:

> I do not consider gender when judging; all judges—men and women—are dedicated to upholding rights and striving for justice. We all wear the same robe, so gender doesn't matter; it's about promoting fairness. I still don't view issues through a gender lens because when a judge presides, they must follow established rules. Regardless of gender, if rules are broken, the case is subject to appeal. Judges have a duty to evaluate cases based on evidence, and their perceptions are shaped by personal experience. Everyone is influenced by their environment, and judges are no exception. When presiding, judges must not reveal personal beliefs; they must stay objective. That's why there are strict legal guidelines for judges. I believe a judge should be unbiased; I trust in their integrity, and they must judge fairly.

Several judges believe they cannot promote women's rights because they feel unable to enforce their decisions. Although the Constitution and other laws may guarantee equality under the law, most judges I interviewed did not identify as feminists or prefer the label of activist judges. However, some adopted strategies could be seen as feminist or activist. One judge described her approach as *judicial creativity*, a process in which a judge uses available legal tools and laws to advocate for women's rights in cases that could significantly change gender norms related to issues such as land and property. A Supreme Court judge in Ghana shared her experience with judicial creativity.

> Rights are not granted by legal documents; judges simply affirm them. All judges are expected to make a difference, but if some fail, it becomes crucial for women lawyers and women judges to step up because when you witness wrongdoing, you must

> acknowledge it. When the law appears to endorse wrongful actions, it's important to analyze it critically and consider whether there is room for judicial creativity. One should never feel embarrassed or ashamed to do what is right; instead, a problem occurs when unjust favoritism is shown. However, regarding fairness in divorce settlements, I would prefer to enhance what a woman deserves because, after examining the equities, it becomes clear that she often contributes more than the man, even if her contributions are usually intangible.

The previous discussion reinforces the antiessentialist argument—that women are different, as are women judges. Women's lived experiences greatly influence their contributions on the bench. These responses also show what the judges have done or believe they would do in various situations. While some may champion women's rights, others feel it is not their duty to defend them; nonetheless, their decision-making approach might unintentionally support this cause. Is it the role or expectation that women judges must solely bear the burden of changing gender norms? All judges need to be aware of the negative social norms and practices that impact women's rights. Another judge noted that a strict, formal application of the law does not stop a judge from referring women for counseling and alternative dispute resolution to encourage family or community harmony. Because women judges are often accused of bias and lack of impartiality in cases involving women and children, they tend to be more conscious of such accusations and may act more cautiously, as some narratives suggest.

3. Changing Institutional Norms and Gendered Perceptions

Demographic shifts in the number of women joining judiciaries are impacting traditional gender norms and practices within these systems and influencing societal views of women's roles as judges. Worldwide, women have entered judiciaries that were historically based on masculine expectations and needs (Kenney, 2013a; Schultz & Shaw, 2003). Besides institutional norms and practices that prioritize a male work ethic, the court infrastructure was not built with women judges in mind. Effie Owuor, the first woman to join the bench in Kenya, had to request a special accommodation for a bathroom because the only restroom in the courthouse was designated for male judges (Institute for African Women in Law Legacy Project, n.d.-e).

Another evolving norm is how judiciaries have adopted inclusive language when referring to women. In Kenya, as in many other parts of the common-law system, phrases like "My Lord" or "Lord Justice" are traditionally used to address male judges. Judiciaries have had to distinguish between male and female judges, leading to the introduction of terms like "My Lady" or "Lady Justice" for women. Women's early interactions with masculine judicial systems have changed over time. As the number of women judges increases, social norms and expectations are slowly shifting, though not consistently or uniformly. For example, in Nigeria, women judges are still addressed as "My Lord." By accepting these labels, are women judges themselves complicit in maintaining gender norms? Should women judges adopt masculine titles and traits to be seen as equals to men? The contrast between Kenya and Nigeria highlights how institutional and social factors within the HISP framework influence this process—specifically, that institutional practices and norms develop gradually and are heavily influenced by various factors.

The gendered impacts of historical colonial gender segregation policies, patriarchal norms, and sociocultural gender expectations continue to be challenged as more women earn law degrees and join the judiciary. Sociocultural and historical factors significantly influence how women judges are perceived and accepted by society. A second-generation woman judge in the Ivory Coast shared her experience of navigating male-dominated structures and highlighted the importance of women speaking out against gendered treatment.

> I initially started my career as a prosecutor and later became a judge. Back then, there were so many men in the field that when litigants came to court, they called me "Mr." I had to correct them, explaining that I was a woman. They responded that they knew I was a woman, but because I was doing the work of men, they called me "Mr." out of respect.

A judge in Cape Verde narrates her experience:

> Some defendants still come to court and show less respect for the female judge. In one case, I noticed that the defendant responded respectfully to the male prosecutor by saying, "Yes, sir," but when he spoke to me, he addressed me as if I were his peer. These subtle behaviors may go unnoticed, yet they reveal certain perceptions of gendered respect. When I observe such actions, I address them directly and assert, "I am the judge here; I am in command." When they do the same to female attorneys, I emphasize the importance of respecting women and everyone involved. You might hear people label a woman judge as "mean," a term often used as a code for being skilled at her job and not allowing lawyers and litigants to manipulate her courtroom.

Women must continuously navigate and challenge gendered power hierarchies to function equally and effectively in their judicial roles. Female judges have found innovative ways to manage their courtrooms, setting the tone for litigants and attorneys alike. When asked if women judges are changing institutional norms and perceptions, a High Court Judge in Ghana responded:

> It all depends on how you manage your courtroom. If you're firm, they will take you seriously; therefore, your gender does not come into play, and they won't try to undermine you. For instance, you must be punctual, avoid adjournments, and refuse bribes. You'll need to run your court effectively to maintain control, establish your ground rules, and ensure they are respected.

The influence of cultural shifts on women's representation in public life affects how much women can bring about change in institutions (Chappell, 2006). As more women serve as judges, societal norms about women's abilities are evolving, leading many to believe that if men can do something, women can too. In some societies, there is a view that women judges are less likely to accept bribes compared to their male counterparts (Cardinal, 2013). This perception fosters respect and caution in how lawyers and litigants interact with women on the bench. Societal views of women's respectability relative to their male colleagues, along with litigants' opinions of their competence, fairness, and integrity, warrant further research.

4. Caseload Management and Court Administration

Hearing and resolving disputes in court is not the only role most judges fulfill. Several administrative duties accompany the cases assigned to them throughout the process. In nearly all the jurisdictions where I conducted my fieldwork, judges described a substantial administrative workload involved in managing their caseloads and collaborating with court clerks to ensure that files remain intact and that all evidence presented by lawyers is available and properly filed. Across all jurisdictions where I conducted interviews, judges reported lacking administrative support or law clerks to assist with research and other administrative tasks. As a result, judges must efficiently manage their caseloads and courtrooms to keep the court running smoothly. In various audits of judiciaries, judges have consistently cited the lack of administrative support as a major challenge that affects the efficiency and timeliness of courtroom management. This challenge is not exclusive to women judges. The interviews aimed to clarify how my respondents handle the added complexities of judicial and administrative duties alongside their home commitments. A judge in Nigeria shared her experiences and insights on managing cases in her courtroom as a woman judge. While she acknowledged that women excel at balancing these responsibilities, she also suggested that this could serve as a strategy for women to counter negative perceptions of inefficiency or incompetence.

> When I practiced law, I noticed that most female judges completed cases more quickly than their male counterparts, and they became my role models. I'm not saying this just because I am a woman. Many people still believe in a man's world, which leads some women to feel the need to prove that we can do it better. In terms of case assessments, we find that women achieve higher success rates.

A senior judge in Nigeria was wary of generalizations suggesting that women managed their courtrooms better. She believed that while some women excelled, others did not, and she cautioned against "making sweeping statements . . . you can see the hardworking ones and the lazy ones, and the litigants and lawyers know them."

Another judge in Nigeria felt that her age and experience provided stronger explanations for how she managed her courtroom and cases than her gender.

> I don't believe my gender determines how I work. When I arrived on the bench with the broad experience I brought, I was able to manage my court. I am usually the one in control of the courtroom. The lawyers may try to test the waters, but once they see that I know what I'm doing, they stop challenging me.

A court of appeal judge in Ghana emphasized the importance of a judge maintaining control over their courtroom while also alluding to the feminine qualities that judges can contribute to the courtroom.

> Court management involves more than just how a judge handles her cases; it also requires creating a supportive environment, especially for witnesses who may feel intimidated. For some witnesses, I offer water at my own expense to help calm them down. To keep the case moving, I also provide light refreshments to the lawyers.

Women judges find that in performing their duties, they must balance societal perceptions with legal demands to accomplish their work effectively. Perceptions of thoroughness and fairness can also be influenced by gender. For example, a male judge might be described as "tough" for managing his courtroom with authority, whereas a female judge could be labeled as "mean" for similar actions. These gendered descriptions stem from the different sociocultural expectations placed on women and men in society. A court of appeal judge in Cape Verde summed it up this way:

> Sometimes, society claims that women judges are tougher and more resolute. In Praia, the capital city, from 2005 to 2009, we needed strong judges to address societal issues. One strength of women judges is our ability to be firm or compassionate when necessary. We possess a deep sense of justice: to punish when appropriate and to support victims whenever possible. I strive to do that every day, although at times it isn't feasible.

Finally, several respondents believed that women judges bring a sense of aesthetics and order to the courtroom, with some even using their own funds to improve courtroom facilities. While this may seem far-fetched to some readers, it should be understood in light of the inadequate infrastructure found in many public buildings, including courtrooms, especially in rural areas. Effectively managing caseloads and courtroom environments is crucial to how a judge fulfills their responsibilities. With the rise of technology and the gradual digitalization of courthouses, there is hope that judges will have efficient systems in place for managing their cases. Caseload management is a key factor in how judges are evaluated and promoted. Further examination of how caseload management impacts the promotion of judges will be essential to assess and compare promotion rates between male and female judges.

5. The "Other Bench:" Women Judges' Associations/Organizations

Women judges recognize the importance of collective mobilization to support one another in their work. In some countries, women have formed associations for female judges with well-defined governance structures and a code of conduct for their members. Similar to the discussion in Chapter 4 regarding the "women's other bar," I see women judges' associations as the "other bench" since they are often created outside the main judicial organizations for all judges. The survey examined women

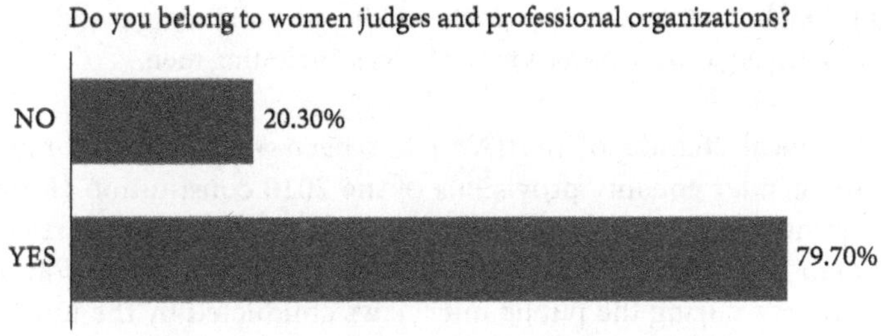

Figure 5.4 *Women Judges Belonging to Professional Organizations*
Source: Survey respondents: 79.

judges' involvement in these "other bench" organizations and other forms of group activity. As shown in Figure 5.4, a substantial 93.7% reported that they belong to these associations.

The International Association of Women Judges (IAWJ), based in Washington, D.C., was established in 1991 as a nonprofit organization consisting of a global network of women judges advocating for the rule of law and equal justice. The organization works with member associations in various countries and holds biennial meetings in different regions worldwide. Several African nations have established local chapters of the main organization to offer professional support to women judges and to address gender-based issues within their communities. For example, the local chapter in Tanzania has been a leader in providing judicial training for women judges in the country (Masabo, 2021; Rukuba-Ngaiza, 2021; Yoon, 2016). The Ghana chapter has partnered with women in local communities, especially through queen mothers, to fight gender discrimination in society (Dawuni, 2016b). In South Africa, the association has launched several training programs for women judges and magistrates, and it also runs a mentoring program for young lawyers and law students aiming to join the judiciary.

In 2023, the South Africa chapter, led by Deputy Chief Justice Mandisa Maya, launched the first *Journal of South African Women Judges*, published in partnership with the publishing house JUTA. In Senegal, the Women Judges and Lawyers Association (*L'Association Juristes Senegalaise* (AJS)), was established in 1974 by female lawyers and judges to address legal issues affecting women in society; the organization adopts a more outward-looking approach. Members of this organization are at the forefront of addressing women's rights issues and advocating for the repeal of gender-insensitive laws (Scales-Trent, 2010). The association has gained national recognition and is often consulted by the government for advice on gender-related matters. However, its focus on societal issues means it has limited resources and time to support its members. In Senegal, I asked respondents whether the association provides professional development opportunities for its members, and one of the organization's executives shared:

> The AJS advocates for women's rights through meetings, raising awareness, and educating our members about recent legal developments. Most of us, the members, have reached the peak of our careers, so we don't see why we should focus only on ourselves. Our mission is to fight for women's rights and change social attitudes.

> While additional training could be beneficial, the men might argue they need it too. Occasionally, we organize seminars for all judges, including men.

In Kenya, the local chapter of the IAWJ has been very active in raising awareness about the gender equality provisions of the 2010 constitution (Kamau, 2013). Following the nomination and confirmation hearing of Justice Martha Koome as the first woman chief justice in 2021, the association sent a delegation of its members to support her during the public interviews conducted by the Judicial Services Commission (Institute for African Women in Law, 2023j). Other countries have yet to establish women judges' associations. More research is needed to map the development of these organizations and to conduct a comparative analysis of the various associations across the continent, focusing on their effectiveness in achieving their goals and expanding access to justice.

V. Challenges: Navigating Gender Hierarchies From the Bench

Women's fair representation in the judiciary across Africa is still developing. While these progress points are important to note, many interconnected factors—including history, institutions, and social systems—affect when women can join judiciaries, their chances for promotion, and the work conditions, such as bullying and harassment, that some face. Despite the growth in gender diversity within judiciaries, women, especially those in leadership roles, continue to encounter challenges, as highlighted by former Deputy Chief Justice of Kenya, Dr. Nancy Baraza, during the launch of the Institute for African Women in Law's reports on women in law and leadership at the Kenyan bar, bench, and legal academy.

> We may have achieved formal equality, [for example] in the judiciary, by virtue of the robust constitution that puts equality and non-discrimination at the center of our governance. For the first time, we have a chief justice who is a woman. The question is, is she home and dry? Are there challenges she faces? These are things that we want to address.

The quantitative data on women's underrepresentation in certain judiciaries show only part of the picture. Women judges' lived experiences provide a more complete view of their professional lives. For example, although women are underrepresented in the Senegalese judiciary and encounter many challenges, the shared perspectives of the women I interviewed reveal a high level of job satisfaction. Many respondents expressed a common feeling about helping their communities and serving their country. This chapter discusses the challenges women face on the bench by using examples from different jurisdictions and incorporating qualitative data from interviews conducted during fieldwork.

1. Challenges in Appointments and Selection Methods

The legal tradition of a country greatly influences how judges are selected. Countries with similar legal traditions tend to modify their selection methods to fit local

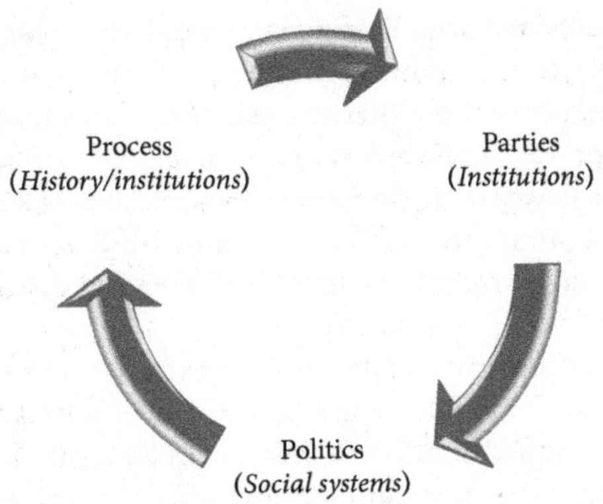

Figure 5.5 *The Impact of HISP on Judicial Selection*

contexts. Judicial selection processes usually involve multiple steps and participants, and the country's political environment also plays a significant role. Research exploring which judicial selection methods or factors contribute to greater representation of women in judicial roles remains inconclusive (Escobar-Lemmon et al., 2021; Kenney, 2018). **Figure 5.5** sorts the challenges women may face in the selection and appointment processes into three categories: process, parties, and politics. Each of these elements connects to the HISP framework, where the appointment process is rooted in history (H), shaped by new institutional (I) appointment rules and policies, and influenced by the politics of social actors overseeing the process (S). These HIS factors collectively influence when and where women will be appointed, ultimately affecting their status (or position) (P) as judges.

A. Process

A key feature of how judges are chosen is the process used to select nominations and appointments. As noted earlier, the civil-law model of judicial exams is known for offering fair representation for women in courts because it depends on a bureaucratic, merit-based system that avoids gatekeeping (Boiegol, 2013; Cohen, 2018; Schultz, 2013). While women perform well at entry-level roles through merit-based standardized exams, they face more stagnation at higher levels, with women not advancing in the judicial hierarchy as quickly as men. This stagnation is caused by persistent patriarchal practices that favor masculine work expectations and results. Following the civil-law model, Francophone African countries use standardized exams to appoint judges and magistrates (Kang, 2016).

In Senegal, a key step to entering the judiciary involves taking an exam and participating in an interview. Once someone earns the necessary undergraduate degree from an accredited university, they can apply to take the judiciary exam. The exam is administered by the judicial training center, which has replaced the National School of Administration and Magistracy (*École Nationale d'Administration et de Magistrature*, or ENAM). Successful candidates are then invited for interviews by a selection committee. As Dawuni and Masengu (2019) noted in their study of judge selection in Nigeria and Zambia, the gender makeup of a selection panel can greatly affect how fairly judicial candidates perform. During my work in Senegal, I tried to learn about the makeup of the selection committee, but none of my respondents could clarify its exact composition. Reports show that women candidates do well on the exam but face challenges during the interview stage. A magistrate in Senegal explained that women tend to perform worse during interviews because of social norms they learn early in life, which discourage them from speaking up publicly. She says women arrive at these interviews with the right knowledge but often feel shy and struggle to express themselves effectively before the selection panel.

While the judiciary remains an attractive career for many women due to factors such as prestige and job benefits, women have historically faced challenges, which explains the low 18% representation of women in Senegal's judiciary. Another key factor contributing to these low numbers in Senegal is religion. It is socially discouraged for women to serve as judges because of the belief that Islamic teachings do not permit women to judge men (Ibrahim, 2016). This religious belief seems to have influenced women's roles and career choices. However, this perception is gradually changing. With more women attending universities and increased awareness of women's representation in public life, women are starting to assert their personal and professional choices. During my fieldwork in Senegal in 2018, data from the Judicial Training Center showed that of 828 candidates who took the judicial exam to join the magistrature, 247 (29.83%) were women. The director of the center noted that although the number of female applicants was smaller, women outperformed men in the last two cohorts of successful candidates appointed to the judiciary. A longitudinal study will be essential to track these developments, identify the factors driving this change, and determine whether these factors will persist over time.

In the Ivory Coast, although current data on the number of women in the judiciary are lacking, interview respondents indicated that this number is increasing. However, they also noted that a major challenge for women trying to enter the judiciary isn't so much the process itself but rather the perception that passing the judicial exam is difficult. In Chapter 6, I discuss the experiences of two women academics who pursued careers in academia after failing the entrance exam for the judiciary.

Data collected during my visit to the *Magistrature of the National Institute of Judicial Training* (INFJ) in 2018 regarding the entrance exam shows that out of 1,192 candidates, 624 (52.35%) were men and 568 (47.65%) were women. Among the successful candidates for the 25 judicial positions, 16 (64%) were men, while 9 (36%) were women. The data from the Ivory Coast support the shared views of interview candidates that women face challenges with the entrance exam. Unlike in Senegal, religion did not affect women's ability to join the judiciary in the Ivory Coast. The findings from the 2018 data on Senegal and the Ivory Coast suggest that the merit-based judicial appointment process through the entrance exam has yet to favor women—a conclusion that contradicts other studies on civil-law countries, which show that women tend to outperform men in entrance exams (Schultz & Shaw, 2013).

This observation should be considered with two caveats: first, the data used in this research were gathered in 2018, which means the situation might have changed before this publication. Second, the ratio of men to women in higher education institutions and the number of candidates taking exams in these Francophone countries should be compared with other civil-law jurisdictions to better understand the outcomes.

The proportion of women judicial candidates, relative to women in higher education in these comparison countries, should also be included in any such analysis.

Besides the two civil-law countries mentioned earlier, common-law countries also have unique entry processes. In several common-law nations, the division of the judiciary into magistrates (lower courts) and judges (higher courts) may explain the lower number of women in higher courts (Escobar-Lemmon et al., 2021). While magistrates can advance in the judicial hierarchy to become judges, this process is slow and requires managing caseloads and completing administrative tasks, which are crucial for promotion evaluations (Mocumie, 2022). As discussed later, women face significant challenges in balancing professional and personal responsibilities, which most profoundly impact female magistrates who join the bench at the peak of their careers—often right after law school or after a few years of practicing at the bar. Additionally, in common-law countries that allow judges to be selected from practicing lawyers, such as Ghana, Nigeria, Zimbabwe, Uganda, Tanzania, and South Africa, the chances for magistrates to advance and join the judiciary decrease, explaining why women tend to remain at the lower levels of the judicial hierarchy in several countries (Dawuni, 2020).

The pool of candidates heavily shapes judicial selection processes. For instance, in South Africa, the distinction between advocates and attorneys often favors appointing judicial candidates from practicing lawyers, mainly advocates. Due to historical exclusionary policies and practices, women, especially Black and Coloured women, are underrepresented among advocates (Andrews, 2021; Chitapi, 2018; Masengu, 2016). This selection process leads to fewer women progressing toward judicial appointments. Additionally, in South Africa, the process of appointing members of the bar or the academy as "Acting Judges"—covering temporary judicial roles—facilitates lateral entry into the judiciary. These acting judge roles tend to be limited and highly competitive, usually favoring practicing advocates, even though the 1998 constitution has introduced reforms permitting the appointment of nonadvocates (Andrews, 2021; Klaaren, 2020).

In Nigeria, a procedural factor that poses a significant challenge for some female judicial aspirants is the impact of the "Federal Character" rule (or Indigeneity Principle), a system designed to ensure equal representation of the 36 states in the federal government. When applying for a federal judicial position, a female candidate must first meet the requirement of belonging to the state where the judicial position is available. To fulfill this requirement, a woman must demonstrate either that she was born in the state or that her parents are indigenous to that area (hence the term "indigeneity rule"). A woman married to another indigene cannot qualify as an indigene by virtue of her marriage, which automatically disqualifies her. Even if a woman has lived her entire life in a state after relocating to join her husband, she is still not recognized as an indigene. This requirement disproportionately impacts women, as it is typically women who move to be with their husbands after marriage (Institute for African Women in Law, 2023*l*). The implications of relocating to different regions of the country and their effects on judicial appointments and promotions are discussed further in this chapter.

Religious beliefs, practices, and procedures can negatively impact women's representation across all levels of the judicial system (Christelow, 1982; Ibrahim, 2016;

Lindbekk & Sonneveld, 2017). In Tanzania, Kenya, The Gambia, and several jurisdictions in the Sahel region (Mali, Niger, Chad), Kadhi courts play important judicial roles in resolving disputes. In some of these countries, religious customs have been used to prevent women from serving on Kadhi courts, creating a major barrier to women's fair representation on the benches of certain courts. In Nigeria, women are barred from being appointed to the Federal Sharia Court (Ibrahim, 2016). Islamic religious beliefs also contribute to the lower number of women judges in northern Nigeria, where Islam is dominant. This historical trend has recently shifted in some countries, allowing women to participate at various levels in these courts in The Gambia, Kenya, and Tanzania (Aura-Odhiambo, 2018; Satang, 2023).

Last, in both common-law and civil-law countries, the intersection of age (biological and career) and family status (as many young women start families during this stage) affects women and can negatively impact their career progression (Anleu & Mack, 2016). The discussions above show the variety of procedural mechanisms used by different jurisdictions in both civil-and common-law countries. Each of these processes presents gendered challenges; some are obvious and rooted in male-centered historical and institutional practices, while others are socially ingrained.

B. Politics

Turning now to the role of politics in judicial appointments, the common-law tradition provides many opportunities for political figures and party ideologies to influence the appointment process. In systems where judicial appointments begin with a nomination by the executive, a president's political ideology or strategic calculations can either promote the rise of women leaders or cause a qualified woman to be overlooked for the position (Ndagire, 2022). Politics' influence on judicial selection produces mixed outcomes. Despite the democratic principles of separation of powers, Africa's long history of judicial politicization has led some scholars to claim that the judiciary is the weakest branch, often with limited ability to effectively check the abuses and overreach of other branches of government (Ellett, 2013; Gathii, 1994; Prempeh, 2007). The political priorities of a government executive may be influenced by constitutional provisions that aim to ensure equal representation of minority groups in decision-making. While enforcing equality provisions within constitutional or legislative frameworks may not explicitly aim for women's equitable representation in the judiciary, it can generate ripple effects as norms shift and perceptions change regarding women's rights to decision-making roles and leadership.

The first example is the South African Constitution of 1996, which includes a provision in Article 174(2) for women's representation in the judiciary. In South Africa's efforts to transform the nation during the postapartheid era, the focus on racial transformation took precedence over other forms of equity, including gender transformation (Alberthyn & Bonthuys, 2016; Andrews, 2021; Bonthuys, 2015; Masengu, 2016). One reason for introducing Judicial Services Commissions was to increase transparency and reduce the historically patriarchal "tap-on-the-shoulder" method of judicial appointments, where male judges recommended candidates from their networks. Additionally, it was suggested that interviews for judicial positions be made public to improve transparency, reduce political interference, and enhance the legitimacy of the process.

The politics of gendered questioning directed at judicial candidates deserves discussion. The establishment of JSCs faced several challenges, including the unequal representation of women as members and the highly gendered and unprofessional nature of questioning aimed at women nominees (Andrews, 2021; Dawuni & Masengu, 2019).

In discussing the experiences of female judicial candidates before the JSC, Andrews (2021) recounts inappropriate questions, such as whether a "boyfriend" might tempt a candidate to return to South Africa or whether a lesbian judge could meet societal expectations (and the commission chair permitted these questions). While these personal inquiries are rarely directed at men, the lives of women candidates are publicly scrutinized, often to disqualify them not on professional criteria but by casting doubt on their credibility or character (Andrews, 2021; Masengu, 2021). In South Africa, the gendered politics of judicial appointments were illustrated in 2022 when President Cyril Ramaphosa chose not to appoint the recommended candidate, Justice Mandisa Maya, as chief justice, instead appointing her as deputy chief justice under a male candidate.

Kenya, on the other hand, presents a different outcome regarding the role of politics. Similar to the South African context, the 2010 Constitution of Kenya, among other equality provisions, states that no public office shall be held by more than two-thirds of the same gender. Analysts have credited this clause with the increase in the number of women holding public office, including in the judiciary (Institute for African Women in Law, 2023j; Murungi & Meroka-Mutua, 2021). The gender transformation agenda in the Kenyan constitution may be responsible for the institutional shifts toward recognizing women's leadership roles and rights, although women's rights groups continue to fight for their enforcement (Aura-Odhiambo, 2018; Mutua, 2016). In 2021, Martha Koome successfully emerged as the recommended candidate, becoming the first woman to serve as Chief Justice of Kenya. In this case, the president followed the recommendation of the JSC and appointed Martha Koome as chief justice.

Although these are just two examples, they show that there is no clear explanation for the role of political leaders and the factors they consider when appointing women to high judicial positions. Both countries are democracies, both have constitutional provisions aimed at achieving women's equal representation in decision-making, and both use JSCs during public hearings. While Dawuni and Kang (2015) explored several factors that explain the rise of women leaders in African courts, more research is needed to understand the political reasons behind why an executive might choose to nominate and appoint either a female or a male candidate.

C. Parties (Actors)

In common-law systems, the process of appointing judges to higher courts involves various key actors and stakeholders. These may include executive nominations, legislative vetting, interviews conducted by judicial service commissions, recommendations from bar associations, and participation from civil society. Each of these parties acts as a potential gatekeeper at different stages of the process, influencing the pathways to the bench for women (Dawuni & Masengu, 2019). Judicial appointments to the supreme courts of Ghana and Nigeria require presidential nominations, while nominations to lower courts start with a nomination by the chief justice (Dawuni, 2020). The selection process for higher courts often begins with the president nominating candidates. In some countries, the bar association may nominate candidates or support those put forth by the president.

In civil-law countries, entry into the lower levels of the judiciary is managed by judicial training institutes or centers, which conduct competitive exams and use panels of experts to interview candidates, although practices vary by country. Existing research (Schultz & Shaw, 2013) indicates that merit-based bureaucratic exams tend to benefit women candidates, who often perform better on written tests. In Senegal, a respondent noted that women's poor interview performances are linked to their limited exposure to developing public-speaking skills. It would be helpful to examine the interview questions to see if they are gendered in a way that favors men. Do the interviewer's gendered experiences influence these questions? Are they designed to align with societal expectations of women in professional settings? Additionally, analyzing the makeup of the interview panels could provide valuable insight. As of early 2023, women made up less than 18% of lawyers and judges in Senegal, which is not surprising given that the interview panels are mostly male.

An example of the belief in civil-law meritocracy is illustrated in the story of Justice Fatima Coronel, the first woman to serve as president of the Supreme Court of Cape Verde:

> I have never faced discrimination in my role as a judge. I have a career as a judge, just like my male colleagues, and we follow the law. Hiring and promotion practices are always fair; this profession is based on competence, and evaluations are regularly conducted using the same standards. I serve as the President of the Supreme Court, elected by my fellow judges, all of whom are men. The judges appointed to this court are at the top of their careers and are selected by a panel of magistrates. The judges themselves make the selection, and the President of the Supreme Court, along with the President of the country, confirms the appointment; the President does not have the authority to change this decision because the judges make that choice. The President of the Supreme Court acts as the head of the judiciary nationwide, combining administrative and judicial roles.

Despite the presumed meritocratic selection process in civil-law countries, executive influence on higher courts, such as the Constitutional Council and administrative courts, can lead to gendered outcomes. For example, when appointing members to the Constitutional Council in Senegal, candidates are often chosen from academia and various public service roles. In his analysis of Senegal's selection process, Schaeffer (2018) concluded that executive nomination opportunities might weaken the Constitutional Council's ability to check executive overreach, as happened under President Abdoulaye Wade. Dawuni and Kang (2015) present strong evidence that, since 2013, civil-law countries have appointed women to senior judicial roles, including presidents of constitutional courts. Data from Senegal's Supreme Court show that by 2022, only a few women had served on the two highest courts. From 1960 to 1997, only men held positions on the court until Judge Andrezia Vaz was appointed in 1997 as the first woman to serve there. Between 1992 and 2022, out of eight court presidents, only two were women—Andrezia Vaz from 1997 to 2001 and Mireille

Ndiaye from 2001 to 2002 (Institute for African Women in Law, 2023o). Evidence from Senegal regarding the limited number of women on the top court reflects the broader issue of female underrepresentation in the Senegalese judiciary. It remains to be seen whether the number of women in higher courts will grow as the overall proportion of women in the judiciary increases.

In Rwanda, various institutional actors have played subtle yet significant roles in increasing women's representation in the legal and judicial sectors. For years, Rwanda has used the civil-law tradition inherited from Belgian colonization combined with a merit-based appointment process. Article 140 of the post-genocide Constitution of 2003 emphasizes merit as the main criterion for judicial appointments. However, as Kamatali (2016) noted, even though gender is not prioritized as a selection criterion, other constitutional provisions guaranteeing gender equality, women's civil society organizations, and the expansion of legal education have been key factors enabling Rwanda to reach over 30% women representation in the judiciary. These lessons are important for other civil-law countries, such as Senegal and the Ivory Coast.

Ultimately, women's organizations can serve as catalysts for institutional change. Active women's legal and judicial groups may leverage their influence and support to endorse women candidates for higher offices. For example, in Rwanda, the active involvement of women's organizations, combined with women already in judicial roles, led to Kamatali's (2016) conclusion that women can serve as both insiders and outsiders by encouraging other women to apply for open positions. In Lesotho, Ellett (2016) highlighted how women's legal associations supported Justice Kelello Mafoso-Guni's nomination and eventual appointment as the first woman judge. In Kenya, members of Federación Internacional de Abogadas (FIDA) and the Women Judges Association supported Justice Martha Koome by participating in her nomination hearings before the JSC (Institute for African Women in Law, 2023j).

The previous discussion about the relationship among *processes*, *politics*, and *parties* does not suggest that one type of variable is more valuable in predicting outcomes than another. These variables influence each other differently depending on the legal system, women's representation in the judiciary, the political motives behind nominating authorities, and the diverse interests and calculations of the parties involved in the selection process. The level of the court may also matter; for example, the stakes for different actors could be greater when it comes to appointments to higher courts rather than lower courts. The challenges faced by women need to be evaluated on a case-by-case, country-specific basis. Ultimately, no matter the current results for women in appointments, constant vigilance is crucial to make sure that gender-sensitive and gender-inclusive norms and judicial selection practices become standard across all jurisdictions and levels of the court system. Additionally, as more women take on leadership roles within the judiciary and as efforts to raise awareness and mentor female law students improve, it is vital to focus on developing a pipeline of women ready to serve in judicial positions.

2. Promotions

A second challenge identified by interview participants is the limited opportunities for promotion within the judicial hierarchy. The position of a court in this hierarchy does not seem to matter when women have the necessary expertise for available roles. As noted earlier in the survey responses, 46.8% of respondents believed women have equal chances for leadership in the judiciary, while 57% indicated they hold judicial positions. Several interviewees expressed confidence that they would be promoted without facing gender-based discrimination. Furthermore, many believed that the selection and promotion processes in their country are fair and equitable. Judiciaries use various methods and procedures to promote judges both within and across judicial ranks. Policies outlining the terms and conditions of promotions are key to ensuring transparency and equal opportunities for all judges. However, based on evidence gathered during interviews, the lack of clear, written, and enforceable promotion policies is the biggest challenge for women. The survey provided respondents with a list of challenges faced as judges, and 31.6% reported experiencing slower promotions.

First, regarding promotion to higher courts or judicial leadership, the political will of the executive or president is crucial. This was previously discussed, especially concerning the appointment of Justice Mandisa Maya as Deputy Chief Justice of South Africa, even though the JSC recommended her for the position of Chief Justice in 2022. Executives or presidents may also choose not to nominate women they view as opposing government policies. In Uganda, Justice Solomy Balungi Bossa was reportedly overlooked for the role of Deputy Chief Justice in 2017 (Kiyonga, 2017; Ndagire, 2022).

In jurisdictions without written policies on judges' promotions, women judges confirmed during interviews that those eligible for promotion are less likely to request it compared to their male counterparts because of fears that such actions might challenge their superiors' authority. In Senegal, several magistrates said that it is the responsibility of women to address the perception that they are unwilling to seek promotions outside the capital city of Dakar. The reluctance to move beyond Dakar—a feeling shared by women judges in other countries—partly comes from the need for women to stay close to their families and caregiving roles, along with the belief that non-urban cities and towns often have more difficult work environments, including resistance against women in leadership roles. Sharing her experience as a newly married and recently appointed magistrate, one magistrate said:

> I began my professional journey in Kaolack in September 1985. There were five judges who received promotions. The president of the Court of Appeal told me to stay in Dakar because I am a woman. I thanked him, stating that I believe equality is essential and that I want to be recognized as a judge, not just as a woman. I asked him to assign me based on need; I do not seek special treatment. He laughed and said to me, "*You are a lion,*" if I wish to leave Dakar. I responded, "Yes, Mr. President, with all due respect, I want to go everywhere because I am a civil servant."

The judge's experience above differs from that of other women regarding relocation. Some respondents noted that the remote locations of certain courts significantly discourage women judges with young children in school. Most of the women judges I interviewed in Senegal shared that limited mobility due to family obligations is a key factor in women's lower chances of promotion, rather than incompetence.

> If a woman accepts a promotion and relocation to a remote area, she must consider her family and the ages of her children and decide whether to take the promotion and leave her family behind. A man typically does not face this dilemma because he likely has a wife to care for the family. Although these issues are often viewed as private and personal, they can impact a woman's professional advancement. I believe women have equal opportunities for promotion. Judicial authorities are increasingly inclined to promote women for their strong work ethic, yet women often decline such promotions due to the requirement of relocating away from their families.

The challenges related to relocation for promotions are connected to women's intersectional positionality—whether they are caring for young children or aging parents. For some women, the challenge arises as they advance through the judicial system, making the decision to pursue a promotion difficult due to their family and caregiving responsibilities for aging parents. An individual's progression from magistrate to circuit court may be impacted by the need to stay in an area with quality schools and amenities for young children. Masengu (2016) found that for some women judges in South Africa, promotions requiring relocation to another part of the country were a major deterrent in their decision to seek advancement.

In Cape Verde, a judge shared the challenge women face in transfers, but also the strategies they adopt to manage:

> We begin from islands outside the capital and gradually approach the main city. When I mention being in Brava, people often seem surprised because it's such a remote island. For some of my colleagues who are newly married, it has been quite challenging, but they understand it's only temporary and they will eventually return to the city. The same applies to the men. I've never heard of anyone getting divorced because of the transfers.

Second, promotions are connected to institutional factors that can negatively impact women, such as using caseloads to evaluate judicial performance. While studies indicate that women handle their caseloads effectively, those balancing private caregiving and professional duties may find it harder to clear their caseloads quickly and efficiently. Mentioning caseload management does not imply that women should not be evaluated on it. Instead, this observation from interviewees highlights the challenges some women judges face.

Third, social factors influence women's promotion and are often deeply rooted in cultural and religious beliefs. A significant majority of interview participants identified cultural factors as key determinants of the negative attitudes and challenges that hinder women's progress within the judiciary. These barriers include persistent informal cultural norms that favor male leadership over female leadership. In Lesotho, the appointment of Justina Kelello Mafoso-Guni as the first woman on the high court was met with public resistance, likely driven by the prevailing public perception that women were unqualified to serve on the high court (Ellett, 2018).

Other factors women identified as obstacles to their promotion included the lack of political networks that can enhance a candidate's chances of being nominated to a higher court. Last, women often lack mentorship and sponsorship opportunities that are crucial for developing the skills needed to succeed in public interviews for judicial positions. This situation has harmed some female candidates for judicial appointments in South Africa, as their lack of interview skills and preparation made them seem incompetent (Masengu, 2016).

3. Managing the Second Docket: The Private Versus Public

Despite women's progress in the professional world, traditional gender roles related to caregiving still mainly fall on women. No matter their age or job title, women are expected to care for their children, grandchildren, and aging parents. In many African cultures, these caregiving duties often extend to include family members who may not be blood relatives. The nonjudicial duties that women judges must handle refer to what I call the second docket, which includes personal, family, and community responsibilities they take on outside the courtroom. Women constantly negotiate the boundaries between work and caregiving, which takes time away from their professional commitments. Women judges have noted that these caregiving demands can affect their ability to meet various time and energy requirements, unlike their male counterparts, who often do not face the same social or cultural expectations regarding caregiving for children, parents, and extended family.

Extended family interference in managing professional and family obligations toward her husband was highlighted as a common challenge faced by working women in Senegal. A young magistrate remarked:

> The family holds significant influence in our society, and often, the issue isn't with the husband. His family may intervene; for example, his sister might complain about the wife—"she has an attitude," which can complicate a marriage. If you are too busy at work to attend social events and ceremonies, it may be seen as a sign of disrespect toward the family. It's important to handle these situations with a smile.

Research has shown that in every profession, women face a double bind—they must work to establish themselves as equal to their male counterparts, and even when they work twice as hard and more effectively, it still isn't enough. Women judges in African countries are not immune to this global phenomenon of double jeopardy, navigating the boundaries between private and public spheres. In Rwanda, despite the growing presence of women as judicial officers, including leadership roles like chief justice and deputy chief justice, they continue to face gendered expectations. According to Kamatali (2016, p. 151), "As much as the judiciary expects them [women] to perform at the same level as their male colleagues, many in Rwandan society expect them to remain traditional Rwandan wives and mothers. This imposes a heavy burden on them that still needs to be alleviated."

Despite deeply rooted patriarchal cultures in their society, women judges in Senegal consistently referred to themselves and other women as "militant women" who fiercely confronted patriarchy. Unlike earlier analyses in this chapter suggesting that some of my respondent judges did not identify as or avoided being called "feminist judges," it remains unclear whether the term "militant judge" signifies that they see themselves and other women's rights advocates as feminist judges. One Senegalese judge's explanation highlights the challenges women judges face and how some use humor to assert their equal roles. She recounted how she asserted her equal role as a judge compared to her husband, who was a prosecutor, and shared:

> When I got married, my husband was also in the judiciary as the Prosecutor General, so we couldn't work at the same court. I was pregnant at the time, and the road conditions were terrible. I met with the Minister of Justice and told him that when I was sent to school, I didn't know this man (pointing to my husband). I struggled, and when I became a judge two years later, I still didn't know him. Now, my entire career is at risk because I married this man, and I refuse to accept that. You must take all necessary steps to resolve this issue; if not, I will consider all legal options. My rights must be respected. If I hadn't done that, they would have left me there suffering simply because I married a prosecutor. He has his professional life, and I have mine. I mention this to emphasize that the situation is not easy.... As a woman, you have to fight every day... if not, even your home life can fall apart. It's not simple, and you must find a balance. In your professional life, you earn respect, but the home situation shifts—you become the wife, and you are told that you "cannot be a judge at home."

Several judges also noted that a judge's work extends beyond the courtroom, including researching cases and writing judgments, the latter of which often takes place at home. Judicial work outside the courtroom blurs the lines between work and home. As a judge in Cape Verde pointed out:

> Women return home to fulfill their roles as wives and mothers, and managing household duties can be challenging, unlike men who usually do not take on domestic responsibilities. My main struggle has been balancing my career with the personal obligations of having a family and children. Being a judge is not a standard 9-to-5 job; as a judge, you are on duty around the clock. The difference is that even when you're at home, your work continues; if I have a sentence or judgment to write, I must finish it. If a trial runs late, I am required to stay until it concludes.

In the wake of the COVID-19 pandemic, as will be discussed later, the need to balance "holding court" at home with other domestic demands increased stress levels for many women judges, particularly those with young children.

4. Gender-Based Stereotypes and Biases

Although women judges began joining the judiciary in the mid-1940s, they still face various sociocultural gender biases that affect their work. These stereotypes impact women at different stages of their judicial careers. In Malawi, women aiming to join the bench have faced challenges from members of the judicial selection commission who still believe women should not hold judicial positions (Ellett, 2022). Even in countries where women have achieved numerical parity and hold top judicial roles, including the appointment of Justice Irene Mambilima as the first female chief justice and Hildah Chibombah as President of the Constitutional Court, women remain seen as illegitimate occupants of the bench (Masengu, 2021). To explore women judges' perceptions of gender bias and stereotypes, the survey examined whether they faced sociocultural discrimination and gender bias at work. Of 79 respondents, 46.8% agreed that women faced sociocultural discrimination, 15.2% disagreed, and 38% were unsure. The high percentage of uncertain responses suggests a lack of understanding of what constitutes sociocultural discrimination in the workplace, as some may be experiencing it but are unsure if it counts as discrimination. **Figure 5.6** shows the respondents' views on their work challenges. Among the options, 43% said they do not receive the same respect as their male colleagues, litigants, and lawyers. This underscores how sociocultural beliefs influence women in their positions.

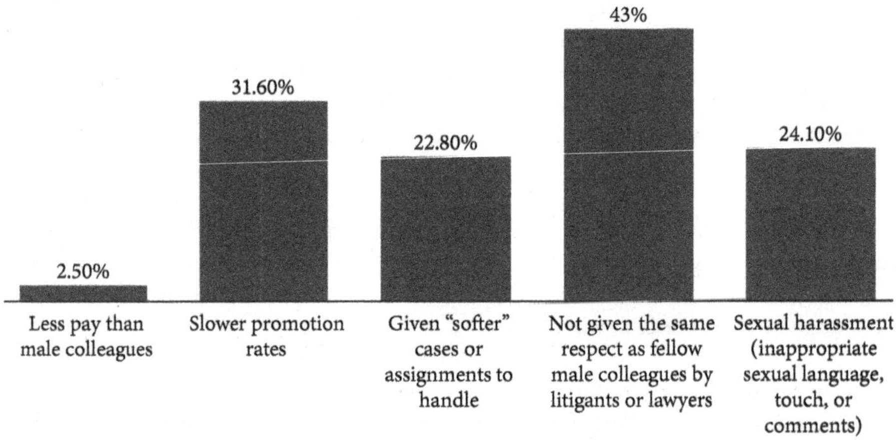

Figure 5.6 *Women Judges and Workplace Challenges*
Source: Survey respondents: 79.

Lower levels of respect shown to women judges may stem from historical continuities rooted in the traditional view of the legal profession as a male-dominated field. The stories of pioneering women judges we have discussed demonstrate that, although acceptance levels vary, masculine institutional cultures—such as in Nigeria, where female judges in higher courts are still addressed as "My Lord"—illustrate the persistent nature of these perceptions. In many countries, the departure of men to more lucrative legal practices has created a vacancy and increased demand for women judges (Uzebu-Imarhiagbe, 2020b). Although women are qualified for these roles, some lawyers appearing before women judges may still see them as "illegitimate" substitutes for their male counterparts. In predominantly Islamic countries like Nigeria, Senegal, and The Gambia, the religious ban on women serving as judges in Sharia courts, combined with cultural beliefs, further diminishes the acceptance of women as legitimate members of the judiciary (Ibrahim, 2016; Yoon, 2016). During my fieldwork, I found no evidence to support the idea that ethnic minority women judges felt more discriminated against than their ethnic majority counterparts. However, in South Africa's racialized context, Black women judges must navigate the intersection of gender and racial biases from both colleagues and lawyers appearing before them (Alberthyn & Bonthuys, 2016; Andrews, 2021; Masengu, 2016).

Pioneer women often confront the greater challenge of dismantling societal stereotypes deeply embedded in society, which also shape institutional policies. In Senegal, these challenges can encompass life-threatening attacks on women judges, as noted by one judge:

> I was the first woman appointed as a judge in that town. My job was very challenging because many could not accept that a woman should send a man to jail. Sometimes, notes were left under my door urging me to find a husband instead of sentencing men to prison. Numerous litigants came to court claiming they would not take orders from a woman. One day, I discovered eggs and other traditional items associated with spiritual beliefs, suggesting that these rituals could bring negative consequences to their targets—but it was merely an attempt to intimidate me. I stepped on the eggs, cracked them, and walked away. It is not easy for a woman in our culture. There were about 25 judges, and I was the only woman. The president of the court and the prosecutor were very kind; they welcomed me. They would come to my hotel to pick me up and bring me back until I found suitable accommodation and moved out.

For many women, challenging these perceptions of authority requires confidence, building trust, and resilience. A second-generation woman judge in Cape Verde shares her challenges and determination to change these perceptions.

> At first, it felt strange to see a woman working in the hinterlands, since it was considered a man's job. I had to challenge these boundaries and perceptions. While working at the Ministry of Justice, I was responsible for overseeing the country's police, which was quite difficult for me; all the directors were men, so I needed a lot of confidence. I overcame this by working hard. At first, there was some reluctance because they couldn't trust a woman, but after they saw my strong work ethic, they started to trust me.

In the neighboring country of The Gambia, the response from a high court judge indicates that, despite the ongoing perceptions and distrust toward women holding positions traditionally viewed as reserved for men, some of these views are evolving:

> Here in The Gambia, I don't believe women judges face difficulties with our male colleagues. However, culturally, because of the strong influence of religion and men holding prominent roles, some men still try to assert their dominance, even though they generally show respect toward women. The role of women has changed in our society, and there is ongoing advocacy for women to get education and take on positions in society.

Several context-specific gender-based stereotypes about women judges have been documented by African scholars studying gender and judging in Ethiopia (Addadzi-Koom & Gage, 2022), Uganda (Ndagire, 2022), Kenya (Kamau, 2013; Murungi & Meroka-Mutua, 2021), Benin (Kang, 2016), Zambia (Masengu, 2021), Nigeria

(Ibrahim, 2016; Uzebu-Imiarhagbe, 2020), and South Africa (Alberthyn & Bonthuys, 2016; Andrews, 2021; Mocumie, 2022). Some respondents noted that societal perceptions of women legal professionals as difficult to handle in relationships contribute to marital challenges in Senegal and Cape Verde. In the Ivory Coast, a judge explained how these perceptions stem from female students taking exams to become magistrates at the university level. In Senegal, a magistrate shared that the increasing belief that women are taking men's roles is causing a backlash against women pursuing professional careers. Additionally, entrenched social expectations in Senegal that women must marry and start families partly explain why some female students do not receive family support to finish their university degrees and qualify for the magistrature.

5. Maintaining Judicial Autonomy vs. Gender Nonconformity

Judicial autonomy and independence are essential for the proper functioning of the judiciary. For example, the United Nations Bangalore Principles of Judicial Conduct include various provisions to safeguard judicial independence. Ongoing political and democratic shortcomings, along with economic underdevelopment in many countries, have created conditions that enable executive authorities to infringe on judicial power, posing a serious threat to judicial independence. Allegations of judicial corruption often target members of the judiciary, and women judges are no exception (Ellett, 2013; Fombad, 2011, 2021; Gathii, 1994).

In the face of executive overreach, some women judges have remained steadfast against political hostility. These judges not only uphold the sanctity of judicial independence but can also be seen as *gender nonconformists*, a concept discussed in Chapter 1. Resisting executive interference comes at a cost, and in some cases, it can even lead to death, as shown by Justice Cecilia Koranteng-Addow, a high court judge in Ghana who was killed along with two male judges for refusing to issue decisions favorable to the ruling military regime (Dawuni, 2016a). Justice Mary Mame Yassin Sey, the first woman high court judge in The Gambia, was also targeted by President Jammeh for resisting his control and for refusing to make decisions that benefited his government. Similarly, Gambia's first woman chief justice, Mabel Agyemang from Ghana, appointed by the Commonwealth Secretariat, had to flee for her life after making a decision unfavorable to Yahya Jammeh (Dawuni, 2020).

Justice Izuako Nkemdilim, a Nigerian judge assigned to The Gambia through the Commonwealth Secretariat program, was forced to flee the country after facing attacks for not ruling in favor of the authoritarian government of President Yahya Jammeh. Justice Nkemdilim also showed heroic acts of defiance when she refused to comply with the demands of a state governor during her time as a judge in Nigeria. When initial attempts to bribe her to change her decision failed, threats to her life ensued. Ultimately, she had to escape for her safety, eventually reaching the United Kingdom as a refugee until she could return home years later (African Women in Law Legacy Project, n.d.-e). In Nigeria, High Court judge Olamide Folahanmi Oloyede was reinstated in 2022 after a ruling by the Supreme Court of Nigeria. Judge Oloyede had resisted numerous attempts to bribe her to influence her decision on a case, which led the state governor to bring false allegations against her, resulting in her suspension as a judge (Bamigbola, 2022). In Uganda, women judges who opposed executive overreach, such as Judge Esther Kisaakye and Justice Solomy Balungi Bossa, have been recognized as judges defending judicial independence (Ndagire, 2022).

Contrary to misconceptions that African women are appointed to judicial leadership positions solely to appear gender-progressive, these women leaders face significant challenges in their roles (Masengu, 2015). Such challenges stem from executive overreach, especially during attempts to amend constitutions that favor incumbents seeking to extend their terms beyond what is legally allowed (Fombad, 2021). In a notable act of defiance, Justice Daniel Darlan, president of the Constitutional Court of the Central African Republic, opposed efforts by the incumbent president to change the constitution so he could run for a third term. Justice Darlan's brave stance earned her international recognition when she was named one of 11 Women of Courage by the United States Department of State (Solomon, 2023).

In 2023, Meaza Ashenafi, the first woman president and chief justice of the Federal Supreme Court of Ethiopia, resigned after serving five years in office. Although no reasons were provided for her resignation, reports of tension between her office and the executive emerged. In Sudan, Nemat Abdullah Khair's appointment in 2019 was brief, ending with her removal from office in 2021, with no public explanation given (Dawuni, 2020). Mathilda Twomey became the first woman chief justice in Seychelles when she was appointed in 2015. The power struggle involving then Acting Chief Justice Karunakaran against Justice Twomey included several false allegations of her abusing her power. In 2018, a three-member Tribunal of Inquiry, established by the Commonwealth Secretariat, dismissed the allegations and exonerated Chief Justice Twomey (Rickard, 2019).

In Kenya, Dr. Nancy Baraza, the first female deputy chief justice, resigned from her position after a constitutional tribunal found that she had exceeded her authority by pointing a gun at a security guard in a mall (Chege, 2017). In an interview, Baraza said, "My experience was bad. It was horrible. I was treated maliciously." She also remarked, "had I been a man, I wouldn't have been treated that way. If you use Nancy to set the standards, then stick to those standards" (Chege, 2017). While many commentators are divided on the incident involving Nancy Baraza, some compare the public outcry against her to a case where a male judge shot someone in public but faced no consequences (Reuters, 2008). These examples highlight some of the challenges women judges face in leadership roles. Through my research and documentation of women leaders' history, I've found that many hesitate to share their challenges. Others confide their stories with me off the record, which is why they cannot be included here. Documenting such experiences is vital to show that women judicial leaders are not merely token appointments and face serious challenges in performing their duties.

The experiences shared in this section show how some women judges have navigated institutional patriarchy and political tensions to maintain their personal and judicial independence. These difficult situations reveal that women are not immune to serious consequences for refusing to conform. Is a woman judge's refusal to engage in corrupt practices more costly than what her male counterparts face? Determining whether male judges have faced similar objections and reprisals is not simple, as the focus here remains on female judges. A comparison of the experiences of both male and female judges asserting their independence and dealing with related repercussions would help evaluate the role of judges in promoting judicial independence. In a study on media coverage of women judges' appointments to higher courts across five democracies, Escobar-Lemmon et al. (2016) found varying emphasis on gender and gender roles in media portrayals of women judges. Comparing male and female judicial leaders, I found fewer reports of challenges faced by male chief justices from the executive branch. This supports the initial idea that women chief justices face a higher risk of backlash from both the executive branch and the judiciary when asserting their autonomy in decision-making or leadership roles. This is an important area for future research.

6. Limited Opportunities for Professional Advancement

Judges often receive training from judicial training institutes or similar organizations established by judicial administrations to educate them. However, ongoing training while on the bench is limited due to financial constraints within judicial budgets (Masabo, 2021). Judges frequently rely on their own networks for professional development and to stay informed about legal developments. Some judges have reported gaining training and professional growth by attending conferences and meetings abroad. These events are usually based on selections made by the head of the judiciary (either the chief justice or judicial secretary), indicating that connections are necessary for nomination. Participation in such meetings also offers benefits like receiving an honorarium or per diem and expanding networks through interactions with other judges. Social capital and networks within the judiciary are vital for accessing these opportunities. Most respondents indicated that male networks, often called "old boys' networks," tend to favor male judges. While opportunities to attend training programs may be limited, judicial training institutes aim to provide equal opportunities for judges both domestically and internationally (Rukuba-Ngaiza, 2021). The survey asked about the types of professional development opportunities respondents need, and **Figure 5.7** shows the responses.

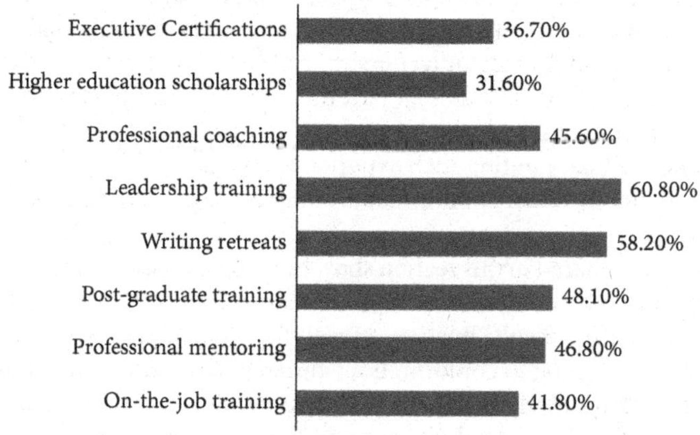

Figure 5.7 *Self-Reported Training Needs of Women Judges*
Source: Survey respondents: 79.

The responses indicate that leadership training is a priority for women judges, reaffirming discussions that they are prepared for leadership roles. The previous discussion has offered thematic analyses of the challenges identified through the quantitative and qualitative tools used in this research. Chapter 7 provides a comparative analysis of the strategies women in law have employed to overcome their individual and collective challenges and suggests solutions to these issues.

VI. Conclusion

Research on women judges in Africa is currently the most advanced among the three sectors of the legal profession discussed in this book. The findings of this chapter are based on qualitative responses from participants in the countries where I conducted fieldwork, supported by quantitative data from survey responses, and enhanced by the growing body of scholarship on African women judges. Overall, the findings in this chapter indicate that, like the other two sectors—the bar and the academy—the increase in the number of women judges has led to positive changes in law, justice, and judicial institutions. Drawing on the HISP framework, the findings in this chapter show that women judges continue to navigate gender-based stereotypes linked to *history* (the lingering impact of colonial practices), persistent gendered *institutional* practices, and *social* norms and expectations that create different *positional* outcomes for different women judges.

The chapter highlights women's contributions to justice and the judiciary in both domestic and international settings. Using a matri-legal framework that explores women's roles as leaders during precolonial and postcolonial times, this chapter expands our understanding of how African women judges manage their professional and personal responsibilities to perform their duties. Overall, it provides strong evidence supporting the conclusion that, despite many challenges, women judges are making important contributions to justice, equity, and the rule of law, and are effectively representing women in leadership roles on the bench.

6
Women in the Legal Academy: The Third Frontier

I. Introduction

Following the pattern set in Chapter 4 on lawyers and Chapter 5 on judges, this chapter uses a comparative framework to discuss and assess the positionality and experiences of women in African legal academies. Situated within the global context of women entering the legal field and specifically within Africa, this chapter applies the HISP (history, institutions, social systems, and positionality) framework from Chapter 1 to analyze women's symbolic and substantive representation in the legal academy across six countries, where primary data were collected through qualitative interviews with 23 women legal academics. It also includes the quantitative findings from 48 survey responses. Finally, it draws on existing literature about women in higher education in Africa (Aura-Odhiambo, 2018; Kwesiga, 2002; Mabokela & Mlambo, 2015; Maphalala & Mpofu, 2017). Using this mixed-methods approach and feminist methodology, the chapter centers on the respondents' voices to identify overall patterns, similarities, and differences in women's experiences within the African legal academy.

The findings confirm the influence of colonial educational policies—some of which banned legal education for Africans, as seen in South Africa and the Congo (Maphalala & Mpofu, 2017), while others limited women's access to legal education. These historical continuities had diverse effects on educational outcomes for women in society, including spillover impacts on women in the legal academy (Tamale, 2021). Such past exclusions and restrictions on women's educational opportunities raise important questions discussed earlier in Chapter 3: Who were the academic and professional gatekeepers, and what strategies did they use to keep women out? How did colonial, racially exclusionary policies create a precedent making the legal academy the third frontier in the trilogy of women's entry into the profession? How have these historical links shaped other mechanisms, norms, and conditions that limit women's access to leadership roles in the academy within a postcolonial context? What has been the effect of democratic and neoliberal policies on women's access to higher education? And what are the ongoing implications of increasing women's representation in the legal academy?

Weighing these questions against the evidence from fieldwork, as this chapter develops, we find that although law faculties and law schools were established later than other faculties in post-independence universities (Mamdani, 2018), women have gradually entered the legal academy. However, women academics face intersectional challenges within the HISP framework. First, they must navigate the *historical* legacies of colonial educational policies, second, they have to contend with

African Women in Law. J. Jarpa Dawuni, Oxford University Press. © Oxford University Press 2026.
DOI: 10.1093/9780197795095.003.0006

patriarchal contexts of higher education (universities), and third, they must deal with *social* factors such as patriarchy, which are embedded within the legal profession as the first frontier of the trilogy discussed in previous chapters. The interaction of these intersectional challenges shapes the position of female legal academics, affecting who can enter, succeed, and rise to leadership roles in the academy.

Structured into six sections, section II provides a brief overview of the structure and trends in legal education, based on models from selected countries. Section III explores women's pathways to the academy by examining personal and motivational factors that lead to joining. Section IV uses the intersectionality framework to analyze women's representation in the academy. Section V highlights women's contributions to the academy, while section VI evaluates ongoing challenges women face. Overall, the chapter shows that, unlike women's experiences at the bar (Chapter 3) and the bench (Chapter 4), women have yet to be fully integrated as equal participants in the legal academy—the final frontier in the trilogy.

II. Structure and Context of Legal Education

The term "legal academy" or "academia," as used in this discussion, refers to undergraduate and postgraduate educational institutions located either within universities (law faculties) or as stand-alone institutions (law schools) that prepare individuals to become legal professionals (lawyers). The terminology and structures of these institutions vary and may change over time in response to shifting national and global academic trends (Dawuni & Badejogbin, 2021). This section briefly outlines the broad patterns emerging from the legal education systems of selected countries across Africa, focusing on the six countries where interviews were conducted to provide a contextual analysis of women in the legal academy. Instead of analyzing specific changes in each country over time, the discussion highlights key features and characteristics of various educational systems that significantly influence the representation and status of women in the legal academies of these countries.

Legal educational structures differ across the continent and are often connected to the type of legal tradition—civil or common law. In civil-law countries like Senegal and the Ivory Coast, earning a law degree at the university level qualifies someone as a *juriste* but doesn't allow them to practice as a lawyer or judge without additional training at a judicial training institute. These educational systems are neither fixed nor uniform; different countries have modified their systems over time to suit their specific needs. Additionally, over the years, both common-law and civil-law countries have integrated elements of the American legal education system through funding initiatives and academic exchanges (Dawuni & Badejogbin, 2021; Harrington & Manji, 2021b).

During colonization, the transplantation and internationalization of educational models to the African context involved adopting key aspects of the structure and form as practiced in the colonial metropole (Basedow, 2014; Harrington & Manji, 2021b; Kwesiga, 2002; Madlalate, 2022; Odhiambo, 2011). In Uganda, as in much of Africa, Tamale (2021) finds that the transplantation of legal education systems was rooted in both gendered and racist perceptions of women's mental capacity to pursue higher education and specialized courses such as law. In England, where the common-law legal education system developed, one could choose whether or not to attend classes to become a lawyer (Auchmuty et al., 2021). The British legal education model allowed individuals to study independently, take the final exam, and gain experience working as an apprentice or pupil under a senior lawyer. The fact that attending classes was not mandatory contributed to diminishing the prestige of the legal academy as an institution that produced knowledgeable individuals (Auchmuty et al., 2021; Garth & Shaffer, 2022; Sommerlad, 2021). Drawing from the British educational model, most common-law countries in Africa offer a law degree, the Bachelor of Laws (LL.B), within a faculty of law at a university. To become a lawyer qualified to practice, one must pursue further education at a law school to acquire the practical knowledge and license required to qualify as a lawyer (Manteaw, 2008; Ndulo, 2002).

The civil-law tradition, on the other hand, emphasizes scientific methods that involve studying jurisprudence and other theoretical subjects. In colonial centers of France and Germany, law professors were highly regarded for their perceived role in training lawyers who understood legal theory and could engage in critical and logical thinking (Schultz, 2021a). Francophone countries are mainly civil-law nations, and access to the legal profession and academia remains highly competitive. The *Conseil Africain et Malgache pour l'Enseignement Supérieur* [African and Malagasy Council for Higher Education] (CAMES), established in 1972, manages the process for selecting entrants to the legal academy. CAMES oversees the competitive exams that determine entry into and advancement within the legal academy (Institute for African Women in Law, 2023o). The general view among interviewees for this project shows strong confidence in the objectivity of the CAMES organization, although this study could not independently verify its structure and functions. These adapted legal education models, whether from civil- or common-law systems, have developed over time. Legal educational institutions aim to address evolving national needs while keeping up with global educational trends. Different countries adopt the models that best suit their specific contexts.

1. Structure of Law Schools and Legal Training—Law Faculty Versus Law School

Legal education offers specialized training for those aiming to become lawyers. Different countries have various systems and models for training attorneys. In common-law countries such as Nigeria, Ghana, Uganda, Kenya, and Sierra Leone, legal education usually starts with an undergraduate degree at a university, which takes three to four years. The university training occurs in what is commonly called the law faculty. After finishing their undergraduate studies, individuals enroll in a specialized institution called law school to earn a postgraduate professional qualification. These general models change over time and may differ from what is currently described.

The time spent in law school varies by country, typically ranging from one to two years. Some countries have created new models and pathways for students studying abroad who want to obtain licensure in their home jurisdiction. The typical law school system in many African countries differs from the system used in the United Kingdom. There, after earning an undergraduate law degree, individuals can either take the solicitors' qualifying exam to become a solicitor or complete an apprenticeship to qualify as a barrister associated with one of the Inns of Court (Schultz, 2021b; Wells, 2021). With some exceptions, such as South Africa—which has a split legal profession between attorneys and advocates—most other common-law countries, including Nigeria, Ghana, Kenya, Uganda, and Tanzania, have a fused legal system where one qualifies as a lawyer and can serve as both a solicitor and an advocate (Burgis-Kasthala, 2022; Oloka-Onyango, 2021).

2. Academic Ranks

The structure of law faculties and law schools determines the types of academic ranks used. Educational institutions are ranked hierarchically, and a survey of the ranking system at the university level (law faculties) in common-law countries shows a general pattern. The ranks include titles such as Lecturer, Assistant Lecturer, Senior Lecturer, Associate Professor, and Full Professor. In civil-law countries, however, the ranks include Assistant, Maître Assistant (assistant professor), Maître de conférences (similar to senior lecturer or associate professor), and Professor titulaire/agrégé (full professor). Each rank has specific requirements for promotion—such as teaching, research, and service—and these requirements vary across institutions. These requirements affect women differently, as discussed later. In Ghana, for example, law schools (where specialized training leads to qualification as a lawyer) do not use these academic rankings, as there is generally no promotion or tenure; many lecturers are part-time employees drawn from practicing lawyers and judges (Dawuni, 2021b).

3. Changes and Challenges of Legal Education

As the demand for legal careers grows, law schools have expanded their capacities and revised their admissions and teaching standards (Garth & Shaffer, 2022; Manteaw, 2008; Ndulo, 2002). As a result, increased interest in legal education has created more opportunities for women seeking academic careers. Additionally, many university law faculties have strengthened their hiring standards for professors. In response to changing accreditation rules in several countries, including Ghana, Kenya, and Uganda (Dawuni, 2021b; Ghai & Ghai, 2014; Tamale, 2021), many law faculties now require their lecturers to hold a doctoral degree. While some current faculty members have been grandfathered in, new hires are given several years to earn a doctorate. This doctoral requirement has gendered implications for younger women seeking to establish a legal career. Women must find innovative ways to balance teaching, caregiving, and pursuing a doctoral degree, often from abroad. The challenges faced by women in obtaining a doctoral degree as a prerequisite for teaching at law schools will be further examined.

Law schools, on the other hand, are considered professional training grounds that emphasize practical skills. As a result, most instructors are practicing lawyers and judges. Generally, a doctoral degree is not required. However, the reality of balancing legal practice with teaching and other family and personal responsibilities increases women's workloads relative to those of their male counterparts in law schools, as discussed further in later sections.

III. Pathways to the Academy

Across many cultures worldwide, the duty of imparting knowledge (teaching) from birth through various life stages has often fallen primarily on women. Women's teaching roles are present in all parts of society—from the domestic sphere, where they educate children, to the public sphere, where women serve as essential custodians and transmitters of morality, values, and norms. In traditional African systems, women play vital roles as educators. I use the term "educators" to encompass the diverse ways and spaces in which women serve as teachers. Beyond domestic teaching or education, women fulfill crucial communal roles as keepers of oral history, conveyed through songs, storytelling, and customary initiation rites. Women also hold important leadership roles in rites of passage—from birth to death, including the naming of newborns, marriage ceremonies, and funeral rites (Ndulo, 2011; Obiora, 1993). Viewed through the matri-legal feminist framework used in this book, women across Africa are valued as teachers of moral codes, custodians of oral history, and guardians of oral traditions and practices. These sociocultural expectations shape women's traditional roles as teachers, arising from these cultural functions and later possibly explaining some of the noneducational roles interviewees were expected to perform in the legal field.

Drawing from these traditional roles, women have historically been limited to teaching—mainly at the early stages of education. In many African countries, following colonial missionary educational policies, teaching was seen as a suitable profession for women, and young girls were encouraged to pursue teaching degrees after high school, with nursing and culinary arts being other popular choices (Tripp, 2004). Several pioneering women lawyers and judges, such as Justice Effie Owuor—who became the first Kenyan woman lawyer and magistrate called to the bar in 1968—were encouraged by missionary teachers to pursue teaching because law was not considered a woman's job. Race also played a crucial role, especially in countries with white settler minorities like Kenya, South Africa, Zambia, Zimbabwe, and Namibia, where racist beliefs held that the Black mind was simply incapable of studying law (Madlalate, 2022; Tshuma, 1991). While this belief was directed broadly at Africans, women in these colonial environments had to contend with both racial and gender restrictions (Andrews, 2018).

In the following discussions, women's personal narratives on why they joined the academy, and the experiences of the first women academics, illustrate that women legal academics have not been spared the underlying currents of patriarchal institutional norms pervasive in higher education (Tamale, 2021).

However, the earlier discussion in Chapter 3 demonstrates that the underrepresentation of women in the legal academy across Africa is not an isolated issue. Global data show that women continue to mainly occupy lower positions in higher education institutions (Auchmuty et al., 2021; Deo, 2019). Universities are at the top of educational institutions, and faculty members often enjoy privileges linked to perceptions of prestige, higher pay, and greater flexibility in managing their roles within institutional rules and structures. Given these higher levels of academic privilege and prestige, it is no surprise that women's path to the top of the educational hierarchy has been more contested and difficult than men's.

Colonial policies favored boys' access to education, investing little to nothing in girls' education, thus beginning centuries of limited opportunities for women's higher education. Coupled with imported colonial patriarchal systems that enforced a strict separation between private and public spheres, women were neither educated nor recruited as teachers. As the movement toward independence advanced and more educational institutions were established at both basic and higher levels, the demand for human resources to teach at these levels led to the training and recruitment of more women as teachers (Tripp, 2004). Therefore, in its own unintended way, employing women as teachers ensured that the next generation of African women was raised by those who desired greater achievements for their children. Importantly, women in academia now stand on the shoulders of those who first entered the teaching profession in primary schools, then high schools, and increasingly into higher education (Stewart & Tsanga, 2011).

Years later, with the establishment of higher education institutions and law faculties at these universities, university teaching emerged as a masculine profession from the beginning. Earlier in Chapter 2, I described the development of legal education in African countries as an "accidental" evolution. This evolution resulted in the transplantation of imperial masculinity into African systems, affecting who qualified and who was deemed capable of teaching. As the legal academy advanced, the gradual entry of women into the academy was significantly shaped by the enduring belief that women could only be prepared for teaching at the elementary and high school levels. The intersection of colonial history and educational institutional policies led to the double exclusion of women at the onset of higher education in nearly all countries across the continent (Mabokela & Mlambo, 2015; Tamale, 2021).

The specialized skills and training needed for university teaching created better opportunities for men with the necessary education to fill open positions (Odhiambo, 2011; Tamale, 2021). Men dominated in fields like law, medicine, and the sciences because the colonial administration had provided them with the means to earn these degrees. Despite the relative privilege African men had over women when most universities in sub-Saharan Africa were first established, many early university educators were foreigners hired during the colonial period (Ghai, 1981; Ndulo, 2002), and several of them continued serving as deans of law schools, shaping and influencing the legal education system that later developed in these countries (Harrington & Manji, 2021b; Karekwaivanane, 2020; Luckham, 1976; Madlalate, 2022; Tshuma, 1991).

The brief summary of the main themes in Chapter 2 about the evolution of the legal professions in Africa provides the reader with a guide for upcoming discussions. While colonial racial and sexist policies limited women's access to the legal academy, their personal choices and decisions to join vary as much as the women themselves. However, the thematic analyses of women's paths to the legal profession (including the academy) in Chapter 3 highlight several common factors that influenced their decision to join. Section IV looks at demographic patterns of women's representation in the academy, identifies key themes, and analyzes the intersectional factors that shape their individual and collective roles within the profession.

IV. Representation in the Academy: Trickle in, Move up, or Stay the Same?

Chapter 1 identified five generational phases to help contextualize women's emergence in African legal professions: phase one (1930–1950: colonial and pre-independence), phase two (1951–1970: independence to state formation), phase three (1971–1990: post-independence resistance to authoritarian rule), phase four (1991–2010: democratization, diffusion, and expansion of education), and phase five (2011–present: globalization and expansionism). The following discussion examines the evolving dynamics within the legal academy, with women's entry beginning in earnest in the early 1970s. The demographic changes since then are interconnected with broader political economy shifts, developments in higher education, and the overall growth and feminization of the legal profession. Although women are gradually entering the academy (*trickle in*), various institutional and social challenges influence whether women's representation as a proportion of all law school faculty is increasing (*trickle up*) or remaining steady. This section explores the changing demographics of legal academics, sex diversification driven by demand and supply factors, academic ranks and promotions, diversity in teaching specialization, research diversity, and women in academic leadership.

1. General Demographic Patterns

The first women law lecturers took different paths to the academy and often started at various ages. Some, like Akua Kuenyehia, who in 1972 became the first woman law lecturer in Ghana at age 25 (Dawuni, 2018a), entered directly from law school into university law faculties. Others, such as Jadesola Akande, Nigeria's first woman law lecturer, joined the academy in 1975 at age 35 after a career as a practicing lawyer, a public prosecutor, and the first woman appointed as a commissioner in Nigeria's Western Province (Cruickshank & Ozobia, 2006).

The demographic patterns from the research survey establish a baseline for future studies to track changes over time. This section highlights three key personal demographic factors: age, marital status, and qualifications. The survey responses show that the earliest graduation was in 1980, with the most recent in 2018. In **Figure 6.1**, respondents are unevenly distributed, with the largest group in the 31–40 age range, indicating that many women may have started their legal careers or continued their education before joining the academy.

The second demographic category of marital status shown in **Figure 6.2** indicates that a majority, 44% of respondents, are married with children. When compared with the data in **Figure 6.1**, these two variables suggest a period when women are heavily involved in family and child caregiving responsibilities, which have different effects on women's career experiences and decisions.

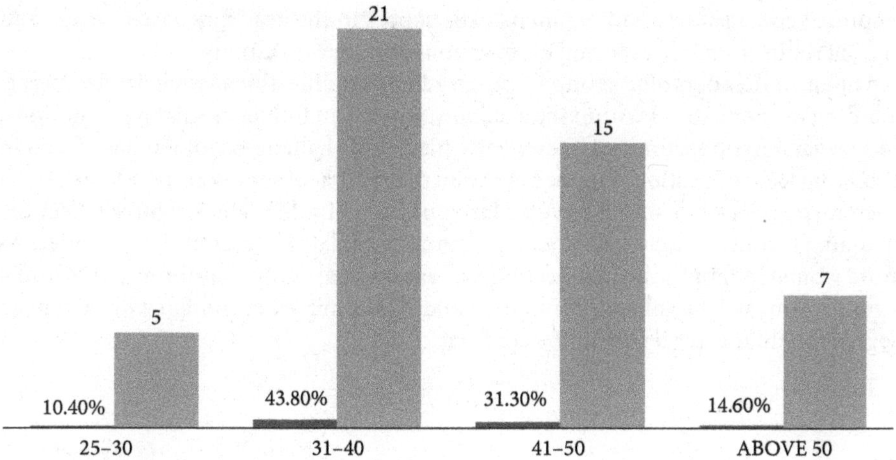

Figure 6.1 *Age of Respondents*
Source: Survey respondents (48).

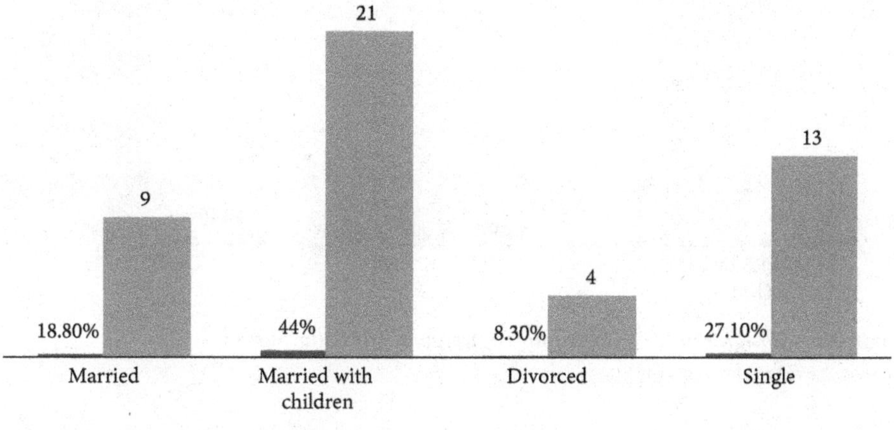

Figure 6.2 *Marital Status of Respondents*
Source: Survey respondents (48).

Figure 6.2 is a bar chart showing marital status of respondents. Categories include: Married with children (44%, 21 respondents), Single (27.1%, 13 respondents), Married (18.8%, 9 respondents), and Divorced (8.3%, 4 respondents).

In *Breaking the Veil of Masculinity: Women and the Legal Academy in Ghana*, which analyzed data from six accredited law schools and the Ghana School of Law between 2017 and 2018, women made up only 34 of the total 153 faculty members, accounting for 22%. This leads me to conclude that "while the current number of women legal academics remains low, the prospects for achieving both descriptive and substantive representation of women and gender issues in the legal academy look promising" (Dawuni, 2021a, p. 150). The challenges I faced in accessing current data across the countries where I conducted research for this study made it impossible to compare women's representation within and across regions. This study draws empirical conclusions about women's experiences in the academy based on age and marital status from self-reported observations and survey responses.

The third demographic group of postgraduate qualifications is crucial for understanding women's status within the academy, which can influence salary, promotions, and leadership opportunities. Despite the historical challenges women have faced in obtaining legal education, **Figure 6.3** shows that 52.1% of survey respondents hold a doctoral degree, while 45.8% have a Master of Laws (LL.M). These figures reflect the changing hiring standards for doctoral degree candidates in various law faculties. As more women attain these qualifications, a longitudinal study examining shifts in the legal academy will be valuable for understanding the impact of women with advanced degrees on their experiences in the academy.

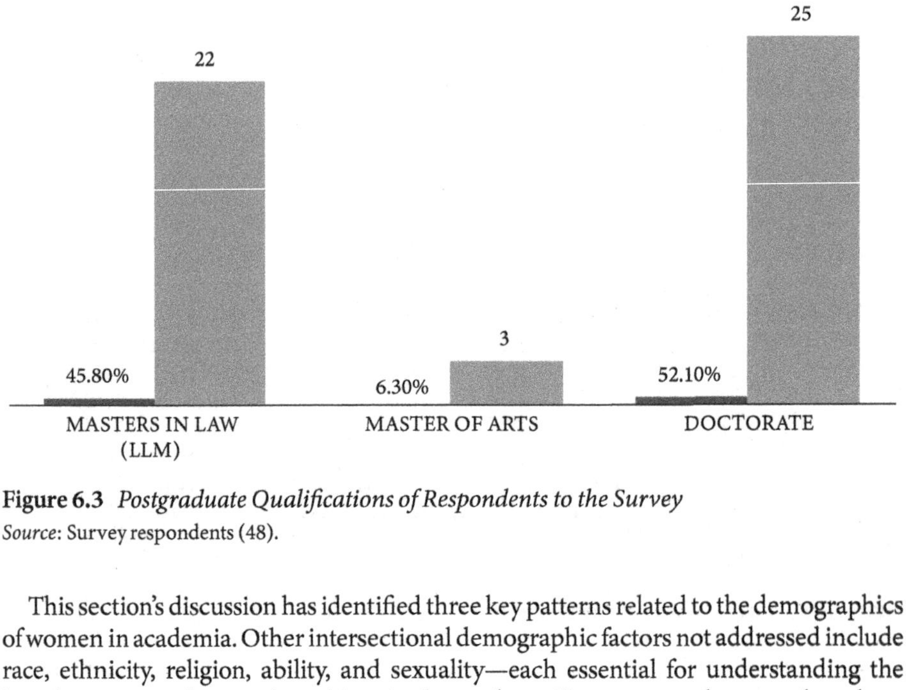

Figure 6.3 *Postgraduate Qualifications of Respondents to the Survey*
Source: Survey respondents (48).

This section's discussion has identified three key patterns related to the demographics of women in academia. Other intersectional demographic factors not addressed include race, ethnicity, religion, ability, and sexuality—each essential for understanding the broader context of women's positions in the academy. Future research can explore these identity categories. The impact of the three demographics studied here and their implications for women's roles in academia will be discussed again when we revisit topics such as workload, rank, promotions, and contributions to the legal academy.

2. Sex Diversification

In Chapter 1, this book used "sex diversification" as a more precise term to describe the changes in the number of males and females, rather than the term "feminization," traditionally used to describe the increase in women's representation in the legal profession (Menkel-Meadow, 1986; Michelson, 2013). Distinguishing between changes in numbers and changes in working conditions, Menkel-Meadow (1986) examined the feminization of the legal field from two perspectives. First, does the growth in numbers relate to the new qualities women bring? Second, is this increase in numbers accompanied by new work arrangements that support women's presence? In a study on the global trend of feminization—defined strictly as the quantitative growth of women at the bar—Michelson (2013) found that an increase in the overall number of lawyers (lawyer density) leads to a rise in the number of women lawyers.

Michelson's (2013) conclusion is based on a sample of 86 countries, using 2010 census data available from only 53 of them. However, only nine African countries are included in his dataset. For the countries listed, the data do not accurately reflect lawyer density at the time of the study because of several missing data points, highlighting challenges in data access. Nonetheless, Michelson (2013) concludes that an increase in the number of lawyers—both female and male—will lead to more women entering the profession. Given the difficulties in obtaining accurate enrollment and graduation data, this chapter relies on descriptive gender diversity in law school classrooms and law firms based on responses from interviewees. The rise in female lawyers represents a demographic shift driven by several previously mentioned factors, such as improved educational opportunities, role model effects, and changing perceptions of women's career options.

Earlier discussions in Chapter 3 about the pathways to the legal profession identified five key variables: family, accidental, intentional, role model, and interest in social justice. For some individuals, family tradition served as a predictive factor in their decision to pursue a career as a lawyer or judge. In contrast, for certain academics in the Ivory Coast, the accidental variable played a more significant role in their paths, with multiple respondents noting they entered academia after failing the competitive magistracy entry exam. **Figure 6.4** shows the main reasons respondents chose

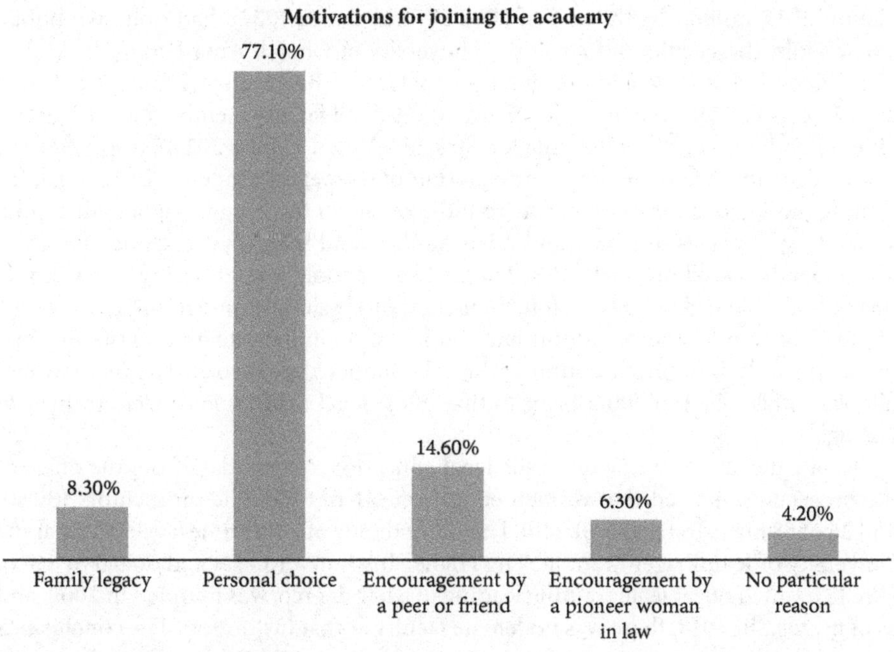

Figure 6.4 *Decision to Pursue an Academic Career*

Source: Survey respondents (48). Respondents had the option to choose more than one option, hence the numbers add up to more than 100%.

an academic career. For 77.1% of them, it was a personal choice, matching interview responses where participants expressed their passion for teaching. For others, the decision was based on the belief that an academic career would offer the flexibility to balance their domestic and caregiving roles as mothers, wives, or in other relational responsibilities.

As the number of lawyers in the bar increases, the number of female candidates choosing to join the academy is expected to rise accordingly. A previous study of women in the Ghanaian legal academy found that newer and private institutions tend to enroll more women than the older public law faculties. This study attributed the trend to ongoing gender stratification and predominantly male hierarchies in older legal education institutions, which are perceived as prestigious (Dawuni, 2021a).

Two factors explain the changes in women's entry into the legal academy: demand and supply. On the demand side, the increase in law schools and the expansion of their campuses indicate a growing need for law lecturers to teach the rising number of law students. Neoliberal political economies have created new opportunities for educational growth through the privatization of legal education (Garth & Shaffer, 2022; Kameri-Mbote, 2014; Madlalate, 2022; Oloka-Onyango, 2021; Tamale, 2021). As more law schools are established, the demand for additional lecturers will continue to grow, thereby increasing opportunities for gender diversity among law faculty and challenging the male-dominated culture in the legal academy (Dawuni, 2021a).

Supply-side factors are influenced by the size of a country's legal profession and the total number of women lawyers. For example, Senegal, with an estimated population of 17 million by the end of 2022 (World Bank, 2022), had only two public law schools: the Faculty of Law at the University of Cheikh Anta Diop (UCAD) in Dakar, founded in 1957, and the University of Gaston Berger in St. Louis, established in 1990. As of 2023, women made up just 10.9% of all faculty members at the law faculties of both universities (Institute for African Women in Law, 2023o, p. 42). Several factors contribute to the underrepresentation of women in academia in Senegal, including the sociocultural context surrounding women teaching in higher education, societal expectations to marry and raise families, and the heavy teaching and grading demands placed on academics. The first law school in neighboring The Gambia was only established in 2007. Before then, legal professionals were trained in Nigeria, Sierra Leone, and other common-law countries. A similar situation exists in Cape Verde, the only Lusophone country where I conducted fieldwork. The first law faculty was established in 2002; prior to that, most legal professionals were trained in Portugal.

Despite the late start of a domestic legal education system, data from the office of the prosecutor showed that women comprised 21 of 69 public prosecutors (30%), and 26 of 68 magistrates (38%). Still, I could find only one full-time law lecturer at the University of Jean Piaget in Praia. The Higher Institute of Legal and Social Sciences (ISCJS), which offers legal training leading to a law degree, was founded in 2009, and as of my visit in 2018, there was no female faculty at that institution. The conclusions drawn from the examples in these three West African countries suggest that the supply of women lawyers as a pathway to the legal academy depends on the availability of legal education (in Cape Verde and The Gambia) as much as it is influenced by other sociocultural factors, as noted in Senegal.

3. Rank and Promotion

The sex diversification discussed earlier also means that women are occupying different academic ranks. The survey results in **Figure 6.5** show that 52.1% of our respondents hold a doctorate degree, but only 8.3% are full professors based on their academic ranks. Most respondents (50%) are lecturers, which is often the entry level at law faculties.

The data show that women still dominate the lower ranks of the legal academy. Some women have reached the mid-level as associate professors, while even fewer have achieved the rank of full professor. The pyramid structure of women at the lower academic levels may also result from women's late entry into the academy and some of the ongoing challenges they face, which will be discussed later in this chapter. In 2022, women made up 37.9% of the faculty at the Nigerian School of Law and 58.8% at the Nigerian Institute for Advanced Studies (Institute for African Women in Law, 2023n).

This study aimed to understand women's perceptions of promotion. When asked whether they experienced slower promotion rates than men, only 27% agreed that women were promoted at slower rates than their male counterparts. The lower number of women in higher academic ranks suggests that women advance more slowly up the academic ladder, and section VI examines reasons women cited for their workplace challenges that contribute to their slower promotion rates.

Academic promotions follow standardized procedures established by national regulatory and accreditation agencies, universities, and the law faculty. Regardless of the

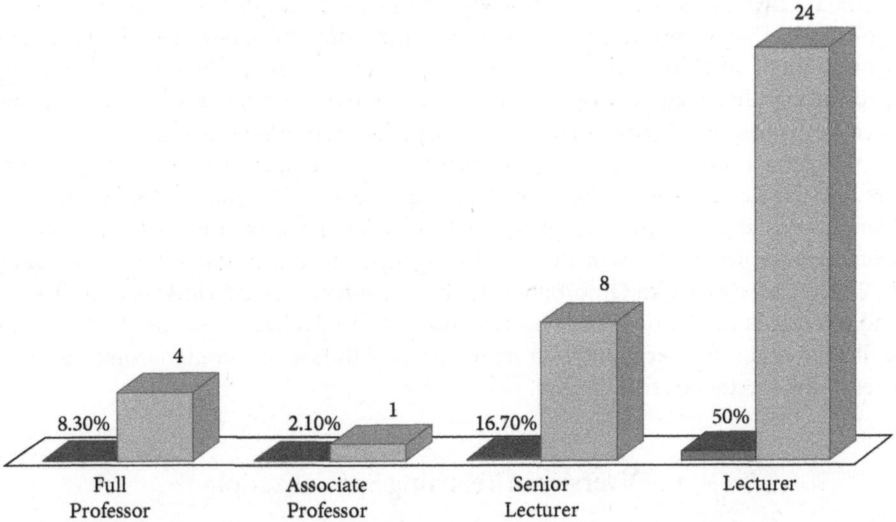

Figure 6.5 *Academic Rank of Respondents*
Source: Survey respondents (48).

legal system—civil or common law—academics are expected to teach, publish, serve the faculty or university, and participate in other activities that support their professional growth. In civil-law countries, an additional step with a more standardized process involves taking the competitive CAMES examination for independent assessment in promotion, as discussed earlier in section III (Institute for African Women In Law, 2023o).

Without transparent institutional norms that promote open merit-based appointments and promotions, women's limited networks, contrasted with the persistent "old boys clubs," may restrict their access to internal and external opportunities that can improve their upward mobility within the profession. Echoing the gender queue argument of Reskin and Roos (1990), if the prestige and quality of legal education decline, then the exodus of men from the academy will stagnate salaries and benefits, leaving women no better off in the academy or in institutions that do not prioritize their needs. Women will become the majority not because of their merit but due to the attrition of men to more lucrative legal practices, a trend already seen in some countries, including South Africa (Institute for African Women in Law, 2023r). Globally, research has shown that women often find themselves at a disadvantage when male flight inadvertently creates opportunities to recruit more women, with little effort dedicated to improving conditions of service and retention (Auchmuty et al., 2021).

Despite the intersectional effects of women's historical exclusions, ongoing institutional challenges, and competing social expectations and roles, women academics continue to transform representation by advancing into ranks and positions once exclusively held by men. In 2011, Professor Kameri-Mbote made history as the first woman promoted to the rank of full professor at the University of Nairobi School of Law. She earned Senior Counsel status in 2012 and served as the first female law dean from 2012 to 2016. In 2019, she attracted attention by earning a higher doctorate—the first of its kind in Kenya and across all of East and Central Africa. In neighboring Uganda, other pioneering women law professors include Professor Justice Lilliam Tibatemwa-Ekirikubinza, who later joined the Supreme Court bench. Professor Sylvia Tamale of Uganda has significantly impacted research, advocacy, and leadership through her focused work in African women and gender studies. In 2004, she became the first female dean of the University of Makerere School of Law.

In Nigeria, Professor Bamgbose, a law professor at the University of Ibadan, became the first female academic to be named a Senior Advocate of Nigeria (SAN) in 2018. Her notable achievement was highlighted by the fact that, at the time of her induction, women made up only 4.9% of all SANs in Nigeria (Dawuni & Abdul-Rahman, 2022). In 2022, Professor Yinka Omorogbe, also a law professor at the University of Ibadan and a research professor at the Nigerian Institute for Advanced Studies (NIALS), as well as an expert in energy and petroleum, became the second woman from academia to earn the prestigious title of SAN.

4. Diversity in Teaching Specialization

Law faculties at universities—both private and public—often introduce students to the theoretical aspects of law. In contrast, law schools provide the practical training and skills needed to join the legal workforce. Law faculties typically offer foundational law courses, including constitutional law, legal systems, legal writing, contracts, and jurisprudence. In common-law countries, the law school curriculum aims to familiarize students with the practical application of legal concepts. Ideally, this stage should involve gaining hands-on experience through courthouse visits and accredited internships with law firms, courts, and other legal sectors. The rise in the number of law students, combined with insufficient infrastructure for practical training, has caused many law schools to focus mainly on theory with little practical application. In civil-law countries, since formal legal education occurs only at the university level (within law faculties), students mostly engage with foundational law courses. Practical legal training happens during a two- or three-year apprenticeship that students pursue while affiliated with a law faculty (Schultz, 2021b).

To understand the teaching loads of male and female academics and how this may influence women's roles, I asked interviewees to clarify the division of labor and how faculty choose courses. The responses varied. In Senegal, a law professor described her department's fair approach to course assignment and selection.

> At the start of the academic year, we hold a meeting about course selection. There is no distinction between men and women; there is no gender-based discrimination. A list of courses is circulated, including which ones we want to teach and our preferred teaching times. We primarily respect the older professors; beyond that, we all choose equally, and a person's gender is not a factor. It's all about your expertise.

This seemingly egalitarian selection of courses, based on expertise and age, reflects the isolated experience of a woman from one of the two universities in Senegal. Therefore, it cannot be generalized, but it remains instructive regarding the existing approaches. In the report *Women in Law and Leadership in the Kenyan Academy*, a Kenyan female academic shared a different and contrasting experience in the course selection process, noting that (Institute for African Women in Law, 2023k, p. 29):

> Women professors are not made to teach specific courses, but you find that during course allocation during faculty board meetings, the men rush to pick the courses that are traditionally perceived to be more masculine and suitable to them. The men are reluctant to take family law, gender, and child law. Men often argue that women have a soft touch and are nurturing, and therefore in a better position to teach those courses. In one scenario, a colleague once said that gender is for women and women should teach the course because they understand women's problems, yet gender encompasses men and women. The perception is that gender is synonymous with feminism/women, and the wrong perception is that feminism is about women who are out to fight men. Perhaps there is a need to debunk this myth about the courses.

In Nigeria, a legal academic at a law school started by explaining that she had not experienced any gender-based discrimination, she noted:

> When it came to teaching, my gender was a factor. The law faculty is mostly male, and teaching international law is even more so. I was hired to teach the jurisprudence

> course, which had been taught solely by men for 42 years. The lead professor told me to teach, and when I entered the classroom, the students thought I was lost. News spread that a woman was teaching jurisprudence, surprising everyone who heard it. Even now, I still face gender issues. Although I no longer feel the need to prove myself, I sometimes encounter resentment from colleagues who question why I am teaching the course. I've developed a thick skin about these matters and remind myself that it's their perspective. Overall, we maintain politeness and respect among those who share similar views.

This interviewee's response offers important historical context for understanding how she started teaching the course. Her expertise in the subject aligned with the need for an instructor, and while there were initial challenges, it ultimately had a positive outcome. A faculty member's academic rank and course requirements partly determine which courses a female academic can teach.

Their interests and qualifications mainly influence the subject a person teaches. If someone has the necessary credentials to teach a specific course that matches the faculty's needs, they are likely assigned to that course. Additionally, most hiring decisions at law schools are based on advertised courses, so faculty typically teach the courses for which they were hired. While faculty may have some flexibility in their teaching preferences or assignments, class size is an important factor. Generally, women did not report any selective assignment of large classes based on gender. However, rank significantly influences whether someone teaches an introductory or a specialized course. As the demand for law degrees grows, most law schools are experiencing larger class sizes, and eventually, all professors may find themselves teaching large classes, especially in introductory courses.

Existing scholarship on law schools shows a disparity in teaching loads based on gender, highlighting the types of courses typically assigned to women, with the "soft" courses often taught by women (Kameri-Mbote & Wekesa, 2018; Neumann, 2000; Schultz, 2021b). Interviews conducted for this study find no evidence suggesting that women are pressured or expected to teach these "soft" courses. Historically, women have often pioneered courses on women and gender at universities, and law faculties follow this trend. For some women, teaching courses on women and gender or gender and the law aligns naturally with their professional interests in women's rights. For others, offering these courses serves as a form of activism, motivated by the desire to showcase feminist perspectives on the law and to illuminate how gendered constructs within it influence citizens' rights.

In Ghana, the first course on gender and the law was introduced by Professor Akua Kuenyehia, who was the first law lecturer and a women's rights activist. The movement to introduce courses on women and gender gained momentum across the continent as universities established centers for women and gender studies. Some of these centers are at universities in Ghana, Nigeria, Kenya, Uganda, and Zimbabwe, among others. These centers have helped increase the importance of women and gender studies courses within the university curriculum (Ampofo et al., 2008; Barnes & Mama, 2007; Mama, 2003; Tamale, 2015).

In Zimbabwe, the Southern and Eastern Africa Regional Center of Women's Law (SEARCWL) plays a vital role in producing research and courses on women and the law for much of southern and eastern Africa (Stewart & Tsanga, 2011). Women faculty also develop and teach innovative courses, such as climate and environmental sustainability, law and technology, intellectual property, and artificial intelligence. The academic advocacy for incorporating women and gender into law courses has become a crucial battleground for women legal scholars, which will be examined later in section VI.

5. Diversity in Research

Women academics have made significant contributions to knowledge production across various subject areas, and law is no exception. However, many of the women interviewees consistently cited a lack of time to engage in active and ongoing research as a major challenge. At underfunded universities, it is common for lecturers (male and female) to supplement their incomes through paid external consultancies, which leaves them with little time to focus on research. The size and prestige of law schools often correlate with faculty requirements to maintain active research agendas. At long-established universities in Nigeria, Ghana, and Senegal, research is a key criterion for academic career advancement. In smaller, newer institutions, these requirements may be less strict, with a greater emphasis on teaching. This is especially clear in countries like The Gambia and Cape Verde, where law faculties were established recently during my visit in 2018.

Respondents observed that there are no rules or conditions governing the research interests of women academics, allowing them to select their research focus based on personal interests. From the interviews, it was clear that some researchers had not considered developing a specialized area for their research, often following whatever research consultancies caught their attention. For many others, their research interests appeared to stem from their teaching areas. Before reaching the height of her career as an international court judge at the International Criminal Court, Professor Akua Kuenyehia of Ghana began her professional journey as a legal academic. Reflecting on how she decided to study law and pursue a career in teaching and research on women, she recounted her accidental path to becoming a women's rights activist (Dawuni, 2018a, pp. 59–60):

> At the time [of her legal education], most courses in the arts prepared people to become teachers, I did not want to become a teacher and, with my good grades, studying the law gave me other options and that was enough for me. Right from the get-go, I realized that the perception that the law was gender-neutral was not accurate. If the laws were gender-neutral, why were there so many discriminatory practices against women? I started to focus on these issues, and that is how my interest in women's rights grew.

A significant number of women academics have made important contributions to the fields of women, gender, and law. Some of the pioneering books and articles on gender-related issues have been written by women academics, both on the continent and in the African diaspora. As academic requirements for promotion have changed, research is increasingly prioritized, and women academics, like their male colleagues, must meet these standards. Data from this study's survey of 48 women academics show a variety of research interests.

A quick review of the web profiles of male academics showed that none listed gender and women's issues as a research focus, even though more male legal scholars are writing about and analyzing legal issues through a gendered perspective. Based on this, it's reasonable to conclude that although not all women research women and gender topics, these issues still mainly fall within the research areas of female legal academics. While women who specialize in gender issues choose this path independently, some female scholars have reported facing institutional challenges, like less emphasis on research related to women and gender issues and a lingering perception that gender research is less scientific (Tamale, 2021). The expectations for women to conduct gender-related research pose a challenge faced by female academics worldwide (Auchmuty et al., 2021; Carle, 2021; Sommerlad, 2021). When these academic gender divisions intersect with racial bias, many female scholars experience double alienation (Deo, 2019; Mabokela & Mawila, 2004).

6. Women in Leadership

Although women entered the legal academic field much later than their male counterparts, they have steadily advanced to leadership positions, including department heads and deans of law schools (Tamale, 2021). The procedures for appointment and selection in these roles differ by country and institution. Formal criteria usually include holding the rank of full professor, demonstrating academic leadership, possessing a higher degree such as a doctorate, and demonstrating leadership skills. Often, the officeholder is chosen from among their peers, but there are also cases in which external candidates are recruited to lead a department. For deans, other individuals involved in the selection process may include the university's vice chancellor or rector. Department heads tend to be younger scholars compared to deans, which means the significant administrative demands of these roles add to the time constraints faced by women. To understand women's chances for leadership roles, the survey asked respondents if they held a leadership position. **Figure 6.6** indicates that 45.8% were in some form of leadership role.

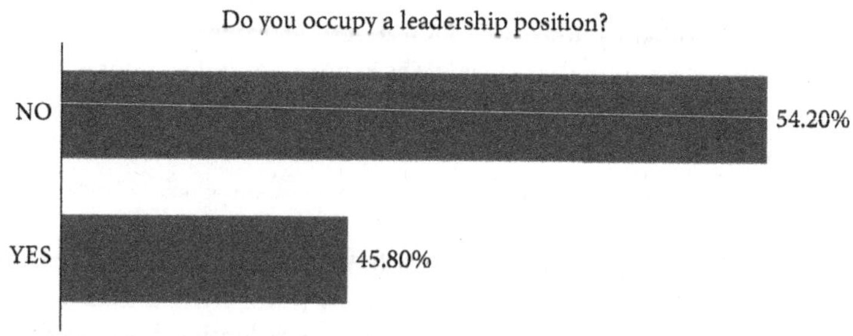

Figure 6.6 *Women in Leadership Positions*
Source: Survey respondents (48).

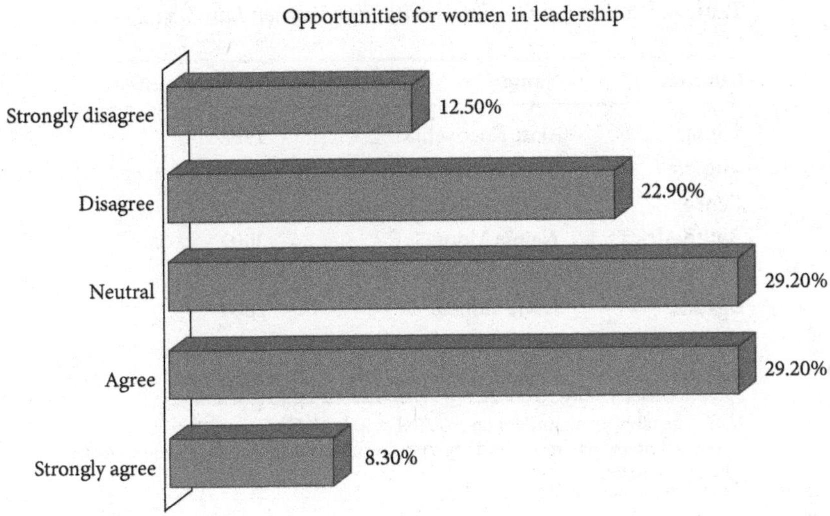

Figure 6.7 *Women's Perceptions of Equal Access to Leadership*
Source: Survey respondents (48).

The survey asked respondents, "Women in my country have equal opportunities for leadership as men in my profession." *How much do you agree with this statement*? The figures in **Figure 6.7** show that while 29.2% agreed with the statement, 22.9% disagreed, and 29.2% remained neutral. This neutrality among respondents suggests they may either be unaware of which leadership positions the survey referred to or lack knowledge about leadership roles within their institutions. This neutral perception of leadership indicates a need for more efforts to promote leadership training among women in law.

Some respondents indicated that they declined offers to assume leadership roles because of the extra burden it places on their personal and professional lives. While the formal criteria may suggest equal opportunities for qualified candidates, numerous informal and hidden factors influence who secures a leadership position. The persistence of "old boys' networks" and favoritism toward male colleagues is a significant factor in who ultimately gets chosen. An increasing number of women have served as deans at various law schools across the continent. **Table 6.1** shows selected data on where women have held deanships (this list is by no means comprehensive of recent developments).

The findings from the *Women in Law and Leadership: Kenyan Legal Academy* (Institute for African Women in Law, 2023k) report show that in 2022, 37% of law faculty deans in Kenya were women. This progress is linked to increased representation of women in public decision-making as mandated by the 2010 Constitution of Kenya, a growth in the number of women in law faculties, and the demand for diverse leadership skills. In contrast, in Senegal, the number of women in leadership roles, including as deans, has decreased. As of 2023, women made up only 14% of legal academics in the country. It is therefore not surprising that the first female law dean, Professor Aminata Cissé Niang, was appointed in 2022 at Cheikh Anta Diop University, the country's first public university. With her appointment as the first

Table 6.1 *Select Law Faculties With First Women Law Deans*

Country	Name	Year appointed
Ghana	Akua Kuenyehia	1996
Nigeria	Chioma Agomo	2004
Senegal	Aminata Cissé Niang	2022
South Africa	Najma Moosa	2002
*Zambia	Margaret Munalula	N/A
Uganda	Sylvia Tamale	2004
*Tanzania	Yitiha Simbeye	N/A
Kenya	Patricia Kameri-Mbote	2012

Note. The table presents data on selected countries. Those with asterisks represent countries where the year of appointment could not be verified after multiple searches.

woman among 13 deans, women account for 5% of all deans since the law faculty was founded in 1957. At the second public university, Gaston Berger in St. Louis, established in 1990, only one woman has served as assistant dean (2017–2020), and no woman has been appointed as dean among the nine who have served in the past (Institute for African Women in Law, 2023o).

The growing gender diversity in leadership roles within law faculties and law schools indicates that institutional norms and practices are becoming more inclusive of women. However, this outward display of institutional inclusivity hides the genuine challenges that women in leadership positions still face. Feminist managerial theory suggests that women in authority must navigate various patriarchal institutional norms, leading some to conform in order to survive within these patriarchal cultures (Abadi & Ayentimi, 2023; Barnes, 2007; Tsikata, 2007). For women to not only survive but thrive in leadership roles, a radical reimagining of contemporary leadership and institutional cultures is necessary (Moodly & Toni, 2017).

These observations raise two related questions: First, what opportunities exist for women to hold leadership positions? Second, what does it take to ascend the academic leadership ladder? A 2023 study on women in law and leadership within the Nigerian legal profession, which surveyed 449 respondents, revealed that 36% believed women had equal opportunities to occupy leadership roles. However, qualitative responses indicated that many respondents were divided, suggesting that formal equal opportunity standards masked the informal challenges preventing women from assuming leadership positions. Even with the 36% who acknowledged equal opportunities for women, 87.5% felt that men found it easier to advance in leadership. A significant 92.5% agreed that men challenge women's leadership roles (Institute for African Women in Law, 2023n). At the Nigerian School of Law, established in 1960, despite an increase in the number of women in academic leadership roles, by 2023, no woman had yet been appointed director general of the law school (Institute for African Women in Law, 2023n).

Personal factors greatly impact how women see themselves as leaders and their willingness to seek leadership roles. My review of past and current deans of law schools and law faculties shows an average age of 50 or older. Age is an important indicator for understanding this aspect for two main reasons. First, by age 50, these women have typically been in the profession long enough to build the necessary academic credentials, qualifications, and experience for leadership positions. Second, after age 50, most women with families—such as a spouse and children—have usually moved past the active child-rearing stage, which demands a lot of time and attention. This shift often allows women, by age 50, to focus more on administrative leadership while managing other family and personal responsibilities.

The analysis of the institutional, social, and positional factors presented here does not indicate that women have it easy or that the doors to leadership are wide open for them. The historical structure of legal academies has naturally developed from the patriarchal nature of the legal profession, which has shaped the gendered formal and informal norms within the legal academy. Women's access to leadership positions is not simple, and the paths vary. The first female dean of a law faculty in Ghana shared her experience (Dawuni, 2021a, p. 160):

> Gender has not been a problem, I have not had a sense that because I am a woman, there is a shortfall [in her capabilities]. I use a different type of management style depending on the context, and I draw more on my expertise in leadership. My appointment process was very, very rigorous, it was open, though none of my male colleagues applied, all other applicants were well known and based abroad [meaning the other applicants resided outside Ghana, in foreign universities and institutions]. So, it was clear that I was very qualified, and they could not bypass me and give the position to anyone even though they could have given the position to a Full Professor which I was not at that time. It was made clear that I got it on merit, so I started on that premise and no one could challenge my appointment. They also recognized my expertise—I have a very active research agenda and they cannot challenge me.

For other women pursuing leadership roles, their experiences are shaped by the intersection of key variables in the IIISP framework (history, institutions, social factors and positionality), creating a triple exclusionary axis. An example of the impact of this intersection is illustrated by the experience of a woman law professor in Nigeria.

> When I joined the faculty in 1987, it was mostly a male-dominated environment. A few women were present, but they held no administrative roles; they were only lecturers. I was the first woman to become head of the department, and the men reacted as if they had never seen a woman in a leadership position before. When I became pregnant with my third child, the men expressed outrage, claiming it was inappropriate for me to be pregnant so soon after my appointment as head of the department. I challenged them on what my pregnancy had to do with my abilities and intelligence. I had to work very hard to pave the way for other women who would follow. Through my dedication and effort, I set a standard for excellence, which led to my reappointment for another two years because of my hard work.

In the narrative above, the respondent faced opposition not only because she was a woman but also because the resistance to her pregnancy highlights the deep-rooted patriarchal beliefs among some men that women cannot lead. The narrow perspective held by some men that a pregnant woman cannot lead or work effectively demonstrates the selective application of gender norms—while men rarely question the realities many pregnant women face in society, such as caring for their families and working in informal sectors like farms and markets. As will be discussed later regarding the challenges women confront and the strategies they use to persevere, this respondent fits into the category of women I identify as *gender-norm disruptors*, as she consistently challenged gender stereotypes throughout her career.

In Senegal, a country with a civil-law system, women made up only 10.9% of legal academics at the two public universities in 2023 (Institute for African Women in Law, 2023o). The legal academy has the lowest representation of women among the three sectors: the bar, the bench, and the academy. This limited representation occurs in the context of the first female law dean being appointed only in 2022. Professor Amsatou Sow Sidibe was the first woman to reach the rank of full professor of law. However, she was not elected dean, likely because she retired from academia to run in the country's presidential elections. A respondent shared that women often do not apply for dean positions because of their time-consuming nature, which conflicts with women's heavy caregiving roles. More often, toxic administrative politics also contribute to the lack of interest from many candidates, even though some men often compete among themselves for power.

The HISP framework highlights the significant challenges women in Senegal face when entering academia. Social, religious, and cultural expectations for women originate from early social conditioning that emphasizes marriage and family. Women have not only struggled to access academia, but those who succeed also face various intersectional challenges that hinder their advancement. In this context, Professor Aminata Cissé Niang was appointed the first female dean of the faculty of law in 2022. Her appointment was celebrated as a sign of the progress women are making in Senegalese society, despite ongoing socioreligious norms. In my interview with her in 2023, she underscored the importance of supporting young women and female academics in climbing the ranks and noted that the young male faculty in the department fully supported her appointment as dean. This strong backing from young male faculty could suggest a shift in gendered perceptions of women's leadership, or it may reflect the traditional view that women, as mothers, can "care for" the department and its demanding administrative challenges and needs. Her mention of "care for" alludes to society's expectations of women's caregiving roles extending into the workplace.

What distinguishes Prof. Aminata Niang's rise to the decanal leadership position from that of the earlier respondent in Nigeria (the head of the department) is attributable to several factors that merit further exploration. Was it due to the country's context, departmental culture, or the institutional expectation for a woman to "clean up" when departments face crises? What explains why Professor Aminata Cissé Niang was appointed as dean instead of Professor Amsatou Sidibe Sow? Could it be their differing personal traits—one seen as a gender-norm conformist exhibiting stereotypically gendered qualities of consensus-building, while the other was regarded as a *gender-norm disruptor* who would not allow the men to uphold masculine institutional practices? In my interviews with both women, they confirmed that students and faculty viewed them as "mothers," a response that aligns with earlier studies on the slippery divide and the blurring of lines between professional and private caregiving obligations (Coetzee & Moosa, 2020; Kipkosgei, 2019; Maphalala & Mpofu, 2017; Nzewi, & Ohia, 2016). Thus, while Professor Sidibe Sow can be seen as a gender-norm disruptor, she still valued motherhood in her role as an academic, dedicating her time to academia:

> The students liked me; they called me "mom" and "aunt." When I teach, I give my best, and many students sign up for my classes. That is my role as a mother, and I enjoy it. I embraced motherhood and treated them as if they were my children. When I taught, they were quiet and attentive. They showed great respect and never insulted me.

However, in describing her time as an academic, she highlighted the challenges she had to face as a woman:

> It wasn't easy. I was constantly competing with my male colleagues due to the rivalry. I was the first and youngest to earn a doctorate, while the younger men were still finishing theirs and aiming for positions of authority. There was always some scheming going on, but I pushed back. I became the first woman to reach the rank of Full Professor. I aimed for the very top, and I can't go any higher. My colleagues said I am a strong woman. I worked very hard and took my responsibilities seriously. I wanted everyone to succeed, and I consistently excelled.

These two experiences—one as a teacher and the other as a leader—confirm the main argument of this book: there is no single story for women in law. Different historical, institutional, social, and positional factors produce a variety of experiences and outcomes. Still, despite these differences in outcomes, women's entry into and advancement to leadership roles indicate growing opportunities for women's representation in decision-making within the legal academy.

Women's representation in top leadership roles in higher education may be improving, but this progress primarily results from changes in institutional policies and, in some cases, advocacy and activism by women. When discussing the challenges encountered during Professor Lillian Tibatemwa-Ekirikubinza's appointment as the first female deputy vice chancellor at Makerere University, Tamale (2021) highlights the obstacles set up to block her appointment and concludes that a gap exists between policy and practice. This gap requires women to stay vigilant and adopt strategic measures to ensure that qualified women have equal opportunities for leadership roles. Although Professor Tibatemwa-Ekirikubinza was ultimately appointed deputy vice chancellor, Tamale (2021) notes that the appointment policy remained inactive after her tenure. Like many others, this Ugandan case underscores the importance of continuous vigilance to prevent fleeting appointments and to maintain progress toward women's right to leadership. Women's paths to leadership and their experiences in these roles can be both challenging and influential. Do women deans lead differently from men? Exploring this question is important because the experiences of women legal academics have not been studied as extensively as those of women at the bar and on the bench. The following section examines some of the contributions women legal academics make within the profession and in the often unseen realm of academic service.

V. Contributions: Changing the Academic Landscape

The previous discussion has outlined the historical and current context of women's symbolic and substantive representation in the legal academy by presenting both qualitative and quantitative findings from this research and citing examples from emerging studies and data on women in the legal academy across Africa. Considering the relatively low number of women in the legal academy, how are women doing in this environment, and to what degree are they changing the academic landscape? This section's analysis provides a comprehensive look at women's contributions both inside and outside the legal academy.

1. Changing Gender Norms and Perceptions

Across the continent, women legal scholars are transforming the field of legal academia—often in subtle ways but also through activist efforts exemplified by gender-norm disruptors. This study's findings suggest that one of the most significant impacts of women's contributions to the legal academy has been to challenge and dismantle the barriers created by masculinized institutional norms that once favored men's entry into the field.

The presence of women who were the "firsts" in the legal academy paved the way for other women to enter the field; these trailblazers served as role models, demonstrating that women could hold prominent positions in higher education. The pioneering women in law were also influential figures beyond the academy. For example, Akua Kuenyehia from Ghana became an international judge at the International Criminal Court. Through her exceptional leadership and vision, Akua Kuenyehia's role as a law lecturer and dean challenged various gender norms. These norms included managing numerous responsibilities as an academic, wife, and mother while actively participating in the women's rights movement both locally and globally. Additionally, she demonstrated a strong work ethic in administration as the first woman dean of the law faculty, leading the effort to build the first permanent structure for the law faculty at the University of Ghana (Dawuni, 2018a).

In Kenya, the first group of women law professors and lecturers—Janet Macharia, Patricia Kameri-Mbote, and Winifred Kamau—were outspoken in their opposition to institutional patriarchal norms, including resisting the introduction of courses on women and the law (Kameri-Mbote & Wekesa, 2018). Female legal academics in Zimbabwe (Stewart, 2012) and Uganda (Tamale, 2021) faced similar challenges as they aimed to introduce gender awareness in legal education, expose institutional patriarchy, and promote the recruitment and inclusion of more women in legal academia. Beyond launching the first courses on gender and the law, these women academics played a vital role in creating anti-sexual harassment and gender equality policies to address the ongoing issues female students faced in higher education (Kameri-Mbote & Wekesa, 2018).

Women's activism aimed at changing gender norms often faces significant costs. The intersection of historical, institutional, and social factors mentioned earlier creates various challenges for individual women in academia. It is during these moments of conflicting influences that gender-norm disruptors stand out. Through their acts of resistance, they dismantle sexist gender norms. Women academics must work to transform these norms, as emphasized by a senior academic in Nigeria:

> When I had my baby while serving as the head of the department, I wrote to the Vice Chancellor to inform them that I would not be taking maternity leave and would instead bring my baby to the faculty. I brought my nanny to work with me; I breastfed my baby while working and demonstrated to the male faculty that the baby was not a disturbance. I continued my research and published in international journals, ensuring that my baby did not hinder my progress. I set a standard for other women to show the men that we, as female faculty, can do it.

The caregiving roles of women go beyond the home and often continue when they enter the workforce, especially during their prime childbearing years. The stages of caregiving and childbearing frequently overlap with the period when many women begin building their careers, as shown by the survey results mentioned earlier. Among the respondents, 43.8% were in the 31–40 age group, and 44% were married with children. Balancing their dual roles as educators and mothers can be difficult for some women, often leaving them with few options. In Ghana, Akua Kuenyehia had to bring her sick child to class when she had no child care at home. Fortunately, unlike in the earlier story, she received support from her male colleagues and supervisors (Dawuni, 2018a).

The narratives above offer insights into how women navigate their public and private lives. The first story describes a toxic masculine environment where the first woman leader chose to skip her maternity leave to demonstrate to her male colleagues that she could balance her roles as a leader, woman, and mother. The second story shows a woman who reported having positive relationships with her colleagues, which helped her manage her multiple intersectional roles—carrying her child on her back while teaching a class because her domestic support system was unavailable at the time.

These two contrasting narratives show that, regardless of women's circumstances, they must find creative ways to fulfill their multiple and intersecting roles. Whether these actions are deliberate or born out of necessity, they do alter perceptions within institutions, indicating that gender or motherhood identities do not serve as barriers to women fulfilling their responsibilities as academics. Although women are developing innovative methods to manage their personal and professional duties, their experiences with masculine gender norms and discriminatory treatment in higher education institutions continue to present significant challenges for women in academia (Aura-Odhiambo, 2011; Obers, 2014; Oladunmi, 2014).

Women in academia are leading the way in proposing solutions for institutional change. Professor Sylvia Tamale (2021, p. 247), a well-known feminist rights advocate and the first female dean of the Makerere School of Law, proposed measures to address the lasting effects of historical and current intersectional factors that exclude women academics, thus reinforcing masculinized gender norms.

> Makerere needs to embark on a serious decolonization/decolonial process that rejects essentializations, stereotypes, and colonial-dominated hegemonies. It should take concrete steps to get rid of its institutional and organizational structures that perpetuate and reproduce sexism, ageism, heterosexism, and other inequalities. Only then will the academy at Makerere become truly gender-sensitive and fully inclusive for female academics, thereby effectively playing its role in the broader democratization process of the country.

Women leaders must constantly assert their leadership roles, often encountering backlash due to a masculinized culture that does not expect women to claim their authority or challenge deeply ingrained patriarchal institutional and social norms. Numerous studies underscore the challenges posed by the insufficient number of women capable of advocating for change within dominant masculine institutional cultures. At the University of Nairobi, Odhiambo (2011) found that women academics were not strongly resisting their relational position within the academy. Women academics must lead efforts to advocate for changes that would positively impact women's working conditions in higher education institutions (Akala & Divala, 2016; Zulu, 2021.

2. The Invisible Theatre of Gendered Performativity

Contrary to what most people outside academia believe, academics wear many hats. These "hats" can include teaching, conducting research, advising students, serving their department and university, and participating in professional development activities like attending and presenting at conferences, workshops, and seminars. I categorize the primary roles of academics in **Figure 6.8**; although not an exhaustive list, it

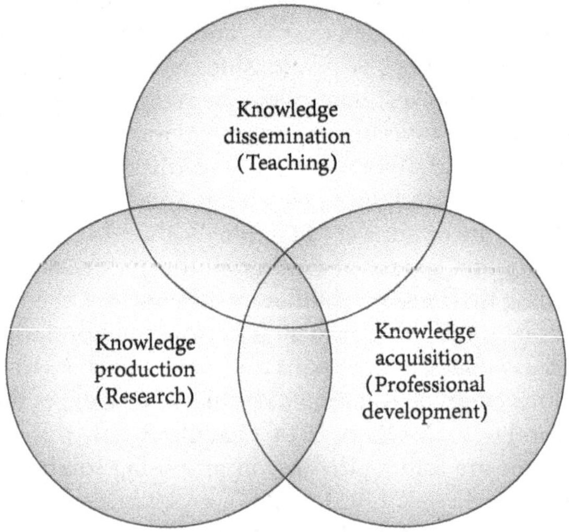

Figure 6.8 *Typology of Primary Academic Functions and Expectations*

effectively illustrates their main functions. Men, who also have commitments outside the academy and in their personal lives, often operate within these clear boundaries, facing minimal to no expectations for caregiving tasks—a responsibility that Wane (2000) describes as the "other-mothering" roles that female faculty fulfill for their students.

On the other hand, women academics often end up in secondary roles, whether due to the demands of their students or personal choices made to support both male and female students. These roles often arise from systemic sociocultural expectations of women as nurturers and caregivers, which develop into informal gendered institutional norms. The creation of these institutional gendered expectations usually places caregiving responsibilities within higher education on the shoulders of women academics (Datta & Lund, 2018). **Figure 6.9** illustrates the expanded roles women take on in academia, which I describe as the invisible theater of gender roles. As shown in this figure, beneath the surface of equal functions and expectations for all academics, women frequently assume additional secondary roles. These secondary roles often impose significant emotional strain, yet they remain unseen and are not recognized as work that contributes to service obligations for evaluation and promotion.

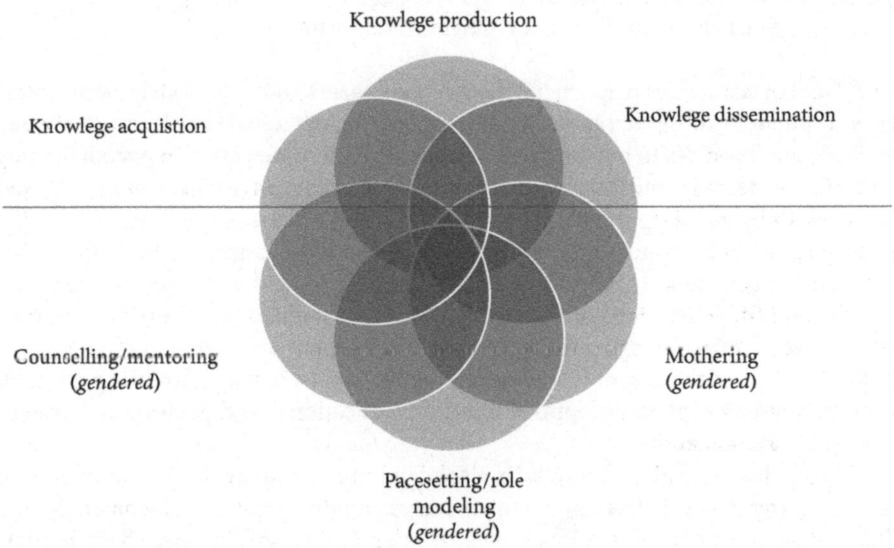

Figure 6.9 *Invisible Theater of Gender Roles in the Academy*

Women academics often unknowingly assume roles as counselors and psychologists, helping students navigate personal and academic challenges both at home and in their lives (Acker & Armenti, 2004; Wane, 2000). Female law students tend to seek help from female faculty when dealing with sexual harassment issues. Additionally, women academics support young female colleagues facing harassment while managing motherhood and pursuing their degrees. A law lecturer in Nigeria shared her experiences in helping female students who are mothers:

> I always encourage my female students not to give up. Once, I had a female student who had a baby and stopped attending class because she lacked support at home. I suggested that she bring the baby to class. I let her sit at the back of the room and care for the baby while listening to the lecture. I also allowed her to bring the baby to my office when she needed to attend other classes.

In Senegal, the high dropout rate among female students greatly contributes to the shortage of women in the legal field. A law lecturer described how she supports her female students (Institute for African Women in Law, Senegal, 2023o, p. 43).

> Two of my exceptional students, who married during their master's program, are contemplating giving up. That's why I feel it is my responsibility to remind them of their true worth by engaging in conversations and motivating them as much as possible about their potential to achieve successful careers. However, I sense they are reluctant to continue fighting. More and more often, men are taking the lead, while women seem to be fading from the spotlight; it's unfortunate.

Last, women academics play crucial roles as trailblazers and role models. Some interview respondents observed how the influence of the first female law lecturers shaped their personal choices to pursue careers in academia. Women are also paving the way for others, especially students, by serving as visible examples of what can be achieved and how to balance a professional career with personal responsibilities. While the early generation of women pioneers had no female law lecturers to look up to, this has changed over time as more women have joined the academy. Over the years, the fourth and fifth generations of women in law have expanded the diversity of women entering academia—bringing different ages, professional ranks, and academic backgrounds. Most of the recent women entering the legal academy also bring doctoral degrees, thereby expanding opportunities for educational and professional growth among female law students.

Women's invisible performativity is also seen in their support for law students and their teaching in law courses. Some interview respondents noted that women bring a different "touch and feel" to how courses are taught, often shifting away from patriarchal, autocratic teaching styles. Others mentioned that women tend to have "a better understanding of what students generally face, especially female students."

Beneath the institutional façade of gender equity in the division of labor at various higher education institutions, a gendered division of labor persists. Women's secondary roles as counselors, "other-mothers," and pacesetters for both students and junior academics add to the extra burden on female academics. Although these roles and responsibilities often go unnoticed and are not officially recognized as academic service duties, women continue to engage in them at different levels. While these actions may not be overtly subversive, they still impact the retention of female students, as shown by the rising number of women graduating from law schools in recent years.

3. Teaching and Research on Women and Gender in the Law

The gender diversification of the legal academy has led to several positive outcomes, including the introduction of courses on women and gender in the law, which previously had not been included in the course offerings at most law faculties and several higher education institutions (Kameri-Mbote & Wekesa, 2018; Oladunni, 2014; Tamale, 2021). Most of these courses focus specifically on the gendered framing of law and how the construction of law through a masculine theoretical lens has contributed to women's subordination in both private and public spheres. The goals of these courses include training students to understand how the gendered nature of law informs, produces, and reproduces gender hierarchies that lead to gender exclusion and discriminatory practices. Overall, the teaching of courses on gender has emerged from the personal interests of women who propose and teach them.

As law schools increasingly confront the rising number of female faculty and students, the demand for courses on gender and the law is becoming more institutionalized. In some regions, this progress may occur more slowly, especially in countries with only one law school and a smaller female student and faculty population, such as The Gambia and Cape Verde. Nevertheless, it wouldn't be surprising if these universities leapfrog ahead to introduce such courses as part of their efforts to promote gender inclusivity. In Senegal, a feminist legal scholar shared the challenges she faced when trying to introduce a course on women and the law, which was unsuccessful. She remains optimistic that the appointment of the first female dean in the law faculty might reduce the opposition she faced. The addition of courses on women and gender studies in Senegal isn't limited to the law faculty alone. Another feminist scholar and historian, Professor Penda Mbow, has detailed her struggles with university administration in her efforts to implement courses on gender and women's studies. Reflecting on the impact of institutional resistance to gender studies in Senegal, she lamented (Mbow, 2000, p. 71):

> Senegalese female academics are significantly lagging behind. They lack women's journals or magazines, and certainly no seminars or updates on gender issues are present. It seems they do not fully grasp the issues, which could explain their minimal engagement with feminist studies. Some male researchers have managed to persuade them that discussing women's issues is secondary and will only further marginalize them, trapping them in a "ghetto." It is crucial that we transform the social dynamics within university institutes, research centers, and civil society, as well as in research and publications.

In Uganda, despite a long history of women's studies at Makerere University and the establishment of an independent Department of Women's Studies, introducing courses on women, gender, and sexualities faced significant opposition. In "'Bitches' at the Academy (Oloka-Onyango and Tamale, 2000), the first female dean of the law faculty at Makerere University, described the sexist academic environment that consistently marginalized women's and gender studies. Despite this, women persisted, leading to the creation of new courses on gender and the law.

Several institutes have also emerged across the continent, primarily within universities, to promote education and research on women in law. A notable example is the University of Zimbabwe's SEARCWL, which has significantly influenced the incorporation of gender into teaching curricula and the development of inclusive research (Stewart & Tsanga, 2011).

The research carried out by these centers has been vital in questioning and challenging perceptions of gender neutrality in law. These studies have also offered recommendations for making the law more gender-inclusive. In Kenya, Kameri-Mbote and Wekesa (2018) highlight the importance of research on women and the law in shaping policies, the constitutional-making process, and establishing gender and women's law courses at various universities. At the University of Nairobi School of Law, gender and law courses were introduced in 1992, with faculty training to teach these subjects (Kameri-Mbote & Wekesa, 2018). However, implementing these courses was difficult, as Kameri-Mbote and Wekesa (2018, p. 69) describe.

> What was conventional was the teaching of law courses from a male-centric viewpoint, as many lecturers, most of [whom] were male, could not really appreciate the need to engender the curriculum. The three women members of the academic staff at the School (then Faculty) fought a bare-knuckle war in the faculty boardroom and after much struggle, the course "Women in the Legal Process" was introduced in 1992. This was a major win in the efforts to have women's perspectives in the law curriculum. The instruction of the course was largely left to the women, and this gave them room to shape it to challenge the dominant narratives in law.

The challenges faced by the three women faculty—Janet Kabeberi-Macharia, Edith Munene, and Patricia Kameri-Mbote—were substantial, including derogatory remarks from their male colleagues. While students, mostly female, welcomed the new course enthusiastically, it took time to convince male students to understand the gendered construction of laws and how these laws discriminate against women. The persistence of these three women faculty members who introduced the course ultimately paid off, as several students enrolled each year, and male faculty began co-teaching alongside their female colleagues (Kameri-Mbote & Wekesa, 2018).

Continuing the path pioneered by the trailblazing faculty who challenged institutional patriarchy, other law schools across Kenya have introduced courses on gender and law, guided by the influential women who initiated this course at Kenya's first public School of Law. These efforts show how women academics remain committed to making gender a core part of the law school curriculum, demonstrating their ability to navigate institutional power to transform systems, increase opportunities for their students, and foster institutional change.

Feminist legal scholars have played a vital role in efforts to decolonize and demasculinize the law, aiming to move away from a colonial patriarchal interpretation of the law that was established when law faculties first emerged (Tamale, 2020). Since the late 1980s, groups of feminist legal scholars have worked to challenge these normative assumptions. In 2013, a project was launched in Zimbabwe, Zambia, Malawi, and Kenya in collaboration with faculty from Norway, titled 'Master's, PhD, and Research Programme for Capacity Building in Law Faculties.' This initiative was funded by the Norwegian Programme for Capacity Development in Higher Education and Research for Development (NORHED) (Hellum et al., 2019). The NORHED project aimed to mainstream and "engender" the law by identifying, critiquing, and evaluating the marginalization of women based on multiple identifiers, including ethnicity, sexual orientation, class, and disability. It operated on the premise that "legal engenderment is linked to substantive rather than formal equality. It requires the integration of theories, methods, and skills that empower students to critique and reshape rights in light of the diverse lived realities of different groups of women across all areas of legal education" (Hellum et al., 2019, p. 476).

The emergence of women, gender, and law courses at universities is commendable, but more needs to be done to fully integrate these courses into the legal curriculum. Conducting a gender audit of these courses could provide valuable insights; for example, what are the main focus areas of these courses? What primary resources are used in teaching them, and how much do they depend on foreign materials and research by women in the Global North? Do any of these courses specifically address the experiences of women in law, or do they mainly cover women's rights issues in society? As one academic told me, while the effort to introduce gender into law courses was important, it has revealed the need to make an introductory course on gender and the law a requirement for all students. Typically, few students choose gender courses as electives, and many male students might pick them because they see them as easier options.

A better way to include women, gender, and the law in the law school curriculum might be to integrate the teaching of gender theories into all courses. This would shift the responsibility away from women, who often tend to teach these specialized courses alone. Such an approach would also help involve other women academics who may not see gender as a key principle shaping the law. The downside of this recommendation is whether faculty members who lack understanding of gender theories will be best suited to incorporate gendered approaches without risking the reinforcement of patriarchal norms and practices. This challenge can be addressed through professional development and unconscious bias training for all legal academics teaching in law faculties and law schools. Some legal scholars (Kameri-Mbote & Wekesa, 2018; Tamale, 2015) have already implemented this approach.

Furthermore, as a respondent explained:

> Those who teach gender may, during the current semester, assist with instruction across various modules and courses. Some courses are more urgent than others for mainstreaming gender. For example, it is crucial for private practice lawyers to have a comprehensive understanding of the gendered aspects of criminal law and family law.

Women's rights and human rights advocates have greatly contributed to current research and understanding of gender and the law in Africa. Although academics usually select their research topics, most people studying women, gender, and the law are women. Law schools, professional organizations, bar associations, and legal societies need to find innovative ways to involve more men in researching and writing about women, gender, and the law.

4. Establishing Women's Legal Clinics

As part of ongoing efforts to improve legal education across Africa, legal academics and scholars have suggested developing practical teaching methods that give students real-world experience with the law (Burgis-Kasthala, 2022; Madlalate, 2022; Manteaw, 2008; Ndulo, 2002; Oloka-Onyango, 2021). Expanding legal instruction to include clinics focused on gender issues is an important strategy adopted by some female law academics (Kamau, 2020; Kameri-Mbote & Wekesa, 2018). In discussing the role of lawyers as agents of change in the globalization of world systems and democratization, scholars have recommended equipping law students with practical skills needed for development (Manteaw, 2008). In several jurisdictions, women academics have led the way in implementing many of these recommendations by establishing legal clinics that address various concerns, mainly related to women and gender issues.

In Ghana, Akua Kuenyehia, the first female law lecturer and later the dean of the law faculty, played a vital role in establishing the Legal Aid Center. At the University of Ibadan in Nigeria, Oluyemisi Bamgbose, the first woman to lead a department and subsequently the first female dean of the law faculty, founded the Women's Law Clinic to address issues impacting women in the community. Other examples include the Zimbabwe Women Lawyers Association (ZWLA) collaborating with female faculty at the University of Zimbabwe to create legal aid programs for disadvantaged women and advocate for changes to marital laws (Stewart, 2012). In Kenya, female law professors were key in developing gender-related courses and legal clinics focused on women's issues (Kameri-Mbote & Wekesa, 2018). These efforts by female legal scholars have been essential in transforming the academic landscape, offering students opportunities to learn beyond the classroom and developing practical skills needed for their careers. The following section provides a detailed discussion of the contributions women academics are making to the legal academic environment.

5. Changing the Academy: Institutional Norms and Practices

Regardless of whether women academics are called pioneers, pacesetters, counselors, mothers, or any other titles, it is clear they are transforming the legal academy. The question Menkel-Meadow raised in 1986 still resonates—does the feminization of the academy lead to greater representation of women? Is this feminization encouraging institutions to change their traditionally masculine practices to better include women? While some of these changes create more opportunities for women to succeed and advance, others do not provide the same benefits. The burden of demonstrating their impact should not fall solely on women in academia, who are already burdened enough. Institutions must take action by establishing frameworks that promote gender diversity, implementing inclusive policies, and ensuring fair opportunities for women's success. Women's contributions to the legal academy go beyond their gender, and a comprehensive approach that addresses institutional and systemic barriers impacting women academics should be the priority for all educational institutions. Reports on women in law and leadership within the legal academy highlight ongoing gendered challenges women face, as shown in this quote (Institute for African Women in Law, 2023k, p. 26):

> The school board meetings were the worst and had many gender slurs. The men would say that women could only do three things: one, cook in the kitchen; two, to be slept with; and three, to bear and take care of children, and therefore implied the females were in the wrong place. Whenever they said that, I would tell them off and insist that the statements are withdrawn before the meeting proceeded, or else I leave. If I did not go through this, there would be no path. I can see the path I have made.

The example above shows how gender-norm disruptors use their voice and agency as forms of feminist resistance against institutional patriarchy. To fight these ongoing stereotypes, women faculty have led efforts to advocate for and develop gender equality and anti-sexual harassment policies, which some universities are gradually adopting. The rise in the number of women has also created more opportunities for mentorship and career guidance for young scholars entering the field. Although most respondents noted a lack of institutional mentoring programs, junior faculty still form mentorship ties with senior women academics. Unsurprisingly, women academics are divided on whether the process of gender diversification makes a meaningful impact within the academy—especially for women. A young female academic in Ghana believes that women are transforming the profession because of their unique understanding, approach, and responses to issues, which differ from men's methods. Citing the experience of the former dean of the law faculty, she emphasized that "you could feel the difference and touch of a woman in that office—she is a woman, a mother, and an academic."

However, some academics are not convinced that increases in the number of women are leading to institutional changes. As one academic in Nigeria noted:

> I am unsure if we, as women academics, are creating change; we are still outnumbered, but over time, things will get better. There is now renewed enthusiasm among women lecturers to pursue further education. Women are realizing they can leverage their law degrees. The few of us here don't meet often to discuss our issues or have meaningful conversations about what to do next. Finding mentors is also tough; there aren't many women available for guidance, so we're all navigating this journey blindly, hoping that someday we will find clarity and carve out our own paths.

To reiterate a key point in this book, women are not all the same, and therefore, not every female academic is a feminist or understands the gendered aspects of social and political life. Highlighting the importance of female academics recognizing their feminist perspective when addressing these issues, a feminist academic remarked:

> To make a meaningful impact, women in leadership roles need to clearly understand, from a feminist perspective, the influence they want to have. Often, women leaders enter a space already shaped by men regarding how things are done. Without a strong ideological foundation about the difference women can make, they often reinforce, rather than challenge, patriarchal and sometimes toxic practices.

To truly make a difference, women in positions of power need to have a feminist perspective on the change they want to create. Often, women leaders enter the workforce shaped by masculine norms and expectations. Without a clear ideological foundation about the difference women can make, what they should accept as normal rules, norms, and practices, and what they should challenge, some women have simply reinforced, rather than challenged, patriarchal and sometimes toxic masculinity within institutional norms. The long-term effects of women's entry into the legal academy require longitudinal studies to evaluate shifts in perceptions among faculty and students, as well as the effective implementation of policies to dismantle masculine cultures that harm women's equal participation as faculty.

6. Collegiality and Social Relations Among Colleagues

Women in the legal academy navigate different social relationships with their male colleagues, and women's intracategorical intersectional differences suggest that their experiences with other women vary (McCall, 2005). Gender roles and relationships have changed over time, resulting in different experiences among women from one generation to the next. A pioneering woman academic reflected on her experiences joining the law faculty, as noted by Dawuni (2021a, p. 160).

> At the time [when she joined the academy in the early 1970s] there was no problem, there was collegiality, interaction and debating legal issues. We did not have a senior common room and we could just sit and have lunch and I created it [the faculty breakroom]. It does not mean we did not have misunderstandings, but it was never acrimonious. You cannot run over me easily. At the Executive Committee of the university, I was the only woman there—I don't believe in confrontation, I believe in consensus for the better of us. Not that they always agreed with me.

Relationships with colleagues can be shaped by intersecting identities like age, marital status, and academic rank. For example, married women might experience different interactions with male colleagues—who are often more distant and respectful—compared to single women, who may have more open and engaging exchanges with coworkers. As mentioned earlier, in many African cultures, age plays a key role in shaping social relationships and interactions. Therefore, a younger woman with a higher academic rank often shows respect and deference to an older man with a lower rank. Similarly, an older woman in academia is likely to be respected by both male and female colleagues, even if they share the same rank. The patterns of vertical (age or rank differences) and horizontal (same age or rank) social hierarchies are flexible and influenced by various factors that can shape these interactions. The expectation is that a woman in a higher social and academic position should earn respect from colleagues of all genders and levels. However, this isn't always true; many respondents point out that sociocultural perceptions of a woman's societal role can cause these respect boundaries to be ignored, simply because of socially constructed gender norms. An academic in Nigeria shared her frustrations about the gendered behaviors and insensitivity women face at the intersection of gender and age.

> When I joined the faculty, many of my former instructors were already part of the staff, which created a complex dynamic. Over the years, those I taught have also become faculty members. However, there still seems to be an assumption that women will be interested in women's or gender issues, leading people to look to you for input on these topics. I believe it's more about socialization and culture.

Overall, respondents reported positive and supportive relationships with their male colleagues, peers, and superiors. Some highlighted that these relationships can differ depending on individual traits, challenging the idea that all men behave or expect the same things, and reinforcing that we should not generalize men. Several respondents mentioned that male colleagues offer support when needed, as one respondent in Senegal explained: "We help one another and work in partnership; for instance, if my child is sick or I have an appointment, I can reach out to my colleagues to cover my class."

The common phrases used by respondents to describe their social relationships with male colleagues included "almost perfect," "professional," and "quite good." These phrases reflect different levels of connection and collegiality that women have experienced through their interactions with men at work. Recruitment patterns may also help explain this shared sense of collegiality. For example, when academic hires come from cohorts who were classmates or present at the university at the same time, it fosters familiarity, reducing tensions, as noted by an academic in Senegal: "We have been mates at some level, so we have known each other for a while, which helps, and everyone is professional."

The examples and themes from this research are not meant to show a universal view of women's experiences in academia—not within any one country, or across the entire continent or its regions. The different experiences may result from culturally influenced social systems, gender norms, institutional practices, or individual traits and interpretations of gender socialization. Some women have said that their interactions with male colleagues are not always welcoming. As one academic in Ghana stated when asked about her relationship with male colleagues, "It is quite good; it is complicated, but overall it is cordial and based on mutual respect. It is professional and fine, but sometimes you get the impression that certain attitudes can feel a bit patronizing." Women who recognize the boundaries between what is considered collegial and what isn't, as reflected in this feedback from an academic:

> It is a very friendly working relationship. We all joke and laugh, but if it goes too far, you can always rein in the guys. Most of the time, they are quite understanding. Usually, they leave the welfare responsibilities—the *"female stuff"*—to the female lecturers.

The previous discussion emphasizes that women are making notable progress in challenging gender-based institutional norms and perceptions. They are balancing their primary and secondary roles and making significant contributions to teaching and research on women and gender issues. However, these insights are confined to the academic world, as women's diverse lives and interests go well beyond the classroom. In common-law systems, the division between legal academia and practice means women contribute in various ways to developing legal principles, jurisprudence, and human rights, whether as scholars or practicing lawyers. These dual roles are common in law schools, where many male and female faculty members juggle their work as full-time practitioners or judges with their duties as part-time instructors.

A review of existing research across the continent shows that women academics continue to play vital roles as women's rights activists by providing both theoretically and empirically informed research that supports advocacy for change and the expansion of women's access to justice (Ampofo et al., 2008; Kameri-Mbote & Wekesa, 2018; Mama, 2020; Stewart & Tsanga, 2011; Tamale, 2021). Women's presence in academia is clearly changing the boundaries of what was once considered a man's world, gradually weakening the masculinized concrete ceiling of the legal academy, one woman at a time. However, more work is needed to create an equal playing field. Section VI discusses ongoing gender-based challenges in the legal academy.

VI. Challenges: Navigating Barriers and Boundaries

Ongoing changes in the legal academy have not yet fully transformed institutions into gender-inclusive and egalitarian spaces for women. The HISP framework shows how interactions among historical, institutional, and social factors create a cycle of challenges that women must navigate. By focusing on the individual stories and experiences of women in the academy, the analysis in this section highlights emerging themes identified through fieldwork. While some common themes emerge from these stories, varying opinions and experiences are also presented, reinforcing a key argument of this book—that we cannot essentialize the experiences of African women in law. **Figure 6.10** displays respondents' views when asked to choose the types of workplace challenges they face.

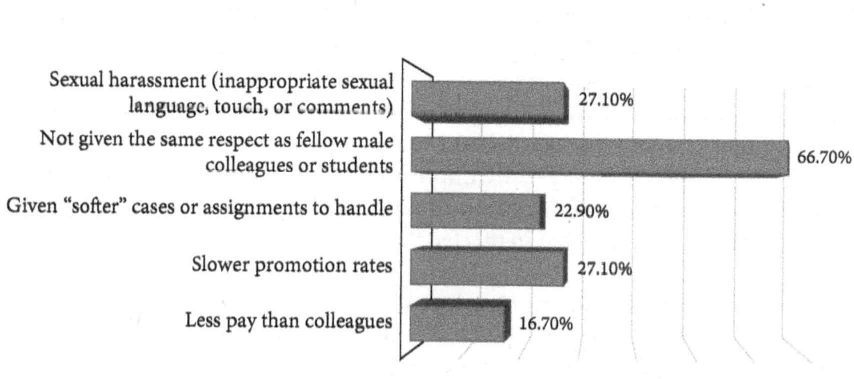

Figure 6.10 *Workplace Challenges for Women in the Academy*
Source: Survey respondents (48).

The challenges women face in academia occur along a spectrum; some are obvious and easy to spot, while many others are subtle and often embedded in institutional norms and practices that exclude women from resources and opportunities. These norms silence those who speak out against gender oppression and can even penalize women who resist these patriarchal standards (Aiston & Fo, 2020). Essentially, women often dominate the invisible theater of gendered performativity by taking on both primary and secondary roles in departmental service and supporting students through mentoring and other forms of assistance. However, their contributions are frequently overlooked, undervalued, and unrewarded. We now turn to this discussion.

1. Persisting Gendered Institutional Norms and Expectations

Although women have made progress in challenging masculinity norms and breaking the patriarchal glass ceiling, higher education institutions, especially the legal academy, still grapple with gendered norms. These ongoing issues force us to reconsider how women are represented both descriptively and symbolically in law. Despite the institutional and demographic shifts discussed earlier, the legal academy often appears to maintain a facade of gender equality. Personal and positional experiences may indicate slight bias, but many formal and informal institutional gendered norms influence women's professional lives. Often, the most severe gender bias, stereotypes, and discrimination occur within these informal norms. Some of these perceptions and insensitivities stem unintentionally from unconscious bias, while others are deliberate and rooted in patriarchal beliefs and practices (Kameri-Mbote & Wekesa, 2018; Tamale, 2021; Tsikata, 2007).

Several scholars have studied the persistent gender inequalities in higher education institutions across Africa and their effects on women's access, retention, and progression in academia (Beoku-Betts & Njambi, 2005; Mabokela & Mlambo, 2015; Mama, 2003; Mbow, 2000; Tamale, 2021; Tsikata, 2007). These studies consistently highlight recurring themes of false gender neutrality in the processes and opportunities available to faculty. Oloka-Onyango and Tamale (2000, p. 3) stress these institutional gender biases and insensitivities that have continued since the founding of higher education institutions.

> An academic was seen as a gender-neutral person with the right qualifications. Therefore, there were no measures in place to support them during the intense period of childbearing and raising young children. The university's apparent neutrality on these issues ignored key differences between men and women, putting women at a disadvantage.

Some of these historical institutional challenges persist. A senior academic in Nigeria describes her fight against gender-insensitive and discriminatory institutional practices:

> When I joined the faculty, I had to challenge some university-wide rules. For example, there was a policy that allowed men on sabbatical leave to bring their wives

> along, but women were not allowed to take their husbands with them. I questioned the cultural assumptions that "men do not follow their wives" and asked, What if a man wanted to follow his wife?

Women have adopted various survival strategies, including downplaying their intersecting identities—such as marital status, motherhood, and age—to align with the masculine academic expectations set by their male colleagues and students. Some women in legal academia have reported altering their appearance or attire to avoid attracting attention. Others refrain from discussing controversial gender-related issues in their classrooms to prevent being labeled as "an angry feminist." Many junior female academics have reported suffering in silence as victims of sexual harassment, unequal pay, and delayed promotions. Regardless of academic rank, a common theme among all interview respondents emphasizes the challenge of balancing personal and family responsibilities with fulfilling their professional obligations in teaching, research, and service. Despite being cut off from the corridors of power and often excluded from recognition and resources, women are still expected to fulfill the essential yet unpaid responsibilities of providing mental and psychological support to students. By extending caregiving roles and expectations from the home to the academy, they confront multiple layers of gendered performativity and engage in unacknowledged, invisible labor (Bennett & Tamale, 2011; Mama, 2003; Tsikata, 2007).

In a previous study of women in Ghana's legal academy, Dawuni (2021a) discussed the overlap of maternal and professional expectations. Male professors are called by their professional titles such as "Dr.," "Mr.," or "Professor." In contrast, women academics are often referred to as "Aunty" or "Mama." While these titles stem from social and cultural norms of respect and affection, they also place caregiving expectations on women that their male colleagues do not face. Despite women's professional roles, there are widespread expectations from students and staff that women will fulfill mothering roles. This gendered view of responsibilities leads some students to confuse women's roles as academics and caregivers. As one respondent in the Ivory Coast noted, "the main thing is to earn the respect of your students—if they see you as a mother or auntie, you have to help them understand that you are a professor, not an aunt or mother." Expectations for women academics may also be embedded in how faculty refer to female colleagues and in their anticipation that these women will be nurturing toward students. Similarly, in a study of women in Ghanaian higher education institutions, Adusah-Karikari (2008, p. 122) observed that "the image of the woman as a mother and wife transcends her duty as an academic or administrator. Women must work hard to survive in the university, and it is unfair, if not irrelevant, to refer to their reproductive roles."

2. Hiring and Appointments

The earlier discussion about pathways into the legal academy highlighted the evolving hiring standards in law schools, where earning a doctoral degree has become a key requirement. Older faculty members who joined before these policies were implemented are often exempt from this requirement, while those who started their positions afterward must obtain a doctorate within a set time frame. For members of this latter group, universities offer various options that allow faculty to take study leave to pursue a doctorate. These requirements and opportunities for study leave have gendered effects that might not be immediately obvious. Ironically, 25 of 48 survey respondents (52.1%) held doctoral degrees, but this is not representative of all jurisdictions. The experiences of those without doctoral degrees provide a compelling explanation for the effects of hiring and appointments in the legal academy.

For many women, marriage and starting families often occur soon after law school, which causes delays in their plans to pursue a doctorate. Historically, this meant that most women entered academia without a doctoral degree. Additionally, choosing to take leave from work to earn a higher degree, such as a doctorate, is a difficult decision, especially for those with families and young children. Being away from their families can be costly, particularly when there is a working spouse, school-aged children, and other caregiving duties for aging parents.

Most doctoral degrees are still obtained from universities outside the continent. For women, the options often involve relocating—disruptively affecting a working partner and children's education. Moving to a foreign country also means disconnecting from the support networks at home, which are crucial for managing work and household responsibilities. Increasingly, more universities on the continent are offering doctoral degrees in law, which may help reduce the burden of location. However, juggling a full- or part-time job, pursuing a doctorate, and providing full-time care for children and aging parents is never easy, regardless of one's social background.

Besides the doctoral degree requirement for entry, the appointment of women to academic leadership roles is, in some cases, limited by the small number of women in the profession. For example, in Senegal, although public universities offer equal employment opportunities in higher education, the shortage of women in the legal field has made it difficult to find female candidates for open positions. Similar challenges are seen in The Gambia and Cape Verde, where respondents highlighted that the small size of the legal profession restricts the pool of lawyer candidates available to fill full-time faculty roles.

The differences women face in hiring are closely linked to the influence of gender biases and stereotypes that some recruiting gatekeepers, often male, bring to the process. In Nigeria, an academic described the obstacles women still encounter in the hiring procedures in certain faculties.

> There are no formal barriers. If you have what it takes, you'll have no problem. However, regarding attitude stereotypes and biases, the dean during my hiring stated that he would not consider a female candidate because women have personal responsibilities that influence their performance. I believe there are subtle prejudices against women. If you want to balance a career and family, it could impact your upward mobility.

Others were unsure whether the challenges women faced in the hiring process came from systemic sociocultural biases or institutional requirements and expectations. When asked about barriers to women's hiring at the law faculty, a senior academic in Ghana responded:

> I am unsure if it relates to any institutional factors. I enrolled before the Ph.D. requirement was introduced. Since then, recruiting has generally been difficult. It is more challenging for women to dedicate the necessary time to obtain a Ph.D., and we have turned away many qualified candidates. We argued that the law faculty did not require a Ph.D., but because of the emphasis on research, they did not make an exception for us. Not many applicants are women. While we receive many requests from women for letters of recommendation to pursue an LLM (Master of Laws), I am unsure why the number of women remains low. There are no obvious systemic barriers. We do not see our recruitment as an effort to increase the number of women; rather, we consider it a matter of merit. Gender does not influence our admission process for law students.

In response to a question about hiring processes, a department head in Nigeria mentioned that targeted efforts are sometimes made to recruit women, and some male deans support their departments' informal affirmative action initiatives to hire more women. The reasons for this support are not immediately clear but may stem from a shift in perceptions of women's abilities and an acknowledgment that diversity improves organizational cultures. She also shared her insights and experiences regarding the hiring process.

> I don't believe there are barriers stopping women from joining the faculty. If such barriers exist, they are unintentional. More women would consider academia if they met the minimum qualifications. It could also relate to the structure of the legal profession; many assume you must be involved in litigation. I think some see you as a lesser lawyer if you don't practice that way. Because there are so few women, search committees may be eager to see if female candidates will succeed, and men often speak more openly about recruiting women.

These narratives highlight the complex challenges in hiring processes—including the earlier discussion of the changing requirements for a doctoral degree and the insufficient focus on diversity initiatives aimed at recruiting more women. While affirmative action policies might not be necessary to increase the number of women, it could require intentional efforts from a dean who actively seeks out and hires women with doctoral degrees, as more women earn those degrees. It remains unclear whether this would be a priority for any dean, especially if the focus is on filling positions to accommodate the growing number of law students. Future research and analysis of diversity efforts in law school faculty recruitment will offer valuable insights.

As more women become lawyers, it is expected that the pool of applicants for legal positions will also grow. The forces of demand and supply will align to create additional opportunities for women to enter academia. However, not all respondents were optimistic about the direct relationship between the rise in female lawyers and the increase in female academics. A senior academic warned:

> In our globalized world, there are now competitive opportunities for top students, such as working with international organizations. However, as long as local conditions are not economically favorable, many of the best students, increasingly women,

> will continue to be drawn elsewhere instead of being channeled into local universities. Retaining local expertise remains one of Africa's biggest challenges.

In other contexts, the presence and enforcement of constitutional provisions are changing gender equality norms, which seem to have helped improve the numerical representation of women academics in South Africa and Kenya (Institute For African Women In Law, 2023r).

3. Academic Promotion

Higher education institutions have established procedures to promote academic staff. These procedures generally require fulfilling obligations in teaching, research, and service. Despite the variety of formal models and criteria for staff promotion, informal rules significantly influence the process. These informal guidelines can be quite subjective, depending on the individuals involved in the academic committees overseeing promotions. The overall pattern of interview responses suggests a combination of factors that may include several key steps. Typically, the Appointments and Promotions Committee (APT) conducts an internal review of the application docket. Once a decision is made, it may be forwarded to the dean of the college or faculty and then to external reviewers. The final authority for appointments may rest with the vice chancellor or university president. In Francophone countries, this process also involves the external promotion body—CAMES, as previously mentioned. These procedures show that many stakeholders and gatekeepers participate in the promotion pathway, providing various checks and balances to ensure transparency. When promotion rules are clearly defined and documented, they can improve transparency in the process, benefiting both women and men; on the other hand, a lack of clear rules can have the opposite effect. When asked if women experienced slower promotions than their male colleagues, 27.1% of survey respondents agreed.

A law faculty academic in Nigeria expressed her concerns about the process:

> Overall, there are concerns about the promotion process. Over the years, the policy has become less transparent, although it is not directly connected to gender. The Faculty Appointments Committee reviews the portfolio and submits it to the University Appointment Board, which makes the final decision based on input from external reviewers. If an application is rejected, the applicant can request a review of the decision. Regarding the weights assigned to teaching, research, and service, we have noticed that the appointment board is not following established procedures.

Most of the challenges identified through the fieldwork can be grouped into two aspects of the HISP framework: institutional and positional factors. While informal institutional barriers stem from social and cultural perceptions of women's abilities, some may originate from personality traits rather than institutional influences. These informal challenges can be tackled when other gatekeepers in the promotion process are committed to enabling change. In the case of a female academic, if the vice chancellor chooses not to endorse a transparent process, her application could be stalled, and she might have to seek legal recourse. She described the challenges she faced:

> My application for full professorship was a tumultuous experience because I was the first female professor to be appointed through promotion at the law faculty of [*name of university redacted*]. At that time, the dean advised me against applying, claiming I was too young to become a full professor. The issue was that he was the only professor and did not want to relinquish the deanship. He informed me that he would not support my application. I decided to follow the university policy, which allows candidates to apply directly to the vice chancellor; only one person in the university's history had taken that route, so others discouraged me from doing the same. I insisted that, as a lawyer, I needed to follow the law. It worked! The process was tumultuous because it was clear that the environment was biased, leading the Vice Chancellor to send my portfolio abroad for external review instead of conducting an internal one within Nigeria. The dean challenged my candidacy based on my youth and lack of international recognition, even though I had served as a visiting professor during my two sabbaticals at various universities in the United States. I included all of the dean's comments in my application dossier.

Many women have faced similar challenges, as described by the respondent above. Due to informal institutional obstacles they encounter, some women have adopted a conflict-avoidance strategy by ensuring they are overprepared before applying for promotions. Another academic shared her approach:

> When competing for a promotion alongside a man, you must produce more than he does, despite the policy stating that you need 12 publications, including one in a foreign journal. For my promotion, I submitted 16 publications, with two in foreign journals, leaving no room for doubt. I have the required qualifications, teaching experience, and research background. You need 22 publications, with six in foreign journals, to achieve full professor status. I already have 32 publications, including ten in foreign journals, so by the time I reach that stage, I will be more than prepared, leaving no justification for denying my promotion.

The experiences described above are supported by research evidence (Chacha, 2021; Deo, 2019). The value assigned to women's portfolios compared to men's is influenced by gender and is subjective; women often face underestimation of their contributions (Bezuidenhout & Cilliers, 2011). As a female academic in Ghana stated, "I feel that my current position [as a lecturer] is unfair; if I were a man, I would have received a higher rank because of all the work and experience I bring."

Women's caregiving and domestic responsibilities significantly impact their ability to balance and focus on academic work. Another respondent observed that while the formal rules seem identical at first glance, women's caregiving and household duties greatly affect the amount of research they can produce to meet the requirements. She further emphasizes the influence of informal rules and gendered expectations, which suggest that women must go beyond the minimum standards. In her words:

> There are no formal barriers to promotion; if you meet the requirements, you should face no obstacles. However, as a woman, you may find yourself falling behind not because of your gender but because of your social circumstances. Based on my experiences, I have great respect for senior women professors, recognizing what they may have endured. As a woman, you often need to perform better or prove yourself superior to men. Men might be able to produce more work because of our double duties as women. With my kids growing up, things are getting easier for me.

In civil-law countries, candidates for promotion, along with some variations in the promotion process discussed earlier, must pass an external exam to demonstrate their readiness for advancement. This exam is administered by CAMES, a regional governing body responsible for making the final decision. Historically, the formal institutional rules regarding promotion requirements in some universities and faculties have been unclear and lacked transparency; in fact, many of these rules have become outdated, allowing for subjective interpretation by gatekeepers. In Senegal, one academic pointed out that the teaching load significantly impacts some women's ability to advance in the academic hierarchy. Consequently, some women choose not to apply for promotion, remaining at a single rank throughout their academic careers. She highlighted large class sizes and inadequate administrative support, including the lack of teaching or research assistants. When asked whether the promotion rules are gender-biased, the respondent noted:

> The rules stay the same, but the social demands in our lives restrict many women from meeting those expectations. We're not complaining about the rules; I think they are fair. It's just that the challenges women face can sometimes hold back our progress up the ladder.

In assessing the difficulties of maintaining the necessary research output for promotion, I asked interviewees about their active research agendas, and some of their responses were revealing.

> Let's not even discuss what I consider "active," because it isn't active at all. First, there's how the course load is structured: teaching three classes each semester, and the administration doesn't pay attention to the numbers—two of my classes have around 70 students each, while the other has 45. That requires a lot of time, leaving you with less opportunity to sit down and truly think about research. Second, there are family responsibilities. However, the bigger problem is class sizes. We don't have teaching or research assistants. What I've done is enlist some of my undergraduate students to do preliminary research for me.

Furthermore, professional networks are vital for building the social capital needed for career advancement. While these networks can develop through various platforms, academic and professional conferences provide important opportunities to expand connections. Women academics often face limited access to international conferences for several reasons. First, most universities do not fund international travel for faculty members (including men), and when such funding exists, it is usually not enough to cover all expenses. Second, women with caregiving responsibilities at home may find it difficult to arrange travel, especially if they lack a supportive partner. Third, the process of writing papers and applying to attend conferences is only beginning to be understood, as women have often been excluded from internal departmental networks that offer insight into these procedures. As younger female academics gain access to mentors and build their academic networks, awareness will increase among women about how to enhance their professional presence. However, many may still need guidance on building effective networks at these conferences. Providing professional development opportunities during graduate studies and early career stages can help address some of these challenges.

4. Leadership Promotion

Alongside promotions within academic ranks, these advancements can also include appointments to administrative positions. Such progress may involve moving from a faculty role to an administrative one, such as department head, dean of a college or faculty, or other university-wide roles. In various professions, leadership is still largely perceived as a male domain. Despite the increasing success of women breaking through the proverbial glass ceiling and assuming leadership roles, many challenges remain due to masculine institutional norms and expectations related to women's leadership (Collier, 2021). The road to leadership is filled with numerous obstacles women must navigate. In *Women in Law and Leadership: Kenyan Legal Academy*, an academic reflected (Institute for African Women in Law, 2023k, p. 34):

> Leadership is tricky. Men have serious wars when it comes to public appointments. Daggers are drawn, and this discourages women. Few women apply for top positions. We must understand that men decide who takes what, and this is discussed at the men's club, which is not within reach of women [to] occupy top leadership. Men still want to be at the apex, with females given symbolic positions to serve male interests. I have applied for [a] position, but despite being qualified, men are still advantaged.

Changing gender norms and perceptions of women's leadership abilities, along with the required years of service, a strong publication record, and overall academic excellence, has helped women become strong candidates for administrative and managerial positions in law schools and faculties across the continent (Moodly & Toni, 2019). Although securing a leadership position can be difficult, women in managerial roles may face significant obstacles, as power hierarchies remain largely male-dominated (Abadi & Ayentimi, 2023).

Institutions often take pride in claiming that promotions are based on merit, fostering the perception that factors such as gender are not considered, thus creating a transparent and fair process. However, merit-based appointments that assume the absence of gendered norms within institutional policies and practices are likely to reinforce exclusionary outcomes that tend to favor men (Moodly & Toni, 2019). While women are gradually advancing in the academic leadership hierarchy, some sectors remain inaccessible to them. Since its founding in 1960, the Nigerian School of Law has yet to have a woman serve as Director General. A respondent shared her insights on the promotion process at the Nigerian School of Law:

> The appointment of the law school head depends on various factors beyond just gender. I believe politics plays a significant role, similar to other parts of the country. If promotions had been based on seniority, as is usually the case, the longest-serving faculty member, who is a woman, would have been chosen as the head. However, she was overlooked in the recent appointment. This raises questions about whether gender influences the decision. Gender discrimination can be subtle, and some women may choose not to discuss it for personal reasons or to avoid being perceived as leveraging gender for special treatment.

Most law schools at public universities require candidates for decanal roles to be full professors. Fewer women reach full professorships, so the pool of female candidates is limited. A thorough comparative study of the promotion rates of women and men in law schools will offer deeper insights into the main factors affecting disparities in promotion outcomes within the academic hierarchy and leadership positions.

5. Salary and Benefits

Gender pay inequity remains a persistent global issue. In the United States, legal academics earn more than faculty in other departments; however, a recent study reveals ongoing pay disparities within the legal profession (Nelson et al., 2023). Black women earn less than both their male counterparts, regardless of race, and less than their white female colleagues (Deo, 2019). A major challenge for this research is the absence of salary data for faculty at the surveyed universities and law schools. In reviewing data and research on pay structures, I found no publicly available information on faculty salaries at these universities.

A former dean of a law faculty noted that men typically negotiate higher salaries during hiring processes than women, implying that women often begin at a disadvantage and on the lower end of the salary scale. In public universities, while employee benefits might be standardized and equal across ranks, additional perks—such as research and travel funds—are often negotiated and heavily influenced by one's internal networks, including access to male gatekeepers and decision makers. Many new faculty members who lack the networks and mentorship necessary for effective negotiations may miss out on these extra perks, and women frequently find themselves in this position.

An academic in Nigeria explained that one key reason some women earn less is that they are often socialized and mentored not to negotiate for higher salaries. Also, deep-rooted sociocultural expectations still suggest that men are the main earners in their households and should be paid more. In Senegal, even though the leading law faculty is part of a public university, one respondent noted that for many years, women did not receive equal pay compared to their male colleagues and had to push for change to address this issue.

In the Ivory Coast, a respondent noted that at public universities, salaries are standardized within each rank but can vary depending on the degree held. As a result, individuals with doctoral degrees generally earn more. However, the lack of accessible salary data makes it difficult to assess whether a higher degree is associated with increased pay or if women with advanced degrees earn as much as men with similar or even lower degrees. Referencing the earlier discussion in Chapter 4, some women lawyers with more qualifications and years of experience were surprised to find they earned less than a junior male colleague. Conducting comprehensive and transparent gender audits of salaries and benefits at universities is the most effective way to assess the extent of gender pay inequality.

Because of low salaries, law lecturers often take on part-time legal work or other consulting projects to supplement their incomes. For female academics, juggling teaching duties and family responsibilities is already overwhelming; adding the extra task of part-time practice can be extremely demanding. Those who take on these additional roles constantly struggle to manage the sacrifices needed to maintain balance. Therefore, low salaries may discourage women from pursuing careers in academia.

6. Managing Social Relations, Perceptions, and Expectations

Gender hierarchies are socially constructed and influence perceptions of various social categories. In many African cultures, the concepts of matriarchy and gender fluidity create spaces of power for women, shaped by cultural views on age, motherhood, and other social factors, such as belonging to a lineage of traditional leaders (Amadiume, 1987; Oyewumi, 1997). Aside from these exceptions, women's professional experiences are greatly affected by socially constructed, gender-based discriminatory perceptions and norms that determine how they are treated in professional settings.

Consequently, sociocultural structures shape the development of both formal and informal institutional norms that influence women's roles in professional settings. As a result, men often receive more respect than women, which can sometimes affect the social dynamics between students and female faculty. However, these general observations about gender-based discriminatory practices and perceptions are not universally true because women in academia have unique identities. What one person sees as discrimination might not be viewed the same way by another. Therefore, the social conditions and circumstances of each individual are important for understanding what qualifies as discrimination in different contexts.

Regarding gender biases and stereotypes, the interview responses varied. Most interviewees stated that they do not experience discriminatory practices. The differing perceptions and experiences may also relate to the intersectional identities discussed earlier in Chapter 4. Consequently, an older, married woman or a member of a sexual minority may face discrimination differently compared to a younger, unmarried, cisgender woman. Most importantly, the foundation for examining gender-based discrimination lies in whether and how effectively women recognize its implications. Throughout my research and discussions with women in law, some have candidly noted a lack of awareness about gender-based discrimination. Although they endure various forms of alienation and exclusion, they do not always identify these experiences as gender-based discrimination. This observation highlights the importance for many women to resocialize and learn to recognize and define what gender-based discrimination involves.

In response to the question of whether she experienced any gender-based discrimination as an academic, a respondent from Nigeria questioned whether men's negative perceptions and actions might stem from unconscious bias and gender insensitivity rather than intentional acts of discrimination. She explained the dichotomy:

> You might hear remarks like "*you're a woman* . . ." or "*as a woman* . . ." These comments may be made in a lighthearted way. I've had to confront male colleagues who make insensitive remarks about other women. When I encounter comments or situations that go beyond my comfort level, I either address them or bring attention to them. When I first joined the faculty, a male colleague was notorious for his remarks and behavior toward female faculty, and no one really spoke up to him since he was a senior faculty member.

In this narrative, women must recognize their own socialization, cultural awareness, and conditioning regarding what defines appropriate statements or actions from certain male colleagues. Women often find themselves caught in a cycle of victimization and need to take the necessary steps to address these actions or remarks. While some male perpetrators may push the limits of what is acceptable, women are burdened with correcting these individuals. However, several respondents felt they had not experienced any discrimination and shared insights into how their social conditioning and positionality influenced or shaped their interpretation of these experiences. An academic in Senegal stated, "I do not see any discrimination based on gender; I believe the women academics worked hard to be here [in the academy]. I would use the term 'difficulty' rather than discrimination to describe my experiences." Another respondent in Ghana remarked, "Personally, I have not faced any discrimination. I have heard about discrimination, but I do not have evidence to support it. In my field of law, there are more men, but as long as you work hard, you should be fine."

Last, a participant in Nigeria observed:

> Generally, I don't see gender bias. On the contrary, men support women because they are proud to see them in the field and respect that. Men actively seek out women's perspectives. This reflects my personal experience, though others may have different experiences with discrimination or gender-based bias.

The responses above confirm that personal experiences cannot be universally applied. While some respondents do not perceive or have not encountered what might be considered gender bias and stereotypes, many others have faced very unpleasant experiences. Some of these incidents have even originated from students. In Senegal, one respondent mentioned that these challenges include students assuming that a female academic is less qualified than her male colleagues; some go so far as to question her competence and may even directly challenge her. Such reactions from students lead some women academics to respond assertively to disrespectful students, risking negative evaluations in return. Women, especially younger academics, often spend extra time "overpreparing" for their classes to avoid any conflicts. All these actions take an emotional and psychological toll on women, often leaving them with less time for their research and professional development tasks.

The racially divided context in South Africa (Moodly & Toni, 2017) mirrors certain experiences of women of color in the United States (Deo, 2019; Gonzalez & Harris, 2012). The ongoing racial tensions and gender stereotypes place women in the South African legal academy at a difficult intersection of race and gender discrimination. Although women are well represented in this legal field, women of color still face negative perceptions, such as being viewed as incompetent (Institute for African Women in Law, 2023r).

7. Sexual Harassment and Workplace Bullying

Sexual harassment in higher education remains a major challenge for many women, including students and faculty. Numerous reports and studies offer strong evidence of explicit acts of sexual harassment, bullying, and other aggressive behaviors toward women (Saungwame et al., 2024). Though several universities have put policies in place to combat sexual harassment and misconduct, a large gap persists between policy and actual practice. Those in authority responsible for enforcing zero-tolerance policies often participate in these behaviors. Even when not directly involved, many protect members of the "old boys' network" by hiding or ignoring victims' complaints. When asked if women in academia face sexual harassment, 41.7% answered yes, 31.3% were unsure, 12.5% thought it was not an issue, and 14.6% expressed doubt. These survey results align closely with findings from studies on women in law and leadership roles across Africa.

In a study on gender equality in the legal profession titled *Gender Equality in Law Across Africa: Is the Glass Half Full?* (Institute for African Women in Law, 2024), 63.4% of the 582 survey respondents reported that they had not experienced sexual harassment in their workplaces. Furthermore, when asked to specify the types of sexual harassment, 41.7% identified verbal harassment as the most prevalent form. In another study on Women in Law and Leadership in the Nigerian Legal Academy, 77% of the 449 legal professionals surveyed indicated that the primary challenge faced by women in law is sexual harassment (Institute for African Women in Law, 2023n). A similar report on Women in Law and Leadership in the Kenyan Legal Academy revealed that several respondents from qualitative interviews affirmed either having been victims of sexual harassment or knowing someone who had been victimized (Institute for African Women in Law, 2023k). Sexual harassment contributes to significant health issues for women, reduces their productivity, and can cause stagnation within the academic environment. The absence of institutional support forces many victims to endure in silence, feeling unable to file complaints or leave their jobs. Those courageous enough to report often encounter additional forms of retaliation, including penalization in course assignments and denial of pay raises or other academic benefits (Kameri-Mbote & Wekesa, 2018).

The actions constituting sexual harassment must be examined within the sociocultural context when addressing this issue. A survey of 16 law students in Senegal (Institute for African Women in Law, 2023o) showed that while 50% agreed that sexual harassment happens, 11% disagreed, and 39% stayed neutral. The neutrality of 39% indicates they either did not understand what counts as sexual harassment or lacked the awareness to recognize it, which is concerning. More empirical research may offer additional insights into these numerical results. When asked if she had experienced sexual harassment, a legal scholar in Senegal said she had never seen or experienced any incidents, despite hearing about harassment between faculty and female students. She believes that any harassment of female faculty is more likely to come from senior faculty members who can use and abuse their authority or experience in academia.

Workplace harassment can take various forms and may include unwanted comments aimed at the intersectional identities of women. A participant in the study on women and the legal academy in Nigeria noted:

> From my experience, harassment often happens secretly and shows society's lack of empathy for women. Asking a female colleague why she isn't married or doesn't have kids is disrespectful, especially when it comes from senior male colleagues who aren't friends or mentors. Doing this in public and expecting a polite response or smile is even more inappropriate. We need to educate everyone about this issue. Additionally, asking women to handle cooking tasks or serve at faculty events not only demeans them but also reinforces the idea that women are not equal to their male colleagues at work. This is a major demotivating factor. These forms of covert harassment are tough to fight because they're often hidden by seniority and cultural norms, which harms women. Greater awareness and empathy are crucial.

Understanding one's positionality is crucial for tackling workplace harassment. Unconscious bias training can effectively educate the academic community about what constitutes bullying and harassment. Women's support groups also play an important role in helping women recognize common perpetrators and patterns. Ultimately, institutional support that offers reporting mechanisms and disciplinary measures against offenders is vital for addressing this issue.

8. Balancing the Professional and Personal

Maintaining a balance between private and public responsibilities remains a constant challenge for many women. Since the COVID-19 pandemic, the distinctions between these spheres have become increasingly unclear. In this analysis, I challenge the simple separation often made between women's private and public lives. Different women have diverse duties and responsibilities based on their positions and the social contexts they are part of. For most women across Africa, these private duties go beyond just caring for immediate family members, like husbands and children, to include various responsibilities toward extended family and the wider community. The survey respondents' views are shown in **Figure 6.11**.

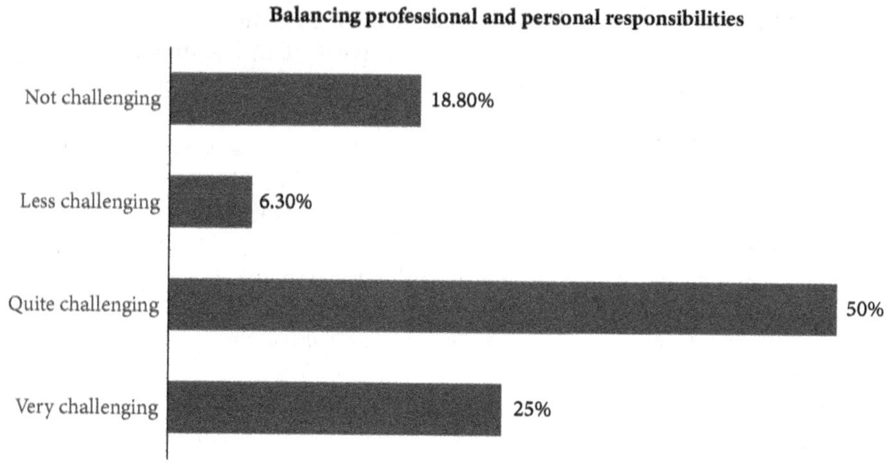

Figure 6.11 *Challenges of Balancing Work and Family*
Source: Survey responses (48).

A respondent summarized it like this:

> It's a constant balancing act. You try to even things out, and sometimes one aspect suffers more than another. You just have to keep up with what you need to do. You don't want to discuss your family obligations at work, so you try to keep them from interfering with your job. It gets easier as you go along, and the responsibilities may lessen as the children grow older. You have to figure it out on your own.

A respondent in Ghana described similar challenges and highlighted the ongoing administrative duties that "steal your time." She acknowledges that her research is affected by this lack of time, which leads her to adopt strategies such as using her summer break as her only chance to complete her research. Some respondents also mentioned the difficulty of meeting all benchmarks and the choices and priorities they must manage to find balance.

> My teaching is non-negotiable, so I stopped everything to focus on it. I can't say the same for my research; I've let that go. Things are getting better, and I'm finding my balance now that I have a good nanny. This gives me the peace of mind to do my work.

For numerous other women, attaining a sense of balance is unattainable. As noted by a scholar in Senegal (Institute for African Women In Law, 2023o, p. 47):

> For me, it didn't work out; I couldn't balance my work life with my married life. Leaving home for two or even three weeks in some cases is challenging, especially for a young couple—it just doesn't work, and it certainly didn't work for me. Right now, regarding my daughter, this is my significant obstacle. As an academic, I need to travel, and my schedule doesn't always align with hers. When I travel, I have to leave her with someone else. I've attempted twice to have her move in with me, but it hasn't

worked out. It's tough because she's so young and doesn't see her mother. It's also difficult to go a month without seeing my daughter. All of this makes me consider exploring other options, like changing careers.

Women often bear the significant responsibility of balancing personal and public caregiving roles. Many respondents have developed strategies to manage and cope with these demands, which are discussed in Chapter 7. For most women, support from family—such as a spouse, mother, or extended network—is vital for their well-being.

9. Limited Opportunities for Professional Development

Women also expressed frustration about limited opportunities for professional growth, such as attending and presenting at conferences, symposia, and workshops. These opportunities are crucial for preparing for promotions, staying current in the field, and building professional networks. However, it seems to be an area where many women face challenges because of the lack of internal institutional networks that could help them build meaningful connections. When asked if they apply for internal or external funding to support their professional development, several respondents said they do not seek funding. Some cited a lack of information about available opportunities, while others pointed to the ongoing issue of time poverty and the significant time commitment needed to write successful grants.

Drawing from my experience, I have successfully applied for several fellowships and research grants. However, the guilt of being away from my family is a constant burden I carry each time I travel. To address this issue, I have tried to bring my family with me on some of these fellowships, but that has also meant I couldn't fully utilize the fellowship period or actively participate in group activities because my time was divided between parenting and fulfilling my fellowship responsibilities. My role as an academic mother with children who can take care of themselves when I need to rush to the office is helpful, but not all women have such arrangements.

10. Mentors, Networks, and Sponsors

There is evidence supporting the positive impact of mentorship and sponsorship opportunities on professional development (Datta & Lund, 2018). Mentoring networks tend to develop naturally for men through the stereotypical "old boys' networks," which help them maintain advantages and dominate power hierarchies through their support systems. While mentoring relationships can form organically, they also require a significant investment of time and effort, such as attending professional conferences, meetings, and events to connect with the right people. Informal networks that arise outside work hours, often in the evenings, are more challenging for women to navigate due to their additional domestic responsibilities. For many women, attending informal networking events may expose them to inappropriate demands from senior colleagues or potential mentors (Dawuni, 2021a). Throughout the countries where I conducted fieldwork for this project, I did not encounter any formal mentoring networks for women academics. Some women reported receiving support and encouragement from male colleagues, confirming that mentorship across genders is possible, despite concerns that some senior male colleagues may seek to exploit junior female colleagues (Tamale, 2021).

11. Ageism vs. Sexism

In African cultures, there is a stronger expectation of respect based on age. The interplay of gender and age makes relationships more complex for women who are junior faculty. Younger female academics encounter challenges from their students and, as a result, must assert more authority to gain respect. In a previous chapter, I described this dynamic as the intersection of ageism and sexism (Dawuni, 2021a, p. 166):

> The concept of ageism must be situated within the socio-cultural context of Ghana where respect for authority is anchored in seniority, as determined by age. This sense of seniority feeds into the hierarchical academic structure and determines workload and committee service.

Younger female academics at this intersection are more vulnerable to senior colleagues who may use their age to exert undue pressure on junior female faculty, including sexual harassment. In describing the complex relational challenges that stem from the intersection of age and gender, Dawuni (2021a, p. 166) noted:

> The concentration of women as junior faculty in the lower academic ranks implies that they will adversely be affected by the impact of age on their relative standing within the faculty, where the most senior are often men. The boundaries between ageism and sexism are further blurred when a junior female faculty must constantly navigate the boundaries of deciphering when unwanted gestures and comments should be regarded as generational and when these should be taken as sexist and discriminatory. Each person must make that call in how they choose to handle such situations, and it is not easy for women faculty confronted with sexual harassment to respond to such negative gestures without being punitively characterized as disrespectful. The fact that women will have to choose between speaking up or keeping quiet is a clear sign of gender inequality.

VII. Conclusion

The previous discussion emphasizes women's experiences in the legal academy by drawing on field data and existing studies. The emerging patterns and themes show how history, institutions, and social context shape women's paths into the academy and continue to influence their experiences, challenges, and contributions. Additionally, the evidence presented in this chapter demonstrates the impact of time spent in the academy, academic rank, educational qualifications, marital and childbearing status, and personal agency on female academics' professional experiences.

Overall, the findings reveal that gender diversity in legal academia enhances institutional practices, teaching methods, and research diversity and shifts socially constructed gender norms regarding women's roles as leaders. The extent to which these changes affect women academics, the gendered hierarchies they navigate, and their survival strategies within the academy could benefit from country-specific studies that expand on this research. Despite ongoing gender inequalities, women academics are transforming institutional practices, social norms, and academic approaches through their presence and actions, contributing to student well-being and increasing diversity in teaching, research, and academic service.

7

A Comparative Framing of Women's Lives in Law

I. Introduction

In the final chapter of the first edited book on women judges in Africa, "Gender and the Judiciary in Africa: From Obscurity to Parity?" Bauer (2016b, p. 249) made a powerful observation:

> One of the main findings of the book is just how much we do not know about women and the judiciary in Africa today. To begin with, we could find no reliable source of comparable data across countries and courts—so any central source of data on women in the highest court in all African countries, or in the higher courts as a group, or in the lower courts as a group. Even data on women chief justices and presidents of constitutional courts in Africa is not readily available. Even within countries, it is difficult to find longitudinal data on women on the bench—at almost any level.

The above statement remains applicable to many other areas and research questions regarding women in law across Africa. In contributing to filling this gap, this book analyzes three interconnected sectors of women in law—the bar, the bench, and the legal academy—to highlight major developments affecting African women in law. By presenting a model that analyzes the influence of history, institutions, and social variables on the positionality (HISP) of women in law, this book offers a comparative narrative analysis of women's experiences and impacts in law across sectors, within countries, and between countries. It weaves a cohesive story of how women's representation in law has evolved. Using a comparative approach, this book highlights key similarities and differences among the bar, the bench, and the legal academy, drawing on 153 informant interviews and 249 survey responses.

Besides providing a comparative analysis of the earlier chapters and key arguments in this book, this chapter evaluates the different strategies women in law have used to survive and succeed as professionals. The findings show that the key to success for African women in law is their personal and collective resistance to historical patriarchy, persistent institutional biases, and social norms that challenge their role as active agents in their professional paths. In essence, the historical and current journey of African women in law demonstrates that these women are not victims but agents in shaping their professional lives.

Section II provides a brief review of the comparative framework that underpins this project. Section III offers a comparative discussion of the key findings regarding the changes that have occurred, the challenges women face, and their contributions to

African Women in Law. J. Jarpa Dawuni, Oxford University Press. © Oxford University Press 2026.
DOI: 10.1093/9780197795095.003.0007

the profession. Section IV connects the findings to the matri-legal feminist framework and presents a detailed discussion of women's strategies for survival; section V offers a broad overview of women's experiences in law during the COVID-19 pandemic, and section VI concludes the chapter.

II. Revisiting the Comparative Framework

The continent of Africa cannot be simplified to a single story. Its diverse geography, history, legal systems, and traditions, along with the complex mix of structures within the legal professions, make it challenging to develop a straightforward comparative framework or model that can accurately reflect the experiences of women in law across all 54 nations. The goal of this book is not to present a simple, uniform narrative about the lives of African women in law. To enhance our understanding, the HISP framework outlined in Chapter 1 was created as a model to situate the comparative approach within a broader, evolving context that connects the past, present, and future. It demonstrates the interactions and links among history, institutions, and social norms and their impact on women's roles in the legal profession. In Chapter 3, tracing the historical development of the legal professions across the continent provided a foundation for analyzing the rise of pioneering African women in law. Breaking down the historical progress of women in law into five generational phases was essential for pinpointing major developments within each phase while also observing continuities over time and in different contexts.

Using the comparative historical method, **Figure 7.1** shows the main variables that frame this study. First, the study recognizes that legal traditions serve as key frameworks for organizing legal systems and the legal professions (Abel & Lewis, 1989). The spread of major legal traditions—civil law and common law—happened through colonization. As the foundation for the development of legal professions, these

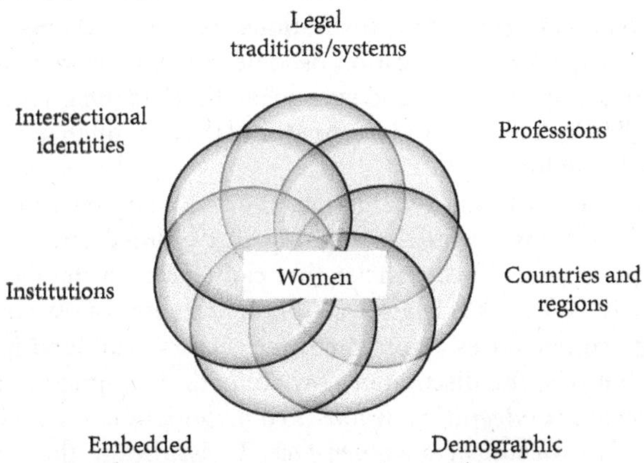

Figure 7.1 *Comparative Model for Measuring Variables/Comparisons*

traditions not only brought over formal legal institutions but also carried informal norms and practices within the profession. Formal and informal norms embedded in patriarchal and gendered practices continue to shape many of the experiences women in law face in Africa, which show both similarities and differences to women's experiences in Western countries (Schultz & Shaw, 2003, 2013).

Building on my earlier argument in Chapter 3 about the "accidental emergence of lawyers" in Africa, the legal profession was often the first to develop, as lawyers were needed for practical administrative and commercial transactions (Adewoye, 1969, Ghai & McAuslan, 1970; Harvey, 1962). Members of the judiciary and the legal academy emerged from the legal profession, establishing a connection that explains the similarities in the structure of the profession and its functions, regulation, and influence. A detailed examination of demographic shifts and changes within each of the three groups was conducted through the three main chapters: the bar, the bench, and the legal academy. The rest of this chapter now shifts to a comparative analysis of the trends and patterns across these three sectors, focusing on changes, contributions, challenges, and the impact of the COVID-19 pandemic.

III. Trends and Patterns

1. Changes, Contributions, and Challenges

Both demand and supply forces drive the global integration of women into the formal sectors of the economy. Supply forces result from years of investing in girls' education, professional training, and upskilling, creating a pool of qualified professionals who are capable and ready to fill available opportunities. As economies open up, the demand for specialized skills generates new opportunities for women to enter the workforce. Studies on women in the workforce show that while the interaction of supply and demand allows women to join traditionally male-dominated fields (*sex integration*), organizations continue to operate based on male-standard roles, leading *to sex-based occupational segregation.* Institutions are slow to change, and over time, the divisions of occupational segregation become evident—women are confined to specific roles within organizations, and even when they are integrated into the workforce, their contributions may be undervalued, and they are often underpaid (Chiu & Leicht, 1999; Reskin & Roos, 1990).

Addressing sex occupational segregation and the ongoing gender-based challenges within institutions requires realigning institutional strategies and adopting women-sensitive or feminist policies that can lead to sustainable system-wide changes (Kenny, 2014; Krook & Mackay, 2011). The degree of *sex integration* versus *occupational segregation* varies across the three sectors examined in this book. To understand these levels, the discussion now shifts to demographic *changes within the profession due to sex integration, women's contributions to the profession, and the persistent gender-based challenges women face.* To synthesize the key findings, the discussion highlights common patterns observed across sectors, with a few examples shown in **Table 7.1**.

Table 7.1 *Representation of Women Across Three Sectors in Selected Countries*

Country	Bar	Bench	Academy
Senegal	**16%** of lawyers. No woman has held the position of president of the bar association.	**18%** of magistrates and judges. **29%** on the Constitutional Council.	**14%** of women law faculty in the two universities. **5%** women in leadership at the two universities since they were founded. The first woman dean of law was appointed in **June 2022.**
Nigeria	**Number of women lawyers unavailable due to lack of gender-disaggregated data. Estimates put it at about **40%.** No woman has held the position of the president of the bar association except for one year in an acting capacity.	**30%** of judges at the Federal level (Supreme Court, Court of Appeal, and High Court).	**18%** of women leaders/ deans at the law faculties covered in this research.
South Africa	**42%** of lawyers. The first woman president of the Law Society was elected in **2022.**	**45%** of judges as of June 2021. **49%** of magistrates as of June 2021. The first woman to hold the position of ***deputy chief justice*** was appointed in 2022.	Women make up **51%** of the law schools and law faculties covered by the study.
Kenya	**44.6%** female lawyers. Two women have served as chairperson of the Law Society **(2001-2003) and (2024-).** Three women have served as vice chairpersons of the law society.	**50%** of magistrates and judges First female Chief Justice appointed in 2022. Three women have served as Deputy Chief Justices. Most heads of courts and the registrar are women.	Women deans make up **18%** of the three law schools and law faculties covered by the study.

Source: Institute for African Women in Law, 2023a

A. Changes

Increasing numbers

The five generational phases outlined in this book cover nearly a century since women started entering the profession. The difficulty in obtaining longitudinal data makes it impossible to precisely measure and visualize the gradual increase in the number of women versus men called to the bar over these years. However, it can be hypothesized that these numbers began to grow with the establishment of law schools and faculties in Africa from the late 1960s onward. For example, although the University of East Africa was later divided into three universities—Dar-es-Salaam in Tanzania, Nairobi in Kenya, and Makerere in Uganda—the first woman lawyer in Kenya, Effie Owuor, was trained at the law faculty at the University of Dar-es-Salaam. As discussed in Chapter 3, pioneering women lawyers in East Africa and much of Southern Africa emerged during the second phase (1951–1970), compared to the first phase (1930–1950) when the earliest women lawyers and judges appeared in West Africa.

Across the three sectors of the legal profession discussed in this book, I refer to the bar as the first battleground because, in many jurisdictions, earning a law degree is the initial step toward entering other parts of the profession. Typically, an increase in lawyer numbers often leads to more women at the bar, but the proportion of female lawyers may still remain low nationwide. For example, as shown in earlier chapters, despite the rising number of lawyers in Senegal and the Ivory Coast, the number of women passing the entrance exam to become lawyers and judges stays low. The judiciary, seen as the middle ground, is also seeing more female judges due to population growth and the rising demand for judicial services and dispute resolution. This increased demand creates more opportunities for women to join the judiciary. Regarding the legal academy as the third sector, even though women entered the academy much later than the first two sectors, the expansion of legal education has driven new demand for legal studies. The opening of new law faculties and schools has resulted in the recruitment of more women into the academy.

Changes in institutional norms and frameworks

Across much of the continent, inherited colonial policies were embedded in national laws that banned women from exercising property rights. In some countries, women needed permission from a husband or male guardian before they could work in the public sector, open a bank account, or apply for a passport (Kamatali, 2016). Thanks to activism from women's rights groups and increased global awareness through the UN Decade for Women and other initiatives, several countries, including South Africa, Kenya, and Senegal, have incorporated gender equality into their new or amended constitutions, expanding women's rights in both public and private spheres (Dawuni, 2022b). Women lawyers have played a key role in advocating for these constitutional and legal reforms (Murungi and Meroka-Mutua, 2022 Scales-Trent, 2010).

Across the continent, women lawyers have actively fought for women's rights at the national, regional, and global levels. Women lawyers and judges such as Annie Jiagge of Ghana, Vera Duarte of Cape Verde, and Reini Alapini-Gansou of Benin have played vital roles in shaping new laws and frameworks like the Convention on the Elimination of All Forms of Discrimination Against Women (CEDAW) and the Maputo Protocol. They have been key figures and leaders in women's rights organizations like Federación Internacional de Abogadas (FIDA), serving as legal counsel in significant cases before the African Court on Human and Peoples' Rights (Ojigho, 2021) and as commissioners on the African Commission on Human and Peoples' Rights (Alapini-Gansou, 2021). Women lawyers have contributed significantly to the successful enactment and enforcement of constitutionally guaranteed rights to equality, which have advanced women's legal rights in countries such as South Africa (Andrews, 2021), Senegal (Scales-Trent, 2010), and Kenya (Aura-Odhiambo, 2018). As discussed in Chapter 3, however, these constitutional and legislative rights alone are not sufficient to transform systems, and progress has been slow at times. For example, Kenya and South Africa have progressive constitutions and laws that promote women's representation in public office, which have been credited with the relatively high number of women in their judiciaries, even though women are still underrepresented in the Kenyan parliament. Rwanda has also made strides in increasing the number of women in its judiciary, a development likely influenced by the higher number of women in its parliament and executive cabinet (Kamatali, 2016).

Changes in domestic institutional frameworks for equality, such as the 1996 South African Constitution and the 2010 Kenyan Constitution, have helped boost women's representation in public spaces (Andrews, 2021; Kamau, 2020). However, despite Senegal's constitutionally mandated provision for gender equality in government and decision-making, which has increased women's presence in the National Assembly, the impact on women's representation at the bar, on the bench, and in the legal academia has not shown significant upward movement. Conversely, countries like Zambia and Zimbabwe do not have constitutional provisions for women in public office, yet their judiciaries have reached and exceeded 50% of women judges (Masengu, 2021). The role of constitutional frameworks in increasing the number and percentage of women in law remains unclear and warrants further research.

Changing cultural norms and perceptions of women's roles

While legal frameworks like constitutions may not always strongly predict changing norms that facilitate women's entry into professions, shifts in cultural norms and perceptions of women's roles in specialized fields seem to have a greater predictive power. The first women in law faced challenges specific to their eras, and each generation of women in the legal profession encountered different obstacles. Some challenges have persisted, such as the difficulty of balancing personal and professional responsibilities. Contrary to the common belief that African women have domestic help, motherhood responsibilities extend beyond the nuclear family, and not all women have domestic help. The increase in the number of women in traditionally male-dominated professions has influenced societal perceptions and attitudes toward women in public and professional roles. Earlier chapters discussed the experiences of several women interviewed for this book, who shared their experiences of being considered "outliers" in their communities when they joined the bar, and some were called "men" and "lions" because they entered a profession viewed as male.

These shifts in cultural and social norms have taken place over a long period and can be partly credited to the role model effect at two levels. First, as more women enter the workforce, they serve as role models for young girls, showing that they too can pursue these careers. Second, as women assume roles traditionally held by men and advance into leadership positions, they challenge the so-called glass ceilings and non-inclusive gender norms, paving the way for more women to follow. These evolving norms are also developing within the institutions where these women work, which this book classifies as gender-norm disruptors. Understanding that change doesn't happen overnight, the acts of resistance by these disruptors have been crucial in reshaping perceptions of women's abilities and in advancing women's fair representation as decision makers. Different women have adopted various strategies to alter gender stereotypes—some revolutionary, others more subtle, like striving to stand out through hard work.

Women in leadership

Changes in the number of women in law across the five generational phases have positively influenced shifting institutional norms and social beliefs, leading to an incremental move toward accepting women as decision makers in law. Using the matrilegal feminist framework, I have argued that women's leadership roles across the continent are not a new phenomenon, and they should not be attributed solely to foreign or international influences, as several African feminist scholars have challenged (Mama, 2020; Tamale, 2021). The past and present decision-making roles women hold trace back to the gender neutrality and matriarchal power present in many African societies. These leadership qualities are evident in the number of African women who have served as chief justices and presidents of constitutional courts (Dawuni & Kang, 2015).

Women's judicial leadership is also evident internationally, with African women judges serving as presidents and vice presidents of major courts, including the African Court on Human and Peoples' Rights, the International Criminal Court, and the International Court of Justice (Dawuni & Kuenyehia, 2018). Although research on women lawyers in Africa is limited, data from Chapter 3 show more women managing partners in law firms across the continent. At the same time, women are advancing to partnership roles within firms, and many are starting their own law practices. Similar progress is seen in academia, with more women becoming deans of law schools, department heads, and vice chancellors of universities. These achievements are significant, yet women leaders still face challenges due to ongoing gender hierarchies, the burdens of being the "first," and difficulties balancing private and professional responsibilities (Institute for African Women in Law, 2023a). Women must navigate shifting power structures, including glass ceilings, labyrinths, cliffs, and sticky floors (Weidenfeller, 2012). Despite these advances, women remain largely at the lower levels of leadership, and the factors behind this situation, along with strategies for change, are discussed in later sections of this chapter.

Expanding areas of specialization

Closely tied to the growth of the legal market is the variety of practice areas at the bar. With the globalization of legal markets, women are branching into specialties such as law and technology, artificial intelligence, mining and construction, and intellectual property, among others. While interview respondents noted no restrictions on the practice area they choose, the main practice areas in law firms can influence where individuals decide to focus or expand their expertise. Once again, the choice of specialization may also depend on age—older lawyers can select their areas of specialization more easily than younger junior associates, and women tend to be more numerous at the associate level. Across different judicial systems, the demand for judicial officers determines which courts female and male judges are assigned to. Although interviewees stated there is no gender-based assignment to courts, the perception was that women are more likely to be assigned to courts handling family law matters because of gender sensitivities involved in those cases.

In the legal academy, women early in their academic careers may have fewer opportunities to choose the courses they teach. Women might be assigned to introductory courses, which are often larger classes that require more time to grade assignments and exams (Dawuni, 2021a). The area of research is where women academics usually have more freedom to decide their focus. However, women tend to dominate research and teaching in subjects like gender, women, and the law, mainly due to personal interest and self-selection. A few men are starting to join those who teach and research in these areas, but overall, research on gender, women, and the law remains largely female-dominated. Increasing diversity in expertise across all three sectors is occurring and is encouraged by the freedom women have to make these choices.

The "other-bar" and "other-bench"

Women have always led the way in challenging gender-biased norms and discriminatory practices. Women's rights advocacy groups often hire women lawyers or seek advice from women lawyers on how to mobilize for social change. Although women have entered these three legal sectors, the full integration and institutionalization of women's issues and concerns into organizational practices remain limited. The bar and bench are where we see the most active mobilization of women by women to promote women's rights within the professions and to continually push for full acceptance of women as equals (Karekwaivanane, 2020; Tamale, 2021). Several countries I visited have established women's fora within the broader frameworks of bar associations or judicial bodies to address gender issues—these organizations I refer to as the *other-bar* and *other-bench*, respectively. These groups serve as support systems for women in the profession, even though they often focus on addressing other gender-based discrimination within society. They have had a meaningful and diverse impact, often operating with little or no financial support and relying on members' voluntary time commitments. However, the legal academy stands out as an outlier in this context.

Across all the countries where data were collected for this research, I did not encounter an organization or group specifically for women legal academics. This may be partly because the legal academy is the third frontier where women joined much later than the other two. It could also mean that the challenges women faced in the early stages at the bar and on the bench have improved the conditions for women in law, from which women in the academy are gaining some indirect benefits. Another possible explanation from the interviews is that women in the academy have not yet formed these coalitions because women academics often belong to other organizations, like the larger bar association and academic bodies. These commitments, along with the responsibilities of teaching, research, and service required of legal academics, further limit the time available for engaging in additional organizational activities.

B. Contributions

Pioneers and pacesetters

From the first groups of women lawyers in several countries to the current rapid increase in women in law, African women are transforming the face of the legal profession. The pioneering women in law were vital agents, not only in opening the path for others but also in symbolically changing societal views on women's roles in law and leadership. As outlined in Chapter 3, these trailblazing women challenged the sex and gender social constructs of their era to enter the legal fields in colonial metropolises, where women's roles were still highly limited. After returning to their home countries, they continued to break new ground, not just in words but in actions. Many served as role models and inspired others to pursue legal education and careers. Additionally, as systematically presented in Chapter 3, several of these women were celebrated women's and human rights advocates who played leading roles in defending the rights of women, children, and the impoverished. The pioneer women shattered the idea that law was a profession only for men; they fought against unequal pay and promotion practices, and many were the first to serve in various other capacities.

Their contributions have transcended national borders, with many representing their governments at international forums such as the United Nations Women's Conferences from Mexico City to Beijing. Several served on global committees, including Justice Annie Jiagge, who helped draft CEDAW (Dawuni, 2012), and Vera Duarte of Cape Verde, the first woman appointed to the African Commission on Human and Peoples' Rights, who led the drafting of the Protocol to the African Charter on Women's Rights in Africa (Maputo Protocol) (Duarte, 2022). Many pioneer women lawyers and judges, like Justice Florence Mwachande Ndepele of Zambia, Navi Pillay of South Africa, and Fatoumata Diarra of Mali, served on international courts and tribunals (Dawuni & Kuenyehia, 2018). Several were also political activists, playing key intermediary roles as civil society members demanding democracy, good governance, and the rule of law. For many of these women, including Vera Chirwa, political activism meant spending time in jail. Women's impact is also evident in academia, where pioneering women academics fiercely challenged entrenched institutional patriarchy to create opportunities for women in the academy, earning recognition as equals in teaching and research across countries like Kenya (Kameri-Mbote & Wekesa, 2018), Uganda (Tamale, 2021), Ghana (Dawuni, 2021a), and Zimbabwe (Stewart & Tsanga, 2011).

Diversity and enrichment within the profession

Evidence across the three sectors shows that gender diversity in the profession is changing how law firms, judiciaries, and academic institutions operate. Interview respondents shared different ways in which the individual contributions of women and the collective mobilization of women in these workspaces have helped create organizations that are more attentive to the needs of a broader section of society. In South Africa, while efforts to overcome the legacy of apartheid have led to initiatives aimed at creating racial diversity and inclusion, gender diversity and inclusion still face ongoing challenges in the legal profession (Klaaren, 2020), legal education (Madlalate, 2022), and the judiciary (Masengu, 2021; Mocumie, 2022). Although this study has not fully explored ethnic diversity and the rights of sexual minorities and people living with disabilities, these are areas that warrant further investigation in future research. Diversity in all its forms must be central to how legal organizations operate and deliver services to their clients and communities.

Expanding access to justice for women

Women in the legal sector have made significant contributions by expanding access to justice for women and other marginalized groups (Dawuni, 2022b; De Souza et al., 2014). Women lawyers have advocated for and contributed to drafting legal instruments that expand women's rights (Aura-Odhiambo, 2018; Murungi and Meroka-Mutua, 2022). Women judges have helped advance gender-sensitive jurisprudence in areas such as women's property rights and inheritance (Gayoye, 2021; Mensa-Bonsu & Mensa-Bonsu, 2021), maternal and reproductive rights (Kyobiika, 2021), violence against women, and women's bodily integrity rights (Ojigho, 2021). Women lawyers have played a key role in the operation of FIDA, a global organization with chapters across Africa. Through FIDA, women have provided free legal advice and representation to impoverished women. Finally, women academics have led the introduction of courses on women and the law and have conducted research on women's rights issues such as property, marriage, inheritance, alimony, violence against women, and many other important studies that highlight gaps in women's rights (Banda, 2005; Kuenyehia, 1998; Stewart & Tsanga, 2011; Tamale, 2020).

Increasing the pool of role models

Last, the rise in the number of women in law and leadership roles within these sectors has served as a positive role model, inspiring younger generations of women to pursue careers in law. When asked about their motivations for choosing a legal career, even though most respondents (71.5% of lawyers, 65.8% of judges, and 77.1% of academics) said they were motivated by personal choice, a combined 15.65% of lawyers, 22.8% of judges, and 20.9% of academics reported being encouraged by a peer or a pioneer woman in law. Women in law serve as role models, setting examples for others to follow, aspiring to become managing partners in law firms, chief justices, or deans of law schools. The symbolic presence of women setting standards in domestic and international law is creating renewed awareness of women's capabilities, challenging gender-biased and negative perceptions, and catalyzing the increasing number of women entering the profession.

C. Challenges

Persisting gender inequities in entry and promotion

Since the passage of the Sex Disqualification Act in 1923, women have been joining the legal professions in increasing numbers in South Africa. In other countries, efforts to promote gender equality have led to the creation of legal frameworks that guarantee equal employment opportunities and equal pay in national constitutions, legislative acts, and international instruments under the International Labor Organization (ILO). Despite these laws, women continue to report persistent inequities in hiring, some of which are influenced by a preference for male workers. As mentioned earlier, the new requirements for doctoral degrees for teaching positions have been a deterrent for some women entering the academy, but this is changing as more women pursue higher education and earn doctoral degrees. In judiciaries, on the other hand, women are catching up in many countries, yet women still occupy lower levels of the judicial hierarchy in several others. Across all three sectors, the data and empirical responses presented in Chapters 3, 4, and 5 show that women still experience slower rates of promotion, resulting in a pyramid shape with women overrepresented at the lower ranks. Clear and accessible policies for hiring and promotion are the first step toward addressing these inequities. However, policies alone are not sufficient; equitable enforcement mechanisms must support them.

Tensions between the private and public realms

The demands on women's time between the public and private spheres mean that women's lives cannot be easily balanced to produce the same outputs as men within male-determined work standards and expectations. A majority of the challenges professional women face result from trying to fit into systems designed to accommodate men's lived realities—the architectures of institutional rules, norms, and practices. This clash between women's private lives and work expectations creates tensions that make it difficult for women to fully participate in the public sphere. Even though the number of women in the legal workforce is increasing and women are advancing into top managerial positions, these changes are not fully matched by shifts in the domestic realm or masculine work expectations (Ely et al., 2013; Haslam & Ryan, 2007).

As a profession primarily focused on applying legal principles for justice and fairness, it has, in several cases, failed to protect and promote the rights of its own members—particularly women. Originating from the depths of Western patriarchy, the current legal professions have preserved historical and institutional norms that foster gender-based discrimination, such as sexual harassment and unequal pay. While changes in constitutional and legislative standards that guarantee gender equality, institutional demands for women's labor, the rising number of women legal professionals, and evolving perceptions of women's competence are contributing to reforms in the legal field, more efforts are necessary to achieve real equality. Globally, scholars have observed that the gendering of the legal profession has yet to lead to meaningful institutional and professional changes that ensure equity, inclusion, and equality for women in law (Auchmuty et al., 2021; Schultz & Shaw, 2013).

Gender-based perceptions of incompetence

Despite the contributions women are making to the profession and society, women across all three sectors constantly navigate gender-based biases and stereotypes about their competence and suitability for employment. The hope that increasing the number of women in the profession would lead to changes in societal and professional acceptance of women as equal participants has been met with an ongoing wave of new challenges (Markovic & Plickert, 2022; Schultz & Shaw, 2013). Overall, most women interviewed believe these persistent perceptions stem from unconscious biases rooted in history, culture, religion, and personal tendencies toward gender bias. A common example I heard was the perception that women lawyers are not suited for courtroom litigation, even though women attribute their aversion to litigation to its aggressive, masculine nature rather than to women's abilities or legal knowledge. Across all three sectors, women must confront these perceptions not only from colleagues but also from clients (lawyers), litigants (judges), and students (academics). Women have devised creative strategies to manage these issues, which will be discussed further in section IV.

The invisible theatre of gender performativity

Across all three sectors, women report constantly juggling their professional and personal lives. This challenge persists throughout women's careers, whether they are mothers, grandmothers, or caregivers to aging parents. The extended family networks in African systems further complicate the available time for professional women. Women's traditional roles as caregivers at home often follow them into their workplaces. For many women, these caregiving responsibilities and expectations become blurred as they are expected to extend their nurturing roles to colleagues, litigants, and students. I categorize these extended caregiving roles as the invisible theatre of gender performativity—actions women perform for the well-being of their workplaces but receive no recognition during evaluations. In law firms, women are expected to handle cases involving women, yet these cases often pay less. Despite their high emotional stress, they are not valued as highly as commercial transaction cases. In court, women judges have had to fight to assert their roles as decision makers, and many respondents reported going the extra mile to protect women and children victims of rape and abuse. Women in academia also face expectations to mentor and perform "other-mothering" duties for students and junior colleagues. While these gendered roles are often invisible or undervalued, they significantly strengthen institutions by providing emotional and mental health support to clients, litigants, and students.

Sexual and workplace harassment

The evidence presented in earlier chapters shows that women in law experience varying levels of workplace bullying and harassment. Younger women are more vulnerable to bullying and sexual harassment partly due to the culture of ageism and workplace expectations of seniority. Cultural stigma attached to sexual abuse often prevents most women from sharing their experiences. While most of my respondents did not share their personal stories, many were willing to discuss the experiences of other women in the profession. This observation prompted me to change my questioning approach and ask in the third person to help respondents distance themselves from any traumatic experiences they might have faced if they were victims. The emphasis on age in African systems also tends to blur the lines between respectful deference to a senior colleague, which could be an abuse of power or bullying, thus complicating the ability to distinguish between ageism and sexism (Dawuni, 2021a). The structure of legal practice, with long hours and client meetings to prepare briefs, exposes young women to sexual harassment from senior colleagues and, in some cases, from clients. Some institutions have implemented antiharassment policies, but their enforcement and implementation vary widely. Women who report abuse are at risk of being publicly shamed or blamed, as seen in some cases discussed in Chapter 3. Women need to support each other to foster a culture where women feel safe sharing their encounters with harassers and bullies openly.

IV. Strategies for Success

1. Stay, Strategize, Succeed

The history of women in the legal professions worldwide is filled with women facing years of professional barriers to entry, unequal pay, the silencing, and sometimes erasure of their contributions and impact. Describing the experiences of women in law from 1890 to 1940, Glazer and Slater (1987) noted that early women lawyers had to be skilled at using various strategies to overcome the prejudices they faced. Unfortunately, many of these challenges still exist in the legal profession today, appearing in different forms and degrees (Chitapi, 2018; Masengu, 2015; Schultz & Shaw, 2003; Sterling & Chanow, 2021). Several of these documented biases remain true for many women now, and even more so for minority and minoritized women in the field (Deo, 2019; Melaku, 2019; Norwood, 2020). Similar to these global trends, in Africa, women in law must contend with both internal challenges within their countries and the broader issues of global patriarchy, exclusion, silencing, and erasure as they work with their international colleagues and clients.

While the number of women in law across the three sectors is increasing, the lack of radical change in persistent gender-biased institutional norms and social expectations means women are continually managing intersecting challenges. The histories of African women's resistance to oppression before colonization, their matriarchal agency, and their capacity to overcome challenges have been discussed in Chapter 2. This section explores strategies women in law have used across different sectors. As shown in **Figure 7.2**, despite many obstacles, women in law have consistently resisted victimization and chosen to persist, strategize, and succeed—even if sometimes at a significant cost to their health, family, and overall well-being. This typology is neither linear nor the only route to career success. The intersectional factors discussed in Chapters 1 and 3, a country's political economy, and the specific norms and practices within institutions can combine to produce different outcomes for women. The experiences of women in law are too varied and complex to fit a single model of survival. Nonetheless, this typology was developed based on responses gathered from informant interviews.

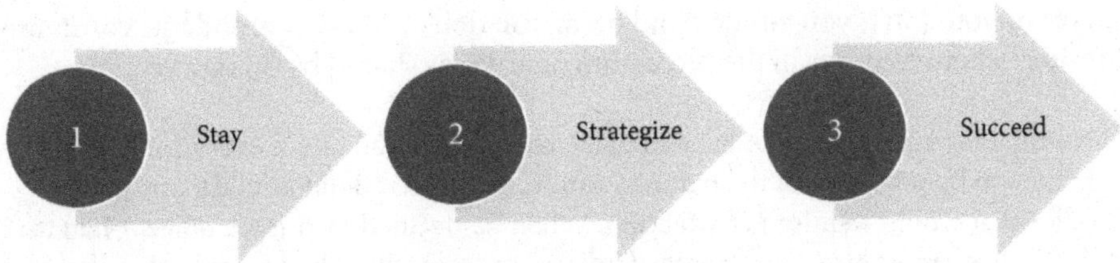

Figure 7.2 *Typology of Women's Paths to Career Growth*

Returning to the *matri-legal feminist framework* outlined in Chapter 2, African women in law are not victims, nor do they adopt roles of victimization waiting to be rescued by external actors. Across the continent, women have challenged systems of oppression at the macro-level of global imperialism, the meso-level of state authoritarianism and institutional gender-based discrimination, and the micro-level of social gendered norms and expectations of conformity within the community and family. At each of these overlapping spheres of oppression, women have consistently developed survival strategies and skills.

Women in law have relied on their agency, drawn on their cultural matrilineal powers, and challenged multiple intersecting systems of oppression. The matri-legal feminist approach broadens our understanding of how women in law have devised success strategies to navigate the challenges embedded in history, institutions, and social structures. This argument does not presuppose a model indicating a linear pathway, nor does it attempt to prescribe this typology as the only model for success. For instance, some women may choose to leave and reenter the profession (e.g., taking time off to start a family or pursue higher education), and this choice not to stay at a particular point during their career does not mean they have failed or not reached the stage of success in the last stage presented in the typology. Alternatively, some may choose not to stay in one profession and join another (from the bar to the bench or academia). Intersecting factors and variables will predict the strategies one chooses to adopt, and success is specific to each person's professional goals and choices. For most women, these strategies are often informed by the will to succeed through acts of resistance to multiple layers of oppression and discrimination. The following discussion combines the shared experiences of women across the three sectors.

A. The Choice to Stay

Stay or leave

Expansion in domestic and global legal markets has provided more options for women to choose their area of practice and which law firm to work with. However, the luxury of choice may not be available to all women. Depending on their career stage, younger lawyers (both men and women) need to first build their expertise and join reputable firms to gain the skills required to become successful lawyers. While the bar may be the initial entry point for most law students, many eventually branch out into other sectors of the profession for various reasons. Being a lawyer is challenging, and as the challenges mentioned above show, women face additional obstacles. As one woman lawyer said during the interview, "As a woman, you either decide to be a lawyer or you don't; you either stand up or you don't." Many respondents constantly consider whether to stay in the profession or leave, as shared by this lawyer.

> Nothing is perfect. Women have to make choices; we can't have everything. When I chose to be president of the bar association, my husband did not take any political office that would require my attention. When he decided to run for office, I had to decide to support him. Our daughter suffered the most. But I had to make that choice and remind myself that I am a mother first. I had to organize everything so I can be a mother first and then a lawyer.

The reality is that most women come into the profession unaware of some of the professional challenges discussed earlier. A third-generation woman lawyer in Ghana shared some practical strategies for women lawyers at the early stages of their careers:

> Young lawyers must be practical and understand the challenges they will face; whether they like it or not, they have to work twice as hard as men. To stand out, they must be very confident in what they are saying. I've noticed that when I discuss issues that interest men, I sometimes fade into the background as a woman. We need to emphasize our differences in ways that will earn their respect. The way some young women dress can divert attention from their intellectual capabilities, but if we also present ourselves well to our clients, they will trust us and recognize our competence.

This statement by the lawyer suggests many issues—some related to the expectation for women to demonstrate their intellectual ability by knowing what they are talking about. However, her reference to "I realize that when I discuss issues that interest the men, after a while I fade away as a woman, we must emphasize our differences in doing that which will earn their respect" shows that the profession is still gendered. Her use of "fade away" implies that women need to adopt masculine traits, and a woman who appears intelligent is equated with a man. The idea that women must engage men and highlight their differences to "earn their respect" is quite problematic and highlights the ongoing challenges women face in a profession that remains masculinized.

Women facing sexual and other forms of harassment are caught in a cycle of violence with mental and physical health consequences. Confronting an abusive work colleague—who likely controls your caseload, paycheck, and promotion—can feel like a nightmare. As interviewees shared, for some women facing sexual harassment and bullying, the choice has often been to leave and seek employment in other sectors, such as the judiciary, a state agency, or as in-house counsel in banks or other corporations, while others may choose to stay and fight. Women should not have to make such choices in a professional setting. Unfortunately, most women lawyers lack support systems in the workplace or within the legal profession to assist victims of harassment. Sexual harassment is widespread, and addressing this issue effectively will require institutional mechanisms and anti-sexual harassment policies adopted by bar associations and law firms to protect women's rights. Women should not have to make such difficult choices due to institutional gaps that hinder their ability to be seen and treated as equals in the legal field.

Gender norm-disruptors versus norm-conformists

Several women interviewed for this book emphasized the fundamental belief that women have a right to be in the legal profession. For these women, standing up, speaking out, and challenging normalized masculine practices are essential strategies for women's representation in the field. Several women rejected the idea that it is women's duty to manage male expectations at work. Members of the legal profession are tasked with defending people's rights. However, as reports of discrimination and bullying faced by women lawyers reveal, women are not immune to victimization. Women in law encounter different institutional biases, and their ability to defend themselves depends on various intersectional factors. Age (both biological and years at the bar) may hinder a woman lawyer from being her best advocate, whether speaking up against unwanted advances from other lawyers or disrespectful treatment from judges in the courtroom. Nevertheless, some women do not hesitate to become their own advocates when necessary—these are women I categorize as gender-norm disruptors. At some point in their careers, women lawyers will find themselves in the disruptors category—whether fighting for equal pay, respectful treatment, deserved promotions, or speaking out against bullying and sexual harassment.

Others have adopted strategies that are more managerial in handling colleagues or unprofessional situations. A woman lawyer in Nigeria shared:

> Men will be men first before they become professionals. Even in a professional setting, men still want to act as they would at home; they want to be the boss making the final decision. I don't get upset about that—just like you manage your husband at home, you manage them. When you go into a meeting, you know they have already made up their minds, so you come prepared, and you also work on convincing your other male colleagues. You deal with them before you actually enter the meeting.

Another group of respondents are what I call gender-norm conformists because they conform to gender-biased norms through their silence and inaction. For these women, the best way to handle workplace masculinity is, in the words of one lawyer, "let things bounce off you." This means smiling and letting unwanted jokes, unpleasant gestures, and sexist language go without challenging them. Other gender-norm conformist strategies are seen in women lawyers who choose to adapt their dress and style to fit in and avoid being a "distraction." As one lawyer said, "I do not put on much makeup—I don't look over-decorated that way, I am not calling attention to myself." I asked her if women need to change their style to suit men, and she responded, "I don't think it is wrong to be toned down, I think we are a profession with standards." There is a thin and slippery line between staying within professional standards and losing the right to express femininity or personal style. It's true that lawyers should present an appearance that aligns with professional ethics, but the fact that such discussions mostly focus on women suggests a gendered view in how these standards are judged.

Supportive and inclusive work environment

A common and recurring theme throughout this book is the slow pace at which law firms and the legal profession are changing to accommodate the increasing number of women joining the bar. Law firms need to adapt to this trend, and the challenges of rigid working hours, unfair promotion practices, and unequal pay should be replaced with inclusive and equitable policies that benefit women lawyers and the firms themselves. Most of my interview respondents believed that organizational support and inclusive work environments that recognize women's needs are key factors in whether women stay or leave. For a female partner in a law firm in Nigeria, policies that allowed her to work while pregnant and on maternity leave were important signs that the firm valued her well-being. Despite the time she needed to care for her child, these arrangements enabled her to continue working and earn enough points for a promotion and a raise. She concluded that when law firms support women at different stages of their careers, women are more likely to stay loyal and work to improve the firm's success.

For several years, gender activists have been urging law firms to promote gender equity and inclusion through a legal framework rooted in laws that guarantee equal rights at work. Recently, researchers and practitioners have been examining the need for gender equality and inclusion in law firms and legal practice more from a business perspective, often called the "business case" for equal representation. Some law firms are making changes to address the needs of working mothers. A managing partner in Ghana shared her experience.

> After several years working at this firm, I have observed that women tend to be more committed and loyal to the company's growth. Since we have more women here, we have made arrangements to support them, such as offering flexible work hours so they can balance work and family commitments. I work from 8 am to 2 pm, pick up my kids, then go home and do some work. I have a house help, but no driver, because taking my kids to school and picking them up is a time I spend bonding with them.

During fieldwork, I was surprised to visit two law firms—one in Ghana and the other in Nigeria—that had a creche for their employees with babies. In both law firms, women made up more than 50% of the junior and senior associates, and most of the women associates were of childbearing age. The law firm in Ghana also prioritized the well-being of all its employees by investing in a workplace gym where associates could work out either before or after work, thereby eliminating the need to leave early or come in late for those who included working out at a public gym as part of their daily routine.

There are advantages and disadvantages to having a day care at the workplace. From a work-life balance perspective, the argument is that by bringing the child to the workplace, women might face additional pressure to work long hours, based on the assumption that their child-care responsibilities are handled by the company. This argument does not fully consider the range of child-care demands. Simply going to breastfeed a child for a few minutes does not constitute full child care. In these cases, child care is typically provided by personal nannies that women bring to the workplace at their own expense. If a woman has more than one child, especially if others are of school age, she still needs to be home in time to care for those children and meet other obligations to a spouse or partner and, in some cases, aging parents. Despite ongoing challenges with workplace creche or day-care arrangements, I believe that overall, this is a positive effort by law firms to support women returning to work after maternity leave.

For other law firms that lack on-site creche or day-care options, some permit women the flexibility to bring their children to work during emergency school closures or when a nanny is unavailable. Although most law firms do not oppose women lawyers bringing their children or leaving early due to child-care emergencies, women often bear the additional burden, feeling they might be judged negatively for doing so. For women in judicial positions and academia, child care challenges are a constant concern, and without institutional support to address these needs, women must find creative ways to manage their maternal responsibilities while working. These solutions sometimes include taking their children to the office or hiring a caregiver at home.

B. The Need to Strategize

Professional networks, mentors, and sponsors

To some extent, the legal profession can be compared to a stock exchange where lawyers *occasionally* trade clients through a referral system. Professional legal networks play a crucial role in the legal referral process. With the legal field still largely male-dominated, women lawyers must break into male-centric structures and hierarchies by building strong networks with both male and female colleagues who have distinguished themselves at the bar. During fieldwork, when I asked respondents how women are navigating the "old boys' networks," a respondent in the Ivory Coast emphasized the importance of building strong networks of both men and women:

> I have never found myself in a situation where I needed help and didn't receive it. It might also be because I've built a strong network over time; when I ask for help, I do so first because they are my friends. I haven't been exposed to the proverbial "bitching" of women.

Mentorship plays a vital role in a person's career journey. People who find role models are more likely to follow their examples when making career decisions. For many law students, the lack of women as law professors probably explains why fewer women consider academic careers after law school. Besides personal interest, the law curriculum still emphasizes litigation. Most women become academics after completing their master's degrees and discovering their passion for teaching, research, or both, along with gender issues. Building a significant presence of women in academia could challenge stereotypes, inspire young women, and offer mentorship opportunities for students and peer support for emerging academics. Some senior women professors actively mentor others, as one interviewee explains.

> When I was the Dean, I made sure all women were encouraged to apply for these grants. I maintained friendly relationships with their husbands and often told them to allow their wives to travel. I co-authored with them and took them to conferences. Once they gained experience, I advised them to mentor new faculty members. That is how women in academia should support each other.

Some women have also received mentorship from male colleagues and passed it on to other women, as shared by this respondent.

> I came from a middle-class family, so I already had international exposure. When I joined the faculty, I didn't know we had local journals. A male colleague called me and told me about local journals, and I started publishing in them. I also made sure to attend at least one international conference each year. I would save up for a conference and spend a two-week holiday in that country afterward. That was how I mentored all the female faculty in my department. If you invest in yourself, nobody can take it away from you. If you invest in yourself, you'll preserve your pride, so don't wait for the university because it may never happen.

In all six countries where fieldwork was conducted for this project, there were no institutionalized mentorship programs between junior and senior faculty. Individuals establish these relationships on an ad hoc basis. In fact, some women shared that they received more help from male mentors than from women mentors, which may be due to several factors. It may be because there are more men than women in the academy; however, some respondents believe that women are not always supportive of other women. Many also indicated that women are often overburdened and stretched thin by intersectional roles, leaving them little time or energy to actively mentor others. Regardless of the reasons, a significant gap remains—the lack of institutionalized or formal mentoring programs for junior women faculty. Due to the intersection of age and gender, junior women faculty are vulnerable to unprofessional demands from senior male faculty. Therefore, there is a need to establish mentorship programs that support women who might otherwise be subjected to power demands from senior male faculty.

Achieve a balance or reach a harmony

The lack of or limited workplace arrangements that support women's caregiving responsibilities means some women must make difficult choices, such as whether to remain in the workforce, find a different job that accommodates their domestic caregiving needs, or stop working entirely. The decision a woman makes depends on various factors. Some respondents share some of these challenges women face; for example, a woman who is married and earns more than her spouse may be too busy with her job to effectively manage her domestic duties, which can increase tensions at home. For single mothers, staying in the workforce often appears to be the only option, even though it involves the added challenge of securing child care and support. For most women who do not fit neatly into these categories—and even those with the option to quit because their spouse or partner earns a higher income—the personal choice to pursue a career can be a key factor in whether they stay.

In all 153 interviews conducted, none of my respondents agreed that they had developed a foolproof strategy or plan for balancing their family (personal) and work (professional) obligations. The overwhelming majority of women shared their strategies for staying balanced, but these were only strategies; sometimes they worked, and other times they did not. Engaging in the balancing act requires a great deal of flexibility and adaptability. A lawyer in the Ivory Coast shared her experience:

> Achieving a balance is about organizing your time. You need to review your tasks for each part of your life and plan accordingly. Generally, I spend weekends interacting with extended family. In the past, I had to sacrifice family time for work, but now I manage to meet my family's needs. One of the strengths of this firm is that we support each other and share the workload when someone needs help finishing a task. However, it can still be challenging; two weeks ago, I was supposed to travel, but my busy work schedule prevented it. Sometimes, work does impact my family.

Another young lawyer noted the challenge of dividing her time between multiple needs. She emphasized that the balancing act is not easy, whether one is married or not:

> It's not easy. I'm a divorcee with two children who live with their father. I'm 33 years old. My husband has custody, and even though it's easier for me not to worry about a husband and children, I now have a new boyfriend and need to take care of everyone's needs.

A senior partner in a law firm in The Gambia shared her views about the role of teamwork in helping one reach an equilibrium:

> I don't think I've achieved balance. Ultimately, it depends on the person you're married to; if he's understanding and willing to work with you, it can work. As a lawyer or professional woman, you can't have a traditional relationship where you do all the expected work of a woman. I do a lot of work for the diplomatic community, so I can't afford to slack off. I must say we can't do what we do without our staff's help—there's no question about that—so it all comes down to teamwork.

These shared experiences from three women at different levels of their careers, with intersecting identities related to marital status (married or divorced) and family needs (older or younger children), all illustrate the unique responsibilities women must balance to achieve harmony. Two of the respondents emphasize the importance of teamwork, which highlights the crucial role that law firms should play in supporting women at work.

For women judges, balancing their professional and personal obligations is what I called *managing the second docket* in Chapter 5. One judge shared her observations on how women handle the second docket: "I have realized that women have to take care of their families, which limits their time for work. Still, you must develop your will and organizational skills to manage your work and personal obligations."

Women academics also shared the tough working conditions of managing large class sizes and how these affect their research, the quality of their teaching, and their personal lives. A former dean of the law faculty discussed the early years of her academic career and how family support was instrumental in her success (Dawuni, 2021a, pp. 163–164):

> My late mother was a headmistress [school principal] who took early retirement and stayed with us to help. It was such a blessing for me and all my siblings, she supervised homework, baths etc. I also had quite an active international presence doing conferences etc.; my husband was also a real support; he would offer to take the children to see a doctor and run other errands and appointments with the children when I was teaching. With my third child I was very busy on various committees and boards. It is never an easy balance, I suppose you work at it and do the best you can, you lose out a bit and the children lose too. Now getting help with children is not easy.

Other respondents believe that women should not let their domestic obligations interfere with their ability to work effectively. When asked if women's personal responsibilities affect their professional progress, a legal academic responded:

> I'll say it's a lie. Based on my experience and what I tell the women in my faculty, I remind them that it depends on your will; you have to make sacrifices to succeed. I believe that you shouldn't succeed academically and fail at home as a mother, wife, or leader in the church. You will need to sacrifice and work late into the night if necessary—you must be disciplined. Compete as if you are competing with a man, and don't ask for less workload just because you are a woman.

For women academics in leadership positions who must deal with extra administrative work, a former female dean provided this advice:

> You can be the best administrator and the worst researcher if you let administrative work consume your thoughts. I didn't allow that to happen. While I was dean, I published two or three papers annually on average. After my meetings, I would go to the library. I made it clear that I shouldn't be disturbed unless there was an emergency. I didn't want to be interrupted.

These narratives reemphasize the point that women are engaged in a constant juggling act of achieving a balance or some semblance of harmony in their professional lives. Several factors influence the strategies one adopts. Each woman must find what works best for her and stick with it.

Planning and compartmentalizing are key to survival

Life as a lawyer is already busy, and for women, it can become more complicated due to the competing demands outside work. To manage this balancing act, some women have mastered the art of planning and compartmentalizing their lives to maintain as smooth a balance as possible. For a managing partner of a law firm in Ghana, the keys to her survival are compartmentalizing her roles and delegating tasks to trustworthy teammates and her family support network.

For some women, compartmentalizing means the following:

> When I am at work, I focus on my tasks and try not to let anything related to my family interfere, but when I leave, I drop everything and pay attention to my family.

> When I have deadlines, I can work on weekends. Sometimes I feel guilty leaving early and letting others work, but that is outside my control. I try to compensate by staying focused and doing my job well, and not letting it bother me.

Personal circumstances will undoubtedly influence the choices individuals make about how they compartmentalize their work. Setting priorities seems to be a key part of what some lawyers do to achieve their goals with minimal stress for themselves and others. Different women have made personal decisions based on their positionality—while some have no option but to be on bed rest during pregnancy, others have been able to work throughout their pregnancy and return to work shortly after delivery. Some have also decided to stay at home to care for their children, while others choose to work and make the most of it.

C. The Will to Succeed

Prove yourself (over and above)

As discussed earlier, women lawyers face numerous socially constructed perceptions of incompetence from their male colleagues, judges, and clients. These perceptions are widespread and affect women regardless of their years of experience or their record of professional success and expertise. While older women lawyers may receive some respect from colleagues and clients, the fact that they must "acquire" this respect and recognition due to their age (biological and years at the bar) is problematic. To succeed in the profession, some women emphasize the need to "be informed and educated" about the law to appear intelligent; in other words, women have to prove themselves repeatedly to gain respect. Women must meet a performance standard that is common across sectors and worldwide, which is not only a gender issue but also a racialized one.

For some women, it starts with the negotiation process when joining a firm or law school. A respondent in Ghana was helpful in giving advice on how women can negotiate their roles with confidence and tact.

> Women often hesitate to negotiate; we tend to give up too quickly, even when it comes to salaries. We should take every opportunity to show our managers how we communicate and negotiate, including how we meet deadlines. I advise my mentees not to expect handouts; you can't rely on your gender to climb the ladder. Nothing will change for you unless you put in the hard work.

Another respondent shared the best way for women to showcase their skills:

> Women need to play it smart too; that's what men do! Build your own pipeline and value chain, and people will rely on you. Surprise your leader, even when you're on leave, by completing some work and creating value for yourself. Some women take their maternity leave without checking in with the office, and they come back to find things have fallen through.

Women have developed their own survival strategies despite doubts and perceptions of incompetence. One respondent advised that women must "show their knowledge and craft, and they will be respected; so when you go into court and announce yourself, the judge will sit up because they have heard about your work and respect you." For men, the default attitude assumes competence, and the extra effort women must make to prove themselves puts them at a gender-based disadvantage. The level of gendered expectations a woman faces largely depends on the type of legal practice or industry she works in. A lawyer at a multinational mining company in Nigeria shared:

> This industry [mining industry] is very male-dominated because of the nature of the work. I am the only woman in management and the first woman to sit on the Executive Committee. The work here is intense—mainly because it revolves around products, with the primary goal being to extract gold, and focus is placed on technical, engineering, and industrial requirements. The legal department is often excluded from meetings and makes decisions without us being informed. It is a true man's world here, and it has taken a lot for me to be recognized as an important part of the business. You literally have to stand your ground to let them know they can't push you out. Even as the head of the legal department, some people still think I am the secretary.

Another lawyer in Nigeria believes that a woman's success heavily depends on her level of confidence (and a hint of intimidation) she brings to the job.

> Going to court is all about confidence. How you present yourself in the courtroom will determine the respect the lawyers and judges give you. In fact, I used to intimidate other people; I would introduce myself as a chief even at that young age.

Women lawyers understand the law; what many may be missing is confidence in their abilities and how to express it—what is commonly called imposter syndrome. For example, during my interviews in Senegal in 2018, I spoke with the director of the law school training institute to explore why fewer women were reaching the bar. During our conversation, he mentioned that in the last two law school graduation cohorts, women outnumbered men, and women continued to excel at the top of their classes. He observed:

> Our profession views women lawyers positively. They are very dynamic and great organizers. I prefer working with women over men because they are committed and know how to organize tasks. The Young Women Lawyers Association should collaborate with women lawyers to help change their mindset and boost their confidence in their abilities. It is women who champion women's causes and advocate for women's education; without such efforts, fewer women and girls will attend law school and become lawyers. Women are extremely valuable, and that is why we encourage their participation in the profession.

Similar sentiments were expressed by a male managing partner of a top law firm in Ghana:

> Women tend to be more structured and theoretical; they are more likely to sit, think, and get the work done. Men tend to be more footloose. I believe women make the best lawyers, but when it comes to litigation, men are more willing and able to travel and stay away from family for longer periods. That's why you'll find more men in that area of practice.

The comments made by two men reflect what many men believe about women lawyers—that they are just as capable, if not more so, than male lawyers. What occurs between the time a woman graduates from law school and her actual experiences in legal practice? Why does the acknowledgment by male leaders that women are hard-working and diligent not translate into work environments that are gender-inclusive? The rising trend of women graduating at the top of their class has yet to make a significant impact on changing the power hierarchies within the legal field, especially in the Nigerian context, where many still cling to the outdated view that "there are no women at the bar," or that women lawyers are "gentlemen in skirts."

The idea that despite women's qualifications and abilities, they still have to "fit in" with the institutional norms of legal practice highlights ongoing institutional sexism. For example, some women noted that measuring work output by the number of billable hours in an office setting is a masculine standard of measuring work. They also pointed out that it creates an uneven playing field, as women often have to consider social and institutional expectations about how to present themselves to clients, judges in the courtroom, and other male colleagues they encounter.

Similar to the experiences shared by women lawyers, women academics also conveyed that they must prove themselves—both to their students and male colleagues. The "prove yourself" standard, or "performance premium," is a gendered expectation, as men typically enter the scene assuming that they know it all and are more likely to be seen as the default in academia. Aware of these perceptions, many women academics intentionally challenge them through their actions by doing everything they can to dispel these negative views. As one respondent stated, "[W]omen have to pull their weight."

The added challenge of proving their worth as the merit-based or rightful owners of the spaces they occupy also involves using multiple strategies and managing their time effectively. A former law school dean shared her survival strategy:

> During the military strikes, I never rested. I still go to work even though there are no classes or meetings. For all the papers I have, I can tell you that when I started writing them, I used the strike moments to begin working on my papers. I take my children to school, so by 8 am, I am at the faculty, usually the first one there, and that is when I teach. I am an early riser. This habit helped me later when I became Dean. We started meetings at 10 am, so I could balance my 8 am teaching and the 10 am meetings. I am actively involved at church and at home: once I come back, I become a wife or mother. Most of my work is done at night. I set targets and go for it.

Women must constantly navigate sociocultural perceptions that question their equality with men. They are also demonstrating that they can perform the work despite intersecting challenges such as age, marital status, sexuality, ability, and more. Encouragement of themselves and others is a strategy shared by many women interviewed, with one noting:

> Joining the faculty is open to everyone, but the time and energy needed for teaching, research, and family responsibilities are what limit women's chances of moving upward. The main point is to encourage women not to settle for what they have; women should keep striving to reach the next level. In my field, one must write articles and publish them to advance. I advise young academics to pursue higher degrees while they are young—it is easier. Women should not create barriers in their minds.

While equal opportunities exist for women to enter the academy, the processes and mechanisms for succeeding and advancing may not always be fair because of the competing demands on a woman's time and energy. Nonetheless, the pursuit of excellence and competing on an equal footing with male colleagues remain consistent goals for many women I interviewed. Increasing the number of women in the academy, and how quickly they can move up the ranks, will depend on individual motivations and other factors that may support or hinder women from pursuing higher degrees.

Support of spouse/partner and extended family

The saying "behind every successful man is a woman" has been used to recognize women's contributions to their male partners' success. I have often wondered why we don't usually hear that phrase when the successful person is a woman. Women must constantly balance competing demands, managing their professional responsibilities along with their personal family duties. Most of the married women I interviewed said they couldn't have achieved their careers without their husbands' support. In one case, I interviewed a managing partner of a law firm and was very impressed by her professional strength, clarity, and innovative thinking. After an hour-long interview and on my way to my next appointment, she sent me a long text message with one additional, very important detail she wanted me to record. She explained in the message that she wanted to acknowledge her husband as a supportive partner in all her work and professional accomplishments.

Other women lawyers expressed similar sentiments, with one remarking, "I have a very, very supportive husband, so that eases a lot of tension. He respects me for my intellect and is very supportive of all I do." Across countries, women consistently credited their partners or husbands for understanding the demands of their work and for being supportive. The consensus is that a spouse or partner can help a woman advance in her career. Having a spouse or partner who knows how to balance their workload to support a wife is important. For some respondents, their extended family also proved helpful at times. Most women mentioned the support they received from their mothers or mothers-in-law who stayed with them and assisted with child care and other domestic responsibilities.

Women supporting women

Women lawyers are finding ways to support each other through women-only professional associations within bar associations and judiciaries. Ironically, most of these women's professional associations still spend much of their time doing what I call "professional care work," by providing support for women's needs. One issue women discussed during interviews was the lack of a consistent support system among women. Will an "old girls' club" be the answer to the "old boys' network"? Several women have suggested that women supporting women through networks, mentoring, and female sponsorship is essential for upward mobility. As the number of women in law (critical mass) grows, more women are speaking out for changes in the norms and practices of the profession (critical actors). However, what might be missing are "critical actions" to actively push for change and engage in deliberate advocacy to alter norms within the profession. Despite efforts by women to challenge gendered institutional norms like sexual harassment—such as suing perpetrators and filing formal complaints—these actions have yet to produce the changes needed to advance women's positions.

Women also emphasized the importance of women supporting each other to lead. The managing partner of a women-led law firm said this about the founding partner of the firm:

> Mrs. A is a strict and demanding boss. She trusted me to handle the office management for a month because she believed in my abilities. She constantly encourages me and tells me to go forward; she offers ongoing support. She pushes you to do your best, and you can rely on her to be there when you need help.

Supporting women also comes through vertical mentoring and peer mentoring. One respondent believes that

> [w]omen can be anything; they should not be intimidated. We have more tenacity than men, but we often let our gender hold us back due to fear of public criticism. When we decide to do something, we can do it well. The court of public opinion is what discourages or stops women's progress. We need to support each other.

Women need to keep building trust and group unity among themselves and intentionally transfer social capital and skills through targeted mentoring of younger women in law. In Senegal, a lawyer highlighted the role of the association of women judges in supporting women but observed that the focus has been more on advocating for women's rights in society than addressing the challenges women face within the profession. Collegial support also exists among women, with some saying they can turn to other women for help when they have a problem. This support is both professional and personal, and some is based more on personal friendships than on formal mentoring networks. Several respondents emphasized the need for women to broaden their networks and not limit themselves to reaching out only to other women. As one lawyer said, "for me it is not about gender; when I have questions, I ask either male or female colleagues. I will not send a case to someone because she is a woman but because she can handle the case well. We help each other but not because we are women per se."

Women judges have also utilized the national chapters of women judges' associations to offer support and guidance to each other. These organizations connect with other regional bodies and hold annual and biennial meetings, providing platforms for cross-national learning about best practices in judicial work. In contrast to women at the bar and on the bench, evidence from fieldwork shows that women in legal academia have not formed collective associations to support one another. Women do belong to large professional organizations, but none are specifically for women. This may be because women academics are part of the main bar association and find the women's *other-bar* groups sufficient for their needs. It could also be because the academy is the frontier with the fewest women, and thus, may not be considering the formation of associations. Once a critical mass is achieved, women might start creating organizations or groups to address the specific needs of women in the legal academy. Establishing organizations or associations for women academics is vital, given the unique institutional and professional challenges, opportunities, and threats that women encounter in higher education (Chacha, 2021; Mabokela & Mlambo, 2015). As the number of women in the bar, on the bench, and in the legal academy continues to grow, developing multiple avenues for meaningful engagement and networking among women is essential for addressing the challenges women face in law.

V. COVID-19 and the Profession

I began collecting data for this book in 2016. My plan to travel during the summer of 2020 to complete my fieldwork in several countries was interrupted by the global outbreak of the COVID-19 pandemic, which radically changed everything. Like many other scholars, my life became filled with long hours of back-to-back Zoom meetings, teaching students in a virtual classroom, managing my children's remote learning, and receiving numerous invitations to speak on virtual panels and discussions. When I started collecting data for this project, I had no idea that by the time I finished writing, the world would have experienced one of the most devastating global pandemics in recent decades.

Realizing the increasing difficulty of traveling, I adopted other strategies to document the experiences of African women in law. Through the Institute for African Women in Law, a nonprofit organization I founded in 2015, I began collecting stories about women's experiences in law and women's rights issues—virtually—during the pandemic. The Institute's blog launched two series focusing on the pandemic; one was called *Women, Law, and Justice: The Feminine Face of Covid-19*. This series was dedicated solely to how women were experiencing the COVID-19 lockdowns, the rise in civil and human rights abuses, and the surge in violence that some women and girls faced from spouses, intimate partners, and, in some cases, parents. The second series, titled *Locking Down Law and Justice*, was broader, focusing on how lawyers, law firms, and the legal and judicial professions were responding to the pandemic.

As the lead editor of this blog series, I review every submission to ensure it meets our publication standards. After two months of reading these pieces, I nearly became despondent. I could no longer tolerate the constant reports of women's rights violations from courts to markets and within their homes. Judges recounted the rising number of cases involving rape, sexual assault, and other violence they encountered in their courtrooms. Some lawyers shared detailed stories of their struggles to get their clients' cases heard, especially when they needed restraining orders to protect female clients from imminent danger by abusive spouses or partners. The issues arising from the COVID-19 pandemic were not solely focused on women's rights. The fluctuating policies of full or partial lockdowns kept lawyers busy defending their clients.

The COVID-19 global pandemic has had devastating long-term effects on people worldwide. Like all other professionals, women lawyers, judges, and academics had to manage their work in ways that considered their physical and mental health, as well as that of their immediate families and communities. Most studies on how the pandemic affected women lawyers reveal common themes and patterns across the globe (Burki, 2020; Offutt, 2021). In a comparative review of 12 countries across Africa, Torvikey and Tsikata (2021) documented the pandemic's impact on women in both the formal and informal sectors. While the authors noted the harmful effects of COVID-19 on national economies and women's lives, they also identified opportunities for innovation and growth.

The discussion in this section offers a comprehensive overview of how the pandemic affected women in the legal field. Since the pandemic had not yet begun when I started conducting interviews for this book, this section mainly relies on the results from the 2021 survey for this project. It is supported by emerging research on the pandemic's impact on women overall, especially women in the workforce. The analysis also examines how the pandemic, as an external factor, interacts with the HISP framework. In this context, the most significant effects are seen in institutions, social systems, and women's intersectional identities. Essentially, as shown in **Figure 7.3**, the pandemic further blurred the lines between private and public life, placing a greater burden on women.

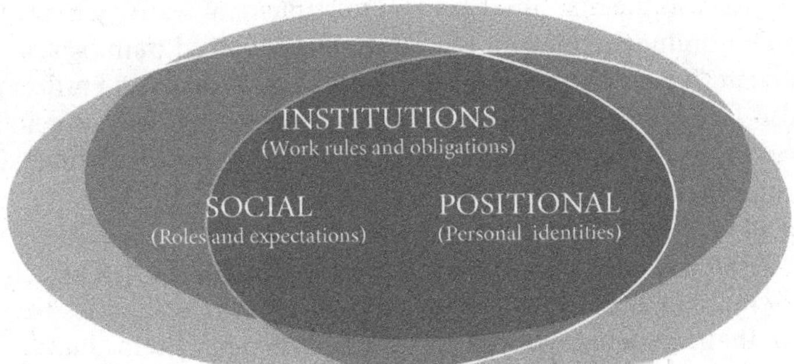

Figure 7.3 *COVID-19 and the Merging of the Three Spheres of Working Women's Lives*

Most lawyers work in law firms, and as the gender scorecard data presented in Chapter 3 shows, a majority of junior associates in law firms are women. The closure of law firms and remote work arrangements were adopted across all law firms, the public sector (judiciaries and ministries of justice), and in the private and corporate legal sectors. Lawyers (both women and men) had to develop new technological skills, adjusting to new methods of filing electronic cases before courts and appearing before judges via electronic platforms such as Zoom and Microsoft Teams (Ndulo, 2021).

Judiciaries had to invest in upgrading their technology and shift to online courts by digitizing court filings, hearings, and evidence collection through digital platforms.

These changes presented several challenges, especially in countries that lacked developed technological infrastructure for basic electronic case management systems. The technological hurdles were even greater in rural areas, where inconsistent electricity and unreliable internet made implementation more difficult. What did these institutional changes mean for judges in general and women judges in particular? For women (and men) judges with limited technology skills, learning and using these new tools was a significant challenge. These initial difficulties increased judges' workloads as more cases were filed electronically, without a corresponding increase in support staff needed to manage the additional workload. This led to a backlog of cases in courts, which took longer to resolve (Tibatemwa-Ekirikubinza, 2021). For judges, the rise in domestic violence and intimate partner abuse cases during the pandemic meant some courts made special arrangements to hear these cases quickly. These cases were often handled by women judges presiding over specialized gender-based violence or family courts. The emotional and psychological toll on women judges grew as they balanced pandemic uncertainties with the increased demands of taking evidence in cases involving violence against women (Ndulo, 2021; Tibatemwa-Ekirikubinza, 2021).

Institutions of higher education, including law schools, were not exempt. Around the world, educational institutions, from day-care centers to universities, had to find ways to adapt to the changes brought by the pandemic. Legal academic institutions across Africa faced numerous challenges. They had to shift online, and access to reliable technology and data was a hurdle for both instructors and students. For most universities, this was the first time they had to implement learning management systems (LMS) for online teaching and learning. This involved training staff and lecturers, often placing a heavy burden on academics' time to learn and utilize these tools. Students also faced many difficulties adjusting to these new learning methods. Law lecturers had to develop innovative strategies to communicate with their students, including using WhatsApp group chats (Addadzi-Koom, 2022).

The impact of these changes across institutions was also gendered. In a study of women academics' experiences during the pandemic, Frehiwot et al. (2022) categorized the increase in additional mothering roles women academics had to socially perform for their students. Supporting women through their churches, community groups, and extended families, these roles included buying food and supplies, helping cover medical bills, and providing social counseling to other women facing hardships from being locked down with abusive partners. "Other-mothering" also involved supporting junior colleagues and international students. The list of "other mothering" roles women have historically performed in academia took on new and intense forms during the pandemic (Arthur & Guy, 2020; Wane, 2000). The overwhelming impact of the pandemic on weak institutions—the judiciary and higher education—required heavy investments in technological resources and support systems, which many of these institutions lacked (Addadzi-Koom, 2022). Supporting women academics, judges, and lawyers was not always feasible, and women had to come up with creative ways to manage their evolving roles (Banaszynski et al., 2021).

The social and positional levels are probably where women felt the most impact from the pandemic. Pre-pandemic sociocultural structures across Africa were highly gendered. The pandemic further increased social expectations placed on women as primary caregivers at home, within their social networks, and in communities (Tsikata & Torvikey, 2021). In most African systems with strong extended family arrangements, this often meant women were at the forefront in attending to the needs of extended family members, including providing physical care for the sick and elderly, and offering financial support for others who were out of work. A major part of the social impact of the pandemic on women across the three sectors includes increased workload at home, managing work expectations, caring for and responding to the needs of clients, litigants, or students, and trying to manage their physical and mental health (Offutt, 2021).

The combined effects of rapidly changing and uncertain developments within the institutional and social spheres became evident in the positional sphere as each woman grappled with the intersection of various factors emerging from her personal experiences. The Institute for African Women in Law's reports on women in law and leadership across four countries—Nigeria, South Africa, Kenya, and Senegal—documented the challenges women in law faced during the pandemic (Institute for African Women in Law, 2023a). **Table 7.2** highlights emerging themes from these countries, based on women's self-reported experiences of the pandemic's positive and negative effects on their personal lives. Keep in mind that the impact of these factors will vary depending on demographic variables such as age, marital or parental status, job rank, and disabilities.

The new work-from-home arrangements posed major challenges for those who did not have a conducive environment at home—especially for young lawyers still staying with their parents; for women lawyers, judges, and academics with young children; and for those who had old and aging parents living with them. Women still made the best out of the situation by devising new strategies to survive and succeed, even if the outcomes were not always optimal.

The long-term effects of the COVID-19 pandemic are still uncertain. A record number of women left the workforce to care for children, sick family members,

Table 7.2 *Respondent Perceptions of the Positive and Negative Impacts of COVID-19*

Positive	Negative
Spending more time with the family	Merged public and private duties
Reduced commute time to work	Increased caregiving—children, aging parents, sick community
Improved time needed for conducting research	Mental health challenges due to increased fear, uncertainty, and anxiety
Lessened the stress of dealing with sexual harassment at work	Increased workload—"other-mothering" of students, domestic violence cases for judges
New opportunities for learning the use of new technology	Longer working hours
Developed new entrepreneurial skills and hobbies	Lawyers unable to meet clients in person

and aging parents (Offutt, 2021). For those with limited options to stay in the formal sector, the boundaries between public and private life became blurred, especially for those with children learning from home due to school closures. The increased need for child care further complicated the already delicate work–home balance. However, for many women, the pandemic also brought some benefits, such as the ability to work from home, which many found helpful, as shown in **Figure 7.2.** Some women also reported saving money on transportation, clothing, and other costs.

The impact of COVID-19 on women in law highlighted the ongoing institutional and social challenges, which had new and recurring negative effects on their work. Personal positionality factors played a key role in producing different experiences for women in law. These insights aim to help legal institutions—such as law firms, courts, and academic organizations—prepare for future global pandemics or other major environmental crises. The future of women in the workforce depends heavily on creating and applying effective policies and systems to eliminate gender-based workplace policies and address the persistent institutional issues women face (Field et al., 2023).

VI. Conclusion

This chapter provides a comparative analysis of the key themes and patterns from earlier chapters. Without repeating the previous analyses, it focuses on identifying major themes across the three sectors. Despite emerging common patterns, the framework and emphasis on interview respondents' voices support the idea that there is no single story that fully captures the experiences of African women in law. What unites these lived experiences is stories of strength, personal agency, and the determination to succeed despite historical, institutional, and social obstacles. The discussion of women's acts of resistance to patriarchy and their creative use of survival strategies affirms the matri-legal feminist belief in women's capacity as active agents within the legal professions. Despite numerous challenges, women in law—like women across the continent—still managed to thrive and balance their personal and professional responsibilities during a pandemic characterized by fewer vaccines, limited government social networks, and less-than-ideal healthcare facilities.

8

Women in Law, Sankofa Futurisms, and Learning From the Past to Move Forward

I. Introduction

"Sankofa" is a mythical bird believed to stretch its neck at a 360-degree angle to reach its back. This imagery is part of the indigenous knowledge systems of the Akan people of Ghana and belongs to the collection known as Adinkra Symbols. These symbols convey wisdom, tell stories, and guide law, morality, courage, and everyday understanding. The Sankofa image illustrates the importance of looking back at history to understand where one is headed (the future). In this chapter, I utilize the Sankofa image to reemphasize the three main objectives of this book, as outlined in Chapter 1: reflecting on the *past,* understanding the *present,* and looking toward the *future.* The first objective examined the history (*looking back*) of African women in law to deepen our understanding of current and ongoing developments. The second objective presented a comparative analysis of the current situation of African women in law, highlighting their demographic diversity, contributions, challenges, and strategies for survival (*present*). The third objective identified new directions (*looking forward*) for future research on African women in law.

II. Looking Back

History influences current institutions, norms, and practices. People can challenge these institutions if they let their collective hopes and aspirations for a fairer world guide their current and future actions. This book thoroughly examines women's representation in law across Africa, focusing on three areas: the bar, the bench, and the legal academy. Through detailed analysis of fieldwork in six countries, 249 survey responses, and a comprehensive review of the existing literature, the book traces the development of legal professions across the continent. The goal of elevating African voices in scholarship on women in law shaped the review of current literature, emphasizing theoretical and methodological frameworks that center the intellectual perspectives of African women in law across these three sectors.

Reflecting on the discussions in the previous chapters, the findings show that since the pioneering first-generation African women in law opened doors to the legal profession in Nigeria, Sierra Leone, and Ghana, many others have followed in their footsteps. Building on these historical roots, a growing number of women continue to hold important positions such as chief justices, attorneys general, and judges in international courts. In the legal field, many women are advancing to managing partner roles in top law firms and serving as deans in law schools. These developments are

African Women in Law. J. Jarpa Dawuni, Oxford University Press. © Oxford University Press 2026.
DOI: 10.1093/9780197795095.003.0008

occurring across various jurisdictions in Africa, south of the Sahara at different levels. Although challenges with data access hinder efforts to systematically assess long-term changes over the past 50 years, reports from interview respondents indicate that women are entering and graduating from law schools at rates comparable to, and sometimes higher than, those of men.

III. The Present

To illuminate the gaps in the literature and expand existing knowledge on African women in law, this volume explored five questions:

1. What are the historical and current **pathways** for women entering the legal profession?
2. What **professional transformations** have occurred with women entering the professions, and what do these **changes signify for the rule of law, access to justice, women's rights, human rights, and good governance**?
3. What intersectional challenges do women in the legal profession face?
4. What strategies have women implemented to navigate gendered power hierarchies in the profession?
5. What factors explain the **positionalities** of women in law, and what **implications do these have for the future of legal professions?**

In answering these questions, the book focused on the experiences of African women in law by heavily relying on survey and interview responses. One of the main goals of centering women's experiences was to explore how women have navigated the challenges of power, patriarchy, and positionality to reshape the dominant narrative of the African woman as someone disconnected from centers of power. Guided by the research questions, the comparative method tracked women's professional journeys through the five major phases outlined in Chapter 1. These questions helped shape the methodology by emphasizing the importance of giving African women a voice in storytelling, aiming to develop narratives and theories rooted in their genuine lived experiences. These stories are shared through their voices rather than being filtered through a Eurocentric perspective, which often diminishes the power of narrative storytelling and embodied agency.

The analyses in the book drew from the existing global and regional discourse on women in law, highlighting similarities and differences to establish a thorough comparative framework. Using a historical comparative methodology, three key variables emerged as essential for answering the research questions—history, institutions, and social systems. These variables, both independently and in their interconnectedness, provide insights and contributions to existing scholarship that deepen African perspectives and lived experiences, as well as understanding, theorization, methodological approaches, and evidence-based arguments. First, it offered a comprehensive historical overview of the legal professions in Africa and the rise of women in law within the broader global context. The book laid a foundation for future studies to explore the complex scenarios within each phase in specific country contexts by outlining five phases of women's symbolic and substantive representation in law.

Second, by building on matri-legal feminist theory, the findings show the influence of matriarchal norms, beliefs, and practices in explaining African women's agency and resistance to historical, institutional, and social norms and practices. Additionally, matri-legal feminism highlights women's relative progress in the legal profession, despite their late entry into a field once globally regarded as reserved for men.

Third, the findings show that different historical factors, various institutional arrangements, sociocultural dynamics, and individual perspectives shape unique experiences, paths, and outcomes for women. Essentially, there is no single story or depiction of the "African woman in law"; instead, a complex mix of individual experiences forms the basis for collective and sometimes broad findings of what can be generally called "African women in law."

Fourth, drawing from the intersectionality framework, the analyses of women's lived experiences show how the intersection of a common factor (gender) combines with identities such as age, marital or familial status, religion, and others to shape women's experiences in law. By highlighting the similarities and differences in women's lives, the interviews emphasize the concept of intracategorical complexity (McCall, 2005), demonstrating that women are not uniform but represent a range of experiences along a diverse spectrum. These differences led to this book's novel binary categorization of "gender-norm conformists" versus "gender-norm disruptors." These terms, which I coined, are used to describe two main opposing forces of women in law. They are not absolute and recognize the existence of other classifications between these two binary points. I leave the task of developing additional classifications to other scholars based on their findings from context-specific studies they conduct.

Through thematic analyses of interviews and survey data, the findings reveal that women in law have developed innovative strategies for successfully navigating gendered and hierarchical structures within the profession. While they encounter intersecting and overlapping historical and contemporary obstacles throughout their careers, women in law continue to adapt to changing institutional norms, cultures, and practices, creatively employing individual and collective strategies to stay engaged and successful.

IV. Looking Forward: A Prognosis

As a scholar–activist, I believe that the greatest value of academic research is in serving the common good of humanity. In each chapter, I provided guideposts for future research questions that later studies can explore. To close the book, I offer two predictions about the future of African women in law. The first prediction highlights the positive trends emerging across the continent and within the profession—the outlook for African women in law is encouraging. As their numbers increase, institutional and social perceptions will change, creating gender-inclusive work environments. However, these changes depend on women recognizing the gendered nature of history, institutions, and social norms that shape their individual and collective situations. Gender-inclusive institutional policies and practices, along with women's decisions to challenge gender norms, are essential for maintaining positive progress.

The second prognosis highlights troubling trends and setbacks for women in the legal field, as the increase in their numbers may provoke a backlash from various sectors within society and the profession. Recent events in certain jurisdictions show that countries with many women in the judiciary, such as Kenya and Zambia, are already experiencing this backlash. Some men see women as "usurpers" of men's "rightful" positions and, in some cases, question women's competence for these roles. The previous chapters have thoroughly discussed some of these setbacks and challenges. While some are common across the three sectors, others are unique to each profession. These setbacks are also rooted in the historical, institutional, and social factors explored. Together, these setbacks and challenges show that progress is not linear. Women in law are aware of these past and current challenges and backlash; therefore, the discussion in Chapter 7 addresses some of women's strategies to counteract the backlash and pursue career growth—*stay, strategize, and succeed.*

These two projections are already unfolding. The first projection will take time to fully materialize and will differ across countries, regions, and sectors. The data presented in this book show that nations are at different stages in addressing and closing the gender gap in women's representation in law. The second projection is apparent in several countries, including Kenya, Zambia, and Zimbabwe, where women have reached or exceeded the 50% threshold in the judiciary. Now and in the future, women must stay vigilant—first, to protect their progress, and second, to counteract the negative effects of backlash. Women did not create gender-discriminatory institutions and should not bear sole responsibility for changing them—sustainable change requires men to play their part. Whether as responsible citizens or male allies, men have a role to play. While the symbolic representation of women positively influences institutions, its full impact is not always recognized. Even in areas where women make up the majority, their rights are at risk of being undermined due to ongoing gender-insensitive institutional practices and cultures reflected in both formal policies and informal norms. Policies and practices hostile to women can impede progress toward a genuinely inclusive and equitable profession.

The legal profession is closely connected to the wider sociocultural contexts in which it operates. Therefore, legal education must serve as a vital gateway for addressing gender inequality in law. However, as discussed in Chapter 6, women legal academics often face institutional challenges when creating courses on women, gender, and the law. The backlash and institutional resistance from male colleagues, especially evident in the Kenyan context, highlight the need for greater awareness of both conscious and unconscious gender biases, as well as common stereotypes in the legal field. Law students should be taught about gender-insensitive laws and practices during their training, and these lessons should be strengthened through ongoing professional development after they enter the profession. Ignoring these issues early on can sustain a harmful cycle of gender-insensitive practices, such as sexual harassment, poor workplace policies, unequal pay, and unequal opportunities for promotion—all of which carry over into their legal careers. If lawyers, who are supposed to defend rights, also continue to perpetuate offenses against their female colleagues, the chances of them being sensitive and responsive to societal issues significantly decrease.

This book explores how history, institutions, and social systems shape women's roles and representation in law. Its main arguments highlight that institutional reforms, such as enforcing antidiscriminatory policies, are vital for advancing gender-inclusive legal fields. Additionally, social and cultural issues impacting women—both inside and outside the workplace—must be addressed by all stakeholders, including men and women alike, through increased public awareness, advocacy, and action. The detailed examples of women's agency and action show that women are not waiting for outside help to rescue them. By linking African women's historical leadership within matriarchal contexts, decision-making power, personal agency, and strategic navigation of unequal gender hierarchies, the book provides strong evidence that, although women legal professionals across Africa still face gendered power structures, they are actively challenging and redefining these dynamics and asserting their roles in the profession.

Most gender equality advocates often define achieving equality by the numerical balance between women and men (parity). In my interactions with women in law, some have questioned whether parity should be the ultimate goal. Should institutions create positions and aim for equal representation of both women and men? Should gender equality or parity be viewed as an aspirational goal and proxy for gender equity? These questions are crucial, especially given the tendency toward superficial efforts, where women may be placed in roles or positions solely to demonstrate gender diversity, equality, and parity, yet they lack the necessary institutional support and resources to succeed. To avoid a shift toward superficial gender equality efforts, I argue that the focus should be on achieving *gender equilibrium* rather than strict parity. I see gender equilibrium as a state of harmony between the sexes, where institutional and sociocultural factors are consistently monitored by everyone in the organizations where women work.

Achieving gender equilibrium, equity, and inclusion in law requires addressing institutional and sociocultural challenges and maintaining constant vigilance from everyone in the workforce. By actively confronting gender biases, stereotypes, workplace harassment, and gender-insensitive practices, processes, and cultures, organizations can foster a professional environment that promotes women's advancement. For example, when gender biases, stereotypes, and other forms of workplace harassment are tackled, practices, processes, and cultures founded on professional respect become the basis for gender equilibrium. This gender equilibrium can, in turn, contribute to the organization's success by increasing women's productivity. Creating a gender-equilibrium environment should not depend on reaching a critical mass of women; instead, it must be actively pursued to build a gender-inclusive setting. A gender-equilibrium organization is one where informed, gender-sensitive awareness influences policies and practices, creating a space where women are respected, appreciated, and evaluated positively for their contributions rather than their gender. In a gender-sensitive workplace, there is no need to wait for a critical mass of women to achieve gender parity. A gender-equitable organization incorporates gender-sensitive awareness into its policies and practices, fostering a space where women feel respected, valued, and fairly assessed based on their work instead of their gender.

This argument might face criticism from those who see it as overly idealistic. Others might question who will establish that equilibrium if there are not enough women or if men and women are not equally represented. Both criticisms are valid. In response to the critique of idealism, the answer lies in the liberal values of inalienable rights to equality, enshrined in constitutions and international conventions. All liberal ideas start as idealistic but can become reality and turn into law if committed individuals and gatekeepers take the necessary steps to push this agenda forward. Regarding the second group of critics who advocate for gender parity as a solution to women's challenges, I agree that numbers matter and that women's presence is essential for addressing gender-blind spots. However, the main point is that women should not bear this burden alone—achieving gender equilibrium benefits everyone, and society (including the legal profession and beyond) must work together to make this happen. When women in law succeed, institutions, societies, and humanity as a whole stand to gain more.

References

Abadi, H. A., & Ayentimi, D. T. (2023). Why are women opting out of academic careers in higher education in Ghana? Implication for policy and practice. *Higher Education Research & Development, 42*(1), 18–32. https://doi.org/10.1080/07294360.2022.2048636

Abdullahi, I. (2017). Ethics, rules of professional conduct and discipline of lawyers in Nigeria: An overview. *International Journal of Public Administration and Management Research, 4*(1), 1–16. https://journals.rcmss.com/index.php/ijpamr/article/view/431

Abdulraheem, I., Adisa, T., & Isiaka, S. B. (2019). Patriarchal hegemony: Investigating the impact of patriarchy on women's work–life balance. *Gender in Management, 34*(1), 19–33. https://doi.org/10.1108/GM-07-2018-0095

Abel, R. L. (1985). Comparative sociology of legal professions: An exploratory essay. *American Bar Foundation Research Journal, 10*(1), 1–79. http://www.jstor.org/stable/828237

Abel, R. L., Hammerslev, O., Sommerlad, H., & Schultz, U. (Eds.). (2020). *Lawyers in 21st-century societies: Volume 1. National reports.* Hart.

Abel, R. L., & Lewis, P. (Eds.). (1988). *Lawyers in society: The civil law world.* Beard Books.

Abel, R. L., & Lewis, P. (Eds.). (1989). *Lawyers in society: Comparative theories.* Beard Books.

Abel, R. L., & Lewis, P. (Eds.). (1995). *Lawyers in society: An overview.* University of California Press.

Achebe, N. (2013). Twenty-five years of African women writing African women's and gendered worlds. *Journal of Women's History, 25*(4), 275–287. https://doi.org/10.1353/jowh.2013.0050

Achebe, N. (2020). *Female monarchs and merchant queens in Africa.* Ohio University Press.

Acker, S., & Armenti, C. (2004). Sleepless in academia. *Gender and Education, 16*(1), 3–24. https://doi.org/10.1080/0954025032000170309

Addadzi-Koom, M. E. (2022). A survey on e-learning experiences of law students during Covid-19 in Ghana. *The Law Teacher, 57*(1), 38–54. https://doi.org/10.1080/03069400.2022.2077517

Addadzi-Koom, M. E., & Gage, B. (2022). Women judges in Ethiopia. In J. J. Dawuni (Ed.), *Intersectionality and women's access to justice in Africa* (pp. 69–94). Lexington Press.

Addadzi-Koom, M. E., & Nkansah, L. A. (2021). Women at the bench: Does it make a difference? Assessing the impact of female judges in addressing gender-based issues in Ghana. *Oñati Socio-Legal Series (OSLS), 13*(3), 1141–1162. https://doi.org/10.35295/OSLS.IISL/0000-0000-0000-1175

Adésínà, J. O. (2010). Re-appropriating matrifocality: Endogeneity and African gender scholarship. *African Sociological Review* [*Revue Africaine de Sociologie*], *14*(1), 2–19. http://www.jstor.org/stable/24487539

Adesinaola, O. M. (2012). *The influence of marital roles and career among female academics in selected universities in Lagos and Ogun State*. [Master's thesis, Covenant University].

Adewoye, O. (1969). Self-taught attorneys in Lagos, 1865–1913. *Journal of the Historical Society of Nigeria, 5*(1), 47–65. http://www.jstor.org/stable/41856822

Adewoye, O. (1977). *The judicial system of southern Nigeria, 1854–1954: Law and justice in a dependency*. Humanities Press.

Adewoye, O. (1982a). *The legal profession in Nigeria, 1865–1962*. Longman.

Adewoye, O. (1982b). Legal practice in Ibadan, 1904–1960. *Journal of the Historical Society of Nigeria, 11*(1–2), 52–66. https://www.jstor.org/stable/41857103

Adjei, P. O., Kyei, P. O., & Afriyie, K. (2014). Global economic crisis and socio-economic vulnerability: Historical experience and lessons from the "lost decade" for Africa in the 1980s. *Ghana Studies, 17*, 39–61. https://doi.org/10.1353/ghs.2014.0009

Adu-Boahen, A. (1989). *African perspectives on colonialism*. Johns Hopkins University Press.

Adusah-Karikari, A. (2008). *Experiences of women in higher education: A study of women faculty and administrators in selected public universities in Ghana*. [Doctoral dissertation, Ohio University]. http://rave.ohiolink.edu/etdc/view?acc_num = ohiou1210704502

African Union. (2005). Protocol to the African Charter on Human and Peoples' Rights on the Rights of Women in Africa. https://au.int/sites/default/files/treaties/37077-treaty-charter_on_rights_of_women_in_africa.pdf; https://www.un.org/en/africa/osaa/pdf/au/protocol_rights_women_africa_2003.pdf

Aina-Pelemo, A. D. (2020). Review of the Nigerian Bar Association sexual harassment policy 2021. *International Journal of Law and Clinical Legal Education, 1*, 122–125.

Aina-Pelemo, A. D., Kulshrestha, P., & Mehanathan, M. C. (2019). Sexual harassment in the workplace: Case study of the Nigerian legal sector. *Journal of Law, Policy and Globalisation, 86*, 121–137.

Aiston, S. J., & Fo, C. K. (2020). The silencing of academic women. *Gender and Education, 33*(2), 138–155. https://doi.org/10.1080/09540253.2020.1716955

Ajayi, D. O. (2017). The Nigerian Bar Association (NBA) under military rule, 1984–1993. *Journal of the Historical Society of Nigeria, 26*, 65–91. https://www.jstor.org/stable/48562079

Akala, B., & Divala, J. J. (2016). Gender equity tensions in South Africa's post-apartheid higher education: In defence of differentiation. *South African Journal of Higher Education, 30*(1), 1–16. https://doi.org/10.20853/30-1-557

Akuffo-Kwapong, B., Etone, D., & Quartey, S. H. (2021). Exploring female lawyers' competence in Ghanaian law firms: Clients' perspective. *International Journal of the Legal Profession, 29*(1), 103–201. https://doi.org/10.1080/09695958.2020.1863218

Akyeampong, E., & Obeng, P. (2005). Spirituality, gender and power in Asante history. In O. Oyěwùmí (Ed.), *African gender studies: A reader* (pp. 23–48). Palgrave Macmillan.

Alapini-Gansou, R. (2021). The feminine face of the African Commission on Human and Peoples' Rights. In J. J. Dawuni (Ed.), *Gender, judging and the courts in Africa: Selected studies* (pp. 161–188). Routledge. https://doi.org/10.4324/9780429327865-12

Albertyn, C. (2005). Defending and securing rights through law: Feminism, law and the courts in South Africa. *Politikon*, 32(2), 217–237. https://doi.org/10.1080/02589340500353474

Albertyn, C., & Bonthuys, E. (2016). South Africa: A transformative constitution and a representative judiciary. In G. Bauer & J. J. Dawuni (Eds.), *Gender and the judiciary in Africa: From obscurity to parity?* (pp. 49–66). Routledge.

Alidou, O. (2002). Gender, narrative space, and modern Hausa literature. *Research in African Literatures, 33*(2), 137–153. http://www.jstor.org/stable/3820978

AllAfrica. (2024). *Ghana: When will the affirmative action bill become law?* Author. https://allafrica.com/stories/202401180172.html

Amadiume, I. (1987). *Male daughters, female husbands: Gender and sex in an African society.* Zed Books.

Amadiume, I. (2000). *Daughters of the goddess, daughters of imperialism: African women, culture, power and democracy.* Zed Books.

American Bar Association. (2006). *Visible invisibility: Women of color in law firms.* ABA. https://judicialstudies.duke.edu/sites/default/files/centers/judicialstudies/panel_1-visible_invisibility_women_of_color_in_law_firms.pdf

American Bar Association. (2019). *Legal profession statistics.* ABA. Retrieved August 16, 2023, from https://www.americanbar.org/about_the_aba/profession_statistics/

Amnesty International. (2022). *Demand Nigeria to pass bills promoting gender equality.* Author. https://www.amnesty.org.ng/2022/03/08/demand-nigeria-to-pass-bills-promoting-gender-equality/

Ampofo, A. A., Beoku-Betts, J., & Osirim, M. J. (2008). Researching African women and gender studies: New social science perspectives. *African and Asian Studies, 7*(4), 327–341. https://doi.org/10.1163/156921008X359560

Andrews, P. (2018). Race, inclusiveness and transformation of legal education in South Africa. In R. Dixon & T. Roux (Eds.), *Constitutional triumphs, constitutional disappointments: A critical assessment of the 1996 South African constitution's local and international influence* (pp. 223–251). Cambridge University Press.

Andrews, P. (2021). Pursuing gender equality through the courts: The role of South Africa's female judges. In J. J. Dawuni (Ed.), *Gender, judging, and the courts in Africa: Selected studies* (pp. 189–208). Routledge.

Anghie, A. (2005). *Imperialism, sovereignty and the making of international law.* Cambridge University Press.

Anleu, S. R., & Mack. K. (2016). Managing work and family in the judiciary: Metaphors and strategies. *Flinders Law Journal, 18*(2), 213–239. http://classic.austlii.edu.au/au/journals/FlinLawJl/2016/8.pdf

Anthias, F. (2013). Intersectional what? Social divisions, intersectionality and levels of analysis. *Ethnicities, 13*(1), 3–19. https://doi.org/10.1177/1468796812463547

Anyidoho, N. A., Crawford, G., & Medie, P. (2020). The role of women's movements in the implementation of gender-based violence. *Politics and Gender, Politics & Gender, 17*(3), 427–453. https://doi.org/10.1017/S1743923X19000849

Apusigah, A. A. (2009). Is gender yet another colonial project? A critique of Oyeronke Oyěwùmí's proposal. *QUEST: An African Journal of Philosophy* [*Revue Africaine de Philosophie*], *20*(1–2), 23–44.

Arowosegbe, J. O. (2016). African scholars, African studies and knowledge production on Africa. *Africa: Journal of the International African Institute 86*(2), 324–338. https://doi.org/10.1017/S0001972016000073

Arrington, N., Bass, L., Delgado, B., Glynn, A., Lindberg, S. I., & Staton, J. K. (2021). Constitutional reform and the gender diversification of peak courts. *American Political Science Review, 115*(3), 851–868. https:doi.org/10.1017/S0003055421000071

Arthur, B., & Guy, B. (2020). Academic motherhood during COVID-19: Navigating our dual roles as educators and mothers. *Gender, Work & Organization, 27*(5), 887–899. https://doi.org/10.1111/gwao.12493

Āse, C., & Wendt, M. (2019). Comparison as feminist method: Denaturalizing gender and nation. In C. Āse & M. Wendt (Eds.), *Gendering military sacrifice: A feminist comparative analysis* (pp. 17–40). Routledge.

Auchmuty, R., Schultz, U., Shaw, G., & Thornton, M. (Eds.). (2021). *Gender and careers in the legal academy*. Hart

Aura-Odhiambo, R. (2018). Gender equality: Integration of women in the judiciary in Kenya. In N. Kabira, W. M. Kabira, P. K. Mbote, & A. Meroka (Eds.), *Changing the mainstream: Celebrating women's resilience* (pp. 123–142). University of Nairobi.

Austin, R. (1987). Access to legal education and the legal profession in Zimbabwe. *The Zimbabwe Law Review, 5*, 172–188. https://hdl.handle.net/20.500.12413/6372

Badejogbin, R. E. (2018). Elsie Nwanwuri-Thompson: The trajectory of a noble passion. In J. J. Dawuni & A. Kuenyehia (Eds.), *International courts and the African woman judge: Unveiled narratives* (pp. 124–141). Routledge.

Baetens, F. (Ed.). (2021). *Identity and diversity on the international bench: Who is the judge?* Oxford University Press.

Bah, B. A. (2022, February 17). Gambia appoints first women cadis. *The Standard.* Retrieved January 5, 2023, from https://standard.gm/gambia-appoints-first-women-cadis/

Baines, B. (2013). Must feminist judges self-identify as feminists? In R. Auchmuty, U. Schultz, G. Shaw, & M. Thornton (Eds.), *Gender and judging* (pp. 379–396). Hart.

Baines, B. (2019). Women judges and constitutional courts: Why not nine women? In Helen Irving (Ed.), *Constitutions and gender* (pp. 290–231). Edward Elgar.

Ballakrishnen, S. S. (2019). Just like global firms: Unintended gender parity and speculative isomorphism in India's elite professions. *Law & Society Review, 53*(1), 108–140. http://www.jstor.org/stable/45093964

Ballakrishnen, S. S. (2021). *Accidental feminism: Gender parity and selective mobility among India's professional elite.* Princeton University Press.

Ballakrishnen, S. S., & Samuel, R. (2021). India's women legal academics: Who they are and where you might find them. In R. Auchmuty, U. Schultz, G. Shaw, & M. Thornton (Eds.), *Gender and careers in the legal academy* (pp. 115–132). Hart.

Balogun, H. A. (2009). *Women in law: The Role of gender difference in the legal profession.* Habiba Balogun Consulting, Libra Law Office.

Bamigbola, B. (2022, June 5). NJC reinstates judge sacked for writing petition against Aregbesola. *Punch Nigeria.* https://punchng.com/njc-reinstates-judge-sacked-for-writing-petition-against-aregbesola/

Banakar, R. (2019). *On socio-legal design.* Lund University Press.

Banaszynski, L. A., Gill, J. G., Harris-Tryon, T. A., & Reese, T. A. (2021). Supporting women in academia during and after a global pandemic. *Science Advances, 7*(9), Article eabg9310. https://advances.sciencemag.org/content/7/9/eabg9310

Banda, F. (2005). *Women, law and human rights: An African perspective.* Hart.

Bar Council UK. (2021). *Race at the bar report.* Retrieved August 16, 2023, from https://www.barcouncil.org.uk/resource/race-at-the-bar-report-2021.html

Bar Council UK (n.d.). Barbara Mills KC inaugural address. Available at https://www.barcouncil.org.uk/resource/barbara-mills-kc-inaugural-address-8-january-2025.html

Bar Standards Board. (2021). *Diversity at the bar 2020.* Retrieved August 16, 2023, from https://www.barstandardsboard.org.uk/uploads/assets/88edd1b1–0edc-4635–9a3dc9497db06972/BSB-Report-on-Diversity-at-the-Bar-2020.pdf

Bar Standards Board. (2022–2023). *Annual Report 2022–2023.* Retrieved August 16, 2023, from chrome-extension://efaidnbmnnnibpcajpcglclefindmkaj/https://www.barstandardsboard.org.uk/static/b3d46689-6a38-4166-a9f6fdd34fa4f315/BSB-Annual-Report-2022-23FINAL.pdf

Barnes, T. (2007). Politics of the mind and body: Gender and institutional culture in African universities. *Feminist Africa, 8,* 8–25.

Barnes, T., & Mama, A. (Eds.). (2007). Rethinking universities I. *Feminist Africa, 8,* 1–7.

Bartie, S. (2021). Oral history and Australia's first women law professors. In R. Auchmuty, U. Schultz, G. Shaw, & M. Thornton (Eds.), *Gender and careers in the legal academy* (pp. 337–345). Hart.

Bartie, S., & Sandomierski, D. (Eds.). (2021). *American legal education abroad: Critical histories.* New York University Press.

Basedow, J. (2014). Breeding lawyers for the global village: The internationalisation of law and legal education. In M. Hiscock & W. Van Caenegem (Eds.), *The internationalisation of legal education: The future practice of law* (pp. 1–18). Edward Elgar.

Bauer, G. (2016). Gender and the judiciary in Africa: Conclusion. In G. Bauer & J. J. Dawuni (Eds.), *Gender and the judiciary in Africa: From obscurity to parity?* (pp. 154–170), Routledge.

Bauer, G. (2021). Women in African parliaments: Progress and prospects. In O. Yacob-Haliso & T. Falola (Eds.), *The Palgrave handbook of African women's studies* (pp. 335–352). Palgrave Macmillan.

Bauer, G. R., Churchill, S. M., Mahendran, M., Walwyn, C., Lizotte, D., & Villa-Rueda, A. A. (2021). Intersectionality in quantitative research: A systematic review of its emergence and applications of theory and methods. *SSM-Population Health, 14,* Article 100798. https://doi.org/10.1016/j.ssmph.2021.100798

Bauer, G., & Dawuni, J. J. (Eds.). (2016). *Gender and the judiciary in Africa: From obscurity to parity?* Routledge.

Bauer, G., & Ellett, R. (2016). Botswana: Delayed indigenization and feminization of the judiciary. In G. Bauer & J. J. Dawuni (Eds.), *Gender and the judiciary in Africa: From obscurity to parity?* (pp. 33–48). Routledge.

Bennett, J., & Tamale, S. (2011). Editorial: Legal voice: Challenges and prospects in the documentation of African legal feminism [Special issue]. *Feminist Africa-Legal Voice, 15,* 1–16. https://nru.uncst.go.ug/handle/123456789/5339

Beoku-Betts, J. A., & Njambi, W. N. (2005). African feminist scholars in women's studies: Negotiating spaces of dislocation and transformation in the study of women. *Meridians: Feminism, Race, Transnationalism, 6*(1), 113–132. https://doi.org/10.1353/mer.2005.0017

Bezuidenhout, A., & Cilliers, F. (2011). Age, burnout, work engagement and sense of coherence in female academics at two South African universities. *South African Journal of Labour Relations, 35*(1), 61–80.

Bilge, S., & Collins, P. H. (2016). *Intersectionality: Key concepts*. Polity Press.

Blackburne-Rigsby, A. (2009). Black women judges: The historical journey of Black women to the nation's highest courts. *Howard Law Journal, 53*, 645.

Blackmore, J. (1999). *Troubling women: Feminism, leadership and educational change*. Open University Press.

Boateng, Francisca (2022). *Of gaudy earrings, bare arms and revealed cleavage: The feminine face of the ills of the bar?* Institute for African Women in Law. https://www.africanwomeninlaw.com/post/of-gaudy-earrings-bare-arms-and-revealed-cleavage-the-feminine-face-of-the-ills-of-the-bar

Boeigol, A. (2013). Feminization of the French "magistrature": Gender and judging in a feminized context. In U. Schultz & G. Shaw (Eds.), *Gender and judging* (pp. 125–142). Hart.

Bond, K. D., Collins, P. H., da Silva, E. C. G., Ergun, E., Furseth, I., & Martínez-Palacios, J. (2021). Intersectionality as critical social theory. *Contemporary Political Theory, 20*, 690–725. https://doi.org/10.1057/s41296-021-00490-0

Bonelli, M. D. G. (2013). Gender and difference among Brazilian lawyers and judges: Public and private practice in the global periphery. *Indiana Journal of Global Legal Studies, 20*(2), 1291–1309. https://www.repository.law.indiana.edu/ijgls/vol20/iss2/24/

Bonelli, M. D. G. (2021). Women, difference and identities in the Brazilian legal professoriate. In R. Auchmuty, U. Schultz, G. Shaw, & M. Thornton (Eds.), *Gender and careers in the legal academy* (pp. 95–114). Hart.

Bonnin, D. (2019). Striking a regulatory bargain. The legal profession, associations and the State in South Africa. *Professions and Professionalism, 9*(3), Article e3113. https://doi.org/10.7577/pp.3113

Bonnin, D., & Maunganidze, F. (2021). An uneven playing field: Experiences of female legal practitioners in Zimbabwe. *Gender Work Organization, 28*, 155–174. https://doi.org/:10.1111/gwao.12535

Bonthuys, E. (2015). Gender and race in South African judicial appointments. *Feminist Legal Studies, 23*(2), 127–148. https://doi.org/10.1007/s10691-015-9285-5

Bosch, A., & Boshoff, N. (2012). Women in South African academia—A statistical profile. In A. Bosch (Ed.), *South African Board for People Practices women's report 2012* (pp. 13–21). SABPP and UJ.

Bourdieu, P. (1987). The force of law: Toward a sociology of the juridical field. *Hastings Law Journal, 38*(5), 814–853.

Brenner, H. (2014). Expanding the pathways to gender equality in the legal profession. *Legal Ethics, 17*(2), 261–280. https://doi.org/10.5235/1460728X.17.2.261

Brodherson, M., McGee, L., & dos Reis, M. P. (2017). *Women in law firms*. McKinsey Publication. https://www.mckinsey.com/~/media/mckinsey/featured%20insights/gender%20equality/women%20in%20law%20firms/women-in-law-firms-final-103017.pdf

Brown, P., Letts, E., & Peery, D. (2020). *Left out and left behind: The hurdles, hassles, and heartaches of achieving long-term legal careers for women of color*. ABA Book Publishing.

https://www.americanbar.org/content/dam/aba/administrative/women/leftoutleftbehind-int-f-web-061020-003.pdf
Bruey, V. (2021). Misogyny, xenophobia, and masculinity in the academy: An epicenter of violence, abuse of power and humiliation. In V. Bruey (Ed.), *Patriarchy and gender in Africa* (pp. 195–226). Rowman & Littlefield.
Bryman, A. (2004). *Social research methods.* Oxford University Press.
Buckett, A., & Ellis, J. (2017). *Women in commercial legal practice.* International Bar Association. https://www.ibanet.org/MediaHandler?id = 9a9d8fe6-347f-4a1d-b441-2900085b197c
Burgis-Kasthala, M. (2022). The transnationalization of legal education on the periphery: Continuities and changes in colonial logics for a "globalizing" Africa. In B. Garth & G. Shaffer (Eds.), *The globalization of legal education: A critical perspective* (pp. 123–148). Oxford University Press.
Burki, T. (2020). The indirect impact of COVID-19 on women. *The Lancet Infectious Diseases, 20*(8), 904–905. https://doi.org/10.1016/S1473-3099(20)30568-5
Carastathis, A. (2008). The invisibility of privilege: A critique of intersectional models of identity. *Les ateliers de l'éthique* [*The Ethics Forum*], 3(2), 23–38. https://doi.org/10.7202/1044594ar
Carastathis, A. (2013). Identity categories as potential coalitions. *Signs: Journal of Women in Culture and Society, 38*(4), 941–965. https://doi.org/10.1086/669573
Carastathis, A. (2016). Intersectionality and decolonial feminism. In A. Carastathis, K. J. Leong, & A. Smith (Eds.), *Intersectionality: origins, contestations, horizons* (pp. 199–232). University of Nebraska Press. https://doi.org/10.2307/j.ctt1fzhfz8.11
Cardinal, M. (2013). The impact of women on the administration of justice in Syria and the judicial selection process. In U. Schultz & G. Shaw (Eds.), *Gender and judging* (pp. 191–209). Hart.
Carle, S. (2021). The way to Barbara Armstrong, first tenure-track law professor in an accredited US law school. In R. Auchmuty, U. Schultz, G. Shaw, & M. Thornton (Eds.), *Gender and careers in the legal academy* (pp. 355–372). Hart.
Carrol, B., & Samoff, J. (2004, March 8–12). *Conditions, coalitions, and influence: The World Bank and higher education in Africa.* [Conference session]. Comparative and International Education Society, Salt Lake City, United States.
Casimiro, I., Kwesiga, J., Mungwa, A., & Tripp, A. (2009). *African women's movements: Transforming political landscapes.* Cambridge University Press.
Centre for Applied Legal Studies. (2014). *Transformation of the legal profession.* Wits University Press. https://www.wits.ac.za/media/wits-university/faculties-and-schools/commerce-law-and-management/research-entities/cals/documents/programmes/gender/Transformation%20of%20the%20Legal%20Profession.pdf
Chacha, B. (2021). Persistence of the glass ceiling in academia globally with a focus on women academics in Kenyan universities. *Journal of International Women's Studies, 22*(1), 215–225. https://vc.bridgew.edu/jiws/vol22/iss1/13
Chadha, G., & Thomas, R. (Eds.). (2023). *Mapping scientific method: Disciplinary narrations.* Routledge.
Chang, R. S., & Culp, J. M. (2002). After intersectionality. *University of Missouri-Kansas City Law Review, 71*(4), 485–492. https://digitalcommons.law.seattleu.edu/faculty/605

Chanock, M. (1982). Making customary law: Men, women and courts in colonial Northern Rhodesia. In M. J. Hay & M. Wright (Eds.), *African women and the law: Historical perspectives* (pp. 53–67). Boston University, African Studies Center.

Chanock, M. (1985). Law, custom, and social order: The colonial experience in Malawi and Zambia. *African Studies Series, 45*. Cambridge University Press.

Chanow, L., & Sterling, J. (2021). *In their own words: Experienced women explain why they are leaving their firms and the profession*. American Bar Association. https://www.americanbar.org/content/dam/aba/administrative/women/intheirownwords-f-4-19-21-final.pdf

Chappell, L. (2006). Comparing political institutions: Revealing the gendered "logic of appropriateness." *Politics & Gender, 2*(2), 223–235. https://doi.org/10.1017/S1743923X06221044

Chappell, L., & Waylen, G. (2013). Gender and the hidden life of institutions. *Public Administration (London), 91*(3), 599–615. https://doi.org/10.1111/j.1467-9299.2012.02104.x

Charlesworth, H., Chinkin, C., & Wright, S. (1991). Feminist approaches to international law. *The American Journal of International Law, 85*(4), 613–645. https://doi.org/10.2307/2203269

Chege, N. (2017). Former deputy CJ gets comfort teaching, farming. *Nation*. https://nation.africa/kenya/news/former-deputy-cj-gets-comfort-in-teaching-farming-374352

Chesterman, S. (2008). The globalisation of legal education. *Singapore Journal of Legal Studies, 2008*, 58–67. http://www.jstor.org/stable/24869351

Chirwa, V. (2007). *Fearless fighter: An autobiography*. Zed Books.

Chitapi, R. (2018). Women in law: Navigating the tensions of gender bias and intersectionality at the Cape and Johannesburg Societies of Advocates (the Bar). *Agenda: Empowering Women for Gender Equality, 32*(2), 43–52. https://doi.org/10.1080/10130950.2018.1460134

Chiu, C., & Leicht, K. T. (1999). When does feminization increase equality? The case of lawyers. *Law & Society Review, 33*(3), 557–593. https://doi.org/10.2307/3115104

Cho, S., Crenshaw, K. W., & McCall, L. (2013). Toward a field of intersectionality studies: Theory, applications, and praxis. *Signs: Intersectionality: Theorizing Power, Empowering Theory, 38*(4), 785–810. https://www.jstor.org/stable/10.1086/669608

Chorev, N., & Schrank, A. (2017). Professionals and the professions in the global south. *Sociology of Development, 3*, 197–210. https://doi.org/10.1525/sod.2017.3.3.197

Christelow, A. (1982). The Muslim judge and municipal politics in colonial Algeria and Senegal. *Comparative Studies in Society and History, 24*(1), 3–24. http://www.jstor.org/stable/178720

Chukwu, G. (2002). Women and nationalist movements in Africa. In T. Falola (Ed.), *The end of colonial rule: Nationalism and decolonization* (Vol. 4, pp. 109–130). Carolina Academic Press.

Cockayne, D., & Mott, C. (2017). Citation matters: Mobilizing the politics of citation toward a practice of "conscientious engagement." *Gender, Place & Culture, 24*(7), 954–973. http:/doi.org/ 10.1080/0966369X.2017.1339022

Coetzee, M., & Moosa, M. (2020). Climbing the illusive ladder: Examining female employees' perceptions of advancement opportunities at a higher education institution. *Journal of Psychology in Africa, 30*(5), 397–402. http:/doi.org/ 10.1080/14330237.2020.1821308

Cohen, M. (2018). Judicial diversity in France: The unspoken and the unspeakable. *Law and Social Inquiry*, *43*(4), 1542–1573. http://www.jstor.org/stable/26630971

Collier, R. (2021). Rethinking masculinities in the legal academy: Men, gender and legal careers (or, whatever happened to the "nutty professor"?). In R. Auchmuty, U. Schultz, G. Shaw, & M. Thornton (Eds.), *Gender and careers in the legal academy* (pp. 513–530). Hart.

Collins, P. H. (2000). *Black feminist thought: Knowledge, consciousness, and the politics of empowerment*. Routledge.

Collins, P. H., & Bilge, S. (2016). *Intersectionality: Key concepts*. Polity Press.

Cooper, B. (2016). Intersectionality. In L. Disch & M. Hawkesworth (Eds.), *The Oxford handbook of feminist theory* (pp. 385–406). Oxford University Press.

Couch, D. L., Malatzky, C., & O'Sullivan, B. (2021). What COVID-19 could mean for the future of "work from home": The provocations of three women in the academy. *Gender, Work & Organization*, *28*, 266–275. https://doi.org/10.1111/gwao.12548

Council of Legal Education, Sierra Leone. (n.d.). *About Sierra Leone law school*. https://lawschoolsierraleone.edu.sl/about

Cowan, R. (2013). Do women in South Africa's courts make a difference? In U. Shultz & G. Shaw (Eds.), *Gender and judging* (pp. 317–333). Hart.

Crenshaw, K. (1989). Demarginalizing the intersection of race and sex: A black feminist critique of antidiscrimination doctrine, feminist theory and antiracist politics. *University of Chicago Legal Forum*, *140*, 139–167. https://chicagounbound.uchicago.edu/uclf/vol1989/iss1/8

Crews-Meyer, K., & Songer, D. (2000). Does judge gender matter? Decision making in state supreme courts. *Social Science Quarterly*, *81*(3), 750–762.

Crocco, M. S. (2001). The missing discourse about gender and sexuality in the social studies. *Theory Into Practice*, *40*(1), 65–71. http://www.jstor.org/stable/1477220

Cruickshank, E., & Ozobia, B. (2006). *Sisters in law: Career choices for Nigerian women lawyers*. Law Society Publishing.

Dalgleish, D. (2005). Pre-colonial criminal justice in West Africa Eurocentric thought versus Africentric evidence. *African Journal of Criminology and Justice Studies*, *1*(1), 55–69. https://digitalscholarship.tsu.edu/ajcjs/vol1/iss1/7

Dalphin, J., Gray, P., Karp, D., & Williamson, J. (Eds.). (2012). *Comparative research methods*. Cambridge University Press.

Dancer, H. (2020). Women in law and justice in Africa. In *Oxford research encyclopedia of African history* (pp. 1–18). Oxford University Press. https://doi.org/10.1093/acrefore/9780190277734.013.556

Dashú, M. (2005). Knocking down straw dolls: A critique of Cynthia Eller's *The myth of matriarchal prehistory: Why an invented past won't give women a future*. *Feminist Theology*, *13*, 185–216. https://doi.org/10.1177/0966735005051947.

Datta, A., & Lund, R. (2018). Mothering, mentoring and journeys towards inspiring spaces. *Emotion, Space and Society*, *26*, 64–71. https://doi.org/10.1016/j.emospa.2017.08.004

Davis, K. (2008). Intersectionality as buzzword: A sociology of science perspective on what makes a feminist theory successful. *Feminist Theory*, *9*(1), 67–85. https://doi.org/:10.1177/1464700108086364

Dawuni, J. J. (2012). Jiagge, Annie Ruth (1918–1996). In K. E. Akyeampong & H. L. Gates, Jr. (Eds.), *Dictionary of African biography* (pp. 207–208). Oxford University Press.

Dawuni, J. J. (2016a). Ghana: The paradox of judicial stagnation. In G. Bauer & J. Dawuni (Eds.), *Gender and the judiciary in Africa: From obscurity to parity?* (pp. 120–136). Routledge.

Dawuni, J. J. (2016b). To "mother" or not to "mother": The representative roles of women judges in Ghana. *Journal of African Law, 60*(3), 419–440. https://doi.org/10.1017/S0021855316000115

Dawuni, J. J. (2017). Valuing diversity in all forms in international courts. *Proceedings of the ASIL Annual Meeting, 111*, 296–299. https://doi.org/10.1017/amp.2017.84

Dawuni, J. J. (2018a). Akua Kuenyehia: Leaving a mark along the journey for human rights. In J. J. Dawuni & A. Kuenyehia (Eds.), *International courts and the African woman judge: Unveiled narratives* (pp. 58–76). Routledge.

Dawuni, J. J. (2018b). African women judges on international courts: Symbolic or substantive gains? *University of Baltimore Law Review, 47*(2), 199–246. https://scholarworks.law.ubalt.edu/ublr/vol47/iss2/3

Dawuni, J. J. (2019). Matri-legal feminism: An African feminist response to international law. In K. Ogg & S. Rimmer (Eds.), *Research handbook on feminist engagement with international law* (pp. 445–462). Edward Elgar. https://doi.org/10.4337/9781785363924.00036

Dawuni, J. J. (2020). Women in judiciaries across Africa. In T. Falola & O. Yacob-Haliso (Eds.), *The Palgrave handbook of African women's studies* (pp. 353–374). Palgrave Macmillan.

Dawuni, J. J. (2021a). Breaking the veil of masculinity? Women and the legal academy in Ghana. In R. Auchmuty, U. Schultz, G. Shaw, & M. Thornton (Eds.), *Gender and careers in the legal academy* (pp. 151–172). Hart.

Dawuni, J. J. (2021b). The legal profession in Ghana: From indigenization to globalization. *International Journal of the Legal Profession, 29*(1), 75–101. https://doi.org/10.1080/09695958.2021.1992283

Dawuni, J. J. (2021c). Gender and judging across Africa: A case of old wine in old wine skins or new wine in old wine skins? In J. J. Dawuni (Ed.), *Gender, judging and the courts in Africa: Selected studies* (pp. 1–22). Routledge.

Dawuni, J. J. (Ed.). (2022a). *Gender, judging and the courts in Africa: Selected studies.* Routledge.

Dawuni, J. J. (2022b). Layered intersectionality and framing feminist legal discourse on access to justice for women. In J. J. Dawuni (Ed.), *Intersectionality and women's access to justice in Africa* (pp. 3–26). Rowman & Littlefield.

Dawuni, J. (2024a). *Is the Ghana Bar Association ready for women leaders?* Institute for African Women in Law. https://www.africanwomeninlaw.com/post/is-the-ghana-bar-association-ready-for-women-leaders

Dawuni, J. (2024b). Victory for women's rights in Ghana as affirmative action law is passed – what must happen next? *The Conversation.* https://theconversation.com/victory-for-womens-rights-in-ghana-as-affirmative-action-law-is-passed-what-must-happen-next-237080

Dawuni, J. (2025). *African women judges: Storytelling as judicial freedom.* Palgrave Macmillan.

Dawuni, J. J., & Abdul-Rahman, R. (2022). *Women senior advocates of Nigeria: Sticky floors or concrete ceilings?* Institute for African Women in Law. https://www.africanwomeninlaw.com/_files/ugd/c889be_b9caa9ba45a647d3945cbb86714d037c.pdf

Dawuni, J., & Badejogbin, R. (2021). Transplantation and domestication of American models of legal education in Nigeria. In S. Bartie & D. Sandomierski (Eds.), *American legal education abroad: Critical histories* (pp. 139–161). New York University Press.

Dawuni, J., & Kang, A. (2015). Her ladyship the chief justice: The rise of female leaders in the judiciary in Africa. *Africa Today, 62*(2), 45–69. https://doi.org/10.2979/africatoday.62.2.45

Dawuni, J. J., & Kuenyehia, A. (Eds.). (2018). *International courts and the African woman judge: Unveiled narratives.* Routledge.

Dawuni, J., & Masengu, T. (2019). Judicial service commissions and the appointment of women to high courts in Nigeria and Zambia. In S. M. Sterett & L. D. Walker (Eds.), *Research handbook on law and courts* (pp. 213–230). Edward Elgar.

Day, L. (2020). African women: Traditional chiefs and rulers. In O. Yacob-Haliso & T. Falola (Eds.), *Palgrave handbook of African women's studies* (pp. 2085–2100). Palgrave Macmillan.

De Groot-van Leeuwen, L. (2021). Compromise, autonomy and courage: Derkje Hazewinkel-Suringa, first female law professor in the Netherlands (1889–1970). In R. Auchmuty, U. Schultz, G. Shaw, & M. Thornton (Eds.), *Gender and careers in the legal academy* (pp. 283–298). Hart.

Deo, M. (2019). *Unequal profession: Race and gender in legal academia.* Stanford University Press.

De Souza, M., Heisch, A., Röhrs, S., & Smythe, D. (Eds.). (2014). *In search of equality: Women, law and society in Africa.* University of Cape Town Press.

De Wit, H., & Sehoole, C. (2014). The regionalisation, internationalisation and globalisation of African higher education. *International Journal of African Higher Education, 1*(1), 217–241. https://doi.org/10.6017/ijahe.v1i1.5648

Dezalay, S. (2017). Lawyers' empire in the (African) colonial margins. *International Journal of the Legal Profession, 24*(1), 25–32. https://doi.org/10.1080/09695958.2016.1232198

Dezalay, S. (2020). Burundi: Middlemen and opponents in the shadow of the ethno-state. In R. L. Abel, O. Hammerslev, U. Schultz, & H. Sommerlad (Eds.), *Lawyers in 21st-Vol. 1. societies: National reports* (pp. 473–494). Hart.

Dezalay, Y., & Garth, B. (2010). *Asian legal revivals: Lawyers in the shadow of empire.* University of Chicago Press.

Dezalay, Y., & Garth, B. (Eds.). (2011). *Lawyers and the rule of law in an era of globalization.* Routledge.

Dezalay, Y., & Garth, B. (2021). *Law as reproduction and revolution: An interconnected history.* University of California Press.

Dias, C. J., Luckham, R., Lynch, D. O. & Paul, J. C. N. (Eds.). (1981). *Lawyers in the third world: Comparative and developmental perspectives.* International Center for Law in Development.

Dijksterhuis, B. (2013). Women judges in the Netherlands. In U. Schultz & G. Shaw (Eds.), *Gender and judging* (pp. 267–282). Hart.

Dillard, C. B. (2018). Let steadfastness have its full effect: (Re)membering (re)search and endarkened feminisms from Ananse to Asantewaa. *Qualitative Inquiry, 24*(9), 617–623. https://doi.org/10.1177/1077800417745103

Dinovitzer, R., & Garth, B. (2020). The new place of corporate law firms in the structuring of elite legal careers. *Law and Social Inquiry, 45*(2), 339–371. https//doi.org/10.1017/lsi.2019.62

Diop, C. A. (1987). *Precolonial Black Africa.* Lawrence Hill Books.

Diop, C. A. (1989). *The cultural unity of Black Africa: The domains of matriarchy & of patriarchy in classical antiquity.* Karnak House.

Diop, C. A. (1991). *Civilization or barbarism: An authentic anthropology.* Lawrence Hill Books.

Diop, C. A. (1996). *Towards the African renaissance: Essays in African culture & development:1946–1960.* Karnak House.

Dipio, D. (2019). African motherhood proverbs and worldview: A matriarchal perspective. *Legon Journal of Humanities, 30*(1), 3–23. https://doi.org/10.4314/ljh.v30i1.1

Diye, J. (2022). Gender and customary justice among the Podoko of the Mandara mountains of the far north region of Cameroon. In J. J. Dawuni (Ed.), *Intersectionality and women's access to justice in Africa* (pp. 311–332). Lexington Press.

Dobbin, F., & Kalev, A. (2022). *Getting to diversity: What works and what doesn't.* Harvard University Press.

Dogan, M., & Pelassy, D. (2001). *How to compare nations: Strategies in comparative politics.* Seven Bridges Press.

Dosekun, S. (2020). African feminisms. In T. Falola & O. Yacob-Haliso (Eds.), *The Palgrave handbook of African women's studies* (pp. 48–61). Palgrave Macmillan.

Dowuona-Hammond, C., Atuguba, R. A., & Tuokuu, F. X. D. (2020). Women's survival in Ghana: What has law got to do with it? *SAGE Open, 10*(3). https://doi.org/10.1177/2158244020941472

Drolshammer, J., & Pfeifer, M. (Eds.). (2021). *The internationalization of the practice of law.* Brill Nijhoff.

Duarte, V. (2022). Opening the door for women in the Cape Verdean Judiciary. In J. J. Dawuni (Ed.), *Intersectionality and women's access to justice in Africa* (pp. 30–50). Lexington Press.

Dubin, J. (2000). Faculty diversity as a clinical legal education imperative. *Hastings Law Journal, 51,* 445–477. https://repository.uclawsf.edu/hastings_law_journal/vol51/iss3/1

Duff, L., & Webley, L. (2021). Gender and the legal academy in the UK: A product of proxies, hiring and promotion practices. In R. Auchmuty, U. Schultz, G. Shaw, & M. Thornton (Eds.), *Gender and careers in the legal academy* (pp. 63–78). Hart.

Duke-Bryant, K. (2020). Education and politics in colonial French West Africa. In *Oxford research encyclopedia of African history.* Oxford University Press. https://doi.org/10.1093/acrefore/9780190277734.013.679

Durojaye, E., & Nabaneh, S. (2023). *Sexual harassment, law and human rights in Africa.* Palgrave Macmillan.

Edsman, B. (1979). *Lawyers in Gold Coast politics, c.1900–1945: From Mensah Sarbah to J.B. Danquah.* Acta Universitatis Upsaliensis.

Ejekwonyilo, A. (2022, April 6). Affirmative action: Court orders government to reserve 35% of public offices for women. *Premium Times Nigeria.* https://www.premiumtimesng.com/news/headlines/522195-affirmative-action-court-orders-nigerian-govt-to-reserve-35-of-public-offices-for-women.html

Elechi, O.O. (2008). The Igbo indigenous justice system. In V. Saleh-Hanna (Ed.), *Colonial systems of control: Criminal justice in Nigeria* (pp. 395–416). University of Ottawa Press [Les Presses de l'Université d'Ottawa].

Escobar-Lemmon, M. C., Hoekstra, V., Kang, A., & Kittilson, M. (2016). Just the facts? Media coverage of female and male high court appointees in five democracies. *Politics and Gender, 12*(2), 254–274. https://doi.org/10.1017/S1743923X16000234

Escobar-Lemmon, M., Hoekstra, V., Kang, A., & Kittilson, M. (2019). Appointing women to high courts. In S. Sterett & L. Walker (Eds.), *Research handbook on law and courts* (pp. 200–212). Edward Elgar.

Escobar-Lemmon, M. C., Hoekstra, V., Kang, A., & Kittilson, M. (2021). *Reimagining the judiciary: Women's representation in high courts worldwide.* Oxford University Press.

Eller, C. (2000). *The myth of matriarchal prehistory: Why an invented past won't give women a future.* Beacon Press.

Ellett, R. (2013). *Pathways to judicial power in transitional states: Perspectives from African courts.* Routledge.

Ellett, R. (2018). Justina Mafoso-Guni: The gendering of judicial appointment processes in African courts. In J. J. Dawuni & A. Kuenyehia (Eds.), *International courts and the African woman judge: Unveiled narratives* (pp. 108–123). Routledge.

Ellett, R. (2022). "Your whole life is an interview to get to the bench:" Gender and judicial appointments in Malawi. In J. J. Dawuni (Ed.), *Intersectionality and women's access to justice in Africa* (pp. 139–160). Lexington Press.

Ely, R., Ibarra, H., & Kolb, D. (2013). Women rising: The unseen barriers. *Harvard Business Review, 91*(9), 60–66.

Epstein, C. F. (1981). *Women in law.* Quid Pro Books.

Epstein, C. F. (2001). Women in the legal profession at the turn of the twenty-first century: Assessing glass ceilings and open doors. *University of Kansas Law Review, 49*(4), 733–760.

Evarista, A. F., & Henry, A. N. (2017). The emergence and history of the "gentlewomen of the bar" into the legal profession in the South West geopolitical zone of Nigeria. *Arts and Social Sciences Journal, 8*(1), 1–5.

Ezeanya, C. (2020). Women and indigenous knowledge in Africa. In T. Falola & O. Yacob-Haliso (Eds.), *Palgrave handbook of African women's studies* (pp. 87–104). Palgrave Macmillan.

Falcon, S., & Nash, J. (2015). Shifting analytics and linking theories: A conversation about the "meaning-making" of intersectionality and transnational feminism. *Women's Studies International Forum, 50*, 1–10. https://doi.org/10.1016/j.wsif.2015.02.010

Fall, A. (2018). President Leopold Sedar Senghor, an exceptional statesman and leader. In S. Acheampong & J. Gordon (Eds.), *African presidential leaders: Selected case studies* (pp. 142–177). New World African Press.

Fanon, F. (1963). *Wretched of the earth.* Présence Africaine.

Farley, C. (1996). Confronting expectations: Women in the legal academy. *Yale Journal of Law & Feminism, 8*, 333–357. https://digitalcommons.wcl.american.edu/facsch_lawrev/902

Federal Judicial Center. (n.d.). *Judiciaries worldwide: Rwanda.* https://judiciariesworldwide.fjc.gov/country-profile/rwanda#:~:text = Rwanda%20now%20has%20a%20hybrid,introduced%20the%20use%20of%20precedent

Field, E., Krivkovich, A., Kügele, S., Robinson, N., & Yee, L. (2023). *Women in the workplace report: 2023.* McKinsey & Company. https://www.mckinsey.com/featured-insights/diversity-and-inclusion/women-in-the-workplace#/

First Hundred Years. (n.d.). *First 100 years project.* Spark 21. https://first100years.org.uk/

Fombad, C. M. (2011). Constitutional reforms and constitutionalism in Africa: Reflections on some current challenges and future prospects. *Buffalo Law Review, 59*(4), 1007–1108. https://digitalcommons.law.buffalo.edu/buffalolawreview/vol59/iss4/4

Fombad, C. M. (2021). The struggle to defend the independence of the judiciary in Africa. In H. Chodosh, H. Eric, & S. Shetreet (Eds.), *Challenged justice; In pursuit of judicial independence* (pp. 223–248). Brill Nijhoff.

Fombad, C., & Murray, C. (Eds.). (2010). *Fostering constitutionalism in Africa.* Pretoria University Law Press.

Fong, B., Trubek, D. M., & Wilkins, D. B. (2019). Globalization, lawyers, and emerging economies: The rise, transformation, and significance of the new corporate legal ecosystem in India, Brazil, and China. *Harvard Law School Center on the Legal Profession Research Paper, 1*, 1–61. http://dx.doi.org/10.2139/ssrn.3453908

Freddie, K., & Koketso, M. (2013). Law and traditional justice system in South Africa: A hybrid of historical and constitutional discourse. *Journal of Global Peace and Conflict, 1*(1), 49–65.

Frehiwote, M., Atobrah, D. & Appeaning-Addo, I. (2022). Negotiating spaces, exercising agency and managing multiple roles: The lived experiences of University of Ghana women academics under COVID-19. *Feminist Africa, 3*(1), 43–70.

Gambia Law School. (n.d.). *About us.* https://gls.gm/

Gathii, J. (1994). *The dream of judicial security of tenure and the reality of executive involvement in Kenya's judicial process.* Kenya Human Rights Commission.

Gathii, J. T. (2011). TWAIL: A brief history of its origins, its decentralized network, and a tentative bibliography. *Trade Law and Development, 3*(1), 26–64. https://ssrn.com/abstract = 1933766

Garth, B., & Shaffer, G. (Eds.). (2022). *The globalization of legal education: A critical perspective.* Oxford University Press.

Gayoye, M. (2021). Why female judges really matter: The impact of female judges on property law outcomes in Kenya. *Social & Legal Studies, 31*(1), 1–27. https://doi.org/10.1177/09646639211007905

Gebeyehu, N. Z. (2015, May 9). How does the case law system fit into the Ethiopian legal system? *Social Science Research Network.* Available at SSRN: https://ssrn.com/abstract=2604475

Geraghty, T. F., & Quansah, E. K. (2007). African legal education: A missed opportunity and suggestions for change: A call for renewed attention to a neglected means of securing human rights and legal predictability. *Loyola University Chicago International Law Review, 5*, 87–105. https://lawecommons.luc.edu/lucilr/vol5/iss1/7

Ghai, Y. (1981). Law and lawyers in Kenya and Tanzania: Some political economy considerations. In C. J. Dias, R. Luckham, D. O. Lynch, & J. C. N. Paul (Eds.), *Lawyers in the third world: Comparative and developmental perspectives* (pp. 144–176). International Center for Law in Development.

Ghai, Y. (1987). Law, development and African scholarship. *The Modern Law Review, 50*(6), 750–776. http://www.jstor.org/stable/1096031

Ghai, J. C., & Ghai, Y. P. (2014). *The legal profession and the new constitutional order.* Strathmore University Press.

Ghai, Y. P., McAuslan, J. P. (1970). *Public law and political change in Kenya: A study of the legal framework of government from colonial times to the present.* Oxford University Press.

Ghana Bar Association. (n.d.). *About us.* https://ghanabar.org/about-us/

Gierczynski-Bocandé, U. (2013). Women in Senegal's politics and society: Priestesses, princesses, presidents? In G. Wahlers (Ed.), *Women in Politics and Society* (pp. 24–47). Konrad Adenauer Stiftung. http://www.jstor.org/stable/resrep10122.5

Gill, R. (2012). A framework for comparative judicial selection research with an application to gender diversity on high courts. *Social Science Research Network.* Available at https://ssrn.com/abstract=1982705

Gillborn, D. (2015). Intersectionality, critical race theory, and the primacy of racism: Race, class, gender, and disability in education. *Qualitative Inquiry, 21*(3), 277–287. https://doi.org/10.1177/1077800414557827

Gilligan, C. (1982). *In a different voice: Psychological theory and women's development.* Harvard University Press.

Glazer, P. M., & Slater, M. (1987). *Unequal colleagues: The entrance of women into the professions, 1890 to 1940.* Rutgers University Press.

Goettner-Abendroth, H. (2012). *Matriarchal societies: Studies on Indigenous cultures across the globe.* Peter Lang.

Gomez-Mazo, D. (2020). *Afro-descendant representation on Latin American courts.* [Doctoral dissertation, Fordham University School of Law]. *SJD Dissertations, 17.* https://ir.lawnet.fordham.edu/sjd/17

Gonzalez, C. G., & Harris, P. H. (2012). Introduction. In G. Gutierrez y Muhs, Y. F. Niemann, C. G. González, & A. P. Harris (Eds.), *Presumed incompetent: The intersections of race and class for women in academia* (pp. 1–14). University Press of Colorado.

Gorman, E. (2006). Work uncertainty and the promotion of professional women: The case of law firm partnership. *Social Forces, 85*, 865–890. http://www.jstor.org/stable/4494942

Gorman, E., & Kay, F. (2008). Women in the legal profession. *Annual Review of Law and Social Sciences, 4*(1), 299–332. https://doi.org/10.1146/annurev.lawsocsci.4.110707.172309

Gouws, A. (2017). Feminist intersectionality and the matrix of domination in South Africa. *Agenda, 31*(1), 19–27. https://doi.org/10.1080/10130950.2017.1338871

Gower, L. C. B. (2014). *Independent Africa: The challenge to the legal profession.* Harvard University Press.

Grossman, N. (2012). Sex on the bench: Do women judges matter to the legitimacy of international courts?, *Chicago Journal of International Law, 12*(2), 647–684. https://chicagounbound.uchicago.edu/cjil/vol12/iss2/9

Grossman, N. (2018). Julia Sebutinde: An unbreakable cloth. In J. J. Dawuni & A. Kuenyehia (Eds.), *International courts and the African woman judge: Unveiled narratives* (pp. 37–57). Routledge.

Haileamlak, A., Magnus, J., & Tushune, K. (2019). From needs assessment to academic leadership training for women in Ethiopia. In T. Halvorsen & S. Orgeret (Eds.), *Sharing knowledge, transforming societies: The NORHED Programme 2013–2020* (pp. 457–473). African Minds.

Halperin-Kaddari, R., & Katvan, E. (2021). Women's entry and integration into Israel's legal academia: History, story, non-story and the men(tor). In R. Auchmuty, U. Schultz, G. Shaw, & M. Thornton (Eds.), *Gender and careers in the legal academy* (pp. 215–2223). Hart.

Hamad, M. (2016). Egypt: The lingering battle for female judgeship. In G. Bauer & J. J. Dawuni (Eds.), *Gender and the judiciary in Africa: From obscurity to parity?* (pp. 16–32). Routledge.

Hammerslev, O., & Sommerlad, H. (2020). Lawyers in a new geopolitical conjuncture: Continuity and change. In R. Abel, O. Hammerslev, U. Schultz, & H. Sommerlad (Eds.), *Lawyers in 21st-century societies: Volume 1. National reports* (pp. 1–41). Hart.

Harrington, J., & Manji, A. (2021a). Africa needs many lawyers trained for the need of their peoples: Struggles over legal education in Kwame Nkrumah's Ghana. In P. Zumbansen (Ed.), *The Oxford handbook of transnational law* (pp. 1109–1136). Oxford Academic. https://doi.org/10.1093/oxfordhb/9780197547410.013.51.

Harrington, J., & Manji, A. (2021b). Conservatives, nationalists, and American romantics debating legal education in Kwame Nkrumah's Ghana. In S. Bartie & D. Sandomierski (Eds.), *American legal education abroad: Critical histories* (pp. 145–172). New York University Press.

Harris, A. (1990). Race and essentialism in feminist legal theory. *Stanford Law Review, 42*, 581–616. https://doi.org/10.2307/1228886

Harvey, W. B. (1962). The evolution of Ghana law since independence. *Law and Contemporary Problems, 27*(4), 581–604. https://www.repository.law.indiana.edu/facpub/1169

Harvey, W. B. (1963). *A value analysis of Ghanaian legal development since independence.* Government Printing Department.

Harvey, W. B. (1966). *Law and social change in Ghana.* Princeton University Press.

Haslam, S. A., & Ryan, M. K. (2007). The glass cliff: Exploring the dynamics surrounding the appointment of women to precarious leadership positions. *Academy of Management Review, 32*(2), 549–572. https://doi.org/10.2307/20159315

Hay, M. J. (1982). Women as owners, occupants, and managers of property in colonial Western Kenya. In M. J. Hay & M. Wright (Eds.), *African women and the law: Historical perspectives* (pp. 110–124). Boston University, African Studies Center.

Hay, M. J., & Wright, M. (Eds.). (1982). *African women and the law: Historical perspectives.* Boston University, African Studies Center.

Hellum, A., Kameri-Mbote, P., Kanyongolo, N., Munalula, M., & Stewart, J. (2019). Engendering and decolonising legal education: South–South and South–North co-operation. In T. Halvorsen, & S. Orgeret (Eds.), *Sharing knowledge, transforming societies: The NORHED Programme 2013–2020* (pp. 474–499). African Minds.

Herbst, T. (2020). Gender differences in self-perception accuracy: The confidence gap and women leaders' underrepresentation in academia. *South African Journal of Industrial Psychology, 46*(1), 1–8. https://doi.org/10.4102/sajip.v46i0.1704

Hesse-Biber, S. (2010). *Mixed methods research: Merging theory with practice.* Guilford Press.

Hoekstra, V. (2010). Increasing the gender diversity of high courts: A comparative view. *Politics and Gender, 6*(3), 474–484. https://doi.org/10.1017/S1743923X10000243

Houghton, B. (1981). Women lawyers in Ghana. In C. J. Dias, R. Luckham, D. O. Lynch, & J. C. N. Paul (Eds.), *Lawyers in the third world: Comparative and developmental perspectives* (pp. 123–143). International Center for Law in Development.

Hunter, R. (2003). Women Barristers and gender difference in Australia. In U. Schultz & G. Shaw (Eds.), *Women in the world's legal professions* (pp.103–122). Hart.

Hunter, R. (2008). Can feminist judges make a difference? *International Journal of the Legal Profession, 15*(1–2), 7–36. https://doi.org/10.1080/09695950802439759

Husa, J. (2022). *Interdisciplinary comparative law: Rubbing shoulders with the neighbors or standing alone in a crowd.* Edward Elgar.

Ibrahim, H. (2016). Nigeria: Women judges enhancing the judiciary. In G. Bauer & J. J. Dawuni (Eds.), *Gender and the judiciary in Africa: From obscurity to parity?* (pp. 67–79). Routledge.

Idahosa, G. (2020). African women in university management and leadership. In T. Falola & O. Yacob-Haliso (Eds.), *Palgrave handbook of African women's studies* (pp. 1619–1638). Palgrave Macmillan.

Igiebor, O. (2021). Historical development of women's underrepresentation in academic leadership in Nigeria: A review of literature. *International Journal of Management Studies and Social Science Research, 3*(15), 142–150.

Imosemi, A. F. (2021). The rights and plights of female lawyers in the legal profession: A paradigm shift from denial to recognition. *African Journal of Law and Human Rights, 5*(1), 237–247.

Inameti, E. E. (2013). The administration of justice in pre-colonial Efik land. *Filosofia Theoretica: Journal of African Philosophy, Culture and Religions, 2*(1), 315–336. https://hdl.handle.net/10520/EJC170623

Ine-Ebi, J. (2020). Gender-based discriminatory and unfair practices in the Nigerian legal profession. *International Journal of Innovative Legal & Political Studies, 8*(3), 37–47.

Inglehart, R., & Norris, P. (2001). Cultural obstacles to equal representation. *Journal of Democracy, 12*(1), 126–146. https://doi.org/10.1353/jod.2001.0054.

International Bar Association. (2022). *50:50 by 2030: A longitudinal study into gender disparity in law.* IBA. https://www.ibanet.org/document?id = Uganda-Report-2022-5050-by-2030

International Bar Association. (2019). *Us too? Bullying and sexual harassment in the legal profession.* IBA. https://www.ibanet.org/MediaHandler?id = B29F6FEA-889F-49CF-8217-F8F7D78C2479

International Commission of Jurists. (2017, November 1–15). *Statement on the independence of judges and lawyers in Africa.* [Conference session]. Sixty-first session of the African Commission on Human and Peoples' Rights, Banjul, Gambia.

International Development Law Organization. (2018). *Women delivering justice: Contributions, barriers, pathways.* IDLO. https://www.idlo.int/publications/women-delivering-justice-contributions-barriers-pathways

Institute for African Women in Law. (n.d.-a). *Women chief justices.* IAWL. https://www.africanwil.org/chiefjustices

Institute for African Women in Law. (n.d.-b). *Pioneer African women in law: Dior fall sow.* IAWL. https://www.africanwomeninlaw.com/african-women-in-law/elisabeth-dior-fall-sow---

Institute for African Women in Law. (n.d.-c). *Pioneer African women in law: Mame Madior Boye.* IAWL.

Institute for African Women in Law. (n.d.-d). *Amandla series: Tujilane Rose Chizumila.* IAWL. https://www.africanwomeninlaw.com/amandla/tujilane-rose-chizumila-

Institute for African Women in Law. (n.d.-e). *Playlist.* African Women in Law Legacy Project. YouTube. Retrieved from https://www.youtube.com/playlist?list = PL0RYeugAXycqHqZPNao92AeYX2wiCWXnS

Institute for African Women in Law. (n.d.-f). Gender scorecards. IAWL. https://www.africanwil.org/genderscorecards

Institute for African Women in Law. (2020). *Unveiling subalternity? Women and the legal professions across Africa.* IAWL. https://www.africanwomeninlaw.com/_files/ugd/dc397a_f4ad148771d44bea826991d7c95e87c4.pdf

Institute for African Women in Law. (2021). *Women in the legal academy.* IAWL. https://www.africanwomeninlaw.com/_files/ugd/dc397a_ae030442fb79476f936073a4f738b816.pdf

Institute for African Women in Law. (2022). *Essi Matilda Foster: First woman lawyer in Ghana.* IAWL. https://www.africanwomeninlaw.com/_files/ugd/c889be_f7f82e5d03f742cd85c4a965d68c8387.pdf

Institute for African Women in Law. (2023a). *High-level summary: Women in law and leadership in Africa in Kenya, Nigeria, Senegal and South Africa.* IAWL. https://www.africanwomeninlaw.com/_files/ugd/229dcd_04c074c8235b40138829028406fbef98.pdf

Institute for African Women in Law. (2023b). *Leadership essentials for women in law.* IAWL. https://www.africanwomeninlaw.com/_files/ugd/229dcd_990e457b98524f729f2b48e65778343b.pdf

Institute for African Women in Law. (2023c). *Making the move from academia to the bench.* IAWL. https://www.africanwomeninlaw.com/_files/ugd/229dcd_86c4f212c817417d882698b54213f4f4.pdf

Institute for African Women in Law. (2023d). *Making the move from the bar to diplomacy.* IAWL. https://www.africanwomeninlaw.com/_files/ugd/229dcd_8a641f4607a640c9b399aea3e87200b0.pdf

Institute for African Women in Law. (2023e). *Moving up! Becoming a partner.* IAWL. https://www.africanwomeninlaw.com/_files/ugd/229dcd_606878b8204c4331945237a3891985d7.pdf

Institute for African Women in Law. (2023f). *New frontiers for women in law.* IAWL. https://www.africanwomeninlaw.com/_files/ugd/229dcd_e275f1c06a244b278a204ad331b1c235.pdf

Institute for African Women in Law. (2023g). *Where are the African women in international law?* IAWL. https://www.africanwomeninlaw.com/_files/ugd/229dcd_88e920f728fc4afa92d4c99e3f367abc.pdf

Institute for African Women in Law. (2023h). *Women and leadership in corporate law practice.* IAWL. https://www.africanwomeninlaw.com/_files/ugd/229dcd_3a5f4b9cccb44c158d64a4f9e3cdb7c3.pdf

Institute for African Women in Law. (2023i). *Women in law and leadership: Kenyan bar.* IAWL. https://www.africanwomeninlaw.com/_files/ugd/229dcd_cefe201bff954472b45a04da6a8c036f.pdf

Institute for African Women in Law. (2023j). *Women in law and leadership: Kenyan judiciary.* IAWL. https://www.africanwomeninlaw.com/_files/ugd/229dcd_0656803a9a77428092cf2b832678b168.pdf

Institute for African Women in Law. (2023k). *Women in law and leadership: Kenyan legal academy.* IAWL. https://www.africanwomeninlaw.com/_files/ugd/229dcd_20d1b28232b8473794f49f28b08616f9.pdf

Institute for African Women in Law. (2023l). *Women in law and leadership: Nigerian bar.* IAWL. https://www.africanwomeninlaw.com/_files/ugd/229dcd_23bdd2444bcd4ddbb3ed3ef572f64218.pdf

Institute for African Women in Law. (2023m). *Women in law and leadership: Nigerian judiciary.* IAWL. https://www.africanwomeninlaw.com/_files/ugd/229dcd_854b02941abe4c65b6d0edac2a960570.pdf

Institute for African Women in Law. (2023n). *Women in law and leadership: Nigerian legal academy.* IAWL. https://www.africanwomeninlaw.com/_files/ugd/229dcd_f27775d4631a4789aa0afa89ac409ba3.pdf

Institute for African Women in Law. (2023o). *Women in law and leadership: Senegalese bar, bench and legal academy.* IAWL. https://www.africanwomeninlaw.com/_files/ugd/229dcd_a625575fee9f42e0889172151858da84.pdf

Institute for African Women in Law. (2023p). *Women in law and leadership: South African bar.* IAWL. https://www.africanwomeninlaw.com/_files/ugd/229dcd_7868ff45ccd343cf8780316977ff9045.pdf

Institute for African Women in Law. (2023q). *Women in law and leadership: South African judiciary.* IAWL. https://www.africanwomeninlaw.com/_files/ugd/229dcd_46623786de7b45cdbcf1a9177b40e691.pdf

Institute for African Women in Law. (2023r). *Women in law and leadership: South African legal academy.* IAWL. https://www.africanwomeninlaw.com/_files/ugd/229dcd_52d85d407e1b4317861b33923e166b75.pdf

Institute for African Women in Law. (2023s). *Women in law and technology.* IAWL. https://www.africanwomeninlaw.com/_files/ugd/229dcd_81bcc6ce8fd44927b06497b2ad6e4d65.pdf

Institute for African Women in Law. (2024). *Gender equality in law across Africa: Is the glass half full?* IAWL. https://www.africanwomeninlaw.com/_files/ugd/e1fb33_e6e48cb3bcc54dd3a62b4279476bce45.pdf

Institute for Security Studies. (2015). *Africa loses a fearless defender of criminal justice.* ISS. https://issafrica.org/about-us/press-releases/africa-loses-a-fearless-defender-of-criminal-justice

Interparliamentary Union. (2024). *Monthly ranking of women in national parliaments.* IPU. https://data.ipu.org/women-ranking?month = 2&year = 2024

Iya, P. F. (2005). Enhancing the teaching of human rights in African universities: What role for law school clinics? *Journal of Clinical Legal Education, 7*, 20–28. https://doi.org/10.19164/ijcle.v7i0.94

Johns, M. L. (2013). Breaking the glass ceiling: Structural, cultural, and organizational barriers preventing women from achieving senior and executive positions. *Perspectives in Health Information Management, 10*(1), 1–11.

Johnson, R. B. (1997). Examining the validity structure of qualitative research. *Education, 118*, 282–292.

Joubert, I. (2022). Breaking the glass ceiling in the legal profession. *De Rebus.* https://www.derebus.org.za/breaking-the-glass-ceiling-in-the-legal-profession/

Jowi, J. O. (2012). African universities in the global knowledge economy: The good and ugly of internationalization. *Journal of Marketing for Higher Education, 22*(1), 153–165. https://doi.org/10.1080/08841241.2012.705799

Kabira, W. (2012). *Time for harvest: Women and constitution making in Kenya.* University of Nairobi Press.

Kamasah, A. (2020, September 17). *Stop displaying cleavage and bare legs in court—Anthony Forson to female lawyers.* Pulse Ghana. https://www.pulse.com.gh/filla/gba-president-anthony-forson-warns-against-display-of-cleavage-bare-legs-in-court/ed35sq5

Kamatali, J. M. (2016). Rwanda: Balancing gender quotas and an independent judiciary. In G. Bauer & J. J. Dawuni (Eds.), *Gender and the judiciary in Africa: From obscurity to parity?* (pp. 137–153). Routledge.

Kamau, N. M. (2011). Outsiders within: Experiences of women academics in Kenya. In O. Oyěwùmí (Ed.), *Gender epistemologies in Africa: Gendering traditions, spaces, social institutions, and identities* (pp. 119–154). Palgrave Macmillan. https://doi.org/10.1057/9780230116276

Kamau, W. (2013). Women judges and magistrates in Kenya: Challenges, opportunities and contributions. In U. Schultz & G. Shaw (Eds.), *Gender and judging* (pp. 167–190). Hart.

Kamau, W. (2020). Kenya: Between globalisation and constitutionalism. In R. Abel, O. Hammerslev, U. Schultz, & H. Sommerlad (Eds.), *Lawyers in 21st-century societies: Volume 1. National reports* (pp. 495–514). Hart.

Kameri-Mbote, P. (2014). Legal education and lawyers. In J. C. Ghai & Y. P. Ghai (Eds.), *The legal profession and the new constitutional order in Kenya* (pp. 121–138). Strathmore University Press. https://docslib.org/doc/8371535/the-legal-profession-and-the-new-constitutional-order-in-kenya

Kameri-Mbote, P., & Wekesa, S. (2018). Reconfiguring legal education to deepen gender equality: Mainstreaming gender through curriculum review at the School of Law University of Nairobi. *East African Law Journal, 18*, 54–81.

Kanake, L. (1997). *Gender disparities among the academic staff in Kenyan universities.* Lyceum Educational Consultants Ltd.

Kang, A. (2015). *Bargaining for women's rights: Activism in an aspiring Muslim democracy.* University of Minnesota Press.

Kang, A. (2016). Benin: Women judges promoting women's rights. In G. Bauer & J. J. Dawuni (Eds.), *Gender and the judiciary in Africa: From obscurity to parity?* (pp. 108–119). Routledge.

Kang'ara, S., Okello, D., & Makokha, K. (2021). Men should be feminists, even if it is hard work. In S. Kang'ara, D. Okello, & K. Makokha (Eds.), *Beacons of judiciary transformation: Selected speeches, writings and judicial opinions of Chief Justice Willy Mutunga.* Sheria.

Kapinga, W. B. L. (1992). The legal profession and social action in the third world: Reflections on Tanzania and Kenya. *African Journal of International and Comparative Law, 4*, 874–891.

Karekwaivanane, G. H. (2015). Lawyers, "Africanization," and political transition: Remaking the legal field in post-colonial Zimbabwe, 1980–1995. *Politique Africaine, 138*(2), 49–70.

Karekwaivanane, G. H. (2016). "Through the narrow door": Narratives of the first generation of African lawyers in Zimbabwe. *Africa, 86*(1), 59–77.

Karekwaivanane, G. H. (2017). *The struggle over state power in Zimbabwe: Law and politics since 1950.* Cambridge University Press.

Karekwaivanane, G. (2020). Zimbabwe: Legal practitioners, politics and transformation since 1980. In R. Abel, O. Hammerslev, U. Schultz, & H. Sommerlad (Eds.), *Lawyers in 21st-century societies: Volume 1. National reports* (547–562) Hart.

Kariseb, K. (2022). The making and unmaking of gender: Reflections on questions of gender and the judiciary in Namibia. In J. J. Dawuni (Ed.), *Intersectionality and women's access to justice in Africa* (pp. 241–258). Lexington Press.

Karki, N. (n.d.). *Mariam Jack-Denton: First woman lawyer in The Gambia.* IAWL. https://www.africanwomeninlaw.com/african-women-in-law/mariam-jack-denton

Kasonde, L. (2023). *Women, resilience, and the will to lead: A memoir.* Author.

Kaunda, K. D. (1971–1972). The functions of the Lawyer in Zambia today. *Zambia Law Journal, 3*, 1–25.

Kay, H. H. (1991). The future of women law professors. *Iowa Law Review, 77*, 5–17.

Kerogo, G., Nyanjong, A., & Milongo, J. (2014). Professional integrity and the disciplining of advocates: Room for improvement. In J. C. Ghai & Y. P. Ghai (Eds.), *The legal profession and the new constitutional order* (pp. 110–120). Strathmore University Press.

Kenney, S. (2013a). *Gender and justice: Why women in the judiciary really matter.* Routledge.

Kenney, S. (2013b). Which judicial selection systems generate the most women judges? Lessons from the United States. In U. Schultz & G. Shaw (Eds.), *Gender and judging* (pp. 461–476). Hart.

Kenney, S. (2018). Measuring women's judicial empowerment as part of political empowerment. In A. Alexander, C. Bolzendahl, & F. Jalalzai (Eds.), *Measuring women's political empowerment across the globe; strategies, challenges and future research* (pp. 207–227). Palgrave Macmillan.

Kenny, M. (2014). A feminist institutionalist approach. *Politics & Gender, 10*(4), 679–684. https://doi.org/10.1017/S1743923X14000488

Khan, M. S., & Ramnund-Mansingh, A. (2020). Move over Ms. Professor! A review of the challenges women experience in academia. *Journal of Higher Education Service Science and Management, 3*(1), 1–14.

Khanna, V., Trubek, D., & Wilkins, D. (Eds.). (2017). *The Indian legal profession in the age of globalization: The rise of the corporate legal sector and its impact on lawyers and society.* Cambridge University Press.

Kiamba J. M. (2008). Women and leadership positions: social and cultural barriers to success. *A Journal of Transnational Women's Gender Studies, 6*(1), 7–27.

Kinyanjui, S. (2009). Restorative justice in traditional pre-colonial criminal justice systems in Kenya. *Tribal Law Journal, 10*(1), 1–16. https://digitalrepository.unm.edu/tlj/vol10/iss1/1

Kipkosgei, E. J. (2019). *A situational analysis of women in higher education in Kenya* [Doctoral dissertation, University of Toronto].

Kiyonga, D. (2017, August 4). Justice Bossa hits out at JSC for denying her Kavuma's job. *The Observer.* https://observer.ug/news/headlines/54226-justice-bossa-hits-out-at-jsc-for-denying-her-kavuma-s-job

Klaaren, J. (2020). South Africa: A profession in transformation. In R. Abel, O. Hammerslev, U. Schultz, & H. Sommerlad (Eds.), *Lawyers in 21st-century societies: Volume 1. National reports* (pp. 535–546). Hart.

Klibi, S. (2016). Tunisia: A new constitution and more women judges. In G. Bauer & J. J. Dawuni (Eds.), *Gender and the judiciary in Africa: From obscurity to parity?* (pp. 80–92). Routledge.

Kluegel, A. J. (2016). The firm as a nexus of organizational theories: Sociological perspectives on the modern law firm. *Annual Review of Law and Social Science, 12*(1), 459–478.

Kohen, B. (2013). What's in a label? Argentine judges' reluctance to call themselves feminists. In U. Schultz & G. Shaw (Eds.), *Gender and judging* (pp. 419–433). Hart.

Koroma, M. (n.d.). *Pioneer African women in law: Justice Mary MamYassin Sey.* Retrieved April 10, 2024, at https://www.africanwomeninlaw.com/african-women-in-law/mary-mamyassin-sey.

Krishnan, J. K. (2012). Academic SAILERS: The Ford Foundation and the efforts to shape legal education in Africa, 1957–1977. *American Journal of Legal History, 52*(3), 261–324.

Krishnan, J., & Ajagbe, K. (2018). Legal activism in the face of political challenges: The Nigerian case. *Journal of the Legal Profession, 42*(2), 197–241.

Krook, M. L., & Mackay, F. (Eds.). (2011). *Gender, politics and institutions: Towards a feminist institutionalism?* Palgrave.

Kuenyehia, A. (1995). Women and law—Current status of teaching and research in Ghana. In M. Prah (Ed.), *Women's studies with a focus on Ghana: Selected readings* (pp. 90–93). Books on African Studies.

Kuenyehia, A. (Ed.). (1998). *Women and law in West Africa: Situational analysis of some key issues affecting women.* Human Rights Study Center.

Kwesiga, J. (2002). *Women's access to higher education in Africa: Uganda's experience.* Fountain.

Kyobiika, W. N. (2021). Judging beyond gender: Maternal and infant mortality as an emerging gender-related issue in Ugandan courts. In J. J. Dawuni (Ed.), *Gender, judging and the courts in Africa: Selected studies* (pp. 99–122). Routledge.

Ladner, Joyce. (1971). Tanzanian women and nation building. *The Black Scholar, 3*(4), 22–28.

Lambert, P., & Scribner, D. (2018). Constitutions and women's rights advocacy: Strategic uses of gender provisions in Argentina, Chile, Botswana, and South Africa. *Politics, Groups, and Identities, 8*(2), 228–247. https://doi.org/10.1080/21565503.2018.1449759

Lamond, A. (2017). The tyranny of low expectations. *Without Prejudice: Women in Law Feature, 17*(1), 16–17.

Lare, D. (2014). Debunking patriarchal legacy in African traditional setting: A reading of Efo Kodjo Mawugbe's *In the Chest of a Woman. Littera Aperta, 2*, 103–123.

Law Society of Kenya. (n.d.). *Senior counsel.* Author. Retrieved August 17, 2023, from https://lsk.or.ke/about-us/organisational-structure/senior-counsel/#1679493466884-9e7bea97-4008.

Law Society of South Africa . (2019). *Statistics for the attorneys' profession.* LSSA. https://www.lssa.org.za/about-us/about-the-attorneys-profession/statistics-for-the-attorneys-profession/#:~:text = the%20attorneys'%20profession-,About%20the%20attorneys'%20profession,at%20the%20Legal%20Practice%20Council

Law Society of the UK. (n.d.). *Becoming a King's Council.* Author. https://www.lawsociety.org.uk/topics/advocacy/becoming-a-kc

Letswaart, H. (2003). Choices in context: Life histories of women lawyers in the Netherlands. In U. Schultz & G. Shaw (Eds.), *Women in the world's legal professions* (pp. 353–369) Hart.

Levit, N. (2001). Keeping feminism in its place: Sex segregation and the domestication of female academics. *University of Kansas Law Review, 49*, 775.

Lewis, G. (2013). Unsafe travel: Experiencing intersectionality and feminist displacements. *Signs, 38*(4), 869–892.

LexisNexis. (2021/2022). *LexisNexis legal tech report.* LexisNexis. https://www.lssa.org.za/wp-content/uploads/2021/12/LSSA-and-LN-Legal-Research-Report.pdf

L'Heureux-Dubè, C. (2001). "Outsiders" on the bench: The continuing struggle for equality. *Wisconsin Women's Law Journal, 16*, 15–30.

Liani, M. L., Nyamongo, I., & Tolhjurst, R. (2020). Understanding intersecting gender inequities in academic scientific research career progression in Sub-Saharan Africa. *International Journal of Gender, Science and Technology, 12*(2), 262–288.

Liebenberg, R. D., & Scharf, S. A. (2019). *Walking out the door: The fact, figures, and future of experienced women lawyers in private practice.* ABA Book Publishing. https://www.americanbar.org/content/dam/aba/administrative/women/walking-out-the-door-4920053.pdf

Lindbekk, M., & Sonneveld, N. (2017). *Women judges in the Muslim world: A comparative study of discourse and practice.* Brill.

Liu S. (2013). The legal profession as a social process: A theory on lawyers and globalization. *Law & Social Inquiry, 38*(3), 670–693.

Liu, X. (2021). Women legal academics in China. In R. Auchmuty, U. Schultz, G. Shaw, & M. Thornton (Eds.), *Gender and careers in the Legal Academy* (pp. 233–248). Hart.

López, A. (1999). A comparative analysis of women's issues: Toward a contextualized methodology. *Hastings Women's Law Journal, 10*(2), 347–368.

Lorde, A. (1984). The master's tools will never dismantle the master's house. In A. Lorde, *Sister outsider: Essays and speeches* (pp. 110–113). Crossing Press.

Lugones, M. (2010). Toward a decolonial feminism. *Hypatia, 25*(4), 742–759. http://www.jstor.org/stable/40928654

Luckham, R. (1976). The Ghana legal profession: The natural history of a research project. *The Journal of Legal Pluralism and Unofficial Law, 8*(13), 106–144. https://doi.org/10.1080/07329113.1976.10756224

Luckham, R. (1981). Imperialism, law and structural dependence: The Ghana legal profession. In C. J. Dias, R. Luckham, D. O. Lynch, & J. C. N. Paul (Eds.), *Lawyers in the third world: Comparative and developmental perspectives* (pp. 201–243). International Center for Law in Development.

Luckham, R. (1994). The military, militarization and democratization in Africa: A survey of literature and issues. *African Studies Review, 37*(2), 13–75. https://doi.org/10.2307/524766

Lumumba, P. L. O. (2014). The legal profession and crisis of ethics. In J. C. Ghai & Y. P. Ghai (Eds.), *The legal profession and the new constitutional order* (pp. 77–100). Strathmore University Press.

Mabokela, R. O. (2000). "We cannot find qualified blacks": Faculty diversification programmes at South African universities. *Comparative Education, 36*(1), 95–112. http://www.jstor.org/stable/3099853

Mabokela, R. O. (Ed.). (2007). *Soaring beyond boundaries: Women breaking education barriers in traditional societies.* Sense.

Mabokela, R. O., & Mawila, K. F. N. (2004). The impact of race, gender, and culture in South African higher education. *Comparative Education Review, 48*(4), 396–416.

Mabokela, R. O., & Mlambo, Y. (2015). The older women are men: Navigating the academic terrain, perspectives from Ghana. *International Journal of Higher Education Research, 69*, 759–778.

Macbeth, D. (2001). On "reflexivity" in qualitative research: Two readings, and a third. *Qualitative Inquiry, 7*(1), 35–68.

Mackenzie, R., Malleson, K., Martin, P., & Sands, P. (2010). *Selecting international judges: Principle, process and politics.* Oxford University Press.

MacKinnon, C. A. (2013). Intersectionality as method: A note. *Signs, 38*(4), 1019–1030.

Madlalate, R. (2022). Legal education in South Africa: Racialized globalizations, crises, and contestations. In B. Garth & G. Shaffer (Eds.), *The globalization of legal education: A critical perspective* (pp. 157–179). Oxford University Press.

Madonsela, T. (1995). Beyond putting women on the agenda. *Agenda, 11*(24), 27–38. https://doi.org/10.1080/10130950.1995.9675392

Maggott, T., & Prah, E. (2020). The role of feminisms in building a transformation framework for institutions of higher learning in South Africa. *Social Dynamics, 46*(3), 515–539.

Mahoney, J. (2004). Comparative-historical methodology. *Annual Review of Sociology, 30*, 81–101. http://www.jstor.org/stable/29737686

Maingi, G. (2011). The Kenyan constitutional reform process: A case study on the work of FIDA Kenya in securing women's rights. *Feminist Africa, 15*, 63–81. http://awdflibrary.org:8080/xmlui/handle/123456789/435

Malleson, K. (2003). Justifying gender equality on the bench: Why difference won't do. *Feminist Legal Studies, 11*(1), 1–24. https://doi.org/10.1023/A:1023231006909

Malleson, K. (2006). Rethinking the merit principle in judicial selection. *Journal of Law and Society, 33*(1), 131–140. https://doi.org/10.1111/j.1467-6478.2006.00351

Malleson, K., & Russell, R. (Eds.). (2006). *Appointing judges in an age of judicial power: critical perspectives from around the world.* University of Toronto Press.

Mama, A. (2003). Restore, reform but do not transform: The gender politics of higher education in Africa. *Journal of Higher Education in Africa [Revue de l'enseignement Supérieur en Afrique]*, *1*(1), 101–125. http://www.jstor.org/stable/24486116

Mama, A. (2020). "We will not be pacified": From freedom fighters to feminists. *European Journal of Women's Studies, 27*(4), 362–380. https://doi.org/10.1177/1350506820953459

Mama. A. (2023). Nkrumah's legacy, feminism and the next generation. *Contemporary Journal of African Studies, 10*(1), 169–200. https://doi.org/10.4314/contjas.v10i1.7.

Mamdani, M. (2018). *Citizen and subject: Contemporary Africa and the legacy of late colonialism* (2nd ed.). Princeton University Press.

Mandela, N. (1995). *Long walk to freedom: The autobiography of Nelson Mandela.* Back Bay Books.

Mann, K., & Roberts, R. (Eds.). (1991). *Law in colonial Africa: Social history of Africa.* Heinemann.

Manteaw, S. O. (2008). Legal education in Africa: What type of lawyer does Africa need? *McGeorge Law Review, 39*(1), 903.

Maphalala, M. C., & Mpofu, N. (2017). Are we there yet? A literature study of the challenges of women academics in institutions of higher education. *Gender and Behaviour, 15*(2), 9216–9224.

Markovic, M., & Plickert, G. (2022). The gender pay gap and high-achieving women in the legal profession. *Law & Social Inquiry, 48*(2), 1–32. https://doi.org/10.1017/lsi.2022.7

Masabo, J. (2021). Unlocking gender inequality through judicial training: Insights from Tanzania. In J. J. Dawuni (Ed.), *Gender, judging and the courts in Africa: Selected studies* (pp. 233–253). Routledge.

Masengu. T. (2015). A perspective on women and leadership in the South African judiciary. *South African. Journal on Human Rights, 31*(3), 655–665.

Masengu, T. (2016). It's a man's world: Barriers to gender transformation in the South African judiciary: Perspectives from women advocates and attorneys. *International Journal of the Legal Profession, 23*(4), 305–319. https://doi.org/10.1080/09695958.2016.1179639

Masengu, T. (2020). *What lies beneath: The complex nature of appointing women judges in Zambia and South Africa.* [Doctoral dissertation, Universiteit Gent]. http://hdl.handle.net/1854/LU8664196

Masengu, T. (2021). One sauce for the goose, another for the gander: Zambian women judges and perceptions of illegitimacy. In J. J. Dawuni (Ed.), *Gender, judging and the courts in Africa: Selected studies* (pp. 209–230). Routledge.

Masola, A. (2020). African women's letters as intellectual history and decolonial knowledge production. In T. Falola & O. Yacob-Haliso (Eds.), *Palgrave handbook of African women's studies* (pp. 1315–1328). Palgrave Macmillan.

May, V. M. (2015). *Pursuing intersectionality, unsettling dominant imaginaries.* Routledge.

Mbow, P. (2000). Academic freedom and the gender issue: A report from Senegal. In E. Sall (Ed.), *Women in academia: Gender and academic freedom in Africa* (pp. 64–78). Council for the Development of Social Science Research in Africa.

McCall, L. (2005). The complexity of intersectionality. *Signs, 30*(3), 1771–1800.

McCleod, J. (2016). *Daughter of the Empire State: The life of Judge Jane Bolin.* University of Illinois Press.

McGlynn, C. (2003). The status of women lawyers in the United Kingdom. In U. Schultz & G. Shaw (Eds.), *Women in the world's legal professions* (pp. 139–156) Hart.

Means, T. (2022). Her Honor: Black women judges' experiences with disrespect and recusal requests in the American judiciary. *Journal of Women, Politics & Policy, 43*(3), 310–327.

Medie, P. (2021). A new agenda for gender and politics scholarship. *American Political Science Review.* https://www.cambridge.org/core/journals/american-political-science-review/an-international-women-s-day-collection-from-apsr

Meer, T., & Müller, A. (2017). Considering intersectionality in Africa. *Agenda, 31*(1), 3–4. https://doi.org/10.1080/10130950.2017.1363583

Mekgwe, P. (2007). Theorizing African feminism(s): The "colonial" question. *Texts, Tasks, and Theories: Versions and Subversions in African Literatures,* 3, 165–174.

Mekgwe, P. (2010). Post-Africa(n) feminism? *Third Text, 24*(2), 189–194. https://doi.org/10.1080/09528821003722116

Melaku, T. M. (2019). *You don't look like a lawyer: Black women and systemic gendered racism.* Rowman & Littlefield.

Melaku, T. M. (2021). The awakening: The impact of COVID-19, racial upheaval, and political polarization on black women lawyers. *Fordham Law Review, 89*, 2519–2540. https://fordhamlawreview.org/wp-content/uploads/2021/05/Melaku-May.pdf.

Menkel-Meadow, C. (1986). The comparative sociology of women lawyers: The "feminization" of the legal profession. *Osgoode Hall Law Journal, 24*(4), 897–918.

Mensa-Bonsu, A. S., & Mensa-Bonsu, M. Y. (2021). To win both the battle and the war: Judicial determination of property rights of spouses in Ghana. In J. J. Dawuni (Ed.), *Gender, judging and the courts in Africa: Selected studies* (pp. 40–56). Routledge.

Meyer, T. (2018). Female attorneys in South Africa: A quantitative analysis. *African Journal of Employee Relations, 42*(1), 1–21. https://doi.org/10.25159/2664-3731/4888

Meyer, T. (2021). *Reaching for partnership: An intersectional study of occupational closure among women attorneys in South Africa* [Doctoral dissertation, Stellenbosch University].

Michelson, E. (2013). Women in the legal profession, 1970–2010: A study of the global supply of lawyers. *Indiana Journal of Global Legal Studies, 20*(2), 1071–1137. https://doi.org/10.2979/indjglolegstu.20.2.1071

Minamino, K. (2014). Introducing gender training in judicial education in Japan to support the judiciary. *International Journal of the Legal Profession, 21*(3), 297–306. https://doi.org/10.1080/09695958.2015.1036869

Miwa, A. (2013). Gender and judicial training—Lessons from the Philippines. In U. Schultz & G. Shaw (Eds.), *Gender and judging* (pp. 167–232). Hart.

Mocumie, C. (2022). Gender transformation of the judiciary in South Africa. In J. J. Dawuni (Ed.), *Intersectionality and women's access to justice in Africa* (pp.161–188). Lexington Press.

Mohammed, W. (2022). Why we need intersectionality in Ghanaian feminist politics and discourses. *Feminist Media Studies, 23*(6), 3031–3047. https://doi.org/10.1080/14680777.2022.2098798

Mohanty, C. T. (1984). Under Western eyes: Feminist scholarship and colonial discourses. *Boundary 2, 12*(3), 333–358. https://doi.org/10.2307/302821

Mohanty, C. T. (2013). Transnational feminist crossings: On neoliberalism and radical critique. *Signs, 38*(4), 967–991.

Mohanty, C. T., Russo, A., & Torres, L. (Eds). (1991). *Third world women and the politics of feminism.* Indiana University Press.

Mokhele, M. (2013). Reflections of Black women academics at South African universities: A narrative case study. *Mediterranean Journal of Social Sciences, 4*(3), 611–619.

Moodly, A., & Toni, N. (2017). Re-imagining higher education leadership—In conversation with South African female deputy vice-chancellors. *Perspectives in Education, 35*(2), 155–167.

Moodly, A., & Toni, N. (2019). Do institutional cultures serve as impediments for women's advancement towards leadership in South African higher education? *South African Journal of Higher Education, 33*(3), 176–191. https://doi.org/10.20853/33-3-3137

Morgan, V. (2013). *Perceptions of career advancement for women in law* [Master's thesis, University of Pretoria].

Mossman, J. (2006). *The first women lawyers: A comparative study of gender, law and the legal professions.* Hart.

Mossman, J. (2013). Becoming the first women judges in Ontario: Women lawyers, gender and the politics of judicial appointment. In U. Schultz & G. Shaw (Eds.), *Gender and judging* (pp. 51–66). Hart.

Mougoué, J-B. (2019). *Gender, separatist politics, and embodied nationalism in Cameroon.* Michigan University Press.

Mugenyi, M. L. (2021). *Unveiling subalternity: Women and the legal professions across Africa.* Institute for African Women in Law. https://www.africanwomeninlaw.com/_files/ugd/dc397a_f4ad148771d44bea826991d7c95e87c4.pdf.

Mumba, F. N. M. (2018). Women judges in international courts and tribunals: The quest for equal opportunities. In J. J. Dawuni & A. Kuenyehia (Eds.), *International courts and the African woman judge: Unveiled narratives* (pp. 28–36). Routledge Press.

Murphy, W. F. (1991). Civil law, common law, and constitutional democracy. *Louisiana Law Review, 52*(1), 91–136. https://digitalcommons.law.lsu.edu/lalrev/vol52/iss1/6

Murungi, A., & Meroka-Mutua, A. (2022). Making gains for women's rights: Using gender quotas to achieve gender equality in the composition of the Supreme Court of Kenya. In J. J. Dawuni (Ed.), *Intersectionality and women's access to justice in Africa* (pp. 117–138). Rowman & Littlefield.

Musoke, L. S. (2024). Silent but pervasive: Sexual harassment against women lawyers in Uganda. In F. Saungweme, C. Ngang, & G. Towl (Eds.), *Sexual harassment and the law in Africa: Country and regional perspectives* (pp. 110–128). Routledge.

Mutua, A. (2006). Gender equality and women's solidarity across religious, ethnic and class difference in the Kenyan constitutional review process. *William & Mary Journal of Women & Law, 13*(1), pp. 1–128.

Mutua, M. W. (2000). "What is TWAIL?" *ASIL Proceedings, 94*, 31–38.

Mutua, M. W. (2001). Justice under siege: The rule of law and judicial subservience in Kenya. *Human Rights Quarterly, 23*(1), 96–118.

Mutunga, W. (2014). The 2010 constitution of Kenya: Its vision of a new bench-bar relationship. In J. C. Ghai & Y. P. Ghai (Eds.), *The legal profession and the new constitutional order* (pp. 59–76). Strathmore University Press.

Nabaneh, S. (2023). Foreign Judges on the Gambian bench: Implications for judicial independence and rule of law. In A. Dziedzi & S. N. M. Young (Eds.), *The Cambridge handbook of foreign judges on domestic courts* (pp. 392–408). Cambridge University Press.

Nabaneh, S. (2025). Mary Mamyassin Sey: Gambia's first of firsts. In J. J. Dawuni (Ed.), *African women judges: Storytelling as judicial freedom* (pp. 181–205). Palgrave Macmillan.

Naidu, S. (2013). *Navi Pillay: Realizing human rights for all.* Quercus.

Nash, J. C. (2008). Re-thinking intersectionality. *Feminist Review, 89*, 1–15.

Natarajan, U., Reynolds, J., Bhatia, A., & Xavier, S. (2016). Introduction: TWAIL—On Praxis and the intellectual, *Third World Quarterly, 37*(11), 1946–1956.

Navarro, S. (2010). Shaking hands and kissing babies: The intersectionality of ethnicity, class and gender and Latina women's decisions to run for judicial office. *A Journal of Chicano Studies, 65*(2), 65–87.

Nayak, B., & Tabassum, N. (2021). Gender stereotypes and their impact on women's career progressions from a managerial perspective. *Society and Management Review, 10*(2), 192–208. https://doi.org/10.1177/2277975220975513

Ndagire, J. (2022). A critical assessment of the status of women judicial officers in Uganda. In J. J. Dawuni (Ed.), *Intersectionality and women's access to justice in Africa* (pp. 189–212). Lexington Press.

Ndulo, M. (2002). Legal education in Africa in the era of globalization and structural adjustment. *Penn State International Law Review, 20*(3), 487–503.

Ndulo, M. (2011). African customary law, customs and women's rights. *Indiana Journal of Global Legal Studies, 18*(1), 87–120.

Ndulo, M. (2021). The COVID-19 pandemic, courts, and the justice system. In J. J. Dawuni (Ed.), *Gender, judging and the courts in Africa: Selected studies* (pp. 279–298). Routledge.

Nelson, R., Dinovitzer, R., Garth, B., Sterling, J., Wilkins, D., Daw, M., & Michelson, E. (2023). *The making of lawyers' careers: Inequality and opportunity in the American legal profession.* University of Chicago Press.

Nesiah, V. (1993). Toward a feminist internationality: A critique of U.S. feminist legal scholarship. *Harvard Women's Law Journal, 6*, 189–210.

Nesiah, V. (2003). The ground beneath her feet: "Third world" feminisms. *Journal of International Women's Studies, 4*(3), 30–38.

Neumann, R. K. (2000). Women in legal education: What the statistics show. *Journal of Legal Education, 50*, 313–357. https://scholarlycommons.law.hofstra.edu/faculty_scholarship/734

Ngambi, H., & Nkomo, S. M. (2009). African women in leadership: Current knowledge and a framework for future studies. *International Journal of African Renaissance Studies–Multi-Inter- and Transdisciplinarity, 4*(1), 49–68.

Ngcukaitobi, T. (2018). *The land is ours: South Africa's first black lawyers and the birth of constitutionalism.* Penguin Press.

Nichols, S., & Stahl, G. (2019). Intersectionality in higher education research: A systematic literature review. *Higher Education Research and Development, 38*(3), 1–14.

Nigerian Bar Association. (n.d.). Nigerian Bar Association leadership. https://www.nigerianbar.org.ng/about. NBA.

Nkrumah, K. (1959). *Ghana: The autobiography of Kwame Nkrumah.* Thomas Nelson and Sons.

Nkrumah, K. (1962). Law in Africa. *Africa Journal of Law, 6*, 103–112.

Nnaemeka, O. (1994). From orality to writing: African women writers and the (re)inscription of womanhood. *Research in African Literatures, 25*(4), 137–157. http://www.jstor.org/stable/3819872.

Nnaemeka, O. (2003). Nego-feminism: Theorizing, practicing, and pruning Africa's way. *Signs: Journal of Women in Culture and Society, 29*(2), 357–385.

Norwood, K. J. (2020). Gender bias as the norm in the legal profession: It's still a [white] man's game. *Washington University Journal of Law & Policy, 62*(1), 25–50. https://openscholarship.wustl.edu/law_journal_law_policy/vol62/iss1/10.

Novak, A. (2018). Capital punishment in precolonial Africa: The authenticity challenge. *The Journal of Legal Pluralism and Unofficial Law, 50*(1), 71–93. https://doi.org/10.1080/07329113.2017.1422586

Nowrojee, P. (2014). The legal profession 1963–2013: All this can happen again—soon. In J. C. Ghai & Y. P. Ghai (Eds.), *The legal profession and the new constitutional order* (pp. 33–58). Strathmore University Press.

Nwankwor, C. (2021). Women cabinet ministers' substantive representation in Africa. *Social Politics: International Studies in Gender, State & Society, 28*(1), 241–264.

Nyamu, C. (2000). How should human rights and development respond to cultural legitimization of gender hierarchy in developing countries? *Harvard International Law Journal, 41*(2), 381–418.

Nzewi, U. M., & Ohia, C. (2016). Socio-cultural challenges of women's development: The case of female academics in Igbo land. *Mediterranean Journal of Social Sciences, 7*(1), 269–278. https://www.mcser.org/journal/index.php/mjss/article/view/8746/8404

Obani, P. (2021). "Judging" lesbians: Prospects for advancing lesbian rights and protection through the courts in Nigeria. In J. J. Dawuni (Ed.), *Gender, judging and the courts in Africa: Selected studies* (pp. 57–76). Routledge.

Obers, N. (2014). Career success for women academics in higher education: Choices and challenges. *South African Journal of Higher Education, 28*(3), 1107–1122.

Obiora, L. A. (1993). Reconsidering African customary law. *Legal Studies Forum, 17*, 217–252.

Obiora, L. A. (2020). Feminist legal theory, human rights and culture in Africa. In O. Yacob-Haliso & T. Falola (Eds.), *Palgrave handbook of African women's studies* (pp. 171–198). Palgrave Macmillan.

Odejide, A. (2003). Navigating the seas: Women in higher education in Nigeria. *McGill Journal of Education, 38*(3), 453–468.

Odejide, A. (2005). "What can a woman do?" Being women in a Nigerian university. *Feminist Africa, 42*(8), 42–59.

Odenyo, A. O. (1979). Professionalization amidst change: The case of the emerging legal profession in Kenya. *African Studies Review, 22*(3), 33–44. https://doi.org/10.2307/523894

Odhiambo, G. (2011). Women and higher education leadership in Kenya: A critical analysis. *Journal of Higher Education Policy and Management, 33*(6), 667–678. https://doi.org/10.1080/1360080X.2011.621192

Offutt, V. (2021). The ugly, the bad, and the good: How COVID-19 restructures the workplace and careers of women in the law. *The Voice, 20*(3), 7–8.

Ogbogu, C. (2016). Engendering gender equality: Building the research capacity of female academics in Nigerian public universities. *West East Journal of Social Sciences, 5*(2), 1–10. https://westeastinstitute.com/journals/wp-content/2018/01/Christiana-O-Ogbogo-.pdf

Ogbomo, O. W. (2005). Women, power and society in pre-colonial Africa. *Lagos Historical Review, 5*, 49–74. https://doi.org/10.4314/lhr.v5i1.32524

Oguamanam, C., & Wesley Pue, W. (2007). Lawyers' professionalism, colonialism, state formation, and national life in Nigeria, 1900–1960: "The fighting brigade of the people." *Social Identities, 13*(6), 769–785.

Ohene, I. (2010). *Gender and leadership in higher educational institutions: Exploring perceptions and practices in University of Cape Coast, Ghana.* [Doctoral dissertation, University of Sussex].

Ojigho, O. (2021). Litigating gender discrimination cases before the ECOWAS Community Court of Justice and the African Court on Human and Peoples' Rights. In J. J. Dawuni (Ed.), *Gender, judging and the courts in Africa: Selected studies* (pp. 142–158). Routledge.

Ojo, A. (1987). *Constitutional law and military rule in Nigeria.* Evans Brothers Limited.

Ojo, I. O., & Ekhator, E. (2020). Pre-colonial legal system in Africa: An assessment of indigenous laws of Benin kingdom before 1897. *Umewaen: Journal of Benin and Edo Studies, 5,* 38–73.

Okafor, O.C. (2008). Critical third world approaches to international law (TWAIL): Theory, methodology, or both? *International Community Law Review, 10,* 371–378.

Okeke-Ihejirika, P. E. (2017). Asserting agency by negotiating patriarchy: Nigerian women's experiences within university administrative structures. *Journal of Global South Studies, 34*(1), 1–21. https://www.jstor.org/stable/48517872

Oko, O. (1994). Contemporary law practice in Nigeria. *Journal of African Law, 38*(2), 104–124. http://www.jstor.org/stable/745390

Oko, O. (1997). Lawyers in chains: Restrictions on human rights advocacy under Nigeria's military regimes. *Harvard Human Rights Journal, 10,* 257–91.

Oko, O. (2008). Lawyers in fragile democracies and the challenges of democratic consolidation: The Nigerian experience. *Fordham Law Review, 77,* 1295.

Okoth-Ogendo, H. W. (1988). *Constitutions without constitutionalism: Reflections on an African paradox.* American Council of Learned Societies.

Okudzeto, S. (2018). *SAM: A life of service to God and country.* Smartline.

Oladunni, T. M. (2014). Best practices in gender mainstreaming in the academia: Lessons from African higher education institutions. *International Journal of Humanities, Social Sciences and Education (IJHSSE), 1*(10), 81–87.

Oloka-Onyango, J. (2017). *When courts do politics: Public interest law and litigation in East Africa.* Cambridge Scholars Publishing.

Oloka-Onyango, J. (Ed.). (2021). *Politics, democratization and academia in Uganda.* Daraja Press.

Oloka-Onyango, J., & Tamale, S. (1995). The personal is political, or why women's rights are indeed human rights: An African perspective on international feminism. *Human Rights Quarterly, 17*(4), 691–731.

Oloka-Onyango, J., & Tamale, S. (2000). "Bitches" at the academy: Gender and academic freedom in Africa. In E. Sall (Ed.), *Women in Academia: gender and academic freedom in Africa* (pp. 1–23). Russell Press.

Omotola, S. J. (2007). What is this gender talk all about after all? Gender, power, and politics in contemporary Nigeria. *African Study Monographs, 28*(1), 33–46.

Osori, A. (2017). *Love does not win elections.* Narrative Landscape Press.

Oxner, S. (2001). The many facets of training. In R. V. Van Puymbroeck (Ed.), *Comprehensive legal and judicial development: Toward an agenda for a just and equitable society in the 21st century* (pp. 273–298).World Bank.

Oyebode, A. (2005). Is the judiciary still the last hope of the common man? In A. Oyebode, (Ed.), *Law and nation building in Nigeria: Selected essays.* Centre for Political and Administrative Research (CEPAR).

Oyěwùmí, O. (1997). *The invention of women: Making an African sense of western gender discourses.* University of Minnesota Press.

Oyěwùmí, O. (Ed.). (2003). *African women and feminism: Reflecting on the politics of sisterhood.* Africa World Press.

Oyěwùmí, O. (2004). Conceptualising gender: Eurocentric foundations of feminist concepts and the challenge of African epistemologies. In S. Arnfred, B. Bakare-Yusuf, & E.

W. Kisiang'ani (Eds.), *African gender scholarship: Concepts, methodologies, and paradigms* (pp. 1–8). Lightning Source.

Pant, S. (2020). Calculating the gender gap in legal scholarship: An empirical study. *Saint Louis University Law Journal, 65*(1), 199–226. https://scholarship.law.slu.edu/lj/vol65/iss1/9

Paquin, J. (2021). The feminisation of legal academia in Quebec: Achievements and challenges. In R. Auchmuty, U. Schultz, G. Shaw, & M. Thornton (Eds.), *Gender and careers in the legal academy* (pp. 79–94). Hart.

Peeples, A. (2019). Women's works: The evolution of Tanzanian women's movements from late colonialism to post-structural adjustment. *Global Africana Review, 3*(1), 21–31. https://doi.org/10.17615/et00-qj71

Pilawa, D. (2019). Sifting through the arbitrators for the woman, the minority, the newcomer, *Case Western Reserve Journal of International Law, 51*(1), 395–435. https://scholarlycommons.law.case.edu/jil/vol51/iss1/14

Pillay, C. (2017). *Sponsorship: An enabler to advancing women in law firms* [Master's thesis, University of Pretoria].

Pimentel, D. (2011). Legal pluralism in post-colonial Africa: Linking statutory and customary adjudication in Mozambique. *Yale Human Rights & Developmental Law Journal, 14*(59). Available at SSRN: https://ssrn.com/abstract=1668063 or https://doi.org/10.2139/ssrn.1668063

Pinnington, A. H., & Sandberg, J. (2013). Lawyers' professional careers: Increasing women's inclusion in the partnership of law firms. *Gender, Work & Organization, 20*(6), 616–631. https://doi.org/10.1111/j.1468-0432.2012.00610.x

Prah, E. (2017). Stratifications of blackness: Meditations on the intersect of gender, race and age. *Agenda, 31*(1), 71–77. https://doi.org/10.1080/10130950.2017.1354441

Prah, M. (2002). Gender issues in Ghanaian tertiary institutions: Women academics and administrators at Cape-Coast University. *Ghana Studies, 5*, 83–122. https://muse.jhu.edu/article/904671

Prah, M. (2004). Chasing illusions and realising visions: Reflections on Ghana's feminist experience. *Gender Activism and Studies in Africa, 3*, 27–40. Council for the Development of Social Science Research in Africa (CODESRIA).

Pratt, C. (2012). Sisters in law: Black women lawyers' struggle for advancement. *Michigan State Law Review, 2012*, 1777–1793.

Prempeh, K. (2007). Africa's "constitutionalism revival": False start or new dawn? *International Journal of Constitutional Law, 5*(3), 469–506. https://doi.org/10.1093/icon/mom016

Pruitt, L. (2002). No Black names on the letterhead? Efficient discrimination and the South African legal profession. *Michigan Journal of International Law, 23*(3), 545–676. https://repository.law.umich.edu/mjil/vol23/iss3/2

Public Broadcasting Service. (2003). *The road north: Hauwa Ibrahim.* PBS. https://www.pbs.org/frontlineworld/stories/nigeria/voice01.html

Rabinowitz, B. (2020). Ethnicity and power in sub-Saharan Africa: Do colonial institutions still matter? *Comparative Politics, 52*(3), 405–431. https://www.jstor.org/stable/26907862

Rackley, E. (2013). *Women, judging and the judiciary: From difference to diversity.* Routledge.

Rasivhetshele, P. (2020). *The sustained success of female executives in elite law firms in South Africa* [Master's thesis, University of Pretoria].
Reskin, B. F, & Roos, P. A. (1990). *Job queues, gender queues: Explaining women's inroads into male occupations.* Temple University Press.
Reuters News. (2008, October 20). *Kenyan judge accused of road rage stabbing.* Reuters. https://www.reuters.com/article/oukoe-uk-kenya-rage-idUKTRE49J1Y120081020/
Rhodes, D. (2003). Gender and the profession: An American perspective. In U. Schultz & G. Shaw (Eds.), *Women in the world's legal professions* (pp. 3–22). Hart.
Rickard, C. (2019, February 22). Seychelles CJ Mathilda Twomey cleared of all charges by top tribunal. *AfricanLii.* https://africanlii.org/articles/2019–02-22/carmel-rickard/seychelles-cj-mathilda-twomey-cleared-of-all-charges-by-top-tribunal
Roberts, R. (2013). Law, crime, and punishment in colonial Africa. In J. Parker & R. Reid (Eds.), *The Oxford handbook of modern African history* (pp. 171–188). Oxford University Press.
Robson, P. (2021). Gender and law teaching in Scotland. In R. Auchmuty, U. Schultz, G. Shaw, & M. Thornton (Eds.), *Gender and careers in the legal academy* (pp. 195–214). Hart.
Rodney, W. (2012). *How Europe underdeveloped Africa.* Pambazuka Press.
Ross, S. D. (1992). The rule of law and lawyers in Kenya. *The Journal of Modern African Studies, 30*(3), 421–442. http://www.jstor.org/stable/161166
Röwekamp, M. (2013). First female judges in the Weimar Republic in Germany: Reflections on difference. In U. Schultz & G. Shaw (Eds.), *Gender and judging* (pp. 103–118). Hart.
Rukuba-Ngaiza, N. (2021). Gender awareness training in judicial training institutes in Kenya and Uganda. In J. J. Dawuni (Ed.), *Gender, judging and the courts in Africa: Selected studies* (pp. 254–276). Routledge.
Rwelamira, M. (1981). The Tanzania legal profession. In C. J. Dias, R. Luckham, D. O. Lynch, & J. C. N. Paul (Eds.), *Lawyers in the third world: Comparative and developmental perspectives* (pp. 204–225). International Center for Law in Development.
Sabharwal, M. (2013). From glass ceiling to glass cliff: Women in senior executive service. *Journal of Public Administration Research and Theory, 25*(2), 399–426. https://doi.org/:10.1093/jopart/mut030.
Said, E. W. (2003). *Orientalism.* Penguin Classics
Salman, S. (1981). The legal profession in Sudan: A study of legal and professional pluralism. In C. J. Dias, R. Luckham, D. O. Lynch, & J. C. N. Paul (Eds.), *Lawyers in the third world: Comparative and developmental perspectives* (pp. 226–248). International Center for Law in Development.
Samararatne, D. (2020). Gendering the legal complex: Women in Sri Lanka's legal profession. *Journal of Law & Society, 47*(4), 666–693. https://doi.org/10.1111/jols.12259
Sanchez Salcedo, E. (2021). Women law teachers in the Philippines then, now and six decades in between: The cheerless transformation of a road less travelled to a path oft-chosen for convenience. In R. Auchmuty, U. Schultz, G. Shaw, & M. Thornton (Eds.), *Gender and careers in the legal academy* (pp. 249–268). Hart.
Sanderson, P., & Sommerlad, H. (1998). *Gender, choice and commitment: Women solicitors in England and Wales and the struggle for equal status.* Ashgate.

Sanneh, S. (2014, March 8). Justice Mabel Agyemang: One more victim of a patently vindictive dictator. *Sidi Sanneh*. https://sidisanneh.blogspot.com/2014/03/one-more-victim-of-patently-vindictive.html

Sasinsky, M. S. (2020). *Understanding the phenomenon of intersectionality and its effect on inclusion and transformation in the South African legal profession* [Master's thesis, University of Pretoria].

Saungweme, F., Ngang, C. & Towl, G. (Eds.). (2024). *Sexual harassment and the law in Africa: Country and regional perspectives*. Routledge.

Scales-Trent, J. (2010). Women lawyers, women's rights in Senegal: The association of Senegalese female lawyers. *Human Rights Quarterly, 32*(1), 115–143. https://doi.org/10.1353/hrq.0.0132

Schoepffer, C. (2018). Judicial review and democratization in Francophone West Africa. *Law and Politics in Africa, Asia, and Latin America, 51*(2), 191–215.

Schultz, U. (2013). Do German judges need gender education? In U. Schultz & G. Shaw (Eds.), *Gender and judging* (pp. 585–598). Hart.

Schultz, U. (2021a). Gender and careers in the legal academy in Germany: Women's difficult path from pioneers to a (still contested) minority. In R. Auchmuty, U. Schultz, G. Shaw, & M. Thornton (Eds.), *Gender and careers in the legal academy* (pp. 39–62). Hart.

Schultz, U. (2021b). Introduction: Gender and careers in the legal academy: Overview and synthesis. In R. Auchmuty, U. Schultz, G. Shaw, & M. Thornton (Eds.), *Gender and careers in the legal academy* (pp. 1–36). Hart.

Schultz, U., & Shaw, G. (Eds.). (2003). *Women in the world's legal professions*. Hart.

Schultz, U., & Shaw, G. (Eds.). (2013). *Gender and judging*. Hart.

Sen, M. (2017). Diversity, qualifications and ideology: How female and minority judges have changed, or not changed, over time. *Wisconsin Law Review, 2*, 367–399. https://tinyurl.com/yb3uxoao

Sesanti, S. (2016). African philosophy in pursuit of an African renaissance for the true liberation of African women. *Journal of Black Studies, 47*(6), 479–496. https://doi.org/10.1177/0021934716645486

Sharif, M. Y. (2015). Glass ceiling, the prime driver of women entrepreneurship in Malaysia: A phenomenological study of women lawyers. *Procedia-Social and Behavioral Sciences, 169*, 329–336.

Shen, Anqi. (2017). *Women judges in contemporary China: Gender, judging and living*. Palgrave Macmillan.

Shetler, J. B. (2015). *Gendering ethnicity in African women's lives*. University of Wisconsin Press.

Shomade, S. (2022). *Colonial legacies and the rule of law in Africa: Ghana, Kenya, Nigeria, South Africa, and Zimbabwe*. Routledge Press.

Silver, C. (2013). Getting real about globalization and legal education: Potential and perspectives for the U.S. *Stanford Law & Policy Review, 24*(2), 457.

Smart, C. (2009). Shifting horizons: Reflections on qualitative methods. *Feminist Theory, 10*(3), 1–14.

Smith, C. Jr. (Ed.). (2000). *Rebels in law: Voices in history of Black women lawyers*. University of Michigan Press.

Solomon, S. (2023, March 31). Woman of iron honored for protecting CAR's constitution. *Voice of America.* https://www.voanews.com/a/woman-of-iron-honored-for-protecting-car-s-constitution-/7030087.html

Sommerlad, H. (1994). The myth of feminization: Women and cultural change in the legal profession. *International Journal of the Legal Profession, 1*, 31–53.

Sommerlad, H. (2013). Let history judge? Gender, race, class and performative identity: A study of women judges in England and Wales. In U. Schultz & G. Shaw (Eds.), *Gender and judging* (pp. 355–373). Hart.

Sommerlad, H. (2021). Patriarchal discourses in the UK legal academy: The case of the reasonable man. In R. Auchmuty, U. Schultz, G. Shaw, & M. Thornton (Eds.), *Gender and careers in the legal academy* (pp. 531–548). Hart.

Sornarajah, M. (2016). On fighting for global justice: The role of a third world international lawyer. *Third World Quarterly, 37*(11), 1972–1989. https://doi.org/10.1080/01436597.2016.1180955

Spivak, G. C. (1988). *Can the subaltern speak*? Die Philosophin.

Stanley, L., & Wise, S. (1993). *Breaking out again: Feminist ontology and epistemology.* Routledge.

Steady, F. (2011). *Women and leadership in West Africa: Mothering the nation and humanizing the state.* Palgrave Macmillan.

Sterling, J., & Chanow, L. (2021). *In their own words: Experienced women lawyers explain why they are leaving their law firms and the profession.* ABA Book Publishing. https://www.americanbar.org/content/dam/aba/administrative/women/intheirownwords-f-4-19-21-final.pdf

Stewart, J. (2012). Lawyers? Women? Women lawyers in Zimbabwe. *Journal of Law & Social Research, 2*(3), 11–28.

Stewart, J., & Tsanga, A. (Eds.). (2011). *Women and law: Innovative regional approaches to teaching, researching and analysing women and law.* Weaver Press.

Subramaniam, B. (2016). Stories we tell: Feminism, science, methodology. *Economic and Political Weekly, 51*(18), 57–63.

Tamale, S. (2015). The context and content of teaching of family law in Uganda: A feminist analysis. *Zambia Law Journal, 46*, 1–51.

Tamale, S. (2020). *Decolonization and Afro-feminism.* Daraja Press.

Tamale, S. (2021). Juggling the personal and the political at Makerere University. In J. Oloko-Onyango (Ed.), *Politics, democratization and academia in Uganda* (pp. 220–266). Daraja Press.

Terretta, M. (2017). Anti-colonial lawyering, postwar human rights, and decolonization across imperial boundaries in Africa. *Canadian Journal of History, 52*(3), 448–478.

Thornton, M. (1989). Hegemonic masculinity and the academy. *International Journal of the Sociology of Law, 17*, 115–130.

Thornton, M. (1996). *Dissonance and distrust: Women in the legal profession.* Oxford University Press.

Tibatemwa-Ekirikubinza, L. (2021). Sexual and gender-based violence in Uganda during the COVID-19 pandemic: New and old lessons for the criminal justice system. In J. J. Dawuni (Ed.), *Gender, judging and the courts in Africa: Selected studies* (pp. 297–320). Routledge.

Tibihikirra-Kalyegira, P. (2010). *Liberalization of legal education in Uganda: policy considerations.* LawAfrica.

Tomlinson, J., Muzio, D., Sommerlad, H., Webley, L., & Duff, L. (2013). Structure, agency and career strategies of white women and black and minority ethnic individuals in the legal profession. *Human Relations, 66*(2), 245–269.

Tøraasen, M. (2017). *Gender parity in Senegal—A continuing struggle.* Chr. Michelsen Institute (CMI Insight 2017:2). https://doi.org/10.2139/ssrn.3648097

Tripp, A. M. (2000). *Women and politics in Uganda.* James Currey Fountain.

Tripp, A. M. (2004). A new look at colonial women: British teachers and activists in Uganda, 1898–1962. *Canadian Journal of African Studies, 38*(1), 123–156

Tripp, A. M. (2016). Women's movements and constitution making after civil unrest and conflict in Africa: The cases of Kenya and Somalia. *Gender and Politics, 12*(1), 78–106. https://doi.org/10.1017/S1743923X16000015

Tshuma, L. (1991). Twelve years of legal education in Zimbabwe. *The Zimbabwe Law Review, 9,* 171–185.

Tsikata, D. (2007). Gender, institutional cultures and the career trajectories of faculty of the University of Ghana. *Feminist Africa: Rethinking Universities, 8,* 26–41.

Tsikata, D. (2009). Women's organizing in Ghana since the 1990s: From individual organizations to three coalitions. *Development, 52*(2), 185–192. https://doi.org/10.1057/dev.2009.8

Tsikata, D., & Torvikey, G. (2021). COVID-19 and Africa: A synthesis of 12 country studies. *INCLUDE: Knowledge Platform on Inclusive Development Policies.* https://includeplatform.net/wp-content/uploads/2022/06/COVID-19-Synthesis-Report.pdf

Tsikata, E. (1989). Women's political organisations, 1951–1987. In E. Hansen & K. Ninsin (Eds.), *The state, development and politics in Ghana* (pp. 73–93). Council for the Development of Economic and Social Research in Africa (CODESRIA).

Ubink, J. (2011). The quest for customary law in African state courts. In J. Fenrich, P. Galizzi, & T. E. Higgins (Eds.), *The future of African customary law* (pp. 83–102). Cambridge University Press.

United Nations Development Programme. 2024. *Women in justice in Africa: A comparative study of women judges in 14 countries.* UNDP. https://reliefweb.int/report/algeria/women-justice-africa-comparative-study-women-judges-14-countries

Uzebu-Imarhiagbe, E. (2020a). Nigeria: An account of adaptation. In R. L. Abel, O. Hammerslev, H. Sommerlad, & U. Schultz (Eds.), *Lawyers in 21st-century societies: Volume 1. National reports* (pp. 515–534). Hart.

Uzebu-Imarhiagbe, E. (2020b). Women in the Nigerian judiciary: Considerable headway or organized progress? *International Journal of the Legal Profession, 27*(2), 2–14. https://doi.org/10.1080/09695958.2020.1750410

Valdini, M., & Shortell, C. (2018). Women's Representation in the highest court: A comparative analysis of the appointment of female justices. *Political Research Quarterly, 69*(4), 865–876.

Vanderveer, S. (2015). *Pursuing equity: How women academics are challenging gender norms and (Re)shaping university culture in Ghana.* [Master's thesis, Simon Fraser University].

VonDoepp, P. (2013). The rule of law and the courts. In D. M. Anderson, N. Cheeseman, & A. Scheibler (Eds.), *Routledge handbook of African politics* (pp. 37–48). Routledge Handbooks Online.

Vrushali, P. (2013). From patriarchy to intersectionality: A transnational feminist assessment of how far we've really come. *Signs, 38*(4), 847–67. https://doi.org/10.1086/669560

Wallace, J. (2001). The benefits of mentoring for female lawyers. *Journal of Vocational Behavior, 58*(3), 366–391. https://doi.org/10.1006/jvbe.2000.1766

Wambua, M. K. (2013). *Challenges facing women legal practitioners in Kenya*. [Master's thesis, University of Nairobi]. http://erepository.uonbi.ac.ke:8080/xmlui/handle/123456789/60018

Wane, N. N. (2000). Reflections on the mutuality of mothering: Women, children, and other-mothering. *Journal of the Motherhood Initiative for Research and Community Involvement, 2*(2), 105–116. https://jarm.journals.yorku.ca/index.php/jarm/article/view/2143

Wangila, Brenda. (n.d.). *Patricia Kameri-Mbote: First woman law professor in Kenya*. Institute for African Women in Law. https://www.africanwomeninlaw.com/african-women-in-law/patricia-kameri-mbote%2C-phd

Weber, M. (1978). *Economy and society*. University of California Press.

Weeks, S. (2022). Transforming traditional justice through gender diversification: Comparing two South African communities. In J. Dawuni (Ed.), *Intersectionality and women's access to justice in Africa* (pp. 353–378). Lexington Press.

Weidenfeller, N. K. (2012). Breaking through the glass wall: The experience of being a woman enterprise leader. *Human Resource Development International, 15*(3), 365–374. https://doi.org/10.1080/13678868.2012.688361

Wells, C. (2001). Working out women in law schools. *Legal Studies, 21*(1), 116–136. https://doi.org/10.1111/j.1748-121X.2001.tb00169.x

Wells, C. (2021). Memories: Becoming a law professor. In R. Auchmuty, U. Schultz, G. Shaw, & M. Thornton (Eds.), *Gender and careers in the legal academy* (pp. 409–424). Hart.

West, R. (2018). Women in the legal academy: A brief history of feminist legal theory. *Fordham Law Review, 87*(3), 977. https://ir.lawnet.fordham.edu/flr/vol87/iss3/8

Whitehead, C. (2005). The historiography of British imperial education policy. *History of Education, 34*(4), 441–454.

Widner, J. (2001). *Building the rule of law: Francis Nyalali and the road to judicial independence in Africa*. W.W. Norton.

Wilkins, D. B. (1992). Who should regulate lawyers? *Harvard Law Review, 105*(4), 799–887. https://doi.org/10.2307/1341608

Wilson, F. (2005). Caught between difference and similarity: The case of women academics. *Women in Management Review, 20*(4), 234–248. https://doi.org/10.1108/09649420510599061

Wing, A. (Ed.). (2000). *Global critical race: An international reader*. New York University Press.

World Bank. (2022). Senegal: Data. https://data.worldbank.org/country/SN

Yoon, M. Y. (2016). Women judges as agents of judicial education. In G. Bauer & J. J. Dawuni (Eds.), *Gender and the judiciary in Africa: From obscurity to parity?* (pp. 93–107). Routledge.

Zeleza, P. T. (2005). Gender biases in African historiography. In O. Oyěwùmí (Ed.), *African gender studies: A reader* (pp. 207–232). Palgrave Macmillan.

Zeleza, P. T. (2016). *The transformation of global higher education.* Palgrave Macmillan.

Zulu, N. T. (2021). The struggles and triumphs of South African Black women professors. *South African Journal of Higher Education, 35*(6), 239–257. https://doi.org/10.20853/35-6-4272

Index

For the benefit of digital users, indexed terms that span two pages (e.g., 52–53) may, on occasion, appear on only one of those pages.

D

J

T

U